EDWARD KENNEDY

AN INTIMATE BIOGRAPHY

Also by Burton Hersh

EDWARD KENNEDY

AN INTIMATE BIOGRAPHY

Burton Hersh

COUNTERPOINT

BERKELEY

Library of Congress Cataloging-in-Publication Data
Hersh, Burton.
Edward Kennedy : an intimate biography / by Burton Hersh.
p. cm.
ISBN-13: 978-1-58243-628-9
ISBN-10: 1-58243-628-2
1. Kennedy, Edward M. (Edward Moore), 1932–2009
2. Legislators—United States—Biography.
3. United States. Congress. Senate—Biography. I. Title.
E840.8.K35H424 2010
973.92092—dc22
[B]
2010017799

Jacket design by Silverander Communications
Printed in the United States of America

COUNTERPOINT
1919 Fifth Street
Berkeley, CA 94710

www.counterpointpress.com

Distributed by Publishers Group West

10 9 8 7 6 5 4 3 2 1

This book is dedicated to our remarkable children,
Leo and Margery,
whose future Edward Kennedy struggled to protect

Contents

BOOK TWO
The Shadow President

Preface

Genuine history is what survives the lies agreed upon. This book comes wrung out of more than half a century of impressions and research, formal interviews and intermittent social exchanges which began in the early fifties, when Ted Kennedy bobbed up as an undergraduate in my class at Harvard College after a couple of years of penance in the military for having been pitched out for cheating in a Spanish exam. By my sophomore year Teddy was back in school, "Cadillac Eddie," dismissed mostly around Harvard Square as a rock-jawed goof-off who was dependable mostly on the football field or chugalugging beers with his fellow lightweights at Pi Eta, a secondary final club. I'd seen Ted here and there, in fact had several times tossed him around in the wrestling room of the Indoor Athletic Building when he'd stopped by during the off season. He struck me in passing as a lanky, freckled Irish-American buckaroo, not strong, particularly; good-natured but empty; unmistakably a legacy admission.

After 1955 I myself was out of the country for six years, until JFK was installed as president, and within months of the inauguration Edward Kennedy had announced that he intended to occupy his brother's Senate seat. Like so many others acquainted with the president's exuberant, handsome, wild-eyed, hard-drinking, risk-loving youngest brother, I felt the Kennedys were pushing it.

By the middle sixties I had started to reconsider. Ted and I both had studied with a prominent teacher in Harvard's Government Department, Professor Samuel Beer. Beer was a hard-bitten, brilliant, iconoclastic fixture on the Harvard faculty, ultimately the Eaton Professor of Government and for many years the head of the department, and always he said what he genuinely thought. One of Sam's enthusiasms in those days was skydiving, usually out of Orange, Massachusetts; every once in a while he took me along for a jump. In 1961 Beer had signed on to help coach Ted prior to his debates in the Massachusetts Democratic primary with Eddie McCormack, and had come away convinced that Kennedy was not only capable of mastering the issues but showed every indication of the finesse and instinct for bringing along his colleagues that was indispensable in the fickle Senate.

Not long after that I spotted a couple of news lines about the effectiveness with which Kennedy had dispatched a bit of special-interest "procedural" legislation: an effort to put off at least into the early seventies court-ordered congressional redistricting. Kennedy's initiative involved taking on the mellifluous Republican Minority Leader from Illinois, Everett McKinley Dirksen, a cornfed reactionary who hated in particular the high court's one-man-one-vote mandate. I already knew Washington well enough to acknowledge that countering anything like Dirksen's lobbyist-financed efforts took parliamentary legerdemain well beyond the imagination of most politicians.

Something must be developing. Not too long afterward, in 1967, I happened to be discussing article ideas with Harold Hayes of *Esquire*. I accepted an assignment to profile Edward M. Kennedy.

I wrote the piece itself just after the opening of that politically tumultuous year. Ted Kennedy himself was generous. I suspect that Kennedy understood that both of us had been hatched from the same collegiate generation, remained committed to familiar principles, shared important mentors. As for his inmost social circle—that would be committed lifelong friends like John Culver and Tim Hatton, John (Varick) Tunney, and Claude Hooten.

But Kennedy was confident all his life when it came to trusting his instincts, and perhaps he saw in me a contemporary he could depend on when it came to exchanging ideas and trading accommodations. Whether I was in or out of favor, the closest of his aides were permitted to speak freely; I got my first look at politics on the state level during one of those barnstorming tours of Massachusetts Kennedy exploited to keep in touch. Well into the night a kind of motorcade of dark, unmarked automobiles proceeded Mafialike from point to point while trusted lieutenants like the implacable young lawyer Paul Kirk fed unruly members of the press in and out of the back seat of the senator's car, each desperate for a few precious minutes to throw questions out and pray for headline potential. Control was paramount.

During interviews that year the Junior Senator from Massachusetts appeared broadly informed and occasionally almost penetrating; he tended to maunder a bit at times; whenever he saw the need he was shamelessly evasive. "I think he's a pasteboard mask. If you can get behind that you're doing something," a colleague who had covered Kennedy for a newsmagazine commented at the time. I finished the article having concluded that for all his booming politician's gestures Edward Kennedy was in fact extraordinarily guarded, that—unlike JFK—he had the makings of an authentic liberal, and that, as much as anybody, he himself was the unlikely Svengali who—in answer to the commonest question I encountered—"did his thinking for him." There was a forced boyishness at times that I suspected was costing him maturity. Bobby had come into the Senate in 1964 and quickly established himself as dominant. *Esquire* bought the piece, printed it, and reprinted it in its anthology of the sixties.

As 1968 moved into spring and summer I began to realize that The Kennedys as a subject needed work. I read Kennedy books—books by aides, books on single events, quick books by journalists as one brother or the next caught a fresh wave of publicity. Fine outside research jobs by writers nobody in the Kennedy organization would talk to. None . . . fit, smelled right. As early as the 1967 days in the Old Senate Office Building the notion of doing a book on Edward Kennedy arose. Richard Drayne, Kennedy's frolicsome press aide, had come to me with the idea; the drawback at that time seemed to be that so much of Kennedy's performance had been very deliberately kept low-keyed in order not to throw a shadow across the increasingly conspicuous Bobby.

What was already fascinating to me was Kennedy's success in establishing himself as an operator, an insider. The fact was, neither John nor Bob had gotten far into the process as senators. Teddy was something else. As early as 1965, once Ted was back on crutches from months in the hospital after his near-fatal plane crash, Lyndon Johnson deputized this light-fingered kid brother of the Kennedys to wangle his important immigration bill through the recalcitrant Senate. Teddy lent a lot of the muscle behind the key Voting Rights Bill. As the ranking expert in the Upper Body on refugee issues, Kennedy was already starting to question openly the rationale behind the war in Vietnam.

How had Ted managed to make his way in so deep so young? That alone, I thought, might justify a book.

By that time, of course, Kennedy's career—if not Edward Kennedy personally—had undergone a shift of modalities. Negotiating with the industrial-state bosses throughout Bob's aborted 1968 spring candidacy, Ted had aroused a lot more affection than his frequently bruising brother the candidate, and narrowly avoided being drafted for the presidential nomination by the Party in Chicago. He was already being "built" as the inescapable Democratic nominee in 1972.

Shaping the publicity was crucial, especially since I was being given unique access to Kennedy's day-by-day operations. After a low-key but determined-enough round of dickering, the Kennedy aides and I agreed that the treatment would be balanced, that they would not to prevent me from interviewing any-one, that I would be under no obligation to let anybody in Kennedy's offices see any manuscript, at any stage.

That got complicated. As my 1972 publication date got closer, and the incident off Chappaquiddick Island threw up a tidal wave, I felt gathering pressures. "Couldn't you give us some . . . at least a hint of what your book is going to be about," one of Kennedy's advisers, the spectral attorney Milton Gwirzman, attempted one day at lunch. By then the tabloids were starting to traffic in Kennedy's extracurricular activities.

"I probably shouldn't," I told Gwirtzman.

"How about . . . maybe . . . the working title?"

"Well, Milton. Since it's you. We're thinking of calling it *The Venereal History of Edward Kennedy*."

Gwirtzman took off his glasses and rubbed his eyes.

What I had not expected as I foraged among generations of retainers was the vivacity of detail, the excited sense of the past I was accumulating. Meanwhile, mishaps and tragedies repeatedly threatened to grind the whole project under. Many Kennedy bystanders had never been approached by a journalist before; access had been tightly controlled. While Joe Kennedy was in charge he arranged for most of the publicity that created the perception of the superhuman Kennedys, from planting the PT-109 narrative that first inflated Jack's national image in *The New Yorker* to purchasing cover stories in *Time* and *Look*. After 1961 Joe was paralyzed, money was more limited, and Ted had to take his chances.

I conceived of the long first section of this book while Bob was still around, researched it when Ted Kennedy had already been all but coronated by millions of Democrats, settled into the drafting that fateful July when Kennedy drove off the Dike Bridge at Chappaquiddick. Preceded by a very full-bodied rendition of the events surrounding the Chappaquiddick acci-dent, which was turned into virtually an entire issue of *Esquire* in 1972—by then I had interviewed just about everybody involved, including Kennedy himself—*The Education of Edward Kennedy* (Morrow) came out in 1972. It was reviewed everywhere. Like its subject, the book was repeatedly blindsided. The afternoon of the book party at The National Press Club, George Wal-lace was gutshot in a Baltimore parking lot, Ted—who had been expected at the party—took fright and disappeared, and, to the horror of the Morrow publicist, the entire D.C. press corps stampeded out to Maryland.

After that, for the next twenty-five years, I concentrated mostly on other subjects. From time to time I did a magazine piece on Ted, usually for *Esquire* or *The Washingtonian*. After he finally decided to run for president I pitched in where I could.

Occasionally I would get a call from his office—the senator knew I had been to D.C., I had been spotted in Paul Young's or The Monocle, why hadn't I stopped by? Whenever I did we would take a walk around the Capitol, or he would lure me into his inner office and torture me as only he could. "See this letter from my mother?" he complained once, taking off the wall a framed note from Rose. She had read my book, and she was annoyed with her son for having been quoted in it for swearing—mildly—in public. Kennedy put the letter back in place. "See what you've done? My own mother! On me about *another* of my bad habits."

Occasionally Kennedy would be miffed at something I had written, and I wouldn't hear for a while. Then, unexpectedly, he would call. He was aware that I was working on a long manuscript dealing with the CIA. What could I tell him about what was behind the Iran-Contra fiasco?

In 1994, when Mitt Romney's run at his Senate seat became serious overnight, on assignment from *Esquire* I spent some time campaigning with Ted and Vicki in Massachusetts. The risk-loving bravo of our youth was aging fast, toddling up and down the factory floors shaking hands, his pewter hair thinning, fighting something of a tremor, never missing—at Victoria's urging—the chance to hit a men's room. The political trappings, the entourage, of so many years earlier were gone. The losses were compiling—he was overwhelmed at that moment by the abrupt loss of Jacqueline Kennedy. He knew about the lymphoma, certainly, but then one day last week he got the call to come attend last rites . . . !

In 1997 a compilation of my pieces on Kennedy after 1972, fortified by a good deal of new, unpublished material, was put out by Steerforth Press as *The Shadow President*. I interviewed Ted extensively at that point to fill in the blanks. By then he was ready to begin to deal with his deeper feelings, on every subject from Joan to the complicated apprehensions of his childhood, the fear of his father and alienation from his family that coexisted with his intense love of his father.

In 2006, while I was completing my embattled treatment of the Kennedy family *Bobby and J. Edgar*, I spoke with Kennedy a final time. He was excited about a project he was working on, a children's book about dogs. He ducked—said he couldn't remember, probably wasn't there—my queries about such incidents as the donnybrook between Bobby and Old Joe the Christmas of 1956, when Bobby decided that political success for him lay in going after the Mob. Family involvement with the underworld was a subject into which Teddy and I had never ventured, beyond his observing to me at one point that "All the way through his existence Dad had relationships and contacts none of the rest of us had." When, in *Bobby and J. Edgar*, I probed too deeply into those, I never heard from Edward Kennedy again. Still struggling to exert as much influence as feasible on the Obama administration while staving off an incurable brain cancer, Kennedy died on August 25, 2009.

Many years earlier, at the beginning of 1971, while I was rounding into the final draft of my first book about Ted, Kennedy's colleagues had dumped him unceremoniously from the Whip's chair. Kennedy's future, as he wrote me at the time, seemed more than precarious. Typically—he was to do this all his life—he objectified catastrophe for himself in terms of sympathy for the victims, his life as penance. Even then he was able to step outside personal responsibility, turn the situation around. "As your letter suggests," Kennedy wrote, "my political fortunes are tied to your book. Every time you think you finished a manuscript, I can think of a way to send you back to the typewriter for another chapter or two. One of us had better put a stop to it, or you won't have any book and I won't have any future." Soldier's humor, as always, if of an increasingly fatalistic veteran.

EDWARD KENNEDY

AN INTIMATE BIOGRAPHY

BOOK ONE

THE INITIATION OF THE MINOTAUR

That men in armour may be born
With serpents' teeth the field is sown;
Rains mould, winds bend, suns gild the corn
Too quickly ripe, too early mown . . .

C. K. SCOTT MONCRIEFF
from the dedication to
Within a Budding Grove (Proust)

The Kennedys are no more the Kennedys because
they've got money, than the Beatles are the Beatles
because they've got hair.

FOSTER FURCOLO

CHAPTER I

Root Systems

1. Origins

July is the month America celebrates itself. Entertainment is traditional, and that may be one overlooked reason why the catastrophe, shock though it was, seemed more than a coincidence. Closer to a curtain-raiser for which the players started gathering, unnoticed, toward twilight a day or so before the moonshot scored—while most of the nation was watching Neil Armstrong watching the chalk-dead satellite grow and preparing his insides to ease the landing module onto the Sea of Tranquillity like a cat's paw onto a scientifically cornered mouse.

Across the tenuous steep void the earth was rising. It was a mid-July Friday night in 1969 on Chappaquiddick Island at the Lawrence Cottage, a listless cookout on a sweltering black evening into which nobody could push much life because Bobby was still dead. Earlier, before people started eating, there had been hopeful, high-jinksy moments. While Ted Kennedy's sidekick cousin Joey Gargan, who prided himself on his kitchen techniques, was trying to get the stony frozen sausage hors d'oeuvres going in the oven, there had been people enough around to prod him with that needling devious gotcha-from-the-flank style of inside humor Kennedy regulars seem to pick up from the Kennedys; jokes about the sailing and even the campaign in '68 went over, reminiscences, cherished private digs. Then—the steaks, once grilled and eaten around the cookout outside—the mood itself seemed to thin out, went away, irrevocably . . .

That night John Kennedy's lunar dream was about to be realized and

Teddy Kennedy's presidential future burned rubber and skidded across forty-seven feet of gravel and planking and pitched off the Dike Bridge to land upside down in that inky midnight tidal pond. It took Ted Kennedy's luck to squirm out and into the opaque night alive; Mary Jo Kopechne didn't. It was a terrible thing to happen, inexplicable finally, and yet—and this the nation grasped immediately—in keeping: This, too, was knowledge between the country and the Kennedys—this also fit. Death, there was always death; the navigating and political engineering of the Kennedys had been perfected to such an extent that only one event, somehow random yet inevitable—only death could make any real difference.

Death was the alternative to winning, finishing first again; death kicked on unexpectedly, when all the instrumentation read perfect. This all the children recognized prematurely, but Teddy was the one who grew up after it had started to happen . . . "Jack Kennedy was really only interested in two things: sex, and death," his carousing buddy George Smathers would insist afterwards. Joseph P. Kennedy, modest before gigantic dooms, had his suspicions early about where, exactly, for each of his profoundly driven children, the weakness for death would start glimmering through.

Certain anxieties are racial: emotional deformations to be watched out for early, like silicosis with a miner or skin cancer in the crosshatching of a farmer's neck. Every Establishment, well aware of its unacknowledged requirements, picks from among the most promising untouchables its necessary Mafia. The gentleman Brahmins of mid-nineteenth-century Boston, who had for generations supported a gene that taught them how to mix rum and slaves to the benefit of their tight-clutched pocketbooks, watched from their neo-Athenian City on a Hill as the Cunarders emptied themselves of Irishmen along the piers of Noodle's Island, survivors of six or eight weeks of an Atlantic passage in a fetid steerage so shallow no adult could stand upright in it. The water had normally gone rank after the earliest days out and, laced with vinegar, mixed brackishness with the communal overflow of stomachs crampy with dysentery and the putrescence from the open privies and the groans of the moribund dried up with "hunger typhus"; a third died outright, or of the after-effects, on landing.

What the native Yankees noticed about these newcomers as the nineteenth century deepened was the way, depleted and sick as they were, they seemed to crawl out of their holds and ship bellies in brawling little clans and gangs, each from its county or village, Cork versus Mayo or Galway, belligerent and struggling noisily for its own. Besides which, as soon as a few pennies came in, they went out immediately for a can or a mug of the homemade rotgut that came closest to the well-remembered burn of their deadly native "poteen."

The arrival of the unspeakable Irish was by no means a historical accident. The Shawmut Bank, already a tired-money repository by 1839, had negotiated that year with Sir Samuel Cunard to make Boston the terminus of his Liverpool Line. A seething pool of the desperate poor was arriving, willing to scrub the narrow brownstone vestibules or unload boats or shovel out stables or—most important—drudge by the hundreds of thousands in the penitentiary-square shoe factories and wool-carding purgatorios of Waltham and Lawrence and Lowell. A city of trade and commerce until that moment, Boston, during the decades that bracketed the Civil War, went industrial, overseen by an unlikely generation of patrician plutocrats in tightly buttoned vests who shuddered to encounter one of their white niggers, their Paddys or Maggies, along Boston's fashionable cobblestone cowpaths. NINA—No Irish Need Apply—became a standard subscript for a job notice. Better a farm girl or a Negro—they could be trusted further. "Dogs and Irishmen keep off the grass," read signs in parks and herbariums.

The pariah has few choices; being the Other, he can permit himself few. In Ireland, a damp green slave colony of the English at least since Pope Adrian gave it to Henry II in 1155, the options were, truly, pitiful: Absentee landlords had kept the sharecroppers and cottiers cut off and pathetic in their mud huts, among their pigs and potatoes, forbidden to own weapons, engage in commerce, learn to read, organize their own snippets of land as they chose, form parties politically, vote openly, or protest.

The invaders found their Celtic victims a scholarly if disputatious people. The Irish fought so bitterly among themselves, hated each other's success, that Joyce's reference to his mother country as "the sow that eats her own farrow" came down through centuries. So many of the stereotype characteristics the immigrants brought over—the need for drink, the love of noise and boasting and self-delusive exaggeration, a sense of whimsy and weakness for deep black superstition, the churchiness in extremity, the acidulous, self-deprecating humor that reconciled itself to defeat before anything was properly attempted, the impulse to spend up what there was because it would be taken anyhow, the physical squalor—these had become a broken people's tactical resort for getting itself emotionally through the misty, anguished historical night.

They transposed into industrial servitude only too easily. The point to work toward about the Kennedys and Fitzgeralds is that, almost on landing, in both families the leadership sought to become, in approach at least, unIrish.

This shows in their earliest purposeful stirrings. Patrick Kennedy the first, who immigrated in 1849, seemed typical of the break-in generation. He had been a half-starved tenant farmer in the Wexford lake country; he was young when he shambled onto the docks at Noodle's Island and he was young still—thirty-five—when he died of cholera and generalized exhaustion. He left four children, three girls and an infant son, the next Patrick Kennedy, an underpaid job as a cooper, a maker of whiskey barrels, and a widow, Bridget, nee Murphy, two years older than himself. Bridget Kennedy was an immigrant like her husband, and she remained for a time in the shanty by the ferryboat pier where Pat had gone and died on her, but she was evidently a woman of no small soft-spoken initiative and considerable délicatesse, because before long she was running a small notions and stationery store at the foot of Broad Street, and after that went along to Boston's already well-established department store Jordan Marsh, where she became chief hairdresser, a notable appointment at a time no gentleman cared to have an Irish close enough to smell when he received a haircut.

Tom and Rosemary Fitzgerald, Rose Kennedy's parents, like the immigrant Kennedys, came out of County Wexford. The Fitzgeralds—by accident, largely, exactly the sort of accident that can save an immigrant family a generation—washed up among Boston's more genteel brick tenements of the North End. Tom started out as a farm laborer but returned to Boston soon, and by the time he died, in 1881, at thirty-three, had arrived at the station of the high-humored proprietor of a North End grocery and liquor store. Tom had outlived his wife, "Mother Roseann," by three years: Their seven growing sons were orphans.

Fortunately for the others, their third son, John, seems to have been born with a combination of unquenchable dervish energies and the natural plotter's eye, before which there are no irreversible setbacks, only unexpected new games. Little Johnny Fitz, as he was dubbed by his amused neighbors, survives in the telling as an exuberant urchin in patched pants and bare feet who couldn't help taking the stairs of the three-decker four at a time, dodge up and down the streets and wharves and behind the pushcarts of the great port city pulsating with its raw, reawakened sense of itself.

This excitement of the City of Boston as the great life-inhaling port was to remain with John Fitzgerald throughout: Imaginatively, he became, from his earliest street years to his dotage at the Bellevue, coexistent with the city, Boston's Biggest Booster, ultimately its showcase mayor. "When I was six years old, and my grandfather, John F. Fitzgerald, was seventy-five, he used to take me around Boston and show me the historic places," Ted Kennedy once wrote, introducing the port and the man overlapping: "He knew everything that went on in the city. 'Have you heard that Mary O'Reilly has left to teach school in New York?' he would say. 'We have to pay our teachers more.' Or, 'They haven't had a squash pie at Hayes-Bickford's restaurant for three days. Can't we get the food to market faster?'" Among the very best of Ted Kennedy's splendid party routines was his version of Honey Fitz: "What! No punkin' pie?"

2. Honey Fitz and P.J.

Anybody interested in how the Kennedys became The Kennedys had better look first at the grandfathers: "Fitzie," as his schoolmates called him, and the much more solemn yet in the end more substantial second Patrick, "P.J.," Joe Kennedy's father. The Mayor, Honey Fitz, is easier to track because his was an extended public life full of perusable documents and thousands of snake-bit voters who were among his closest personal friends. John Fitzgerald was a reasonably well-educated man, for his own time and nowadays. In an era when the school was good enough to start on their astral way such promising poor boys as George Santayana and Bernard Berenson, the bantamweight Fitzgerald attended Boston's rigorous Latin School, played baseball and managed the football team, served as sports editor of the magazine, and hurried upon graduation right on to Harvard Medical School; he had a year in which his father died suddenly of pneumonia. Fitzgerald quit to support his brothers—accepting this, too, with the apparently puncture-proof good humor that became one of his earliest political assets, and claimed to have cooked, made beds, washed the faces of older and younger brothers equally, until all of them were men on the street. There is here a strain of rather unusual male tenderness, a kind of unabashed motherliness, that crops up later on among the Kennedy men—in Ted, certainly in Joey Gargan, and, very often and more undisguisedly, as he grew old enough to dare reveal himself, in the unpredictable Bobby.

Although doing well enough at first selling insurance, John Fitzgerald felt the need of a position; he took the local civil service examination, passed easily, and was appointed a clerk of the Customs House beneath an early Leverett Saltonstall. Step Two was politics. By then the landslide of immigrants was irresistible. Tutored by the wily Martin Lomansky, Fitzgerald worked the Catholic solidarity and singing club circuits and easily glad-handed his way up the political ladder—the Boston Common Council, the State Senate, and before the nineteenth century was over three terms in the U.S. House of Representatives.

By the time the effervescent young "Fitzie" came along, the great majority of the Irish families who were ever to arrive had already landed in the pit of Boston's delicate patrician stomach like a supertrencherload of overpeppered corned beef. Four million Irish had already emigrated; by the 1900 census Boston alone, glutted, with a population approaching 561,000, had managed to garner 246,101 people who were either Irish immigrants themselves or of immediate Irish ancestry. At the same time the "number of white Bostonians who might be considered of traditional New England origin"—Brahmin stock—ran to a meager 59,071. The regnant Yankee minority, whose collective hold had been assured for generations on the significant real estate, the seminal banking houses and cultural temples and hospitals and institutions of professional education within the community, clutched.

Boston stagnated. The port of Boston died little by little; the financial marketplace shrank as New York expanded. The mills were relocated to cheap Southern labor markets or even—in the case of one hemp producer—directly to India: Even the ununionized South couldn't underbid the pitiful wages offered along the polluted Merrimack.

The overall deterioration was well along when John Fitzgerald remarked to a reporter around the turn of the century in a personal rhetoric laced with an unmistakable pungency: "Many of the rich people of the Back Bay are not worthy. They have plenty of money, yet they invest little of it in their own city." Fitzgerald liked to boast, as he made his inexhaustible rounds from wake to dance to convocation, from toast-mastering dinners of the Ancient Order of Hibernians to haranguing as many as thirty street-corner rallies the last night before an election, that he was Boston's first mayor to have been born of immigrant Irish parents. Meanwhile, it seemed to Boston's WASP investment community that every bit of integrity Government had to have was being destroyed overnight by the blarney-spouting riffraff who now infested city hall and liked to pinch your shoulder affectionately and explain how things weren't open to question at all, if you only knew the details; still, it did get pretty complicated, and it was obvious that you were too busy a fellow to take the time to hear all about that . . .

It was, in fact, a raid, a tarpaper revolution. The loot was tangible, right there, extracted in purloined spittoons or the appearance of new nitwit relatives every day in one of the already proliferating agencies and commissions, cases of scotch whiskey, a touch of graft for an advanced look at the bids on a highway-paving competition, furniture stolen in broad daylight from public anterooms, massive derelictions in appropriated funds . . .

Everything was gross, bald—none of the civilized arrangements that led to an exchange of directors' fees or private information confided discreetly in the Somerset Club in advance of a major offering. No respect at all for the decent, time-honored procedures the Yankee overlordship had evolved over its hundreds of years to make sure the important money remained in Responsible Hands.

Alongside the performances of Fitzie's perennial rival James Michael Curley—who was himself about to release upon the Nice Persons of Boston unshirted Social Justice with a Gaelic tongue and a roll of nickels in its fist—the mayoralties of John Fitzgerald assumed, once the storms of office were over, a political rainbow quality, the world through carefully cut second-generation glass. Little Johnny Fitz was forty-three when he assumed the long-anticipated mayoralty for the first time. To the arms-across double-handshake of the "Irish switch," the mayor added a move of his own, a hot expectant look of enthusiasm directly into the eyes of the next constituent along. He softened up the men in recalcitrant electoral pockets by playing to the wives. "He got me through the women," a ward leader lamented. "Every time I went to their houses and tried to tell the men the truth, the women would pipe up and 'Johnny Fitz this' and 'Johnny Fitz that' until they simply talked me down and out." Prematurely sensitive to the impact of his publicity image, Fitzgerald had a knack for the politics of the underdog, a theme his grandson Teddy would pick up early and make his own. "Manhood against Money," keynoted Fitzie's second mayoral campaign against the brittle James J. Storrow: He let it speak for itself beneath a full-blown family portrait—the mayor and his wife and their three appealing boys and three blooming girls.

"You are an impudent young man," Senator Henry Cabot Lodge exclaimed upon spotting Fitzgerald just after the nervy little Fitzie, the single Catholic ever elected to the U.S. House of Representatives, had broken in one Sunday afternoon unannounced on Grover Cleveland. He talked with and at and around the president until the weary man agreed to veto the recently passed Immigration Bill that limited the immigration rolls to foreigners who read and wrote the language. "Do you think Jews or Italians have any rights in this country?" demanded Lodge.

"As much right as your father or mine," Fitzgerald popped immediately. "It was only a difference of a few ships."

"I was born of poor but honest parents," the mayor once remarked, running for reelection in 1910 and finding his starchy opponent, James J. Storrow, awkward and snobbish enough to walk away from his handshake before a roomful of dinner guests, "but I was always instinctively a gentleman."

Fitzie had discovered that political survival depended on arousing the faithful, who soon came to include his followers of earliest conviction—one of his brothers became a policeman in Charlestown; another, Joe, got $1,100 annually for carrying the daily traffic report from the Warren Avenue Bridge and the respectful nickname, among the initiates, of the "Human Postage Stamp."

His Honor himself, however, didn't take. He didn't have to: Long before he ever became mayor of Boston John Fitzgerald figured out for himself the difference between the way the poor enriched themselves at the public expense—properly called stealing—and the way people of means in situations of influence made sure they were appropriately remunerated for their valuable services. In 1901, employing a straw buyer, Fitzgerald purchased for $500 a defunct neighborhood weekly called *The Republic*. As he improved himself politically, and as his became the hand through which appointments and contracts invariably passed, the ad revenue in Fitzie's seemingly unimportant local gossip sheet mounted unimaginably: Virtually all the local public service corporations felt it suddenly mandatory to announce, in a massive advertising campaign only *The Republic* carried, that they were there.

The paper was shortly recapitalized at $300,000. Brothers Jim, Edward, George, and Henry were all involved in one end or another of the reliable liquor business; Henry, while honored as the president of the Ward Six "Total Abstinence Society," also ran a barroom and handled the patronage of his brother the mayor.

Along with his polo team and his Dorchester mansion with its window leaded to the coat of arms of Shawn a Boo—John the Bold—Fitzgerald's approach to taking showed that he had already discovered that, once your position in society is secured, the money soon becomes an insolently accepted byproduct. "The old conception of His Honor as a republicanized copy of His Lordship has disappeared," little Johnny Fitz announced at his inaugural. "A less formal and decorative personage seems to satisfy the requirements . . ."

Unlike his primary rival, the sarcastic James Michael Curley, whose virtually every quip was a slap that left a bone bruise, Fitzgerald's humor tended to be sly, rococo, and light. When a Philadelphia visitor, sniffing about the fact that Boston's serpentine streets were hard to navigate, ended with the wish that "Boston was laid out the same way as Philadelphia," the mayor observed good-naturedly that "When Boston is as dead as Philadelphia we'll have her laid out the same way." He seldom if ever needed a drink; he played the piano nicely and was forever threatening to sing "Sweet Adeline" unaccompanied; and he lived a life throughout which both sunrises and sunsets were predictably magnificent.

To a great extent the reputation Fitzgerald nourished as a family man would prove his political undoing. In 1914 Jim Curley decided he wanted the mayor's job in Boston for himself and announced publicly his intention to review the performances of great lovemakers "from Cleopatra to Toodles." "Toodles" Ryan was a well-founded blonde cigarette girl at the Ferncroft Inn, a regular stopover of His Honor's along the Newburyport Turnpike, and although the mayor insisted in later years that he had done no more than kiss the sympathetic Toodles casually at a party while his wife stood watching, Curley's brutal threat was evidently enough. His Honor stepped down.

If Boston's candy-dancing little mayor seemed to have a temperamental antipode among the Irish over the decade of his political flowering, that man would probably have been the somber, reliable Patrick Kennedy the second, P.J., son of Patrick Kennedy the immigrant cooper and father of Joseph P. Kennedy, banker, financier, ambassador, and Adviser to Presidents. P.J., Bridget's youngest, after a schooling at the hands of the Sisters of Notre Dame, helped his mother in the notions store, put time in on the docks as a longshoreman, and, starting with a barroom in Haymarket Square, worked himself bit by bit into the retail liquor business. He acquired finally a half-interest in three saloons and a wholesale liquor operation. He himself never drank. A watchful man with just enough vanity to cultivate a soup-strainer mustache, curled and waxed up at the tips, pleasant in a reserved way, he was not one to raise his voice or very often have to; his name for shrewdness, fairness, and freedom with the dollar to the needy spread among his customers, then throughout East Boston, finally throughout Massachusetts.

Power tended to come to him, often while he was looking over Boston Harbor from his baronial mansion on Webster Street or relaxing with his spectacles perched across his forehead as he perused the American history that fascinated him. He served as a Massachusetts legislator and state senator and, more often than he would have preferred, in those touchy civic commission posts—he was, over the years, election, fire, and wire commissioner—where the opportunities to line the pocket were many and appointees to emerge clean were few. P.J. emerged, clean, and was never opposed for any office.

He was a charter member of the Irish "Strategy Board," the "Mayor Makers," along with Joe Corbett and Jim Donovan and—when out of office temporarily and persuasive enough to talk his way back in among them one more time—little Johnnie Fitz. Politicians of every coloration relied on P.J. for disinterested advice.

Pat Kennedy was by no means impervious to the benefits from his increasing means. He kept a sixty-foot cabin cruiser, *The Eleanor*, for excursions to Peddock's Island with cronies on a Sunday afternoon; he returned from a political trip to New Orleans with a taste for sauce Bordelaise, each portion of which required two glasses of sparkling burgundy. Yet he remained inconspicuous, the child of mudflat East Boston. Joe Dinneen, an early Kennedy chronicler and newspaperman with immediate lines to that earlier, post-immigrant generation, deduced a "code" that P.J. passed along to his children and grandchildren explicitly: "Come in first; second place is failure. Don't make mistakes. Do nothing that will reflect upon your moral character or reputation for honesty or integrity." P.J. was a block to chip from.

Rose Kennedy, who remembered her father-in-law as "wonderful, a very calm, quiet man, not nearly so vociferous as my father. A man very well respected in the neighborhood," warned me against underestimating Mary Hickey Kennedy. "My husband's mother was more aggressive than his father, and I should think may have had more influence on him. She was a very charming woman, terribly interested in whatever was going on, especially in the church or in politics. She was a very big woman and she didn't move around very much. An influence, a definite force."

Along with two daughters, Loretta and Margaret, Mary and P.J. produced one son, Joe. His sisters, notes one biographer, "treated their brother like an Irish prince." Ambitions for the next generation were definitely concentrated in Joe, a tall, well groomed lad with a hint of the feral to his close-cut features and—even as a boy—a scrambler. His mother cherished Joe especially. Mary Kennedy's daughter, Mrs. George Connelly, remembers, along with her mother's love of religion and "delightful sense of humor" and kindness and fairness, "a driving force that was instrumental [in] having her Family reach the heights of their ambitions and abilities." "All the family have self-confidence," Sargent Shriver says, "which principally came from Mr. Kennedy, who said many times that his mother developed it in him."

Family values were under construction. Both Kennedy parents betray themselves slowly, reluctantly. There is that wet-plate photographic impression of P.J. and Johnnie Fitz, uneasy friends as early as 1896, sitting horses before a fox hunt in Asheville, North Carolina. One runs across the occasional family snapshots and dignified-dramatic, locket-style portraiture: P.J. with his vest buttoned and his hair parted magisterially in the middle and those ears fully meated out for Teddy to inherit in time. There are the reveries in later years of Joe Kennedy's two adoring younger sisters: scenes like the Sunday-afternoon atmosphere inflated with the ever-poignant aroma of bread baking and Boston-style beans and meat in careful slices and those cut-glass side dishes and the stained-glass lampshade catching a sheen across the floral damask in the parlor of the house in Winthrop, the gathering around the baby grand Steinway while young Joe Kennedy, Harvard Undergraduate, "a mischievous smile on his handsome and open face," leads his sisters through "Danny Boy" and "Peg O' My Heart."

Not alluded to directly but most certainly a presence, out a little beyond the opal glow of the leaded Tiffany chandelier, the Kennedy parents seem solider in some way, more formidable, thrown into relief by the historical half-light. Mother Mary, a bit more socially aware than her husband, perhaps, what with one brother a doctor and another the Mayor of Brockton, pausing to wipe her hands on the hem of her apron and beam at her tall proud son Joe before having a look into the kitchen to make very sure the girl isn't breaking up too much crockery. P.J., settled into his reading chair, half-hearing the hammed-up music, muses, baleful walrus, on the brashness and pride of youth and what the years coming up will do, inevitably, to all that, especially in the case of this boy, who, the father knows, hurts easily behind the push and cocksureness and feel for enterprise. Mary indulges the boy. Harvard is her idea.

3. Joe

Even inside the frame, the tableau—young Joe P. Kennedy himself, behind the handsomeness, basking in the admiration of his two adoring sisters, needing Sunday to recover that "mischievous smile" a little. The rusty Irish hair is trained in a neat slab to the right by two decades of Mary Hickey Kennedy's tirelessly loving hand. The long, preternaturally composed, rather insolently vulpine face and the extraordinarily pale wolf-cub eyes seem to have opened themselves a little wider to linger on what they saw—without embarrassment, without the need at all to look away—longer than anybody else's: then, done, moving on, hunting further. Classmates remember that about Joe Kennedy first: his wiliness about where exactly a particular effort is going to leave him off. He is a born position player. Kennedy drinks no alcohol, neither does he smoke. Overhearing that a German A classmate was out for freshman football Kennedy introduces himself and arranges, on a tip from P.J, to meet Bob Fisher, touted up already around the City as the one to watch among the upcoming freshmen, and charms and impresses the agreeable future All-American into rooming with him. Joe personally is no better than a mediocre student, yet there still is something about this persuasive, slow-footed Irish kid that sticks with people; once he reaches Harvard he himself knows this and seems to be everywhere around the place merchandising his enthusiasms.

Everybody isn't buying, and this exposes that reflex which, young as Kennedy still is, will again and again jam up his career: Rejection sickens him. Literally makes him sick. Once Kennedy has made it clear that he wants something from somebody, the elusive answer, the half-raised eyebrow, the telephone call unreturned—any gesture that involves being put down at all by people in a position to affect his own, to whom he has revealed enough of himself to make clear his need—the smallest turning-away is . . . excruciating. So many of Joe Kennedy's quirks and characteristics to come—the brusqueness, the brutal slangy frankness, the insatiate ambition, the impulsive empathy with the completely helpless—so much of Kennedy is a complex of strategies to avoid the unbearable turndown. Harvard University before the First World War, still very much the lily pond on which floated easily the children of the Brahmins, must have proved toxic wherever Joe turned.

This was a terrible surprise after the breakthrough years at Boston Latin— also Protestant, also formalized, where Kennedy had done so badly academically that he had to repeat his last year to make up courses but nevertheless had shouldered himself into position to emerge as the unmistakable leader, the hero his mother always assured him he would be: president of the senior class, colonel of the ROTC marching unit, successful pigeon breeder, batting champion of the City of Boston. He was already dependent on a trademark brash charm and a lot of push to secure for himself whatever he wanted. But adolescence recognizes tribal values largely, and civilization begins for Americans at the university.

Furious, upset, convinced that background was frustrating his efforts to make his way at Harvard socially, Joe Kennedy fell back. While evidencing a certain amount of polish—for an Irishman—the need to prevail tended to overcome restraint. When something was important there were no compunctions. His glass always seemed half-empty. While selected early for the more ecumenical Hasty Pudding, and even—if late—for D.U. (a secondary final club), most of Kennedy's operative friendships at Harvard were with other Irish-American undergraduates.

As a child he had always appointed himself the organizer, the sort of kid who demanded to be captain of the baseball team because he owned the bat and ball. At Harvard the system was again and again too entrenched for him to manipulate. When, in 1911, he found himself benchsitting for the second year straight, he did not scruple to make sure "his influential father threatened to withhold a theater franchise from the Harvard team captain unless Joe was allowed to play in the Yale game." It was not merit but rather pull that determined how things came out. Control, the whole secret was obviously control.

And, although he was in the end awarded his letter, one senses the unhappy discovery of the third-generation outsider here. *They* worked things around so as to help one another along, *they* weren't hesitant about doing each other favors; why not use pull and capitalize on advantages? Scruples were a waste of time.

Ambition ate at Joe; ulcers and periodic nervous exhaustion were starting to be a problem. An older friend at Harvard and, subsequently, a rival for Rose Fitzgerald's hand, remembers discussing careers with Joe while he was still a sophomore. "Joe's reaction was that he felt he wanted to be on his own, in a business of greater opportunities and diversification, possibly in the banking field." The organizational drive and initiative were unmistakable—Joe had already put together a semiprofessional baseball team and a tour bus service while still an undergraduate. Given his mentality, it could not have come as too much of a surprise to his classmates that after a year and a half as a Massachusetts bank examiner and aided by a big financial boost from the patient P.J., a founder and onetime president of the bank himself, Joe Kennedy took advantage of a wave of panic mergers that endangered the Columbia Trust Company and, playing the major institutions of the community off against one another, borrowing and maneuvering everywhere, Joe appointed himself America's youngest bank president, at twenty-five.

In September of 1914, after one of those long on-again-off-again courtships that so often suggest, or once suggested, that hesitations are greater between the families involved than between the young people, Joe Kennedy married Honey Fitz's daughter Rose. Remarks survive to suggest that P.J. viewed Boston's sitting mayor and sometime fellow "Strategy Board" member as "insufferable." To Fitzgerald, of course, the Kennedys looked respectable but on balance a little stodgy.

The main point about Joe Kennedy, banker, is not that he was uncommonly young but that Joe Kennedy, the son of Pat the Barkeep, should be in a position to count anybody else's money at all. A wit of the period, accosted by Mayor Fitzgerald and charged that the Irish could simply not seem to get into the banks of Boston, responded with a nice Brahmin dryness, "No, the police are too vigilant."

It was a charge his son-in-law would never have bothered to bring. The mayor—with his handsomely gardened mansion in Dorchester, his three sprightly musical daughters who "came out" one after the next at enormous parties, his weakness for Palm Beach and Newport and the public company of the world-famous yachtsman and tea producer Sir Thomas Lipton—reflected a hopeful social accommodation with the Yankee hegemony. The crafty Joe Kennedy played to his father-in-law's pretensions. He introduced Fitzie to the parents of an acquaintance he had made on his bachelor trip around the Continent, Mr. and Mrs. Samuel Rea—he was the president of the Pennsylvania Railroad. Kennedy invited the whole family to Boston for the Harvard-Princeton game; the Reas arrived in their own private railroad car, the ne plus ultra of the era.

Rose worked hard to placate both styles of men at once. For all her religious preparation at the Sacred Heart Convent and the aristocratic finishing school at Aix-la-Chapelle and her piano studies at the New England Conservatory of Music, she was hardheaded enough to recognize about her husband from the day they fell in love as teenagers that Joe Kennedy was geared up for something serious, major. She took Joe on well prepared to contribute her crooked smile and untiringly updated card catalogs and steadiness and persistence and hard, all-surviving sensibility to rearing the master generation she and Joe were about to attempt. They took a lease on Destiny early.

CHAPTER II

Political Lullabies

My babies were rocked to political lullabies.
Rose Kennedy

1. Fortune-building

Any youngster born late and perhaps a little unexpectedly into a freshly rich American family once it has pushed beyond the primary convulsion—beyond the wet-palm stages, unsleeping nights through which greed and opportunity pop the ears like too much adrenaline—this wide-eyed newcomer will experience quite another father indeed from that avid fortune builder of the start-up years. By the time this final baby is a part of the thing—by the time Teddy is born and scrambles in training pants—by then being included on the sponsorship list for an important charity function, the excitement when the doyen of the New York Financial Community recognizes the father and comes across the first-class dining salon of the *Queen Mary* to snap off a nod and a handshake hello—these rewards have been . . . not so much tarnished, really, as . . . familiar . . .

Nineteen-thirty-two, the year in which his youngest was born, broke a new direction in the sweep of Joseph P. Kennedy's career. In the twenty-year yearbook report he sent his Harvard class representative, Kennedy listed his profession as "capitalist": It was characteristic uppercut humor.

"Capitalist" of itself barely implied what Kennedy had actually been up to: roving the commercial Outback, pulling off, one after the next, a two-decade linked sequence of closely calculated sorties. Each had its immediate as well as long-term purposes; each was set aside or turned over to subordinates soon after the critical turn was executed. Whatever the intended reorganization—raid, refinancing, a well-concealed if immensely profitable sideline as Mafia godfather Frank Costello's stealth partner in the bootlegging cartel, the infatuated flyer at moviemaking in California, the brilliantly orchestrated public-relations campaign while Joe furtively sanitized previously undeclared assets or buried the arms-length killings he brought off through straw partners while plundering successive stock pools . . . By 1932 Joe was primarily legitimate. He was the esteemed Chairman of Somerset Importers, about to become America's primary distributor of Haig and Haig while shouldering himself onto the FDR express as ramrod of Franklin Roosevelt's drive toward the presidency.

And why not? How could anybody expect him to escape the common cravings of the Great Age of the Secondary Carnivores in America? The résumé Kennedy admitted to was improbable enough. Having survived his precocious glamor as the boy president of Boston's little Columbia Trust, Joe Kennedy put in a stint as straw boss of the Fall River Shipyards for Bethlehem Steel during the First World War, ducking out from under the draft throughout World War I by means of a shifting array of exemptions based on his indispensability to the war effort.

Finally, the chance came to acquire a touch with securities by understudying the portly, low-keyed technician Galen Stone. By the middle twenties, Kennedy was well into the parlay that moved him by stages from the ownership of a small chain of New England movie theaters to ultimate control of the producing elements that came together as the behemoth R.K.O. Through even the hanging-garden Hollywood atmosphere of the era the young Kennedy moved with hallmarked bluffness, evoking finally the admiration—sometimes even the affection—of the semiliterate garment district Jews who were soldering together that capricious industry, primitive capitalists whom Joe would later credit with having taught him the value of emphasizing the family.

After twenty-two months that involved Kennedy in everything from a fling at directing films himself to cannibalizing financially his very good friend Gloria Swanson, Joe Kennedy was back East thirty pounds underweight, ulcers and neuritis acting up, perhaps $5 million heavier around the bank account. Back home in the Bronxville mansion Rose Kennedy, busy with her lists and constant travel and her beautifully ordered household, really hadn't a very precise idea of what her husband was doing out West so long. "Business," she presumed serenely— "money" was a word neither parent thought proper to mention much around the house, particularly if the children were eating.

"I had no idea we were worth that much," an older Rose Kennedy is reported to have said, mildly annoyed when the figure $250 million somehow came up. That—money—was "not important," her husband the financier insisted; money was out there, in jungle cities, beyond the well-clipped hedges of Brookline and Bronxville, an unbridgeable remove from where the lawns went down to the sea at Hyannis Port. The older children apprehended that a lot of this fortune of Joe's was coming from sources the parental generation didn't care to talk about. "I was amazed to hear such warm praise from anyone who has done business with my father!" John Kennedy was later quoted as having observed after a banquet in 1960.

No doubt the children seldom met commercial people from "outside." This went beyond a newly rich family's squeamishness before its origins. Throughout those twenty years of piecemeal scavenging inside the great walled institutions of American commerce, Kennedy began to marshal his family life through a staged social withdrawal. After a trial residence in the quiet suburban streets of Brookline, commenting in 1926 to a reporter that his daughters would never have been invited into the debutante clubs, "not that our girls would have joined anyway," Joe Kennedy loaded family and servants into a private railroad car and relocated in Riverdale, New York. From there the expanding family moved on soon to the Pondfield Road house in Bronxville, the family's formal urban residence as long as the smaller children were still involved with private preschooling.

At about this time, starting in the spring of 1926, the family began to rent, then after several years bought, the rambling frame Malcolm Cottage at Hyannis Port. The building was subsequently remodeled to include fifteen rooms, nine baths, a tennis court, and a moving picture theater in the basement. Two and a half oceanside acres rolled down toward a beach and a breakwater. Before long the clapboard house became, to all the Kennedys, their true emotional address: home.

It is important to realize what the Hyannis Port place meant. The village itself, although an appealing enough Cape Cod summer community, certainly did not support anything like the *Social Register* trade of oceanside colonies like Bar Harbor, Maine, or Newport, Rhode Island. The Kennedy family had, in 1922, tried vacationing at Cohasset, a favorite among Boston's patrician families; there, a local historian reports, they were "brutally snubbed," and Joseph Kennedy was himself blackballed for country club membership. At awakening Hyannis Port, back a bit and out of the gusts of Cape Cod land speculation, new money was quietly made welcome. The up-and-coming financier had himself selected the area to meet his evolving purposes: This was to be the playpen, the schoolyard, the seminar room, and battleground. Here he set about to raise the family of children to which he was coming to attach his most profound aspirations.

2. Teddy

That unlikely medley of urgencies, lacks, bromides, considerations, callousness, forced skills, ignorances, stresses, appetites, courage, shrillness—the essential and much-marveled-over Kennedy ethos, in fact—became recognizable during those Playpen Hyannis Port years. Early testimony is particularly revealing. Kirk Lemoyne Billings was an equally feckless friend Jack Kennedy made at Choate while "healing the brief" (putting out the yearbook, that refuge so many congenital misfits at boarding school). The sickly, outrageous JFK teased his big, clumsy, earnest admirer from Pittsburgh mercilessly, and soon the two adolescents were roommates as well as fellow troublemakers in "The Muckers Club," a gob in the eye of the starchy Choate headmaster George St. John.

Billings would recount to me his introduction to the Kennedy household during the Christmas break of 1933. His Pittsburgh doctor father had already died, the family money had evaporated, and his mother was reorienting herself, preoccupied with making new friends. Lem would develop into a kind of gentle, tall, gossipy, unmarried schoolmaster of a man, a de facto uncle to several generations of Kennedys, undisguisedly gay, with an endearing ungainliness and a mood that passed unaware from stiff to forlorn, broke back from tears into a characteristic excitement giggle.

At breakfast a few days before the 1960 inauguration, Evelyn Lincoln reports, the president-elect wondered of Billings, a White House fixture, "whether he wasn't thrilled to be having breakfast with the President of the United States." Billings replied that he had no feeling about it. Having established that Mrs. Lincoln was "overjoyed" to be working for the president, John Kennedy told him, "with a twinkle in his eye," that it was "a privilege for you to be eating with the president." Billings, who had eaten breakfast with John Kennedy for more than twenty-eight years, is not on record as convinced.

As he would later describe it, the scene that Billings encountered his first Christmas at Hyannis Port, in 1932, suggests the backdrop for an early-Victorian drama: lowering skies, the boom of the Atlantic winter tides heaving across the beaches beneath the high porch windows, the saturnine, intimidating figure of Joseph P. Kennedy, who often scheduled a stay-over when the older children, the Golden Three—Joe Jr., Jack, and Kathleen— were in residence, briefly.

The house itself Billings remembers as unadorned but sensible, full of "summer furniture" with lots of the warm scuffed kicked-around, left- wherever-the-game-ended feeling chairs and sofas and sideboards take on when a lot of children are swarming back and forth across the public areas. Each had to battle for position—no child came back to an established room of his or her own, so each time the swarm descended on Hyannis Port there was a scramble to grab off the better accommodations. Especially when there were guests, it would be the good-natured last-born, Teddy, who was most likely to find himself sleeping in the bathtub. Status—at some level, member- ship in the family—remained provisional, constantly readjusted according to the momentary parental assessment of each anxious child's most recent performance.

The youngest of the children, Teddy, had arrived the previous spring, on George Washington's birthday, as he would regularly remind acquaintances. Ted had been conceived during one of the increasingly rare marital interludes that punctuated Joe's extended, semi-public affair with Gloria Swanson, the soigné queen of Tinsel Town and Joe's sometime business partner. Pundits have pointed out that, even by his siblings, pudgy little Teddy was regarded as something of an afterthought. Unlike the other boys, who commemorated distinguished family predecessors, Ted got his name from Edward Moore, a flunky Joe acquired from Honey Fitz; Moore took on the custodial role with the youngest children when the parents were out of town on holidays or otherwise too busy. Ed Moore would get a lot of credit from Joe for having talked Rose around during the Swanson embarrassment.

Little Teddy had appeared at a point in Rose's life when she was frank to admit that she was tired of reading bedtime stories to one infant after another. Father Joe, if anybody, would show up once in a while and read the funny papers to Teddy.

As with the earlier children, Rose had insisted that she avoid serious dis- comfort, and retained the controversial obstetrician Dr. Frederick Good, who specialized in "painless" if on occasion precarious deliveries. Rose had made up her mind not to "lose her figure," which meant a lot of ether and in most cases a high-forceps delivery, a procedure which may well have produced Jack Kennedy's truncated leg and lead to a lifetime of back problems. Family insiders remember that Teddy's delivery was very slow and dragged-out and that it ripped up Rose, who was forty-two, so badly that she would remain in the hospital for close to a month. Ted was her last baby. His appearance had been extremely trying, and there was an unvoiced suspicion around the household that he was one more than the family really needed. Little Teddy would do well to justify himself.

Joe Kennedy—Kennedy's life—was in something of a doldrum just then: With his uncanny sense of the wind the financier had smelled presidency on Franklin Roosevelt by the middle 1920s, waited, then selected exactly the breaking moment to elbow past the disapproving reformers around FDR and flummox the 1932 convention fight by bluffing the decisive, final-second support out of the quixotic old press tyrant William Randolph Hearst, one of Joe Kennedy's mentors. A display of legerdemain as sure-handed as that persuaded FDR to let Kennedy handle tactics throughout the campaign itself. Kennedy took hold of his job, as always, from the top down: He managed Roosevelt's speechmaking tours, dealt knowledgeably with everything from briefings by local Democratic chieftains to press conferences.

Roosevelt received his mandate; Joe Kennedy, anticipating his political reward, fell into the first of a decade of increasingly depressed vigils. As long as Roosevelt stayed alive, the president remained one of the few men whose guile and coquettish force of personality were more than Kennedy could counter. An awkwardly inquiring telegram of congratulation to the newly inaugurated president brought a return telegram of thanks that ended with Roosevelt's heartbreakingly vague hope that Kennedy "be sure to let us know when you are going through Washington and stop off and see us."

Desultorily, Kennedy returned to business. He participated in a pool of Libby-Owens-Ford stock—the kind of manipulation he himself was shortly to prosecute as founding chairman of the Securities and Exchange Commission. Tipped off that Prohibition was about to end, Kennedy lured the ever-susceptible Jimmy Roosevelt to Scotland as bait for the New England distribution franchise on Dewars and Haig and Haig scotch and Gordon's Gin. Even before Prohibition was repealed Kennedy's warehouses at Somerset Importers were piled to the rafters with liquor imported under special license for "medicinal" purposes.

Fortune-building was not enough. Billings had discovered the senior Kennedy to be preoccupied, not awfully interested in this new friend his sickly and disgruntled second son dragged home for the holidays, rooted and unmoving in a chair to mend a recently broken leg, which Joe was able to prevent his doctor from setting in a cast by stating very firmly that he was never going to let it stir throughout the healing months. Joe rarely listened to doctors.

There was an established atmosphere about the household. Everything was in place: boats in various categories and sailors with the best references to teach the children how to sail, the basement studio-type screening room, the tennis court, horses, the power launch . . .

Visitors as such were rather unusual, but the arrival and departure of cronies was constant—the father's cronies, lesser men like Joe Timilty, the Boston commissioner of police, or Phil Riesman, or the ever-present Edward Moore, that smooth-worn, old-fashioned amanuensis who ran the business errands and quietly indulged the younger ones and was even permitted to pull the father's leg once in a while because he knew exactly when enough was enough. Joe and Rose Kennedy eased away from regular community involvements, said no politely to most dinner-party invitations, rode secluded bridle paths, played the very-nearly-daily game of golf entirely for the exercise, then dressed quickly and slipped away from the Wianno Club before people realized they were around. Playmates, other children, visited *them*. "Years ago we decided," Rose Kennedy remarked in the thirties, "that our children were going to be our best friends and that we never could see too much of them. Since we couldn't do both, it was better to bring up our family than go out to dinners." In that all the children were shipped off to boarding school from first grade on and the privately disillusioned Rose preferred to spend much of her year plying the Atlantic on the *Queen*s and Joe was gone most of the time, such proclamations deserve a cautious second look.

As early as this there was a well-thought-through way to do most things. Kennedy's financial concerns were already tightly enough organized to permit him to see after most of the day-to-day administering by telephone. He was routinely absent for long stretches—he maintained several apartments in Manhattan, where he entertained generations of lady friends, the Palm Beach mansion on North Ocean Drive, a pied-à-terre in Chicago and—over the years—favorite getaway destinations from the Cal-Neva, on Lake Tahoe, to the Cote d'Azur. Whenever Joe was home, quiet around the house was enforced. The young were alerted whenever the father was asleep. An awareness that seven-fifteen was the precise time the father liked to begin his meal in the evening was wired so deep into the Kennedy circuitry that thirty years later a gang of very famous grown children, some with almost-grown children of their own, would rush on impulse into the dining room at the Palm Beach estate, breathless not to disappoint the glassy-eyed paralytic in the wheelchair at the head of the table.

About the time of Billings's Christmas visit the rites of Kennedy conversation were barely emerging; the father was establishing the protocol of table talk. "Mr. Kennedy is one of the most brilliant men I've ever met," Sargent Shriver later explained to a reporter curious about those educative years. "He told me that at dinner every night there were always subjects of discussion, and it might start with something about a new Supreme Court decision about censorship that Justice William Douglas had written—and Douglas might be there at dinner to talk about it, or the situation in the Middle East and what kind of guy Ibn Saud was, as explained perhaps by Jim Landis who might have just returned from there, or else a book somebody had just read. And every child would be expected to give his opinion on everything."

Jack Kennedy's memory differed. "At first, in the early years, they were mostly monologues by my father . . . well, not exactly monologues. But we didn't have opinions in those days. Later, the discussions included us more, but mostly about personalities, not debates on issues and things." The truth was, friends at table during the formative decades insist, that after the children reached adolescence and moved, one by one, to the adult table, there was a long, long incubation period of watchful listening until enough of a background sense of political affairs filled in to permit a child to venture an opinion unselfconsciously.

Unimportant friends from outside were not much moved—or invited— to participate, nor were the younger girls; Rose Kennedy would normally remain, sweetly, still. The Golden Three were quieried about world events and invited to contribute, wittily if possible. They were permitted to sit at the adults' table; the younger children moved up in time. The financier himself liked to force the argument personally sometimes, push the older boys vigorously to come up with documentation for whatever facts they used, ambush their lines of reasoning from surprise premises to see how supple they were in repelling the unexpected, ask several of the children to look up the same information and play off their memories one against the other. Perhaps it wasn't surprising that most of the children wound up with ulcers.

"There was always a tremendous excitement around when the old man was in the house," a survivor remembers. During the extended early absences of the father, the lulls, Rose Kennedy would keep her medical-history card catalog up to date, see after the Catholicism, and instruct the younger children unknowingly in that peculiar sort of elongated death-row elocution—neither Cape Cod nor Long Island Society, really, nor East Boston nor Patrician Cambridge and certainly not Harvard—which became the extremely infectious dialect of all the Kennedys except Joe. Whenever she was in residence Rose was the drill mistress of civilized manners.

That introductory visit, trapped in a stuck shower in one of those jammed-in little Hyannis Port bathrooms, Billings scalded himself terribly. What remained most poignant to Billings about the visit was his remembrance of the troupe that Mrs. Kennedy led dutifully past his hospital bed every afternoon as soon as his bandages were changed: Joe Jr.—a bit over-earnest about himself just then, conscious of the demands of eldest brother manhood—through the line of hushed compassionate small girls all the way down to pudgy little Teddy, scowling out from beneath his baby helmet of shiny bobbed hair. As family snapshots will, this one is beginning to yellow, noticeably.

Whenever he got a chance throughout the years of intermittent government service coming up, Joseph P. Kennedy took pains personally to drag a footing or two of familial principle into place. His messages were simple and extremely complicated: Win; worry about how or why secondarily. Throughout decades of regattas the boys would attempt to ignore the financier leaning over the fantail of his cruiser, "The Honey Fitz," alternately exhorting and chewing them out at the top of his voice whenever they appeared to lag or neglected some corner-cutting maneuver.

The bromides were incessant. "If it's on your plate, eat it." (Ted never forgot that.) Control, never depend for anything on the loyalty or good intentions of people better placed than you. You have a wholly legitimate claim to absolute loyalty, unstinted performance, complete self-sacrifice from menials—superheat their atmosphere to make them fervid with the ultimate importance of what you are doing for yourself. Afterward, you owe them very little. They were being paid.

The boys were introduced early to the presumptions of the predatory. There is no truly authentic counterclaim to what you are after except your own unanswerable insistence. Take whatever you want and deal with the consequences later—attractive women are there for you. The financier did not scruple to bring his heartthrob of the moment—actress, secretary, whatever—home for the weekend to meet the older boys. Rose would have to cope.

The mentality Joe was after, becoming a Kennedy, remained first and foremost. Never let your children or the world at large discover the intensity of your involvement. Mask weaknesses like your love of the spongier passages of nineteenth-century keyboard music or the atonement implicit in your charities. Conceal your illimitable hopes and incapacitating seizures of dread. Better rough than lachrymose. Nothing here the Corleones wouldn't rubber-stamp.

Finally—the operative principle—get the details straight. "The Kennedys never shit themselves," a cool-eyed legislative assistant, who worked a little while for Ted, had told me early. "There are no daydreams." This is a reflex with a pedigree. "Carroll, that's a crazy deal," a member of the family over-heard Joe Kennedy tell his close friend Carroll Rosenbloom, the mobbed-up owner of the Baltimore Colts, on reviewing one business proposition. "Crazy. You know, I used to eat guys like you for breakfast . . ." This became a Kennedy birthright, too: the ability to bring an opinion up all the way from the floor and stun somebody with it; that, and inherited jawbone enough to shake off the counterblow.

For all the financier's evasiveness, worry about his children's destiny put him into a sanitarium as early as the twenties. They remained his secret obses-sion, his shot at immortality. Close to the beginning of his New Deal jour-nal, Franklin Roosevelt's carbuncular Secretary of the Interior Harold Ickes notes Roosevelt's selection of Joseph P. Kennedy, "a stock market plunger," to the founding chairmanship of the Securities and Exchange Commission. "Apparently he is going on the assumption that Kennedy would now like to make a name for himself for the sake of his family, but I have never known many of these cases to work out as expected."

Kennedy served briefly as head of the Maritime Commission. Years later, when Kennedy's tenure as Ambassador to Great Britain (1937–1940) approached its calamitous end, Ickes mentions a Washington press interview at which "Joe Kennedy unexpectedly came in and planted himself down. He cheerfully entered into the conversation and before long he was saying that Germany would win, that everything in France and England would go to hell, and that his one interest was in saving his money for his children."

Government figures remembered statements like his much-quoted claim, deep in the early Depression, that he would gladly give up half his fortune to keep the other half for his family, or his open efforts, late in the Lend-Lease period, to speculate against the collapsing Czech currency and to propagandize against American involvement at a time he was bemoaning to acquaintances that the struggle coming up would cost him "one of my children." He advocated a deal with Hitler as late as 1943. In time of larger peril Kennedy's thinking was easily ignored in the hurry to condemn him for "dynastic" motives. As soon as people pushed in too close he liked to throw them off with bombast or a lot of droll caricature profanity or leg-pull cyni-cism. Always, better a low motive than a phony one.

Most parents love their offspring, but there were compulsions here. "If Teddy came in second in a sailing race," Sargent Shriver recalls, "Mr. Ken-nedy would say, 'What do you mean coming in second? What was wrong?

If the sail was too loose, tighten it; if the hull isn't good enough, change it, but the next time come in first.'" Friends of the Kennedys' when Jack was a senator remember the old man appearing unexpectedly and throwing his sons out of porch chairs, admonishing them to "go do something." "What is the big idea of sitting around up here on the Cape when you should be at your job in Washington?" his father demanded of an exhausted Bob Kennedy when he caught him taking an extra day off after three unbroken months spent milling through labor records after evidence for Senator McClellan's Rackets Committee.

A friend of the children's can still summon up "those eyes, that's how he did his disciplining, with that glare, those eyes." During the early years Mother Rose concerned herself with whatever minor nagging and reprimanding was needed, the pulling and paddling; the knitting of an eyebrow, the implication of disappointment, of displeasure from the father—these were usually enough.

The financier suffered outside influence unhappily. Lecturers of the day at the Kennedy dinner table had a way of being—like the Douglases and Landises whom Shriver mentioned—earlier Kennedy discoveries, ex-proteges, bearers of the family imprimatur. Relations fell off with grandfather Fitzgerald. Once the family celebrity, during later years the infatuated old Fitzie would arrive to visit his adoring grandchildren, peep through the porch windows cagily, shuffle off quietly for a while if he happened to spot his icy son-in-law.

However oversolicitous or overbearing, Kennedy's children loved him. They feared him and they loved him. When their dysfunctional sister, Rosemary, disappeared in 1941 after a botched lobotomy, not a word was said. Once he was gone the children would remember the Joe Kennedy unpretentious enough to meet a new employee in his bathrobe and stocking feet while eating Corn Flakes out of a bowl as he leaned against his apartment kitchen counter, the father beaming in triumph at another of the family celebrations as he stirred the daiquiris—one per adult child—ritually, with his extended little finger. The archives of family legend are full of tales of the father's forbearance as still another borrowed Kennedy automobile came home behind a tow truck, mashed up by one more friend of the children. He infiltrated his children's childhoods—they lived by his charm and his largesse—but at the same time he put them out into the widest of privileged worlds, to travel, to experience, to disagree. People closest to Kennedy say that he probably despised stupidity more than any other shortcoming, yet whenever a child of his showed pathetically poor judgment in public he ran on impulse to his externally reassuring father. "You lucky mush!" Kennedy exploded at JFK after the Bay of Pigs, pointing out how much worse it might actually have been had it come later in his presidency. Teddy especially depended on his father's ultimate forbearance.

"If I had slipped and fallen flat on the floor, [my father] would have said, 'The graceful way you picked yourself up was terrific,'" Jack Kennedy told Ted Sorensen just after the lackluster second Kennedy-Nixon debate. "Mr. Kennedy had a great generosity about the average human failure made in the course of a great effort," his son-in-law and business understudy, Stephen Smith, remarked to me in fond recollection. "It was one of the great pleasures I discovered . . ."

His credentials for forgiveness hung out like a psychiatrist's waiting-room diploma, Joseph Kennedy assumed his patriarchal right to become a party to his children's decisions, beguile them into confessing their preferences and mistakes and impulsively protected secrets. "The father liked to get together with the elder boys, and he'd draw the details of their peccadilloes out of them, and they'd all laugh," one early friend recalls; another comments privately, "the old man kept track of everything they did. If he sensed something, if he had some kind of clue but not the story complete, he'd pretend he knew all about it and more often than not he'd worm the rest out of them fast enough." Empathize with them, and compete with them.

"I fixed it so that any of my children, financially speaking, could look me in the eye and tell me to go to hell," a Kennedy legend has the father telling Bernard Baruch as he set up those original million-dollar trust funds in 1929; the legend neglects to indicate how the funds were themselves administered through the business offices of Joseph P. Kennedy, Inc. There, as the children's checks cleared, flurry by flurry, Kennedy educated his guesswork. Meanwhile, taxes eroded principal.

"My children won't be able to live up to the scale I do, that's for sure," he told a crony just before his stroke. This much the old man knows for certain—maybe too well. Wealth, which Kennedy as a young man had intended to bestow as a benediction, had become mostly a worry to him finally, a faltering control technique.

"Mr. Kennedy was very understanding," insists the ubiquitous Joey Gargan, the orphaned cousin, Ted's age, who finished growing up as a ward of the Kennedy family and would provide me with perhaps my most trenchant insights into Teddy's formulative years. "I'd say he's probably, outside of my own father, the most understanding man I know. He never second-guessed you, and he always gave the responsibility right back to the person it belonged to—you."

"My father always made it a point to be identified with his children, involved in their lives at any particularly important moment," Edward Kennedy himself would recall to me; Kennedy puff literature is murmurous with rumors of transcontinental train rides undergone for the sake of a lacrosse match or the quiet, fatherly word or two secured as expertly as a guy wire at precisely the point an emerging personality begins to go awry. Whatever has been published suggests the tone of the cache of unpublished letters Kennedy wrote over many many years to all his children: painstaking, straight, shrewd, and inspirational. Whereas Rose would write one letter periodically to all her children and then mail carbons around, Joe wrote long, searching letters to each of them, regularly.

To this most central and revealing of investments, his family, the one by which he announced himself willing to be judged, Joseph P. Kennedy brought the sharp appraising eye that made him his legend as a speculator: No child of his ever saw the father flustered into uncertainty or panic or sensed his belief that any mistake was final, damning, or—dumb symbol—beat the old man at a sport.

"I think there was a real sense of direction coming from him," Kennedy brother-in-law Steve Smith ruminated aloud—fine-boned little Knight of the Bath, fiduciary understudy of Joseph. P. Kennedy, tilted back in his chair, gray-shot hair overgrown to a razor-cut bob in back, appearing to search his recollection before the plate-glass prow of his corner office beyond the labyrinth of bookkeepers behind door 3012 in the Pan American Building.

"In my book he is the greatest practicing psychologist. He had a focus all the time, was way ahead of things, even in his hopes, and he had the judgment to come off it while there was still some choice. He had a talent for judging horses. When there was a shortcoming, he would try to protect it in what was then asked . . . This business of talking something over with him, before you decided . . . there was always something in his advice—not that you did it. It was . . . afterwards, when you had decided, he was the . . . the enforcer, because after that, when you started to equivocate, be unsure, there is the push . . ."

Until, in the end, after the stroke and the stubborn failed efforts at partial recovery, the fact that he lived still remained enough: Underlings flew him bundled beneath his coverlets in his special wheelchair to sit in on business meetings at the Merchandise Mart; Jack, that last year, and Bobby conferred across his lap robe in the back of limousines, below the hairless mummified profile pointed toward the chauffeur's neckline; unfamiliar guests at lunch in Hyannis Port found the wheelchair at the table, the nurse in attendance to spoon-feed the unspeaking patron of the house. "You'll see a tremendous change in Teddy when his father dies," Joey Gargan muttered to me again and again after drink after drink. What the father is, what the father has meant . . . Clear.

3. The Superior Older Brothers

The adjective "strapping" comes so often when people summon up or write about Joseph P. Kennedy Jr., the eldest of Rose's brood, that it begins to look custom-tailored. Joe Junior was unmistakably the head-boy type: the kind of long-muscled good-humored locker-room-Irish kid with powerful legs cobbled prematurely with heavy black hairs along the front of his thighs, foot up on the bench and still in his jockstrap as he takes pains to stretch his fetid T-shirt over his hip pads so that it will be at least soggy-dry before the scrimmage tomorrow. Railing out a happy insult or two at the quarterback while underclassmen up and down the benches file by quietly, reverentially, towels dangling, en route to the showers. Already he resembled his absolutely adoring father: perhaps a touch huskier but every bit as much of the bluff-ness and the unexamined belief in himself: the heir primary, the handmade prototype.

"Bring up the oldest the way you want them all to go," Mrs. Joseph P. Kennedy suggested to a television interviewer a great many years later: Joe Jr. was oldest. The nuns who taught him as a child remember him as "a very wholesome boy who . . . couldn't pass a hat without squashing it in or leave an unprotected shin unkicked." Others found him hot-tempered, a bit intol-erant, and willing to go to great pains to help almost anybody, and especially his brothers and sisters.

"He had a pugnacious personality," John F. Kennedy was to remember. "Later on it smoothed out, but it was a problem in my boyhood." "It wasn't their father they were afraid of," a family friend has said of the brothers and sisters, "it was Joe Jr. The real reason they didn't drink or sneak a smoke here and there was that they were afraid young Joe would find out and beat the hell out of them." Jack remembered evenings his older brother would register his annoyance by banging his head against a wall for a while.

Lem Billings, durable omnipresent Billings, remembered Joe Jr. as the archetype who "did terribly well, won the Saint Andrews prize for being the best athlete-scholar at Choate during those years"; Jack, eighteen months younger, remained "quite unhealthy," kept a messy room, spelled poorly, and had a way of answering the teachers back they "didn't appreciate." There were the unavoidable concussions; Robert, a boy child marooned chronologically among the sisters, hid and held his ears whenever his two older brothers fought their problems out. It was a poorly made match: Closed in his room with books and friends, visited occasionally while he recovered from a life-long series of illnesses that ran from scarlet fever to colitis to a chronic adrenal insufficiency, Jack Kennedy evolved little by little into the beguiling and skeptical young politician the world was to discover late in the forties.

In the ideological line of succession, Jack was, to some extent, bypassed: When Bobby learned his scrambling, gouging game of touch football, he learned it directly from Joe Jr. For all the gratitude and express affection Jack Kennedy felt for his older brother, he obviously viewed him as perhaps too good an example, a parental stand-in. Jack, hoping to slide out from under, followed Lem Billings to Princeton; this feeble initial escape attempt aborted when another of those suspicious malaises of his, jaundice this time, wiped his first semester out by Christmas; he took the spring off and followed Joe to Harvard during the fall of 1936.

Kennedy procedure at Harvard was established: Fight through to reasonably good grades despite what appears to be a generic slowness to come of academic age, break your heart going out for teams you don't really have the speed or coordination to make, hobnob with important athletes, fix with a disapproving post-proletarian eye the liberal associations and the whole final-club life and cotillion-oriented post-prep scene. His last two years in particular—Joe Jr. in graduate school by then and the father out of the way in London—Jack Kennedy at Harvard began to discover himself in his slowly improving work (became, as his father said, "The only one of us who really liked the place").

The honors thesis Jack Kennedy came up with his final year at Harvard, a kid-glove autopsy of the bloated hopes and futile appeasements of Baldwin and Chamberlain, got fuller treatment as the precocious bestseller *Why England Slept*. Joe Kennedy filled the basement at Hyannis Port with copies. Kennedy regular Arthur Krock helped with the title and publishing contacts; Henry Luce, Joe's good friend, wrote the introduction. "You would be surprised how a book that really makes the grade with high-class people stands you in good stead for years to come," the Ambassador wrote his son enthusiastically. "I remember that in the report you are asked to make after twenty-five years to the Committee at Harvard, one of the questions is 'What books have you written?' and there is no doubt you will have done yourself a great deal of good."

By mid-March of 1938, when he and all his sisters and Bobby arrived in London to take up residence at the Grosvenor Square Embassy, Teddy Kennedy at six is already a fat little study inside his pouchy camel's-hair coat, dubbed "Biscuits and Muffins" and "Fat Stuff" by his adoring—and condescending—siblings, especially the sisters. At six he keeps his socks pulled up carefully to where his short pants end, the band of the Buster Brown mushroom pod of a hat he drags everyplace with him tugged down to where those protrusive question-mark ears of his begin. For all the spatter of freckles the elements of the face—the broad-skull widow's peak hairline, the cave of the eyes, the narrow lips inclined to wrinkle together thoughtfully, to push out in repose, the promise of meatiness at the hinges of the jaw—the look of the man is ordained.

Backed up to an elephant beneath twelve-year-old Robert's mild fond eye, young Ted assists with the honorific opening of the London Children's Zoo, waits with his Brownie to snap the Guard at Buckingham Palace when it finally changes . . . The feel of the embassy itself arouses him, the lorries and pigeons of Grosvenor Square outside, the vistas of marble and walnut, the niches with busts, paintings, six floors and thirty-six rooms: the family's preposterous own hotel.

"His first day in the elegant six-story embassy he commandeered the servants," a journalist of the period writes, and "with whoops and imperious orders" ran "elevator loads of them between cellar and attic, playing what he calls 'department store.'" Whoops and imperious orders, charged with a mad native gusto struggling to find an acceptable place to explode.

The journalist, subjecting Mother Rose to a gentlemanly interview, picks up a final clue. "Every now and then Teddy popped in to report on a very serious illness in the family. One of his goldfish had been found gasping on its back and he had it in a bathtub of cold water, trying desperately to revive it."

Desperately, already: his early life, a keen and sometimes panic-stricken sense of who he is, of obligation to family, to people, to life. "Can I hit Romney over the head?" the six-year-old asks his surprised governess one afternoon when he gets home from a session at London's Gibbs School. "Every day when I come to school," the child explains earnestly, "Romney hits me in the stomach. Mother says I must be polite to everyone and I mustn't do anything that would reflect on us; so I can't hit him back because my father's the ambassador . . ."

The historical instant, a moment of puissance when "Jolly Joe Kennedy," as the British tabloids dubbed him immediately, could refer to the Queen of England as a "cute trick" and amuse her—that level of public indulgence sputtered out in rancor and counterclaims that broke into the media as early as November of 1940.

"There is a time for Kennedys . . ." a death-haunted overworked Edward Kennedy was to sigh to a reporter in a darkened airplane nearly thirty years later, weeks before his car bounced off the humpbacked bridge at Chappaquiddick Island. In 1940 the tide for Kennedys went out, and with the family's communal apprehension of this there ensued a period of repair, of bracing for that mountain of backwash they sensed in their Druidic hearts was certain to break across their lives. Joseph P. Kennedy, after months of flouting the Roosevelt State Department and pushing openly for an accommodation with Hitler, having already sent the disgusted president his written resignation, sat still for a shirtsleeve interview in his suite at Boston's Ritz-Carlton in which he scattergunned comments ranging from his opinion that "Democracy is finished in England" to "Our Congressmen are dopes who don't understand the war or our relationship to it . . ." Suspect as an appeaser anyhow, damned already by the emergent liberal conclave as an isolationist, Joe Kennedy had delivered his own freestyle political eulogy.

The years of exuberant international nose-rubbing ended: sessions at the London School of Economics during which Harold Laski himself explained Fabianism; Joe Jr., entranced and naive, sightseeing around a sullen Moscow still bleeding in the aftermath of the NKVD purges; balls in Belgravia; the stripling John Kennedy ushered through the lines of the German Army and into besieged 1938 Prague by unhappy State Department officials as he presumed to make his own "fact finding" tour; afternoons at Lady Cunard's. Before long the Ambassador in his own limousine would be blasted out of the street by a German bomb (the financier had already started to sleep in a rented country house, away from the Blitz, to the disgust of the English).

Teddy, seven, informed the Roman press at the coronation of Pius XII that he "wasn't frightened at all." The new pope was long since a friend of the family's; Joe had conducted him around America while Pacelli was still the Papal Secretary of State. "He [the Holy Father] patted my head and told me I was a smart little fellow," little Teddy reported. "He gave me the first rosary beads from the table before he gave my sister any." It was a final gust of supercelebrity for the Kennedys; by then there was no talk whatsoever of Joseph P. Kennedy for president.

Once the war started Joe attempted to push his services on the overtaxed

Roosevelt. Roosevelt, who had months earlier had come to agree with his advisers that Kennedy was a man "whose hand you always had to hold," feared Kennedy's outright political opposition. He stalled off the financier by alternately pretending he hadn't received Kennedy's offer, then asking Massachusetts Congressman John McCormack why he hadn't, then languorously tendering Kennedy a nebulous situation working with the shipbuilding industry in which he would have surely been immobilized by the wartime Lilliputia of bureaucrats. The wily Roosevelt had vamped Kennedy one final time, and he had embittered him. The parvenu newsreel was over.

The war heated up, the deeply dreaded war, and with the war the damages came. All three of the older boys went, even Bobby, adenoidal post-teenager frustratedly chipping paint in the Panama Canal Zone. Late in the fighting, as the Ambassador had dreaded, Joseph P. Kennedy Jr. was blown to pieces approaching the English Channel in his dynamite-packed PB4Y Liberator just short of the Belgian submarine pens. The worst happened, the most feared, most unimaginable worst. Under heavy pressure from the strategically minded Ambassador, who foresaw political advantages coming out of a heroic war record, young Joe had volunteered to return to England for a last, potentially suicidal flight after his allotment of sorties for the Navy was over. The renown the Ambassador had generated in the media over Jack's *PT-109* heroism had rattled his older brother, and Joe Jr.'s final letter from England clearly amounted to an attempt to mollify his father after a painful tiff. It wouldn't matter.

"His worldly success," Jack Kennedy wrote privately of his hero brother from his hospital bed in the Chelsea Naval Hospital, "was so assured and inevitable that his death seems to have cut into the natural order of things." Two priests came to inform the father: His face when he returned to his family was drained, and it was all he could do to drag himself up the stairs to his room, and close his door, and lock it behind himself.

It is a shock so deep Kennedy will never come back, really. As the lull deepens he remembers—the plunger in his carpet slippers at three in the morning riffling through his personal telephone book of debentures and municipals, the essence and distillation of everything so far: Those closeted months of short-selling over a telephone in a hotel room, ulcers, the decades of secret trafficking with top-drawer hoodlums, the whiskey-dealing and ice-blooded boardroom amputation of another man's career with an offhand "Didn't you know, Ed? You're washed up, you're through," the era of top hats and again finding himself snubbed by the Everglades Club, punching Harry Bridges in the mouth while maritime commissioner, interrupting Franklin Roosevelt with "Listen, boy, if we do that we'll land in the outhouse where we belong," the affection of a string of movie queens.

When Arthur Krock indicated his amazement that Hugo Black would accept a Supreme Court appointment without mentioning his past Ku Klux Klan membership, Kennedy responded, and later reported to a Franklin Roosevelt "collapsed in laughter," "If Marlene Dietrich asked you to make love to her, would you tell her you weren't much good at making love?" Time has hollowed the laughter out utterly now for the aging ambassador-defunct. Private losses mount: his Protestant son-in-law, "Billy," the Duke of Harting-ton, dead two weeks after his son and—in 1948, just as the religious rips in the fabric of the family had begun to heal—the body of the beloved Kathleen, the ebullient "Kick," she of the Golden Three, brought down on a peasant's cart after her private plane crashed in the mountains of the Ardeche, flying down from England to meet her father for a Riviera holiday.

Hanging on, the seizures of apprehension closer and closer together as he aged more quickly now, Joseph Kennedy's attention turned from collecting wealth to securing wealth: He sold Somerset Importers, became as liquid as he could, and conducted the disposition of much of his fortune into real estate. Property values in New York City especially were depressed in the immediate postwar capital shortage. Kennedy founded Park Agency, Inc., dabbled in oil and Coca-Cola franchises and—with arms-length underworld partners—casino gambling, and soon acquired the Merchandise Mart in Chicago with an insurance company's money, through which he augmented his fortune enormously in the onsetting real-estate boom.

It lacked the exhilaration, the joy of studied rampage. Ennui was setting in. "I have to [see after the fortune]," the father would tell a reporter in 1960. "Business doesn't interest me either, that's for sure. I don't give a tinker's damn about it."

4. Last-born

Little Edward Kennedy, back in the United States by 1940 to go to grade school, felt silence closing around him after the din of parental ambition gratified that had been ringing through his seven-year lifetime. In that the parents were not available much of the time, Rose used her connections to the Church to wangle a slot for the baby of the family in a Benedictine boarding school, Portsmouth Priory, which otherwise accepted thirteen-year-olds to start in the eighth grade. Bobby was enrolled there. Teddy reportedly "seemed young and immature," according to one of the priests who taught him, "and didn't get along particularly well." Kennedy's grades were poor, and remained poor as he was dragged through a total of nine schools before he turned fourteen and was enrolled in Milton Academy, again tracking Bobby. Among Robert Kennedy's childhood letters are notes to Rose complaining that he and Ted had no place to go over the Thanksgiving holidays. Joe McGinnis quotes Ted—"Fat Ted," as he jokingly called himself—as alleging that "Bobby was the one who used to call me up to see how I was getting along. On the two or three weekends I was able to get off from the boarding school outside Boston, he'd spend the weekend with me. I'll never forget how we used to go to the big, empty house at Cape Cod—just the two of us, rattling around all alone. Bobby was in charge, taking care of me, and always making sure I had something to do."

In 1941 the Kennedys had sold the mansion in Bronxville—vestigial memento to newly married hopes of acceptance among the "nice people" of Eastern Seaboard Society—and took up residence for the rest of their lives in beach resorts. Even in Hyannis Port the children were expected to retain a measure of that tentativeness children can't help but feel toward a residence their family has landed in for the season. Nobody in the younger generation was permitted to lay claim to any particular bedroom of his or her own, so each time they converged on the Cape they erupted into squabbling over who would get the most desirable quarters. Here, too, they were to consider themselves *in* the community but not of it, privileged vagrants. Joe and Rose each maintained suites of their own in opposite ends of this sprawling Colonial country seat on the beach, as well as separate apartments in Manhattan. As the older boys came into adolescence, the household assumed something of a nomadic quality, elements of the sheikdoms maintained by Howard Hughes or William Randolph Hearst: the long separations that the rich so often take from one another to refresh their feelings.

Employees, squeezing for favor, became "Kennedy oriented," pecking tidbits about the children out of newspapers and magazines to feed the patriarch during the innumerable drives back from airports and docks and railroad stations. There were already signs of that subtle identity-confusion which was to make all three of Kennedy's surviving sons at once stronger and more vulnerable than their generational contemporaries, more precocious and later to mature, more realistic within their ranges but blinder at the margins, freer to choose but less able to hazard independent choices. The risks of destiny were set.

Little Teddy, the baby, budded to his sense of himself during the lull. The world as he experienced it must have seemed particularly final, finished—

fewer of the father's long, long empire-building absences, tensions of the sort that the older brothers had known at the same stage of their own coming-to-awareness, then the overstimulation of the return of the financier worn by the exhaustions of the avid months, sick sometimes, temper ragged sometimes. None of the New Deal ideological soul-searching, the anguish of waiting on the guileful imperious Rooseveltian mood. Rest, at last, and, if not the ultimate celebrity, position of a sort. Cholly Knickerbocker, at least, lists Joseph P. Kennedy, along with Joe DiMaggio and Louella Parsons, as part of America's "Aristocracy of Achievement."

It remained a problem that before he started at Milton Academy Edward Kennedy had attended nine different private schools as his repatriated parents settled and resettled. He tended to travel light emotionally. He himself would credit this constant uprooting with developing his huge gregariousness and constant willingness—need, even—to meet people and win them over quickly. His private sense lingered of himself as a child constantly planted and transplanted. He refused to blame his parents. Portsmouth Priory? "It was too late to enter me anywhere else," Kennedy reminisced once to me, "and my mother didn't have a permanent place to live, so she sent me to Bobby's school, which began with the seventh grade. I went to classes, slept in my own little cubicle, learned something about geography, and was completely mystified by Latin."

Shortly before he passed away, Kennedy himself memorialized this hellhole administered by monks, in which his only friend was a turtle, which died. The child buried it, solemnly; older boys dug it up and reburied it in his bed.

By 1941, at nine, Kennedy was a boarder at Riverdale Country School for Boys. His dorm master was a pervert who insisted on playing a kind of sadistic strip poker with the more vulnerable among his charges, followed by a humiliating "inspection" during which the dorm master might take a "private interest" in certain of his favorites; almost seventy years later Kennedy would recall having spent "many terror-filled nights under my bunk, hiding lest I too become one of those victims."

Home would remain his haven, whenever his peripatetic parents might accord him a few weeks of relief. Rose was on and off the ocean liners, bustling in and out of world capitals, exploiting the family's cachet with the Holy See to demand audiences with prominent Catholic despots from Generalissimo Franco to Haile Selassie. Joe, at least, stayed in touch, wrote letters, telephoned, showed up during the longer vacations at Hyannis Port. Exile from the protection of his indulgent if demanding father was unthinkable, terrifying, whatever the requirements. Little Teddy understood early that he must validate himself as a Kennedy before anything else.

There is the germ of self-conception here: the doughty waif, persistent to find his own situation somewhere, caught in the midst of the much older, much more self-assured boys swarming the halls around him, willing always but frightened and dizzy with the bewilderment of declensions and conjugations. And even after that the years kept changing, and the schools kept changing; still, in response to a question of mine: "I don't think I felt anything particular about it." Then, unprompted, turning on me: "I don't have any complexes, if that's what you mean."

None to be seen just then, as a little assurance appeared quickly, and after that he had the advantage of seeming so . . . so receptive, so affable. He had already learned how to meet each new conclave of class leaders as an equal. Like the deceased Joe Jr., he seemed to have been born clubbable—the sort who instinctively minded Kipling's warning to "let all men count with you, but none too much." Out of these political abilities nourished early came the traits that were to make Kennedy—unlike both his surviving brothers— a much more acceptable senator than money could buy, a compromiser, and a trustworthy bedrock liberal.

None too much. Except the family, of course; by now the weight of three omnipresent generations of all those brothers and sisters is bearing down formulatively on this malleable last-born. The most important lines, the Kennedy imprint, are long since identifiable. There is a tendency already, one in common with Jack and his immaculate and precise mother, to judge what he encountered slowly and watchfully, in stages, in slow cuts of day-by-day experience. When she was around, Mother Rose was forever pinning clippings and headlines to the kitchen bulletin board, pestering the younger ones to tell her why so many places in California had Spanish names and how it was the United States never had a king.

She battered his catechism into Teddy over luncheon, taught him to dance, bothered him about his grammar, helped him to express himself in an expansive, gently personalizing way of ribbing people back, which enabled him to confront the chronic needling of his older siblings without the risk of scars. "I remember him when he was seven or eight," his sister Eunice says, "as being overweight, terribly good-natured, laughing constantly and an incessant tease, particularly when I was entertaining." His sisters and brothers warmed themselves in his cheerfulness, spoiled him when they could get away with it, took advantage of his easy admiration by offloading their chores, and provoked him lovingly. Jack, who doted on him especially, had the patience to lie in wait for his stocky little godson and catch him on the side of the head with a pillow whenever he poked his muffin of a face outside the bedroom door.

Loved—loved to such an extent that even much later, when Ted was attempting his coltish beginnings in politics and his brother Jack was following his progress from the White House, the president would go "weak with pleasure," in Billings's phrase, listening to his baby brother up there speechmaking. "Even as a child, Ted had a terrific animal energy. You never had to push Ted, you always had to hold him back," Jean Smith, the closest to Teddy in age, later said.

And holding Teddy back could get pretty involved sometimes. It is the father in particular, with his speculator's nose for the direction of a problem, who takes the trouble to prowl very, very close to his scampering youngest. The adult Ted Kennedy often recurred both to his father's immediacy and warmth—his real, literal warmth, the warmth so profusely felt as an infant snuggled in next to the father on a Sunday morning to listen devoutly to Donald Duck—and to the persistence with which the aging financier made sure the rudiments of discipline were nourished properly.

Teddy as a kindergartner slips away from the chauffeur waiting to pick him up and walks home naughtily, by himself. There, a walloping with a coat hanger, "the usual punishment," awaits. As the boy grows older the parents expect him to be in the house, his bike stowed already, as soon as the streetlights blink on across the Cape. His allowance, as late as the years at Milton, remains below the scale of his classmates': a dollar-fifty. Edward remembers his father as determined that, financially, at least, he not regard himself as privileged.

"My father—was always very sensitive—to considerations like that," Kennedy explained to me decades later in that square-cornered delivery, between puffs on one of those nauseating little cigars he loved, musing in the gloom of his nondescript inner office in the Old Senate Office Building. "For example, he didn't feel I ought to have a bicycle of my own unless my classmates did. That sort of thing. He kept this up until these things were . . . were sort of . . . self . . . self generating . . ."

"Dear Teddy," the father one day writes in a note that accompanies a snapshot of himself, five perhaps, and with a gigantic silk bow beneath his chin. "This is a copy that some old friends of the family sent me. I don't know how old I was. It is a rather striking costume. What I would particularly like you to observe is the sharp piercing eyes, the very set jaw and the clenched left fist. Maybe all of this meant something! Dad." The mood of the note is unalloyed, absolute Kennedy-facetious: The cast of the lips is serene at exactly the moment the bite is set. The father knows—pierces, forgives—but knows, what is there already and what is still to nourish in yourself, to develop.

Even then the child was undoubtedly aware that the Kennedys were . . . different, that the "nice people," as Rose observed, didn't want them around. Joe routinely attributed this to the anti–Irish Catholic bias of the era. Gore Vidal, a remote Kennedy in-law, flatly ascribed the "scorn" the financier aroused in "that old Protestant patricate" to the well-known fact "that he was so exuberantly and successfully a crook."

Vidal maintains that "once a week, until Joe's stroke," Frank Costello, "the boss of the [New York] mob and the president's father had dinner together in Joe's Central Park South Kennedy apartment," preceded by a rubdown from an "ancient Teamster." As I was able to document in my earlier book, *Bobby and J. Edgar*, organized crime came into play early in Joseph P. Kennedy's rise. John F. Kennedy—cold, sick, congenitally detached so much of the time—both appreciated and quite openly resented the financier's chronic demands, his unabashed cultivation of humiliating sexual rivalries, not infrequently with his older boys. At times the pressure eroded judgment. Before too much longer, two more of Joe's sons would pay the price.

For the developing Teddy, already aware that he at best amounted to a kind of afterthought in a family in which the serious investment was going into the brothers who preceded him, the perception that his family *itself* was rejected in so many important places ate at him the rest of his life. Sometimes he would joke about that. It would inform his politics.

By 1941, with all the others scattered around the world while Joe himself has been consigned to oblivion by FDR, the father and his pudgy youngest find themselves spending weekends together on the Cape. Teddy has secured the priviledge of bouncing alongside his father during the Ambassador's morning rides on one of the big Irish hunters the Ambassador prefers. "Most typically," Edward Kennedy would later write, "Dad liked to wax philosophical, thinking out loud about the family."

Early—early—the father catches hold of the fascination this youngest has with water, with the land's edge and weather and the ocean—the ocean especially—and with this he is able to establish something too. "One summer," the son will tell an observer, "I wanted a kayak, and I asked him for the necessary five dollars. He felt it was a bad investment, that I'd quickly lose interest in it. In the end, he gave me the money with the understanding if I did lose interest before the summer was over, I'd have to pay him back out of my allowance.

"For two weeks I practically lived in the boat, and then I just forgot about it. I spent most of the next winter paying him back." When, at eleven, Teddy and his cousin Joey gave up on a rained-out overnight sailing trip and rowed the dinghy to shore to call the chauffeur to get them, "we ran into my father at home, and he asked us what happened. I told him, adding that we hadn't slept all night, but he sent us back immediately to sail the boat home." Through years, through maturity, through appreciation of the old man's tenacity one somehow feels here . . . not resentment so much as, that morning . . . astonishment!

5. Joey

"This is really important," cousin Joseph Gargan intones, getting me ready, but at the same time he decides to smile that nostalgic little smile he has, lets his expression float away into a kind of Gioconda dreaminess I've already seen by then a couple of times. "Mister Kennedy he . . . he could read minds," Joey Gargan says. "Just as clear as hell. And," Gargan waits again, for effect: "he was very kindly because of it——."

Our cocktail waitress, until just now rather a motherly seeming little person and something of a kidder, has got that I'd-like-to-cash-in-now way of planting the glasses with a finality. Gargan, unpushable, decides on another round. It takes an effort not to sit there assessing Joey Gargan from a bloodline standpoint: There is a suggestion of that goshawk bump that runs to the Kennedy nose, but in the case of Joey it wants to blunt a little too much, snubs into a bill. The eyes behind the spectacles are willing, gentle: The inflection, that flat Kennedy bleat, is perfect. There are family resemblances, although Joey will admit that in his case those famous genes Honey Fitz passed around got knocked out of line a little. "Not that I'm the same cut as a Kennedy," Joey Gargan drawls—reading my mind—winding down his story about a touch game at the Cape the previous weekend, during which his cousin Ted, after dumping him into the brambles, trots over to demand, "Jesus, Joey, for Christ sake, will you please get off my goddamn rosebush!" Then Joe Gargan smiles that dreamy, dreamy smile again, as if he has now established exactly what he is and what he is not.

Time, after the Chappaquiddick incident, would identify Gargan as a lawyer who hung around his cousin Edward largely "as companion for carrying out miscellaneous chores—making reservations, ordering food, emptying glasses and drawing baths." Gargan undoubtedly did such things, but out of affection, dedication. The two were children together. The fact is, until he moved down to Hyannis Port the fall of 1969 to take an important position in a new bank on the Cape, Joey Gargan had a well-grounded reputation around Court Street in Boston as a thoroughly competent courtroom attorney with a touch for liability cases. Gargan has been one person who was very, *very* close in. When their father died, in 1941, Gargan and his sister Ann turned into regulars, trusted support personnel, inside the Kennedy household. Ann had hopes of becoming a nun; when she seemed to develop a form of multiple sclerosis, the entire family—the financier especially, who hated to see her deteriorate like this—fussed over her with anything that might help. The disease paused, then remitted. When the Ambassador had his stroke the niece insisted on devoting what health she had recovered to nursing her uncle throughout his final, paralyzed years.

Teddy, nine in 1941 and pleased to be home from a world full of elevators in your house and people who came and fitted you for your personal gas mask in case of air raids, merged life with this perpetually breathless eleven-year-old cousin into his seaside summers. Here was somebody who was family and trustworthy but at the same time did what you wanted and knew enough to keep quiet about it. Unlike Bobby, who got so worried sometimes.

Bobby was like that, a worrier—a serious sort the priests depended on when they needed altar boys, if with a sharp nervous self-deriding humor Bobby's adolescent moralism couldn't really cover. There was another aspect to that: Bobby was already the one the others took their genuine difficulties to, and when his oversize little brother gave everybody a turn by trying out, for a few months, life behind the cold, self-satisfied expression of the hulking prepubescent who was hell in a fight at recess, Bobby dealt with him the way he was to deal with children until the evening he died. He tried to interpret whatever it was Ted needed as something he felt honestly, kidded him (hard, sometimes, but watchful of his feelings), and helped him however he was able.

"Bob, quite frankly, was interested in having us participate. He taught us sailing and he wanted Ted to do—he wanted one to do well," Gargan recalls. "He worked very hard—he was very helpful, he sailed to win, quite frankly, and he taught us everything he knew. He'd take the time, he created that kind of an atmosphere, he was always able to get Ted to make the extra effort." This kind of devoted older-brothering survived childhood and became a regular adult thing, a constant. When Ted was out for football at Harvard and Bob was weekending, they renewed their feelings with hour after hour after hour of one-on-one in bathing suits on the Kennedy beach sand, pass patterns, varying which leg ended up in front when you left your feet laying down a cross-body block—anything that might make a difference.

There was an exhilaration about this, but—yet—how not to regret in a way how everything eased off, normalized, the moment Bobby went back and Teddy and Joey could take a larking little sail together in Jack's old sloop the *Victura*—fool around, try things, make a few of those dangerous dumb unsuperintended mistakes that nobody would have to know about. Puppy-dog fun, sniping twigs and bouncing deadfalls at each other's feet to get them out of the bridle path before the Ambassador's ride in the morning, tossing a little swill at each other whenever they were slopping the pigs for a nearby farmer. Or the occasion, sawing up trees and trimming things after a hurricane, that Joey managed to lay a tree trunk down so that it flattened Teddy, an incident that led to the two of them having to stand there sheepishly and absorb a sarcastic and humiliating word or two from the Ambassador himself, who found out somehow and hadn't thought much of woodsmanship like that.

Middle-boyhood years, overshadowed: Throughout this sun-warmed, spray-soaked decade there is the Steady Recuperating Presence, the Easter Island Head faced off permanently by now in the direction from which the new day is expected to dawn—Joseph P. Kennedy. Visitors come away reporting the expression on the Ambassadorial visage fearsome—"The old man scared me," one admits outright. The raider suggested to one of Jack Kennedy's better-looking one-night-stands to go "Get youself a real man"— Joe meant himself. Yet somehow this domed and towering presence in the horn-rimmed glasses turned into a pushover in the presence of genuine helplessness.

So to the badly shaken Gargan children vacation life in the "big house" represented balm and reassurance, an awakening and a stimulation. "It was a delight to go to lunch with him, it was an opportunity, it was an exciting event," Joe Gargan maintains twenty years later: Through everything he says, through awe of years and position and the uncomfortable poor-relation-grown-old-enough-to-appreciate mouthings there comes . . . tenderness. Tenderness!

This is the secret emotion here—it is to become the deepest secret of the Kennedys altogether—being so excruciatingly moved by a glimpse of the old man's vision that the hunger comes, the groping, a desperation just for the chance to serve. It is something one can very nearly hear, urgent and soundless, beneath the clomp-clomp-clomp-clomp of Joey Gargan, gangling teenager, owner and operator of two prematurely big wide feet, going out for a pass in new shoes that pinch him awfully because he is breaking them in for his uncle the Ambassador. Ear to the ground: It is the future running at you and by.

One incident plays itself out devastatingly in Gargan's overstimulated recollection. As one of those innumerable services, the by-then rather stringy eighteen-year-old had taken delivery for his uncle in Boston on a Cadillac convertible. He has the heavy lustrous car almost back to the village when a panel truck bursts out of a blind crossroad just above the canal and smashes into the convertible with force enough to drive both the Cadillac and its petrified driver into a stand of trees beyond the opposite embankment. When composure of a sort returns, Gargan feels the wreck back onto the road, drives with a funereal attentiveness into Hyannis Port itself, and pulls the car up before the estate's garages. Jack Fitzgerald, Joey's uncle and Aunt Rose's brother, a passenger since Boston, disappears in the direction of Craigville without venturing a word.

The trembling Joey gets out to inspect: Both front fenders of the convertible are pushed in completely. Bobby appears, and behind him that perennial Kennedy butler-chauffeur Dave, and both urge this hapless cousin of theirs to get the damned thing out of sight at least, put it in a body shop possibly and get it fixed before the father gets a look at this disaster. Gargan—there is that hangdog honesty of his—trudges up to the big house and asks the nearest servant to go and inquire as to whether it would be possible for him to have a moment of discussion with his uncle. Joseph P. Kennedy appears, and listens to Gargan's rendition gravely. The profound fear that every one of them can't help but feel in the presence of this generalissimo of their destinies touches every nerve.

Silently, the two of them walk down the steps, still without a word, and stand together *very* silently over the automotive remains. The Ambassador looks austerely at his shattered nephew. "Joey," he begins when the time has come finally—the words go into Gargan's memory like a tattoo—"You're-very-lucky-to-be-alive." Then, carefully, Joseph Kennedy suggests that his nephew might like to go join the touch game the others have gotten into below on the lawn. One can very nearly hear, twenty years later, Gargan letting his breath out very very slowly for, say, fifteen or twenty minutes uninterruptedly.

There is an intriguing postscript. That evening at dinner Congressman John F. Kennedy, well known inside the family for his delicate but unsparing needle, offers, very lightly, "Dad, I understand Joey had a little accident with the new car——."

The glare that terrifies intercepts that. "Joey and I have discussed the car," Joseph Kennedy says, "and I don't want the car mentioned again." A week or so later, despite his nephew's protestations that, quite frankly, he'd just as soon not, the financier makes plain his wish that his yet-unsteady nephew drive Aunt Rose up to Logan Airport in Boston to catch the plane for Paris. This Joey Gargan understands and does, and from the moment he agrees to drive his confidence begins to come back to him.

6. *Atonement*

Edward, writing about his father much later, commented with a felt hesitation that "he said he was anti-clerical," and hurried to explain that the financier didn't really mean anything by that. It is the disclaimer that looks most dubious. Joe maintained excellent political relations his whole adult life with the Holy See—Cardinal Spellman was a fellow conspirator on a number of occasions, and Eugenio Pacelli was a friend of the family's long before he became Pius XII. To the pragmatic financier, Church connections were like Mafia connections—links to an indispensable constituency. Where religion was concerned, what Joe Kennedy undoubtedly intended to say was exactly what he meant.

As the Kennedy fortune accrued, and with it the extent of the Kennedy philanthropies, there continued to be something of the quality, the redolence of . . . of the b*urnt offering* coming off the sacrifices and generosities. Good works—good works offered in uncertain hope. With Rose and Joe there developed almost a compulsion at times to help this depleted newspaperman remembered from the earliest Boston promotions, or that aging pediatrician Rose spotted across an avenue shuffling hatless beneath a pummeling of snowflakes . . . . Helped, if as deviously as possible, because one is—because *he* was, finally—P.J.'s son, and because . . . because . . . sooner or later, it happens to you too. Even you.

Beyond death, worse than death—Rosemary, grayed decade by decade in the Kennedy shadows, alive for the most part in photographs that release, in an unexpected burst, that uncomprehending grin-of-a-Kennedy that squeezes the heartbeat tighter and tighter and tighter until you only have to look away, in the end, and just . . . have to . . . quit on it. A few things: the bewildered determined courage of the presentation to the Queen, the glimpse of this wild-eyed creature panicky as she is hustled in fright and confusion among the rabble of sisters and brothers to her place along a block of seats to sit before two hours of incomprehensible hockey. Until, unavoidably, she had receded slowly into a senseless truculence that forced the decision to—really, for her own good, happier like that . . . quit on it. Joe's decision to quit on it.

7. Adolescence

"I remember Teddy at ten or eleven," says the solemn Lem Billings, "and he was a kind of a wiseass fresh kid, kind of fat, not terribly appealing—then suddenly, when he was twelve or so, this terrific appeal, his personality emerged and overcame the rest. His sense of humor couldn't be equaled, it was very adult for his age, he took part in everything, the family games you always played after dinner. He became . . . just damned good company. His older brothers and sisters began to appreciate him. I don't think the president loved anybody the way he did Ted——."

Because, when you think about it, there was a position opening up around the family just then. Enough personality had already emerged to indicate that Ted was going to be . . . hearty, but in a very considerate and soothing fashion. And this was something the others were ready to appreciate by that time. The honeyed tones, that way of joking around that invited you in—these were already emerging. There were harsh rhythms around the table sometimes—Jack, mortaring you from the blue-green intellectual distance, and Bobby with those Celtic mood storms of his . . . . "When you have older brothers and sisters," Mrs. Kennedy observed "they're the ones that seem to be more important in a family, and always get the best rooms and the first choice of boats and all, those kinds of things, but Ted never seemed to resent it." "We used to sail together," JFK commented, and Teddy was the one who was "always willing to put up the boat"—meaningful from a brother who was slipshod enough himself to leave a sail out between races on a gusty afternoon and return to tatters. Younger, weaker until his growth arrived, Teddy became the conciliatory one, very generous, very thoughtful of people, eager to push himself as soon as he saw what any of them wanted and, footnotes Joey Gargan hesitantly, "impatient on occasion with those who were not."

Conciliatory, yes, but not—never—in an unctuous fashion. More and more, in fact, the older ones begin to notice, a touch for the Irish-laddie style. Boisterous—Christ, riotous sometimes—but almost never wholly forgetful of what being a Kennedy was supposed to mean. A nudge by the wised-up father suffices. Polo, for example, was "all right for certain people on the island," the old man stormed when he found out about pony talk between Teddy and the stable groom; and that did it. Kennedys weren't polo society;

now Teddy knew that. Overhearing Jack and Eunice planning a memoir to Joseph Jr., Teddy—twelve—kept bothering them with his insistence that he had something of his own to include.

"Eunice started to explain to Teddy what he should write," Jack reported. "She told him to say how wonderful and strong and calm Joe was. Teddy said to her 'but Joe wasn't calm—one day he threw me in the ocean.' I told Teddy to go ahead and write about it in his own words and we published it just as Teddy wrote it. I think it's one of the nicest things in the book."

Teddy wrote: "I recall the day the year before we went to England. It was in the summer and I asked Joe if I could race with him. He agreed to this so we started down to the pier about five minutes before the race. We had our sails up just as the gun went for the start. This was the first race I had ever been in. We were going along very nicely until suddenly he told me to pull in the jib. I had know Idea what he was talking about. He repeated the command again in a little louder tone, meanwhile we were slowly getting further and further away from the other boats. Joe suddenly leaped up and grabed the jib. I was a little scared but suddenly he zeized me by the pants and through me into the cold water.

"I was scared to death practully. I then heard a splash and felt his hand grab my shirt and he lifted me into the boat. We continued the race and came in second. On the way home from the pier he told me to be quiet about what happened in that afternoon. One falt Joe had was that he got very easily mad in a race as you have witnessed. But he always meant well and was a very good sailor and swimmer."

It was a foresighted inclusion. The boy was becoming, already, servitor of the heritage. "Shortly after Jack first got elected to Congress, that first time," Mark Dalton, the soft-spoken attorney who managed John Kennedy's early campaigns, recalled for me, "I was invited to lunch at Hyannis Port one Sunday. It was John Kennedy's birthday, and all the brothers and sisters were there, and a lot of toasts were drunk, and then finally the father asked Teddy, who was sitting at the end of the table on the right, whether he happened to have a toast to something. Teddy got to his feet very somberly, I remember. 'Yes, I would like to drink a toast,' Teddy said, 'to our brother who is not here.' Everybody drank, I saw, but the effect he had was of a stunned silence, and I remember it took several minutes before any of them could really say anything . . ."

CHAPTER III

Whelping the Juggernaut

1. Congress

One enduring point of dispute among Kennedy scholars is whether Jack Kennedy went into political life because he chose to, or because his father wanted him to, or because his father absolutely insisted on it. Well over half a century after the skinny lieutenant (j.g.) took off his uniform for good and hung it in the closet at 122 Bowdoin for Teddy to find seventeen years later, the roots of the decision remain snarled in and out of the brickfill of an earlier Massachusetts politics. "I got Jack into politics. I was the one . . . He didn't want to. He felt he didn't have the ability and he still feels that way. But I told him he had to," the Ambassador informed a magazine reporter as early as 1957; Clem Norton, a pal of the Honey Fitz–Joe Kane era, remembers the exhausted candidate the afternoon he repaired to the back room of his campaign headquarters at the Bellevue Hotel—dustbag address for politicians on the make since Honey Fitz—and wept with fatigue and disgust at what he found himself jobbed into agreeing to.

Jack Kennedy was twenty-nine but—war, schooling, diplomatic errands notwithstanding—he was an inexperienced and unassured twenty-nine. Despite what little book reviewing and newspaper work Kennedy had done since leaving the hospital—his "special correspondent" status for International News Service at the founding of the United Nations, his dispatches from England about the Labour upset of Churchill's regime—his prose was stilted, lifeless, the off-hour deadline-beating of the dabbler. He toyed with the idea of academics, briefly.

The operation the Naval surgeons had performed on his spine in 1944 wasn't really successful enough to ease the pain, and now those fourteen-hour days dragging himself up the steps of one musty stinking three-decker Charlestown stairwell after another, climbing the banisters by handholds and trailing one leg because he couldn't really bear to put much weight on it, to solicit the vote—beyond the stench of cabbage boiling, of astonished scowling people so poor that the toilet and the gas heater shared their living room with them—week following week of this cost the depleted new veteran whatever enthusiasm he had attempted to muster. "Sometimes we all have to do things we don't want to do," Kennedy told young fellow veteran John Droney, recruiting him in Honey Fitz's apartment: His brother was dead now, and his family "seemed to feel he was best fitted to carry on."

The tapping of nonchalant young Jack was not a decision the Ambassador made so much as one he accepted. The side of Jack Kennedy that by the end of things came so to enchant a generation—his irony, his tantalizing archness, his subtle and abiding eighteenth-century sense of man as a limited figure against the historical landscape—Kennedy's charms came tainted by his practical limitations. He tended to forget appointments and turn up tardily for the ones he kept. He was forever without cash, and borrowed from whomever was around—his half-tolerant, half-annoyed father usually—without ever bothering to repay anybody.

Like rich men's children universally—like all his brothers and sisters after him—Jack Kennedy regarded the money problems of workaday people with very little interest. "Good God, Jack," his father exploded at him one day when his son observed that the $5,000 a year an ex-aide was earning at night while putting himself through law school ought to be "more than enough." "How can you say a thing like that? Do you realize that you've been spending fifty thousand dollars a year on incidentals!" You could follow Jack Kennedy's progress along a trail of flooded hotel bathrooms and wads of wet towels and underwear and stockings and shirts for underlings to recover or room service managers to dry and mail to his Washington offices.

He had a way of walking around even at political rallies with his head down; ideas and issues interested him far more than personalities or the mousetrap skulduggeries of the eternal Irish gutter politics. His abilities with a prepared speech, in the opinion of one who knew him early and loved him long, were so marginal when he started that he sounded like "one of those runners-up in some American Legion declamation contest in Brockton or some place like that."

The Massachusetts district that opened up when Jack Kennedy was looking for a political base was the giant eleventh, a sprawl of rotting masonry, glued together by a hundred years of soot. Kennedy's district was squalor gerrymandered. On humid dirty evenings the summer of that first Kennedy campaign the candidate made his way beneath a rusty jungle of fire escapes from which the heavy wives of Italian warehousemen and Irish stevedores oversaw the streets. Robert, a tense bony kid notable for his big ever-bobbing Adam's apple, worked Cambridge's East End: Jim Curley's district, ethnic Asian.

" 'Red,'" Kennedy's Navy buddy Paul Fay reports him to have ventured during the opening months of 1945, "'I can feel Pappy's eyes on the back of my neck.'" Then, and "with no special enthusiasm," "'when the war is over and you are out there in sunny California giving them agood solid five and a half inches for a six-inch pavement, I'll be back here with Dad trying to parlay a lost PT boat and a bad back into a political advantage. I tell you, Dad is ready right now and can't understand why Johnny boy isn't "all engines ahead full."'" Fay, who had a father with a business too, understood.

By the time Fay and Lem Billings and John Droney and Eddie McLaughlin and Mark Dalton and all the other clean-limbed recently discharged Navy officers and political greenhorns had rushed from everywhere to the Kennedy suite at the Bellevue that spring of 1946 to help "Shafty" out with his political debut, the financier had planted two figures of his own choosing in his emaciated son's camp. One was Joe Kane, the son of P.J.'s sister and therefore the financier's first cousin. "At precisely the right time he'd come up with one of his Rembrandts or Degas," in the words of Billy Sutton, JFK's early secretary. Kane disliked Honey Fitz. "Get that sonofabitch out of here," Kane growled, to the shock of the babyfaced candidate himself, when the former mayor blundered into the headquarters.

The financier's other find and gift to his son's campaign was the redoubtable Francis Xavier Morrissey. Frank Morrissey, while quite a young man in 1946, was technically still the secretary of Massachusetts Governor Maurice Tobin. "We threw him out of the room," both Sutton and Kane reported subsequently. What nobody could mistake before long was the fact that Frank Morrissey settled into the campaign early as "the old man's eyes and ears," and stayed on to run the Boston office once Jack went along to Washington. "Frank's job in life was holding the Ambassador's coat and bag," one worker of the period says in cold summation.

"Morrissey's detractors were afraid of him because he had direct access to Joe Kennedy," Gerry Doherty, the lobbyist who ran the Massachusetts Democratic Party for Ted after 1962, later insisted. "An inveterate medal-giver-outer, and he'd even let you choose your own color ribbon. He's always known where all the bodies are buried, probably because he's helped bury quite a few himself.

"Morrissey was disgusting. Really, a professional tattletale, d'you know? Because actually the one absolutely certain way you could always entertain Mister Kennedy, get his complete interest, was to feed him stuff about his children. And it was more interesting to him if it was something worthwhile to chastise them with. And I assure you, Morrissey really knew how to feed the old man, help his ego along. But of course Teddy was not exposed to the Morrissey Jack was, and I assume Teddy simply regarded him as a friend of his father and of his brother . . ."

The campaign manager of record was Mark Dalton, a tall, rather courtly attorney from a family of high regard in the district, who was barely out of the Navy just then and setting himself up in legal practice. The Ambassador was directly in touch with Dalton constantly from his own power center at the Ritz-Carlton: Dalton remembers telephone calls that caught him changing diapers early Sunday mornings and lasted hours. Joe Kennedy pounded away particularly at the importance of keeping up with the appearance schedule— a problem with his lackadaisical son, who had barely remembered to register as a Democrat in time to attempt the primary. When Dalton—who had been known as an experienced public speaker since his B.U. days and came into the campaign to help Jack Kennedy with his initial radio address—delivered an eloquent long introduction at a rally and was immediately succeeded by the badly faltering candidate, the financier made it clear that the two must never share a podium again.

It was probably in publicity that the financier had the most effect. He brainpicked the local press constantly, conferring on larger issues with the doyen of *The New York Times*'s Washington bureau, his confederate Arthur Krock. When a *Boston Post* poll showed, midway in the campaigning, that Jack was already taking a preponderant lead, the doubtful financier flew up the celebrated "straw" pollsters of the *New York Daily News* to confirm the results. Reprints by the thousands of John Hersey's *New Yorker* piece on the *PT-109* incident appeared behind the District's innumerable screen doors. There were house parties all over the District, but it was at the reception at the Commodore in Cambridge, just out of Harvard Square, that the Kennedys began knowingly to market a calculated projection of themselves as something more than people.

At the time the idea of the "Kennedy Teas" came up, the whole idea seemed absurd to the regulars in the organization—a kind of costume

put-on to which fifteen hundred local scrubwomen and taxi drivers were
asked by embossed invitation along with a sprinkling of openly tongue-
in-cheek Harvard faculty, all filing together in confusion along a protocol-
ordered reception line headed by the Ambassador himself in white tie and
tails before fanning out to play hell among the teacups and petits fours; the
line of communicants stretched across the lobby of the Commodore Hotel
and out the door, across the street and into a park nearby. With the "Kennedy Teas" their organization had stumbled onto what was to remain their
most successful publicity device, the introduction of pop class to ox-tongued
ethnics across America.

"I never thought Jack had it in him," the father muttered from limousine-
side to the faithful Morrissey as his son handshook his way into a crowd of
Sicilians around P.J.'s old base of operation at Maverick Square. This kind
of thing, week after week after week of sixteen hours a day, street corner
beyond street corner and ducking in and out of candy stores and barber-
shops and a quick shave in the mirror of the men's room of a pool hall above
the resinated stink of pine soap melting into a backed-up urinal . . . politics,
the initiation ceremonial. "He was not a speaker at that stage of the game,"
Dalton said later.

"I don't think he ever developed into an orator in the Churchillian sense,
and by that I mean a person whose emotions show strongly, who has the
capacity to bring an audience to its feet.

"What he was, even in those early years in Congress, was a fine debater.
I remember when he had that debate with Norman Thomas—I got a call to
come over to 122 Bowdoin for a few minutes, I did, and I found him stretched
out on the die-van, a pile of books by Thomas beside him—I think he had
read everything Norman Thomas had ever written, he had made up his mind
as to the weaknesses in Thomas's thinking and he had already established
answers to the positions Thomas had taken . . . so that later everybody felt
that he had easily defeated Thomas." One of the high spots of the primary
battle was an outdoor rally at which Major (retired) Catherine Falvey, who
liked to campaign in her dress whites and refer to Kennedy as the "poor little
rich kid candidate," leaned over the sallow ex-lieutenant (j.g.)—having just a
moment before razored him with accusations—and whispered, "Don't pay
any attention; it's just politics." Jack smiled back obligingly, waited his turn,
and savaged her.

Weekends, that rare day off wedged into a tighter and tighter schedule,
a lot of this found its way back to summer Hyannis Port. Teddy was coming into his growth, the braces were off and the Fitzgerald French curve of

his jawline accentuated the long-toothed Kennedy smile, he wore his hair in a smooth auburn wing parted in a perfect furrow on the left, and he was already starting to show up for ceremonial occasions in a pinstripe blue suit. Once, plotting with staff people in the appropriate patois—a language that modulates from profanity to obscenity, pausing for relief sometimes with a burst of scatology—Jack Kennedy got a call from the clerk at the Bellevue informing him that his baby brother was on the way up in the elevator. The candidate put his hand over the receiver: "Let's watch our swearing and our language," he cautioned his co-collaborators. "Remember—he's not a part of this yet, he wouldn't understand."

The candidate himself now understood better and better. "Trust nobody completely; never take anything for granted," Kennedy boilerplate read. Jack visited his District whenever it was convenient and fraternized pretty widely; about the time Jack Kennedy was inaugurated as president some townie contacts of his—a high-humored crowd with whom the new president had been known to drop out and go boating on occasion—were shipped off to the penitentiary for having engineered the Brinks robbery.

The candidate was exploring this new world in his characteristically oblique way. The Ambassador was still skittish about hinting to his children when something involved his own Mob connections, and the odds are top-heavy that he never really picked up on a lot of this. "Jack tended to be a little bit fey, a little offhand around his father," Steve Smith recalled. Jacqueline Kennedy was later to identify the young president as an "idealist without illusions"—after 1946 he was divesting himself at an accelerating rate. Teddy, standing by and pitching in more and more those break-in days, was beginning to absorb the generational experience.

2. Cold War

As the postwar years stretched out, the Ambassador understood that his own political resuscitation was unlikely. Joe Kennedy, ran the consensus around Harry Truman, had deteriorated, along with Henry Wallace and Father Coughlin, into an ideological Kewpie doll. Speaking in Fulton, Missouri, in March of 1946, Winston Churchill attacked the Soviets in the Iron Curtain address that is commonly regarded as the opening trumpet of the Cold War. Writing the same month in *Life*, Joe Kennedy's observations underlined Churchill's. ("I remember as kids," Joey Gargan would muse, watching his glass fill up, "when he would go down for a swim, and everybody was welcoming the Russian victories, he constantly said then, the great problem was going to be with Russia . . .") As Joe Kennedy saw the situation, the Russians were already there, with seasoned well-equipped troops in place much beyond even their pre-1914 imperial borders, and the United States had established its hegemony over much of both the Atlantic and the Pacific communities, and—the pattern of a speculative lifetime—there are near-term dangers and risks and long-term dangers and risks. The crucial danger now—the financier is out with it, almost at once—is the collision of Russian and American interests with force enough to blow off World War III.

This risk of immediate oncoming embroilment the Ambassador would mitigate by, in effect, breaking the world map down into graded spheres of influence. The United States would regard such steps as Soviet annexation of the Baltic States, Bessarabia, and the Kuriles as "accepted as beyond review"; incursions already in the works like the Soviet policy in Poland and Prussia would be objected to on principle but not made an issue of; encroachment on such states as Rumania and Bulgaria would be more strongly opposed, but "military action is impracticable." Kennedy's spectrum ranges all the way through outright Soviet aggression against Western Europe, Great Britain, the Philippines, the Western Pacific, or the Western Hemisphere, any of which would lead to outright war.

Most intriguing about Joe Kennedy's geopolitical observations, tossing into view again and again like a restless sleeper's arm above the blanket of his argument, is his underlying anguish about what he perceives to be the presuppositions of the unsteady new Truman foreign policy. We are throughout assuming, says the financier, that "by pressing steadily and persistently to establish liberal democracy throughout the world, the world will eventually reach such a state of advanced civilization that there will be no more war or fear of war." This is a policy which is "ardent, sincere, active, and optimistic," but it is one which "would involve the nation in a program of minding other people's business on a global scale, never previously attempted or seriously considered," which imagines, against history, that "advanced" nations wouldn't fight wars, at least against us, and is "in no practical way specifically designed to prevent a major war or win it if it should occur."

Already, the Ambassador insists, we have begun to come away bleeding a little from the first nettles of our international "meddling." "Elections in Greece; racial crisis in Palestine; ideological and political conflicts in the Balkans, India, Spain, and the Argentine; problems of 'dependent people' wherever found . . ." Our very optimism, which makes us so eager to involve ourselves, hides the cost and discipline such obligations carry: "The postwar military policy of the United States is not yet announced or determined. However, when one contemplates how popular demand and the lack of strong leadership to control that demand have wrecked our vast military machine of a few months ago, the prospects are not bright for a military policy strong enough to give much insurance against war."

Before long Joe's congressman son would appear to embrace, then repudiate, the Ambassador's misgivings about the fast-emerging national security state. Joe began to complain that year by year his son Jack was more and more enthusiastic about the projection of military power to accommodate every momentary challenge. Our commitments were already outstripping our long-term capacities. Bobby tended to agree with Jack, but many of the old speculator's apprehensions would reappear in Edward Kennedy's thinking as decade by decade we revamped our priorities to establish the New World Order.

In 1946 Joe Kennedy was still regarded, by many conservatives, as a statesman from the near past prescient enough to have urged America to jump free of the phony-war writhings and utter collapse of a European system bankrupted by blank-check interinvolvements. The financier was dismissed on the left as a neo-isolationist, but his warnings attracted serious interest throughout that raucous public debate that opened Harry Truman's presidency. By December of 1950, when Joseph Kennedy acceded to his son Bobby's request to speak publicly at the University of Virginia Law School Forum, the outbreak of the Korean War had pushed holdouts as venerated as Republican Senator Arthur Vandenberg and even the reluctant Robert Taft to support a monolithic "bipartisan" foreign policy. Weeks before the Ambassador spoke, the Chinese had infiltrated a million regulars into the fight, and the holy grapple was finally on.

If the financier sensed the national mood at all, he was very grand about ignoring it. The Truman foreign policy the Ambassador pronounced "suicidal," a means "to accomplish some unknown objective," "politically and morally a bankrupt policy." The United Nations was "hopeless"; we must, quite simply, "get out of Korea—indeed . . . get out of every point in Asia which we do not plan realistically to hold in our own defense." Our approach to Europe was poorly considered, too: "Today it is idle to talk of being able to hold the line of the Elbe or the line of the Rhine . . . What have we gained by staying in Berlin? . . . The truth is that our only real hope is to keep Russia, if she chooses to march, on the other side of the Atlantic, and make Communism much too costly for her to try and cross the seas. It may be that Europe for a decade or a generation or more will turn Communist. But in doing so, it may break of itself as a united force. Communism still has to prove itself to its peoples as a government that will achieve for them a better way of living . . . the more people that are under its yoke, the greater are the possibilities of revolt . . . Is it appeasement to withdraw from unwise commitments, to arm yourself to the teeth and to make clear just exactly how and for what you will fight?"

3. The Congressman

For all the Ambassador's disclaimers, the speech was treated everywhere as autumnal America-Firstism. Kennedy's preoccupations remained personal. While corporative America was buying up Europe—and on such a scale that by the mid-sixties the United States's collective holding in Western Europe was, of itself, the third largest industrial complex in the world—Kennedy (never the boardroom type, exactly) was, emphatically, not involved. If Chile expropriated the copper mines of Anaconda, or the jute crop in Thailand failed—all this was far from the interests of Joseph P. Kennedy, Incorporated. If Joseph P. Kennedy was prepared patiently to watch Europe succumb to Communism in hope that the new regime might, one day, "break of itself," the administrators of Esso or IBM in Europe took a historically shorter view.

Later on, musing to the ADA professors and Jewish libertarians who wanted so much to believe in this incandescent young politician, Jack Kennedy liked to throw out a wry, all-sufficing allusion to the views of his well-known—awfully well-known—father. "Some people have their liberalism 'made' by the time they reach their late twenties," he said, "almost wistfully," to his early biographer James MacGregor Burns. "I didn't. I was caught in cross currents and eddies. It was only later that I got into the stream of things."

Inexperienced as Kennedy was those years, just another "worm" in Congress, the way he was already voting and talking privately marked the force of many of those "crosscurrents and eddies." The malarial young congressman was prickly, if in his increasingly suave way, from the day he had to prove to guards that he was not a page to get himself into the chamber of the House. He advocated the inclusion of Franco's Spain—bugbear of the principled Left forever, the Catholic Menace incarnadine—into the armory of NATO. He was skeptical publicly of the U.S. involvement in Korea. Despite his earlier attack on the "Lattimores and Fairbankses" whose advice had lost mainland China to the Communists ("What our strong men had saved, our Diplomats and our President have frittered away"), Jack Kennedy set Defense and State Department teeth grinding, year after year, with cogent and murderously detailed attacks on the approaches, funding, and administrative effectiveness of both NATO and the Foreign Aid Programs: "Our resources are not limitless. We must make no broad, unlimited grant to any government."

Returning from a round-the-world trip with Bobby and Patricia in 1951, Kennedy assailed United States policy in Indochina, "where we have allied ourselves to the desperate efforts of a French regime to hang onto the remnants of empire." He went on to question "our intervention in behalf of England's oil investments in Iran, directed more at the preservation of interests outside Iran than at Iran's own development." Sixty years later his kid brother Edward would voice the same qualms.

If the boy congressman's nitpicking raised ever-ready liberal eyebrows, he subjected himself to far more serious damages with his appetite for the kind of political sweetmeats available from "redbaiting." The incident that most affected the young JFK was his nonparticipation in the Senate initiative to censure the rampaging Joe McCarthy, a pal of old Joe's, one of Bobby's first employers, and the suitor, for a time, of Ted's sister Eunice.

Students of the Kennedy record stutter unhappily at mention of Kennedy's flailing tarbrush style while, as an investigating member of the House Labor Committee, he attempted to back into a corner his old Harvard economics instructor Russ Nixon, by then the legislative representative of the United Electrical Workers, with citations from Lenin about the utility of fellow-traveling organizations. Such publicity nullified a lot of the impact of Kennedy's dogged fight against the Taft-Hartley Bill, both in Committee and on the floor of the House. "I'd be very happy to tell them I'm not a liberal at all," Kennedy informed a reporter in 1952. "I never joined the Americans for Democratic Action or the American Veterans Committee. I'm not comfortable with those people."

The fact is, John Fitzgerald Kennedy was never to be truly "comfortable" with people in any of the clearly labeled categories. Kennedy owed nobody. For all his slope-shouldered way of shrugging along the corridors and all the wired-puppet arm gestures, Richard Nixon was only too well aware all along of what it was exactly he had to sell, and what his services were worth, and who, precisely, was interested in buying. From the beginning it seemed clear enough the young JFK was playing both to and against an audience of one-the financier himself.

Moving around the cloakrooms arguing for a piece of legislation he had devised that would divert federal funds into local agencies willing to plan their own slum-clearance and public housing projects, Jack Kennedy bumped again and again into the paid lobbyists of the American Legion. Kennedy was well aware of the squalor in which recently returned veterans were necessarily living. One day on the floor of the House, listening to yet one more proposal of one more sop bonus to be thrown to the veteran in the name of a grateful nation at the behest of Legion officials, the congressman forgot himself: "I am a member of the American Legion," he insisted in open exchange. "I was never consulted about this plan. Who in the American Legion was consulted?" That, together with his unsheathed public observation that the Legion had become the "drummer boy for the real estate lobby" intent on "wrapping the flag around the veteran"—this was the kind of indecent self-exposure that destroys careers.

"Jack, if I were you, starting in down here, I'd marry [Massachusetts-based Majority Leader] John McCormack," a sound Boston pol advised the congressman just after he had taken his seat. "I'd hang around with him in the House, eat dinner with him a couple of nights a week, listen to everything he had to say and ask for his advice." The politician pauses. "You know what Jack did when I told him that? He backed away from me in horror as if I had pointed a gun at him."

"I never felt I needed Truman," Jack Kennedy later remarked privately; his naivete seemed universal. When, in 1947, McCormack approached Kennedy on the floor of the House and asked him to sign a presidential release petition for that sick old roustabout orator James Michael Curley, who was just then simultaneously serving one term as mayor of Boston and another in the Danbury penitentiary for mail fraud, the congressman stared back without speaking an uncomfortably long time. "Has anyone talked with the president or anything?" Kennedy finally asked.

"No," McCormack said. "If you don't want to sign it, don't sign it."

"Well, I'm not going to sign it," the touchy Kennedy decided.

Kennedy had stood alone in this: All the other Massachusetts representatives, both Republican and Democratic, had signed McCormack's petition unhesitatingly. One congressional colleague, Foster Furcolo, would broach to me the subject of Kennedy's congressional performance in that flowing soft-edged old-time politician's way of circling and touch-sparring with the subject: "Jack was . . . as a congressman, you have to say he was completely . . . indifferent, partly because he wasn't there so much of the time. I remember we were both on the Labor and Education Committee, and I had this plan for a Federal Scholarship Program, more or less what became the law through the National Defense Education Act. I took it to him, and I don't think he knew really what I was talking about—that, or he knew, and he just wasn't interested . . ."

Tiny orange-yellow moons the size of BB shot drift into the glaze of Furcolo's brown warm Italian eyes. From 1957 to 1961 Furcolo was the governor of Massachusetts, the countervailing influence within the Democratic Party to John F. Kennedy himself. He challenged the Kennedys and wound up one of nineteen assistant district attorneys for Boston's Middlesex County, the kind of job normally available to a recent local law school graduate.

"And Jack was naive in this sense," Furcolo continues. "Once, I remember, he asked that I go in a group, five of the six of us from the state, to go to the White House to talk about more patronage. We got together—we were in the car, and I looked around and asked, 'Jack, where is McCormack?' And it turned out that he was having a squabble with McCormack about the post office appointments. And he was going to the White House to complain about that! Well, after all, John McCormack was Rayburn's Majority Leader, and one thing was for sure—we weren't going to be in the White House ten seconds before somebody there was going to put through a call to McCormack——." Furcolo's eyes shifted perceptibly. "Jack wasn't much of a congressman, but as a senator he did a little more . . ." Ted Kennedy, who revered his brother, was very lucky not to be watching.

4. *The Kennedy Machine*

The 1952 decision for Jack to go after Henry Cabot Lodge's Massachusetts Senate seat was arrived at late. Part of the rush developed because of the hesitation of the state's presiding Democrat, Paul A. Dever, Massachusetts's stumpy bachelor governor, to decide whether to run for reelection or try for the Lodge seat himself. Lodge was admittedly formidable: He had spent the largest part of the winter and spring engineering the Republican nomination of the politically irresistible Eisenhower, and now had taken public root, in the opinion of a waggish Kennedy lieutenant, "like a well-cared-for house plant in the beaming general's navel."

The decisive conclusions here, as all along, stemmed from the seismic intuitions of Joseph P. Kennedy about which way the political earth was about to slide. Over the same years his son was taking those four-day weekends away from Congress to crisscross Massachusetts, ultimately to speak in 311 of the state's 351 registered cities and towns, hunting out and addressing eight groups in a single day, pollsters in the employ of the father were reconnoitering the back counties and milltown wards to discover that the elegant, liberally attuned Lodge had significantly shallower support than the more homespun Leverett Saltonstall. Especially in the campaign's earliest stages, even the smallest decisions underwent the financier's ultrasensitive scrutiny. Mark Dalton, Jack Kennedy's longtime collaborator by then, himself wrote the formal announcement of the congressman's entrance into the race, read it to the financier, and, on his insistence, cleared every phrase of it through ex–SEC chairman Jim Landis, by then an employee of Joseph P. Kennedy, Inc., and the venerable Arthur Krock.

John Ford, of the New York office, fine-chopped the gigantic expenditures; the father now took it upon himself to approach the crusty, bristling James Michael Curley and ask whether Curley might possibly speak for Jack; when the enraged Curley quieted down, the Ambassador somehow persuaded him at least not to speak *against* the candidate.

Perhaps the most overpublicized incident of the campaign occurred when the financier arrived at 122 Bowdoin Street to find a group of Massachusetts liberals headed by Pat Jackson putting the last touches to a newspaper advertisement headlined COMMUNISM AND MCCARTHY: BOTH WRONG. Joe Kennedy reportedly blew: "You are trying to ruin Jack. You and your sheeny friends are trying to ruin my son's career," the upset financier is supposed to have shouted, exploding the project forever. Just then Tail Gunner Joe McCarthy was a regular weekend visitor to Hyannis Port.

It was the kind of performance reminiscent of the scene during which the financier fired Mark Dalton—"The old man spread all the books on the desk in front of him, studied them for about five minutes without saying a word, then shoved his finger in Dalton's face and yelled: 'Dalton, you've spent ten thousand dollars of my money and you haven't accomplished a damn thing.'" Dalton was out.

In fact, for all the bucksaw touch of the aroused financier's personality, the amputations were probably necessary if the career of the candidate was to survive. "Jack Kennedy in 1952? He was engaging, even then," one liberal Kennedy won over early says, "but he was very immature." Joe McCarthy might have seemed beneath contempt to both the aloof Lodge and the aloof John F. Kennedy, but to the Catholic mobocracy of Boston just then he was their hero and Commie-fighter, above attack: The financier had contrived by means of privately conveyed campaign funds to keep McCarthy out of Massachusetts.

Dalton, who remembered the father as a man of "unquestionably vast abilities," "extraordinarily sentimental where his own family was concerned," spoke as if being relieved of his managerial duties came none too soon: "The pressure was beyond belief, morning, noon, night—organizing the whole state, trying to get decisions from so many people . . . after five or six months it was clear to me that I just could not handle it, and I told him so, and Bobby came into the picture."

The appearance of the reluctant Bobby: It is 1952 now, and that moment has come at last when perfervid self-doubting little Bobby Kennedy appeared like an alligator in a swimming pool to roil Eisenhower-era politics. A lot of the sourness and that curt, disdainful way of handing out orders and putting an emery edge to even an inquiry in passing owed something to the fact that Bobby had been happy enough unearthing the scandals of the Truman administration as a government attorney in Brooklyn.

"All this business about Jack and Bobby being blood brothers has been exaggerated," Eunice Shriver insisted. "First there was a big difference in years. They had different tastes in men, different tastes in women. They didn't really become close until 1952, and it was politics that brought them together. That's a business full of knives. Jack needed somebody he could trust, someone who had loyalty to him. Jack knew he had a person like that with Bobby around." There were similarities: Both brothers were brutally hard self-drivers when they had to be, both rather openly and arrogantly detested the bibulous courthouse hypocrites still in style around Massachusetts politics, and they both were either painfully candid or painfully shy in their back-room dealings.

Temperamentally, the gap was enormous. The John Kennedy of the latter enchantment was already evident: increasingly subtle and polished in his social turnings, easy and amorous privately, irritable sometimes but steeled by the years of intense daily pain to hold himself within studied psychological limits—rational ultimately, his fine wit attended by a self-assured Whig dryness and a remote mocking note that sometimes was reminiscent of Franklin Roosevelt's in many of its surprising junctures.

The Bobby of his detractors was recognizable, too: narrow-minded, pensive, moralistic, settled into his prolific marriage. Leo Damore, among his Cape Cod cullings, has come up with a secondhand episode that reveals the state of things a few years before. Jack Kennedy and a friend, bumming around Hyannis Port while the lieutenant (j.g.) was recuperating from his first back operation, picked up a pair of local girls and brought them back to the family homestead the evening of a major Atlantic storm. The four were singing songs around the piano when Bob Kennedy came through the living room. There was a perfunctory introduction: After several minutes Bob said he thought it was time for him to go along upstairs to bed. At the top of the staircase landing, one of the girls recalled, he paused and looked down and asked "troubled and hurt," "'Aren't you glad to see me?'"

"I remember we all stopped what we were doing and Jack sort of smiled and passed it off. 'I'm always glad to see you,'" the offhand young naval hero said in a level voice.

As late as 1952, when Bob turned up at 122 Bowdoin, it wasn't a question of Jack's having summoned him, exactly—"We don't have that," Bobby later said. "When Bobby came in we knew it was the old man taking over," one of the disgruntled organizers of the time has noted.

The campaign effort had begun early in the year; by June, when Bobby arrived, the effort was effectively jammed. "Joe and Jack—the two of them fought like cats and dogs," Helen Keyes, that close-mouthed grand-aunt to all of the Kennedys who ran the digs at 122 Bowdoin, slipped once and admitted to me frankly. What evidently occurred was that the taciturn Bobby was informed of the deteriorating situation, and arrived, and unlocked those generational gears. JFK had taken to referring to his brother as "Black Robert."

The pinning figure at this point was twenty-five-year-old Kenneth P. O'Donnell. Still young and back from the war already with a Purple Heart after a stint as a bombardier-navigator in the Army Air Force and recently the captain of the Harvard football team, O'Donnell was already halfway a hero to start with to the rude, shy, self-deprecating Bobby. O'Donnell saw something from the outset in the sheer force of character with which his ex-teammate drove himself beyond his talents. Bob introduced his friend to Jack; Kenny went onto the payroll as a follow-up organizer.

Paul Dever had already indicated that he would not himself oppose Lodge for the Senate, but rather would stand for reelection as Massachusetts's governor; he made very clear to the Kennedys that he himself intended to co-opt the Party apparatus—the Kennedys would have to put together their own organization and fund it themselves.

They threw together the 286 "Secretaries"—businessmen, housewives, PTA officials, schoolteachers—who recognized in John Kennedy a more enlightened type of politician than the usual fast-talking, graft-loving, party wheel horses.

Another subtle move was to try to find for any locality Secretaries who lived and worked outside it, and so were not caught up in local factionalism. The Secretaries, supported through the Boston headquarters, became the area directors of a statewide pattern of thousands of volunteers. Potential rivals were scared out easily by the abrupt appearance of this formidable grid of organization rising out of the Massachusetts landscape. Kennedy entered the party primary unopposed: His headquarters tried out the loose new muscles of this political yearling by amassing signatures for his nomination papers—2,500 were mandatory; 262,324 were amassed.

The difficulty was, as soon as the young men who had begun to put this prodigious thing together began to haul it up, the creature turned out to be extremely wobbly. John Galvin was still involved at this stage, Dalton came back, Frank Morrissey and now O'Donnell as well as the more phlegmatic Larry O'Brien (who had worked for the ambitious Foster Furcolo, fallen out with him, and so come over to the Kennedys).

"Six people," O'Donnell recalled in that level soft gray echo of a voice, such a surprise sometimes coming out of so lipless a man. "Six confused people. Because the organization was coming together by degrees, Dalton had been appointed the campaign manager technically, and he was a good man, but his nature was that of a speechwriter, not a head-knocker. And the head-knocking part is a tough job, especially when you are dealing with a Kennedy. The old man running around . . . We had reached the point where we had all the groundwork done, and John Kennedy himself was reluctant to make the selections, appoint some people and lose others, because Dever would resent the new people.

"So Robert Kennedy arrived at my behest. I had been in touch with him and I told him, 'Things are so screwed up; no one here is prepared to deal with your father; the old horses of Massachusetts simply won't understand that we're trying to grope our way into a new situation; we've reached the point where we have to decide who is going to run the campaign in the city of Worcester . . .' The father, actually, when he would come in and visit, had some of the most sensible criticisms of stupid things we were doing, but in a way he could never really trust himself because people kowtowed to him. He knew the older fellows like Kane, and Johnny Powers, and he had a real rapport with Dever——."

Bobby arrived. "I know you're an important man around here and all that," the furious governor told the Ambassador in a much-quoted telephone call very soon after that, "but I'm telling you this and I mean it. Keep that fresh kid of yours out of my sight from here on in."

Jack Kennedy himself, that disk grinding deeper into his back as each campaign day passed, managed through the uproar and the back-room taffy-pulling to stagger on stalwartly toward the eventual victory. "A cold champion with a touch of class," in the opinion of his handler O'Donnell, he found the strength somewhere to show up at a meeting hall or auditorium on crutches, leave them at the entrance with one of the advance people and march down the center aisle like a guardsman. The first time Jackie, whom the candidate was courting by then, showed up in Massachusetts political annals she was sitting on the steps of the Masonic Lodge at Quincy while her overfatigued date, the candidate, dealt straight talk back and forth in the basement among the neighborhood wire pullers. "I didn't think he was going to live through the campaign," Jim King, Ted's manager in Boston and a political stripling at the time, concluded from Jack's exhausted looks. But the candidate absolutely had to; he had to show his father, and, winning, he did.

As early as the first planning conference at Hyannis Port, the financier came in and told everybody where to sit—"They [were] just children in that house," a participant reports—and was about to take over the proceedings completely when Jack Kennedy, as neatly as he was able, suggested that his father concentrate his efforts on providing the necessary money: "We concede you that role." The realization Jack had of the shambles his father made as Ambassador to the Court of Saint James's kept the candidate skeptical. When Pat Jackson bridled with indignation at the financier's anti-Semitic blast—"those sheeny friends of yours"—Jack supposedly remarked in explanation of his father: "I guess there isn't a motive in it which I think you'd respect except love of family." Then, after a pause, "And more often than not, I think that's just pride."

Joe Kennedy held up his end of this struggle for self-esteem. His father had a way, Jack told friends, of suggesting to the press that he "made" his son do whatever worked out, that his supreme alertness and his imported downtown specialists supplied the shadow management. Jack was, the Ambassador implied, a dilettante in all things: When a fatuous admirer attributed part of Jack's success to his appeal to women, the father was reported to have responded that, yes, women liked Jack—older women. It is Joe Kennedy versus the silken Roosevelt all over again, and again the consequences of the match are pretty much foregone. "Bobby is soft—soft on people," the father commented shortly. "He has the capacity to be emotionally involved, to feel things deeply, as compared with Jack and that amazing detachment of his."

So Bobby, brought in of necessity to take over the middle of things, became the center. That pepperpot old father, recognizing that he had become something of an embarrassment to his ascendant son, stepped back into the flats of the political landscape and began to make a completely new reputation as the possessor of a willing shoulder on which an opposing politician could cry. Bobby would become the heavy. The Ambassador called in John McCormack to help with the intractable Jewish liberals of Brookline and Newton. Influential Boston Jews liked McCormack—he owed his nickname, Rabbi John, to sentiments that antedated his support for Israel—and Kennedy's colleague Jacob Javits, up to help Lodge at a Blue Hill Avenue rally, was doing the Kennedy cause no good by reportedly referring to Jack as "the son of his father." Jack Kennedy was charged, in the House of Representatives, with putting forth an amendment intended to strike much of the allocated aid to Israel. The amendment in fact amounted to a shrewd move to shortstop even deeper cuts, the sly McCormack divulged to audience after audience.

"That was, of course, a figment of McCormack's imagination," Tip O'Neill, a House colleague, would tell me. The father was forever "making a few calls" to people he just happens to know—big-city machine bosses, new governors, congressmen, unhappy statesmen of the trade union movement. "He had a fantastic ability to be the most charming man you ever met," an associate of the period insists, "for hours sometimes—but then in the snap of a finger he could turn into the most hard-nosed guy there ever was—capable of taking your head off. He was a tough tough guy. You made a deal with him, you kept your deal—otherwise, get out of the way."

Having purportedly stepped back, Joe left a lot of the details to his stand-in Frank Morrissey. "He used a self-proclaimed 'pol' named Francis X. Morrissey as a political confidence man and buffer in Boston," Jack Kennedy's alter ego and biographer, Ted Sorensen, would write in caustic dismissal of Morrissey's functions, ". . . but he depended on his brothers and others of whom the 'pros' had barely heard to run his Massachusetts campaign." A longtime buddy of Jack's sums up the association a little less obliquely: "Jack absolutely hated Morrissey. He'd go out of his way to eat his ass out in front of everybody . . ." The first true Kennedy cell division was completing itself.

5. *School Days*

While Jack Kennedy was thus coming into his own in Washington and Boston, Teddy was in school. More about Edward Kennedy's preparatory years comes to life going through his senior yearbook than conferring with the mild calm benign scarcely aging Old Boys who were his masters at Milton Academy. Their after-impression remains that he was good-humored, unusually considerate of others for a teenager, willing, reasonably hard-working, and, at best, a so-so student. John Torney, in time the dean of the boys' school at Milton and Teddy's English teacher, noted with the suggestive arch of an eyebrow that he had been to "so many schools before he got here, and one simply can't do that with younger people . . ."

Comments in Milton's year-by-year dossier on Kennedy make clear that Ted was trying hard with his studies and that there was at least measurable self-betterment: "conscientious and eager worker throughout the year," his math teacher indicates. "For the year Teddy has shown considerable improvement in grasping the implications of the material. His difficulties with spelling and punctuation are disappearing also," an English teacher comments hopefully. He was not then, nor will he ever be, as he himself often remarked to me and many others, a "quick study." Acquiring the network of facts and theory with which to construct the sense of a field on his own went ploddingly at first. Foreign languages were especially slow-going; he undertook the least demanding, Spanish, and didn't do at all well even with that.

The feeling the masters carried away about Kennedy was that there was a lot to this one that experience will begin to sharpen. Debating was an important activity at Milton, and Kennedy, who didn't have a varsity sport in winter, joined the team and emerged as a starter his last several years. Albert Norris, who coached him, regarded Kennedy as one of his strongest and most versatile rebuttal men, unusually well poised and with an exceptional knowledge of his subject and ability to organize his thoughts as the argument turned. "He always knew what he was talking about," Norris said. "And even when he was in school he could speak more intelligently, with great concern and feeling and knowledge of public affairs—more than a great many bigwigs from Washington who came here——." When Milton Academy debated the Harvard freshmen, Kennedy was a member of the team that brought back victory.

"Smilin' Ed," as his yearbook editor dubs Kennedy, seems to turn up in one picture or another on almost every page. He was class secretary; he stands in there with the glee club, among the tennis and football players, grinning enormously next to the director among the dramatic club personae, although the part he had was decidedly minor. Here and there he managed to include himself in one of the group shots of an extracurricular activity he hadn't even joined: This pleases the evolving taste for the delicately absurd that he and his brother and godfather John are coming to appreciate in each other. He is a member of a group called the Boogies, which has no recollected reason for convening at all, and in their candid yearbook shot they are poised before the usual library backdrop naked to the waist, all striking hand-seductively-behind-the-scalp-and-a-leg-up poses, joke cheesecake.

Teddy was a football player too, of course—and, as in everything else just then, dependable, a regular. He was Milton's left end his final two years. He specialized in the "pop pass": The quarterback would hit him quickly about five yards beyond scrimmage and as a wall of linebackers fell on him he would drive doggedly for five or six more yards until too many safety men were up and on top of him even for his surging beefiness. This role was by no means one anybody on the team envied Kennedy: He would find himself too often the recipient of what his teammates referred to as the "lumbago pass." Bobby, who had played Milton's blocking back in a single wing to Dave Hackett's tailback, was remembered for his ability to capitalize on Hackett's setup fakes and execute the sharp off-angle blocks that sprang Hackett for yardage. Ted, too slow for razzle-dazzle, absorbed a lot more punishment.

A team player, willing. One yearbook vignette catches Ted while he sprawls in one of the dorm rooms, juggling "a piece of dry ice into the wastebasket and mumbles 'if you want to stick around, my man, you might get some.' Immediately a quart of milk appears from behind his back and the party gathers momentum." This, too—this engulfing gregariousness—draws attention, but by the time Ted Kennedy left Milton he had made no permanent close friends, as Bob had with Dave Hackett.

Preoccupied—haunted, at times—with the expectations of his unremitting father, Edward Kennedy had very little emotional room for the commitments genuine friendship requires outside his family. Episodes like the sudden, utterly unexplained disappearance when he was nine of his lobotomized sister Rosemary—the warmest and most accessible of all his siblings, as he would explain to me many years later—would leave him apprehensive underneath. He, too, might drop out of sight. Important to remain an accredited Kennedy.

Ted Kennedy's four years at Milton, like Bob's year and a half, had gone by easily, free of the cliquing and the obeisances to society pecking orders that made miserable so many of Jack Kennedy's days at Choate. Ted's associations remain loose and comfortable. When college loomed he talked a little about Stanford, but applied and went along dutifully to Harvard, like Bobby a legacy.

No doubt a lot of cheerful acquaintanceships were to be preferred to one or two deathlock associations. Rose Kennedy, whose views came out as a scrupulously calculated needlepoint of opinions, told me that while Teddy was at Milton he and the president-to-be developed a very full and relaxed friendship. This works out: Bob was in college and law school at the time, courting, marrying, and setting up housekeeping with Ethel Skakel while working on a steady accretion of friendships with highly independent and outspoken classmates of his generation—Hackett, Dean Markham, Ken O'Donnell—whose lives, and to an extent whose identities, would soon be tangled into his own.

Jack Kennedy, recuperating from hospital stays for months at a stretch, got back to the big house often: Bob's friends remember Jack as stretched out rather glumly in the movie theater, or reading in a rocking chair on the side porch that overlooked the Atlantic. The parents were gone most of the time, generally in different directions; even when the children were in residence Rose had taken to spending most of her time by herself—she had a kind of shack set up for herself not far from the water's edge—or with acquaintances from her exalted childhood. One pal of Jack's passed along to me the future president's complaint that, over his many hospital convalescences, Rose never visited him once.

Rose prized her midlife independence; her observations remained objective, precisely targeted. "The president adored Teddy," their mother responded to my question as to why Jack and Ted became so close, "because he was so strong. He really envied him his good health. He could do everything the president himself would have wanted to do, with his great towering strength . . ."

The day the news reached Milton that Kathleen Kennedy had died in an airplane crash, and Teddy's whole impulse had driven him to take the next train for Hyannis Port, the masters at Milton confronted an "irate" Jack Kennedy, arrived to break the terrible news to Ted himself and furious that the school should have released his distraught kid brother unaccompanied. They shared a gaiety, a sense of the ridiculous. "There was always a lot of play between the two of them," Ted's streetwise aide Ed Martin remembered. Unlike the more austere young Bobby, who simply could not help feeling every human involvement deeply, Jack and Teddy both admitted to an easygoing fascination with good-looking women which regularly led to sexual episodes as piquant as they were momentary, and generated spirited badinage afterward.

They liked to travel together; Ted flew down weekends to sit with his recuperating brother in Palm Beach and was most frequently delegated to pick Jack up in a wheelchair when he was finally finished with one of his many postoperative hospital confinements. They sailed together constantly. Ted was by most accounts the best sailor in the family: He liked to race *Tenovus* especially and won with regularity. "Read all you can and remain jealous of your time," Ted says his older brother repeatedly told him—stretch, push yourself. Exertion hung in the Kennedy air: The years themselves were passing, passing, passing, and where were the profits destiny expected?

More disconcerting even, how to explain the way the seams of character tore open at unexpected moments? Then a Kennedy really had to stand up. "The toughness was important," John Kennedy explained to Arthur Schlesinger one night at the White House. "If it hadn't been for that, Teddy might be just a playboy today. But my father cracked down on him at a crucial time in his life, and this brought out in Teddy the discipline and seriousness which will make him an important political figure."

6. The Cheating Scandal

The crucial time the president alluded to was, presumably, the lapse that resulted in his younger brother's "connection," in Harvard's sweet phrase, having been "severed" the spring of 1951. The facts of the disgrace are certainly routine enough. But to schoolboys, fallout is everything, and what takes the explaining is the mentality that produced Kennedy's never-to-be-forgotten earliest disgrace.

The background was Cambridge still vibrating a little from World War II and clamorous with geopolitical self-examination as the Korean War expanded beyond its police-action origins. Swaggering veterans of combat in Europe and the Southern Pacific theater were still in residence nursing their G.I. Bill money, hanging around the Yard at Harvard to impress the hell out of susceptible incoming underclassmen, hustle pool in the Freshman Union, appear at meals with neckties above the necklines of their T-shirts to show what they thought of the dress regulations. It was a quirky, transitional period; Harvard was settling down again, but the exhilarated, capering, tomorrow-we-die undertone of the later forties lingered. With three brothers who had served in the military, Ted Kennedy was especially vulnerable.

He'd signed up the day he registered at Harvard for freshman football; incoming athletes were especially susceptible. Anti-sports-minded as Cambridge is traditionally, it would have taken an exceptionally self-assured youngster not to resent the put-downs directed routinely at Varsity Material by Senior Tutors and entry proctors who wore black silk stockings with garters and carried their umbrellas furled. Jocks reacted, tipped one another off about "gut" courses, traded notes, crammed desperately before tests in self-conscious little groups that dismissed academic work as something to be tolerated at best and—wherever this was possible—circumvented. Respect went to the teammate who snagged a "gentleman C" in a course without "cracking a book."

One team member who was known to have absorbed a lot of physics in high school found himself confronting his natural-science hour-long exam in the amphitheater of the new Allston Burr science building; at the insistence of his buddies, he allowed himself to be planted under good light in the bottom row; his friends fanned out, above and around. "I had no sooner started the test," this jock related later, "when the whispers started in behind me. 'Write Bigger!' This kept on. So I printed, and the letters got larger, and larger, until at times individual symbols got two and three inches high. I remember it took me fourteen blue books to get through that fifty-minute test. Then I remembered how worried I was when my section man called me in. When I got there, he asked me whether I had considered getting my eyes examined. I remember Ted was three rows back. All that was probably on the way to the Spanish exam."

The desperation it took to produce a blunder that dumb was in the air. For weeks, hanging around the room of Kenny O'Donnell's kid brother, Warren, Kennedy had been fretting about doing well enough in his Spanish course to relieve himself of the colleges's language requirement; languages still came hardest. Two qualities about Kennedy interested his friends: He was a daredevil, and he was somebody who would do anything if you challenged him properly. In jockstrapping circles he had a reputation as something of a secret grind, always grubbing away at his studies if he had a chance at a B in a course.

Playing on these peculiarities, the crowd that hung around O'Donnell's room started working on another roommate, Bill Frate—a big lumbering freshman from Connecticut the roommates liked to needle as a "Master of Spanish" because he had done so well at the language in his College Boards. Why not go help Ted out and take Kennedy's test for him? Just . . . slip into that auditorium, and . . . pick up Kennedy's blue book, and . . . and . . . . It was a spontaneous joke, something far-fetched enough to laugh about.

The morning of the test it was a joke still. Kennedy had been up early, as always, going over the material; not long before the exam was scheduled to start he stopped by O'Donnell's room. Bill Frate was still asleep. Full of jollity, the rest of them went and woke him up, pushed him to get dressed.

"Isn't this the day you're going to go over and take Ted's test?" one said.

The Master of Spanish was impulsive. "Hell, why don't I go over and take it? If this is what you want . . ."

It just happened. Kennedy didn't protest; he didn't say anything. Nerve under the building pressure was being tested all around. So Kennedy's classmate proceeded to the examination hall; Kennedy made his way back to his room at Wigglesworth.

When Kennedy next saw his stand-in the news was alarming. "It was an easy test," his benefactor began. "And I think you did very well. But I think we're caught." Unhappily, the examination proctor that morning had been a teaching fellow who was also Warren O'Donnell's freshman adviser and, Frate was aware, like Ted, "hung around that room a lot. I could see him all through that exam going up and down the roster; several times our eyes met," Kennedy's unhappy co-conspirator remembered twenty years later. "I dropped it on the desk in front of him and looked him square in the eye. He practically had an orgasm. He saw the name on it and he was out of the room before the test was over. I think he made it up from Emerson to University Hall in three bounds." The best hope was that the teaching fellow would stop by and offer to talk the whole thing over; that notion was amputated soon enough: Officials at University Hall telephoned Kennedy's room within minutes. Sentence was handed out in Dean Delmar Leighton's office: Out. If either man cared to attempt to reenter the institution, the University would observe his subsequent conduct and reconsider after a year.

Furthermore, Frate recalls, "the father was terribly disappointed in Ted's doing something as foolish as that when there was so little at stake." Typically, Joe Kennedy had offered all the help the family could muster to the unfortunate dupe his son had gotten into trouble; knowing that the boy had been struggling to get through school on a Rotary Club athletic scholarship, Joe offered cash if that was going to help at all, Jack's assistance with a service academy appointment, whatever the boy needed. When nothing was taken the Ambassador—superstitious as he was, Joe Kennedy now privately subsidized the members of Earl Blaik's Army team who had just been thrown out of West Point for cheating—recognized character. He encouraged Frate to drop in around Hyannis Port and spend a little time with him, even while Ted was in the Army in France: Something of a cross-generational friendship resulted. Tribal ethics held: Nobody was repudiating anybody.

A performance like his youngest son's was all but certain to bring down the furies at Hyannis Port. The financier himself remained hurt and annoyed with Ted, and continued to be, once he thought about it, perplexed: A clean-cut attempt at cheating was unanticipated from his unpromising last-born, out of character. "There are people who can mess up in life and not get caught," the Ambassador fumed at this misbegotten youngest, "but you're not one of them, Teddy." Leave guile and deception to your betters. By every report the financier was able to restrain his temper, but the sustained disapproval he emanated throughout that miserable spring of 1951 kept Edward subdued and brooding. "He made no bones about it," one of Ted's old teachers at Milton, to whom the recent graduate went back for advice, recalled of their melancholy session. "Again and again he reiterated how rotten he felt for the other boy, the one he got to take that exam for him." This was to become perhaps the least attractive feature of Kennedy's maturing personality, the instinct to displace the guilt, push compassion and concern about the price the *victim* now had to pay after his own bad judgment and lack of self-control had precipitated a disaster.

It was an easier stance for the badly shaken Kennedy to live with, this solemn passacaglia of piety, the overriding concern for the situation of others. A happier, a more aristocratic-seeming note, one Kennedy will again and again strike while backing off from a bad mistake, one which will sound trumped-up to outsiders sometimes, will come across the nerves of doubters with a disastrous falsity. At home he dated, exchanged confidences with his ever-loving sisters—"'Do girls ever bite you when they kiss you?'" a horrified maid, telling all to a tabloid, recalled Eunice's having asked her baby brother—but the Ambassador was waiting for the disgraced one to begin the redemptive process himself.

One afternoon Teddy paid an unannounced visit on his local recruiter and signed himself into the U.S. Army. He brought his enlistment papers home; the Ambassador's restraint finally burst its limits as he examined the documents. "Don't you ever look at what you're signing?" The Korean War was blazing like an oil fire just then, a recruiter had talked Ted into accepting a four-year enlistment, and the old man evidently felt the family had sacrificed enough: He telephoned the captain in charge of local recruitment and was able to cut back Teddy's commitment to the more usual two-year draftee stint. With that the Ambassador was able to pull strings in Washington and get his prodigal assigned to the honor guard at NATO headquarters in Paris, much safer along with being well stocked with the French women for whom Ted soon developed a lifelong appreciation.

"Do the best you're able and after that the devil take it," the father had told his son often enough—even at Kennedy depths the principles have escape hatches. Pressure eases. "Bye bye baby, remember you're our baby, when the girls give you the eye," sang his family assembled to see Ted off. For twenty-two months now it would be Teddy Kennedy, private first class.

Sweating infantry basic helped, but disgrace had settled in around the humiliated Kennedy, tincturing everything. "Sixteen of the most worthwhile months of my life," the newly enlisted GI wrote hopefully to his friend the Milton headmaster Arthur B. Perry. But "an experience I never want to duplicate. As I informed Mister Norris, basic training is the answer for any problem youngster you might encounter." He added that he is now in favor, after this, of Universal Military Training—a favorite debate topic of the era. As early as his last semesters at Milton Ted Kennedy had confided to people that he saw a career for himself somewhere in public service. It was already his habit to generalize from his own experience, try to apply what he himself had picked up to public policy.

"You are exposed as an enlisted man to a great deal," the problem-youngster-become-a-senator would remember to me, trying to think back and bring up a little of the emotional tenor of the two years in exile that had obviously dropped pretty much out of memory as soon as they were satisfactorily served. "The difficulties, yes, when riding on troop ships. At the time, though, it didn't bother me at all, didn't give me a deep feeling of the practical inequities, although in a way I had the feelings on me, of course, it had given me the chance to follow the system on out . . ." A typical Edward Kennedy answer, as I already knew by then, the syntax bridging that of Dwight Eisenhower caught off guard and Molly Bloom contesting the superhots.

In fact, Kennedy—whose life was obviously proceeding at much more mundane levels than that of his two older officer-class brothers—seemed to relish slumming while putting in his PFC time at Fort Dix, then in Germany and finally as part of the SHAPE Honor Guard near Paris. Over those military months his morale was touched up gradually: He went on pass to Switzerland once, entered the one-man-bobsled races—a brand-new thrill for Kennedy, speed in an extraordinarily pure form, always welcome to the velocity-loving private—and won. One of the few memorabilia the magazine press has dredged up about Teddy during this two years in suspension was the fact that, in Germany, he made it his business to find out that there were eight Massachusetts absentee voters in camp with him, approach them all, and line up every vote for Jack.

Kennedy returned without incident to Harvard College in 1953 (undergraduate memory is disinterested and short), worked hard at everything he did, and graduated in 1956. "He was no aristocrat at college," a sometime aide who knew him there observes; friends from his freshman days who remembered him as a good-humored happy-go-lucky Irish kid did detect, without finding it objectionable, a certain subtle stiffening and self-awareness: "He now regarded himself as a Kennedy," one says outright, ascribing this to his brother's having become, in the meanwhile, a senator from Massachusetts.

Fred Holborn, a Harvard teaching fellow at the time, makes the distinction between the earlier Ted Kennedy, with his "large and diversified curiosity and a spread of interests that was pretty disorganized," and the returned veteran who, having stumbled onto an undergraduate course in public speaking, used the techniques that helped him organize a speech to gain some intellectual control of his courses, especially in his area of specialization, government.

Always a plugger, Teddy was free pretty largely of Bob's tendency to let the studies slide and just sit around with the other football people and "talk and argue a lot, mostly about sports and politics." Friends of the period like John Culver remember Ted as one who would invariably steal away after a while, often to the underpopulated business school library, to frown over the books. Even then Kennedy's motivation went well beyond simple grade-getting.

Robert Wood, later Lyndon Johnson's Secretary of HUD but in 1953–54 a lecturer at Harvard in problems of state and local government, summons up the tall, quiet, pleasant Teddy sitting in his little course as an auditor, "sensitive enough to realize that I was probing intellectual material that reinforced family conversations. Ted had an appreciation for material not immediately useful to him." Kennedy's grades, never really outstanding, moved up to honor—B—levels: Significantly, he did better than anybody expected in the mandatory general examinations in government. Without the deep affection for the shadows and crisscrossing tints of the historical that distinguished Jack Kennedy's emerging mind or any of Bobby's spring-cocked incisiveness, Ted was beginning to show, intellectually, exceptional breadth, range, the kind of placid determination that moved him slowly and consumingly across a wide area of knowledge, leaving amazingly little unlearned finally, the larger ideas stripped and the very footnotes defoliated. A passage of locusts at noon.

The public man was beginning to emerge. The regular end on Harvard's 1956 football team, down home and addressing a dinner of the Barnstable Boosters' Club in honor of the local high school's Red Raiders, intones to the boys and fathers his discovery that it was a mistake to believe that the "toughest characters are those who drink the most, smoke the most, or have the biggest vocabulary," since, in college, the insight will arrive that "the toughest are those who block and tackle the hardest." Even from an undergraduate at a football dinner this is a remark of memorable fatuousness; it goes by half-applauded in a banquet room of Boosters, very few of whom are likely to be burdened uncomfortably with vocabulary bloat.

On the football field itself Ted Kennedy stood out more for his overall good-tempered drive than any unusual assertiveness. He labored for years to make it up to the varsity. "Bobby was more a defensive type," Harvard freshman coach Henry Lamar would say. "He didn't have the size that makes for a blocker, but boy, was he mean. All those kids were battlers. Teddy was good at everything. The outstanding thing about Ted was that he'd do everything you asked him to do. If you gave him a job to do, he'd do it, exactly as you asked it to be done."

Lamar recalls the series during which Ted laid an opposing quarterback out. The next play the quarterback waited for Ted and caught him with a forearm across the jaw; the play after that Ted flattened the quarterback after "carefully avoiding the forearm. He was that kind of kid." Kennedy kept his temper always, but once his feelings were roused he had a way of exploding: A player on the JV of the period, against whom the varsity often walked through new plays, remembers that he had to watch out for Teddy, who forgot himself sometimes and hit hard even without pads. Beneath the seemingly phlegmatic good humor there was the volcanic capability; it could be touched off unexpectedly.

On a family vacation cruise off the Maine coast, Ted and Dave Hackett, rowing ashore in a dinghy for supplies, passed a large yacht. A man hung over the rail and advised them to row a little faster; Ted yelled back suggesting that he mind his own business. "Come back here and say that again," the man on the yacht suggested.

"Teddy spun the dinghy around so fast I almost fell out of it," Hackett told someone later. "The next thing I knew, Teddy was on the yacht and the man was being thrown overboard and all the women were screaming and running below to hide in the cabins. Their husbands were running with them, to see that they were safely tucked away, I guess. By this time, I'm on the yacht with Teddy. The men start to come back up on the deck to deal with us, but it's a narrow hatchway and they have to come up through it one at a time. As each guy appears, I grab him and spin him around and throw him to Teddy, and Teddy throws him overboard. In no time, all of the men—there were about eight of them—were in the water, I never saw anything like it."

Even unpushed, Kennedy radiated vigor, two Honey Fitzes in one: College girls who went out with him reported that he made his expectations clear early and with great undisguised feeling, and took it more as a curiosity than an affront if his willingness to extend himself was not instantly accepted. Like Bob, he was a clubman in moderation—Hasty Pudding, AD, Pi Eta—and lived with the jocks in Winthrop House. He took up skiing; James McGregor

Burns, who would join him a few years later, marveled at Teddy's tendency to desert the packed slopes and rip down through the brambles, dodging trees and reappearing at the bottom, scratched up and red-faced.

Ted remained well taken among his classmates despite an occasional undergraduate prank: A rugby player in spring, Ted joined the team one year for an extramural match in Bermuda. The opposing team bivouacked the Harvard squad in outlying Army barracks, and, evidently bored, Ted managed somehow to cajole a large woolly sheep into wandering among the bunks and left him tethered there. By the time the players had returned from their match the sheep had evacuated enormously, and the irrepressible Kennedy faced a circle of sharply annoyed fellow Harvardians.

Perhaps the high point of Ted Kennedy's career at college—if not for him, certainly for the Ambassador—was the football schedule of 1955–56. Three of Joe Kennedy's sons played varsity football for the school: The first of them, the cynosure Joe Jr., did not get into the all-important Yale game for all three seasons he played and never, therefore, lettered. When the final gun sounded that last autumn of 1937, a raving angry Joseph P. Kennedy rushed down onto the playing field himself and let the impassive coach Richard Harlow know exactly what he thought of an omission like that. The rumor survives that so many obviously inspired telephone calls had reached the coach's rooms that he felt he had to keep young Joe Kennedy benched as a testimony to personal integrity. Bobby lettered, but barely, playing the vital game on a broken leg.

Ted, to the Ambassador's joy, was a regular. A Kennedy employee recalls the rain-soaked day, sitting beside the financier throughout the game against Columbia, they watched Ted dive for and hold a ball in the end zone after it had bounced away from two Columbia defenders and another Harvard: The associate feared the overwrought father was about to scramble down onto the field, oblivious to the ongoing game, to "pummel Teddy in his joy and pride." In the final play of one Yale game Teddy picked up the ball in the air as it bounced off the goalposts to destroy Yale's pathetic last hope that year; the next year he caught Harvard's only touchdown. It was a climactic resurrection.

Possibly it was those draftee years, the trapped stench of the bunkroom and perimeter guard—whatever it was, by this time there was to Teddy Kennedy a street-corner quality, a need to move around more and more without the driver and the fanfare and the lap robes and the retinue. "The Army obviously makes a rather dramatic kind of impression on the maturing process," he told me once, "the kinds of high emotions that exist on racial questions. It's a broader kind of experience—individuals become more important, events become more important, causes become more important . . . the uniqueness of our sort of experience compared with others."

Returned to the listless undergraduate grip of Harvard College, Kennedy undertook some unprecedented forays. He volunteered to coach basketball at a settlement house in Boston's Puerto Rican South End. He moved quietly away from the patterned summers at Hyannis Port to try a stint as a forest ranger one year; another summer he served as a crewman on a trans-Pacific yacht race to Honolulu. One vacation he and his live-wire classmate Claude Hooten taught water-skiing at Acapulco and, halfway back, cooled down in a New Orleans jail when police questioned the title to the used car the two were driving. It was an exploratory time: The imminence of parental judgment relaxed for a semester or two, suspended.

7. Vice President

The early fifties were tempering Ted's brother, the freshman senator Jack. "We all have fathers," Jack Kennedy was later to sigh when he discovered that Martin Luther King's father was a bigot; along with his own ubiquitous father, his crushed vertebrae were keeping Jack Kennedy in increasing agony. In 1953 John Kennedy married. "At least one good friend doubts that Kennedy would be married today if he had lost his Senate battle," James Burns has written in an early biography of the senator. Domesticity wasn't Jack's focus.

More significant was establishing his political identity. The Democratic Party in Massachusetts was being incessantly goaded from the left, especially by the hyperliberal Americans for Democratic Action. When the party's rising state treasurer, Foster Furcolo, advised the ADA that " 'those are good programs you believe in but ADA support hurts them. The best thing you can do is disband . . .' It was as if I'd come to dinner and threw up on the tablecloth," Furcolo explained to me later. "It was too bad, a misunderstanding, really, and I regretted it. Because one ADA person will do the hard political work of fifty others . . ."

"The enemy of my enemy," the Arab insists, "is my friend"; even in the political bazaars of backroom Boston, however, Jack Kennedy and the ADA sniffed one another's merchandise dubiously. It was a predictable hesitation. The tendency among the sensible-shoe, twilight-burnished New Deal liberals of the period—the Eleanor Roosevelts, the Thomas Finletters and Paul Butlers and Archibald MacLeishes—was to see this standard-bearer of a second-generation Kennedy bid for political power as callow and opportunistic, able to summon up a little too self-consciously a suitable ironic aside or a quote from Burke or Stendhal or Dante or Duff Cooper: The lacquer peeled readily, a gentleman's education which never penetrated deeply enough to ensure concern with individual liberties or social betterment.

It was that same John Kennedy recent congressman, after all, who had redbaited Russ Nixon, repeatedly voted for Pat McCarran's insidious Internal Security Act in 1950, himself dragged the names of such theretofore unhectored academics as John Fairbanks and Owen Lattimore into the slipstream of recriminations over George Marshall's China Policy throughout the early fifties. Jack Kennedy continued to equivocate about Joe McCarthy and refused to join the posse that strung the collapsing McCarthy up by a censure motion in November of 1954.

In Massachusetts, though, and especially in the academic community, individuals were beginning to pick up on the often-unrecorded committee votes and seemingly minor personnel shifts that, in combination, so often have more to do with the way the government is administered than open floor votes on inflammatory public issues. On appointments especially Kennedy bucked Joe McCarthy so consistently that in the end they passed in the Cloakroom with no more than the briefest of exchanges. Kennedy voted for James Conant as Ambassador to Germany, Charles Bohlen to the Soviet Union, opposed Robert Lee of the Federal Communications Commission, Owen Brewster to the Investigative Subcommittee, and—bellwether of the progressive nightwatch—resisted an ambassadorship for McCarthy's primary succubus in the State Department R. W. S. (Scotty) McLeod.

At the same time Kennedy's doubts about the witch-hunting of the period were becoming evident to the liberal community, his lines to the national— i.e., the "presidential"—Democratic Party pulled tighter. Adlai Stevenson, the dome from Illinois the Democratic Left adored unceasingly, had campaigned in Massachusetts in 1952 for John Kennedy: Here was a primary laying on of hands no one could ignore.

In fact, back as far as the SEC days, in the early thirties, Joe Kennedy had been aware of Stevenson as an articulate young lawyer with excellent local connections and offered him the chance to run the SEC Chicago field office: Stevenson had turned the offer down, but ever after in Joe Kennedy's mind Stevenson was talent he himself had discovered early, and his career was one the older Kennedy began to follow. When Stevenson got the Democratic presidential nomination initially, the financier had contributed generously to Stevenson's support. By that time Kennedy had long owned the Merchandise Mart, hands down the largest of the Kennedy assets, and the financier was on cordial and productive terms with such Illinois kingmakers as Jake Arvey, a political henchman of the regnant mobster Sam Giancana— himself on a serviceable basis with Joe. Arvey functioned to a great extent as Adlai Stevenson's mentor and nut-cutter while Stevenson was governor of Illinois. Like Chicago's high-handed mayor, Richard Daley, whom Joe had spotted and patronized while Daley was little more than a clerk in city hall, the financier regarded Stephenson as a maturing prospect off his transcontinental bench.

As a little of the luster of the Stevensonian aura began to gleam on John Kennedy's cheek—Stevenson had called him "my kind of guy," then and now a code phrase of political anointment—ADA liberals close to Stevenson like Arthur Schlesinger Jr. and John Kenneth Galbraith were forced to reevaluate Jack Kennedy. Kennedy in turn began, warily, to "sponsor" ADA functions.

By 1954 Foster Furcolo had decided to go after the seat of Massachusetts Republican Senator Leverett Saltonstall. At that point Saltonstall had taken political root in Massachusetts—there was that swamp-Yankee integrity to the man, what with those unstraightened splay teeth and snow-white patrician's hair.

As it happened, Leverett and Jack "played well," one to the other. Since Saltonstall's freshman colleague was almost incessantly either in excruciating pain or recovering from an operation, Kennedy welcomed Leverett's willingness, Saltonstall told me, to "put in his name along with my name on bills that related to Massachusetts especially. The fishing industry, or the textile industry, or shoes . . . I think he appreciated that a graddeal . . ." As a Republican Saltonstall had all the prerogatives, since his was the sitting president, in dividing up the postmasterships and marshal appointments that are the rewards of the federal patronage system.

By September of 1954 Foster Furcolo had chosen to climb all over the unassertive Saltonstall in speech after speech. As a Democrat Jack Kennedy was obliged to support Furcolo. Nasty incidents piled up. Before a joint television appearance in Boston—up from Hyannis Port with a light fever the night before local surgeons were to perform a lumbar fusion on his incessantly torturous spine—Kennedy had sat waiting between his upright crutches an hour for the belated Furcolo, who arrived less than five minutes prior to camera time, looked Kennedy's script over, and complained at once that Kennedy's endorsement was not convincing enough.

"Foster, you have a hell of a nerve coming in here and asking for these last-minute changes," Kennedy exclaimed in open anger; he hobbled out of the studio and into the television station's men's room. Kennedy reappeared to endorse Bob Murphy, the Democratic candidate for governor, without mentioning Furcolo. Worse, Kennedy secretly sent Ted Sorensen, most trusted of his speechwriters and advisers, to explain to Saltonstall how to appeal to the Kennedy electorate. Saltonstall was reelected to the Senate by a narrow margin of some twenty-eight thousand votes. This became a Democratic insiders' eyebrow-raiser. Ted Kennedy, already in and out of his brother's operations, couldn't miss the extent to which his temperamental brother was likely to wreck havoc on his own political hopes by moves as rough as these.

One who grasped that was the Ambassador. When Furcolo then announced for governor, a scheduled meeting in Hyannis Port miscarried. Furcolo arrived; only the Ambassador, filling in for his son, was around the vast, empty house. "Paul Dever always used to like to talk to the father," Furcolo would recall to me. "We spoke for several hours. He sounded and talked like a man of sound judgment and common sense. Somehow I had thought he only knew the national situation, the money side as far as Massachusetts went, but I found that he knew the state in incredible detail. Also, I had the feeling he thought very very highly of Bobby . . ."

As 1956 approached there was a party-wide disagreement as to the wisdom of again nominating Adlai Stevenson for president at the convention in Chicago. The feeling was gathering among the older, more establishmentarian figures within the party—Harry Truman, Sam Rayburn, Averell Harriman, John McCormack—that, while Stevenson was an able man and eloquent, he did not have the grit or fundamental political savvy to give the ideologically sterile but hugely popular Eisenhower opposition that stood any genuine chance. John Kennedy, who appreciated Stevenson's standards and was not unhearing—or unprompting, for that matter—of talk that he would himself be a decorative, politically attractive vice-presidential candidate, especially compared with the detested Nixon, alongside the Orator from Illinois.

Kennedy's certification was compounding: After a little backroom trading of favors with Joe, Jack's collection of historical sketches *Profiles in Courage* had won the Pulitzer Prize—an event that broke up at least one historian in the Kennedy's camp. Harvard awarded the rising senator an honorary L.L.D. that spring. One problem of workaday politics presented itself immediately: Titular leadership of the Democratic Party of Massachusetts, adrift since the defeat of the strong-minded Dever, was firmly in the hands of John McCormack, the majority leader of the House of Representatives and an artful and widely connected fixture of the party. If Kennedy wanted to go to the convention with the votes of the delegates at least of Massachusetts under his control and available to barter to the Stevenson managers, he would have to engineer a coup and effectively take over the Massachusetts party machinery.

Prospects of the sort of fight this promised to be were unappetizing to Kennedy—to have any chance at all he would need to hold his aristocratically bridged nose and belly-flop into the mire of Massachusetts backroom politics.

The prize just then was the Democratic State Committee. John C. Carr, chairman of the committee since 1952, was suddenly expelled by court order in favor of the notorious William H. (Onions) Burke, a big bald heedless grunt-groan veteran of generations of the patronage grab, crony of James Michael Curley and onetime collector of customs for the Port of Boston. The Ambassador advised his son to pull shy of what was already shaping up as an embarrassing Irish brawl.

Joe Kennedy remained dubious about his son's involvement in what he saw as a doomed Stevensonian presidential effort. He had been tipped off by Richard Daley through Sarge Shriver that the vice-presidential choice was likely to be thrown to the convention. "Bobby and I felt the senator had no right to walk away from it," Kenny O'Donnell told me years later. "The party machinery was already a shambles, Eddie McCormack, the speaker's nephew, pointing toward the attorney generalship, was clearly attempting to take advantage of the situation to seize control of the machinery, and Foster Furcolo was about to be elected Governor of Massachusetts. I said, 'It's nice for your father to sit in Palm Beach and say to hell with it. But when the nut cutting comes, you'd better have the troops.' John Kennedy was a very elusive man sometimes, but when he said 'how many votes in the Committee have we got?' I knew he was going in that direction. Until that time he had not lifted a finger . . ."

The afternoon of the vote Jack Kennedy was himself at the wedding of his sister Jean and Steve Smith, and sent the still-impressionable Sorensen up from Washington to blood him a little in Massachusetts. Sorensen would report fistfights, the repeated half-serious threat by that colorful bartender, "Knocko" McCormack, the Speaker's brother and father of Eddie, to settle a disagreement cleanly by braining his opponent with a chair, booing, shoving, name-calling, contests for the gavel, people packed so tight they couldn't get their hands up from their sides if they were down, or down if they were up, and one McCormack fancier snake-hipping his way through the packed conference room, hands over his head to interest the "ups" and a thick wad of ten-dollar bills in his hands, from which he peeled the number that a wavering delegate seemed to require to reaffirm his convictions.

The room grew sulphurous with cigar smoke. The Kennedy forces won 47 to 31, a setdown for John McCormack. That summer Jack Kennedy went to Chicago with the Democratic delegation from Massachusetts firmly and permanently under his control. The hope among professional ethnics around the state that Kennedy was there primarily to look after their interests was shattered permanently; much of the senator's greatest strength had been drawn openly from union leaders, ADA intellectuals, and League of Women Voter activists. The Kennedys had replaced the apparatus of the Democratic Party in Massachusetts with one of their own. With or without his father's encouragement, there was little doubt then or afterwards where Jack Kennedy's debts and his deepest identification were going to lie.

The story of Jack Kennedy's vice-presidential candidacy in 1956 in Chicago has been told often enough: Kennedy came tantalizingly close, but Estes Kefauver got the bid from an open convention. The experience was painful, on balance, for all the Kennedys. Pain is an unrivaled teacher sometimes, and kept Bobby furious as he worked the floor delegates, a twenty-five-year-old part-time politician struggling through an impotence nightmare of uncoordinated planning and compounding nonrecognition.

The far more skeptical, much less viscerally involved candidate himself, immersed to the neck in bathwater at the nearby Stockyard Inn, continued to make a series of critical strategy mistakes, languidly. The Kennedy people simply didn't know anybody. The Ambassador didn't like the idea, and wasn't involved pulling strings. Hubert Humphrey (Jack Kennedy's own candidate for vice president, should he himself fail) found himself summoned, through his manager Congressman Eugene McCarthy, to appear before Kennedy for a conference; Jack Kennedy at once provoked in the thin-skinned McCarthy a reflux of disgust: "Not a chance. Up in Minnesota we're Protestants and Farmers."

Years afterward, Gene McCarthy was still steaming when I interviewed him at the effrontery of the Kennedys: ". . . and in comes this young man [Sorensen] with the announcement that Senator Kennedy would like Senator Humphrey to come across to the Stockyard Inn to see him, almost as if you were being offered an audience with Kennedy."

The footwork was clumsier still on the convention floor. Following the expenditure of enormous political muscle, old John McCormack, "literally propelled toward the platform at the last minute by Bob Kennedy," in Sorensen's words, "gave a politically oriented seconding speech ('It is time to go East') that was identifiable as a Kennedy speech only by its closing lines." But the generous-minded old wheel horse had been humiliated in Massachusetts;

for all the disclaimers in every camp, there is no denying that it was McCormack who was whispering in Chairman Rayburn's ear at precisely the moment Rayburn recognized the Tennessee delegation, which, in turning its votes to Estes Kefauver, permanently stemmed the Kennedy tide.

As far as Jack Kennedy was concerned the convention was over; he climbed out of his bathtub at the Stockyard Inn, leaving the ever-devoted Mrs. Lincoln to quiet the alarmed management—with all that bathwater the suite was flooded—and dry out and pack his clothes and send them after him. He stopped by the convention and made a graceful curtain speech.

"We did our best," he told his father in the Riviera over the long-distance wire. "I had fun and I didn't make a fool of myself." With which he himself flew to the Cap d'Antibes—Jacqueline had retired to Newport to visit her mother and await her imminent first baby—to see the Ambassador, who bucked up his tired-out son ("I told him that God was still with him, that he could be president if he wanted to be and worked hard") and shortly after explained how he himself would have won that nomination ("If I had been there . . . I would have had a recess after the first ballot, and that would have given us enough time to organize and win").

The old financier was implying a judgment here somewhere, and it is doubtful if the dejected senator missed it by much as he thought over the previous year while cruising the Mediterranean between Capri and Elba with his boisterous kid brother Teddy and Florida Senator George Smathers, Jack's regular humping companion, and a brace of juicy Mediterranean bimbos. This was the first time Jack had gone after something political, and failed. As the politicians retraced the ins and outs of Jack's run at the Democratic ticket, Ted was receiving a cram course on how up-from-the-precincts politics worked—or didn't—on the national level. Furthermore, the recent Harvard graduate couldn't mistake what was likely to happen when the Ambassador— and his invaluable "contacts"—*refused* to get involved.

The party was several days out when word got through by radio that Jacqueline had miscarried and now was in an emergency room. The unsuccessful candidate himself was hesitant to break off such a relaxing jaunt, but Smathers finally convinced Jack that he had better get back. How would this look, politically? Meanwhile, Robert Kennedy was camping at the hospital beside his sister-in-law's bed. What would turn into a deeply felt mutual dependency between Bobby and Jackie was being established.

Bobby—never graceful, least of all after losing—accepted defeat the way an eel accepts an electric prod. With some political aforethought he volunteered himself as an aide to Stevenson's campaign manager Jim Finnegan, rode the Stevenson campaign train, and analyzed the Kennedy camp's behavior at the recent lamented Chicago convention.

"It really struck me then that it wasn't the issues that mattered so much, it was the friendships," he said later. "So many people . . . were going to vote for Estes Kefauver because he had sent them a card or visited their home. I said right there that as well as paying attention to the issues we should send Christmas cards next time." Also, it hadn't escaped Bobby that Kefauver had ridden into the vice-presidential nomination on a tide of televised Senate hearings which projected the Tennessee populist as the lion-tamer with guts enough to cow the nation's top mobsters. Bobby had guts. Before the year was out he was imploring Senator John McClellan to let him and his brother preside over hearings before what became the Rackets Committee and take the battle to organized crime.

A silent figure on the Stevenson train, Bob watched the often-bored candidate read his speeches perfunctorily, ignore impatient crowds, duck away from reporters, underexploit television. Robert Kennedy, who knew his older brother's proclivities well enough, recognized the potential parallels. It was not enough to organize meticulously; one had to break out of the familial self-absorption somehow, experience the moods and exasperations of everyday people. Watching, remembering, the touchy middle brother began to backfile.

8. Law School

Throughout the spring and summer of political infighting which ended for Jack Kennedy in that sudden-death floor battle with Estes Kefauver, the senator's recently graduated kid brother was disporting himself abroad. Freshly out of college, Teddy had managed to sign himself on as an International News Service stringer with the French Army in Algeria. "I'd been interested in that part of the world in school," the senator told me later, harking back in phrases to the summer he and his knowledgeable instructor Fred Holborn wandered the post-colonial chaos of Berber Africa. "Tunisia was just beginning to turn into some kind of country on its own, and Morocco—that was exciting, the country was just getting together under Mohammed V, and it was on the verge of civil war, that El Glaoui . . . And of course Algeria was fascinating. So that at the time I talked with my brother I think that out of our opportunities to talk, the conversation, came the idea for the speech he gave in the Senate urging the French to get out of Algeria . . ." Europe, for the Kennedys, had long before become a lure, a pleasure garden of shadows and foliage and concealment beyond the perennial fluorescence of their all-too-public American lives: Edward Kennedy was to remember his father's admonition not to spend "too much time" among the Old World's graces and fleshpots.

The brothers were close. There was a sauna at the big house in Hyannis Port, and after a long afternoon of hauling at the sails the three liked to perspire together and compare notes. Rose never hesitated to send in a pitcher of something wet with one of the girls who came and went as servants, and later several went on record complaining that the Kennedy boys never took the trouble to cover themselves. Modesty was for the working classes.

That summer Teddy savored, with an unusual fullness, the boon of wealth and early young manhood. Ted's grades, while sound enough his last several years in college—later he would brag about his B in Spanish—were not quite at a level to get him into the law school at Harvard; he proceeded without thinking it over much, largely because "Bobby recommended it," to begin his legal training at the University of Virginia at Charlottesville. Administrators of the law school, an "honor system" institution, were forewarned of the reasons behind the two-year break in Edward Kennedy's college work; they reviewed his undergraduate record and let this eager youngest among the Kennedy offspring in anyway.

Teddy buckled down hard. For establishmentarian children of the mid-fifties the graduate trade schools of law and business administration amounted, as often as otherwise, to a kind of demonstration of maturity. Law school is a test, six grueling bourgeois semesters of initiation between the dress-up horseplay of subscription dances, assing off whole afternoons in the club, athletic snapshots—between that and life.

For Ted Kennedy—who even in college, according to his fullback friend John Culver, "worked like hell"—learning the law was one unbroken three-year pick-and-shovel enterprise. "I've got to go at a thing four times as hard and four times as long as some other fellow," Kennedy himself insisted. "I remember at law school, I used to be up early and late, hitting the books. I had to, just to keep up with some of the other guys. It's hard work, and you keep at it, and, after a while, you begin to understand the thing and then to see a way to do something about influencing it."

"Bob had lots on the ball," Professor Charles Gregory of the University of Virginia Law School remembered, " . . . but then he had lots of other activities so it was hard to judge what he could have been like if he had given more time to work. He was not so hard-working as Teddy." Worked hard, hard—

a Percheron dragging a broad slow deep harrow of a conventional mind forever and ever beneath eternally dulled skies.

Will, doggedness, perseverance. That scholarly horse-faced giant John Varick
Tunney, son of the boxer and a senator from California, would unclamp his
pipe from teeth that look as if they might have belonged to one of the larger
ruminants and recall the law student with whom he shared a three-room
house on Barracks Road in Charlottesville. "Ted worked very hard learning
the law," Tunney says—Tunney is an earnest person, judicial by instinct, a
man to weigh the merits carefully and make his decision—exactly as, worked
on those roommate years, reading the theology books Ted pushed on him, he
was converted to a dutiful Catholicism—and now Tunney wanted to tell me
exactly how those three years went. "He wasn't a great student, I wouldn't
pretend that he was, but he wasn't a dummy either: He was always pretty
much in the middle, sometimes the lower-middle segment of the class . . .
What was unusual about him then was that he seemed to know exactly what
he wanted out of life. Jack influenced him especially—he'd constantly say
Jack did this, Jack did that. And he wanted to live up to it. I think he already
thought largely in terms of politics. I remember when we entered the moot
court competition . . ."

The moot court competition is manifestly an ego-marker, a thing Kennedy did that confirmed his slowly evolving self-assurance and seated one
side of his massive character. Like the Ames at Harvard, the moot court at the
University of Virginia is a series of round-robin debating exchanges, centered
on a hypothetical case and turning on a point of constitutional law, with the
field of entrance narrowing semester by semester until, toward the end of
each senior year, two teams of winners arrive at the finals and argue it out
before a panel of nationally distinguished jurists.

"Ted asked me to go into it with him," John Tunney recalled, "and we
made a great effort, a great effort. Really, up early every morning. And, to
tell the truth, we never expected to win—there were so many others, the best
students, people who were much higher in the class . . . The subject that year
was a section of the Taft-Hartley Act that prohibited company officials from
contributing to political campaigns. The question was whether a corporation
executive was denied his constitutional right to free speech by this kind of
prohibition. A lot of work went into writing the briefs, and you had to have
forensic skills, a lot of ability with argument . . . The fact was, between the
two of us Ted was by far the outstanding one. He had great energy, great
ability to succinctly phrase an argument, an excellent voice and timbre, one

that projected a lot of vitality and dynamism. For that ultimate round the law school brought in Stanley Reed of the Supreme Court and the Lord Chancellor of England, their highest legal officer."

"Ted put more energy into preparing his case than he did into his lessons," Joan Kennedy remembers. "He particularly loved the oral arguments. And the work paid off—he and Varick won the competition." Energy. The oral arguments. Newly married in 1958, Joan Kennedy gets right at the gist of what was most promising here: presentation, the readying of material for public display, debate before the public forum—this is what pulls it into some kind of meaning for Teddy. It is as if hunched over those thick legal tomes that lie open of their own weight, with his eyes itching from page after page of scrapings from some forgotten Circuit Court opinion here, filings of interpretations as codified to a fare-thee-well by some pointy-headed dervish of a kid editor in another law school's Review columns—suddenly, at even the prospect of talking about the material: Shazam—order, a sense of pattern surges through the whole dumbfounding myriad, as if some horseshoe magnet of the pragmatic were clamped in under all these details.

So unlike either of his older brothers, really—Jack with that eighteenth-century-rationalist intellect of his, stirring in its marinade of history. Bobby's little auger of a mind battered into an ever wider eccentric by displacements from the moral and (finally) the existential outrages breaking upon his lifetime.

By the end of law school Teddy had come upon a way of processing what he needed appropriate to the slowly dawning computer age. He was learning to take information in exactly ("Teddy takes in everything you tell him and gives it back, exactly as you told it to him," one professional adviser comments privately. "Bobby takes it in, and you get that and something more back," the professor sighs. "With John Kennedy, of course, you had a discussion"), and retrieve it according to the program indicated: counter-statistics all prepared for rebuttal in floor debate, demonstration of logical inconsistency, secondary information to buttress an argument more securely on the exposed side.

Edward Kennedy liked the rhythms and much of the feel of rhetoric—born orators have to—but tended to prefer the more sinewy, more lightly inflected short line pulled tight as cable fact-to-fact as compared with the wider, more fanciful, often more augustly balanced diction of his brother Jack. The effect Ted has will vary with the audience he gets—university people especially will pinch down an eyebrow sometimes at the density and flatness of the argument and the hyperearnest choirboy inflections, the elocution-lesson poise, the drone of opinions taken from people grateful for the warmth of Kennedy's personal welcome. Inflamed by his argument, he has a tendency to bellow. But this is caviling, this early at least—what well-disposed professors and friends of his brothers and professionals around the Kennedys are beginning to notice about Ted by now is the way he is developing the touch. He reaches people. He has the tact for situations. He has demonstrated himself to be—ahh—a hard worker. And—relievingly, and to his closely attendant father especially—he takes his future seriously.

Usually. Even at law school, that haute-bourgeoise Siberia, there has been, from time to time, a nip in the Kennedy heavens, a flash of that sharp self-forgetful psychological heat-lightning. However late it happens to be: By the time the heavy back straightens above the library table and that ever more leonine head begins to raise itself, there is as likely as not a gleam of expectation touching those half-hooded Kennedy eyes. "He turns into quite a different person when he isn't working," Varick Tunney said, with a noticeable obliqueness, thinking back over any number of occasions, although reserving the details. "Effervescent, a great person to have fun with."

Kennedy had a name all over that gentleman's campus as a bonfire of gregariousness at a party, arms-around joviality and chin-chucking and game ideas in every direction once he has had a few. Acquaintances prod him to show off his gifts as a mimic, his range of dialects from Honey Fitz's East Boston near-brogue to back-country seacoast Yankee. Telling, invariably, but never really piercing or cruel or contemptuous.

"We used to play touch football on Saturday afternoons," Tunney says, "and the thing that impressed me about Ted was his leadership. He got people together so effortlessly. Then he became head of the legal forum. He did these things so naturally, met people so well. He's always had the ability, under heavy pressure, to keep cool. I've climbed mountains with him——." Between semesters Kennedy and Tunney had climbed the Matterhorn together: On Rimpfischhorn Kennedy slipped and dangled over a 3,000-foot abyss, fell onto a ledge, took five minutes to eat an orange for energy and collect himself, and immediately after that the two of them struggled on the rest of the way to the Matterhorn summit.

But even then there were occasions, as he and the Ambassador knew, when adrenaline tended to swamp restraint. Thomas Whitten, the Virginia police lieutenant who patrolled the university end of Charlottesville, has documented to reporters what amounted to a personal duel he had in March of 1958 with the high-spirited law student. First noticing Kennedy's ragged convertible, its plastic back window half torn away, when he shot through a red light on the 250 bypass, the lieutenant chased Kennedy until Kennedy's powerful Oldsmobile outran his patrol car.

Whitten himself tracked down the "rough-looking" Oldsmobile finally—its hood still hot from the engine—and lay in wait for Kennedy on the Saturday night following. The Oldsmobile shot through the bypass intersection on schedule, at ninety miles per hour and again against the light, swerved in and out of the same series of streets as before, and stopped in front of the Barracks Road cottage just as it had a few days earlier; this time the patrolman was in knowledgeable pursuit, and pulled up immediately. Whitten stepped out of the patrol car; Kennedy was not around, but "I knew he hadn't had time to get out," Whitten says: He found his man doubled up and hiding in the darkness below the steering wheel. "He came out weak as a cat. He gave me no lip," the lieutenant reports.

Kennedy picked up one more speeding ticket, and he and his then-fiancée Joan Bennett flew down to Charlottesville that summer so he could stand trial and pay the fines for his violations. Not long before he graduated, in 1959, as if to leave one more memento for Charlottesville's hard-worked patrolmen, Kennedy ran a last red light and paid a final violation.

This was to remain a cherished personal ineptitude Kennedy would never outgrow. Always in a hurry, oblivious to surroundings, loving speed and completely unafraid of it, always preferring to drive or fly an airplane himself, Ted Kennedy's performances behind the wheel were to provoke a drumbeat of anxious inside humor among his friends and, especially, members of his staff over the years coming up just then.

One other quirk. If he crashed or even sideswiped a car he would walk away, grab a cab, turn over the consequences to some flunky or lawyer. It was already Ted's instinct to slide out from under responsibility, lay the consequences off.

9. Campaign Manager

If Edward Kennedy's debating skills were keen that final law-school winter of 1958–59, perhaps it was the summer of speechmaking that preceded it that stropped them to such a brightness. In Massachusetts, Jack Kennedy was up for reelection to the Senate in 1958, and well before the preliminaries began the decision came out of Hyannis Port that his campaign manager this time out was to be his politically uninitiated twenty-six-year-old brother Teddy. Politicians and newspaper commentators around the state treated this decision as one more perversity of the unpredictable

Kennedys; the *Boston Globe*'s C. R. Owens depicted Edward during his maiden political appearance as a schoolboy in nominal charge of "the most plush political headquarters Boston has ever seen," a youthful figure "customarily surrounded by a flock of young beauties."

The assumption almost everywhere was that O'Brien and O'Donnell were in fact operating the campaign, and this was the case. "We dry-ran everything we were going to do during the primary fights in 1960. We tuned everything, set up and tried out our advance people," O'Donnell would concede later on, bluntly. But there have never been any honorific positions during any of the Kennedy fights for office, and there were none in 1958. Neither Edward Kennedy nor the sophisticated young Steve Smith, during that summer Kennedy sister Jean's two-year bridegroom and listed in the campaign schematic as "comptroller of the currency," were included for display purposes: They were around to learn and work, and the demands were incessant.

The inclusion of Smith in the operations was unmistakably an effort to form a closer, more umbilical relationship between the political side of the family enterprise and the Park Avenue financial clearinghouse that Joseph Kennedy had overseen in 1952 but the details of which had required the intervention of operatives like Lynn Johnson and Jim Fayne. Smith, who before very long was slated to take over the directorship of the Park Avenue offices himself, needed to be familiarized with the cost-accounting problems of a political endeavor in the expectation that, as a member of the family, he would assume the administrative role in subsequent campaigns that the financier had played—everything from approving and signing the larger checks to breaking the advertising budget down.

Listening to the matter-of-fact Smith reminisce about that half-forgotten reelection, I would be struck by the concerns to which his attention had unmistakably been directed: "I was frankly an observer, it was more of an education for me . . . I guess I learned something about media in the course of that . . . compared with New York, Massachusetts is easier to deal with—in terms of sheer size the mix is more manageable, not the equivalent of the city versus the rest of the state there is in New York . . ." Smith's head rocked back a moment in recall; light from the corner of plate glass pinpointed the pupils of his milk-blue eyes. "Edward Kennedy, of course, took to the campaign with a great deal of ease. The easiest part for him was the straight politics, dealing with people, he was very effective with people. He worked like hell. I don't think he had formed in his own mind anything definitive about his own future at that point . . ."

His own future. Behind that expansive grin at all the weddings of all the brothers and sisters throughout the fifties, throughout the afternoons and evenings above the books in Virginia—for all that impulse to cut up unexpectedly his father so deplored, knife through an intersection or abruptly dump a snifter of champagne onto his own head just as the bride was cutting the cake: The future is beginning to pluck at Edward now. His future. He is beginning to evidence a half-muffled, quickly explained-away urge to find his way out from under. Over the next four years he will confide to intimates his thoughts of moving to the West somewhere, practicing law, buying and running a newspaper somewhere. While still in law school he develops, and is treated for, an ulcer.

Inside the family he is still the clown, the one they pull to his feet to bray out his version of "Hooray for Hollywood," the afterthought. There is a lot of apprehension at the thought of breaking loose, and there is a lot of apprehension at the thought of staying where he is, the baby brother, the last. His omniscient father picks up on a lot of this and regards it with a well-practiced tolerance: fancies.

That reelection summer of 1958 Teddy got his chance to work off some of these random promptings, move into the undusted universe of spittoons and cold chicken-and-peas luncheons in Holy Name Society auditoriums, help out the family.

Talent emerged. "Edward Kennedy is the most naturally gifted political person I've ever met," Frank Morrissey opines; Morrissey, in ever-deeper disfavor, had been resurrected to lead this inexperienced campaign manager in and out of back rooms throughout the wards: Morrissey's opinion becomes the maxim. "Teddy is the best politician in the family," both Jack and the Ambassador are regularly quoted as having insisted thereafter: The citation is accurate, but "politician" is a term nobody wants to press too hard. Not a compliment, entirely.

What everyone meant at the time, presumably, was that the big frolicking law student did indeed impress people around the state with an immediacy that went beyond good cheer. This much, at least, the Kennedy strategists depended on. By 1958 Jack Kennedy was on the make for the presidency in 1960—unhesitantly, and with a minimum of the kind of highly flattered disavowals serious hopefuls for major elective office attempted normally. His efforts to establish a claim for himself through accomplishment within the Senate itself had remained frustrating, unproductive, but it was clear enough both to JFK and the people he and his father brought in to forward his presidential chances that there was an exceptional amount of box office out there for their wealthy, urbane young candidate: This meant the earliest manageable start with an exhaustive campaign of transcontinental promotion to sell the idea and "the name of Kennedy," in the Ambassador's characteristically undressed phraseology, "like soap flakes."

The realization of this projected presidential campaign would cost the family an estimated $17.5 million and involve the cultivation of people ranging from committeewomen insignificant even at county levels to international press lords. For four rugged years, beginning with his 150 speeches and appearances for Stevenson in 24 states in 1956, Jack Kennedy called home his sloppily packed suitcase, mapped and remapped the American political lands in airplane hops and $100-a-night testimonials. The mood and tenor of most of these expeditions was hectic—groggy eight-hour transcontinental airliner rides with Sorensen, bumping down in a field in Iowa to address a corn-picking contest. Not anything like the network of "paid operatives" the concerned Eleanor Roosevelt suspected. Then, at precisely the worst possible time, the frontrunning Democratic hopeful had to go home temporarily to get himself reelected in Massachusetts.

So Teddy received greetings. He took the role without illusions: By 1958 Theodore Sorensen had been well established as Jack Kennedy's almost spookily attuned alter ego; Jack's kid brother Teddy walked into American politics in 1958 with scarcely a line of coaching or more than a suggestion or two about footwork, a kind of younger, huskier, more affable, and friskier stand-in for the ephemeral candidate himself.

Bringing Ted in amounted to guesswork. Ted Kennedy was involved in the planning stages early, put in charge at once—although under the tutelage at first of the tall, seasoned, ever-agreeable Mike Feldman—of the policy group that helped work out the responses to the more ticklish issues—the South, Civil Rights, Labor—with which the senator was embroiled just them. Empowered to authorize decisions one would otherwise clear with the candidate, he—this primarily—moved in and out of dozens and dozens and dozens of situations all over the state where a spokesman for the family was needed. "It was obvious from the beginning that if we could get one of the brothers to say something somewhere, either Bobby or Ted, we would get three or four times more turnout for any political meeting than if any of us went," Kenny O'Donnell would say. "I don't see how we could have run that campaign without Teddy. We would have had a helluva time."

For Ted Kennedy himself that summer of 1958 every minute was delicious punishment and a line-by-line education in that artistic mixture of force, charm, and fraud that energized political life in Massachusetts.

"I think I was the one who took Ted to his first factory gate," insisted the omnipresent Jim King, the jumbo cherub who ran the Boston office. It was the Fisk Factory gate in Chicopee, meeting and handshaking the workers as they streamed through the mists of four-thirty in the morning, an important rite in anybody's political initiation. Ted Kennedy's took place at the end of August that summer, on an unseasonable darkened morning so cold "I froze my ass off," King remembers. "O'Brien was with Ted, and we could see immediately that he could communicate with those people—pols, cops, guys going in a gate. They gave him a helluva greeting, although at least a third thought he was Jack—he kept saying, 'No, no, Ted Kennedy, the senator's brother'"—he knew how to talk with them, no hail-fellow-well-met crap. He was interested in them, interested in their lives, and people caught it.

"After that when Ted came to the western part of the state everybody was glad to get him out, keep him busy. I myself found him challenging and delightful. Partly, I think, because he was such an eager campaigner, he really loved the pace of campaigning. You'd go to one fire station in Springfield, and then he had to go to all the others. So you'd have fourteen hours of visiting fire stations that day. I remember once we got stalled in a traffic jam and he jumped out and started going from car to car shaking hands and attaching bumper stickers to every car they'd let him. He loved campaigning, you couldn't hold him down——."

Early in a five-week state tour with O'Brien and O'Donnell, Ted Kennedy—not out of law school yet—explained that he was abroad in the Commonwealth to "put our finger on the pulse of the people in every section of Massachusetts," to "determine the position of the senator in the minds of the voters . . . We want to know what the voters are thinking and their feelings on the vital issues of the day. We are going directly to the people to find out and by the middle of August I plan to speak with voters in every part of Massachusetts."

Jack Kennedy's Republican opponent, Vincent Celeste, who had no chance of winning from the outset and must certainly have known that and thus was freed of the danger of having later to live down whatever he said, slashed all around himself like a bear on a chain. There were the savagely ominous references to the Kennedy "financial steamroller," powered by the "breathtaking sums the Kennedys are dumping into this campaign." There were the predictable charges that the senator was cold-bloodedly putting the Commonwealth to service as a fulcrum to pry open the Democratic Party nationally. There was the allegation that Kennedy was an absentee officeholder—not around Washington enough anymore to represent the state's best interest there, nor even, goaded by these new presidential cravings, willing to campaign full time in Massachusetts even to assure his own reelection.

Filling in for the absentee candidate was "a relatively easy transition to the campaign itself," Ted Kennedy reminisced to me years later. "By late September, of course, it was more a matter of issues, approaches, how everything was going over. For instance, my brother had a slogan, 'Make Your Vote Count.' He wanted to suggest that your vote was needed for his reelection, but there was some . . . overtone in that, we felt, of . . . of 1960. Also, we found the Italians were upset because they seemed to feel that there was an implication there—an awful lot goes into these things, really—that because Foster Furcolo was running, if you made your vote count for John Kennedy it wouldn't . . . somehow it wouldn't count so much for Foster Furcolo. Resentments built up, and I . . . we . . . it was decided to modify this in another direction, the slogan was changed to 'He Has Served All Massachusetts With Distinction.'"

"Ted Kennedy was better with people he didn't even know than Jack Kennedy was ever to be," maintained Eddie McCormack, the Speaker's flamboyant nephew, before long to prove Edward Kennedy's most dangerous opponent but just then moving into his first term as Massachusetts's attorney general and already the one important Democrat of stature whom the Kennedys actually invited to join the senator—a clear move of cross-family reconciliation—at a scattering of political receptions. "Jack didn't really like adulation, open flattery embarrassed him, but Teddy was already a . . . a freewheeler, a swinger, he liked to be with people, good with the glad hand, the big smile, the slap on the back . . . I think they brought him into the campaign for that, and even more than that because if they chose Teddy campaign manager they didn't have to choose among the factions . . ."

The factions. The danger is evident this early, there is a kind of morning sickness within the organization, and the Kennedys themselves are aware of what a stumble is possible if major personnel mistakes are made at this point. If there is clumsiness in controlling the altercations within the staff. Who ranks whom, how do you decide what, when their opposite numbers in Massachusetts, regulars like O'Brien and—when Bobby could spare him from the Rackets Committee—the plain-spoken likes of Kenny O'Donnell and Ted Reardon and the sometimes savagely profane Eddie McLaughlin are working the back room of the political shop at 122 Bowdoin?

With this much national attention the approach was critical. Money, you have to be a little bit cute about the way you allocate the money, too many billboards or a season of television too choked with Madison Avenue–crafted spots and however well the candidate does is going to look like the aftermath of that "financial steamroller" Celeste keeps wailing about. Better to push the Secretaries, mount an intense but unpublicized canvass for "pledge cards" that will get the volunteers out talking Kennedy around the neighborhoods— Bobby's Principle: A lot of people doing a little work is better than a few people pushing themselves daily to the margins of exhaustion.

It was already time by 1958 to ease off on the tea parties, too: that apparently endless queue of four-and-a-half-foot ladies with swollen ankles from Chelsea who thumbtacked antimacassars to their porch furniture and tottered to keep from swooning as they waddled beneath the Ambassador's white tie . . . The end of the queue has appeared, finally, and it did not turn out to extend to Wellesley, let alone Shaker Heights or Telegraph Hill, and by now it is increasingly evident that the market of ticket-takers for the Kennedys' Theater of the Socially Absurd, while large enough still, was going to have to be won over with an array of somewhat more indirect effects.

The theme of the 1958 campaign was understate. Jack Kennedy was "*sincerely* convinced," Sorensen wrote an aide, italicizing *sincerely* himself, "that it will be tough to beat Dever's old record of 250,000 in an off year. Can you see," he added with afterthought, "that everybody gets the word?" It was to be a return to political basics: Keep the costs low, keep the troops hustling, mend the political fences in anticipation of 1960, and build support for the inevitable victory out of the enthusiasm and help of honestly convinced plain people.

The perfect candidate for a campaign conceived along the lines of this one, of course, would be neither the diffident Jack nor the self-conscious Bobby. Better somebody with an air of the street-corner to him and the knack for making himself comfortable eating ice cream and bullshitting sports with one foot wrapped around the leg of somebody else's kitchen chair, and laughing his boomer Irish laugh, and listening and talking.

What that campaign needed—and got—was Teddy.

"It was the old man who really ran those goddamned campaigns, you know," divulges one political confidant of the period. "Both of them, in 1952 with the tea parties and that last one in 1958." And in fact, the hand of the untiring old manipulator was omnipresent. If occasionally the financier was brusque, overwhelming, autocratic, in 1958 he exerted a lighter and more indirect administrative touch. He was stepping back, according to the script.

"My father is a wonderful businessman, but as a politician he's—well— that's something else," Jack now told people: The Ambassador—it would appear, at least—acknowledged his limitations; like Teddy, Joseph P. Kennedy was supposedly in there to spell the candidate.

"Betty, what are you doing with all those newspapers?" Jack Kennedy demanded of liberal spokeswoman Betty Taymor when he walked in on her laboring over a bale of the specially printed *Boston Record American* edition extolling the candidate.

Betty's answer was irrepressible. "Do you really want to know what we're doing with the newspapers?"

"Well, that's another fine idea my father has," Jack Kennedy said, less convinced than anybody else of the need for so uninspired a return to political basics.

Personalities rubbed wrong. There was an incessant, often a fierce clash between the hard-bitten Bobby, worried whenever he did get up from Washington about what might be gone aglimmering on the Rackets Committee, and such volunteers as the volcanic Eddie McLaughlin, himself on the rise politically.

The Ambassador heard all complaints, assuaged, decided, drew backed-up venom. There remained an inveterate bristling on both sides whenever Jack Kennedy and Foster Furcolo, standing for reelection as Massachusetts's governor in 1958, collided. Out of the older generation's determined effort to run an old-fashioned personal-appearance political-Model-T campaign came the decision to utilize the candidate's wife, Jacqueline, who with every human instinct detested the exposure. Bored numb each time she was required to stand there in some high-school gymnasium reception beneath a basketball hoop, a perfumed, remote *Vogue* cutout before whom the seemingly unbroken files of scrubwomen seemed each to suppress a curtsy while choking out "O Missus Kennedy, and when will we see you in the White House?" The concerned aides would have to remind the candidate's wife that her handshake seemed to have gone a little bit limp, and perhaps it would improve the impression were she to remove her . . . glove . . . ?

The wife of the candidate had a way, halfway through a session when things went on like this, of disappearing, later to reappear, when the caravan formed up, still leafing through her magazine in the back seat of one of the limousines in the parking lot. "I don't believe the president spent more than eighteen or nineteen days in Massachusetts between September and November that fall," Edward Kennedy remembered. "But people felt he was there, it made it appear he was there most of the time. But of course there were enormous demands on him in other parts of the country most of the time."

It was a stunt, expertly handled. John Kennedy won reelection by a margin of 874,608, close to twice the vote of the undergunned Celeste and the most impressive victory for the office not only in the history of Massachusetts politics but also in the country at large that year. With the nation watching, the professionals were dazzled.

Missing, much of the time, was Bobby. Busy establishing himself on the Senate Select Committee on Improper Activities in the Labor and Management Field (better known right away as the McClellan Rackets Committee), Robert Kennedy simply did not dare absent himself for too long in case the investigation should render up its overdue prize: the labor vote. Having been struck by the extent to which beating up mobsters on television had propelled Estes Kefauver, Bob had promoted himself—to his father's horror—into the limelight as Chief Counsel of the Rackets Committee. With Jack as a highly visible committee member, Bobby felt that his brother would garner enough attention to attract a national following.

Robert Kennedy had begun to get his Select Committee taken seriously by turning up evidence so graphic that the members seemed to be lined up in the alley to watch Jimmy Hoffa's hoods working over an organizer who wouldn't take, or sniffing the malodorous "sweetheart" exchanges between open-handed Teamster bosses and open-minded business executives. Unfortunately, those years of headlines consequent to fleaing the rump of labor were slipping away into court cases and contempt-of-Congress proceedings by 1958.

"From what I understood," a newspaperman, one who covered the Kennedys closely through the end of the fifties, maintains with the innocence of the trade, "Bobby used that enormous staff he had to get the dirt on everybody in the Labor Movement. I remember a room they had in particular—it was a large room, and it was absolutely packed with filing cases. From what I understand, in every city they'd go and look up the local Labor guy and say, 'Look, we've got this, and this, we *could* prosecute, hold hearings, but—what interests us now is that you people help out, stand ready to do a little work for us.' A typical Bobby operation—tough, uncompromising, unassailable——."

This cattle drive would culminate with the Ambassador's convening the leadership of Al Capone's old Outfit and several East Coast Commission members at Felix Young's restaurant in Manhattan, to demand a lot of cash and motivated volunteers to work the precincts during the coming campaign. The constituencies Joe Kennedy was out there endeavoring to wrangle into line for Jack were coming into view: the moguls out of Hollywood and big-league wise guys and the magazine lords and the figureheads of the Church and the older, less publicized but massively influential urban court-house powers, the Crottys and the Buckleys and the Daleys, who controlled the delegates and worked the crucial unit swap-offs at national conventions. Add to this Jack's people, the League of Women Voters chairwomen and first-term congressmen still aching with gratitude that this acknowledged presidential hopeful would come as far as Great Falls, Montana, or Prince-ton, New Jersey, merely to appear at a luncheon with them. And dominat-ing almost everything, grunting, Labor, big rich all-overlapping Labor, with its savvy, well-connected lobbyists wandering around Capitol Hill all day, its high-priced top-quality legal people like Arthur Goldberg and Joseph Rauh, Walter Reuther, its brain-bank of political action committee experts, its heavy old muscles still aching a little from the violence of its unforgotten past, its nose for who loved it truly—and why—impossible to fool.

The troops line up. By now, the game is mostly about power.

CHAPTER IV

The Castle

1. Joe

Theodore Sorensen, aware by 1969 that infatuated legend was beginning to do for Jack Kennedy's political reputation what cortisone had done to his profile, admits in passing that, even as he became president, Kennedy was "not motivated by any special tasks he wanted to accomplish in the White House." Kennedy's Senate performance prefigures this.

Probably Jack Kennedy's keystone effort was his repeated attempt, at the end of his senatorial career, to push through the Senate the bill he and Irving Ives of New York developed to reform union practices and expose union-management "arrangments." When a somewhat stiffer form of the legislation, the Landrum-Griffin Act, came out of the House-Senate Conference, Kennedy regretted the more repressive measures the bill now included, removed his own name from sponsorship, and voted for it with a well-advertised reluctance. Big Labor swallowed hard but understood.

Overall, the book on Jack Kennedy, Senator, had been filled in sketchily: Eight years is little more than a flicker of the eye to the oligarchs of committee legislation up on the Hill; Kennedy's expertise was restricted—labor reform was his issue—and, besides being gone so much, and sick, there was something not completely . . . not completely . . . clubworthy about this unpredictable boyish man. "He was like that, both he and Bobby," Senator Thruston Morton later complained. "They both had a way of being . . . they were impatient, arrogant sometimes, they had a way of talking down to the rest of us . . ."

Years earlier, another colleague observed, "The thing that bothers me most about Jack is this attitude that everybody is on earth for the sole purpose of helping him." Not that Jack Kennedy was unpopular—he was liked widely, too widely to suit a good many of the liberal devoted. Even when he was brusque it was clear no offense was seriously intended: The tone was to some extent a byproduct of Kennedy's steadily accelerating speed of mind. Jack Kennedy was, by impulse, brilliantly scattered often, unsystematic, a man of appreciations more than precepts. He appreciated ideas with a connoisseur's fingertips for the distinctions, but how deeply he felt about the individuals and groups behind the issues was guesswork. At every level of his public life he remained accessible—Massachusetts businessmen and exurban Republicans with problems often found him easier to see than the plainer Saltonstall.

Kennedy's credentials had taken on weight. He appeared to have matured beyond the kind of impulse that had led Kennedy as late as 1952 to vote for a $14 million cut in funds for the Tennessee Valley Authority and later characterize his vote with a shrug as a kowtow to his father and his "Economic Royalist" luncheon partners. James MacGregor Burns, in his 1960 pre-campaign biography, caught an aspect of Kennedy's inherent skepticism in that characterization that so outraged Sorensen when Burns called Jack Kennedy a "serious, driven man, about as casual as a cash register." Burns touches another when he quotes Kennedy quoting Lord Falkland as having said, "When it is not necessary to change it is necessary not to change," and Robert Frost, more succinctly, "Don't take down a fence until you know why it was put up." Jack operated out of a fatalistic recognition of society as a deeply and organically corrupt thing, in which governing inevitably involved a series of lesser-evil choices, the manipulation of the War of All Against All. The best hope was to inch forward without breaking up the interiors and civilized techniques, the elegances and balances, of a more settled and achieved age. At very deep and wholly honorable levels, Jack Kennedy was a conservative.

With the possible exception of his traditionalistic mother, Jack Kennedy was alone among the members of his family in his intuition of the past as well as his apprehension before the oncoming barbarism—which took the imaginative form for him, as for his father, of holocaust and war. The same qualities that made Kennedy perhaps the most aesthetically appealing American statesman worldwide since Woodrow Wilson were exactly the ones that limited his sense of what was possible and meaningful in government, crimped his moral alternatives, and reduced his promising presidency in the end to a three-year extension of Cold War Conventional.

If Jack Kennedy and that insuppressible old father of his shared a recurrent nightmare, their ideological overlapping was small enough when they came to discuss policy. "Fifty percent of what Jack thinks these days I am opposed to—and that's true entirely of foreign policy. We discuss it—but I don't expect to convert him," the elder Kennedy told an interviewer late in the fifties. Easy to imagine the aging capitalist's bemusement and pride and rue as his son the senator stood up to rail on the floor against those exact same tax loopholes—oil carve-out and depletion advantages, tax-free municipal bonds—through which the Park Avenue retainers marched daily en route to the Kennedy vaults.

Some of the father's doubts may have been stirred as he—he, intimate of Joe McCarthy's—found his son in the vanguard of legislators pushing for the repeal of loyalty oaths and anti-Communist affidavits, or developing as a major preelection theme the missile gap and the need for air-mobile divisions the very availability of which could only drag the United States deeper into a Cold War the Ambassador had never seen the logic of entering in the first place.

"I knew vaguely of the development of some of my husband's ideas," Rose Kennedy told me. "As early as 1914 and 1915 he felt that the government would involve itself more in the lives of the people. I can remember his saying in the thirties that as we got older there was going to be a little money and perhaps the children could go to England, to Oxford, even to Russia. He saw these things evolving." The patriarch was railing privately at the way authority was so scattered among the departments and commissions and boards that nobody had power enough to affect events at all by the time the claims and jealousies and petty accommodations had absorbed whatever unsmothered energy there originally was.

Politically and philanthropically, Joe Kennedy's deployment of his assets had been unpredictable. He contributed generously to Harlem community centers and Negro colleges long before *Brown v. Topeka* in 1954. As late as the Christmas holidays of 1960, rambling on in his knockabout style to a couple of reporters, the Ambassador insisted that some of the things he would like to see his newly elected son push for first would be cheaper and better medical care for everybody, involving some kind of national health insurance, a better program for the unemployed, and a radically improved Social Security system. "It makes no sense in a country as rich as this to work your tail off most of your life, then virtually starve to death once you hit sixty-five—no sense at all," the financier told the UPI's Merriman Smith.

"Dammit, Jack has to succeed if the country is going to succeed."

No doubt Merriman Smith was surprised. This from one of the nation's most outspoken Tory businessmen? A cry for social justice? How could the developing Teddy not have heard that too?

The old buccaneer was obviously starting to think about political trade-offs. A month or so earlier, a matter of days after Jack Kennedy had gotten himself elected president, Charles Lewin—the editor of that same conservative *New Bedford Standard-Times* whose Cape Cod editorial support had probably delivered his seat to Senator John Kennedy in 1952—telephoned the Ambassador in Hyannis Port to relay a report that certain Louisiana delegates were going to attempt to swap electoral votes to his son for a softer civil-rights position. "To hell with it," Joe Kennedy responded immediately. "If you have to make deals for these electoral votes you couldn't get the right start with the American people."

"And then he said something which amazed me," Lewin goes on. "Joe said he prayed every night that Jack would 'get out of this thing,' the presidency. He said, with the state of the country as bad as it was, Jack wouldn't engage in any deals to go in as president and he went on to say Jack would always remain as a senator. Joe said he got down on his knees every night and prayed Jack wouldn't have to take the job." This was perhaps a faltering and uncharacteristic moment, but it was a moment of revelation.

For Teddy Kennedy, starting to hear all this, whatever impression the father's thinking made was obviously quite different from what Joe's Economic Royalist friends might have expected. Something of the old financier's up-from-the-streets conditioning had a way of resonating in Teddy, whose insecurities and daily struggle to be taken seriously had carried him much closer to the miseries of the common man than his older brothers ever experienced. Joe Jr. and Jack traveled officer-class; Bobby and Ted were noncoms.

"All the way through his existence Dad had relationships and contacts none of the rest of us had," Ted Kennedy conceded to me years after his father died, and after this there was a second or so of lapse. It was the hour of the dog in Washington by now, the secretary who poured the cranberry juice we both were sipping had long before looked in on us and slipped away in hopes of a taxi, and beyond the shelter and pastels of the Whip's Office the Senate continued into evening session.

Nobody said anything. The Ambassador had died, finally, twenty-two

days previously, with this last-surviving, self-tortured youngest of his tossing through the terminal night in a sleeping bag next to his deathbed, and
whether it is the cranberry juice on an empty stomach, or simply the newness
and rawness of his world following the Chappaquiddick disaster, Ted Kennedy now had a kind of ragged, patchy look, the whites of his Minotaurus
eyes looked scalded, and there was no way for either of us to ease around
the mention of the father's name. "Paul Dever, of course—" the senator is
forcing— "and . . . other associations, of course he had some contacts in
Massachusetts with individuals, groups, newspaper editors—"

We both backed into this talking about the pre-primary scavenging for
boss support that gave some context to Jack Kennedy's subsequent push
toward the Democratic nomination. "I remember in 1960," Ted Kennedy
said, risking timbre, but an instant later he has it smoothed out again. "I
remember in 1960 my brother saying to Dad, almost jokingly, 'The states
you have are Illinois, New Jersey, Pennsylvania, New York,'" and after that
the memories came easier—

Bringing up 1960 is hard. As recently as the afternoon previously, squirming on the leather Turkish mohair guest chair to keep straight in my notebook
what was to be quoted and what was not among the guarded confidences
offered around his fresh-lit cigar by that sprightly, aging Irish stork John
McCormack, Speaker of the House of Representatives, I sensed the ghost
of the financier putting it together for one last time—propping up, cross-
checking, reinforcing, undermining—before 1960 opened and with it the
oceanic Kennedy decade.

Lyndon Johnson's own memories push everything a little further. "In the
fall of '55 when I was here at the ranch, Senator Kennedy's father, Joe Kennedy, called me and said that he had talked to Senator John Kennedy and
that they had concluded that they would like to support me for president,
and they wanted the go-ahead to do it. I told them I had no ambitions to be
president . . ." Lyndon Johnson, in retirement, had confided this early pass
by Joe to a fascinated Walter Cronkite. As characteristically with the financier
there was the quick profit to skim from an unexpected combination—it was
the vain if readily punctured Johnson, after all, who rose in Chicago in 1956
to cast Texas's delegate count for "the fighting sailor who wears the scars of
battle."

"I liked the idea of getting Kennedy and Johnson together for more
than the two years prior to the 1960 convention," the Speaker himself had
divulged to me, and fervently. "I felt that was the only ticket that could win.
The only way the Democrats had a chance . . ." The routing is clearer by now:

Johnson to his longtime mentor Speaker Sam Rayburn to *his* then Majority Leader McCormack to McCormack's durable political intimate Joe Kennedy at home—if not completely at rest—in Hyannis Port-by-the-Sea. "I told Joe Kennedy that I thought Lyndon Johnson would be the strongest running mate Jack could find," the light-footed McCormack insisted to me, "and both the president and his father knew my views on this."

McCormack's opinion became an important ledger entry on the Kennedy side by the spring of 1960 when the financier requested McCormack personally to get in touch with Bill Green of Philadelphia, Charley Buckley of the Bronx, and Pat Brown of California, and confer upon the strenuously canvassing Jack the benediction of the Congressional Power Structure. The obliging Speaker did.

As with so many other key background assignments, the Kennedys sent out another downfield political blocker just in case. "It was on January 7, 1960," Massachusetts Congressman Thomas P. (Tip) O'Neill recalled precisely when I came around, "and Jack came over to the House side to see me. 'I've got two assignments for you,'" he informed O'Neill immediately. " 'I have a hard time talking with City Bosses. Do what you can with Dave Lawrence and Bill Green'—he thought they opposed the whole idea of a Roman Catholic candidate as impossible to win with—'and try and butter up Speaker Rayburn, tell him I'm a Democrat and a decent fellow.'" O'Neill worked on Rayburn; he pestered Green to "get on the bus" until the powerful Pennsylvania boss roared, "You can get off my back—I'm not only on the bus, I'm drivin' it." O'Neill proceeded to Art Rooney, another Pennsylvania playmaker, who drew him aside and told him that the real boss in Pennsylvania was a Joe Clark—not the senator—who operated as the State Party's treasurer and was the power behind Green. O'Neill reported to Jack Kennedy; Kennedy, who had never heard of Clark, telephoned his father. "Within forty-eight hours the father had Clark as his guest at the Waldorf," O'Neill says. "That was the real turning of the attack." The financier was ubiquitous; years later good political detail men like Harry Truman were still smoldering at how cheaply a critical delegation-controlling politician had reportedly been bought, "with $14,500 . . ."

By the end of the fifties Bill Green and shrunken little Charley Buckley were used to the Ambassador and his plain-spoken, out-of-the-way lunches and bursts of thousand-watt charm, but Pat Brown and California were terra incognita: The Senior Scout of Park Avenue Incorporated went West. Fred Dutton (onetime Special Assistant to John F. Kennedy, President, the adviser who more than anybody else probably kept the candidate Robert Kennedy

sane the last two tumultuous months of his abbreviated life)—cheerful, balding, initial Director of the Robert F. Kennedy Memorial Foundation—Fred
Dutton remembers the Senior Scout's appearance well. "I had a brief exposure," Dutton says, "and of course you had heard he was a bastard—soft on
Hitler, an anti-Semite, things like that. I was quite young at the time, but I
could see immediately that he was obviously a very sophisticated guy. He had
come out to California two months before the convention. At the time Pat
Brown was the governor and I was his executive secretary. I had originally
been a Stevenson guy in '56, but after that I had started to feel that John Kennedy made more sense, and particularly that it made more sense for Pat to
go with him. Pat, meanwhile, was starting to go the other way.

"The old man was up at Tahoe, and one day he called down and we talked
and he came to Sacramento and all of us had lunch together—Pat, Mrs.
Brown, Hy Raskin, and Mr. Kennedy and I. Somehow we expected him to
break arms and twist spines, but in fact the old man was charming, persuasive; he never pushed it and he never crowded it. He went away without getting what he wanted, a commitment, but everybody felt, here was this rich
old guy who took the time to have dinner with just us——."

Characteristic testimony from Kennedy conscripts coming closer who
expected, from the kind of press the old man got, a gasoline-sloppy Irish
blowtorch in horn-rimmed owl glasses and discovered themselves beguiled.
Watching those beautifully manicured old hands accomplishing the close
ones, the heads you had to turn, finally, because there was nothing in the files
to bust them with. James Burns had written in 1959 that the Kennedy administration was going to be run by men as "young, dedicated, tough-minded,
hard-working, informed, alert, and passionless" as the candidate himself.
Efficient, that certainly, but Joe could provide a less abrasive interface with
which to meet District bosses and up-from-the-farm press tycoons. Old Joe
might lay it on the line sometimes, but that was where the older operatives
were accustomed to reading.

As evocative an anecdote as any came out of Manchester, New Hampshire, publisher William Loeb, unshakable old land crab of ultra-Reaction.
Loeb reconstituted in his obituary the blustery November day, not long
before John Kennedy's pre-presidential drive, when Loeb and his brother-
in-law Charles Scripps, Chairman of the Board of the Scripps-Howard and
United Press Monoliths, telephoned Hyannis Port to ask something related
to the Hearst operations. Joseph Kennedy invited the two men down. The
Ambassador was pretty well laid up at the time with grippe and a fever. When
Scripps, an amateur pilot, brought his private plane down at the Hyannis

Port airport, the heavily bundled financier was standing there himself, out on the windswept landing pad, all heartiness to grab and pump the influential Scripps's hand. "Charles," the elderly mind reader boomed as the publisher alighted. "That is the best landing I've seen anybody make here at the Hyannis Port airport." He remained an extremely tough act to follow.

Probably it's no accident that after 1961, when Joe Kennedy succumbed to his irreversible stroke, neither Robert Kennedy nor Ted ever came close to winning the Democratic nomination, let alone the election.

2. *The Proconsul*

Insofar as the chronicles pick up at all on Edward Kennedy in 1960 the recognition is nodding, inclusion in this list of advisers at a strategy meeting or as the front man for that little mission to a recalcitrant county chairman. Much of the time he is a page to the realm—nobody hides this—licking envelopes and handing out leaflets one day and cheering up his played-out Arthurian brother as Jack lay in his tub the next. Willing, Christ knows, liking whatever he does, and inexperienced.

This is a vision of himself the senator-to-be nurses along personally: the burden of those giddily elaborated tales he loves to tell people, hovering in the updraft of his raconteur's imagination. One anecdote the future senator has worked on concerns the bitterly disputed West Virginia primary. The point of entering was to demonstrate that Jack could carry a state of unemployed Baptist coal miners and backwoods moonshiners. Anti-Catholic sentiment was endemic, and the boilerplate answer was to buy votes. Joe leaned on his friends in the Chicago Outfit, who kicked in a lot of cash and recruited Paul (Skinny) D'Amato from the New Jersey affiliate to oversee the distribution of a great deal of currency from the Las Vegas skim among judges and county assessors and sheriffs and flexible black preachers.

Among Teddy's initial duties was to transport this money to regional party chairmen, butter up the locals, and make some friends. Within that generation, Ted was without question the last to know when it came to the origins of the fortune, but he was catching up fast. It was at a Kennedy family party at the Sands in Las Vegas sponsored by Frank Sinatra during the primaries in 1960 that JFK had accepted as a party favor the apprenticing demimondaine Judith Exner; Ted had reportedly made a pass at her that night only to discover that it was the candidate the susceptible beauty had in mind. Within a few months, without relinquishing the recently inaugurated president, Exner was to share her favors with Sam Giancana, honcho of the Mob in Chicago.

West Virginia epitomized hardscrabble politics among Edward Kennedy's reminiscences. He liked to recall the day he was reaching the weary end of more than a month of donkey work in the extremities of West Virginia's stripped-out boondocks, passing out Kennedy literature at the mouth of some mineshaft, when a big black limousine loomed into view and slid into place beside his station. One of the heavyset unknowns inside announced that Kennedy was to climb into the car and come along with them. Wordlessly, the group proceeded to the nearest airstrip; young Kennedy was led aboard a small rented airplane, which took off and landed shortly just outside of Wheeling. John Kennedy, Edward discovered, had lost his voice a couple of hours before he was to deliver a significant policy speech: Ted would have to deliver it for him.

Edward Kennedy looked the typescript over, took his place beside the principal behind the lectern, stepped forward, and enunciated the opening—"Do you want a man who will give the country leadership? Do you want a man with vigor and vision?"—with such force and self-assurance that his brother the candidate broke in to croak that it was important for Ted to remember that constitutionally he was ineligible to run for president until he turned thirty-five.

Edward finished to heavy applause and the feeling that now that he had demonstrated his talents he would be allowed a central role in the policy planning; he began reevaluating at five the morning afterward, when there was a knock on his motel-room door and the band of saturnine operatives marched in and informed him that the candidate had recovered the use of his vocal cords. Within an hour or so the ever-obliging youngest brother was back in position next to the mineshaft door distributing whatever was left of the Kennedy propaganda flyers.

This is a turn Edward liked to reserve for himself: the afterthought youngest, out there, legging it, lugging the familial politics door to door while back at the Esso Building, at the end of the corridor at 200 Park Avenue or inside the Oval Office the more refined calculations, the bluffs and gains and losses and expenditures and limitations are talked through to the option stage, prepared. West Virginia was make or break: Joe pulled the plug and Mafia money and operatives came in and flooded the state.

At Ted's level, all this was need-to-know. Kennedy himself once played out

for me the endless tantalizing intermittent telephone call during which he
learned the results of that fail-safe West Virginia primary finally: The night
before the election itself the brainplex had sent him West again to work on the
leadership factions in his original territory, the Rocky Mountain West, where
Lyndon Johnson was entrenched and support for his brother was thinnest.
By the middle of the evening his energy and persuasiveness with whatever
delegates were around Thermopolis, Wyoming, were spent, he knew that at
least the first West Virginia results would be in, and when he called Kennedy
headquarters in that basement barbershop in the Hotel Kanawha in Charleston there was this waiting and waiting for a line to open up, somebody would
answer momentarily and he would hear a raucous medley of shouts, cheers,
laughter through which he would over and over again ask whoever it was
on the other end whether he might speak with Bobby, possibly . . . Bedlam
persisted, with an abrupt chorus from time to time of "Haven't you heard?
Haven't you heard?" and it was nearly an hour before a message reached
Bobby, who made his way to a public telephone booth and returned his
younger brother's call: John Kennedy, on the short end of a final 60–40 poll
prediction, had carried Southern Protestant West Virginia overwhelmingly.

What Teddy hadn't been around to feel were the cold-sweat strategy sessions that led his older brothers to import Franklin Roosevelt, Junior, and
ship him around this hardscrabble state that reverenced his father's memory
to read a speech that climbed all over the underfinanced Hubert Humphrey,
certainly Eleanor Roosevelt's choice by now, with clear allegations that Humphrey draft-dodged his way through World War II. This maneuver not only
bruised Humphrey badly among the chauvinistic West Virginia poor but
resulted in the washout of young Frank Roosevelt's own dangerously promising political prospects.

"A borrowed saw cuts anything," as the Irish proverb insists. Pieces of that
desperation campaign keep surfacing, like armament fragments tilled back
into air on a forgotten battlefield: Kenny O'Donnell's reply, when charged
that the Kennedys had spread $10 bills all around West Virginia, that none
of them would even have thought of anything like that—cases of whiskey
were election currency down there; the way Jack Kennedy, everything tried
and defeat still looming, flew back to Washington to await the results so as
not to let the setback soil him where he had suffered it; Muriel Humphrey's
explosion of primary-night contempt for of Bobby.

What Ted Kennedy heard was simple results. One feels the frustration
and the pride, the thinness and fragility of that transcontinental strand of
telephone wire. This last-born's sense of himself as the eternal advance man,

the lifelong supporting player most of a world away when the moment of triumph or calamity comes. Out catching one final unnecessary lumbago pass. On trial forever.

By now Ted was starting to pick up the walk-on player's trick of catching the eye of the audience from the edge of the wing. The entire truth told— Edward Kennedy had far more of a part than all his wistfulness makes clear. That afternoon of October 28, 1959, when all the Kennedys sat carving up political America, Edward Kennedy had caught the unpromising briskets of the West. Hyman Raskin, a silver-haired onetime tactical fine-tuner for Adlai Stevenson out of a liberal Chicago law office, caught up with this barely graduated University of Virginia attorney from time to time to advise and introduce and help, but most of the bullwork and tests and blunders Ted Kennedy had to contend with on his own.

In front of fifteen Young Democrats in a YMCA lounge at the University of Denver Ted was overheard volunteering that the Democrats would be foolish to nominate Adlai Stevenson again; Stevenson was a "brilliant but ineffectual man," who would make an "admirable Secretary of State." A newsman picked up on this youngest Kennedy's remark somehow, a blooper of majesty, and printed it—to the chagrin of the front-runner, who needed Adlai's people. The hyperactive Edward must have been apprised forthwith because—mobbed at his next assignment by aggressive reporters—the Kennedy Proconsul West listened to his alleged statement read back at him, got up that grin he depended on, and suggested, with aplomb, "Why, I can't imagine my saying" anything like that.

What struck John Kennedy, much more than a misdirected lunge or two, was his kid brother's talent with sticky political combinations. "He's the hardest political worker I've ever known," John Kennedy said subsequently, and, given space and chance, Ted was demonstrating what his brother meant. After a post-graduation deferred honeymoon with Joan to South America the summer of 1959, Edward had returned, checked in with Bobby and Steve, and put together a personal pre-convention Western campaign that kept him ricocheting across deserts and mountain ranges from Nogales, Arizona, to Nome, Alaska, speechmaking, screening and selecting local Kennedy managers, scaling the organization up and down until he himself knew who could handle what, fixing assignments, jiggling and patching and charming and cutting free what he had to until the people and the operations felt right, at least to him. "Ted doesn't have exactly the quickness of John Kennedy or Robert Kennedy," Dick Goodwin has confided to a friend. "But he has a shrewdness about human motivation."

Lumps, streaks, breakthroughs, and setbacks—it all shuffled up together, that first year out of school. Anybody who cares to measure the adrenaline these weeks required has only to glance at snapshots out of the photo morgue to catch this exuberant Proconsul at exactly the instant the Montana bronco he has been talked into getting onto in Miles City breaks up out of the rodeo gate in one pure horseflesh gusher of unbroken meanness—eyes dull, scrag of a mane bristling and both ears twitching that hair-trigger instant before they lay back for real—while Edward Moore Kennedy arches his shoulder blades back powerfully, his right hand a paddle in the air, and shoves that peatspade of a jaw out, supergrinning. He lasts five seconds.

This is a year of new configurations; there is the leap of nerve as, beginning to descend in a chartered aircraft above starlit Las Vegas with his brother the candidate next to him, Edward hears John Kennedy lean across and ask in that nerveless prodding intimate way of his whether he, Eddie—isn't he supposed to have learned to fly a plane recently? Why doesn't he bring this airplane in? And this, too, the possessor of one of the most recently issued pilot's licenses in the West contrives to perform. The feelings of the regular pilot remain unrecorded.

It is a year in the air. Foraging for auditors at a ski meet near Madison, Wisconsin in the midst of his brother's break-in primary push, Edward is invited (later he is never sure how seriously) to go off the tremendous jump by college boys who have been soaring all afternoon—if he wants them to stand still and listen to whatever he is there to say. There is good humor to this, but there is an edge to the challenge as well, what with plenty of newsmen and cameras all around, and there is the apprehension that if he backs away from this challenge something will be lost, something that has been carrying them all will give up on all of them, his brother will hear, perhaps the primary will falter and he will himself be blamed—Ted Kennedy puts boots on and selects jumping skis for himself.

"I went to the top of the 180-foot jump," he said later, "and watched the first three jumps. Then I heard the announcer say, 'And now at the top of the jump is Ted Kennedy, brother of Senator John F. Kennedy. Maybe if we give him a round of applause, he will make his first jump.'

"I wanted to get off the jump, take off my skis, or even go down the side. But if I did, I was afraid my brother would hear of it. And if he heard of it, I knew I would be back in Washington licking stamps and addressing envelopes for the rest of the campaign." Ted Kennedy has never come close even to going off a thing like this before—he is a good, social, recreational skier, with guts enough to leave a trail and try the brush and rocks sometimes, but going off a full-size ski jump for him is as if, to somebody who likes to do a half-gainer off the board above the pool, the unwelcome opportunity came to execute a plummet off the cliffs above Acapulco. Never before or since, Ted Kennedy was to divulge to friends, had he been as deeply terrified in a simple physical way as when he fastened on the jumping skis at the top of that chute of a lift, looked over the anthill crowd, and watched his tips drop over the edge: He remembered enough to straighten as much as he could in the air and, seventy-five feet out and away, touch down on snow and crash finally, ecstatic to feel the earth again, into a whorl of unwary spectators.

The Wisconsin primary was a scramble anyhow, a frozen ordeal that started in February and cost the whole of March until the voting on the fifth of April. The Kennedys needed Wisconsin to prove that they could win in white-bread America. March is a lion of a month that far north among the Great Lakes prairies. There are no white-tie receptions in Wisconsin. All Hubert Humphrey, the straw opponent, had, really, was his bus to ride in and the fact that he seemed to understand these Finnish ice fishermen and Croatian-Slovene brewery workers, knew dairy politics and resort problems: This might be enough.

Bob Healy, subsequently the executive editor of *The Boston Globe*, tells the story of the winter afternoon, shortly before the primary ended, when John Fitzgerald Kennedy was soaking his aching back and swollen right hand in bathwater in a motel: Teddy was around the suite, fidgeting, sure that there was still something he could do, some way to spend the time effectively. John Kennedy asked Healy to keep Ted company while he distributed whatever handbills were around out there wherever he found a likely place to use them up. Ted Kennedy and Healy put coats on, drove around the sanded and pot-holed network of the local Class A road system for a while, and wound up in a shopping center parking lot. Ted Kennedy grabbed an armload of leaflets, prowled among the cars while snapping the material under windshield wiper blades or through whatever windows he found open.

Most of the windows were snowy or frosted, and just as Kennedy was running out of enthusiasm he was able to get the back door of a four-door sedan ajar a little and was reaching across to drop a leaflet on an inside seat when—Healy tells it best—"The biggest goddamn bulldog in the world appeared from behind the transmission tunnel and just about took Ted's arm off cleanly at the elbow. He jerked his forearm out of there in a hell of a hurry, of course, but I could see that the bulldog had just about torn off the sleeve and had sunk his teeth pretty nicely into Ted. I said, 'Jesus, let's get you to a doctor or something,' but he mumbled something about no, we don't have time, it doesn't hurt anyway . . . What he was really saying was that he was a Kennedy, and you can't hurt one of them, of course. But I'll tell you something . . ." the impish Healy, feet on his desk, finished his story off with one of those smothered Irish smiles. "It would have hurt Jawn all right. He wasn't that much of a Kennedy."

Of course by this time—Ted Kennedy is twenty-seven—this Kennedy business, the being a Kennedy, this being roped up with the father and the brothers on this perilous, often terrifying ascent—there is, has to be, a forced quality to this. Early ripe—the spotlight is white hot a lot of the time, the personality grows luxuriously. Too luxuriously. The overblown super-gregarious hyper-energetic extra-courteous precociously political Kid Brother with his jawbreaker grin-and-a-half, who has his role in the family . . . all this is already getting harder to sustain. Smilin' Ed, yearbook hero. "Easy to meet" goes the word on Ted among the pols—John Kennedy and Robert Kennedy were fundamentally harder to meet, disliked being handled, poked, grabbed, armed-around. Ted—or, at least the Ted Kennedy available to the public—this one grabs back, doesn't seem to mind at all.

He just isn't letting anybody in. Ted Kennedy is already enough of his iron-handed old father's son to understand that before long he is going to have to ask for whatever it is he wants himself, and insist on authority enough to produce his own triumphs and mistakes. He has already started to look ahead. "I had gone to school in the East and in the South," Edward Kennedy would tell me apropos of the way he happened to volunteer, sample case in hand, to open up the Western territories for the Kennedys, "and I was interested in the West. I wanted to get to know that part of the country better. We were all starting pretty well from scratch there, which made it interesting, a challenging opportunity. I was delighted to help, of course," Kennedy pauses, "but I wanted an area of my own responsibility . . ."

Sometimes a conjunction is everything, and Edward Kennedy's hesitatingly phrased *but* is everything here. Grown up now, but still the one who puts the sails up after the races are over and sleeps in the bathtub when the vacation crowd is one bed short—Teddy has begun to temper his constitutional need to oblige people with a premonition that he had better establish himself.

Ted Sorensen has alluded to the Kennedy family as a club, and there are important connotations here: If much of their strength derives from the way they stick together and help each other, a great deal of their effectiveness owes to the intervals they keep. Intimates suggest that it is rare that any of them will ask a favor directly from any one of the others—"We don't have that," as Bobby said in 1952—but once a service is proffered, a familial mission undertaken, the performance will be scrutinized, adjudged ruthlessly. A kind of pan-Kennedy efficiency report gets posted: Regard—and self-regard—tend to be readjusted to that.

There is a stimulant and a spur to this, of course, but there are times, when a misstep or failure is imminent, already apprehended, when the uncontrollable rush of fear and self-rejection this involves can be overstimulating, paralyzing. Hands shake, knees knock.

Now, still very young that airplane winter of 1960, the stakes of his Western responsibility give zest and daring to Edward as he flies in and out of the Rockies, above the Grand Canyon, experiencing for the first time himself what was involved in spending prestige and money, eating barbecue, charming delegates' wives, sorting out the individuals his brother and Sorensen had unearthed and bringing in outsiders where the local party is at loggerheads, dealing, pacifying, enthusing, back-checking.

His touch is precociously dextrous. In Arizona (its Democratic delegation unit-ruled by Ernest McFarland, former governor and senator and onetime Democratic Majority Leader until Barry Goldwater took his seat away), a combination of what Kennedy refers to as "machinations" by Stewart Udall and himself picked out all seventeen votes for John Kennedy. Although both the Democratic governor and senator from Colorado preferred other candidates, Ted Kennedy and Byron (Whizzer) White came in low and everywhere and organized the county chairmen and wound up with thirteen and a half of Colorado's twenty-one delegate votes. In New Mexico, solid Johnson country, John Kennedy himself was imported and four of New Mexico's seventeen went over to the front-runner.

Guerrilla actions invariably shred the rulebook. Improvisation, the bold stroke—this was something Ted Kennedy seemed to have reflex enough to handle. "There were situations in which we didn't know the broad issues well enough—water, power, land—and this was presented to me dramatically on my first night in Billings, Montana," Kennedy subsequently confessed. "I went to a meeting of people whose names we had, farmers, mostly, and when I finished my prepared comment I asked for questions. The first question was 'How does your brother stand on 90 percent of parity on wheat on controlled acreage?' And naturally I had no *idear*——.

"But just then I remembered a story my brother the president told me about the time he was instructing personnel in the Navy about fire control. He'd told them that if it was a wood fire you wanted to put it out with water, and if it was an oil fire you wanted to use foam on it. And then one fellow ahhsked, 'How do we know if we find a fire burning already whether the fire was caused by wood, or oil, or electricity . . . ?' And my brother said, 'That's a very good question, and there will be a fellow here next week who will be able to answer——.' And he stepped down. And so I ended the questioning with that."

It was a graceful save. Throughout the months of that unending winter-spring Ted worked the Montana delegation, Jack Kennedy himself flew out and turned on maximum candlepower as late as June 27, just before the convention, and in Los Angeles a few weeks later Montana delivered up ten of its seventeen delegates to John Fitzgerald Kennedy. Overall—excluding New Mexico and Utah, out of which sizable bites were taken, and Idaho, which the Kennedys lost narrowly—better than half the delegates of Ted's enormous Western territory came in for Jack on the first ballot of the Los Angeles convention. It had been a sweeping effort, rough sometimes but effective, and attention was paid duly in Hyannis Port and around the Esso Building and by the financial people on middle Park Avenue.

By far the most absorbing image Jack Kennedy was to see of Teddy in Los Angeles in August 1960 came over the television set at the candidate's hide-away on North Rossmore Street as the first round of balloting tailed out. The enormously publicized Kennedy Juggernaut most of the delegates and news-papermen expected to roll over Los Angeles—like every other Juggernaut the Kennedys ever stuck together politically—was at essence a Chinese New Year's Dragon: a paper and spangles dreadnought intimidating as a locomo-tive in front that exhaled a gigantic orange balsa-wood flame-tongue from time to time and weighed an ounce and a half with all the aides and advisers pedaling furiously inside.

The fascination remains that it could appear at all: the Eleanor Roosevelt–Harry Truman liberals were dubious during their kindest moments, the commercial interests weren't attracted, the South was skeptical, what unpre-dictable black leadership there was—the Jackie Robinson–style moderates of the era—found Kennedy impossible to pin down on Civil Rights. Major labor spokesmen—including by now Joseph Rauh and Arthur Goldberg and Walter Reuther—had finally come around. But even the Catholic urban bosses—the Dave Lawrences and John Baileys and William Daleys—moved into the Kennedy vanguard nervously, fearful of sacrificing party support if they appeared too Catholic, and Catholic ward support if they were too Party.

Commitments had been made to Kennedy, but many of them were fright-eningly contingent, this leader willing to go along because that leader was said to have agreed: One important maverick breaking out against expectations could panic this carefully wrangled herd. The vice-presidential "consideration" had been ambiguously tendered to a number of important Democratic governors. The fire-breather on Kennedy, of course, was his late-starting Majority Leader Lyndon Johnson. The strategy of the savvy old-timers who preferred Johnson—"Mister Sam" Rayburn and the legislative party, largely—was to break the force of the Kennedy onslaught by tossing in the Juggernaut's way the ambivalent but—to his devotees—nostalgia-provoking Adlai Stevenson.

That initial convention ballot was, accordingly, everything: If John Kennedy could be denied that the bosses might split and run for it, the half-convinced Kennedy liberals might recoil to Stevenson, and the party regulars could take over the convention and do business as usual with the more predictable Lyndon Johnson.

As the convention played through, the flashpoint event of 1960—the equivalent of the booing of Nelson Rockefeller by the Republicans four years later in San Francisco—was the addition of Lyndon Johnson as the vice-presidential candidate to Kennedy's ticket. From behind the scenes, Johnson was dumped on board through the intercession of the wily Ambassador, who understood that support for Jack among the bosses was unenthusiastic and that Johnson could probably carry the Southwest for Jack in the close election he foresaw. To almost everybody else around Jack Kennedy—and especially to the nerved-up Bobby—Johnson appeared on the Kennedy ticket like an infected abscess.

Aides close in would later write of Lyndon Johnson's selection as "inevitable" or "a stroke of genius to balance the ticket," but at the time the selection of Johnson represented a betrayal of every principle with which Jack Kennedy, however late in life, seemed to have identified himself.

Revisiting the suite of the Majority Leader, reports Arthur Schlesinger—who must have been swallowing hard throughout those seesaw hours himself—Robert Kennedy assured Johnson that in view of the "ugly floor fight" shaping up, should Johnson prefer to withdraw, the candidate would make him whole by designating him Chairman of the Democratic National Committee. Johnson reaffirmed his decision; invisible tears of frustration streaming down all four walls, Philip Graham, Johnson's champion and liaison just then, telephoned Jack Kennedy to tell him that "Bobby is down here and is telling the Speaker [Rayburn] and Lyndon that there is opposition and that Lyndon should withdraw."

"Oh," Jack Kennedy replied, in the voice of a man interested just enough in what was going on to prefer to be kept abreast of things. "That's all right. Bobby's been out of touch and doesn't know what's been happening." History's die was cast.

"Don't worry, Jack," Arthur Schlesinger reports Joe having advised his son as the Ambassador appeared, happy and in a "fancy smoking jacket" at poolside behind the Davies villa in Beverly Hills, "in two weeks everyone will be saying that this was the smartest thing you ever did." And presumably, by then, everybody was.

That critical Wednesday evening featured the giddying sight of Edward Kennedy (standing exceptionally tall next to the Wyoming chairman, Tracy S. McCraken), his grin enormous and telltale. "This could do it," John Kennedy said hopefully as he watched television from his hideaway—the balloting was almost out of states by now, with the uncertain Virgin Islands, Puerto Rico, the Canal Zone, and the District of Columbia left—and with the exhilarated Teddy right in there beside Wyoming's McCraken he laid his state's fifteen votes down in a block for Kennedy: That solidified the nomination.

Immediately before Wyoming voted Jack Kennedy had been eleven votes short. "We held a review on the states every morning to determine our gains and losses," Edward Kennedy would recall for me, "and we knew where we stood to within a vote and a half. We also knew"—Kennedy measures his words—"that it was going to be Wyoming." It must have been a precise calculation, and early: Wyoming had been tenderized with special attention; over the pre-convention months Edward had managed seven tours of that much neglected sagebrush state in his personally chartered DC-3. "We had ten of the fifteen delegates for sure," Kennedy claims, "and before the balloting started I went to Tracy McCraken, whom I knew quite well by that time, and I said, 'Tell me, if it comes down to where Wyoming can make the difference would you be willing to commit all fifteen in your delegation?' 'Are you dreaming?' McCraken asked me. 'You've got to be. Because it's hard for me to believe our last five delegates are going to make that much difference. If it comes to that, though, I will——.' Of course we realized," Kennedy continues dryly, "it was probably going to come down to that, but there wasn't anybody more surprised to find it out than Tracy McCraken . . ."

Edward Kennedy came out of the convention with a perfectly matched set of observations about the way an assault on a major-party nomination went together, a solid star beside his name on the familial political roster, and an official title going into the election battle—Campaign Coordinator for the Rocky Mountain and Western States, Alaska, and Hawaii. Kennedy brought to the campaign itself every single bit as much energy, personableness, and even that publicity-penetrating derring-do as connoted his performance earlier. But voters aren't necessarily Party loyalists, hope is not delivery, and the West is not the East. Of the thirteen states within Edward Kennedy's suzerainty Nixon carried ten, California included, a loss that nagged at Jack especially. "If we had carried California," Edward confessed to an interviewer a few years later, "I could have done no wrong." But the Kennedys never bullshit themselves, and that new gold star beside the kid brother's entry tarnished a shade overnight.

Some losses were closer than expected. Ted Kennedy, with his months of battering away at the state, had pulled his brother's outcome to within 14,000 votes of Nixon's in Wyoming, far better than any return Stevenson had gotten; Kennedy came closer in Utah too. John Kennedy actually carried Nevada and New Mexico. What seemed most disappointing and ominous to the Kennedy managers as early as 1960 was the recognition that large numbers of influential people in politically awakened areas, many of them Stevenson enthusiasts, to whom the Kennedys felt they had pitched their appeal and language especially, seemed deaf or indifferent. Hard to convince, glamorize, sway, and particularly those "emancipated middle-class Americans who fit into no neat category of occupation, traditions or pressure blocs," in Theodore White's astute phrase, who himself found John Kennedy unconvincing.

Along the increasingly prosperous and de-ethnicized West Coast, people like this had become the political makeweight. Edward and John Kennedy in 1960—like Robert Kennedy in 1968 and Edward Kennedy in 1980—were never quite able to apprehend the shifts of sensibility likely to move this New American Burgher. For all three Kennedy brothers, places like Oregon and California continued to present political problems they never quite got their minds around effectively.

Not that Ted Kennedy got everything else right. The publisher of *The Denver Post* was deflated and discouraged enough when Colorado went for Nixon to charge Ten Kennedy personally with losing Colorado out of "inexperience." Football star and Rhodes Scholar Byron (Whizzer) White was moved up to function as a roving national volunteer-organization troubleshooter for John Kennedy; neither Washington Senator Magnuson nor the figurehead National Chairman Senator Henry (Scoop) Jackson was able to deliver his wealthy, liberal constituency to John F. Kennedy.

In California Kennedy ran a million votes behind the Democratic registration. What the California campaign needed, unmistakably, was somebody with blood all over his smock, somebody frowning Bobby-style in the back room and wielding a meat cleaver. This Teddy wasn't doing. In the scramble for responsibility the lines of authority blurred; critical oversights like the ignoring of absentee voters (most of whom were hiding out in hospitals and nursing homes, and whom the Nixon organizers reached and won in numbers high enough to ensure a final Republican victory in California) pained the Kennedy people especially.

Worried, John Kennedy flew West to have a look for himself. Ted Kennedy, reverting to his stand-in role of 1958, was working the West in exuberant motorized cavalcades. "He had a public relations role primarily," said the ever-smiling Bill Evans, on leave just then from Aerojet General to help Ted. Claude Hooten, a Texan from Ted Kennedy's undergraduate years helped, along with John Tunney, still in the Air Force then, John Goemans, Tim Hannon . . . "Everybody was young then," Evans remembers, "and very idealistic . . ."

Ted Kennedy, as always, loved the rallying and showboating especially, the buttons and noise and bumper stickers and Gay Caballero aspects. Kennedy caravans tooted in great looping swings across the desert, Los Angeles to San Luis Obispo to Palmdale to Palm Springs to San Diego, up early to catch the factory gates, to watch them swarm into the squares in the little Mexican-American filling-station stops at the sound of the four-piece ensemble of Russ Arno, with the candidate's enthusiastic brother—outgoing, *outgo-ing,* belting out "Jalisco" in Spanish (never a specialty exactly) and "Sweet Adeline" in a voice roaming further off key with every hypervibrant bar. As dawn approached he'd fall into a motel bed someplace, enjoying even the long sweaty rides between the oases, the grabbing and grinning, eating the piece of cake the obese señoras would push through his no-draft after tearing a chunk off for the driver, immediately, writing on the back of something the name of a ragged old man who'd pressed against the half-closed rear car door to mumble something about a particular grievance, his problem, some doomed hope——.

"I'm supporting my brother and we would appreciate your help," the set speech would open. If he ducked around the central issues of the campaign, deferred them to the brother he insisted "had the qualifications America needs if we are going to move ahead in the sixties"—if Ted Kennedy looked always to higher authority there was this undeniable warmth, the charge of feeling . . .

It had been a sun-struck, ten-gallon-hat political daydream, a touch of desert euphoria. Nevertheless, in the end, California itself was lost to Richard Nixon and his better-organized Republicans. And, of course, that had to be taken into the Kennedy assessments, too.

"Can I come back if I promise to carry the Western States in 1964?" went the cable from Teddy to That Brother in The White House: military humor, a bump to find out how delicate the bruise felt now. The thing is over and accomplished, there is time to sleep in and sail and party, see friends and read desultorily and let the swelling go down: In this lag of destiny Edward Kennedy has joined—and at his own expense, publicity releases emphasize—members of the Senate Foreign Relations Committee, on whom the president has been able to foist his antsy little brother for a five-week, sixteen-nation fact-finding tour of awakening Africa.

Here, too, Ted exerts an unexpected personal impact. In Lagos at the International Labor Federation reception, introduced around by the U.S. Government's young George Lodge, Ted gets into a heated discussion with an Egyptian, a touring Minister for Labor, which he climaxes grandly by whipping off his own *PT-109* tie clasp and presenting it to his conversation partner. Lodge—the son of Henry Cabot Lodge, and shortly to be Kennedy's Republican Senate opponent in Massachusetts—remembers how impressed he was at the gesture and that he was even more impressed when, a few minutes later, escorting Teddy out, he saw him fish another *PT-109* tie clasp out of his suitcoat pocket and slide it smoothly into place.

Even the society columnists were onto the signs and portents by now. Joan Kennedy was marching her fine long model's legs through the cobblestone tangles around the State House and Beacon Hill. When Teddy got home new arrangements were under way. There was the narrow half-furnished convenient brownstone at Charles River Square. An accommodating fish processor from Gloucester, Massachusetts, Benjamin A. Smith, whose main virtue as far as the Kennedys were concerned was that he was avowedly and unswayably "for the family" had been propped up in Jack's old Massachusetts Senate seat. The bar examination for the State of Massachusetts had to be crammed for, endured, and passed. That ordeal accomplished on the first try, Ted, twenty-eight now, would need some sort of a holdover job. Meanwhile, and for the first time in their several years of unavoidably disrupted and geographically scattered married life, Ted and Joan Kennedy settled into something like regular housekeeping.

3. Joan

At this point, on schedule, Joan Bennett Kennedy has started to invite lady reporters over to talk, to fill in personal background in re her marriage to this baby among the Kennedys. It becomes quite evident she has been delegated to help reinforce Ted's image, in and among the rushes of birthday-party cheeriness, the heartthrobbers—"I felt so little and the mountain looked so big. I kept falling down and getting snow in my boots and up my sleeves; I was aching, cold, and miserable. But I really fell in love with Ted on that ski weekend; he was always there to pick me up and urge me on, with such patient, sweet encouragement. Now I really enjoy skiing and can tackle any slope he can; only a lot slower, of course."

Yet amidst the adoring flow, the breathless appreciation of campaigning clothes from Jackie and what's left of a china service from Mother Rose, slip one-day-sensation gaffes: Ted is amazingly robust and "the president used to be the same way, but now his back is a problem. He can barely pick up his own son." The campaign veterans run for cover, issue disclaimers.

Along with the bubbly sincerity there is this undertow of surprise. A puzzlement that creatures this colossal and hectic should make the attempt with her at all, that there should be a bowl for Joansie as well when chowder is ladled and handed around at table at the big house as this generation of politically allied men settle in for a long meal of opinions and lapses, spiked by that unexpected way they seem to like to gibe one another, and big-toothed sisters pass their iron comment back and forth, in undertones, flatly. "In this family you follow the crowd," this ingenue Kennedy wife tells some interviewer. "I remember once I was returning from Palm Beach to Boston, and the president offered me a ride in his plane as far as Washington. Before I knew it, I was being landed in a helicopter on the White House lawn. There was no one home, so one of the maids asked me in and showed me around. And there I was, like any tourist, rubbernecking in my very own sister-in-law's house."

Rubbernecking, precisely. The days are disjunct with surprise, the proportions and methods and those astonishing Kennedy gaps and intervals. There is that heart-stopping afternoon, a novice on trembly legs water-skiing in a tentative straight line behind a motorboat her husband is steering gingerly, when Joan Kennedy's brother-in-law the president slides in there behind the wheel, throttles down hard, and cuts the speedboat out to sea leaving the astonished press and security people bobbing behind the swells and his completely terrified sister-in-law bouncing hard and holding tight, desperately: "I was scared to death, and worried if Jack knew what he was doing"—then, quickly, the publicity reflex developing, "I'd forgotten that Jack once handled a PT boat."

There is a naivete, but besides this—the inexperienced see sharpest— there is this dangerous and irreducible candor about Joan Kennedy. "I grew up and went to public school in Bronxville," Joan Kennedy says, "which means I had as cloistered a background as you can imagine. The community is highly restricted, and I grew up knowing mostly people pretty much like myself. Both my mother and my father, who is in the advertising business, are Republicans, but I knew nothing about politics when I met Ted. Politics and public affairs were never discussed in my family." Bronxville revisited by marriage: a stony few hundred acres between the lawns of Westchester and the abiding ethnic turmoil of the Bronx. Bronxville, like Palm Beach: sociological panic, an artificial uptown fastness of elaborately zoned chateaux the almost-very-rich would provide to sequester their less adventurous children.

The Kennedy family had put in their decade in Bronxville, too, of course, tried mansion existence awhile, and found themselves unacceptable before long there too, if largely for reasons so arcane that Joe Kennedy left instructions that he was to be buried in a graveyard in Brookline, Massachusetts, where he at least understood the grounds of his exclusion.

Somebody who was a child in Bronxville during the Kennedy residence remembers the way the parents of a playmate who lived across one of those windy Bronxville roads from the Kennedys would pull their curtains aside just enough to watch the train of big black chauffeur-driven limousines disgorge and engorge the occupants of the household, the aides to the financier, who, it was rumored, had moved into their reserve, after purchasing his house insidiously through a previously reputable agent, because there were no Catholic schools he might be pressed to support

The noisy, flashy, lucky, slangy Joseph P. Kennedy had materialized among them like an eternally menacing and demonic Daddy Warbucks, flanked by the Asp and Punjab and coolly and ominously determined, through his intimate association with the totalitarian Red-lining Franklin Roosevelt, to wrench from them, as they sat in their clubs and behind their fieldstone facades before their Early American hearths, what God and Grace and Grandfather had determined for theirs.

There is no record of exactly how warmly their friends congratulated Mister and Missus Harry Wiggin Bennett—good sedate family people, the mother a pleasant enough matron known to appreciate a cocktail—when the news broke about the engagement to Edward Kennedy of this rather fragile-seeming younger of their daughters, recently the Virgin Mary in the high-school pageant, no student but a lovely, *lovely* young person now that the braces were off and she was beyond her teenage gangliness.

Joan Bennett had married the baby of the Kennedys at Saint Joseph's in

Bronxville on November 29, 1958, with Cardinal Spellman officiating and cameramen and soundmen the Kennedys had employed setting angles and grinding away with their machinery throughout. One microphone in the wrong place during the home movie the family made caught Jack Kennedy advising his baby brother that marriage certainly did not require him to curtail his appetite for hit-and-run sexual foraging.

Friends of the Bennetts' adopted a wait-and-see approach. Even during their Bronxville stopover the Kennedys were rough—whatever they wanted, they took. Like both her parents, the bride was known to ward off pressure with an extra drink or two. If doubts were general around the well-appointed tables of afternoon bridge when Joan went off to the Barracks Road cottage at Charlottesville, Virginia, to struggle all morning with the breakfast dishes before giving in to tennis and an afternoon of sun with new friends like John Tunney's wife, Miekel—well, the ladies of Bronxville are ingrained doubters anyhow.

What made it easier than predicted those break-in years was that actor's ultrasensitivity of Ted's, his nose for what exactly the role required. In the Land of the Giants the two of them are miniatures for a season, innocents on a giggle together. At the country club reception they might as well be on top of the multitiered cake, rococo with sugar moldings, that she is cutting while he towers protectively in the shadowless instant of the flash and covers her hand with his, the lopsided Kennedy grin noticeably muted for once and edelweiss sprigging along his cutaway lapel. "When I started spending time with the Kennedys at Cape Cod," the bride reveals thoughtfully, " . . . Ted . . . taught me to play tennis and golf, to water-ski and be a much better skier than I was. He spent hours on the tennis court hitting balls to me, something I suspect most husbands would hate. Now"— it is 1962, early— "I can do everything that is required."

An early Kennedy assessment is in on Joan by this time, first findings: She is all right. None of the temperamental backlashes of Jacqueline, although, of course, lacking the wacky drive of that most fortunate and earliest acquisition, Bob's Ethel; still, satisfactory, willing. Ted has the knack for keeping her moving. "I get awfully tired after a day of campaigning," she tells somebody, "but then he leans over and whispers, 'You're a hit' or 'You're a wonderful help' or 'Everybody loves you.' Then I feel so good. I'm really sharing this campaign with him; when his tummy gets upset mine does too."

For these two, late children of the financier's postimperial mood, expectations, after all, were presumably . . . more . . . modest. Joan Kennedy is the sweetest girl anybody could ever want for a daughter-in-law, but she isn't by any means the rambunctious heiress to the gigantic Skakel Great Lakes Carbon Corporation Holdings, nor was her girlhood ear tuned to the sublimities of the Auchinclosses, those astral "little foxes," as John Kennedy remarked, pleased with himself, skinning the lot of them. She was no moving picture star; neither was she a Duke. But even the most majestic tissue gets crepey in time; the most enormous mouth closes.

"The disadvantage of my position," Ted Kennedy says quite slowly to an interviewer, "is being constantly compared with two brothers of such superior ability." "We've been married four years," Joan Kennedy says in 1962, "and Ted can't understand why we don't have four children. He wants nine . . ." But when the Ambassador in his dinner jacket pitches his tantrum about the way the bills flood into the Park Avenue bookkeepers, Joan and Ted get singled out as the only ones who seem to have any conception as to where and why the money they've been throwing around goes.

In fact, Joan Kennedy has never been particularly excited about the jewelry and boutique offerings, the falls and wigs and eyelashes and gowns for which her sisters-in-law have such a widely publicized appetite. Teddy drives himself, usually in a Plymouth he trades like an insurance man after two years, and although he tried a Chrysler once he found it unwieldy in heavy urban traffic and went back to something smaller.

"Rose Kennedy is a string saver, the way I am," Joan Kennedy reports, and she and her enterprising mother-in-law exchange valuable hints as to when apples are cheapest on the Cape. "I like to go glamorous at night," this sister-in-law of the president divulges to an interviewer early in 1963. She likes the clothes of Oleg Cassini in particular, who "gives me 50 percent off, which I think is terribly nice." This is a remark only the honey-blond onetime Virgin Mary in the Bronxville High Pageant could get away with, but Joan Kennedy is like that, so nobody notices. By 1962 there are two children—Kara, Gaelic for dear little one, and Edward Kennedy Jr. Ted Kennedy's marriage settles in.

4. Career

Unburdened personally between the time of his brother's election to the presidency and the resettlement of his family at Charles River Square, Ted Kennedy feels for a moment the germination of the conceivable, the destiny-buried bulbs of other lives he could imagine living. There is that inexplicable restlessness; he and Joan think seriously about relocating to the West. "His main reason for wanting to move was a feeling that in a new state he would have to succeed or fail on his own. Eventually, of course, we both decided that you can't run away from being the president's brother," Joan told one interviewer. Wyoming, the mesa country, so surcharged with that same feeling of elemental space the ocean stirs—a corner of the universe he has himself discovered, broken to his impulses, a place in which Ted Kennedy has first heard—first recognized—echoes of his own young meaningful voice. Country lawyering, or buying and operating a newspaper somewhere, possibly, or—the occupational daydreaming tries another direction—he recognizes just then a reawakened interest in disarmament, part of a fascination that teachers like Hardy Dillard at the University of Virginia stirred up and which a summer between his first and second year of law school at the World Court in the Hague made specific.

This is a pronounced, demonstrable trait by now, this tendency to get interested in something almost in passing, poke around the new subject quietly, reading and asking questions, follow the subject silently for years after a quicker, flashier mind would have pulled just enough together to talk about authoritatively for a season before letting the whole business go forever. Edward, responsible for what he knows, updates.

The alternative possibility remains, of course, Something in Government. He could have gone to Washington and taken some kind of job in his brother's administration, the moonstruck Joan lashes back when the news of her husband's senatorial ambitions releases such a gentry uproar: There was a lot more to this than cynics of the moment realized. Getting Teddy elected the Senator from Massachusetts was, politically, exactly the kind of investment Joseph P. Kennedy, Inc., avoided financially: an undertaking of enormous risk, very little profitability under the most advantageous circumstances, and the omnipresent possibility of the kind of reversals that could send cataclysmic resonances rippling through the more settled holdings.

"Nobody forced me to run—I wanted to," Ted Kennedy told me years ago. "It wasn't a situation of my father pressing me into the breach. That story people keep printing about my father having said to the others that now that they had what they wanted I was to be given what I wanted—I never heard him say that." Not exactly say; those long-smouldering presidential aspirations realized now, the Ambassador needed only to indicate that resources enough to install Teddy would be made available.

What unmistakably happened here was that Ted Kennedy drifted for several months, entertained options, talked to the others in the family, and let the decision make itself little by little. There was a delay; finally, discussing things generally with his father, the ring-wise old uppercutter let his youngest have what's what: "Listen, if you want to get into politics, you ought to go back to Massachusetts and get involved." "My father's logic made a lot of sense to me," Kennedy told an aide subsequently. Kennedy biographer Lester David would have it that Joe was a lot less indirect: "Look, I paid for it [the Massachusetts Senate seat]. It belongs in the family." In his autobiography, Kennedy conceded that his father had, in fact, opened up the possibility: Out on the *Honey Fitz* with Dad the summer of 1961, Ted found the Ambassador, after recurring to Jack and Bob, abruptly changing the subject: "Well, Teddy, now these boys are well set in terms of their political lives, and now it's your turn. I'll make sure they understand it."

Either way, on a visit to Washington, after he brought up his interest in disarmament, Ted sounded the president himself out. JFK would only recommend that if he was "interested in running to go back to Massachusetts right away and start talking, you'll get a feeling, a playback, a sense of the state . . ."

At precisely this point in the Kennedy chronicle, lumbering genially up out of the wardrobe trunk of Eisenhower-era politics, Governor Foster Furcolo reappeared on the Massachusetts stage. Furcolo's final term had been cankered with scandal—Edward Brooke was shortly to make his way in Massachusetts as attorney general by obtaining indictments and convictions of a number of Furcolo's top councilors and very nearly sending up the ex-governor himself for "conspiracy to arrange a bribe."

It had been Furcolo's hope to resign his gubernatorial post a little early and persuade his presumptive successor, Joe Ward, to appoint *him* to John Kennedy's Senate seat. When Ward pulled away, Furcolo evaded the blandishments of the president-elect, who had some preferences of his own. Teddy's name was surfacing as a possibility, especially with Governor Furcolo breathing down the family's neck. "I hope to have a chance to talk with [Ted] about the matter," John Kennedy hinted to the press. There were several subsequent talks with all the principals, during the most heated of which the incoming president threatened to defer his own resignation from the Senate until Furcolo's term expired, on January 4, 1961, and then prevail upon the incoming Republican, John Volpe, to appoint the malleable Ben Smith, whom the president-elect had already picked as his placeholder.

The jostling got serious enough to require the president-elect to summon the cagey and recalcitrant Furcolo to Georgetown. Furcolo was in Georgetown when Kennedy announced Bob Kennedy's appointment as attorney general. The word was already around the Commonwealth that Jack Kennedy was going before too long to appoint his brother Robert to replace him as senator from Massachusetts; throughout the extremely frank give-and-take with Furcolo the president repeatedly used the words "my brother" when alluding to the potential new senatorial incumbent. Furcolo came back again and again with a reference to "Bobby," to which Kennedy regularly, Furcolo noticed, avoided responding. Immediately upon leaving, Furcolo told a friend that it must definitely be Teddy. As early as that, during those tender pre-presidential months, the idea of Ted still seemed, to anybody politically sophisticated, preposterous.

Somehow, in political America, what is unimaginable today is unavoidable tomorrow, and the youngest of the Kennedys had not been around Boston long before pundits were hovering. Meanwhile, Ted Kennedy had arranged for himself a position appropriate to his experience—in February 1961 he signed on at a dollar a year as one of twenty-six assistant district attorneys working for Suffolk County DA Garrett Byrne. "He happened to be looking for a job so I gave him one," the taciturn Byrne remembered; on another occasion Byrne remarked to a neighbor that his recent hireling had the makings of a "great trial lawyer."

It was no secret that Ted had political aspirations of his own. "He's going to run for something," Byrne was guessing to acquaintances within months: By now his energetic trainee was working the Commonwealth like a hyperthyroid census-taker, showing up at firemen's balls in Pioneer Valley and bar mitzvahs in Dorchester with a well-memorized, highly adjustable set speech, replete with longer sections on Latin America and Africa and physical fitness, a quick brushing-over of Massachusetts issues. He liked to open with the inevitable Kennedy leg-pull joke about two brothers who went fishing together, one with expensive gear and one with hook and worms, and when the hook-and-worms brother seemed to do all the fish-catching the brother who wasn't catching anything borrowed the pole next morning and tried the worms himself, and still no luck—and just as he was giving up a fish jumped out of the pond nearby, and said, "Where's your brother?" So, "I hope none of you wonderful people is going to ask me, 'Where's my brother?' "

Ted's effort to establish himself started early and took on momentum steadily. The noteworthy fact here is that throughout that hard-running year of familiarizing himself with the state and waiting to turn thirty Ted Kennedy isn't just getting his dollar a year from Byrne's office while working on his campaign: For forty hours a week Kennedy is tearing into the public prosecution business with care and fervor.

"The president calls and wants to know how he is doing," Byrne reports. "And Bobby has called and I see his father at the Cape. I give them a regular report and it's always the same. Teddy's the hardest worker I've got." Ted has an office of his own at the courthouse, which is a little unusual and which the other employees can't help mentioning, and every time he gets an indictment some overeager reporter turns it into a conviction; but overall, around that grubby world of chipped marble and bald, prematurely morose men who never take their big hats off, the kid gets a name within months, weeks, as . . . OK. Not too bad, for a Kennedy.

Al Hutton, a well-experienced criminal lawyer who worked for the public defender's office while Teddy was breaking in and opposed him in a couple of felony cases, found himself surprised about several characteristics of this closely watched young prosecutor. It was already evident that Ted was on his way toward some much higher office. But it was apparent, too, that far from conniving to get himself assigned cases with which he could easily run out a string of convictions to give some context to his empty courtroom record, Ted Kennedy was willing to take whatever was handed him (including many that his colleagues wouldn't touch because they would require painstaking preparation), work them up with exceptional thoroughness, and lose a great many more than he would have had to had he decided to pick and choose.

After representing a pickpocket against Kennedy and losing to him—in good part, Hutton felt, because the prosecutor sounded so much like his president brother—Hutton found himself defending a client accused of raping an elderly woman on the Notre Dame Church grounds. Hutton was convinced that the county had arrested an innocent man; talking the evidence over with Kennedy before the case came into court, he convinced the green prosecuting attorney of the advisability of exchanging whatever hard information either of them had so as to give the accused the best chance possible to clear his name. "Ted was open and fair about everything," Hutton remembers, "and I never got the impression that the conviction was more important to him than that justice itself prevail."

It was an interlude in the street. "I enjoyed the work," Kennedy would remember. After preparing a skillfully argued case against a couple of armed robbers who specialized in knocking over package stores around Lynn, Kennedy had the novice lawyer's thrill of watching his convictions stand up in higher courts. "I'm never going to vote for you," one growled at Kennedy as he was led away from the courtroom. "Where you're going, lad, you'd nivver get the chance," the courtroom guard assured his prisoner. The convicted man appealed, and Kennedy remembers that the appeals court raised his sentence from 12–50 to 15–80 years.

The Suffolk County courtrooms closed at four in the afternoon, and that left the late afternoons and evenings as well as weekends for Edward to dig away at getting the "feeling, playback, sense of the state" that his brother the president had recommended. Apart from the necessity for preparing the ground for himself, speaking up publicly, the entire backslapping handshaking ritual of the politico was tremendously revivifying to Kennedy; it opened his circuits.

As Ted's intention clarified and he began to organize and take possession of that murky little suite at 122 Bowdoin, in a closet of which Jack Kennedy's dress uniform still hung unattended, down the dumbwaiter of the tiny kitchen of which Jack and his buddies used to shout on too-early (and sometimes slightly hungover) mornings in 1946 to get the superintendent's wife to send up some orange juice, Pleeeeze—in this grimy permanent good-luck-charm rental, with its ghostly political echoes, Teddy began to piece together the beginnings of a campaign. Six secretaries helped, several full time and the rest from Katharine Gibbs or Manpower or Kelly Girls, and two office assistants. One was Kennedy's Harvard classmate John Culver, just out of the Marines and attending Harvard Law School, the other Bill Evans, who had left Aerojet General to spend a season working for the Department of Defense and came along to Boston, on Bob Kennedy's call, once Ted was ready.

After telephoning all over the Harvard-MIT liberal community, and discovering very quickly that the very idea of his running for high public office horrified and disgusted some of his brother's most enthusiastic academic admirers, Teddy—reportedly cowed somewhat by the fervor of the rejections he was getting—inveigled that Mother Superior of Massachusetts liberals, Betty Taymor, up to see him in his Bowdoin Street office. "I thought he had a big fat nerve too, of course," admits Betty, who remembered Ted as the football-hero-type stand-in for Jack in 1958, and sweating and happy and a little bit out of the center of things at Los Angeles in 1960.

Two details struck Betty at the time: Behind Ted in his impromptu office was a Napoleonic map of the Commonwealth perforated with hundreds of pins, both black and red, indicating Massachusetts commnities the pre-candidate had visited in his pre-candidacy year. Many he had dropped in on as a part of his at-large effort to familiarize himself with the state, many in his capacity as the general chairman of the 1961 Cancer Crusade (there is very little waste motion, however constant it seems, to the activity of the Kennedys). Idly—uncommitted yet—Betty asked the pre-candidate what his brother thought of this Senate idea.

"My brother is a very practical man," Edward said. "So he's for it."

Betty asked when that important thirtieth birthday was expected. "The same day as Washington's Birthday," her brash young football hero responded at once. "Only two hundred years later."

My God, Betty remembers thinking weakly. *Ted! You're already running for president!*

As early a recruit as any to the intended blitzkrieg was battle-scarred John (Jack) Crimmins. Crimmins, a bachelor, had driven for years for Massachusetts's bachelor Governor Paul Dever, an experience that meant so much to Crimmins that he unselfconsciously divided all events in Commonwealth history into Before Dever and After Dever epochs. Jack Crimmins soon came to play a role in Ted Kennedy's entourage that the celebrated Muggsy O'Leary—that outspoken professional Irishman who was supposed to drive and see after the baggage of Jack, but insisted on occupying the back seat during Jack's notorious dashes for the airport—held down for the president. As the organization developed, both Ted and his aides came to prize, during those innumerable rides in from Logan Airport or down to the Cape, the marinated wisdoms and sour, thoughtful profanities of their taciturn driver.

"That guy couldn't get you out if your time was up," Crimmins might remark of an ineffective attorney, or—this when the academics were pelting Ted's 1962 candidacy—"That professor is as soft as a sneaker full of puppy shit." Passing an MIT building and overhearing a remark that the staff had been relocated many months earlier, Crimmins reportedly observed, "Yeah, and not one of 'em has taken a bath since." Every politician needs a peephole into the mundane, and Crimmins, an absolutely straight man, was Ted's: a spy come back from the bars and corned-beef-and-cabbage houses to give the word about what the guys were saying.

Idealistic Harvard-polished liberals on the Kennedy staff were fascinated to hear, as early as 1962, Crimmins expostulate bitterly about the way his boss seemed to be sympathetic at the way the "smokes" wanted to take over their own Roxbury wards—"Just the other day there was a carload of those coons ridin' through Southie yellin' at our women"—at his boss's seemingly incontrollable interest in world affairs—"Why does he have to talk about China, he can't even handle things in Massachusetts"—at all this truck with foreigners. On the day of the Arab-Israeli war in 1967, "He should take care of our own dearos first." To Edward Kennedy, who from the start had built his political life upon a matrix of classically balanced, closely reasoned-through contemporary liberalism, Crimmins served over the years as a sort

of permanent grounding wire, a means of measuring the ever-growing distance between his precepts and approaches and the parochial impulses of his
blue-collar constituents.

"I knew he was running for something," Crimmins would admit to me,
thinking back to the months when Ted seemed to be campaigning pretty much
at large, addressing Knights of Columbus annuals and PTA evening meetings
at an over-a-hundred-a-month clip. One event might go better or worse than
another, but—and Crimmins had seen a political hopeful or two before—"I
knew the kid was going to come." The way he threw himself open to questions impressed Crimmins: Ted Kennedy had an unmistakable confidence
in his own public presence, understood his own appeal with the calmness of
a natural matinee idol. "You have to know your audience," Kennedy told a
reporter of the period. "You can't give women too much. They get confused.
Besides, if they've seen you on TV, they can't think anything bad about you."

This was by no means the assessment a more sophisticated political
observer would have attempted, even before feminism marched the corridors,
but it tells more than a little about the Edward Kennedy of that moment, his
sense of the uses and limits of the opposite sex, and his presumptions as to
what he himself was prepared to merchandise just then.

One soapbox those years for politicians looking to take on stature overnight
was High Level World Travel, and Ted Kennedy made sure to improve his
global diplomacy file a little before turning it over to his incipient electorate.
An extended tour of South America in the late fall of 1961 with John Plank
of the Fletcher School of Law and Diplomacy, besides reportedly disrupt-
ing a Caribbean consulate or two as the result of this energetic young man's
insistence on reopening the bordellos after hours, furnished Kennedy with a
much more specific backgrounding in politics throughout the hemisphere.

Having learned Bobby's 1956 lesson, Ted sent personal Christmas cards
from Caracas to every delegate to the last three Massachusetts Democratic
conventions, the first personal communication most had ever gotten from
a Kennedy. He marketed the vast contributions of the Catholic missions
in Latin America to the Holy Name groups, pushed Israel's example to the
B'nai B'rith bagel-and-lox Sunday brunches, extolled Latin America as an
untapped market to chambers of commerce—a pitch Honey Fitz had long
before developed nicely, having left a memory of "Dolce Adelino" throughout
the Banana Republics.

As always, Edward's interest, once aroused, was voracious. Noticing his
audiences begin to rock back, eyes closed, or fiddle distractedly with napery,

Ted mentioned the phenomenon to his brother the president. "How long does your address last?" Jack Kennedy asked. Upon learning that it went something more than an hour and that his kid brother felt he couldn't do the subject justice in less, the president reminded Teddy, perhaps a bit sharply, that he had been able to hold down his own first State of the Union Message, a speech of a somewhat wider orbit, to thirty minutes.

Another trip the candidate-presumptive enjoyed, one that was to turn into a kind of half-buried political land mine during the years coming up, was his May 1961 excursion to Italy. Massachusetts has a sizable Italian electorate, and this youngest Kennedy, who arranged to be "Chairman of the Massachusetts Delegation to Italy in Commemoration of the First Centennial of Italian Unification," received the Order of Merit-Republic of Italy, for which he was promptly reviled by right-wing columnists. Overall, his tour seemed, at the time, all in his political best interests. One companion was that congenital optimist Francis X. Morrissey, recently rewarded for his years as a Joe Kennedy flunky with a Boston municipal judgeship.

The Ambassador, queried by an interviewer as to what problems his youngest son might expect in this premature bid for office, steepled his fingertips thoughtfully, paused for effect, and replied: "None." Joe still had his own angle. The watchful father suggested—unsuccessfully—to his youngest that perhaps he should stay away from events like that notorious party of Bob's over the course of which a large proportion of the new administration's top aides found themselves, cigars in mouths, bobbing in the swimming pool; Ted, a gentleman always, was reported dancing in black-tie and chlorinated with Bob's secretary Angela Novello in her dripping ball gown.

Image was already central. When Ted won some money betting on Jack in Las Vegas and muttered about picking up a snazzy Aston Martin DB4, his father "hit the roof," Teddy later wrote. "Foolish! I'm appalled that you'd get into this kind of thing! You're never going to collect that money." Well connected as the financier remained around the casinos, he made sure Ted was unable to pick up the cash. "Dad was right, of course—as usual," Kennedy conceded. Expensive cars were too ostentatious; during much of his career in the Senate Kennedy drove his own battered Pontiac convertible, the butt of a great deal of insider ribbing. The financier's iron directive was intended to last a lifetime.

The Ambassador had cherished an idea or two about Massachusetts long before he scurried offstage for Jack in 1959 and 1960. "From 1952 on," one politician intimate with the old man's practices notes, "whenever the Democrats of Massachusetts nominated a man for governor, the nominee went to New York, and met Joe Kennedy, and expected to take home maybe $50,000 or $60,000 in his valise. In 1960 the Democrats nominated Joe Ward. When he and Howard Fitzpatrick arrived at the Waldorf, Joe asked Ward whom, should he win, he was going to support for the Senate seat. Ward's mind was made up. "Jack's old friend Fitzpatrick" was his man. So Joe sent him home empty-handed; as far as the Kennedys were concerned Ward was through.

So far as Frank Morrissey could determine, the elderly Ambassador's approaches to politics in Massachusetts were proved out thoroughly, and so the busy little ruddy-faced municipal court judge was soon disrobing himself early to lead this most amiable youngest Kennedy around the backdoors and lace-curtain parlors of his historical diocese. Frank Morrissey could see that the inexperienced Teddy understood. "I think," Eddie McCormack later summed it up for me, "Frank Morrissey was a little cute; sometimes people make up for any intellectual deficiencies with animal cunning, and he was certainly loyal to the point of personal sacrifice."

Ted appreciated all the trouble Morrissey was going to, overlooked all limitations, didn't mind particularly the flow of dispatches to the concerned financier in Hyannis Port. "Frank was very helpful to me," Ted Kennedy later reminisced, "in that he provided me with the chance to get the ball rolling. In terms of people. Through Frank I met the fellow most helpful to me in that campaign, Gerry Doherty."

Gerard Doherty—a plain-spoken, hard-knuckled young legislator and lobbyist from that sea cove of Charlestown four-deckers from which have issued every ten years or so for a century a fresh extremely ambitious generation of political spawn. Doherty had caught the commonsensical Morrissey's nose for upcoming talent early. It could have been Doherty's glacial, street-wary, take-no-shit-from-you-or-anybody presentation. Doherty was a closet Russian scholar. Perhaps it was that he looked so much like—the resemblance was there, unavoidable—Joseph P. Kennedy, with that domey head, the nerveless face, flat eyes behind those strange little tortoiseshell rims. Doherty was invited to Washington in September of 1961. "This man knows what he's talking about," John Kennedy decided aloud after a session of hard-nosed delegate counting. "You seem to know more about the Massachusetts situation than anybody," Bobby Kennedy decided after one more day of interrogation. "You're in charge."

It turned out to be just as well that at least a spectre of an organization was visible before winter, because on the afternoon of December 19, 1961, pushing himself a little harder than he should have to get through the back nine of the Palm Beach Country Club before dinnertime, Joseph P. Kennedy sat down suddenly on the fairway of the sixteenth hole and felt extremely ill. Ann Gargan got the old man home, but by the middle of the afternoon the intracranial blood clot that precipitated the stroke had reduced the financier to such a condition that a priest had already been in to administer last rites. The Ambassador survived to fight his stroke for eight more years, helpless throughout and able to make himself, understood, if at all, in a sibylline way, a totem half-alive yet urgent, ultimately a mystery.

"You can see the emotion in his eyes," Ted Kennedy told me in 1967, bleakly enough. "Especially when he watches his grandchildren play." For Ted, whose greatest booster he was, and who needed the old man so much still, it was an incalculable loss.

The seat of power itself now began its inevitable precession.

Journalists of the moment wrote articles predicated on the notion that this business of getting Ted into the Senate involved no more than rolling out the Kennedy siege apparatus and turning the monster loose. In fact, there was no evading the terribly hard work, huge expenditure, and painstaking organization that would have to begin with the simplest human approaches: patching up defunct alliances, dusting off card catalogs.

There were special political problems involved. "Nobody could possibly overestimate the hatred of the idea of Edward Kennedy's candidacy by the intellectual community and, especially, by the professional Irish politicians around here," says Murray Levin, whose analysis of this effort, *Kennedy Campaigning*, remains an essential document. "They regarded Ted Kennedy as an obscene projection into the political arena." Civic-minded local academics had found Jack Kennedy, even when his national stance began to seem enlightened, evasive, and disinterested in getting caught up in the endemically corrupt party in Massachusetts; political hopefuls had long ago discovered the Kennedy coattails too short to grasp—or, once grasped, liable to backlash. "The Kennedys run solo," in the pungent phrasing of Massachusetts Senate President Maurice Donahue, Ted Kennedy's pro forma campaign manager in 1962: They were so rich and skillful at organizing for themselves that there was very little a rival politician had to trade them for whatever he wanted from them. Also—this was true generally—the affront that Kennedy's candidacy caused was almost universal: The intellectuals felt Ted Kennedy had no intellectual credentials; the pols felt he had no political credentials—at least Jack Kennedy had gone up through the chairs a little. And so, for once, the Harvard liberals and the downtown politicians shared an intense—and, to Edward Kennedy—very ominous emotion.

Meanwhile, the cannonade from the responsible press was audible throughout the spring of 1962. "It was sporting of Teddy to wait until he was 30 instead of asking for an act of Congress or maybe a constitutional amendment to lower the qualifying age . . ." Inez Robb wrote. *The Washington Post* remarked that Edward Kennedy was a modest young man, with much to be modest about. *The New York Times*'s James Reston, after observing with a special sageness that this could be the first Kennedy blunder, decided, "One Kennedy is a triumph, two Kennedys at the same time are a miracle, but three could easily be regarded by many voters as an invasion."

A somewhat quieter but equally persistent resistance to this Kennedy candidacy had already caught hold in Washington, D.C. Advisers well positioned to know insist that the fledgling president toyed rather unhappily with the idea of his kid brother's candidacy, not willing during the early stages to venture much of a comment really about the wisdom of pursuing it; he reportedly regarded the whole idea as "gimmicky."

Robert was opposed. There were some enormous political difficulties.

After extensive prepolling, the Kennedy forces in Massachusetts had convinced themselves that—against the rising public uproar and generalized political pandemonium breaking out just then as the great underlying graft-and-payoff cesspool beneath the Furcolo administration began to seep through floorboards all over the Commonwealth—no Democratic leader inside the state's political establishment had much chance of holding Jack Kennedy's seat for the Democrats. This nobody liked.

Ted, his own advance polling suggested, could.

5. The Cheating Scandal

However, if Ted Kennedy did run he could look forward to engaging in an active—probably a ferocious—contest for the nomination with Edward McCormack, the Massachusetts attorney general since 1958, the nephew and much-anointed political heir of the recently promoted Speaker of the U.S. House of Representatives himself. This meant that Edward Kennedy, if he wanted to establish himself properly from the outset in Massachusetts, was going to have to put himself through two bloodily fought preliminary campaigns—a pre-convention effort and a Democratic primary—against the thirty-eight-year-old Eddie McCormack. Both fights could pretty well be depended upon to produce, however tight the caucus room doors were bolted, shrieks and countercharges and desperate last-second flurries of character assassination and gouts of political gore, the overspray of which might redden at the very least the porticos of the White House.

Rickety as the whole business appeared just then, it made excellent sense to cut the worst of any anticipated losses cleanly and ahead of time. Feelers went out tenuously. "I came back to the Boston office of the *Globe* from Washington early in 1962," Bob Healy recalls, "and one day Dick McGuire, the Democratic Treasurer nationally, called and asked me if I could come down and see him at the Parker House. In essence, he asked me, 'Do you know anything about Teddy that could hurt him in the campaign?' I said, 'Yeah, I know why he was thrown out of Harvard. Harvard keeps its doors closed, I realize that, but ultimately it's going to come out.' So not long after that somebody in the White House called and asked me to come down and see the president."

Healy went. There is some disagreement over the details of what happened in the Oval Office after Healy arrived, but all agree that the language was straight and the bargaining bitter, that Healy stood up for his right to get and play his story "above the fold," as page-one hard news, rather than inserting it quietly in a back-page biographical sketch, as the journalist-president was knowledgable enough to prefer. Contacts were so arranged that special presidential assistant McGeorge Bundy, until recently the Dean of Harvard College and influential enough there still to get at The Harvard Corporation's inviolate records, released to Healy's perusal Ted Kennedy's undergraduate dossier. Sorensen was present, and Kenny O'Donnell, and O'Donnell in particular was anxious about the reverberations of a Kennedy story like this breaking in Massachusetts.

As feet began to cool Healy was summoned to Washington again. Another attempt was made to soften the newspaper impact of the revelation; Healy hung tough. Reconciling himself, John Kennedy raised his back with his usual difficulty out of his rocker and reportedly remarked, heavily, "We're having more fucking trouble with this than we did with the Bay of Pigs."

"Yes," observed the immaculate Bundy, "and with just about the same results."

Healy returned to Boston, conferred with a fully cooperative Edward Kennedy, and wrote his one-day-wonder of a story and printed it on March 30, 1962. At the same time, two weeks after he announced his candidacy formally, Ted Kennedy explained the incident in his own way in a release to the national press:

"I entered Harvard in 1950 at the age of 18. During the second semester of my freshman year I made a mistake. I was having difficulty in one course, a foreign language. I became so apprehensive about it that I arranged for a fellow freshman friend of mine to take the examination for me in that course.

"The dean learned of this, and my friend and I were asked to withdraw with the understanding that we might reapply for admission after a period of absence, provided that during that time we could demonstrate a record of constructive and responsible citizenship.

"Upon my return, I made my application to Harvard and was accepted for readmission. My friend, who was also readmitted, and I later represented Harvard in intercollegiate athletics. I worked hard, passed all my courses— some with honors—and was graduated in good standing in 1956.

"The authorities at that institution were fully aware of all the facts surrounding the Harvard incident. They have an honor system at the law school of the University of Virginia. I was accepted at that institution and graduated in good standing three years later.

"What I did was wrong. I have regretted it ever since. The unhappiness I caused my family and friends, even though eleven years ago, has been a bitter experience for me, but it has also been a very valuable lesson. That is the story."

There is a plangency, an I'm-only-human quality to the way Edward explains himself here that is completely new to the documents of the Kennedys, neither abrasively wised-up like the father's writings, nor brought to a wary self-protective balance between the classical and the sardonic like the incumbent president's. This readiness to toss himself unwrapped and prideless onto the raucous multitudes required either more insides and a profound self-assurance or a good deal less cool and "style" than anybody expected from a Kennedy. Whichever it was, evidence keeps turning up that resistance of at least a passive sort was consolidating around the White House. "Hi, glad to see you down here, what do you think about Teddy?" one Boston visitor to the mansion on Pennsylvania Avenue reports the president having stuck his head out his office door to ask. Nineteen sixty-two was wearing into spring.

"Not so good. He's just sitting in that Bowdoin Street office. The liberal crowd at home simply will not buy the idea of Teddy's candidacy."

"Well, get back there and help," the president suggested, disappearing.

"I know," Kenny O'Donnell supposedly muttered. "I was death against it from the beginning . . ."

For a few weeks—longer, possibly—it appears that Teddy is . . . stymied, shut off. The financier, normally a kind of low-key arbitrator and clearing-house among the boys, has been gagged permanently by his untimely stroke. It's like the Thermopolis scene: You can keep telephoning, but making a connection is . . . evasive, difficult. "They were having an awful time with the White House staff," one insider remembers. "They were going to use their strength to prevent the thing from getting under way. Finally, the people in Boston came down altogether—John Culver, Evans, Ted—and they got the president and O'Donnell together, and the president read the riot act to the Washington people. Told them to cut the shit about no telephone calls being answered, that he wanted them to cooperate with the people up in Massachusetts . . . At least that was understood, and it made quite a difference, I understand——."

"I never held it against anybody in the White House who opposed my candidacy," Ted Kennedy told me several years later. "I realized they were just trying to protect the president, trying to act in his best interest. In fact, if I'd been somebody else I'm not at all sure I would have supported the idea." (This last is typical of the mature senator, illustrative more of his extraordinary political realism than any personal generosity—although the latter battens in its way on the former. Even among the constitutionally soured survivors of Massachusetts State–House politics, Edward Kennedy is known as exceptionally forgiving "for a Kennedy.")

What bothered nose-counters like O'Donnell, who was still running the Massachusetts patronage franchise from his White House office, was the extent of the probable breakages within the state itself. The Harvard-MIT intellectual community, which it had taken John Kennedy so many years to bring around, was banded together and baying in unison at the idea. "Reckless . . . childishly irresponsible . . . Perhaps the candidate . . . is willing to let the public assume that he has received a fraternal blessing. To foster this assumption is in itself an outrage . . ." according to the widely circulated statement of Mark DeWolfe Howe, professor at the Harvard Law School and occasional adviser to the president himself. When academics like Sam Beer of Harvard, Bob Wood of MIT, and James MacGregor Burns of Williams, all of whom had been involved for years in the struggle to retool the corrupt and dilapidated Massachusetts Democratic Party, struck a quiet deal with the youthful Kennedy that traded their help and support for his promise to help assist with Massachusetts party reform, the acrimony at public forums and private Cambridge dinner parties was astonishing to Ted Kennedy's unprepared little brain trust.

"Well, you know, it's only for the last two years of JFK's term; it's not as if it were something permanent," Bob Wood remembers attempting jovially with a crowd of colleagues. They included longstanding Kennedy loyalists like Eddie McLaughlin, Massachusetts's lieutenant governor just then, an ally of John Kennedy's since their PT boat days together.

"I want you to meet my Navy friend," the Democratic candidate for the presidency had opened before the excited mob packing the dank chiaroscuro of Boston Garden the fall of 1960, "my political friend, and, more important, my personal friend the lieutenant governor of Massachusetts." Then, behind one hand and away from the microphone's hard magnetic twinkle to the exalted Eddie, "Stand up, you son of a bitch——." McLaughlin's hopes for the governorship took a shock and began to die forever as Edward Kennedy's back-room people realized that their man was going to need an untainted WASP to run with if they were going to balance the ticket effectively, and started circling Endicott (Chub) Peabody.

6. McCormack

The prospect that was turning stomachs all over the White House, of course, was filching the Democratic nomination from the Speaker's nephew, Massachusetts Attorney General Eddie McCormack. Partly it was a matter of placating somehow the strong-willed old Speaker, whose help the president needed badly to get a respectable program of legislation through a balky Congress. The president and the Speaker joked warily about the oncoming Massachusetts Democratic Convention, and the pipeline suggested that the old man had been pushing his nephew to try for the governorship and let Ted have his place in the Senate if he wanted it that badly. Eddie McCormack, the rumors insisted, wouldn't wait. There was talk that while he himself seemed to have jumped free of the muck and scandal just then surfacing, good friends and political affiliates of Eddie McCormack's like iron-handed old William Callahan, head of the Turnpike Authority, were implicated: As governor that could put him in a much-compromised position.

Whatever his reasoning, Eddie McCormack was after that place in the Senate. On paper—and the McCormack backers lost no time in getting it all on paper—it looked like no contest whatsoever: One early and crushing campaign leaflet of theirs itemized McCormack's many qualifications on the left-hand margin, Edward Kennedy's ("brother of the President") on the right. Eddie McCormack at thirty-eight seemed exactly the style of homegrown politician, apparently straight but wardwise, who could move in under the publicity panoply the Kennedys were certain to throw up and take the Democratic nomination. He was a bona fide local—a child of Southie, the auld sod transplanted onto Boston Harbor and picking up freshets from Galway direct. An Annapolis graduate who had come back to Boston and finished first in his class at the mightily improving Boston University Law School in 1952, Eddie had run for the Boston City Council that same year and showed such an instinct for when to bend and when to stand firm that by 1958 he was council president; shortly, the Massachusetts legislature appointed him interim attorney general of the Commonwealth. McCormack won election to the politically powerful post a few months later on his own, and bucked the reaction in 1960 that gave John Volpe his first term as Massachusetts's republican governor to return to office by a 432,000-vote plurality, an exceptional show of force in a ticket-splitting year.

As attorney general, Eddie McCormack began to draw the close attention, and increasingly the approval, of unexpected elements in the Massachusetts electorate. He seemed to have something of a knack for staying half a generation ahead of his colleagues on significant issues. He had established within his own office a Division of Civil Rights and a Consumers' Council—both models for state governments all over the country—supported legislation designed to curb wiretapping, fight discrimination in housing, establish a firm code of ethics for public employees, and abolish capital punishment.

Edward McCormack—who pitched for John Kennedy whenever the various state attorneys general got together—remembers getting into one of those savagely exasperated Boston-style exchanges with Attorney General Robert Kennedy, new at his cabinet post at the time, about the way Bob was sending his chief civil-rights lawyers around to liberal caucuses in Congress to expend their influence pleading for an expanded authorization for the Justice Department to wiretap. "What you are really talking about is exposure for exposure's sake," the provoked McCormack broke out at one point.

"What's wrong with that?" Bobby demanded.

"If you don't understand that by this time you'll never know," Eddie McCormack allegedly replied.

To people in the high-power Boston legal-academic community, many of whom McCormack had taken to consulting as he put his program together, there was a fascination in watching this townie politician work into law their most reformist proposals. "Eddie McCormack and Mark DeWolfe Howe— that's like the South Boston Chippewas playing the Myopia Hunt Club," gibed one hardened newspaperman. A lot of Eddie McCormack's appeal, of course, was that precisely: Here you have loose-jointed South Boston Eddie McCormack, showing up hours after he is expected at a factory gate in his

Cadillac wearing a dark shirt and a loud wonderful tie, a natural little wave in his flaxen pompadour and never the smallest effort to tone those politicians' obscenities down. ("That's the way politics is," he is shortly reported to have remarked before a small crowd to an aide, airily, when his effort to maul Ted Kennedy in public debates generated an ungovernable sympathy backlash. "You have to do that sometimes," then, reaching around his assistant, "grab the other guy by the balls and squeeze——.")

Hiding nothing—certainly not trying to hide his father Edward McCormack Sr.—"Knocko"—the brother of the Speaker but certainly no lookalike, quite hard to hide, in fact, what with his placid jowly bulk approaching three hundred pounds. There is a kind of quirky pride to Eddie McCormack—no elocution teacher is going to change that funny little bubble of a brogue lisp that sometimes takes phrase definition off what he says; nobody is permitted to coach him out of that "unfortunate slouch" a magazine journalist notices about McCormack's lower lip, or thaw that frozen cockeyed leer with which McCormack habitually meets public trouble.

By 1962 Edward McCormack is . . . Edward McCormack, a born and bred alley fighter who swings from the balls of his feet one moment and passes around handshakes he doesn't bother to firm up for anybody the next. Beneath one of the many award plaques that decorate his walnut-paneled command center Eddie McCormack is eager to greet a new generation of favor-seekers and petitioners, wearing his jet-black sauna belt, patting the visitor good-naturedly in front to see if perhaps he too might need to reproportion his physique, breaking off the interview from time to time to do a deal or two on the telephone he never puts down: "Coach! How's our building? What kindova price they talking about? Not at that price. Make me the bad guy there. What? Eight-thirty? Listen, I like to stay in bed until eight-thirty . . ." Or put his hand over the mouthpiece to place a wager in passing with an associate putting a golf ball into an ashtray across the carpet—"A fin you miss!"

Besides all this, Eddie McCormack had marched into the wide-sweeping delegate roundup of the spring of 1962 with what should have been the cadre, at least, of an army of experienced Democratic professionals. There were the remains of John McCormack's band of loyalists, the "pals" Eddie himself had pulled together when he went for the attorney generalship hell-for-leather in 1958. There was his own personal praetorian guard of twenty-four assistant attorneys general around the Commonwealth. There was a vast assortment of due bills run up over forty or so years of favors done good-humoredly by the Speaker himself for constituents varying from powerful industrialists to minor county commissioners.

It was no wonder that professionals like Kenny O'Donnell, who knew Massachusetts, were dubious about watching the inexperienced Edward Kennedy risk his brother's reputation by getting into the convention. "The Massachusetts Democratic convention really is a whore's paradise," O'Donnell remarked to me years afterward. Jack Kennedy in Massachusetts had gotten his party's nomination without ever getting into a convention.

Nevertheless, Teddy was convinced he could win it.

It made sense initially, of course, to try and discover what . . . what else the garrulous McCormack might like, whether there was some substitute for that inconvenient Senate seat that also might mean something to Eddie. During the winter of 1960, through an intermediary, "Tip" O'Neill, who was well acquainted with both state and federal politics, Edward Kennedy attempted an approach. He proposed a mutually conducted poll: if McCormack came to within 5 percent of his own results he promised to pull out in McCormack's favor. Ted's own polling suggested that he would beat the attorney general 2–1, results with which he was trying to establish his case around the White House. Ted sent the information over to Speaker McCormack, who showed them to his nephew gravely; Eddie laughed, and insisted he had the convention locked up.

The White House, sucked into the situation, stacked up the ante. If Ed McCormack had financial obligations of an overwhelming sort, perhaps a partnership in a large New York law firm? An ambassadorship? Something like . . . Assistant Secretary of the Navy? Eddie McCormack walked away.

The professionals were puzzled. Obviously, if the Kennedys wanted that seat they were going to have it whatever it cost. The Speaker, while requesting the members of the Massachusetts congressional delegation to stay neutral as a courtesy to him, was heard to mutter that his nephew accepted his help willingly enough, if never his advice . . .

The Speaker's desperation had surfaced during a conciliatory meeting among Tip O'Neill, Ed McCormack's secretary, Charlie Hamilton, Eddie McCormack, and McCormack's wife, Emilie. "I don't want my children to have a quitter for a father," Emilie reportedly shrieked; furthermore, she wouldn't accept a quitter for a husband. The only concession the McCormacks would consider would be a telephone call from the President of the United States, specifically and formally requesting Eddie to give up his candidacy. But the presidential neck was out far enough already; that was out of the question.

So Teddy prepared to enter the convention. There was an easy newspeg for journalists from the butcher-paper weeklies in the idea that the Massachusetts Democratic Convention in Springfield on June 7 was rigged out of the Justice Department in Washington or bought with Park Avenue funds. Actually, given the worldwide attention, the presence of those regulars from the Japanese news service and the man from the *National Review* and the stringer for *Tass* and the omnipresent *Times* men, there was probably less opportunity for a favor to be offered or extracted around the Commonwealth than anywhere else in John Kennedy's America. A favorite opening was to refer to the gathering as a "delegation of postmasters." But out of 1,800 delegates there were liable to be fewer than fifteen spots available—or, as far as that goes, people who wanted to become their village or suburbs' postmasters—than there were insurance men, say.

What carried the convention for Ted was his tireless personal campaigning.

"You know, Mary,"—easy enough to hear that timbre dropping to confidentiality as this Kennedy stripling sounds out a stubborn female legislator—"down in Washington they all say: When you want to know something about Southeastern Massachusetts just ask Mary."

One aide of the period remembers grasping unsuccessfully at this husky hyperenergetic candidate as he springs out of his reach to swing onto a scaffolding and climb it and teeter across a ridgepole to grab the hand of a delegate laying down a roof, unable to answer for all the flat galvanized nail-heads dotted along his lips; another remembers halting atop an open manhole while contact is made below. A holdout in the Nahant area finds the candidate on his doorstep at five in the morning, happy to come in for coffee and bounce one of the children in the family on his knee—"My brother Bobby has one just this age"—hours later the delegate's wife gets a call from Joan Kennedy inviting her to lunch nearby with "a few of the girls."

After that, resistance is out of the question. "I can vote against the Kennedys, damn it, but I can't vote against my wife," sighs the targeted delegate, caving in. Another man is involved in Little League; Ted Kennedy, sliding into his place at the kitchen table with one of those perfect natural moves of his, averting his glance from the sticky oilcloth seat of the chrome-legged chair, talks Little League.

It's Honey Fitz's approach half a century later: Walk away leaving the men hesitant but admiring, the women adamant, and let domestic dynamics carry the rest of the distance.

Not that there are not . . . other possibilities. "All right," a journalist quotes Kennedy, both charm and enthusiasm played out for once against an experienced east-Massachusetts professional. "But remember: Win or lose, I'm handling the patronage in Massachusetts." This is pure desperation stuff, and unusual. There were gentler inducements in the Kennedy files: Each delegate card mentioned whether the uncommitted might like to meet the president before long, have his picture taken with him, perhaps, or might just have a relative in the service who had been passed over for a promotion. Rumors spread of vindictive tax investigations: By convention day Springfield itself surged with unverifiable rumors. By now the unsleeping Kennedy has personally visited, worked on, beguiled, pressed an incredible 1,300 delegates. As soon as a delegate came over onto the list of the freshly devoted, whether busted or enchanted, the name was entered into a back-room roll call kept current by five dedicated employment-agency girls who called every delegate every week thereafter; there was a count each morning, and at the first sign of wavering or the changing of a mind the appropriate reinforcements moved in.

Close contacts persisted all the way into the Springfield convention floor: The delegate checkers moved their twelve-circuit switchboard into an upstairs room at the Civic Auditorium and kept the numbers abreast.

No pressure or ruse went unremembered. The Berkshire delegate committed to McCormack passes around a personal letter from Kennedy headquarters declaring—incorrectly—that it is illegal to arrive at the convention pledged. As the delegates mill into the steamy, mausoleum-like Civic Auditorium they find in charge of the proceedings that incorruptible leader of the Democratic Committee John (Pat) Lynch, whom John Kennedy himself hand-picked to replace the fractious "Onions" Burke in 1956. The aisles are patrolled by Kennedy operatives on the floor feeding still another twelve-circuit walkie-talkie system; upstairs, masterminding them and watching everything on a TV monitor, Steve Smith is scratching symbols in next to the 13 percent still categorized "unpredictable."

Well into the first ballot the Kennedy surge pauses, drops back; Congressman Eddie Boland, a Kennedy reliable, hustles among the delegates, reminding one of a favor, another of some exceedingly grim possibilities he might have forgotten. The Kennedy tally resumes its climb. "They're cold, they're cold," old Knocko grumbles of the Kennedy invasion to a reporter. "I got here at twelve-thirty last night, and I got in an elevator with an old friend from Northampton. He's been in the American Legion with me for years, and I say, 'Hello, Commander.' And he hangs his head and he says, 'I can't be with you, Knocko.' 'What do you mean?' says I. 'I've been offered a good federal job if I go with Kennedy,' says he . . . It's pressure, pressure, pressure, post office, post office, post office."

As morning begins, with the delegate count 691 to 360, McCormack gives up, but savagely. With a tight smile, uncharacteristically sardonic, McCormack promises to take his case "to the people" in the September primary.

However irrepressible Kennedy's flicker of satisfaction while he stood, arms folded Mussolini-like, before the television screen in his suite and watched the convention collapse, the damage McCormack could still contrive was more than enough to roil Ted Kennedy's mood that spring. "If his name was Edward Moore . . ." the quiet tough-minded Steve Smith mused to me years later, thinking back. "Now that was the question. Was there anybody there?" Smith smiled his careful, pregnant little smile. "Turned out there was."

The Kennedy organization people, at least, were evidently none too sure. When Assistant Postmaster General Hartigan volunteered to go back to Massachusetts and help out, Kenneth P. O'Donnell came down cleanly and hard: no leaves of absence; if you want "to go back to Massachusetts and help the kid, quit." Ted did or didn't cop the endorsement.

The Man in the White House was keeping at least one quiet eye on things, that was unmistakable, but partly because the president himself could obviously be hurt so badly so easily, and partly because John Kennedy was precisely low-key enough to be curious about what Ted would do on his own up there, especially after defying the strong countersuggestions of O'Donnell, O'Brien, and—one insider insists on this—gyroscopic little Bobby himself, and jumping into that cockpit of a convention. Regular contact tended to be brushing: On Sunday, often, Ted, leaving Hyannis Port, would stop his car and stand at the roadside next to the limousine of his brother, just arriving, and exchange a joke and perhaps a word or two. But the president's detachment was unsettling to a young man who had fallen into the habit of referring the tough ones to his older brother and was never quite able to forget—then, or later—that his own career must be continue to be locked into the larger political intentions of his family. A Kennedy must win to survive.

"I was present at the first real public confrontation of the candidates," a local political scientist recalls. "On the Boston Educational Channel. Ted was in a state of shock. Sweating profusely, every bone in his body shaking. He was so nervous he could barely get sound out of his body. When he was able to speak you saw that it was all memorized questions and answers, often the wrong answer to the wrong question—as if he were the other end of a computer that was really someplace else, in Sam Beer's office, probably."

"The Qualified Candidate" was Eddie McCormack's warcry, and beside it Ted Kennedy's own, "He Can Do More for Massachusetts," sounded a little piping, as if he were offering to carry the entire Commonwealth out of his trust fund income. When it came to a knowledge of the great political issues of the moment—from the multilateral force to federal aid to parochial schools—Ted Kennedy was pretty much one large unspoiled blank. In fact, excepting only his opportune espousal of Washington aid to parochial schools, Ted Kennedy's platform pretty much reiterated mechanically whatever he was aware of among his older brother's own policy positions.

"My concept of a liberal is one who has a concern about the public interest," the boy politician told a magazine reporter, aware that in Massachusetts just then being caught among the liberals could lead directly to an unmarked political burial. "One who believes the government must serve and not merely regulate the public, and one who approaches all new issues with an open mind. I don't believe in labels," young Kennedy concluded, executing one last little dancing step, "but in that sense I'd call myself a liberal." This was an important gesture from a fledgling politician whose brother the president continued to defend Joe McCarthy as a patriot and stated quite unabashedly that he himself was *not* a liberal.

"He was a little callow at the time," admitted Sam Beer of Harvard's Government Department to me soon afterward. Sam was quite happily force-feeding his candidate answers and concepts wholesale. "But he had it."

Pre-convention and afterwards, the problem of experience, the chutzpah issue, remained an open minefield—which if it blew could reverberate well beyond Ted Kennedy and the Commonwealth of Massachusetts. "Lay off that goddamn experience," longtime Kennedy friend and ally Edward McLaughlin remembers Ted all but hissing at him in the Men's Bar of the Parker House.

"I can't help it, Teddy, that's what I've got to sell," the politically doomed McLaughlin replied, perhaps a little plaintively, already aware that the Kennedy people were certain to scuttle him—as they did at the convention, and openly—to balance the ticket with the maladroit Chub Peabody.

The knives were out all around. The outrider in this senatorial race was H. Stuart Hughes, perhaps the country's first bona fide "peace" candidate, whose credentials included: a position at Harvard teaching history, the help of a horde of noisy willing kids, Charles Evans Hughes for a grandfather and a father who was U.S. Solicitor General for a time, and an awe-inspiring assortment of Harris tweed jackets.

"I was the first, sort of your John the Baptist," Hughes told his friend Eugene McCarthy after 1968; McCarthy accepted his due. Hughes's support in 1962 was rather localized: The ban-the-bombers and the more upwrought members of the Women's Strike for Peace claqued throughout for Hughes, and out West in Worcester, where Hughes threw away his schedule one afternoon when somebody told him there was a wonderful collection of medieval armory in a nearby museum.

"Teddy would arrive with his bodyguard at the functions," Hughes remarked to me little ruefully, "and of course they would have nothing to do with the entourages of the other candidates."

The candidates very rarely, in fact, all turned up at the same place together, but Hughes himself remembered one behemoth chamber of commerce luncheon, to which all the major pre-convention hopefuls were invited and to which all came. "My attitude toward Ted, whom I regarded as a kid, was, frankly, somewhat supercilious," Hughes admitted. "When we were introduced he called me Mister Hughes, and I called him Teddy, and then he went into a sort of regulation political handshake. I was somewhat taken aback. Teddy's performance at this point was, actually, somewhat ragged. His speech seemed to be a sequence of lines he'd learned without getting them together—he leapt from the fishing industry to getting a man on the moon without a real transition.

"It happened that Eddie McCormack was seated next to me, and just as Teddy was getting into his text McCormack leaned over and remarked, you know, a little bit behind his hand, 'Don't you think this kid is a fresh son-ovabitch?' Well"—both Stuart Hughes's eyebrows elevated at the recollection alone—"I thought that was rather frank, since I had just met McCormack, and so he could have no idea of what my views were . . ."

By midsummer even Eddie McCormack's handlers had to admit among themselves that the big well-organized heavily financed Kennedy campaign was pushing Ted further into the lead all the time. Word infiltrated the barriers that McCormack was feeling more and more cornered, cut off, desperate, and dangerous. "His people didn't really do too much, but McCormack did a little more," one blasé Kennedy aide, himself accustomed to leaving skin all over the precincts in the rush of a Kennedy effort, observed, yawning.

That personal following Eddie McCormack had among the professionals stirred listlessly for a few weeks and then sank back, discouraged, as the summer wore into dog days. The intriguing melange of liquor wholesalers and bookies and major contractors who provide such a lot of campaign money in Massachusetts was holding funds back by now.

"He had a magnificent inefficiency in the organization," one colleague says baldly, a "dreadful choice of people to do specific jobs; I cannot think of one person in the campaign, with the possible exception of his own personal secretary up at the State House, who was well chosen for the job she did."

To the electorate at large the Kennedy campaign looked like a familiar tent show. Kennedy retainers were shortly all over the Commonwealth handing around lapel pins and pamphlets, buying television spots by the dozens, running off a bracing little film to groups in the North End featuring selected moments throughout Ted Kennedy's visit to Italy in May of 1961, renting billboards, sticking bumper stickers to everything smooth in Massachusetts, watering the necessary elephants.

Steve Smith—who moved into the traditional Park Avenue Annex North at the Ritz-Carlton in April to make sure the office management, money-raising, and expenditure-control was what the financier would have demanded—was the only real regular coordinator. "[Ted] left the scheduling and things like that to me," Smith later told me. "Once the candidate has agreed to the general direction, made the important decisions in terms of what the theme is going to be and how you present it, he should be leaving the mechanics to other people." Smith was busy enough. Lester Hyman, a spruce young attorney well initiated in Massachusetts politics, who was working as Endicott Peabody's campaign manager in 1962, remembers stopping by Smith's office to arrange an exchange privately. Hyman had always found Smith a "tough-minded guy, but for good purposes"; that day Hyman, whose candidate was chronically short of funds, proposed that the two campaigns save a little money by Smith's including in the polls they were taking a question about Peabody, and the Peabody organization would include a question about Kennedy. "We don't use polls," Smith told Hyman without a crack in his expression while he removed his most recent poll results from a drawer and passed it, largely to let the aroma rise, beneath Lester's nose.

"What sticks in my mind," recalled Ed Martin, the compact, wire-haired press aide who took over the multifaceted dealings with reporters ranging from the team from *Epoca* to Earl Mazo, "was watching Teddy himself, observing his ability to work. Jesus he could work. I don't think fatigue is part of their physique. There were alotta days on the campaign trail when we would average forty or fifty stops. It wasn't unusual for Ted to leave his home at Charles River Square at four-thirty in the morning, be at a plant gate at five-fifteen, turn up sometime in the early afternoon and say, 'We've got an hour to spare, let's walk through Filene's, or catch the commuters at Ashmont.' On a warm Sunday sometimes we'd find him out walking the beaches in a blue serge suit, shaking hands with bathers."

The candidate would shake very nearly anything: hands covered with grease, hands covered with mud and sweat, one hand—withdrawn squishing from a long deep conveyor trough in a pie-making factory by a spunky old man who insisted, "If you want my vote, Kennedy, you're going to have to shake my hand"—covered to the stringy old elbow with globs and clots of blueberries. It was an education, Kennedy told me later, a *Beggar's Opera* of the daily industrial.

"For Christ's sake," Bobby telephoned to tell Larry Laughlin, who was handling the schedule and shooing the three young advance men ahead of their seven-days-a-week candidate, "you had better start giving Ted Sunday off pretty soon or you'll kill him." It took some restraining. "We brought the street-corner rally back in style just for Ted," Laughlin insists. "He was the ideal candidate. He's a bit of a showman, you know, like Honey Fitz and his mother. They were a hell of a deal—cheap, you hired a sound truck and a searchlight and a local band you pay a few bucks to and print a lot of pamphlets to throw around in the streets, and then you go anywhere you feel you're weak—suburban shopping centers, subway entrances—and let the candidate go at it without drawing the regular political crowd. Kennedy liked that.

"Of course," Laughlin primed his pipe a moment, "a campaign that lasts that long puts a strain on anybody, and you get pretty raggy. I remember one spell where he flew his own airplane for a while and almost reduced all of us to complete nervous breakdowns until finally somebody got to the president, who convinced him not to do this. Ted . . . he . . . wasn't the greatest pilot in the world." When he was especially edgy or tired, or raw, Kennedy liked to relax by "hitting a convent" to spend a few quiet moments among the hush of the sisters.

"And these things—things nobody could help that bothered him," Laughlin says, "one night we had a policeman who, against the senator's wishes, attached himself to the escort from Fitchburg to Boston . . . killed. Got killed at an intersection. It bothered Ted a lot."

"I remember one fine sunny day," begins Charlie Tretter—one of the whelps, along with Ed King's boy Jim and Andy Vitali, whom Joey Gargan was trying to convert into effective advance men—"I remember the day all of us were riding around in a panel truck, Ed Moss was driving, and Andy Vitali and I were in back, and Kennedy had promised somebody for some reason that he would stop off and see a fellow in a veterans' hospital who was dying of a cancer. When he got back into the truck he looked all washed out, physically ill, and we drove for a while, and then we got a little lost, and Moss and I started a kind of silly bantering—'Should we go right?' so we'd go right, and that was wrong, so he'd say, 'Should we go left?' and we'd go left a while . . . Then all of a sudden Ted turns around and looks right at me, and he really roars: 'WILL YOU GET THE FUCK UP HERE AND TELL ME THE WAY TO GO?' So I got out and asked somebody, and found out, and we went wherever we were supposed to. That was not characteristic language for him at all, of course, and later he apologized . . ." The cancer victim had upset Ted. This is a part of the thing by now: the pain, the tears of things—.

The emotions were simpler sometimes: impatience, annoyance, rage, anger. "I figured he might have been the guy with the silver spoon in his mouth," says Gerard Doherty, "But he wasn't. I began to find him bright, intellectually very very resourceful, and with an unfounded fear of academics. I think what bothered him most in 1962 was the almost total boycott by the liberal establishment of his candidacy." Then—later—this was to become a bone to Kennedy: he insistently worried it. Beryl Cohen, one of the few converts Ted had been able to raise in largely Jewish Brookline, gave a little party and held a meeting in a hotel there; almost nobody came; Kennedy was openly furious.

Before the primary Betty Taymor arranged a reception at the Sidney Hill Country Club, in Brookline; Mrs. Joseph P. Kennedy, after asking personally that the lights be dimmed a bit, appeared on Judge Morrissey's arm and attracted eight hundred people: nothing; applause, but no voter support. All of which might have had something to do with why, in September and ahead in the polls mightily, Edward Kennedy—against practice, common sense, and the advice of virtually everybody who got close enough to give him any—agreed to take on Eddie McCormack in a series of head-on televised debate-debacles.

"In Massachusetts they only really go for a politician once," Gerry Doherty said, "but that time they go for his throat." Ted Kennedy's *once* came at the first of the two debates he had agreed to participate in, one-on-one, with seven minutes each for opening and closing statements and the rest of the time devoted to answering questions alternately from a panel of newsmen, each participant's answer open to a rebuttal from the other.

"Ted Kennedy doesn't necessarily do or not do a thing because that was the way John Kennedy did it, wear a blue tie on Saint Patrick's Day because his brother did; that isn't enough to convince him all by itself," says Milton S. Gwirtzman, an oncoming Kennedy speechwriter and administrative assistant just then to Benjamin Smith II, senatorial seatholder. "But mentioning the fact that the president did it helps." Jack Kennedy had gone the convention route; Jack Kennedy debated. Edward Kennedy would debate.

Even a healthy body gives off most of its waste through the pores, and true desperation is something that politicians in particular can smell. All over Basic Boston that summer, as Ted Kennedy's advancing kids vied with one another to see how many people their man could speak to or handshake as they alternately led him through a day of schedule, pushed the totals up to 7,000, 8,000, 10,000 people at the frenetic peak, the confusion and anguish of Eddie and Knocko McCormack and the pals was on the air.

There were forewarnings. "You are going to win anyhow, so why use all this muscle on me?" McCormack asked John Riley, an assistant of Bobby's.

"Because we've got it," was Riley's alleged reply.

Addressing one of those innumerable chamber of commerce gatherings, this one at Lynn, McCormack played to his audience of Republican businessmen. It wasn't very many months since JFK had faced Big Steel down, allegedly calling the top industrialists sons of bitches. Eddie opened his remarks with the observation that he had "never seen so many SOBs in one room in my life." Ted Kennedy, sharing the speakers' table, blew up. The word among the McCormack headknockers after that was that Teddy had a helpfully "shaht fuse"; the trick was finding the right public moment to put the proper insult to the tip and let the kid himself blow his candidacy apart.

Another opening seemed to be this young Kennedy's way, in the enthusiasm of the moment, of slurring over or distorting facts relating to himself and to the Kennedy family. Ted was forever referring to his grandfather The Mayor, who, he seemed to think, had never lost an election; most of the oldsters he was about to polka with at Polish weddings, or second-generation Sicilians he greeted on the dawn piers, could personally remember Honey Fitz's three decades of losses.

"Fitzy beat Lodge?" one old-timer muttered to a reporter at a milling autumn street-corner rally, while searchlights swung through the clouds and the candidate stabbed away presidentially with his left-hand index finger. "Ha, ha, ha. Don't make me laugh. My lips are chapped."

McCormack had hoped to slip the noose around the gawky Kennedy neck a day or so before the balloting at Springfield: Alluding to young Kennedy's assertion at a press conference that he had voted in every Massachusetts election and primary since he was twenty-one, the attorney general came up with photostats of Edward Kennedy's voting records to show that only in two elections and one primary—all elections in which his brother was involved—had Ted taken the trouble to vote. When Kennedy himself claimed that he had been misinterpreted, McCormack produced a tape recording made at the press conference during which Edward Kennedy's unmistakable voice insisted that he had voted in Massachusetts "Since I have been twenty-one. I have voted every time."

That short a time before the convention balloting, of course, most of the delegates were locked in; the charge affected few. In two open debates, however, with most of the footage certain to wind up on nationwide television, there was likely to be all kinds of time and opportunity for ambushes and blunders.

Influential friends in very high places indeed got worried. "Have no fee-uh, we ah hee-uh," one aide, helping get Teddy's ideological portfolio into shape, remembers Bobby snapping happily to his kid brother as he and Sorensen breezed in just before the August confrontation to run the nominee through his material. That summer the first U-2 overflights had started to alarm the administration at the possibility that the Soviets might actually have started building missile sites in Cuba. Purportedly to alert Ted to the compounding national danger so that he would not touch on dangerous material during his impending "Meet the Press" session, Sorensen deserted Ex-Comm and flew up to catechize the senatorial nominee one more time.

The president himself loved to check his brother out on local situations. "How are things in Brockton?" he might begin, then—finding Ted a little too smug and pat in his positions—"What is your standpoint in Massachusetts on the uniform divorce proposal?" As the August 27 debate loomed, the pressures increased constantly. Red Fay remembered the cocktail hour in Hyannis Port a few days before the first debate when Ted Kennedy, forewarned about McCormack's impending personal attack, went through a fiery ten-minute rebuttal before the family.

"Now listen," John Kennedy reportedly said, "you forget any personal attack on Eddie McCormack. You're going to need all the supporters that McCormack has right after the primary. Let McCormack attack you as much as he wants. You're running for United States Senator. Stay on the issues and leave the personal attacks out."

Joseph Kennedy, struggling for some speech, reportedly forced out the words: "You do what Jack says."

Ted Kennedy managed that, but it may have been the greatest effort of self-control he ever attempted. The first debate was staged in the South High auditorium, a focus in "Southie," at the suggestion of the Kennedy representatives. McCormack accepted with alacrity: He himself was something of a hero in his home neighborhood, and he expected to be able to pack the auditorium with his own enthusiasts. In fact, picking the South Boston hall was as clever a piece of entrapment as the Kennedy aides could possibly devise.

"Southie" was shanty to the lace-curtain Irish, lace-curtain to the cut-glass Irish, a ghetto abandoned for the most part, and feared and detested accordingly. The Kennedy handlers were gambling that before the debate itself the courthouse regulars around McCormack would push him, against his naturally generous impulses, to attack Ted Kennedy with uncharacteristic savagery, ride up on the surge of mob enthusiasm to a level of invective that would make Ted Kennedy into the popular underdog. McCormack's advisers—even, according to reports, his wife—had indeed been working him, poking him with rumors that one Kennedy man had been telling his friends that McCormack was lazy, another that he could have been bought out of the race. McCormack reportedly held on to his intention to keep his part somber and temperate, and it was only on the rostrum itself that the incendiary mood and the feeling of mass support coming off the audience seems to have swept him as far as it did.

After the moderator, Erwin Canham, had introduced the participants, Edward Kennedy made the opening statement. It was a flat thing, completely expected, invoking as it did such local engineering triumphs as Raytheon's Thor missile, his grandfather, the need for government money in industrial Massachusetts; he referred respectfully to his opponent as "Mister" McCormack.

McCormack, after a nod to the sweet religiosity and traditional hard work typical of his South Boston audience—having by this time supposedly rejected his own speechwriters' "stinging indictment" approach—felt murder coming out of his audience and went beyond his most impulsive advisers as he laid his statement in fusillades, blast after blast of verbal buckshot intended to tear the senatorial hopes of Edward Kennedy to rags.

". . . I say," McCormack ripped out, digging in, "let's discuss the issues. And the issues basically are not the issues where Democrats disagree because we agree on the program of this administration, but those issues that are raised by the slogan of the two candidates. I say that I am the qualified candidate and I point to three years in city government, three terms with one term as president of that body. I point to three terms as attorney general of this Commonwealth, the second most important office in this state, and I ask my opponent, 'What are your qualifications?' You graduated from law school three years ago. You never worked for a living. You have never run or held an elective office. You are not running on qualifications. You are running on a slogan: 'You Can Do More for Massachusetts.' . . . and I say, 'Do more, how?' Because of experience? Because of maturity of judgment? Because of qualifications? I say no! This is the most insulting slogan I have seen in Massachusetts politics, because this slogan means: Vote for this man because he has influence, he has connections, he has relations. And I say no. I say that we do not vote on influence or favoritism or connections. We vote for people who will serve.

"This is a slogan that insults the President of the United States. He can do more—that means the president is not now doing enough—or that the president will discriminate against someone other than his brother if he is the senator from this state. And again I say no. I say that the people of Massachusetts will not buy a slogan. And suddenly, my opponent wants men who will serve, who will care. I listened to him the other night and he said, 'I want to serve because I care.' Well, he didn't care very much in 1960 when he thought of living out West. Massachusetts is not my second choice. You didn't care very much, Ted, when you could have voted between 1953 and 1960 on sixteen occasions, and you only voted three times . . . three out of sixteen . . . and on those three occasions, your brother was a candidate. You don't care very much about aid to education. While I was serving on the City Council, trying to bring good schools here in Boston for our public-school children, not once between the period of 1953 and 1960 did you vote for our school committee. You don't care very much about the 186,000 youngsters who attend parochial schools, because while I want to raise the educational standards of all our children, you have said that you will not vote to extend and expand federal aid to parochial schools.

"These are important issues . . . these and issues like civil rights. Do you really care about civil rights? I have been a champion of civil rights. And while I was fighting to eliminate the black belts and the ghettos, you were attending a school that is almost totally segregated, at the University of Virginia.

"I say that we don't need slogans. I say that power and money is not the key to getting elected to public office. I say we need a senator with experience, not arrogance . . . and the office of United States senator should be merited and not inherited."

Pandemonium was general.

The newspapermen panelists now began the questioning: A. A. Michelson of *The Berkshire Eagle* pointedly asked the candidates about their positions on other issues. McCormack announced himself for a tax cut, against wiretapping, "where I feel that if we're going to invade another's right of privacy that all of the law enforcement officials should be required to go to the courts and get a search warrant"—a backhander to Bobby—and thus "bring wiretapping into the purview of the Fourth Amendment."

Edward Kennedy, his syntax not quite joining at the corners much of the time, was Solid Administration: He opposed a tax cut, preferring to see the money spent by Washington on education, job retraining, and limitation of the deficit to control inflation. He was, he insisted, for a "total revamping of the tax system, the closing of many loopholes which exist under our 1954 Act." He defined his brother the attorney general's bill as one that would be a "limitation on the United States Attorney General's power," except for the "wiretaps which would be in cases of national security."

There was enough content and intellectual control of the details and issues here—both Hughes and Lodge were to remark about this to me, that by midsummer Ted Kennedy had a much more solid handle on matters, the discussion of which had been largely a memory exercise to him the spring before—as to give McCormack pause in his hopes of shredding Ted Kennedy publicly by exposing his ineptness with ideas alone.

As the exchange continued Kennedy was clearly gaining confidence, taking verbal excursions into such complexities as the politics of tariff as they affected the shoe-manufacturing companies of Peabody and Salem (dropping such names as "Mister Hallstein," the impresario of the Common Market, to point up his brochure slogan, "He is personally known by every major figure in government—when he speaks, they listen")—so that by that time McCormack felt ground slipping back beneath himself. McCormack came out for stopping nuclear arms production and atmospheric testing; Ted Kennedy reiterated his support for "our strong position of military posture," taking the popular position in a jingoistic state full of militant anti-Communists. More ground slid backward under the attorney general.

In reply to another question Kennedy referred in clear—if conspicuously ready—detail about events in the Congo "in the last few hours." He produced tax-reform proposals again, sailing into the oil-depletion allowance. He touched on the problems of the Lowell factory worker, the Wisconsin dairy farmer, the Upper Volta project in Ghana, and his support for the regime of Sekou Toure in Guinea.

McCormack, increasingly alarmed as this snowfall of heavy briefing landed all around himself, found himself reduced to a panic-stricken inventory of rumors and overstatements, of minor mishaps, condescension and secondhand allegations grabbed all around himself and thrown too hard and faster than the audience could follow:

"But the thing that fascinates me is Teddy's constant reference to his trips, and the fact that he grew up in an atmosphere where they dealt at the international level. He did make some trips around the world. He made two European trips and he visited eleven countries in twenty-four days. In Latin America he visited nine countries in twenty-seven days. In Africa, he spent fifteen days visiting nine African countries. Well, certainly spending one or two days might not make you or I experts, but he picks things up more quickly than perhaps I would. What has developed from his trips? In Israel he almost caused—he caused an international incident by straggling across the border. In East Germany he caused embarrassment by giving recognition to the East German government. In London, he caused a taxi strike. In Panama, the ambassador said to one of the reporters, or reportedly to him, 'It will take me five months to undo what you have done in two days.' And the Irish, typical of the Irish . . ."

There was a short detour into the advisability of the thirty-five-hour week, the population explosion, and the expected Common Market competition, and then another swing for the kidneys:

"Let me just finish with the trip to Ireland, because the Irish, I think characteristically visualize the trip or saw the trip of Teddy for just what it was. This is a quote in the *Sunday Independent* of Dublin, 25th of February, 1962: 'Arriving in Ireland today is Mr. Edward 'Ted' Kennedy, age thirty, a younger brother of President John Fitzgerald Kennedy. Why is he coming to Ireland? He's coming because later this year he is due to be involved in a political fight back home in Massachusetts. He is playing the game political in what has now come to be known as the Kennedy method. You do not spend your time in campaigning in your own little patch . . . you go out into the world far far afield, hit the headlines, hit the American voters in the right way. I think the trips are more political than fact-finding.'"

Edward Kennedy was by now, in the words of one aide, "livid and shaking" with the effort to hold himself in. As McCormack, heavily made up, alternated that sideways grin and an eagerness to drive out a point with a waggle of the forefinger, perspiration began to stand on Kennedy's forehead and both his massive jawlines. He kept his voice level, pumping out statistics, informing his audience that the U.S. steel industry was working at between 60 and 70 percent of capacity, cited precisely the number of farms in Poland that were independently owned, and rang with defense of our support of Yugoslavia.

McCormack, in one incomprehensible lapse, evidently hopeful that maybe he could try some of that ethnic footnoting too, told his audience of his foreboding now that the Polish government was about to take over all religious nursery schools. McCormack then cited the number of criminal prosecutions he had managed; Ted Kennedy, in a moment of authentic poise, remarked that "I think the attorney general should speak for himself about fulfilling the responsibilities of investigating crime and wrongdoing in this state during the last four years." There was, reportedly, wild applause; it had been the only true riposte of the day, reminding the far-flung television audience of the deeply despised corruption of the administration of which the attorney general had been a member, throwing that South Boston auditorium into statewide relief, and fitting the abusive attorney general into it as a principal. The whole "experience" attack was now—permanently—driven back upon itself. "You just didn't attack one of our own on TV like a common goddamn slob," as Andy Vitali, a Kennedy aide, put it much later. The walls were moving in on McCormack steadily.

It had become closing-statement time. Edward Kennedy referred to the convoys starting down the Autobahn to test the building Berlin crisis, indicated his unwillingness to talk about "personalities or families," and quoted Oliver Wendell Holmes on the free traditions of Boston. By now tears were reportedly starting down his cheeks and his rich voice cracked, audibly: The audience, moving over, applauded him tremendously.

McCormack, time escaping him, assaulted one final time. "I'm not starting at the top," he insisted, rounding into an attack shriller and shriller as he realized his final minute was upon him; then: "I ask, since the question of name and families has been injected, if his name was Edward Moore, with his qualifications, with your qualifications, Teddy, if it was Edward Moore, your candidacy would be a joke, but nobody's laughing because his name is not Edward Moore. It's Edward Moore Kennedy, and I say it makes no difference what your name is, in a democracy you stand on your own two feet and you say to the people. You have the right to vote. You go behind that curtain, and you vote without fear, without favor, and you vote for the candidate whom you feel is the qualified candidate, and I place my case in your hands."

Edward Kennedy was ashen. "Ted told me once that he had everything he could do to keep himself from punching McCormack in the mouth when he brought up Eddie Moore," Charlie Tretter, who was there, insists: To spring the name of the cheerful little bald personal secretary to his father, a kind of honorary uncle after whom he himself was named, on Teddy when he was that upset was—was almost more, truly, than flesh could bear. But flesh bore it.

For hours—a day or so even—handlers in both camps apparently believed that McCormack, by showing the strength of his own personality and the flimsiness of Ted Kennedy's claims, had dealt Kennedy's high-riding campaign a belly-blow. "The guys around the White House thought that Teddy got whacked all over the stage in front of the entire country," one insider insists. It took a day, the pulling in of impressions and perhaps a foray or two of polling, to convince the Kennedy people that McCormack had, by the very ferocity of his charge, managed to impale himself and his political hopes permanently.

People who had never noticed either characteristic before saw that Ted Kennedy had an impressive jawline, and Eddie McCormack's head was small. There was another debate on September 5, on foreign policy and in Worcester, better tempered but listless, and when the primary votes were counted on September 18 Ted Kennedy received 559,303 votes to McCormack's 257,403.

For six more weeks Ted Kennedy waged his campaign against the Republican nominee, George Lodge, Henry Cabot Lodge's son. It was a relatively patrician affair after the primary: Lodge, a tall scholarly man of thirty-four at the time who had been an Assistant Secretary of Labor in the Eisenhower administration and was a touch-football friend of Bobby's, was very concerned about the underdeveloped countries and used his campaign as the medium for expressing a body of ideas he was working out at the time pertaining to foreign assistance, the race issue, and chronic unemployment. "George was a very attractive candidate," Steve Smith said, "and in the end the thing was going away a little."

Lodge worked very hard, partly out of a deep gratitude to the people who believed in him and themselves worked hard to support his candidacy. He made an effort to at least appear partisan—"If Father had been elected vice president in nineteen sixty, of course I wouldn't have run," he remarked, publicly and pointedly; the ladies with scrollwork ankles were unlikely to catch the relevancy of that. "He was never really able to put it together politically the way his father had," Larry Laughlin said, remembering the French-Canadian patois the senior Lodge learned exclusively to appeal to the working crowd around Lowell.

Ted took Lowell too, although his brother never had. When somebody in the Lodge camp quoted George as having said that the Kennedys should be concerned that an inexperienced member of the family was going before the voters, Edward Kennedy grinned that grin he has that meant he really liked it when somebody throws out a hooker because it gave him his chance to use his bobbing and weaving muscles and replied that, well, he had no "comment except to express his belief that the Lodges have made great contributions, not only to Massachusetts but to the nation."

"Ted ran a perfect campaign," George Lodge told me a few years later, sighing a little, the sigh of a man well-bred enough to lose on his feet and live with it afterward. The vote on November 6 went 1,162,611 for Kennedy, 877,669 for Lodge, and 50,013 for H. Stuart Hughes. The moment he knew for sure Ted Kennedy telephoned his very excited old father; it was their moment of absolute highest water. Then Edward prepared to join his brothers in Washington.

CHAPTER V

The Senate

1. Apprenticeship

The November 22 Friday afternoon John Kennedy was shot and killed in Dallas in 1963 his kid brother Edward, putting in duty-roster time presiding over the Senate, glanced up from a round of mail-signing and noticed Richard Riedel, a press liaison officer, hurrying toward the dais across the largely empty pre-weekend chamber while Winston Prouty of Vermont delivered a speech in behalf of a federal library service. Arriving at the dais Riedel broke out, "The most horrible thing has happened! It's terrible. Terrible!"

Kennedy lifted his pen. "What is it?"

"Your brother the President. He's been shot."

"No!" Ted Kennedy reportedly exclaimed, grabbing his papers and standing; by then Spessard Holland of Florida was already on the dais beside him to unburden him of the gavel.

Washington has a delicate metabolism: Its consciousness is government, but its nervous system is the unceasing surge and reflux of news; the danger here is that an item can become overwhelming, a Major Story, too much for the Capitol to take in with one shock of acceptance and so may short out the ordinary day-by-day circuits. Hordes of newsmen who have been lounging in and around their bureaus for months, drinking lunches, gossiping, reflexively battering the reputations of public figures with all the sullen cynicism that seems to come with the trade like cigarette breath—when word of the Major Story surges these people invade the bureaucracy from every imaginable direction, the TV guys and extra-aggressive lady investigative broadcasters, the freelancer snooping for an instant history book contract, columnists after inspiration for a week. This could be the breakthrough that eventuates in a Pulitzer! Jack Kennedy's assassination was a national tragedy, but it was also a Generational News Event.

By the time Edward Kennedy had left the Senate chamber and crossed to the press gallery with his fistful of correspondence, the reformulation of history was frenetically under way. That hour after word of the shooting was passed to Kennedy was a kind of nightmare replication of the 1960 telephone call from Thermopolis: Finding out was urgent, but getting through to Bobby, who would be able to tell his brother what ought to be done now, was beyond his competence suddenly. Teddy paused in the press lobby to see what the teletype machines were spewing up but the reporters were knotted too thick to push close enough.

Cutting into Lyndon Johnson's office he dialed the attorney general's extension: the line was dead; he dialed again: busy. Arriving at his suite in the Old Senate Office Building he tried again to get to Bobby, first at the attorney general's office, then at the White House: All lines were busy initially, then tied up with traffic to Dallas. Ted, who had no way of patching into the White House switchboard, was hopelessly outside.

Secretaries in his outer office, gathered around the garble of transistor radios, knew more than he did.

Claude Hooten, a college friend from Houston who was in town to join Ted and Joan for their fifth anniversary dinner that night, stayed close while Kennedy called for his car—it was his Chrysler phase— found that an aide was running around in it, and started home to 1607 28th Street in the Mercedes of his assistant and chief speechwriter Milton S. Gwirtzman. Joan wasn't home; Gwirtzman went to pick her up at the Elizabeth Arden on Connecticut Avenue.

Meanwhile, Kennedy and Hooten had been roaming Kennedy's residence trying to come up with an extension that worked: Every line was dead. They rushed out to the street, ringing and banging on the doors of neighbor after neighbor to beg for the use of an operative telephone. At one of the nearby houses Claude got a dial tone finally; he was still explaining to the woman of the house what they were up to when Ted Kennedy finally reached the attorney general, who told him that the president was dead.

"You'd better call your mother and our sisters," Robert Kennedy told his younger brother, and Teddy, relieved for the moment to at least know, hurried to the Executive Mansion, clanked helplessly at a locked visitors' gate—"Doesn't anything work?" he suddenly cried out, denied genuine access to the Castle even now—but found an open gate finally, and began to place his telephone calls from the office of his brother's physician, Janet Travell. "I'm worried about your father," his mother opened; Ted rushed to Hyannis Port.

What he was supposed to do when he got there, Ted discovered during a walk on the chilly beach with his mother and Joey Gargan, was to tell the Ambassador. The complexities of this two-day effort to break the news to the paralyzed old man are set out in all their poignancy and horror in William Manchester's *The Death of a President*.

Four decades afterwards, dredging through literally hundreds of pounds of recently declassified FBI documents and long-unavailable Kennedy family papers and the late-in-life confessions of mobsters and attending surgeons and coroners and flunkies too terrified to talk throughout the twentieth century, I myself ultimately came to terms with the fact that John Kennedy's assassination really was the Crime of the Century. It enlisted the darkest forces inside and outside the American Establishment, the denouement consequent to forty-plus years of covert favor-trading by the unscrupulous financier. I laid the details out in *Bobby and J. Edgar*.

In the immediate aftermath of the shooting, only one survivor among the Kennedys had been party to the arrangements that brought down this catastrophe, and he was locked into the enduring paralysis of a massive stroke. Afraid, apparently, that the shock of too-unprepared a disclosure would set the emotional old patriarch back irretrievably, Rose Kennedy had stopped Ann Gargan from following up on her opening comment to him that there had "been an accident."

By the time Ted arrived the father was alert to the existence of some very large misfortune, more and more restive as the people around him seemed to want to prevent him from watching his usual television newscasts. The seasoned old plunger was openly dubious of Ted's explanation that the set was broken and a repairman would be by in the morning. When his father motioned toward the unplugged cord, Ted, after plugging it in, ripped it out of the set itself by the wires. As the father's agitation became visible, his full-time nurse, Rita Dallas, began to give him compounds to get him to sleep, doping first his milkshake, then his evening milk. Finally, wary and suspicious and desultorily fighting the drug, the patriarch slept.

By morning—the financier's physician was in attendance by now—Ted nerved himself for the disclosure after breakfast. "There's been a bad accident. The president has been hurt very badly," Teddy attempted. Eyes in the shriveled face stared into the uncertain youngest's own. "As a matter of fact,"

Edward Kennedy admitted, "he died." It was a very nearly insufferable blow, but it was cleanly and wholly the truth. Between bouts of inconsolable sobbing, the old man read the Boston papers, followed events on his repaired television set, and—raw pain backed up—at one point made clear to Ann Gargan that he, too, must appear in Washington; she found him thrashing around alone in the effort to climb into his clothes and was commandeered to drive him to the airport. Finding the *Caroline* unavailable, he permitted himself to be returned to the Compound, and his room, and his covers.

Afterwards, since Bobby couldn't do it, Ted met with Earl Warren and reviewed the conclusions of the Warren Commission. "I'm satisfied that the Warren Commission got it right: satisfied then, satisfied now," Kennedy wrote in *True Compass* months before his death. That made it no doubt easier to deal with. But it wouldn't take long once the assassination began to settle before the less compromised insiders throughout the power structure began to acknowledge the unavoidable. In his 1995 memoir Gore Vidal, who shared a stepmother with Jacqueline Kennedy Onassis, wrote of the JFK murder that "The ultimate irony is that the elements that did him in—the Marcello mob in New Orleans and so on—were the kind of people that his father had comfortably done business with all his life."

Nobody needs much of a reminder of the funeral of John F. Kennedy, the cortege and the rainy, sullen day and the stately marching all of us seemed to need to calm the nerves after one more shrill moment had pierced us from our unhappy history. It was an event so grand and large and public as to seem to swallow its personalities, but here and there Ted Kennedy made a contribution. To pick the quotes and citations for the service a typical little impromptu committee gathered, Jackie and Mac Bundy and Bobby and Sorensen and Ted, and since a feeling for oratory, the music in language, was little by little becoming Ted Kennedy's domain now he seemed to be the one whose suggestions stuck. They needed an opening for Bishop Hannan's main script: Ted, riffling through Ecclesiastes, said, "Well, this mightn't be wrong at all," and read:

"To everything there is a season, and a time to every purpose under the heaven: A time to be born, and a time to die . . ." and that stuck too.

There were other contributions. Joey Gargan rented a full-dress suit for Teddy, but it arrived without hat, gloves, and pants. None could be located during the final minutes. George Thomas, a Kennedy valet since time unremembered, let out a pair of Jack's dress pants—way out, since "Ted's waistline was already a family joke." Ted carried a pair of the president's gloves.

But Edward Kennedy had a very large, tousled head, no top hat was forth-coming, and finally not only the Kennedys, but the legion of arrived heads of state, cabinet members, members of the diplomatic corps—they all of them marched hatless in the rain, heads bowed a bit, somberly, and this was viewed by the more sensitive among the press as symbolic of their collective grief, emblematic of all human vulnerability before fate. And perhaps it was.

It was no rarity those break-in years to catch Edward Kennedy—as indeed the news of his brother's murder had—presiding pro tem over some som-nolent pre-recess session of the Senate. Sitting in for the vice president, or dropping whatever was at hand and rushing onto the floor to help make up a quorum, or attending every one of a series of tedious subcommittee hearings and boning up carefully on the intent of the inquiry and the backgrounds of the witnesses, and remaining useful and available to the subcommittee chairman and, after that, the full committee when the time came to hash the results into proposals and piece together a bill likely to hold its own once it arrived on the open Senate floor—these are the chores people at home have very little notion about. No feature writer takes much of an interest in who shows up regularly at, say, the dragged-out seemingly uneventful testimony before the Subcommittee on Employment Manpower of the Committee on Labor and Public Welfare, Ted Kennedy's first major appointment.

But merely by getting there most of the time, sitting there and picking up on the questions and doubts and thrusts of older men concerned with the great unalterable problems of working people, poor people, who got drafted and who starved—for somebody with Edward Kennedy's kind of mind, quiet but broadly receptive, which accumulated slowly but retained almost totally, it was a slow primary seminar. First nourishment, the cold dawn gruel of the legislative process.

"Jack, when things weren't going well in the Senate, used to get disgusted and go down the list of his colleagues and call every second one a meathead," a Washington journalist close to the then-senator remembers. Bob, to whom the Senate was largely a forum, a platform on which he could alight and begin to recoup his destiny, was reported on at least one occasion to get so impa-tient and disgusted with the rhetoric and ineffectually of things during a com-mittee meeting that he threw his sheaf of documents into the air and stalked out of the chamber before they settled onto the carpet.

Edward Kennedy—who, from the outset, thought and talked to his friends of his career in the Senate in terms of decades, took his seat in the back quietly in January of 1963, made no major speech for an unusual sixteen months, watched out for usages, studied the parliamentary moves and strategies, acquainted himself with each of his colleagues—and foible by talent, thoroughly, waited.

He took his place—this he himself had anticipated—beneath a thunderhead. The legislative branch overall had floated during the Eisenhower fifties into the stagnant backwashes of unreconstructed Southern control. Its mood was defensive now, panicked in the face of a more dynamic administration and inclined by its ancient Dixie reflexes to harp on Calhoun's Doctrine of the Concurrent Majority, which postulates that ours is a nation of such various and savagely opposed interests and backgrounds that what is central to the practice of politics is the ability to accommodate and balm and combine purposes—the often-cited "art of the possible"—with skill enough to keep the Republic from tearing itself apart.

In practice, this meant a devotion to the lowest common legislative denominator. We could run aground—the Civil War proved it—and to the Southerners the legislative branch had now become their fallback line. Seniority controlled the circuits. It would be hard to imagine the archons of the Senate preparing to receive this towering, fresh-faced baby of the Kennedys with any emotion more generous than disgust at the effrontery behind his arrival at such an early age. Permitted an interview with the influential Richard Russell, Chairman of the key Armed Services Committee, who alluded with evident disapproval to his visitor's years, Edward Kennedy summoned up the temerity to remind the Chairman that he, too, had been thirty when he took his Senate seat.

"Yes, but you have to keep in mind that I had already been Governor of Joe-juh," the Chairman reminded his visitor, not taking the trouble to smile.

"You . . . don't . . . you just don't do certain things," an old congressional hand observes. "Lord, here you have Harry Byrd Sr. of Virginia operating that rickety but uncontested gothic machinery of his, and Harry Byrd Jr., he's a good old boy and he's certainly as well prepared as young Kennedy, nobody would dispute that, and the Yankees still allow Virginia two seats in the Senate, but you don't think Harry Byrd would dream . . ."

But Edward Kennedy dreamed, and he arrived in Washington to find both cloakrooms buzzing.

The Senate is supposed to be a club, and it certainly demonstrates its share of fraternity-attic smugness from time to time. A member on arrival was like a green young instrumentalist trying out for a venerable symphony orchestra. Some hear properly early; some never. "I think Teddy Kennedy's younger-brother characteristics stood him in unusually good stead that first couple of years in the Senate," says somebody who helped him out during the breaking-in months. This big hearty inexperienced boy brought with him into the Upper Body—and this the touchy old preceptors of the place began to pick up on well before Kennedy's opening session expired—a kind of finesse that went well beyond the walk-through courtesies, a quiet respectful interested attitude his very mannerisms communicated.

Whereas Jack would so often sit there half-listening to a colleague, drumming on his front teeth with two fingers or tugging absent-mindedly at a knuckle, there was a calm to Teddy, those half-hooded eyes kept watching you, often a little pensively, above a hand scrolled around that compressed lower face. Willing, he seemed to soak up detail. He recognized the fact that he had come into the Senate prematurely, and so began things compromised, and—this his colleagues saw from the way those thin expressive Irish lips winced involuntarily when somebody let slip something perhaps a mite too caustic—this Kennedy bruised easily.

"This used to be Bobby Baker's office," Ted Kennedy pointed out to me, walking me around the Assistant Majority Leader's suite where it was tucked conveniently into a quiet corner of the Capitol labyrinth behind the deteriorated surviving wall. There was a soupçon of warmth to Kennedy's reference to the feline little Baker, the nod of one who knew enough to appreciate the expertise and cajolery enabling that soft, sweet legislative errand boy and part-time pimp for Robert Kerr and Lyndon Johnson. One of those phrases that made its way into most of the early magazine articles about Edward Kennedy was the allegation that he was a "Senate man," as opposed, by implication, to his more aggressive, impatient older brothers, one who "did his homework" and was polite as hell to his senatorial elders.

What this baby of all the Kennedys seemed to realize from the day he took his seat in the back was that there was a yesterday and a tomorrow to every political day, that roles shifted, and that a lot of what he or anybody did was territorial to the job.

"Ted, Ted," Allen Ellender of Louisiana hailed him as he hobbled into the corridor one day just after he got back from his months in the Stryker frame recuperating from his plane crash, balancing his cane, a sack of books, and the shabby twenty-pound briefcase—"The Bag"—in his hurry to catch the Washington-Boston shuttle. "I want y'all to meet our great young friend from Massachusetts," Ellender insisted, presenting a dozen or so important constituents, each of whom shook Kennedy's hand ardently and tied Teddy up—Kennedy's assistant along to drive remembers, fuming—at least ten minutes. "Ted just doesn't spin people off," Ellender emphasized. "You find a lot of the people in the Senate establishment are Southerners, and you just can't get anything done by picking up a phone and saying, 'Where's my rug?' You've got to be civil, almost highly mannered, to get along."

The ultimate demonstration of grace—this Kennedy's first generation of aides leaked in small hushed voices, like children pointing out the big kid who crawled in the porcupine hole—was the way Ted had of stopping 'round for a long scotch in the early afternoon with his Judiciary Committee Chairman, curmurgeonly James O. Eastland of Mississippi. Eastland carried two briefs in the Senate of the fifties: segregation, and reaction. His Internal Security Subcommittee, administered by the bureaucratic hangman Jay Sourwine, worked over the lefties whom J. Edgar Hoover routinely fed to Joe McCarthy.

An unreconstructed oligarch like Eastland presented himself as the Upper Body's preeminent fire eater. Yet Teddy Kennedy soon found himself knocking back a drop or two with the influential Chairman of the Judiciary Committee; Kennedy had discovered on arrival that with each refill he was able to coax another subcommittee appointment out of the lonely old bigot. In his memoirs Kennedy would maintain that each time the tall, stooped, aging archon retired to the lavatory Kennedy dumped half his glass into a handy planter. The times were changing, and Jim Eastland was learning to coexist with the Kennedys more than he cared to admit around the filling stations and courthouse steps of the Delta Country.

The Kennedys were realists at least, Eastland was overheard regaling a somewhat slow-learning Southern statesman; Jack, after all, had voted against ripping the 1957 civil-rights measures out of Judiciary by main force (this was the period when Eastland liked to brag around Washington that he had over a hundred such measures permanently "sewed up" in his rear pocket). When irate Southern legislators called at the Oval Office to complain about what the government in Washington was trying to force on their constituents, a lovely little light would come into JFK's eye, he would try to look at least partially concerned, and he would suggest, tactfully, that the complaint must involve something to do with Bobby. Were they sure they had the right office, actually?

But even Bobby—Bobby could be quite understanding too; Eastland himself had nominated Bobby before the full Senate as the new administration's attorney general. Once installed in the cabinet Bobby had, after all, gone along with the appointment of Eastland's old college roommate and protégé, Harold Cox, to a critical Southern Federal Circuit Court seat. "Tell your brother that if he will give me Harold Cox I will give him the nigger" (i.e., Thurgood Marshall, at that time being held up for the Second Circuit Court of Appeals), Eastland supposedly proposed to Bob Kennedy in a corridor.

Cox turned out to be plain-spoken enough himself—he referred to Negro civil-rights defendants as "chimpanzees," and threatened Bob's successor as attorney general, Nicolas Katzenbach, with jail for contempt—but Marshall went along to the Supreme Court in due course, and, impediment though he turned out to be, it was a matter of time before Cox' redneck decisions were bound to be overturned.

By 1964, as Ted Kennedy was adjusting to his first important assignment, to the prestigious Judiciary Committee, holdovers from the Kennedy administration were learning to submit a bill with a due-date-out prominently affixed, so there was no bottling things up any more. Even Chairman Eastland confessed he liked this youngest Kennedy around. "Wha chu wan' now, Kin-idy," Eastland was heard to sigh as his most junior member turned up with yet another request. "I don't agree with Senator Eastland about much that concerns his philosophical position on the issues," Ted's colleague Birch Bayh told me in re intracommittee hassles, "but I feel he is fair in his treatment of the younger members . . ."

There was a mutual regard. A magazine journalist, attempting to interview Eastland in 1968 from the awkward side of the soles of a pair of shoes, asked the Chairman whether special security provisions were being made to protect Ted Kennedy when the subcommittees traveled for hearings. It had been the journalist's final question; in less than the time it took the man to take the stairs down in the New Senate Office Building, cross a street, and ascend to the fourth floor and across to Edward Kennedy's suite in the Old Senate Office Building a telephone call had preceded him, Kennedy's agitated press aide Dick Drayne was waiting, and the journalist was bearded for presuming to ask *anybody* a question like that.

At the same time Kennedy was acclimating himself, pulling his office together. "I appreciate the wisdom of the saying that a freshman should be seen and not heard," the Senate's youngest member told a reporter in January of 1963, tacking out a cardboard sign with Mister Kennedy lettered on it, making sure the wall-to-wall in the suite he had been assigned got ripped out and replaced by an oval braided Colonial rug, and adding a Simon Willard banjo clock, an M-14 manufactured in Worcester, and photographs of the nuclear warships *Long Beach* and *Bainbridge,* reminders to the constituents that they strolled here, spiritually at least, in territorial Massachusetts.

As Ben Smith II receded wordlessly to let Teddy fill out that last two years of the '58 term, he left at least the beginnings of a staff operation. Joe McIntyre, a man nearly fifty who had spent his whole adult life taking care of those touchy little favors and patronage assignments the public never hears about and the politician never forgets, stayed on to help evade the more embarrassing snafus. Milton S. Gwirtzman, a lawyer and overall Kennedy liaison, who kept after the broader sorts of constituency problems, wrote speeches, chewed away on issues and chipped out the wider-ranging policy statements, was in and out of the office according to his own strange metabolic patterns. Bill Evans came down as overall administrative assistant; John Culver, his Harvard law degree barely dry by that time, helped with the legislative side. The sometimes hectic but ever-active Ed Moss, on leave of absence from the New England Telephone Company and paid out of the Department of the Army, became to Teddy what Dave Powers was to the president, much favored as a foil and regular travel companion.

This was a hurriedly assembled model, pulled together without much prior managerial experience anywhere, and there were rubs and errors enough until events throttled down. Even before 1962 was over the Kennedy staff was leaking word to the press that their man was "very prudent" but pointing "with pride at the wide range of contracts and projects he is proving able to line up in Washington for his home state." Kennedy's office almost immediately announced loans, grants, and federal contracts totaling $135 million. What Kennedy was doing was raiding, most notably in nearby New York State, where he unabashedly approached the Grumman Aircraft executives on Long Island, who were subcontracting the lunar module, to make clear how much more likely the special technology and skilled workers the job needed were to be found in the Commonwealth; Kennedy's New York colleague, Kenneth Keating, boiled over publicly.

Patronage involved special problems: Kenny O'Donnell had been running the patronage in the Commonwealth through his White House desk; he was known to have long-term ambitions in the state himself. And Ted, as the senator from the president's own party in Massachusetts, wanted—and got—the right to oversee federal appointments.

The shakedown problems extended to the staff. The group was polymorphous enough so that the disagreements and frictions were compounded often with real misunderstandings. "One characteristic of Ted's I respected in those days especially was the fact that he would never entertain criticism by someone working for him of another person working in his behalf," John Culver remarked. Like his father and brothers, Edward Kennedy had a knack for never letting any one man get too close, too powerful: The atmosphere became such that staffers watched one another to make sure all balances were retained.

He very seldom commented, but it was clear "The Boss," as the aides soon came to refer to him, missed very little below stairs. "Charlie and Bill are at it again," their traveling employer scrawled across a postcard from Hong Kong that pictured two fire-breathing dragons circling each other. That well-advertised "shaht fuse" still tended to blow from time to time, but usually, even when an aide bolixed things up, Kennedy's impulse was to be considerate, indirect, to frown momentarily and say, "This doesn't look right" or "It's not going to seem right," rather than discourage the man lastingly with an outright reprimand.

This youngest senator's touch was light enough that the question starting around was when would this low-keyed, youngest of the Kennedy boys start to get a grip of his own on something? "A lot of the time that first couple of years, socially at least, I thought Ted wasn't much more than a really happy-go-lucky arrogant brash kid, always out for a good time, one who liked to go out with the boys, John Culver in particular, lots of parties, laughs . . ." one early onlooker admitted.

Decisions often came hard: "He's got one of those Machiavellian quotes: 'Power not used is power saved,'" Gerry Doherty commented. There were times then, as later, when a tough determination would have to be made, and everybody would wait for the Boss to decide, and the last minute would come, and go, and nothing would be resolved. He liked to "preserve his options."

The difficulty was not that Kennedy didn't understand each situation: "He likes to break everything down to X number of alternatives: There are six things you can do, these are the advantages, these are the costs, these are the short-range consequences, and these are the problems you are going to have in each case later," Doherty noted. "If you send him a memo he can cite the appropriate section back to you and indicate the paragraph by number. You can get more real work done with Ted in half an hour than with the staff guys in a week. I think some great work simplifier must have hit him on the head sometime."

All this was wonderful when whatever it was he dealt with was impersonal and remote; where human feelings came into it—and family concerns in particular—he seemed very often to be pulled irresolutely in every direction at once, to evidence too much mind, at times, to make up easily. Pushed hard just then, emotion only too evidently choked up judgment; when things got hopelessly bottled up Bobby often stopped by to nudge matters into the appropriate direction.

A lot of this began to be felt around Massachusetts. "There are only two emotions that move the pols around this place, greed and fear," a Kennedy organizer insists. McCormack people who had been cowering ever since their man lost the primary now started to look up, warily: The anticipated blows were simply not descending. "Teddy is very good to his friends," one who helped handle the Massachusetts side says, "and he appreciates it if you don't abuse the privileges." The other side of that read: Payoffs will be few, well earned, and meager. He raised money and campaigned hard in behalf of candidates like Beryl Cohen for the Massachusetts Senate. To the surprise of the hardened, Kennedy very shortly made good his voucher to the few beleaguered academics who helped him campaign: He pulled together a Massachusetts Democratic Advisory Council, filled it with progressives from the academic and enlightened commercial communities, and made a great effort to get to Boston for almost every meeting. Party activists like Sam Beer, who only halfway joked about the years when they attended political caucuses anonymously, sneaking in the servants' entrance to talk with John Kennedy's political strongarm men like Dan Fenn and Pat Lynch, now used the front door and got their names in the newspapers.

All these were politically risky approaches in Boston, like introducing Quaker Meeting rules of procedure to conclaves of the Mafia. But there were early, and very often unanticipated, dividends. Gerry Doherty, who took over the chairmanship of the Democratic State Committee from the Pat Lynch and so became Ted's man in Massachusetts for the next four and a half years, remembers the afternoon, several weeks after John Kennedy was assassinated, when he was summoned to Washington so that he and Ted could stop by the United States House of Representatives to see the trenchant old Speaker.

The jackals were gathering in Massachusetts already, and John McCormack and Lyndon Johnson had long been allies. McCormack broached the delicate subject himself. "Senator, you've been down here two years, and you've always come and sought my advice, and treated me like the Speaker. You are the leader of my party in Massachusetts, and if this man is your leader, he is my leader." One imagines that fresh cigar turning once, like a ratchet, in John McCormack's lean old face: That subject was closed now forever.

2. The Crash

Probably it was just as well that Edward Kennedy's Massachusetts fences were in exceptional order, because throughout the summer and early autumn immediately after that, when he went before the state to get elected to a full senatorial term on his own in November of 1964, whatever hands he shook had to be the few he could get hold of from his rotating frame at New England Baptist Hospital. The luck was that he could use his body at all—for hours after the five-passenger Aero Commander, in which Kennedy had come in too low on a late, foggy approach to the little Western-Massachusetts Barnes Municipal Airport, crashed and tore itself apart in Walter Bashista's apple orchard at ten-fifty at night, the first question was, Was Kennedy alive? Then, where? Then—once the great world discovered him in the blowzy dark, laid out beneath a tree with a flashlight beam muffled in the high grass just beyond his feet so that the rescue people advancing from every direction through the darkness wouldn't continue to kick into his legs, twisted unnaturally beneath Marvella Bayh's raincoat—was he going to be paralyzed permanently from the neck down?

This disaster came—they always came this way, so that there was never really any point in trying to forestall anything—out of one more ordinary, rushed, overscheduled day arranged to end in personal triumph at one more pseudo-event. Everything was long ago in order, that 1964 evening on June 19, for his party in Massachusetts to nominate Edward Kennedy by acclamation. The West Springfield fairgrounds Coliseum, a kind of big drafty hippodrome of a place that looked like an overscale oil drum inside—the most enclosed space for the least money anybody could engineer—was packed with thousands of Democrats perspiring together from the almost total humidity and the tier above tier of klieg lights.

Edward Kennedy himself was expected along with the convention keynoter, Indiana Senator Birch Bayh. Both of them were necessarily delayed, held up for hours to cast critical votes in the Senate—Kennedy himself had

arranged to address the Springfield Convention from the floor of the Senate in Washington, assuring the thousands waiting that he wanted "everyone to know that I am a candidate this year, even though I am hundreds
of miles away. We are now fifteen minutes away from the vote for civil
rights," he had continued, alluding to the historic bill Lyndon Johnson had
jockeyed through Congress greased heavily with guilty nostalgia subsequent to the assassination, and the voice of Edward Kennedy concluded by
emphasizing that he was going to put in an appearance still, and—as usual
the lame little backspun family joke—"not to nominate Joan until I get
there."

Drizzles battered the Coliseum outside; inside, the milling delegations
went about the party's business. The excitement that summer centered
around the bare-naked grapple for the gubernatorial nomination between
the sitting governor, Chub Peabody, and his own 1962 ticket mate Frank Bellotti, an Italian who knew how to talk Irish and who had become the state's
lieutenant governor in 1962. A lot of the thrust behind Bellotti's challenges
now derived, in fact, from the encouragement he got that spring from Eddie
McCormack, who had determined that a serviceable base for his own political resurrection would be the powerful chairmanship of the Massachusetts
Turnpike Authority, which William Callahan had relinquished by dying in
April.

Ted Kennedy, whose political impulses were charitable but not suicidal,
had arranged with Governor Peabody to turn the post over to State Treasurer
John Driscoll, a Kennedy loyalist.

Virtually from the day he was sworn in as governor, Peabody had parlayed
painful honesty, a numb hand for political manipulation, and homespun bad
luck into a reputation such that the party regulars viewed him by 1964 with
bemused abhorrence. In no way shadowy or venal himself, Peabody had
funded richly the Crime Commission under the leadership of the Republican
attorney general Edward Brooke, well knowing what the commission would
find but determined that "we must eliminate corruption wherever it festers,"
and before the able Brooke was finished Democrats were staggering out of
their commission and agency and legislative subcommittee hearing rooms
and expiring before the public like freshly poisoned moles.

Peabody went out handshaking: A local political organizer well remembers
attempting to flee Boston exhausted on a Friday afternoon and getting
trapped in his car in the Sumner Tunnel for hours; when he emerged finally
he realized that the bottleneck was the governor himself, reaching into every

stopped car to introduce himself, presumably alienating at least one voter for every palm he caught.

And all this was working among the delegates that sultry nineteenth of June in the West Springfield Convention Hall. The Bellotti people were talking fast among the committed and Peabody people were trying to fight it off when a disjunct announcement came over the loudspeaker that Senator Edward Kennedy's plane had crashed somewhere in the vicinity. Word got around the floor, while the insiders rushed to the press trailers, that there were not any survivors.

There very nearly weren't. The Aero Commander that crashed had been a charter, owned and flown out of Lawrence, Massachusetts, by Daniel E. Hogan, the president of Standard International Corporation, manufacturer of Lestoil. Hogan had planned to fly Kennedy up himself that night, but had decided late to go to a Yale alumni reunion and let his regular pilot, Edwin Zimny, who ran the Lawrence Municipal Airport, fly down to get the senator and his party and run them up. As soon as the Civil Rights Bill was pulled through, Kennedy, his regular traveling aide Ed Moss, and Indiana Senator Birch Bayh and his wife, Marvella, after stopping for a moment at John Kennedy's grave, hurried to the airport where the Aero Commander was gassed and waiting. Weather was moving in all along the Eastern Seaboard. The five of them settled into the two-engine airplane with Moss next to the pilot, Kennedy on the seat immediately behind the pilot facing backward, and the Bayhs just inside the tail so they could make conversation with Ted.

The five of them were well out of New York before airborne conditions looked at all serious: There was a scattering of thunderstorms, and Zimny kept zigzagging to detour around pockets of turbulence. This dropped them behind their ten-thirty estimated time of arrival a bit, but the heavier and heavier fog hanging in the rolling hollows of Pioneer Valley was obviously something of a surprise. Zimny evidently didn't say much about it, at least not in such a way as to alarm the easygoing Bayh, and perhaps the first hint that anything unusual was happening came when Ted Kennedy, who had flown a small aircraft around the state himself and had a sense of the terrain, tightened his safety belt without commenting and twisted around to watch the instruments over Zimny's shoulder.

Kennedy himself, whom no flying conditions ever seemed to intimidate, was reportedly determined to set down at Barnes, the landing strip nearest to West Springfield. Fog blotted every window; the Westover approach control spotter reported back to Zimny that ground visibility was badly obscured, two miles at most, the minimum acceptability for any kind of landing, and after several exchanges an instrument approach was agreed on, a procedure turn inbound, to set the aircraft down onto runway 20, the runway lights at high intensity and radar spotting closely coordinated.

The key to the procedure was for Zimny to come in over the Z marker, well beyond the runway and no lower than 800 feet, where radar contact could be maintained virtually until touchdown. Zimny was an excellent pilot who had flown charter and combat aircraft since 1937, and the word among the personnel around Westfield was that he was a little mavericky, likely to fly an aircraft the way he saw fit.

"Let's give the pilot every chance," Kennedy reportedly cautioned the others as the Aero Commander shuddered, low, and pushed through fog; the altimeter reading already startled him.

As the pilot banked and began his approach, much can be read between the lines of the exchange among Zimny, the radar, and the Barnes control tower spotter:

Control 1: 44 Sugar [Zimny's code name]—report the Z marker inbound please.
Zimny: Ah—Roger.
Control 2: He hasn't reported the Z marker inbound yet.
Radar: He disappeared on our radar, so he should be over it.
Control 2: O.K.
Radar: Better duck.
Zimny: Over the "Z" [Z half spoken].

The rest, except for the increasingly frantic exchanges among the ground-control people, was a terrifying radio silence. The Civil Aeronautics Board's probable-cause finding, after reconstructing the accident and picking for months among the instruments and wreckage, was that Zimny had taken a chance and made the approach well under the permitted minimum, grazed treetops along a ridge two hundred feet higher than the runway approach, and lost this final gamble permanently.

Ted Kennedy, half-up and twisted in his seat as the landing gear and wing flaps went down at 1,100 feet, saw impenetrable fog: After that the altimeter dropped to 1,000, 900, 800, 700, 600 feet—still fog then trees, then a frozen second or so while Zimny gunned both engines as the tips of pine trees brushed the belly of the plane, the sky was milk-white and the trees all around were engulfing, and then the nose hit with a paralyzing concussion and apple trees tore both the engines half-off and the fuselage shredded open and only the tail, on which a tiny red landing light kept rotating slowly in the fog all through the remainder of the night, seemed to have survived the demolition.

Marvella Bayh started yelling; this brought Birch around. The rear window of the Aero Commander had broken away into the profound velvet darkness and everything stank of gasoline. Birch shoved his wife out a window, yelled up at Kennedy but got no answer, then followed his wife out and down the hill to escape any explosion. Halfway down he stopped, took in enough breath to keep going and turned around, limped back uphill through the gasoline-soaked grass and groped into the Aero Commander; Ted Kennedy mumbled something. Bayh told him to push his hand out—the whiteness of his cuff was enough to see, to grab hold of—and after working Kennedy's 220-odd pounds in and out the opening got enough through to stagger in under him, taking the weight as well as he could off one hip, down to where the orchard leveled out and Ted could be stretched to length out of the way in case the mangled carcass of the aircraft blew itself apart.

People were already arriving—a farmer from nearby, Robert Shauer, then police and rescue people and newspapermen. Middle June was in-between agriculturally. The apple blossoms were down already but it was too early for the sweet putrefaction of early hay and silage, and around a twist in Southampton's East Street road an elderly collie was barking. The roadside was jamming up, first cars and pickup trucks, then official vehicles with their fishbowls rotating in the way that always means disaster. The apple orchard that tore the Kennedy plane apart was an across-the-road tract that belonged to Walter Bashista, who dairied mostly, and he was just getting in for the evening when his teenage girl, Joanne, who had been watching a little television in the big frame house but not really paying much attention, heard the soft sputter of something that sounded to her like a motorboat in the nearby fog, and then some kind of collision, not so loud that she jumped but with a special tearing quality to it that just "seemed different" to her. She caught her father coming in, and by the time the two of them were out of the house and across the road the Bayhs were out in the fog yelling something, Marvella stumbling because somehow she lost a shoe, and Walter and his daughter hurried back to the house and called an ambulance.

Men were already out there when the two got back; Walter helped with getting the pilot and Eddie Moss out of the wreckage—Zimny had been killed at once, Moss seemed to be more or less alive, his skull crushed and slowly coagulating blood all over his face and clothes, so that the rescuers' hands kept sliding as they attempted to ease him out. Joanne stayed with Kennedy. He lay there, muttering into awareness, eyes closing, then jolted awake again for a moment or two to blue the wet air with profanity whenever somebody stepped into him or kicked the sole of a foot.

There were voices demanding to move him away from the wreck; he demanded that doctors do that. He asked for a drink and Joanne Bashista went back to the house and got him water, folding up an armful of blankets and an extra flashlight to keep everybody away from his exposed feet, and she attempted to make some sort of rough handkerchief compresses to drape along the peak of his forehead. Muzzy, bone pain harder and harder to suppress inside the bloated hemorrhaging, Kennedy managed in gasps and grunting to assure himself that Moss, then Bayh and Marvella had been loaded into the first ambulance that arrived. Then—then only—when the big Cadillac ambulance Easthampton sent was there, did Kennedy permit a stretcher to be worked into place beneath him for the bumpy, backroad dash to the Cooley Dickenson Hospital in Northampton.

The landing light in the Aero Commander's tail was still blinking its slow way around and around in air so wet you could wring it out when the last ambulance left, and Walter Bashista, who got to bed around four for an hour, before he had to be up and milking, remembers that he fell asleep and awoke to the slow all-night shuffle of strangers' feet outside his window "like a funeral procession." That night, and for a good many days afterwards, people he never heard of from every place kept telephoning his farmhouse.

Arrival at a hospital emergency entrance in extremis, wavering in and out of consciousness, with a negligible pulse and lips set grimly, hair matted and tousled above saturated red and green blankets—the moment is anguish enough to whatever consciousness there was for Kennedy without the explosion of flashbulbs and the scratching, somewhere behind the nurses and orderlies, of a reporter getting the detail into his proper notebook. "I worked on him for two and a half days," Dr. Thomas Corriden said. "It was about a week before we were sure he was going to live." For eighteen hours the surgeons probed, relying on the fact that there was awareness enough left to answer and not daring to administer painkillers until they were sure they knew the extent of damage internally. They established finally that three vertebrae in Kennedy's lower back had been smashed, two ribs cracked, the left lung punctured and partially collapsed, and although the spleen and left kidney did not appear to have ruptured, the massive internal hemorrhaging forced the surgeons to keep probing until they were absolutely convinced.

The first person in the family to arrive was Joan, still in the pink suit she had on for the convention and had been wearing at the private home reception where she saw the news flash on television coverage of the convention itself; Jack Crimmins drove her there immediately. Ed Martin had arrived ahead of the second big Cadillac ambulance, but when Joan got there he was already making sure the doctors gave no statement to the press prematurely, and Joan found nobody to direct her to the emergency ward. Maintaining perfect apparent composure—numb, during the silent ride to the hospital she had been getting herself ready for the idea that her husband was dying—she strode directly by the reception desk, up the wrong corridor, back, and asked the nurse on duty to show her where Senator Kennedy was.

The receptionist, young but true to her orders, refused to leave her post without instructions from her supervisor. When Joan found her husband a few minutes afterward he was under an oxygen tent receiving the first of a number of blood transfusions, tubes up his nose and inserted in his arms, but, recognizing the pink blur through the cellulose of the tent, was able to manage at least a phrase. "Hi, Joansie," the survivor said. "Don't worry!"

Among Ted Kennedy's visitors that night was Bill Vanden Heuvel. "How are you?" Vanden Heuvel asked tentatively. The figure in the oxygen tent seemed troubled; Vanden Heuvel bent closer; Kennedy was scheduled to address a group in upper New York State hours after the Massachusetts convention. Would Vanden Heuvel fill in for him? At that moment, Kennedy's own survival looked, at the most hopeful, problematic.

By four in the morning Bobby had arrived. He went directly to Teddy's bedside for twenty minutes or so, then sought out Martin where the press was accumulating and led him aside. "What's the condition of Eddie Moss?" Bob asked. It was bad, surgeons were working on him but he looked certain to die, hard, and shortly. "Is his wife Katie here?" Bobby asked. Bob found her and made her go out for a walk with him on the parking apron of the hospital; light was coming into the sky. The two talked quietly for half an hour or so. By six in the morning Moss was already dead. A team of surgeons from Walter Reed arrived, bringing a Foster Frame bed. Bobby stayed two days.

Those hours that first morning he gritted himself. A press man asked Robert whether the Kennedys intended, now, to retire from politics. "The Kennedys intend to stay in public life," Bobby snapped. "Good luck is something you make, and bad luck is something you endure." It was a brittleness characteristic of Robert in crisis; he spent the following forenoon throwing photographers, who thought they had the patient's permission, out of the emergency ward.

Edward himself seemed detached. "Is it true," he asked his anxious brother once when Bob darted in to see how the doctors were doing now, "that you are ruthless?"

As noon came a more relaxed melancholia softened Bob's tiring mood. "Is it ever going to end for you people?" a reporter asked.

"I was just thinking out there—if my mother hadn't had any more children after her first four, she would have nothing now . . . I guess the only reason we've survived is that there are more of us than there is trouble."

Ted Kennedy's next six months, the bulk of which he spent strapped tight into the Foster frame and Stryker frame rotisserie beds that held his torso rigid so that his vertebrae could mend, are either blank to his biographer or teeming with leads. He took up painting, watercolors mostly. George Lodge, looking in on his recuperating ex-rival at Boston's New England Baptist Hospital, noticed the piles and piles of books stacked up among the water glasses and prismatic reading and shaving apparatus and leg-exercising weights. "Teddy's reading all the books he should have read in college," Joan Kennedy gibed.

Joan tried to stop by three or four days a week for lunch, bringing little Teddy and Kara when she could, but it was a packed schedule for her that summer and autumn. The Massachusetts Organization—Larry Laughlin, Jim King, Doherty, Joey Gargan, Ray LaRosa, with Bob Fitzgerald helping out and Charlie Tretter keeping after the spot advance and legwork—moved her around the state to all the critical checkpoints to say a friendly little speech Ted had helped her with, be nervous, impress crowds with her candor and sincerity. Her voice a bit singsongy with the strain sometimes, occasionally a drink helped. She exhibited overall an interest in people on the street and a golden personal radiance no camera ever captured. It made for punishing days handshaking through the lobbies of banks and the aisles of supermarkets, her skinny knees atremble before receptions for up to five thousand people, women mostly, in overlit milltown auditoriums. There are few people with antibodies enough to resist celebrity sustained, but Joan Kennedy was one. Her wit—her being—stabilized to its natural balance and clarity: Revelation by revelation, Joan saw.

"Joan's sense of humor is really a sense of proportion. She has the ability to see—and give to others—the more positive and lighter side of the situation," a friend says; this was Ted's fundamental outlook, too. Three weeks before her husband's plane crashed she had miscarried again; throughout the rugged months of campaigning she scarcely alluded to that. Sally Fitzgerald, Bob Fitzgerald's wife and herself the niece of Governor Dever, who helped out with the advance details and accompanied Joan through much of the western Massachusetts junketeering, remembers the sunrise awakenings in motels through which she would drag herself wearily but to which Joan woke in "a gorgeous good humor," maddeningly, sometimes.

"Chahhr-lee," Joan would twit the dutiful but occasionally maladroit Tretter as the projector broke down for the third or fourth time in an afternoon and the He-is-doing-more-for-Massachusetts campaign film squawked and fluttered out of focus. "Didn't you say you were going to fix that?" There was a girlishness for people she trusted—she seldom saw Gerry Doherty but that she punched him amiably in the stomach, then made sure, at the mammoth receptions the Massachusetts Democrats liked to stand around drinking through, to spend the bulk of her time "fooling and playing" with Doherty's "little people," the Charlestown fry and lady precinct workers all excited to get invited at all.

"You didn't win in 1964; Joan won in 1964," Jim King was never to grow weary of reminding his boss. On November 3 she—and/or her husband—beat his Republican challenger, former state representative Howard Whitmore Jr., by 1,716,908 to 587,663, winning 75.6 percent of the total votes cast, crushingly.

A fellow female member of the Massachusetts delegation to the 1964 Democratic Convention in Atlantic City remembers, with special admiration, how Joan withstood without bristling or flinching the way "my pals, the Massachusetts Democrats, would paw her, put their hands all over her arms and back every time the cameras came around," while chivalric Maurice Donahue struggled to ward them off a little.

Another remembers noticing Joan, when the convention rose at the mention of John F. Kennedy's name, take advantage of the license allowed beautiful women everywhere and reach across the back of the chair ahead of her and playfully grab a sluggish delegate, still sitting, beneath the arms and haul him up, all sheepishness, to waver onto his feet.

The 1964 Democratic National Convention was, throughout, an anguish for the near-in Kennedy entourage anyhow. Bob wept introducing the official film about his brother the president, an emotion harmless to Lyndon Johnson since he had run his and Hubert Humphrey's nominations through first. Unable to put it away, the Kennedys had rented the ballroom of the Hotel Deauville to stage what one participant called a "delayed funeral for the folks." Jacqueline was there, the widow-bride in a white dress and a paralyzed smile, and joined Bobby in the reception line while many of the women who had known Jack bustled around in black serving as ushers. It was a waxworks, macabre, with three sittings and a speech Bobby made at which Joan Kennedy cried each time. The scene was 1952 at the Commodore in blacklight, camp legend, and ominous.

All this Joan did uncomplaining, willing, never pretending to enjoy it much. "I'm improving a little bit," she confided after a while, referring to those tightly scheduled brush-through appearances her husband's constituency demands, "but I dislike being propelled through a crowd. I feel like a store mannequin. It's so unreal and so impersonal." "I don't do that kind of thing for fun," she replied when an interviewer mentioned a columnist's report that she had enjoyed herself campaigning for Birch Bayh in 1968. "I do it for love of Ted."

Joan's drop-in lunches at the hospital, during which she and Ted discussed the campaign while Teddy Jr. peeped under the sheet to see where, exactly, Daddy's back was broke and Kara drifted out into the corridor in hope that the doctor was coming so she could watch him give her father his shot—these were easy intervals in what became, soon after Ted's bumpy ambulance ride from Cooley Dickenson to New England Baptist Hospital, hard-working senatorial days. Angelique Voutselas, Kennedy's warm, peppy, discreet, and thoroughly able personal secretary, had started working for him six weeks before; she and Eddie Martin, who saw after the incessant curiosities of the press, and busy bustling Andy Vitali, comprised the permanent Kennedy secretariat in an adjacent hospital room.

The days fell into a routine. Kennedy spent the mornings on the telephone, dealing with constituents, checking out campaign details, obliging the Washington and Boston offices. Periodically he did a fifteen-minute television show, and toward the end, stronger, held a daily forty-five minute press conference. Every three hours his two Army male nurses, Sergeants Roger Eckert and Clayton Booth, rolled him over in his Stryker frame to relieve or strengthen his back. He insisted on shaving and feeding himself. Visitors stopped by steadily.

"Watch out now, he has a prepared address," Ted warned the crowd around his bed when Bobby waved to a crowd of nurses in the courtyard. One day Martin got a call from the admissions desk that a little priest had arrived to see the senator. Kennedy was at work, so Martin suggested that maybe he might come down instead; what was the Father's name? "He says his name is Spellman," the nurse replied. The Cardinal went right up.

Another visitor was Lyndon Johnson. Johnson's association with Edward Kennedy was recent in 1964, little over a year, but it was already evident that it was going to lack the underlying rancor and envy that roughened Johnson's feelings about Ted's two older brothers.

After little more than a year in the Senate then, Johnson saw— and heard—every indication in Edward Kennedy's approach to dealing in the Upper House a devotion to the slow, careful, accretive process of learning and building prestige that made Ted Kennedy, uniquely in his family, a "Senate man" to Johnson.

At one point in 1963, overshadowed and muffled, Kennedy had reportedly considered resigning his Senate seat when 1964 came and running for the governorship of Massachusetts; this mood passed quickly, but it gave him a basis for commiseration. In October of 1963, on hearing that the boxed-in vice president had agreed rather reluctantly to fly to Boston to address the Associated Ministries of Massachusetts, Ted Kennedy had got his staff together and arranged a cocktail reception to brighten the depressed Johnson's visit and a tour of historic sites for Lady Bird: Johnson, who never forgot a slight, never forgot a favor either. "Senator, how's my campaign going up there in Massachusetts?" the president called weekly to ask throughout Kennedy's recuperation. In October of 1964, en route to campaigning in New Hampshire, Lyndon Johnson stopped over one early afternoon to spend an exuberant hour with Teddy. Ted understood how effective this heavy-handed Texan was proving to be.

"In my nearly fifty years of public life, we have not had a president as successful as FDR," Kennedy concluded in his memoirs. "The closest we've come (family relations excluded) is Lyndon Johnson." No doubt the reference to Jack was necessary to placate his sisters. Politician that he was, Kennedy was attempting to point up Johnson's unrivaled skills.

One regular was the Ambassador himself. The father, struggling through his own routines of hydrotherapy and exercise, was just then at one of those wavering peaks of deceptive near-recovery his raw will periodically brought him to; he was able to stand unassisted, and even attempted—to inevitable confusion, but with the old determination—to answer his Hyannis Port telephones. He, his wheelchair, and Ann Gargan arrived early and often.

His son's spinal fractures were jagged and unstable: After studying the X-rays, his Army doctors recommended that Ted let his strength come back for six or eight weeks, then let them operate so as to clench the splinters of bone and let them heal properly.

Ted was himself willing, but a witness relates that when the financier heard about this proposal he "stormed at the doctors" in such a way that it was clear that no operation was to be permitted. Two spinal operations had nearly killed Jack; "Dad doesn't like doctors and doesn't believe half what they say," as Ted remarked afterward; so that was that. Ted joined his father for weeks of therapy in a surging Jacuzzi, which resulted in fresh bonding to which Ted would refer fondly. Actually, as the Cooley Dickenson's orthopedic surgeon, Dr. Donald Chrisman, remarked a year later, Kennedy shuffled in his walk for a long time as a result of "paralytic involvement" in one leg, and experts doubted that he would ever walk without a cane. Teddy had no doubt: He had a name for his cane. "I call it temporary," he reported, and it was.

The lump of gristle in the small of Kennedy's back, an egg of a thing at first, flattened out slowly. Every vertebra was reportedly cracked. In time the telltale shuffle eased, and year by year he continued to heal.

His goal, he soon announced, was to be out by Christmas. By early December, when his father and Ann Gargan arrived to have another look, Ted was already in a wheelchair prepared to attempt to stand alone. There was a tense moment; Ted worked his legs beneath him and started to rise, while an orderly stayed poised with the wheelchair to catch him. Noticing this, the story goes, the financier gestured at the orderly furiously: Get that thing back and out of the way—Ted will stand up, or collapse. Teddy stood. Moved. He and the Ambassador moved cautiously to the balcony of his suite; the ambassador stood, too, with Ann gripping him gently in case he lost his footing on the tiles. Father and son were photographed, standing.

One day not long after that Martin and Angelique looked up in their private office and "this character was waiting there in his bathrobe," Martin remembers. "Our privacy was shattered." As the bones knitted and flexibility returned to Kennedy's back it became comfortable for him to move his upper arms. Bob Maury, the same person who had interested Jack Kennedy in painting, showed Ted the rudiments of handling watercolors and oils, and started him out on a hobby that, especially in time of crisis or extended anguish, was to restore him often over the years coming up.

"You have to stand back to appreciate it properly," Teddy ribbed Ed Martin, whose face was puckering at one of Kennedy's very earliest efforts. Martin couldn't seem to get back far enough, and a few days later, hoping that some good might come out of this aberration, suggested that he bring his last year's license plates around and let his employer touch them up a little in next year's colors.

Angelique Voutselas, whose tongue was never *never* known to overrun her perceptions, remarked to me once that the half-year Ted spent recuperating at the New England Baptist was perhaps the only time in his adult life he was utterly by himself. "He never really had any time alone before," she says, "to really think." One impulse he had was to try to produce something durable, tangible for his career, like John Kennedy's *Profiles in Courage*, written during Jack's recovery in 1955. Ted did manage to subscribe and put together a book of appreciations by friends and relatives of the Ambassador's, *The Fruitful Bough. He* wrote an essay on extremism. But, on the emphatic suggestion of people in the academic community like Sam Beer and Bob Wood, he devoted the heart of those long empty stretches of recuperating time to an accelerated bout of post-graduate directed study. The format of the bedside Academic Seminars, as Kennedy referred to them, was actually a kind of round-robin tutorial, the instructors changing constantly and the pace remorseless. Three days after the crash Kennedy was already in a recovery regimen, with angle-rotating and grip-tension apparatus, already doing more exercises, longer, than his therapist, Mrs. Birte Thomasen, asked.

He pushed his intellectual calisthenics even harder. Beer, preparing his tutee for one of those twice-a-week seminars, this one on federal-state relationships at about the time the Heller plan was under consideration, dropped off Graves's enormous tome on intragovernmental relations and came back to find that Kennedy had picked its great hulk empty. "It was quite astonishing to go to that funny little hospital and find what he had done in a week, lying there in that rack of a brace," Beer remembers. Karl Keysen termed the extent to which Ted grasped abstract economics material amazing. Kenneth Galbraith briefed him on balance of payments problems; Alain Enthoven, McNamara's top Whiz Kid, flew up to Boston to answer some questions on weapons systems. Jarrold Zacharias and Jerome Wiesner of MIT worked on science education. Mark DeWolfe Howe, who two years before had publicly labeled Edward Kennedy's ambitions "reckless" and "childishly irresponsible," had grudgingly to admit, after a bedside session, that Ted was unexpectedly well versed in the complicated precedents and legislative entanglements of civil-rights law.

Kennedy worked on Latin American problems, the tax structure, the vagaries of antitrust. Mrs. Thomasen gradually accustomed herself to kneading and stretching a body the face of which was persistently in one book or another, a hand jotting notes while a leg continued flexing and unflexing automatically. The television set seemed never to be on. Nights often found him bundled up in a bathrobe against the chill, out on his little balcony, studying quietly for hours.

The nights were excruciating. "I would lie there for two or three hours

before I drifted off, then I'd wake up again in a half-hour or so," Kennedy
said soon afterward. "I never really slept the whole night through. Nothing
looked better than dawn coming up and the chance to do something again."
Pain teaches, and solitude lends proportion. "In my judgment that was a
very important period for Ted," Bob Wood says now. "I remember we talked
together about very basic things—what kind of a Senate career should he
have, should he follow the trail of notoriety? He wanted something different,
something with more substance . . ."

"I'm not of the opinion that it took the airplane crash to make Ted Kennedy," Birch Bayh told me defensively, anticipating my unintended question;
Bayh's point is indisputable. Well before the accident, appearing at a dinner
party for the newly returned Kenneth Galbraith attended by a number of
dubious tutors, Ted Kennedy had acquitted himself beneath a generalized
grilling so neatly that Galbraith and Beer had winked at each other as their
assortment of nonplussed colleagues filed out.

Ted knew much detail already; what those hothouse months in New
England Baptist meant, besides the chance to study formally, develop some
self-assurance in a number of fields and trace the intellectual connections,
was the appearance of a personal philosophical context, formed out into
the darks and lights of emphasis. In 1964 Kennedy began to think about,
and rough in for himself, his own positions on what little by little were to
become, over the next five or six years, the issues and legislative proposals
with which he would most identify himself: The deterioration of our national
health provisions, our eroded and unfair tax laws, the inequities of the draft,
the extent to which local power groups had been able to nullify the voting
rights of the weak and poor by means of back-room tinkering with the very
conditions on the basis of which the franchise became available.

Ted Kennedy was to get involved with more transient issues—
immigration, for example, or gun control, or Indians (for emotional reasons,
very often)—but again and again throughout his post-convalescent years he
was to keep going back to his concentration on these structural disconnects
throughout public policy that drew his attention while he lay strapped in
his Stryker frame in 1964. They seemed all related finally: the symptomatic
problems of institutions breaking down as the American system dragged
itself into an alien age.

Understanding the problems more deeply month to month, Kennedy,
who grasped the politics from the outset, was developing a specialist's anxiety about the issues. "When he went to the Senate in the first place," Gerry
Doherty says, "the spotlight was on him to prove he was a hard worker. The

crash put him on another plateau. He didn't have to prove himself now, and he had a chance to be reflective, make something of himself. He became somewhat more introspective. He began to understand that the U.S. Senate was not some great honorific for him, it was a place to do some good for some people. He felt he had some time to make up for."

"I had a lot of time," Kennedy said not long after he was on his feet again, "to think about what was important and what was not and about what I wanted to do with my life." On December 16, 1964, the snowy morning on which he was supposed to be discharged at nine, Ted and Ray LaRosa and Eddie Martin sneaked down the back stairs and out the side entrance of New England Baptist at daybreak, drove to Andover, Massachusetts, and struggled—Ted largely on his cane—up the icy grass hillock beneath which lay Eddie Moss's still unstoned grave. They stood together ten minutes silently, then drove to Moss's house for an hour or so of hanging around the kitchen with Katie Moss and her children, then fought the commuter traffic back to the hospital for Ted's formal discharging; the press was there; after that Kennedy took a plane to spend the holidays with his surviving family in Florida.

The midday sun over West Palm Beach was hot and raised a perspiration along the shoulders that welcome winter intersession when the Ambassador and his youngest went wading together along the edge of the surf. Robert Kennedy, despairing of Lyndon Johnson, had resigned the attorney generalship and made it into the Senate from New York beneath a barrage of carpetbagger charges. After the most terrible year of all their lives, some kind of a corner—they all sensed, certainly they hoped—had finally been turned. Nineteen sixty-five opened.

Teddy and Bob—Part One

1. *Status*

Edward Moore Kennedy (Dem., Massachusetts), reelected to his first full term, walked back onto the floor of the Senate chamber in January 1965, dragging one leg noticeably and hunching back his opposite shoulder to compensate. The changes this session went well beyond the addition of his silver-headed cane *temporary* and his brain for new issues saturation-briefed by six months of hanging there thinking Government over. Now, there, among the colleagues, where for two years already Ted had been listening, watching, restraining himself—Bobby had arrived.

Late in his recuperation, when Robert Kennedy turned up and permitted a few bedside photographs of the two senators-elect, the photographer requested that Robert "Step back a little, you're casting a shadow on Ted." Ted Kennedy smiled his baby-brother smile: "It'll be the same in Washington," he commented, not completely without that touch of wistfulness natural to this perennial kid brother, who, whenever accommodations were short, still slept without complaint in bathtubs.

Robert Kennedy lived four and a half more years; the relationship between the brothers developed into something ballasted very heavily with suppressed emotion for both of them: a matter of the old simplicities and wider and wider veinings of ambiguity, unexpected and often quite complicated hesitancies of feeling. The largest fact here is that Robert Kennedy was, by now, not merely the head of the family but the unchallenged General Direktor of the Enterprise, and there was a sinew to his fiat his youngest brother could never bring himself consciously to resist.

"Well before I went to work for Teddy," remarked Dun Gifford, the Old Family legislative aide who summered in Nantucket and was a longstanding social friend, "I used to fly up to the Cape with Bobby and Ted in the *Caroline*. We'd leave right after the Friday voting in the Senate ended. Jack Kennedy was dead, and there was a seat in the plane towards the middle that everybody called the President's Chair. Nobody ever mentioned it, but I noticed that whenever Bobby was along he sat in that seat, and whenever he wasn't Ted sat there. It was the clearest example of—what is that word reporters like so much, primogeniture?—anybody could ever want."

Another aide of the period has commented that, whatever their differences of approach, their substantive positions moved along in "lockstep"; there were overpublicized little discrepancies between their voting records—Ted disagreed with his brother's advocacy of new post offices when the economy was inflating, or permitting draft exemptions to police officers—but these were nits to pick out of a close general congruence. "Whenever Ted felt even the beginning of a genuine disagreement with his brother he had a tendency to slide his opinion under Bobby's," another aide admits; although in fact the surviving brothers saw each other very infrequently during the Washington work week, telephone calls went back and forth continually.

One truism that was starting to make the rounds was the observation that, while Edward Kennedy aspired to a seat in the Senate, Robert Kennedy descended to one. Descended, here, not condescended: The problem was that Bobby had arrived from such turbulent fierce altitudes that the air of the Senate, with its unshakable deliberative ways, its stress on procedures, its sleepers' rhythms, bulked thick in his quick little lungs. He knew too much already. "I'd sleep nights if Robert Kennedy became president," a reporter Bobby jarred on personally once told me. "Because he is one guy who has the brutality to elbow his way to the top of the heap and the instincts to keep the heap under him."

This is the observation of somebody who understood not merely the mercurial Robert Kennedy but, and much more, the rampaging appetites of the national bureaucracy. Robert Kennedy's salient talent, that about him his father regarded most highly, was his capacity to isolate a fixed-boundary problem, assign values to the participants, determine what constituted success, then pull people together in combinations that ranged from a clutch of bookkeepers to an invasion Army competent to break into the situation and reorder things to his liking. The greatest triumphs—and a number of the most pronounced blunders—of his late brother's administration had depended on Bobby's instincts.

By 1965 Robert Kennedy's well-remarked constellation of talents, his constant interplay of verve, mood-shifts, fierce hatreds and fiercer loyalties, bouts of impulsiveness and immaculately prepared judgments—the effects he got were beginning to look more than a little problematical to millions Out There. Even to his intimates Bob Kennedy was a layer cake of ice and fire. You took a bite and hoped.

There comes to mind the half-open, half-closed eyes of Senator John Kennedy at the 1957 Rackets Committee Hearings, pupils darting back and forth, back and forth as if the whole thing was hammering along faster than he himself cared to go while the Committee's impudent Chief Counsel Robert Kennedy set pick after pick into the hide of truculent Jimmy Hoffa. Touchy, mobbed up, in iron control of America's biggest labor union, Hoffa was a target Bobby regarded as heaven-sent on the way to fulfilling Jack Kennedy's presidential hopes.

Yet three years later Bob Kennedy was attorney general in his brother's administration and, for all the press-heralded, high-priced talent he was able to recruit, "the best man I know," Jack Kennedy would confess, almost ruefully, "is Bobby." It required no great gifts of analysis on John Kennedy's part to make out the operational differences between such early kerfuffles as the Bay of Pigs and the skillful modulations of power and reaction with which Bob Kennedy, functioning as chief of staff for his brother the president, directed the missile crisis.

John Kennedy much loved his cutting-torch younger brother and needed him, but the omnipresent Lem Billings, who knew, questioned very much whether the attorney general and Ethel were ever invited, for purely social reasons, to dinner at the White House. Billings ascribed this to Jacqueline Kennedy's quirky mood those years, her hesitations about Ethel. But wives, like aides, tend to be successful insofar as they are able to gauge, unspoken, the intentions of their principals.

Clubbable or otherwise, Robert was central; the assassination in 1963 left him the Kennedy heir apparent. Bobby had a way of collecting and fitting people in, listening with unmistakably flattering attention to figures as divergent as Maxwell Taylor and Tom Hayden, Allen Ginsberg and the singer Andy Williams and A. J. Ayers. Within the Kennedy administration itself Bobby was, at times, something of a mollifier: He was the one available to hear the foreign policy reservations of Arthur Schlesinger, the buffer between the somewhat thin-skinned Sorensen, worried always and despondent at times about his relationship with his beloved John Kennedy, and the "Irish Mafia" operatives, O'Donnell and O'Brien especially, who distrusted half-articulated liberal yearnings as much as they esteemed careful nose-counting.

Finally, after the president was killed, this was what the Kennedys carried away from the wreckage: that melange of talents, contacts and energies and loyalties. "With the Kennedys everything was a kind of huge magnetic grid, everybody in touch with everybody," Fred Dutton later reflected. "With Lyndon everything came down from the mountain . . ." That loose-knit but already recognizable group of men the press was shortly to begin refer-ring to as the "advisers," who were convened in Steve Smith's Fifth Avenue apartment across from the Metropolitan, or at the Cape, or, often, at Hick-ory Hill—this shadow organization was taking shape. Bob himself, barely a senator-elect, was already recruiting another generation of talent as the older Trusted moved into Board situations. One of his lures was shyness, that strange side-mood of self-effacement that drew the unwary out. "You going to come to work for me?" he asked Peter Edelman over his shoulder late in 1964; one of Bobby's feet was up on the hood of a car in the White House parking lot so that a doctor could examine a gash on his knee.

"How much are you going to pay me?" Edelman wondered; Kennedys are famously stingy with the help. "I have this problem. I've been out of law school three and a half years and I've never practiced."

"I know," Bob said. "I have this problem too." He could be irresistible.

The "advisers," meanwhile, were shaking out. A number of the officials John and Robert Kennedy had esteemed most unreservedly—such talents as McGeorge Bundy, Nicholas Katzenbach, Robert McNamara proved careerists after all, hung on with the succeeding president with an enthu-siasm that struck stalwarts within the "government-in-exile," as the press soon started to call the "cabal" around Robert, as unacceptably self-serving. Genuine believers soon quit the Johnson administration. Many felt them-selves called—dozens, hundreds, it seemed, as doubts about Lyndon John-son's Vietnam policy set in; within the family itself a relative handful were trusted, close, chosen.

Ted Sorensen was one, balance wheel and political doppelgänger of JFK himself, listened to with a kind of superstitious respect. Burke Marshall, Robert Kennedy's Assistant Attorney General in charge of Civil Rights—of whom Bob said, and Teddy never forgot, "He has the best judgment of any man I've ever met"—and by then an IBM vice president, weighed in quiet but incomparably heavy. Stephen Smith retained his comptroller position.

Whenever money or a bit of inspired guesswork about where, exactly, the tipoff lay in anybody else's books was concerned, tough, thorough Carmine Bellino was discreet and available. Bob McNamara, once Lyndon tired finally of his "stay-comb" genius, got a considered hearing; Dick Goodwin had proved-out talents with speechwriting and hypersensitive political antennae Bobby couldn't help admiring, dark as Bob's mood grew at times as he reflected on the loquacious Goodwin's independence.

What was beginning to happen, although everybody involved hated and refused to admit such a thing, was that the Kennedy family was undergoing a land-change. The days when Kenny and Larry got $100 a week each, and Joe telephoned his friends, and Robert Kennedy insisted without blushing to a caucus of New York State reform leaders that "I don't give a damn if the state and county organization survives after November, and I don't care if you survive. I want to elect John F. Kennedy"—that ruthlessly simple mood was behind them permanently.

So many *many* people were involved in everything now; each decision seemed more complicated than the last. For Bob politics was turning into a relentless and not completely successful search for issues, problems, human dilemmas clean-cut enough to justify his indignation. The legacy rose around him.

2. Prerogatives

For Ted, Bobby's presence in the Senate was at the same time complicated, a pressure on everything he did, and a beloved protection. Any subtle organism overshadowed long enough must adapt most creatively to shade. "Which way do I drive, Eddie?" Robert Kennedy at the wheel wondered that first January morning as the two of them threaded through Washington traffic toward Capitol Hill. "You know this routine now." Reporters in the press gallery remember how Robert Kennedy, about to make his opening appearance in the well of the Senate as a Member, stopped meaningfully a moment and let his younger brother and senior colleague limp forward and hold open the Cloakroom door.

Respect for Ted Kennedy's determined recovery sparked much of the enthusiasm in the Caucus Room when he appeared—John Stennis was "mighty glad to have you back, boy," and to Clinton Anderson his younger colleague's return was "the best news of the session"; still, to the touchy Bobby, drained still by the shock of his brother's assassination, his own rather perfunctory reception had to be something of a depressant. Kenneth Keating had been well regarded among the members, Ted had been reelected in medium-size Massachusetts by 1,200,000 votes, and the rather hasty, blotchy campaign the Robert Kennedy–Steve Smith organization mounted the previous summer in New York State, although managing a win, finally, by 719,693 votes, had forced on its principals an unstylish descent into personal invective and the humiliating request for presidential campaign support from a smirking Lyndon Johnson. Johnson had done much better. Political coattails make bumpy riding, and votes are the wampum of Kennedy self-regard. Bobby began his Senate career bad-humoredly out of pocket.

"Is this the way I become a good senator?" Milton Gwirtzman remembers Bobby hissing at a committee meeting. "Sitting here and waiting my turn?"

"Yes," Edward said.

"How many hours do I have to sit here to be a good Senator?"

"As long as necessary, Robbie" his kid brother murmured.

Another time, drumming up support for a bill, Robert Kennedy approached a colleague who offered to trade his vote for a home-state speaking engagement. No haggler or favor-seeker by temperament, Bobby confronted his brother: "Is that what you have to do to get votes?"

"You're learning, Robbie."

By every knowing account Ted Kennedy liked having Bobby around. "There was a certain competitiveness," John Culver acknowledges, "but it was a healthy competition. They kidded each other a lot. It was a happy time for Ted. The brothers had a lot of respect for each other's advice; they depended on each other, called back and forth a lot. I don't think there was a major decision either of them made after JFK's death they didn't discuss." Deciding was something else.

"Once Bobby decided something that was it," an aide to both of them remembers. "On the other hand, Ted certainly wasn't by any means Bobby's Court of Last Resort." Who gave the orders in any final way remained unequivocal, whether on a rented sloop cruising the fjord-like coastline off Maine or dragging clear in time from an ill-advised judgeship endorsement.

Whatever rubs there were, the moments in which the accustomed Kennedy intervals narrowed threateningly, tended to release in patches of atmospheric heat-lightning the family called "kidding," or "needling."

In a telegram read aloud at a testimonial banquet for longtime JFK ally Governor Docking of Kansas, Bobby regretted that he hadn't been able to address the group but pointed out that he had sent his little brother, Teddy, and requested the Kansas loyalists to send him "right home" as soon as he finished.

"I thought that was a nasty telegram," Edward remarked. "But at least when I go home I know which state it's in." Worried enough, or preoccupied or frustrated or buoyant or squeezed enough, a trace of that about Bobby his day-by-day employees refer to, quite affectionately, as his tendency to "mild sadism" could play into Ted's mood too. A friend remembers a private plane ride the brothers took with Claiborne Pell, the aristocratic young senator from Rhode Island. Pell, not overly concerned about attending floor sessions at the time, had been the major sponsor of legislation to reform the East Coast intercity transit system. Once the plane was aloft Robert and Edward Kennedy fell into a somber exchange about the floor fight a day or two earlier, in which a piece of major legislation, which sounded to the increasingly alarmed Pell more and more like his own cherished transit bill, had been rushed to a vote and decisively defeated for lack of last-second lobbying. The brothers kept the exchange going for half an hour or so, freely inventing snatches of floor debate and amendments and Cloakroom byplay until Claiborne Pell belatedly, to his unspeakable relief, caught on.

Underneath the horsing around and bouts of impromptu playmaking, the fact that Bob was in there overseeing the legacy allowed the less pugnacious Edward to protract his own senatorial breaking in. The financier had always counseled his yeasty and flamboyant youngest to avoid publicity: This Teddy worked at after he took his seat in the Senate. Once his kid brother was elected, in 1962, the president too had admonished him, specifically, to keep out of the papers.

Ted bit his tongue and waited. After 1964, with Bobby installed as his New York colleague, and unmistakably intending to employ his Senate desk as a forum, Edward Kennedy attempted to interpret his own role as supportive, behind-the-scenes. Talking over his own career with friends he projected his goals in the Senate in terms of decades.

Whereas John Kennedy hesitated five months into 1953 before delivering his important "maiden" speech to his colleagues in the Senate, Edward Kennedy had put off any major presentation an exceptional sixteen full months. Bobby delayed a bare three weeks. If Teddy Kennedy seemed slower about hurrying along to market a quick political "identity" for himself, the omission went unnoticed.

What the public knew, for the most part, about this youngest Kennedy had plenty of superficial outline—the Teddy America recognized was tall, and husky, and grinned when he grinned quite blindingly, and joked around with his delightful mother—and almost no content at all. He professed himself one of and voted among the Northeastern liberals. He turned up at and disappeared abruptly from Georgetown parties a lot. He avoided reporters. He knew he needed time badly.

Needed and—much more important—had. At a loss by his own admission for the wit of John and most of the bite of Robert, Edward presented himself to himself as a ruminative. While Ted Kennedy was in no way a "quick study," as he put it himself, he was determined to put in the hours, months, years required to be a surpassingly *thorough* study. If piercing, erratic little Robert tended to personalize—one traces the stepping stones of Bob Kennedy's career across the heads he stepped on, Roy Cohn's to Jimmy Hoffa's to J. Edgar Hoover's to Albert Anastasia's to Lyndon Baines Johnson's—Ted Kennedy went about things by working through expanses of detail until he felt ready to propose a legislative remedy. It became as hard to come up with anybody on bad personal terms with him as it was to discover anybody with whom he was truly, ultimately, intimate.

"If you ask him about something, he can tell you much more than you could ever possibly use about the subject," an aide of Kennedy's told me once. "Yeah, and then he is put out as hell if you don't have the time to hear it all," another aide gibes. For all his occasional public gusto, the Edward Kennedy, the big extraordinarily courteous rather quiet man liable to fetch the facts out of other people with his seductive curiosity, responding with appreciation to whatever he heard, forever feeding what he heard into what he already knew—the inner-circle senator of the later sixties was already emerging.

Careful to keep close to the guidelines recommended by the well experienced Joe McIntyre, Kennedy rounded out his earliest senatorial months by concerning himself mostly with matters that pertained to Massachusetts. Like . . . fisheries: Representatives from the Bay State have been groaning away about Massachusetts's maritime drawbacks since Increase Mather. Teddy all of a sudden seemed to take the whole talked-to-death business seriously. In his debutante year, 1963, he introduced and pushed actively for a fishing research bill, a bill to correct the inequities of subsidies for construction of fishing vessels, a bill to prohibit foreign fishing vessels from U.S. territorial waters, a bill to promote state commercial research and development projects, and—surprised himself when this one rode through without effective opposition—a bill that resulted in fish products' being included in the Food for Peace program.

No North Shore or Cape Cod publisher, however conservative, could avoid a word of praise on a previously neglected belly issue like this.

By midsummer that same year Kennedy had landed swinging in the midst of the fierce behind-the-scenes fight over the awarding of a renewed license to Northeast Airlines for the Boston–Miami run; only Kennedy, as his Harvard classmate and recently acquired legislative aide, Jerry Marsh, remembers, "had the guts to fight the thing out in the open. Everybody else just complained to the Speaker or copped out one way or another."

Typically, this early, Kennedy moved from the specific to the most bedrock of principles involved. "I wish to say one final word. The CAB was created by Congress. It is completely appropriate, therefore, that we in Congress should have the opportunity to review the consequences of what has been undertaken by the Civil Aeronautics Board."

Unattended by the press that summer and fall of 1963, Kennedy's tangle with the CAB caromed in and out of a sequence of moves and countermoves that would again and again characterize his way with the parliamentary. His immediate purpose was evident—he simply wanted to get a locally unfavorable CAB ruling reversed—but before he finished he had pulled in the major banking interests, the Justice Department, the judiciary, and any number of unhappy colleagues who couldn't avoid involving themselves with the issue once it departed closed-up meeting rooms. A very large—a very sensitive—problem, the appropriateness of congressional review of the work of the shadowy federal agencies and commissions, now caught the young senator's attention.

At about this time, selecting among the subcommittees of the Judiciary Committee, Kennedy had chosen the pallid Administrative Practices and Procedures Subcommittee. The mandate of the committee seemed a bit obscure—to investigate the bureaucratic proliferation of the "shadow government" and the special regulatory agencies that have so multiplied in Washington since 1933–35. But Jerry Marsh, who had been involved in litigation practice before he came to Washington to help out his onetime teammates Kennedy and Culver, realized how much waited promisingly for a natural technician like Kennedy in such a tangled issue.

3. Immigration

Political 1965 turned out to be a year for strategists, for personalities colliding, for harsh pitched battles. Ted Kennedy started it with something of a walk-through, the opportunity he requested of Johnson to floor-manage S:500, a bill to amend the Immigration and Naturalization Act.

Then, executing one of those turnabouts that made the bland-appearing Kennedy exceedingly dangerous at times, he led a revolt that defied the administration by conspiring to load an anti-poll-tax amendment onto the fragile, top-priority 1965 Voting Rights Act. Then, flushed, Kennedy abruptly found himself grabbing for whatever he could lay legislative hands on to somehow prop up his surprise candidate for the federal district bench, vulnerable Francis Xavier Morrissey, while Everett McKinley Dirksen arranged to teach his fellow senator the same lesson a porcupine reserves for an impetuous puppy. Nineteen sixty-five was educative.

Immigration reform, like Medicare and an effective broad-scale aid-to-education bill, was one of those legislative updatings already at least four presidencies overdue by Lyndon Johnson's time. Like so many other items he wrangled into law throughout the Great Congressional Drive, the ideas and much of the language came out of staff work prepared during the Kennedy administration.

The situation of immigrants in America had been a fascination to the Kennedy family for generations. Impudent little Congressman Honey Fitz, after all, had outraged the elder Henry Cabot Lodge over exactly that. Rose Kennedy debated the issue as a high school girl in Dorchester. The last book John Kennedy wrote, *A Nation of Immigrants*, dealt with their unequal statutory treatment and proposed, in largest outline, the substantial reform that Adam Walinsky, then a young lawyer in Robert Kennedy's Justice Department, updated in what became S:500.

Well aware of the special interest of the Kennedy family in a piece of legislation from which, after all, no unreasonable political capital was to be expected, President Johnson had nothing against giving Edward Kennedy the chance to manipulate the bill through Congress. Kennedy regarded immigration as, to him, a "great scorching issue"; also, as an aide of the period remembers, he saw it as one that carried "a lot of plus with the Massachusetts Italians" just then. Johnson's OK was on the assumption that Kennedy would be able to wheedle the temporary chairmanship of the Immigration Subcommittee out of curmudgeonly Jim Eastland, who was known to have very little use for the reformist proposals but liked Ted. Eastland acquiesced. Kennedy's obligation after that required him to chair the hearings, keep an eye on the full Judiciary and the floor debate, work liaison with the legislation's sponsors in the House of Representatives to make sure it did not become unacceptably altered or perforated with amendments there, and defend it in the joint Senate-House conference should that be needed.

The import of the bill was straightforward. While the total of new immigrants permitted into the United States was to remain at 160,000–170,000 annually, the quota of those from any other nation applying was no longer to be determined percentage-wise according to that nation's representation already here—a system that left such nations as England, Ireland, and Germany with enormous unfilled quotas while ruling out long waiting lists from such poverty areas as Greece and Italy. Instead, with short-term exceptions, the immigration was to be relatively open, up to the prescribed limitation of 10 percent from any single nation. The newcomer, instead of having a specific job in advance, must fall into an occupational category within which, in the judgment of the Department of Labor, there were not enough Americans to meet the national need. The unabashed discrimination against Asians that dated from the Burlingame and Lansing-Ishii "Gentlemen's Agreements" was to be dropped finally out of our immigration procedures.

Compared with a good deal of the rushed and sloppily drawn legislation of Lyndon Johnson's cyclonic first presidential year, the Immigration Bill was solid, well thought through, and limited enough in application for even the purists. It was in no way a difficult bill to manage.

One pothole developed: Bobby. A few of the exchanges during the March 4 hearing between Bob Kennedy, appearing as a witness, and Sam Ervin, the showboat constitutionalist who at the time was fighting more than his share of the Southern rear-guard actions as the Johnson Drive rolled over the conservatives, illustrate Bobby's problems with life as a Senator and the Senate establishment's problems with Bobby. Sam Ervin was there to object to the legislation, pick at it publicly, get his complaints on the record; at one point, when Ervin couldn't make a meeting, Ted Kennedy, as a personal courtesy, took it upon himself to pursue the hypercritical line of interrogation he knew Ervin would have.

Bobby saw his personal role differently. When Bob Kennedy and his single-minded aide Adam Walinsky appeared before the Immigration and Naturalization Subcommittee to defend S:500 in detail, the exchanges between Ervin and Robert Kennedy commenced to tear skin off both men's egos instantly. Ervin's main complaint, in his exchanges with Senators Fong and Scott, had been about the way S:500 substituted a "mathematical" division for the first-come, first-served basis of the 1952 McCarran-Walters Act. He saw, as a probable consequence of this, dangerous temptations to the politicians in power, who were at any time administering the law, to admit or not admit immigrants, or gerrymander among job categories, so as to confirm or broaden their own party's hold on a particular locality. This is a cleverly projected point, calculated to appeal to moderates; the exchange about this had been serious but mutually respectful, even playful. With Robert Kennedy's appearance the mood turned, at once:

> *Senator Ervin:* I would like to say that you have made the most eloquent argument for the passage of an unwise piece of legislation I have ever heard.
>
> *Senator Kennedy of New York [Coldly]:* Thank you, Senator.

A little later on, after an explanation of how the reform should work in practice:

> *Senator Ervin:* Is not the way you are doing it more or less throwing out the baby with the bath water?
>
> *Senator Kennedy of New York:* Who is the baby?
>
> *Senator Ervin:* Or burning down the barn to kill the mouse . . . But there is another provision of this bill which gives fourth preference to anybody who is capable of exercising any specific function, where there is an insufficient number of Americans who are employable for that purpose or are willing to work for that purpose?
>
> *Senator Kennedy of New York:* Yes.
>
> *Senator Ervin:* My dictionary teaches me that a function is any action or activity which is proper for a human being to engage in.
>
> *Senator Kennedy of New York:* I will accept that for the moment.
>
> *Senator Ervin:* I will read you what the dictionary—
>
> *Senator Kennedy of New York:* I will accept it. I do not know what it is leading me to.
>
> *Senator Ervin:* I will read it exactly into the record. Here's the way my dictionary defines it, which is one of Webster's. He was another immigrant, though to Massachusetts, not to the United States. He says, and I quote—

There was a presentiment already of onsetting apoplexy all round. A few minutes later, cross-checking Robert Kennedy's answers against the previous testimony of Willard Wirtz, Ervin challenges Kennedy's reading of the "fourth preference" among the subclauses. The inevitable happens:

Senator Kennedy of New York: I might say, Senator, we wrote the bill in the Department of Justice, so I know what is in it.

Senator Ervin: I have a high respect for your memory and your knowledge, but despite my high respect for your ability and your knowledge, and my great respect for you, I do not admit your infallibility.

Bob Kennedy's blunt, scrupulously unemotional answers, without resonances, with none of the give or the fond among-us-colleagues railleries as native to the Capitol as those miles and miles of Byzantine-mosaic corridors, break Ervin down to the point of voicing what is, obviously, his own central difficulty with the bill in hand.

Senator Ervin: . . . But you would certainly not deny the honesty of the opinion of those who say they prefer some national origins quota system on the theory that it will admit to this country as immigrants the people from those nations that have made the greatest contribution to the population of the United States and to the development of the United States?

Senator Kennedy from New York: I do not agree with that, Senator.

Senator Ervin: I know you do not.

At one point, gritted and despairing, Robert Kennedy gives up all hope of imparting even the most technical of detail:

Senator Kennedy of New York: Could I just suggest, Senator, that if it is clarified, I would think that the members of the committee could straighten it out. You have one position and I have given mine.

Senator Ervin: Thank you. I appreciate your testimony. I deeply regret that you do not entertain the same sound views on this bill that I do.

Senator Kennedy of New York: Could I say, Senator, it is mutual.

U.S. Government Printing Offices do not include stage directions, but suspicions mount that, if they did, the hearings transcript at this point would have to include the release of pent-up breath by Senator Kennedy (Massachusetts) audible all the way to the back.

S:500 proceeded. Unnoticed mostly, Edward Kennedy and his legislative people scurried in and out of offices to ward off any unexpected challenge and turnabout. Kennedy ostentatiously pinned a shamrock on Sam Ervin's lapel on Saint Patrick's Day, very soon after Bobby had riled up the old Dixie autocrat. A single turbulent moment remained. Having favor-traded and connived among his more conservative elders to certify that they, however grumpily, would leave his beloved bill alone, once it arrived for presentation on the floor of the Senate, Kennedy was astonished one slumberous afternoon (by which time S:500 had already been through its third rendition and now was procedurally beyond amendment) to hear absent-minded old Spessard Holland of Florida request a minute or two to inquire crabbily of his youthful colleague as to "exactly how many nigruhs" this legislation was likely to inflict on the Republic; there followed an immediate stampede among the Southerners for the anonymity of the Cloakroom. The moment blew over: S:500 steered through without amendment, by an impressive 78–18. On October 3, with pens all round, Lyndon Johnson signed S:500 into the nation's lawbooks.

4. Voting Rights

The Immigration Subcommittee hearings ended on the eleventh of March. Before March was out Ted Kennedy was well advanced on a legislative flanking action that couldn't help but embroil him in the onrush of what was already shaping up as the legislative testing ground, the great embittering domestic issue of Lyndon Johnson's presidency: the 1965 Voting Rights Act.

The voting-rights struggle, involving as it did the concussion of enormous interest groups, huge areas, irreconcilable human approaches, looked to perspicacious members of both Houses of Congress like the struggle Southerners had better win; otherwise, they had better acknowledge that the era of delay and guile in racial matters had passed. Much of the lawmaking accomplished during the Johnson administration depended both in social outline and, often, in detail, on well-worked-through proposals that had been sandbagged by the segregationist old guard in the Congress at least since Fair Deal days. The 1965 Voting Rights Bill had teeth, long, sharp, expertly filed teeth, teeth that demanded a shrewd seasoned legislator like Lyndon Johnson to get it by the Dixie-chaired world of closed-door subcommittees and the filibuster-prone Confederate and Conservative alliance without having important bite extracted.

Johnson, typically, began things by "isolating the problem"—boxing in the die-hard Confederate loyalists and tearing away from behind them their cautiously maintained unburned bridges. He posed the frame by dramatizing the issue nationally: Against the unfolding tableau of Selma marching,

Jim Clark and his cattle prods and fire hoses and bullwhips and police dogs savaging black men and women who refused to defend themselves, Johnson convened a joint televised session of Congress on March 15 at 9 PM, the first public plea of its type since Harry Truman faced down the railroad strike in 1946. The goad here was already far fiercer than conscience; once alerted, liberal enthusiasm was back-pressuring the president: Robert Kennedy, who got Joe Rauh and Peter Edelman together to do the drafting, submitted to the White House a strong, publicly supported measure that cut Johnson's maneuvering room on the left. Invoking Lexington and Concord and Appomattox, the president presented the issue of Negro voting as one, finally, as momentous as the survival of the national soul. The oratory took powerfully. Even moderate and conservative Northern politicians felt heavy constituent pressure.

The voting-rights proposals themselves came out of rugged working sessions among Nicholas Katzenbach and his then-deputy Ramsey Clark, Mike Mansfield, and the wind-sniffing Minority Leader Everett Dirksen. Dirksen demanded and got, reportedly, a stiff advance payment for his indispensable aid: He abhorred in particular the Supreme Court's recent one-man-one-vote ruling, and evidently secured the administration's promise to look away while he ran through the Senate a resolution intended to delay at worst—and dump overboard permanently, if things worked out at all—the reapportionment of state legislatures, on whose imbalance toward the rural so many of Dirksen's fellow Midwestern conservatives depended. Also, he himself saw no reason to jettison what vestigial local poll taxes survived. The concordat achieved, each provision of the closely drafted bill went exactly into place like an expertly driven coffin nail.

By states-rights standards the bill was rawboned and unorthodox, bypassing utterly the conventional heavy-footed trek of the put-upon local complainant through layer after layer of courts to some retreating redress. The Deep South howled. This revolutionary legislation was to pertain to those counties where, on November 1, 1964, literacy tests or similar voting restrictions obtained and where less than 50 percent of the voting-age citizens had been registered and voted in the 1964 elections: This worked out to mean Alabama, Georgia, Louisiana, Mississippi, South Carolina, Virginia, most of North Carolina, but not, oddly enough, Texas.

Johnson, anticipating an effort to suffocate the legislation in that deep back pocket Jim Eastland reserved for civil-rights legislation in his Judiciary Committee, prearranged with Mansfield and Dirksen to surrender the bill to Judiciary only after an open-floor vote had specified that Judiciary report it out and back to the floor by April 9. The president's nose-counting was scrupulous: He knew that after a decent political delay to let the South register oratorically the depth of its indignation, he would have the two-thirds necessary to invoke cloture in the event of a filibuster and push this bitter dosage down.

What Johnson and his attorney general feared most was an unexpected obstruction, a meaningful delay, during which the "fever . . . in the air" Dirksen thought he smelt might settle itself. The danger was that zealots, riding the moment, would attempt to load amendments and reforms into this already overloaded legislation, slow its passage, and so tender the fundamentally unconvinced Conservatives time enough to rejoin their natural Southern allies and pull Johnson's crisis coalition apart. Most heatedly urged, and so most threatening among the amendments pending, was the argument that Martin Luther King was using his widespread influence to promote legislation to outlaw the poll tax in state and local elections.

It was the administration's view that whatever survived of the old poll tax was doomed momentarily anyhow; the year before, the Twenty-Fourth Amendment had invalidated the device in contests on the federal level. So there was concern, alarm even, when the Katzenbach Justice Department discovered that there was indeed a strong, well-organized anti-poll-tax insurgency centered in the Judiciary Committee, and that its leadership was enthusiastically bucking the leadership of both major parties, and that its ringleader in the Senate was Edward M. Kennedy.

Those late-March hearings into the particulars of the voting-rights controversy, while Edward Kennedy appeared to be slogging deeper and deeper into something only he seemed very sure about, formed a series of unshakable first impressions on his newly hired legislative assistant, David Burke. Burke himself had come into Kennedy's staff earlier the same month and was still trying to determine the rhythms, at least, of that interplay of drift and decisiveness by which Kennedy operated. The staff was experiencing a shakeout—Ed Moss had died in the plane crash; Joe McIntyre had collapsed in the Washington office the previous December of a premature, fatal coronary; John Culver had gotten himself elected to Congress from Iowa; Jerry Marsh was back in Illinois; and the mercurial Bill Evans had a new job troubleshooting for Pan American Airlines. Milton Gwirtzman was in and out.

This left Kennedy pretty much dependent on whatever he himself knew: For Burke, helping Kennedy get started again, those typical Kennedy-family gaps, elisions, unspoken judgments and leaps of studied impulse took getting used to. David Burke managed: By the time he himself moved over to administrative assistant, his natural mixture of office competence and the exceptionally pure moral instinct he brought to the major political issues had jibed so well with his employer's talents that he and Edward, like Sorensen with John Kennedy, played wonderfully together.

All this came later; in March of 1965 Burke listened and watched carefully, learned. He found himself involved initially in the probes, the assessment stage, sat in on long and detailed conferences with experts on civil-rights legislation like Paul Freund and Mark DeWolfe Howe—sharp critic, tutor, now adviser to Edward, as he had been to his brother in 1957. Ted Kennedy had always been the sort to keep any final doubts to himself, but Burke was already picking up on the drift of his worries. James O. Eastland and the Judiciary Committee conservatives had shown great consideration for him virtually since the morning Kennedy came into the Senate: Would the many kindnesses extended be nullified going forward by a more spontaneous move, especially on a symbolic mechanism of segregation like the hallowed Dixie poll tax? Kennedy was instinctively anxious, Burke discovered, about making any decision that did not consider something, some unnoticed aspect or unlooked-for operative consequence that reversed the effect of a measure bloodily enacted. Burke found himself cross-checking all over the bureaucracy for answers to questions his boss had about such things as exactly how, procedurally, those federal examiners were to move in and collaborate with local officials in an area, what each involved state's potential situation was, whose figures were to be used to pull that proposed 50 percent trigger.

"We went to our first executive session of the Judiciary Committee, and the senator already had a whole pile of amendments devised for the purpose of perfecting and cleansing the bill," Burke remembers. Kennedy limited himself to these. He subjected the attorney general, Nicholas Katzenbach, to a pinpoint crossfire that was in many ways harder to evade than the big booming constitutional-question mortar blasts that his central protagonist, Sam Ervin, lobbed throughout. His colleagues on both sides of the aisle were becoming aware that Kennedy was likely to prepare himself more exhaustively on any of the complex issues he expected to champion than anybody else on the left. Already, fellow senators tended to wait until Kennedy registered his preferences before commiting their own votes.

Why must a complaint pass through two levels of discretion, the examiner and the local U.S. Attorney, before an injunction could be assured, Kennedy wanted to know. Why should the potential unit of delinquency be the county? Why not any political subdivision in which less than 25 percent of the Negro vote is recorded? Why is there no provision providing for protection of office seekers—what is the use of having an open franchise when no meaningful opponent of the status quo dares run? Yes, Katzenbach admits, ". . . we might, as a practical matter, easily get it in."

The Judiciary Committee hearings meandered toward their April deadline, the atmosphere cut from time to time by an unmistakable whiff, whenever the Southerners panicked, of flashfired brimstone. How did the administration happen to pick that April 9 cutoff date, Charles Bloch of Georgia wonders. "That was Appomattox, was it not?" Judge Leander Perez of Plaquemines Parish, Louisiana, tyrannosaurus of white supremacy, lashes all around himself with assurances that he can, in fact, "smell" the "Black Belt" conspiracy between the Reds and the Supreme Court that has already resulted in a wave of stabbings, clubbings, and, with sticky repeated emphasis, buck Negroes raping white women, including—Perez is country-clever as to his audience— "a fine young Jewish woman I believe in a New York elevator . . ."

Kennedy perseveres. He was concerned about what unpredictably long paper-shuffling bureaucratic delays would do to this newest among a number of heretofore dead-letter voting-rights bills, specifically about from whom, and when, the Justice Department was going to get that breakdown that is supposed to activate this legislation. From Dixie courthouse officials? He pushes the evasive Katzenbach, already edgy, as to the feasibility of having the U.S. director of the census compile unbiased early figures; Katzenbach replies, unhappily, "There is a time lag . . . if the State has not gotten the figures, you would have to go out and get the figures, and that is a fairly expensive proposition."

When A. Ross Eckler, the Acting Director of the Bureau of the Census, appears, Kennedy chivvies him a little as to what the delays would amount to, how much money the additional appropriations and staff that business of getting the information with which to spring the "triggering device" would involve. Why not, Kennedy proposes, proceed on the findings of the Civil Rights Commission, chaired by Father Hesburgh: What, professionally speaking, does Mister Eckler think of their figures? Sam Ervin, who sees where all this is liable to take them, tries to shoulder in; Kennedy blinks that slow polite emotion-repressing blink he cultivates and repeats his question of Eckler. Eckler admits that his "general background and contacts do not suggest any reasons for discrediting these figures . . ." When James Kilpatrick of Richmond, Virginia, testifies, Kennedy asks the editor for the official figures of the local registrars of Fauquier, Mecklenburg and Montgomery Counties, Virginia, then produces figures from which to demonstrate that all these agree substantially with the Civil Rights Commission's statistics.

Judiciary's well-practiced little clutch of Southerners, who had for twenty years dumped just enough weakening legal sand into lawmaking like this, watch glumly as block slides into place beside block. Senator Tydings is having his chance at Kilpatrick when an exchange concerning the efficacy of the Virginia poll tax itself comes up. Kilpatrick was justifying the device, not awfully enthusiastically, as a citizen's "token of membership, his involvement in the community that he lives in." In Virginia itself the law had been written so that anybody dropping behind must pay as much as three years of poll-tax arrears, plus interest, to register and vote. "I would say it is certainly no longer a deterrent in the State of Virginia for voting as far as the Negro population is concerned, because they pay their poll taxes now, or have them paid for them in droves, and turn up pretty actively at the polls."

Edward Kennedy broke in immediately: "Could I ask what you mean, 'having them paid for them'?"

Mr. Kilpatrick: "This is a regrettably familiar political device in certain parts of our state, and I believe in other parts of the Union, not unknown in certain parts of Boston and New York . . ."

To anybody with Kennedy's background a vision had to be forming of how the poll tax must function in Virginia, carloads of blacks, trip after trip, helter-skelter, all day to the polls, each clutching six dollars to reinstate his name, winked at when he holds onto the change by tolerant county registrars loyal to the Byrd machine.

The hearing testimony wobbled on, but Kennedy had now discovered his exact direction. "He was sitting at the table in the hearing room one afternoon," David Burke remembers, "and he called me over and said, 'Where is my poll-tax amendment?' I had been around, involved when we talked to our civil-rights experts Howe and Freund, who felt there wasn't any need for an amendment to the Constitution to outlaw local poll taxes, that it could go right into the bill, and libertarians like Joe Rauh and Charlie Haar, but somehow we never got around to discussing it specifically, and—well, I'm not a lawyer, and I remember leaving the hearing room in a sort of panic. I came back to the office, and got one of the lawyers around, and I was back there inside of twenty minutes or so with a simple amendment, a line or two that would pass for that day. Then the senator—and this was very surprising to me—he had his arguments all marshaled, and that's how the poll-tax fight began. He's that way though: He assumes that what he has been doing and thinking about has leaked out all over the office."

Kennedy's amendment to S:1564 read, "No state or political subdivision shall deny or deprive any person of the right to register or to vote because of his failure to pay a poll tax or any other tax or payment as a precondition of registering or voting." Kennedy argued powerfully for his amendment with a quiet but fascinating assist from suave old Sam Ervin when it came to a vote in the Judiciary and—to the surprise of both the administration and the more retrograde conservatives—Judiciary bought, agreed, and passed it.

Now, *that* had been a cute display for a senator not in his mid-thirties yet; The leadership on both sides of the aisle, plotting tactics together in that rag-picker's paradise Everett Dirksen kept as a Minority Leader's Office, chuckled as they devised their countermove. The administration and its supporters, who had framed most of the language in the first place, now decided to bypass it altogether and present directly to the floor a completely new piece of voting rights legislation, waggishly termed around the Hill the "Dirksenbach Bill" or the "Ev, Mike and Nick Substitute." This lacked Edward Kennedy's amendment nullifying the poll tax; it did, however, include the proposal of Everett Dirksen that, wherever the poll tax survived, the federal registrars collect it, a situation sure to be so obnoxious to most Southern politicians that the tax itself was likely to fall into abeyance rather than involve the interlopers from Washington.

But Kennedy wouldn't bite. Instead he plowed into one of his typically long, wide, deep, flavorless, comprehensive studies, this one of the entire constitutional history and parliamentary status of the poll tax wherever it had come into use, nibbled away at the fine points, assessed the record and predilections of every other senator to try to estimate accurately how convincing he might prove against White House blandishments.

"One day he asked for a list breaking down the Senate into who was for and who was against him," Burke remembers. "He got a big white pasteboard chart on a tripod, and he lived with it. He knew each man, what his position was, what he needed."

His office telephone lines were alive for weeks reawakening Kennedy contacts with church groups and Labor, he hobbled from office to office leaning on his silver-headed cane to lever and charm his colleagues, following up whoever wavered with an arranged barrage of letters from outside, a call from somebody at the top of an important pressure group, advice from a world-famous lawyer. With moderates or borderline Southerners he marshaled such convincing arguments as his discovery when researching that, once, in some cases the poll tax had been a liberalizing measure, removing from the franchise the requirement that the voter own property.

Now it was deadwood, beyond its proper time; he hoped whichever listener he was working on would help him to drag it out of the way, permanently. He briefed and rebriefed himself with Howard University experts. His sympathetic Judiciary colleague, Jake Javits, worked the Republican side hard; support flowed back and forth. Teddy persuaded the incorruptible Ralph Yarborough of Texas, where local poll taxes were still collected. At the same time Edward Kennedy floor-managed the liberal opposition to Dirksen's dream of repealing the one-man-one-vote decision, seeing after the backstairs politics while Bobby blasted the retrogressive measure to obscurity on the floor. "I brought three lost sheep back to the fold," Dirksen wheezed to a reporter just before the floor vote on Kennedy's amendment, "and I'll get another one tomorrow morning."

By the time Kennedy sprang his major poll-tax address on the Senate floor he nearly had his ultimate thirty-eight co-sponsors. Bobby, lobbying quietly for his brother, avoided the sponsor list. Edward's timing was calculated; he picked the session just preceding the spring recess, when nobody could get right back at him, when there would be time for all his colleagues to work through his comprehensive, expertly reasoned lawyer's brief in defense of the constitutionality of the poll-tax prohibition, and hometown opinion would have its chance at the vacationing members themselves. He reportedly gave Hubert Humphrey bleak nights by assuring him, days before the voting, in that deadpan way, that he thought he had fifty votes, total, sewed up: Humphrey, as vice president, would probably have to break the tie and undercut a lifetime of brilliant service to the civil-rights movement by voting for the continuance of the poll tax.

One member of the Democratic leadership abruptly stood with Kennedy—old Jawn McCormack. The speaker of the House of Representatives ignited a powerful side fire by coming out publicly and carrying the Lower Body against his own administration.

The day the poll-tax amendment came to a vote Joan, Eunice Shriver, and Ethel were in the gallery. Bobby's more limited, less controversial amendment, which enfranchised the Puerto Rican community by waiving the English literacy requirement for anyone with a sixth-grade education under the American flag, went through without important incident. By then Edward Kennedy was well aware that he probably didn't have the votes, but refused to bluff the administration with the threat that he might fall back on his heavy support to filibuster the Voting Rights Bill itself, tie the Senate up single-handedly for weeks and jeopardize the cloture motion. About to lose and realizing it, Kennedy retained control. Mike Mansfield handled the administration's opposition; an expert close to the situation, who found that, being no lawyer, Mansfield was "out of his depth," remarks that, in debate, "Teddy

1. ABOVE LEFT: Mary Hickey Kennedy. "A driving force that was instrumental in having [her] Family reach the heights." 2. ABOVE RIGHT: P.J. Kennedy. "His name for shrewdness, fairness, and freedom with the dollar for the needy spread among his customers." 3. BELOW: 1928. The president of First National Pictures, Joseph P. Kennedy, disembarks from the SS *Aquitania* accompanied by his wife, Rose.

4. ABOVE: A generation foregathered. Left to right: Joe Jr., Eunice, Rose Kennedy, Bobby, John, Teddy, Joseph P. Kennedy Sr., Kathleen, Patricia, Rosemary, and Jean. 5. BELOW LEFT: Young Edward photographing the Changing of the Guard outside Buckingham Palace while the Ambassador and his wife meet the king and queen. 6. BELOW RIGHT: Home again, 1940. Rose Kennedy, Pat, Teddy.

7. ABOVE: The new Marchioness of Hartington, née Kathleen Kennedy, with U.S. Navy Captain Joe Jr. **8.** BELOW: A frieze of heroes from the P.T. boats gathers in 1944 above the Hyannis Port lawns, overshadowing the twelve-year-old Edward and muscular cousin Joseph Gargan.

9. Breaking ground with Cardinal Cushing for the Joseph P. Kennedy Jr., Foundation, 1947.

10. Harvard end Ted Kennedy watches the ball sail over his head while Yalies converge, 1955.

11. ABOVE: 1946. Honey Fitz and grandson John strike poses while Rose and her mother, Mary, appear suitably impressed. **12.** BELOW: The brothers Kennedy, 1959.

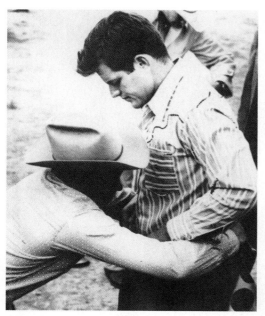

13a & 13b. Easy rider.

14a & 14b. Impact. June 19, 1962.

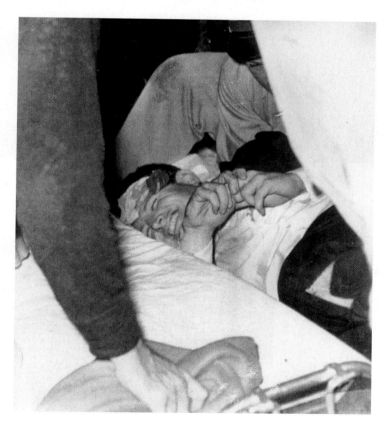

15. LEFT: May 1962. Edward Kennedy attacks issues while Edward McCormack concentrates on personalities. **16.** BELOW: Press conference, October 1962, Joan Kennedy presiding.

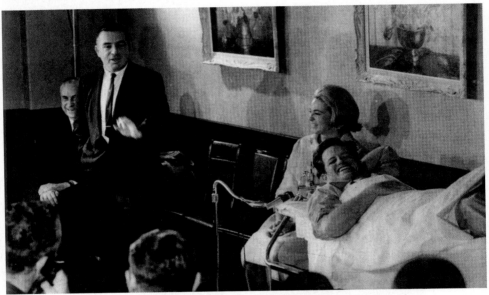

17. Paying calls again, late 1964.

could have torn Mike's heart out. He wouldn't." It came in the middle of May; Kennedy lost, 49–45.

It was the kind of vote no adroit president dares ignore. Dirksen's federal registrar measure drove the abuse to the brink; Katzenbach was instructed "forthwith" to file the government's suit before the Supreme Court; before the end of the year, in a test case involving Virginia, the Supreme Court ruled the local poll tax unconstitutional.

On August 6, when Lyndon Johnson signed the Voting Rights Act, it had Ted Kennedy's fingerprints all over it.

5. *Morrissey*

However the poll-tax amendment went, Ted Kennedy would have had to take one hell of a stumble tactically to weaken himself politically jousting in behalf of principle. The project he undertook after that—the long-deferred Kennedy attempt to secure an appointment to the federal bench for Francis Xavier Morrissey—here was a chore no oratory or sentiment would perfume.

Why push the appointment? "Frank had a great desire to go on the federal court," Kennedy mused to me later on, regarding the event from such an internal distance that wonder and charity seem to have bleached away his personal involvement. "Perhaps that too was . . . the rags to riches part of things . . . His wife was very insistent. Also, it was something he had my father's approval on. I felt in my own relationship with Frank that he had that feeling. My father was sick at this time, and I simply felt it was something that had to be put forward. So I asked the president to support Frank. I expected him to."

Kennedy may in fact have expected Lyndon Johnson to approve the Morrissey nomination; if he expected that, he must have expected more, judging by the rocks and bottles the faintest of whispers concerning a judgeship for Frank Morrissey had years before brought down on the Kennedy administration. As early as 1961, pinched between the cravings of Morrissey and the wishes of the financier himself, Robert Kennedy as attorney general had requested of the American Bar Association an "informal" investigation of the fitness of Francis Xavier Morrissey for a seat on the Massachusetts federal district bench.

Robert Meserve, a prominent attorney in the Boston area and board member of the ABA's Committee on the Federal Judiciary, hadn't needed to ask around long before submitting his appraisal: Morrissey was "not qualified." As Albert Jenner was to recollect at the 1965 hearing, despite Meserve's finding, the U.S. attorney general returned to the ABA "within a very few months" to request a final investigation. The investigation "in depth" was undertaken, in detail; the conclusions were equally detailed: ". . . it was found that Judge Morrissey was lacking in intellectual capacity to become an efficient judge of the U.S. district court . . . he was lacking in scholarship and legal knowledge; he lacked . . . legal experience, trial practice, and general practice of the law" to qualify him for inclusion on a federal bench whose decisions ramified very often high-court points of interpretation and rough-cutting of important jurisprudential doctrines. Morrissey was a stiff, a cheerful flunky whose greatest accomplishment had been to hold Joe Kennedy's coat.

As early as 1961 the working press of Massachusetts—its collective nose bobbing along the spoor of a payoff as juicy as elevating Frank Morrissey— was already howling. "There had been a rumor of a judgeship for Morrissey anyhow," recalls the inquisitive Robert Healy, who was himself still running the Globe's Washington Bureau at that time, "and then we heard about an FBI check, so we went ahead and put through a biography of Morrissey that kicked his balls off. Pretty soon we got word from the White House that it wasn't going to happen. Then, just before JFK died, word came up again through Bobby that he was working on both Teddy and Bobby, claiming, you know, 'Your father promised me this before he went into deep shock . . .' Then, in November of 1963, there was a going-away party at the White House for Dick Donahue, an ex–White House Assistant, and the matter came up, and Bobby came up to me and what he said gave me an indication that they might still put the name in . . ." Then John Kennedy was assassinated in Dallas; Frank Morrissey's persistent judicial daydreams evaporated.

Two rounds within two years of disdainful sniffs at the prospect of Morrissey on the federal bench? The very fact that the Kennedys continued to pick away at the idea, showily ignoring every canon of workaday politics, suggests that to them, too, by this time, this matter of elevating the unsquelchable municipal jurist was surfacing deep, buried emotions. Ted Kennedy in particular, who had by no means forgotten that bleak autumn and early winter of 1961–62, when the reception within even his own family to the idea of a seat for *him* in the Senate wasn't arousing much enthusiasm—Teddy hadn't forgotten the way the chipper, enthusiastic municipal judge ushered him around the parish parlors and in and out the basement clubhouse doors where the husky novice could make the contacts that produced a Massachusetts political organization of his own.

Ted had remained well aware of Morrissey's years of scrambling in the

Massachusetts political shadows, first as a Welfare Department social worker, then in the Department of Corrections, then—his Massachusetts bar exam passed finally after sixteen years of disheartening patchwork study—his emergence as a lacky of the financier while doubling as an unabashed political errand runner first for Governor Tobin and after that for Congressman and Senator John F. Kennedy. The strain and abuse undergone throughout a life like this touched Edward Kennedy, initiated a wave of street-corner fellow feeling just as it had in the plain-spoken financier. More, Dad wanted this.

The legal establishment was down on Morrissey largely because he was "shanty Irish," the Kennedys flared publicly; their determination deepened. Frank Morrissey, for all his unexpurgated poor-boy Charlestown bleat, his need to soft-soap and trim and exaggerate—Frank had been an asset, he had been loyal and available and, always, "one of our own." Himself a loyalist, he had discovered and pushed forward other loyalists from Gerry Doherty to David Harrison, who helped make sure Ted Kennedy was able to maintain a grip he trusted on the Democratic Party all over the Commonwealth.

In sum, the Kennedys owed Morrissey. They intended to recommend his appointment, at least go that far, whether Judge Wyzanski, or the snobs at Harvard Law, or the editorialists at the *Globe*, or the mandarins on the executive committee of anybody's bar association liked it or not. They had been poorly advised before; Ted Kennedy couldn't help remembering the way the same crowd had massed to spout polysyllables and float rumors when his own dubious hopes first surfaced.

In fact, district court benches all over the country were heavy-burdened with political appointees a good deal less world-wise—less law-wise—than Francis X. Morrissey. In mid-July Edward Kennedy himself had sat through two days of perfunctory hearings into the fitness of James P. Coleman, ex-Governor of Mississippi, for a seat on that prestigious and—to the Justice Department—troublesome Deep South Fifth Circuit Court of Appeals. Coleman, an urbane segregationist, had justified his entire political career by citing his skill at circumventing the intent of federal court rulings. "Any legislature can pass an act faster than the Supreme Court can erase it" had been Coleman's most serviceable quotation. But Coleman had marched Mississippi into the Atlantic City convention foursquare for Lyndon Baines Johnson, and the newly elected president, like the Kennedys, understood when a favor was due.

Jim Coleman, of course, had been without any question Lyndon B. Johnson's choice. Recommending Frank Morrissey had been a gesture, a handful of patronage thrown to the earnest young senator who had guided his immigration bill through the Senate with such a precocious touch. That, or something this Borgia of a president, impatient with an unnecessary poll-tax battle the ever-suspicious Chief Executive had regarded as a "Kennedy-Johnson test of strength," handed to the Kennedy brothers to slow them down.

One off-the-record comment by an aide very close to Ted Kennedy just then underlines the president's motivation: "For the most part most of the staff guys were not involved. It was largely a personal fight. It's my understanding that the Morrissey proposal was on the president's desk a long time. It's not my understanding that the president was bombarded with calls to push it. We had assumed all along that the president had his own political fish to fry in Massachusetts. The—remember?—the way the president called a special press conference to announce the nomination? You know, that's very unusual . . ."

Another aide, Charlie Tretter, a Boston lawyer on Ted Kennedy's payroll whose days and nights throughout the weeks just then coming up were to be frenzied with the effort to gift-wrap Frank Morrissey for his Washington delivery, remembers hearing the news on his car radio. "I was driving down the street one Sunday and I heard that Johnson had submitted the nomination. I couldn't believe it. It was out of . . . nowhere, nobody around the office had ever discussed the idea . . ."

Whatever his motivation, the president delivered the Morrissey nomination over to the Junior Senator from Massachusetts that fateful late-September Sunday; Kennedy swallowed, hard. There are precautions a sponsoring legislator can take in the case of chancy appointments, and all these Edward Kennedy took. "Ted sure as hell worked his ass off with those other senators on that one," an aide remembers. "He was all over the Hill trying to get advance commitments from people, trying to hold people . . ." Leverett Saltonstall was, as virtually always, his agreeable, unprotesting self and, as the Senior Senator from Massachusetts, filed his necessary "no objection" well enough ahead of time to give Kennedy that much to talk up with other moderates—many of whom were starting to get a little anxious, what with the heavier and heavier background barrage of unfavorable publicity and such an unexpected onset of unhappy constituent mail.

By early October the general publication of a bitterly upset letter from Judge Wyzanski, the presiding judge on the district bench to which Morrissey aspired, dragged into the open the widespread displeasure among Massachusetts lawyers at the prospect of Morrissey's elevation. It was an issue that all but wrote editorials for itself: Where were the self-consciously high-minded Kennedys, whose brother the president, signing the Omnibus Judges' Act in 1961, had emphasized his intention to choose "men of unquestioned ability"?

More fearful day by day that he was setting himself up, Edward Kennedy "took the opportunity to go around and talk to three of the judges of the [Massachusetts District] Court, that knew Morrissey, to see whether he could handle it," Kennedy told me afterwards. "They indicated to me that it was their belief that he could. Not that he was going to be distinguished, but Morrissey certainly deserved better than he received at the hands of Jenner and the Bar Association."

Morrissey's appearance before the Judiciary Subcommittee that was to review his credentials and recommend to the Senate itself on the appointment was scheduled for October 12. The little group worrying the prospect through decided first to try to spruce the intellectually plain Morrissey up somehow, "brief" him, in more or less the way the Kennedys were wont to undergo briefing, through a combination of grilling and heckling, to prepare him emotionally for the Subcommittee pummeling itself.

The ineffable Milton S. Gwirtzman—thirty-two at the time but involved with close-quarter strategy and research since, as a schoolboy, he wrote campaign speeches for Harry S. Truman and later tuned up John F. Kennedy before the Nixon debates—soon found himself locked up in a hotel room attempting somehow to insinuate an awareness of the political dangers Morrissey faced into the always-cheery little ward politician. The entire exercise was very like a Japanese Zen Master trying to explicate the spiritual implications of the asanas to a more-than-willing basset hound.

Gwirtzman conveys through implication—there is a saying among Kennedy people that Milton is somebody "you can see only if you believe in him." One of Milton's talents was with nostalgic phrasemaking, not really the sort of language anybody would believe coming out of Frank Morrissey.

Afterwards, Gwirtzman caught more elbows than he deserved because of the Morrissey incident; another Kennedy aide remembers Milton's murmurs, the Monday word of the appointment descended on the senator's office, "that this was going to be a hard thing to sell." Others, like Al Novak, freshly hired and about to share much of the Morrissey duty too, commented to the effect that, after all, the Southerners always seemed to be running one stiff or another through, so there shouldn't be that much of a problem . . .

"Morrissey's crime was that he was a small-time coat holder," David Burke observed later in that nervous mournful bass of his, the intonation of a man who has learned more than he cares to admit, and suspects the rest. "It was nobody's fault that in the wheels of history he was caught in the gears——."

And indeed the dreaded moment came soon enough when Morrissey, briefed and buffed up and as well put together as anybody could arrange, arrived finally at the Capitol. And for a day or two it looked as if the Kennedys' longstanding bantam retainer, with his waxen dark hair and apple cheeks and ever-ready smile and black shoes wonderfully polished—as if . . . maybe . . . conceivably, the Morrissey appointment was a pushover. Jim Doyle of *The Boston Globe*'s Washington office barely made the edition with a back-page piece headlined SENATE EXPECTED TO APPROVE MORRISSEY'S NOMINATION WITHOUT DISSENT.

Morrissey's primary exposure came early, on October 12, before the Special Subcommittee on the Nomination, first session; beneath the unblinking lights, the little police court judge from Charlestown couldn't seem to prevent himself, steadily and horrifyingly, from melting. With the kindly disposed Tom Dodd chairing what was certainly to develop into Francis X. Morrissey's longest day, the initial hour or so of testimony seemed to open auspiciously. Edward Kennedy delivered a full, resounding presentation of the virtues of his hard-working selection, paving his introduction with a list of no fewer than fifty Massachusetts judges and statements from a horde of legal and educational and banking and business notables, every one of whom seemed eager to attest to Morrissey's courtesy, his geniality, his personal morals, and his upright character.

The rest of his time Kennedy spent spiking the opposing guns and rigging his own defenses: He pointed out percentage parallels between the contract and tort cases Morrissey had been hearing as an inhabitant of the municipal bench and those he would quite soon be hearing, presumably, as a district judge; solemnly, Kennedy laid emphasis on his statement that Morrissey "has been a practicing attorney for fourteen years and a judge for seven. As a judge he has never been overruled by a higher tribunal."

Kennedy was openly willing to "concede that Judge Morrissey has not had experience in antitrust cases . . . I admit that he has not presided over patent or copyright cases," and quoted Judge Simon Rifkind's comment that ". . . every judge who comes to the court must necessarily learn a number of branches of the law to which he has not been previously exposed."

Yet somehow it came as a surprise, provided a momentary thrill and a sense that something was coming that would be . . . dramatic, out-of-the-ordinary, when, within moments, the Republican on the three-man reviewing group, Minority Leader Everett Dirksen, sidled up to Edward Kennedy and, indifferently almost but terrifyingly, began to stick his quill into the sorest imaginable places:

"Senator Kennedy, you mention that experience is one of those things that can be acquired as time goes on. Do you regard the federal court as an in-training course where you train after you are appointed?"

"My statement," Kennedy began, shrugging despite himself, "was concerned with . . . the type of caseload that that court handles . . . this background . . . extremely useful and important to the Federal bar——."

"Under Massachusetts law," rejoined Dirksen, "does this court have the jurisdiction to try jury cases?"

"No."

"I have noticed you mentioned a number of endorsements from various bar associations; do you have a bar association in Massachusetts?"

Senator Kennedy: "That is correct."

Senator Dirksen: "Namely, the Boston bar?"

There is the Massachusetts Bar Association, Kennedy explains, and the Boston Bar Association. When Dirksen asks which is larger Kennedy stresses that the Massachusetts Bar Association, which has reversed itself since 1963 and now favors the appointment, "more broadly reflects the jurisdiction of the Federal district court."

But, Dirksen points out, with Morrissey's being a Boston municipal judge, "The members of the Boston bar . . . would naturally be expected to know him better than those around the State . . . How," Dirksen seems barely curious, "do you account for the fact that he was not endorsed by the Boston Bar Association?"

Kennedy prefers to "let those who are here representing it respond to that. I am not prepared to answer that."

Dirksen's delicate and colloquial cross-examination has already worked its damages; there are already welts on Kennedy's presentation swelling it out of shape, noticeable places where doubts can gather. Dirksen very wisely says nothing while John McCormack, ever a Kennedy reliable, makes an unusual appearance on the Senate side of the Hill to urge Morrissey's selection primarily because he is a man whose "family life is exemplary . . . a gentleman in every respect of the word." McCormack seems to feel that the important objection to Morrissey's candidacy lies in the fact that he on several occasions flunked the Massachusetts bar examination; he refers to his own trepidation more than forty years earlier, his astounded relief subsequently.

Once the venerable McCormack is out of the way Dirksen moves in again immediately. The next witness is Robert Sullivan, an associate justice of the Massachusetts Superior Court. Dirksen first satisfies himself that in Massachusetts the Superior Court falls between the State Supreme Court and the lower district and municipal courts. Sullivan describes Morrissey as cautious and fair on the bench and describes his jurisdiction as effectively unlimited in civil cases and encompassing all criminal proceedings involving misdemeanors and felonies where the maximum penalty does not exceed five years. In addition, more serious felonies receive probable cause hearings to determine whether to bind them over to a grand jury.

This seemed an enormous mandate; Dirksen proceeds to constrict it. His questions soon established that if a defendant demanded a jury trial he could not be tried in the municipal court and that a great many of the sessions of the municipal court have mostly to do with trivial concerns, like assigning fines for parking tickets. By now others among the senators are on to the direction of things: Senator Quentin Burdick of North Dakota pushes Sullivan to admit that, as respects appeals, most of the criminal court appeals are on driving-under-the-influence charges; where the charge is serious defendants request and automatically receive a first hearing in the state Superior Court. By now a strong point Kennedy has made for his nominee, that none of his decisions had ever been overturned on appeal, fades, all but disappears.

Word has already begun to leak back to the office that Dirksen had Bernie Segal, who handled the investigations of the [American] Bar Association, poking around all over the place, into everything. Before Albert Jenner of the ABA was even properly into his thunderous indictment of Morrissey's legal competence, Everett Dirksen has picked him up on an apparently minor point, to which he must himself have been tipped off in advance. Jenner had just referred a bit loftily to the diploma of graduation Morrissey had got in September of 1933 from "a law school called the Southern Law School which had been authorized by the Supreme Court of Georgia to issue diplomas on study of law" during a period Morrissey was "a resident of and living in Boston."

"Mr. Jenner," Dirksen interjected theatrically, "I wonder if you would stop at that point."

"I would like to know a little more about this Southern Law School at Athens, Georgia."

Under examination it turned out that Morrissey had, on September 8, 1933, formally petitioned to practice law in the Northern District Court of the State of Georgia, on the basis of having been admitted, if newly, to the

Georgia bar, and professing himself at the time an attorney at law, practicing in the Georgia court. Dirksen recurred to his well-practiced tone of orotund surprise at Morrissey's overnight appearance among Georgia's barristers, compounded by his astonishment that "the next day" Morrissey had returned to Massachusetts.

The afternoon deepened. Subcommittee Chairman Dodd, openly out to help Kennedy, ventured a defense of Morrissey by mentioning other municipal judges who had proved fine federal judges, other ABA rejects who worked out.

But Dirksen wasn't ready to move on: "Before you get too far away from it. If you allege that you live in one state for the purpose of being admitted to the state bar, when in fact you are not, there is a rather unpleasant word for that, as you know. I will not use it, but it bothers me a little."

"It bothers me, Senator," Segal, who knew his lines, jumped in to agree. "It bothers me."

By the time the frazzled Francis Morrissey himself, after a day of listening to his entire experience in life pulled like so much jurisprudential taffy, got the opportunity to speak for himself, Everett McKinley Dirksen had already vanished. Kennedy and company had urged Morrissey to remain as courteous and helpful to his interlocutors as he could possibly be; oozing gratitude like perspiration, Morrissey crawled. Dirksen had so red-penciled and underlined and scrawled question marks in the margin of Morrissey's spotty legal background, and especially the episode in Georgia, that he himself seemed to feel compelled to elaborate on that: After the unavoidable reference to his eleven brothers and sisters and his return, "without any judgment, I suppose, to . . . evening law school at Boston College," he indicated how it was that he met "Charles Crowley, who was ten years older than I was, who suggested that I could go down to Georgia and there take an intensive review in the Southern Law School . . . Now, I have said, Senator, that I showed poor judgment at that particular age. Perhaps I did not show proper maturity."

"How old were you?" Chairman Eastland asked, following Dirksen's well-smashed-down route.

"Now, I had never placed any weight on the degree . . . nor did I try in any way, if I understood the very able and fine men who appeared before me in the opposition this afternoon, to try and get into the practice of law in Massachusetts on a reciprocal arrangement . . . I was there about three months in Athens . . ." Morrissey followed with his repeated later attempts to learn the law, prompted by his "burning desire" to become an attorney, of which he had been reminded by "that fine presentation of Mister Segal." Perhaps no man ever skinned in public so admired his executioners' technique with a blade.

But his questions were after the hard information itself, sadly: Here Morrissey's certainty wavered, his total stay in Georgia, he thought, had amounted to "a little less than a year or about a year," begun in June of 1933. This shortened itself on Senator Tydings's inquiry to "about nine months"; after Southern Law Morrissey and the very fine Mister Crowley had allegedly gone to Atlanta, tried to get work, and engaged in "some part-time selling." The hearing ended at 6 PM with Morrissey requesting, and receiving permission, to "kindly express" his sincerest appreciations all around.

The sparks flying up from the Morrissey hearings drove the whole affair the top of the headlines at a time when the reformist flagship *New York Times* had just resumed going to press after a twenty-five-day strike. Dirksen now deliberately permitted himself to surface as the central antagonist of the appointment: Support for his opposition within his own party now became crucial if he wanted to continue to lead its legislative wing. He was angling for a vote of confidence.

Dirksen needed one just then. From across his badly shattered party following the 1964 landslide against Goldwater, the Republican Minority Leader heard squawks that he was becoming the thumb to Lyndon Johnson's forefinger as bill after bill of progressive legislation—the Civil Rights Bill, Medicare, the voting-rights legislation, the War on Poverty—got plucked out of the dead-letter file of committee lockup and hurried now from stage to stage toward nerve-racking quick passage. Was Dirksen a patsy? Conservative doubts were gathering

It had been an unconscionably long time between kills for the heavily outnumbered Minority Leader by late in 1965. Accordingly, still playing the Cowardly Lion, Dirksen opened his famous rubber mouth to its utmost extent; the ever-accommodating Morrissey, the lamb of Boston Harbor, walked in as requested and curled up, baaing.

What constituted his day-by-day experience on the municipal bench, Dirksen now inquired of Morrissey. Prodded, Morrissey admitted that "my real experience has been very limited," mostly "driving under the influence . . . simple assault and battery and shoplifting and leaving the scene . . . Now, on the civil side . . . building law violations . . ."

> *Dirksen:* "So practically all of your trial experience has been on minor felonies and misdemeanors . . ."
>
> *Morrissey:* "Well, I would say that was a fair statement."

Dirksen: "Yes. And if there were civil cases, they were rather inconsequential? . . ."

Morrissey: "I would say that was a fair statement."

Dirksen continued to epitomize Morrissey's inconsequential career on the bench, and Morrissey continued to agree that he was being awfully fair about the thing. Finally, the Judiciary Committee voted on whether to recommend Morrissey's appointment. The vote was yes, 9–3, but a significant seven members of the committee, including such reliable allies of the Kennedys as Joseph Tydings, were conspicuously absent that afternoon and remain unrecorded. Francis X. Morrissey was the first to emerge from a get-together in Dirksen's office in his honor; the TV cameramen and reporters shoved a mike under his nose and Morrissey—exhausted, ripped, his psychological innards hanging around his knees—made a good-tempered, short statement announcing that he had "no ill feeling towards anyone."

Even then the expectation was general that enough Kennedy support survived in the Senate to drag the amiable retainer through. Then, precisely when he needed to have it most, the embarrassingly committed Everett Dirksen caught a break. Bob Healy, back home to serve as the political editor in the editorial offices of *The Boston Globe*, who had been working through the hearing record minutely and considering—not happily—the prospect of Frank Morrissey on the federal bench, got a telephone tip from a minor pol in South Boston, a hanger-on who happened to remember a typically abrasive exchange between Frank Morrissey and his then-employer, John F. Kennedy. Somebody had asked the ever-amiable Morrissey why he himself had never run for office; Morrissey was expatiating to the effect that he had done so many things, been so busy, etc., that there just had not been either the time or the opportunity——. JFK cut him off: "Frank, you're a liar and you know it. You ran in 1934, you received a total of 427 votes, and you were 14th in a field of 16."

Healy's quick excitable yapping laugh at just that moment must have filled the newsroom. Healy hated the idea of promoting Morrissey all along, and had in fact flown to Washington as soon as the news of Morrissey's appointment had come to the *Globe* out of Katzenbach's office, and sat down with Ted Kennedy on a bench in the Senate Cloakroom. He told the senator, who heard him out, glum and silent—it had been Healy, after all, who shaped the cheating-scandal publicity that almost finished Ted's original Senate campaign—that the *Globe* intended definitely to fight the nomination; still, until his tip came there was very little Healy could really do.

He now checked closely, and had within hours come up with documentation of the fact that in 1934, during a period that overlapped the months
in which Morrissey had sworn himself to be a resident of Georgia, he had
also run for the Massachusetts State Legislature from Ward 2 in Charlestown and accordingly sworn himself to be from January 1, 1934, a legal resident there. Peeling away at Morrissey's résumé, Healy, who was to receive
a Pulitzer Prize for his concentration, next discovered that the "evening law
school at Boston College," which Morrissey had testified to having attended
in 1932–1933, hadn't actually existed; no prelaw courses had been offered at
the Extension School during those early years.

Once this was front page news there was no expectation anymore among
even the most unseasoned of Kennedy's aides of picking the Morrissey
appointment off the hearing-room floor. Few senators were going to get away
unrecorded on this issue. Southerners, even certain Republicans whom the
Kennedys sometimes had shown a quiet knack for reaching—very few were
inclined to pay the cost.

The bedridden President Johnson, recuperating from his gallbladder
operation at Bethesda Hospital and watching with mixed emotions his nominee taking unprecedented abuse from the bar association and the Republicans and, more and more, moderates in his own party, was now boxed in.
Nicholas Katzenbach, who had himself originally attempted to persuade
Edward Kennedy not to push for the Morrissey nomination, lunched with
him that Friday, October 15, and divulged the results of a quickie FBI check
on Morrissey's 1934 whereabouts. By this time, rambling around the subject
with reporters, the Minority Leader was sliding out, one after the next, hints
about what was yet to come that were gummy with innuendo. Queried about
a floor fight, he explained that "I have some ideas, but I will not prophesy.
I will have something to say." "I have my lines out, I'm trying to promote
something," he confided by the end of the week.

Kennedy returned early the following week to discover that his docile
fellow senator from the Mother Commonwealth, Leverett Saltonstall, was
suddenly getting starchy about the Morrissey appointment, had publicly
withdrawn his "no objection," citing "doubts about the accuracy of the judge's
testimony" and trusting that "the matter will be referred back to the Judiciary
Committee." The politically initiated around Massachusetts began to speculate aloud, and correctly, that Saltonstall would not be running for another
Senate term in 1966.

Any hope of "riding this right through" disappeared. Kennedy, who had
not known anything in advance about the Georgia conflicts, now based his

pleas among the colleagues on the complete exoneration the upcoming FBI check of Morrissey's whereabouts was expected to provide. That embattled formal report, a copy of which the increasingly desperate Kennedy sent to each of his colleagues along with his own supercharged defense of his nominee, indicated that the FBI was able to corroborate Morrissey's presence in Georgia at least from June through September of 1933, treated Morrissey's demonstrable registration as a voter in Massachusetts during the period as more or less customary among out-of-state students, and slipped back and forth apparently without specifics over Morrissey's 1934 candidacy for the Massachusetts legislature. Healy had gotten it right.

"Probably no judicial nomination has created such agitation in the press since the leaders of the American Bar Association opposed the nomination of Justice Brandeis to the Supreme Court," Kennedy wrote—inaccurately—to his colleagues. "We cannot permit the Senate's role in confirming Judicial appointments to be turned into an instrument of character assassination of decent and able men." Kennedy was nose-counting, ferociously, "collecting all his [political] coupons . . . and writing quite a few new ones. Don't ask me why, but he is," a well-placed Senate source revealed; noses were blinking out like defective Christmas tree lights.

The central problem now, of course, was not so much with what Morrissey was not, did wrong, fudged, hadn't had trial experience with, as with what he indeed, indisputably, was. A "veteran Boston politician" was quoted in the papers as having compared Morrissey with Ditto Boland, the "jovial ward-heeler" of Edwin O'Connor's *The Last Hurrah*, "except that, on reflection, Ditto had more on the ball." As to the possibility of Morrissey's withdrawing on his own, to help the Kennedys off the hotspot, ". . . that's not Frank Morrissey," the veteran had observed.

This sense of Morrissey personally, the artificially hearty toady to an improper ambition, was certain to repel the better-groomed colleagues. Extra-genial, too accommodating; nominating Morrissey amounted ultimately to a sop to the imprisoned Ambassador. The Kennedys, all the Kennedys, saw all the limitations attached to the little judge. But they saw more, understood his limited hopes, his lifelong dream. Their sympathies went deeper than repayment or noblesse.

With neither side all that sure as to where a floor fight would take the voting, the actual vote, scheduled for Tuesday, October 19, got pushed back session by session. By Wednesday it was apparent that Ted Kennedy couldn't run the usual pattern of salesmanship crisscrossed by finesses alone; Hubert Humphrey attempted to lobby. Katzenbach organized a telephone campaign.

The Kennedys' own marvelous shadow-apparatus went overnight into Red Alert: senators who had made clear their inclination to vote against the nominee found major fund raisers and political fixers in their own districts calling in to divulge their urgent concern that Frank Morrissey receive his place on the bench.

And now, inevitably, Bobby stepped in. Until the vote was pending Bobby had remained conspicuously uninvolved, word already having been spread around that, as attorney general, he was influential in blocking Judge Morrissey's appointment to the longed-for federal judgeship in 1961, when the seat first fell vacant and when that first bruiting-about of Frank's name took place. Having answered a 1:30 PM call to Humphrey's Senate offices, Edward met Robert and the two of them arrived shortly in Everett Dirksen's hideout.

The large very visible holes in the Katzenbach-FBI report, to which the widely read hearing testimony as well as *The Washington Post* had drawn exceptionally close attention, left it flopping and sputtering all over the Chamber of the Senate like a leaking balloon; Representative H.R. Gross labeled it a desecration of the good name of the FBI and "an absurd interpretation." Dirksen had earlier, and convincingly, denigrated the brief for Morrissey as a "confession and avoidance," a "legal plea where you confess and at the same time you avoid . . . it did not add up to much." Most colleagues agreed.

Doors closed, Dirksen was uncommonly to the point. "I'm not interested in you or Teddy," he told Robert bluntly enough, "but I'm out to get Morrissey. You think I'm out to cut your neck—to ax you." He pointed to the bust of JFK. "You see that bust on the mantle? That was one of the best friends I ever had." A few minutes later, chewing the Illinois fat with reporters, Dirksen was to let slip the hint of a "bombshell" he was holding in reserve in case of need; asked about that the following day he remarked, with calculated blankness, that he was "just a country lawyer, but when I prepare a case I try to get everything."

One of the things Dirksen's research had been thoroughgoing enough to get him was a clipping from a 1961 Italian newspaper that noted, somewhere on its yellowed society pages, a larky little luncheon party in Capri composed of Frank Morrissey, Edward Kennedy, and a deported Italo-American gangster, Michael Spinella. In fact, the congenitally friendly judge had allegedly, in all innocence, struck up a casual momentary acquaintance with his fellow American, invited him to lunch, and forgotten the incident a day or two afterwards: trussed together with half-explicit allegations of undiscovered Kennedy-Mafia relationships, it was material guaranteed to blister tabloid headlines for months and months. Edward Kennedy knew—and Bobby knew much better—that an explicit and protracted investigation of the decades of cross-connection between the Ambassador and organized crime in America could dynamite all their dreams.

At the time, hating as he did to be coerced or threatened, Bobby refused to renege on Morrissey; the brothers left soberly and hashed the political consequences of the whole affair over together for the rest of the afternoon and evening. They had no easy choice, and they both knew it. That evening Ted called Jim Eastland, Thomas Dodd, and—it was approaching midnight—Lyndon Johnson at Bethesda.

Thus, Ted Kennedy's famous speech that Thursday in executive session on the Senate floor was anticlimactic. Just before he withdrew the nomination he informed Dirksen of what he was about. Teddy delivered the speech itself—with its Gwirtzman-crafted, choked-up references to Morrissey as one of twelve children of a dockworker whose "old shoes [were] held together with wooden pegs their father made"—as a Hail and Farewell brief in behalf of this horribly pounded family loyalist. "I would want any nominee of mine to be confirmed on a record clear and complete enough so that any fairminded person, after study, would conclude from the record that the judge has the necessary integrity and qualifications . . ."

And that ended that. Kennedy saved what face he could by repeatedly insisting that, had the matter come to a show of votes, he definitely would have had enough. Nobody will ever know; the fact is, that morning there were fourteen absentees, all Democrats, including such Kennedy regulars as Church, Bayh, and McGovern; all Dirksen's troops showed. Relief at Kennedy's decision was, of course, widespread: For or against Morrissey, absent or present, anybody involved would suffer some kind of serious political damage. The buzzwords that session were "judgment" and "statesmanship." "It takes something for a young man to subdue his pride," Everett Dirksen rumbled with all the equanimity of the mature predator whose appetite has at last been satisfied. "It doesn't bother an old bastard like me. But in a young man it takes courage."

Mercifully, that same afternoon Kennedy left on his already delayed inspection tour of the refugee camps in Vietnam; if his good humor had been abraded for the moment, it repaired itself by the time his aide, Charlie Tretter, drove him to the airport. "For Christ's sake," he opened after a short, brooding delay. "Can't you get this thing going any faster?"

Tretter pointed out that he was already going a hundred miles an hour.

"Charlie," Kennedy woke up to observe as they reached the approaches to Dulles, "I hope you never put me through this when I try and make you a federal judge." Tretter had flunked his bar exam the first time around. "I can see myself now: 'Why *shouldn't* Charlie Tretter be a federal judge . . . ?'"

When Kennedy got back from Southeast Asia, Vietnam had already assumed a size, a moral meaning, that softened and shrank much of what had happened earlier. He had read—and talked with—the prescient French journalist Bernard Fall, who chronicled the French collapse in Vietnam and predicted the American. The sort of considerations that would have concerned his father—was this thing manageable, did we have accurate intelligence, what would we have to pay to offset the costs?—had started to bother him. And on the ground? The thousands and thousands of refugees?

Not that Kennedy had forgotten anything or anybody back home. During his first return trip to Boston after that he took the trouble to book a very conspicuous table for himself, right in the middle of the Parker House dining room, and there took Municipal Judge Francis X. Morrissey to lunch.

CHAPTER VII

Teddy and Bob—Part Two

1. A Sniffer for Issues

Locked as securely as he himself could arrange inside Edward Kennedy floor strategist, and Edward Kennedy diligent bland Child of the Senate who does his extra-credit reading, and Edward Kennedy worrier over the worldwide unprotected—inside this array of personae all taking their public places slowly, there comes the dazzle and report sometimes, like lightning through the bars, of unchanging old Teddy Kennedy the Kid.

Something about the Kid is ageless—not immature, ageless—and appears unalloyed most often when Kennedy is off duty for a couple of hours, playing games or drinking or dropped out of view and perhaps a bit desperate in his way for the chance to blow off the sours and stinks of too many committee sessions, give his sequestered daemon a helluva lungful.

Chance-taking appears a necessity. "As a sailor Ted is a real Captain Bligh," a neighbor who sails with him observed. "Joey Gargan is usually the chief member of his crew, and they then pick some unfortunate—and he is an unfortunate—and from the time you leave the dock until the race is over it is one constant harassment. Ted's very aggressive—get the jib, get that up, where are the charts? Look OUT! Move over . . . He seems to want to sail it all by himself. The air is a little blue, the language a little rough.

"Actually, Joey is a better sailor, he knows how to handle a boat, other people better. Ted is more daring, he'll take the chance in a particular situation where Joey won't——."

Kennedy cousin Joe Gargan. Joey Gargan in middle-manhood, grown up but still the half-preoccupied relative in the family business whose responsibilities seem to exceed the information he has. Who formed the habit long ago without being told of sitting in one of the outer rooms during one of the important planning sessions, hearing out Jack Crimmins's foulmouthed complaints, running the significant errands. Bareheaded always—the eternal Almost-Kennedy, a lawyer by profession though favoring the long black overcoat of the Operative, his head carried a little bit distractedly to one side . . .

Joe Gargan is a gentleman. He adores Ted Kennedy; Teddy, for his part, obviously reciprocates, in part by making an unusual effort, when Joey is around, to exemplify that decisiveness, toughness, courage, determination that Joe Gargan looks for in the authentic Kennedys . . .

If, between Ted Kennedy and Joey Gargan, there is this need to play to each other with something inherently competitive, something that bruises in its odd rough Irish tenderness, one senses in Kennedy's own by then twelve-year-old marriage nothing very much like this. What problems there are, reduced finally, appear to owe their tensions and consequences to uncommunicated matters, lacks. There is a Perfect Escort quality about the public attention Ted Kennedy pays to his wife, the emptiness of which, one suspects, carries into their rare private moments. From the beginning of their marriage Kennedy has suggested to his bride that she go ahead and pick decor and color schemes and architectural details she likes for the Squaw Island and Charles River Square and Georgetown and McLean residences: He won't be around that much.

In McLean he authorizes the construction, under the guidance of society architect Jack Warnecke, of a 12,500-square-foot residence off the Potomac on Chain Bridge Road, where different decorators had furnished different sections. The bedroom suite offered a den as well as separate bedrooms and dressing areas. Under the same roof, they were leading separate lives. Apart from the weakness for alcohol that had bedeviled her parents, "Joan was private, contemplative, and artistic," Kennedy would explain in his memoirs, "while I was public, political, and on the go . . . We remained together for many years longer than we were happy . . ."

Whether in person or in spirit, Kennedy has been in and out; even when he's there so many, many evenings go into his slow, frowning perusals of the contents of The Bag, into sessions of dictation to Angelique Voutselas that fill the hours until bedtime.

Instead of any dependable routine his days tend to fall into a series of episodes: He may come home late after a late meeting in the office, eat quickly, and drop in at a party for a few hours of high jinks and excited fun and a good many drinks sometimes, then leave without ado at ten or eleven and turn up shortly in his office or at home to put in a last couple of hours with some experts or an aide who a few minutes before found himself climbing back into his clothes an hour after he'd gone to bed.

For long periods Kennedy may get to sleep at any hour; by five or six, restless, he is up to hear the earliest newscast and perhaps telephone another aide to check back on something he has seen in the early editions of the Boston papers. After weeks or months of this he tends to wear himself down and sleep, eat, drink wherever he finds himself: Transatlantic aircraft are a favorite place to doze off for five or six straight hours, often beside his exasperated wife, who has been waiting months for the chance simply to talk with her overscheduled husband.

So that a great deal of her life is necessarily a lonely thing for Joan Kennedy, a lot of missing Ted. Her music, the piano-playing with which she disciplines herself very seriously, takes up a lot of her energies, and tennis, and of course the children, and domestic responsibilities that include a household staff and keeping the checkbook straight. Little by little, even through the most Pollyannaish of magazine interviews, hollows give back echoes. "He expressed his appreciation for what I'd done in one sentence. But what he said meant— 'I'm so glad you performed; you did something on your own; you did a professional job,'" Joan tells a reporter, who writes it up along with all the other quotations. "I cherish my girlfriends more than I ever did . . . These friends to whom I can and do tell almost everything. Most of them are friends from my days at Manhattanville College," she tells another. Into the exurban New York/Birthday Party uptips of her phrasings a husky throatiness, something tear-soaked, now darkens her beautiful musician's tones.

The second half of the sixties are by no means the best years for any of the Kennedys. "You can tell when either of the Kennedys has been drinking a lot," somebody who knows them both well observes. "Their faces get awfully puffy." "Now we know our good and bad traits; we have seen one another at rock bottom," Joan confided, candor still her touchstone.

Ted is naturally gargantuan when he lets himself loosen up, gets a little cocky; there is the fireworks of nerves discharging. It doesn't show up much in the news photos yet, but on close inspection there is something alarmingly overblown, taurine about his appearance these days: the blood-flagged whites of his eyes, the mottled swollen cheeks. He betrays the desperation of the Minotaur, frustrated, imprisoned in his labyrinthine schedule.

With a tendency to put on weight anyway, he loves to eat, defiantly. "He spends a great deal of time worrying about his weight, usually while he's eating ice cream," observes his ever-piquant mother. These years he often has, close up, the out-of-sorts ectoplasmic look of the fourth-grade fat boy too slow for kick-the-can. "Isn't there another course, a dessert of some kind?" he asks his wife rather pointedly when associates are around one Sunday night.

"*Pamplemousse, s'il vous plait,*" Joan suggests to Andree, onetime cook for the Duchess of Windsor and Mr. and Mrs. Joseph P. Kennedy, whom the financier took pains specifically to present to the Edward Kennedy household.

"What's *pamplemousse?*"

"Grapefruit," Joan breathes.

"No, no, haven't you got cake of some kind, with some sort of ice cream, chocolate chip?"

The emotional effect of all this on Kennedy, into whose makeup plays so much of the self-awareness of the natural actor with much of the actor's vanity, leads to recurrent episodes of unadmitted discouragement. Something is wrong, unfulfilled, for each of them that neither can quite identify. Upbeat as she consistently attempts to be, stubbornly attending the Senate galleries for all Ted's important speeches, Joan Kennedy still has that schoolgirl frankness to her as well; Kennedy's tendency to wander off verbally sometimes, meander into abstracted phrasemaking, throws Joan off. "I'm his worst critic," she admits to an interviewer. "I'm always after him to put his thoughts in human terms, because if he can't make *me* understand, who will?"

Certainly there are times, periods, when things seem stymied, during which there are new friends, newly impressed, surprised and flattered to find behind such a famous name somebody so alert and at the same time boyish, puckish, fun-loving . . . "You know you look just like Senator Kennedy," says a woman whose suitcase is so heavy that she has been kicking it ahead of herself along one of those seemingly endless corridors of the Los Angeles airport; Kennedy has noticed this and is now carrying her bag for her to the taxi stands.

"You're the second person today who's told me that," Kennedy observes.

"My husband and I worked for Bob," she continues—it is 1969, and Kennedy is arriving on an impulse to speak for Cesar Chavez—"and we're getting ready to work for Ted. His ideas appeal to us . . ."

"Oh I don't knowwww—" the husky man rejoins, drawing his fellow traveler into a spirited argument; as he drops the bag off for her he introduces himself with a grin and lopes off before she recovers herself.

There is quick energy for the exhausted ego in encounters like this; if Ted Kennedy can't always resist a nibble or two, who, actually, could? An emotional intensity underlies a good deal of this, an access, very unexpected sometimes, to an unarticulated strong, utterly conveyed feeling for people. "Teddy is almost always very good to his friends," one of them remarks: Whether he is roughhousing with Teddy Jr. and John Tunney's kids in one of the parks in Georgetown, or hugely embracing an aide's wife in his pleasure that she is pregnant with her first baby, or doing all the voices successively in a wild complicated running animal fantasy for his children over the telephone at six in the evening because he won't be able to make it home, or breaking up a game of tennis with a Hyannis Port visitor he discovers to be embarrassingly inept by suggesting that if they don't hurry they'll miss their last chance at the sailboat—unless he himself is pushed, challenged, the childhood considerateness abides.

Milt Gwirtzman remembers the choppy seaside afternoon when Ted tried to teach him to water-ski. Bereft of his fifty-carat spectacles the world goes gelatinous to Milton; Kennedy was holding Gwirtzman up from behind to help him learn, and through the spray and tension and intense backsplattering blast of the motorboat, Gwirtzman recollects Kennedy's vast hairy form behind him and his warmth and his arms coming around to steady him "almost as if he were my . . . my father or something," Gwirtzman, who seldom lacks predicates, half-stammers to remember.

"He has that, this great capacity for whatever he's doing—work, drink, fun," notes a lawyer intimate with official Washington overall—and the Kennedys especially. "It's the Brendan Behan side of his personality. They're all a little that way, politicians. It's been my observation that politicians who are successful all have a tremendous sexual drive. They're flesh-pressers. A lot of this gets sublimated during the campaign, that satisfies the thing in its way, you can actually feel it, the emotion rippling through the crowds when they're stirred, responding, it's almost as if the crowd is rising and falling under you, almost like a woman . . ." In Edward Kennedy a full rich timbre and a highly musical ear combine to give his oratory a rhythm and substance neither his brother Jack (with his flatness and harshness of inflection at times) nor Bobby (with his reedy insistence) ever really approached.

Late at night or before the light is properly in the sky he often reads compilations of great English-language oratory, plays them inside his head like violin sonatas. "President Kennedy had a bound edition of the world's great speeches," Ted Kennedy told me once, "and I've gotten through about eight of the volumes. Just the other evening I was looking at a speech Charles Francis

Adams made in eighteen sixty-eight, and I could see in the music of that speech, the rhythm, something I thought I recognized in the inaugural . . ."

Thus the antipodes persist: the long determined exhaustive months beyond months of work, thinking, careful rather defensive maneuvering; the breaking out, the great muscle flexed so long it kinks of itself, trembles with the imposition of its last scintilla of self-discipline and then cuts loose, often at odd times or on quick trips. Fatigue erupts in strangely unguarded episodes, a terrible uncoiled to-hell-with-it mood oblivious to the anxious track-coverings of the morning to follow, the lifetime to follow. "I know he loves his wife, I know he loves his children, I know he's very good-looking," a friend remarks, not quite ready to more than hint at the exorbitant philandering about which the insiders are beginning to buzz. "Draw your own conclusions——." Bobby remains the worrier.

David Burke worries, too. "We use private planes an awful lot," Burke raises the subject himself one lunch at the perpetual clublike gloom of Washington's Carroll Arms. Burke is by now Kennedy's administrative assistant and by every reading the first among equals around the office "and I hate little planes. My palms get wet. So he does things to drive me crazy. Whenever we're in any kind of turbulence he uses his hands—you know, palms up for the wings—to demonstrate to me what's going on. Then he tells me that when a plane banks, it slides. So—one day we're coming into Morgantown, and it's rough, and he's playing with a deck of cards, and he holds it out to me and he says, 'Take a card.'

"I do, and he says, 'Isn't it too bad nobody is going to know the last thing you did?'"

"'. . . *You* did.'": Edward Kennedy contemplating the demise of his workaday alter ego Burke. This is—what, exactly? Diffidence? This peculiar identification Ted Kennedy sometimes makes with himself as someone who is at the same instant there and, puzzlingly, not there at all. The cunning dreamer hoarding his omnipresent awakening, liable to pop out of any event once it has begun to pinch him close enough to be—inacceptable, intolerable.

To an extent, of course, this is the carried-over existential fantasy of the baby brother for whom the older ones must still do the important deciding, remain more real. More, as the terrible sixties deepen, it is the emotional hideaway within which to curl at times against the well-apprehended probability of Edward Kennedy's own premature death.

Death, the huge surrounding ash-saturated stink of death. The important thing is to carry oneself as if, to believe, that what is hovering at all times can never intrude, isn't there at all. For oneself. This must be tested, flirted with, to maintain the nerve: If Joe Gargan's chin trembles when the necessary risks are taken, or Dave Burke's palms slide up and down the Learjet seat arms— these are—what?—aberrations, evidence of an incomplete grace? Not very important anymore. The testing must continue, Kennedy must—he knows it himself, this terminality—lose. He chases pathetic protectors away, angrily, tall men in blue suits who shoulder all around him in public places, the Secret Service people who knock on his door in McLean pretending to want to sell him brooms. "Forget about 1980," he cautions an aide who in 1968 is unwise enough to project presidential elections Kennedy will still be young enough to enter. "Because by that time I'll probably be dead——."

"You mean——."

"Shot? Maybe, or more likely an airplane or an automobile." The identity of Edward Kennedy, inside the radiant Teddiness that is wearing thinner and thinner and thinner now, is arriving in very dark colors indeed.

"Isn't it too bad nobody is going to know the last thing you did?" Kennedy humor, old certainties made likable somehow by this delightful exploitation of personality. Because who would notice—more, judge—the destruction or survival of the estimable Burke, that young-old administrative assistant of Kennedy's who, ever since Ted Kennedy's career began to get serious at all, has put Kennedy's days together as staff housekeeper, issue tenderizer, and—most needed—social-conscience-in-residence. Burke is normally to be glimpsed just beyond Andy Vitali's side door inside the Kennedy Senate offices, rumpled shirtsleeves blousing beyond his titmouse-brown, front-buttoned vest, cocked back in his swivel chair, the heavy lips uttering something impossible to overhear through Vitali's telephone guffaws as he rug-trades patronage all day.

Burke comes in earth colors. David Burke is witty enough, his intelligent gaunt face lined already at thirty-four from grimacing through his keen appreciation of the unavoidable political ironies, straining to keep practical things around Washington and whatever ethics pertain in some kind of composed congruity. There is the inquiring perplexity sometimes of a bony friar who never got far in monastery affairs because he never really recognized the necessary bribe when it was finally offered. Dave's skin is muddy, pitted by an acne that must have made him decide a great deal about himself early; his voice is muddy, too, arising . . . arising nervously, brisker than it ought to be from detail-worrying a lot of the time—out of a register that approaches croaking.

In marble Washington, where power is sunlight, David Burke is a toad of integrity among butterflies. "He's never flown a jet," Burke reminisces typically, "and we're going to Topeka, and he's saying, 'If that guy had a heart attack I bet I could bring this jet in. Except that——.'" Burke can already feel himself blanching across the forehead, the wetness in his palms—"'I've got to admit to you, David, that I really don't know what that one little red light there is supposed to indicate . . .'"

"What happened to your hair, Andy?" a secretary around the office coos as she comes across Andy Vitali, sneaked away from the telephone to Boston, just standing there in his yellow shirt and extraordinarily fat necktie, leafing through the mid-morning editions. Vitali is the Washington Office's bachelor. He appears to be letting his hair grow a little bit long this winter, get fashionably shaggy. "It looks nice," the secretary decides. "Like a little girl's. When are you going to wash it?"

Vitali looks up. "Thanks, Barbara. You're all right. You're all heart." He scrutinizes the sports page. Andy has a hedgehog's face; his eyes gleam yellow. "Tell me, Barbara," he continues a little too slowly. "What happened to your leg?"

Deskside banter, a Kennedy undertone to help get the fatigue kinks out toward the end of those extra-hour afternoons, along with the nicely picked-over box of chocolates somebody's mother in Fall River sent last week, which has been going around ever since five o'clock and which the Boss, looming above the Xerox machine, appreciates too. Not "informality": The place is such a sweatshop for paperwork, with orders coming in so fast nobody seems to be bothering about whether a press release has crept out of a drawer, whether one leg of the scraped old oak desk that probably has been lugged from office to office since the administration of Millard Fillmore is so short that when Kennedy's press man, Dick Drayne, glides in and perches on a corner, an afternoon's correspondence dumps onto the floor and snaps up a mousetrap that bounces once and lands in an ashtray immediately. Loretta Cubberly may have a ladder running up her stocking and carbon-paper smudges all over the back of her left hand, and Nance Lyons always gets rather a pasty look to her by three o'clock the afternoons she is so busy she misses lunch, but nobody complains: a huge rimless blow-up of the swollen face of John F. Kennedy overlooks the commotion.

Ted Kennedy's legislation sweatshop, a plain-pine-racks operation well shaken down and putting out the paperwork by the last three or four years of the 1960s. People are helpful—the girl with the hastily applied eye shadow deepening her meaty face and the Sassoon bangs and the early miniskirt runs to get the NRA Gun Control speech out of the files. Angelique Voutselas walks the intruder watchfully, for all her grace, around the senator's office, but there is almost always an abstractedness. That Kennedy clock is ticking louder and louder for these people too. All prospects remain open, everything is there to be improvised still.

"We, the staff guys, we can say, do, get into anything," Dave Burke volunteers. "We're free to offer an opinion. It's very fluid."

"That doesn't mean he appreciates your thinking out loud. He doesn't. You think before you go in. Everybody's measured on the conciseness of a decision that is supportable. When you suggest that he do something, and he does it, he says, 'You are on record.' The other day he came in and said, 'You know your suggestion?' And then he stands there, imaginary bat in his hand, and whiffed three times. Then he went back to his office, without a word.

"Then there's the game played where he's gotten the answer in advance, and you have to produce it and you have to defend it. Or—you come up with a great idea and he finds the one hole in it." It is 1967; the newsmagazine reporter I'd lunched with has just tipped me off that once an issue is isolated, Burke is the one who works through the intellectual part; Kennedy feels the politics out. Not so at all, Burke suggests, getting at something else: "He's got a sniffer for issues and directions that I'd never have . . ."

"It's that timing he has," somebody else says. "Wasn't it last week he walks in, and, apropos of nothing at all, says, 'You know we're just going to have to do something about the noise.'

"And I said, 'You mean, here? In the office?'

"And he said, 'No, not here, out there, everyplace, in society.'"

Issues, yes! Burke is correct—he seems to have been born with a . . . sniffer for when they're migrating and where and how they're about to expose themselves. For years and years and years bright colleagues—brighter colleagues, maybe—like Ribicoff and Gaylord Nelson and Muskie have been blatantly, urgently worried, placing broadsides into the general-circulation magazines and prodding among the colleagues for legislative support on their proposals to do something about the way environmental pollutions of all kinds are ruining everything . . . and then one day in 1968 Ted Kennedy ambles into his office and drops The Bag into a chair, and sighs about the noise, and, as if he had called it up himself, noise pollution becomes political.

The Bag. "It's fantastic, an institution," David Burke laughs. "Everybody throws everything into it. He not only reads the stuff, when he gets to work he's got notes on everything. Then we all push more stuff in there for him. An hour after he gets in it's filling up again, and he'll say, 'Gee, I thought I did my homework last night.' When he takes the plane to Geneva we have to fly a second Bag over for him to get at on the airplane home."

"I remember once he left his briefcase in his father's apartment," Gwirtzman says, "I retrieved the goddamned thing. It must have weighed twenty pounds. There must have been books in there. Books or gold bars . . ."

"When you're working on an issue," Burke says, "and you're involved, and he doesn't want to get all his eggs on that issue, he'll say, quietly, Well, it's a long road, it's a long road . . ."

2. Two Senators Kennedy

One reason the road looked so long to Ted Kennedy during the mid-sixties was, of course, the priorities of the insurgent Robert. "He was forever getting out of the way of things, forever giving them to his brother," Ted Kennedy's straw boss in Massachusetts, Gerry Doherty, remembers. "We found a guy who had all this issue information on very current stuff, LSD especially, and we got the material to Ted in Washington. Nothing happens, and then the guy calls me four or five weeks later and says, 'I just got through watching Robert Kennedy on *Huntley-Brinkley* and there he was, being interviewed on drugs, and what he had was all my stuff . . .' I think Ted had a real fear of center stage."

If sometimes Ted had a way of prodding a hot topic toward Bobby to knock over beneath the National Lights—well, the fact was that most of the time the big fleshy Major Trophy Issues seemed perhaps a little . . . theatrical possibly—trivial, even—to the maturing senator. As Milton Gwirtzman once phrased it in his gradual near-whisper, Ted preferred to "get hold of issues that interested him, especially things concerned with the political process, and cast a very wide net of experts, immerse himself, so that when he had to fulfill himself he really had all the facts. Then he seems to apply what amounts to an intuitive political genius to as many facts and opinions as he can get to involve a position that can be made into a public law."

The headline of tomorrow, the warm issue getting hotter, has become interesting to Kennedy primarily as something likely to point up something in his own areas of legislative concern. By the later sixties Edward Kennedy's primary areas of focus included, along with a variety of special problems particular to the Massachusetts constituency, almost anything that concerned refugees or immigrants, the updating and making more universally fair the chances of individuals to vote, reform of our antiquated health system, and overhauling the already inequitable workings of the draft. Immigrants, and an expanded franchise, and offsetting the disasters of illness had long been scorchers around his father's household.

As a onetime draftee himself, he regarded service as a "compulsion that is abhorrent," at the same time he felt himself "enough of a traditionalist to think that service in the Army is a citizen's responsibility." Musing on these matters between turnovers in his Stryker frame, and thinking them through aloud with Al Novak once he was halfway onto his feet a few months later, he roughed together the Kennedy draft proposals and shouldered them hard at the successive administrations until the Nixon administration backed them, if in a typically weakened version, into policy. Like so many of Kennedy's backdoor contributions, Ted Kennedy's reworking of the military exemption bylaws, for example, turned out to have a very convulsive ripple effect: It set in motion the sequence of events that ended the Vietnam War.

During this initial decade, a lot depended on Kennedy's perpetual homage to the obsessively territorial committee chairmen and his continuing pains to take the long way around almost any manner of headline-grabbing publicity. Having come to understand wholly the ins and outs of General Hershey's tacky little Selective Service shop, Kennedy nudged open its back door a crack and found himself peering, patting the top of his hair thoughtfully, across the endless vistas of the military-industrial complex. Fretting about where the budgeting for a national health subsidy was supposed to come from, Kennedy discovered himself beginning to examine the raggedness and inequities of the tax structure. One year now followed the next of persistent, cautious outcreep.

The hint likely to activate Kennedy's Sniffer for Issues was liable to come off virtually anybody, anywhere. The slip an overzealous witness at a hearing makes, the problems of the cross-eyed lady in the cafeteria line, frequently— most frequently, probably—local complaints that have begun to take on a regularity, as they come into the senator's Boston and D.C. offices.

"Right, yeah, yeah, he says he's a retired postal——. Exactly, and now he's working for the school department . . . it's a violation of——." It's not ten in the morning yet, and Andy Vitali in Washington is already juggling two telephone receivers, one caller hanging on while Andy struggles to work something out with one of the Massachusetts provincials inflamed enough so that his incessant half-apologetic voice is almost audible. "You got it, so now she's so mad because of that superintendent of schools up there she's going to strangle . . . of course, and the political mail from there is awful enough anyway. The guy must have friends for Chrissake who——. Rii-gt. You know, he drives a bus. Y'know, of all things to——."

Ten minutes later, Dun Gifford, one of the legislative aides, is conjectur-
ing in his curt ultradefinite way that "The president will put in a bill, and we'll
have a bill of our own in a week or so, with, I should judge, great support—
there is a confluence of personal interest of a good many Senators here——."
When the natty Vitali dawdles through the door and volunteers "You know,
we're running out of money. These towns just don't have it, and what can
I——? I can tell 'em it might be worthwhile to get in touch with the Public
Works Committee. There just isn't . . . they don't have a proposal, a program
. . . You know Mike Joy in Hollings's office; he has a damn good formula for
those city-state tangles——."

"I'd be glad to write a speech," Gifford says.

Vitali sort of nods, and rolls his eyebrows once, and drifts toward his warren of telephones to whoever is expiring behind his hold button.

"You may have just heard the inception of a bill," Gifford says. K. Dun
Gifford is one of those extremely rare "social" friends of the Kennedys'
willing to work at the shirtsleeve level for any of them between elections.
Nineteen sixty-seven was still Gifford's first year around the offices; he
had come immediately out of the excitement of lobbying around the Hill
for Robert Weaver's showcase new Department for Housing and Urban
Development, and any chance at all to pull out those bright unforgotten
town-planning concepts causes a glint to catch for an instant in Gifford's
otherwise glacial round pale-blue eyes. Unhappily for Dun, housing has
remained largely a Bobby issue. Gifford is an exceptionally big man, but softening along his heavy oarsman's hands and under his dimpled Presbyterian
chin.

"A proposal around here can start out any possible way," Gifford says.
"Today—Andy in the office thinks that because of the pressures on cities
and towns and their tax collection facilities a need has developed. It can
begin there, Andy Vitali talking with his friends, with his friend who works
for Senator X from another state . . ."

"Then we'll start to get together the materials. I'll talk with some people,
some big thinkers. Talk about it politically with the union people. In this
situation there is already the tax-sharing plan called the Heller-Peckman
plan—Joe Peckman from the Brookings Institute here—I may talk to him,
or talk to the economists at Harvard, or Yale, MIT. I might write ahead and
visit Cambridge, and then I write a long ten- or twelve-page memorandum
about what I think, what other people think, what the bill will look like, what
it will do, who for——.

"Then the senator will look at that, maybe get some people to fly down for lunch and we sit around there and he will ask a lot of questions to try and find out what the hell this is———."

There: Ted Kennedy's personal sanctorum. Nothing seems exactly decorated—that scuffed-up old sea-desk John Kennedy resurrected is flanked by what appears to be a smudgy little discount-house TV, a coat tree that might or might not have all of its arms unsplintered; instead of works of art, or even citations, there are, year after year, mostly Kennedy memorabilia: a photograph of Ted Kennedy's mother framed with an old report card of hers; Kennedy has written a note pointing out "some trouble with geometry which you obviously have been careful to conceal from your children," to which his mother writes back, with the usual untarnishable Kennedy brass, "Never had any trouble. Your record must have been incorrect. Always A in everything." Ted as a five-year-old is overseen with affection by his balding father. A manifesto the morning after an embattled session of homework from the then seven-year-old Teddy: "You are not asking me questions about the 5 pages. You are not creating my home work, it is a free world," spelling reminiscent of Jack's—whose picture hangs signed, "From one coattail rider to another, JFK." And—until 1968, the only non-Kennedy represented—an exuberantly inscribed photograph from Hubert H. Humphrey.

The back-and-forth in Kennedy's knockabout parlor falls of itself into a kind of low-keyed Socratic exchange. Kennedy eases that tortured back of his into a chair half-supporting himself with one of those freckled little hands, shuts up, as he invariably will when he is truly serious, and puts his staff through firehoops. Bobby generally wondered *why*; Teddy is usually after *how*, not nearly so deep a question but wider and more productive of data. Any one of the four or five aides he respects enough to pester this way finds himself treated as interchangeable, loaded arbitrarily with things to check out or draft a statement about, frowned at over Kennedy's curled scroll of fingers, lured along a line of recommendation quite the opposite of the one he started with and startled to discover that Kennedy has deliberately switched viewpoints to push free of an overrepetitive argument a little or devil's-advocate himself in close enough to determine how deep the preparation goes.

An aide not quite that sure of his facts is likely to get anxious as Kennedy just sits there, blinking his heavy impatient blink, drumming on his front teeth with his forefinger and middle finger, or on his legal pad with his pencil, waiting. The shades of Joseph P. Kennedy and John F. Kennedy overhang.

Then—nobody knows quite when to expect it—"He'll say, 'OK, let's go with this.'" Gifford shrugs. "And that's it. Or—'This is crazy, change it or dump it.'"

"If he likes it I'll work some language out and then start to check with others on the Hill, get co-sponsors if that is important. Then there is the process of trying to get hearings scheduled—"

"Hello, speaking, yeah, yeah, yeah"—the hard political cackle of Andy Vitali on the trunkline to the Commonwealth half-drowns Dun out—"we had everybody on the phone for that one. Yeah, Kenny O'Donnell—sure, well, you know, we *had* to in Boston. The disclosure bill, we drew it up and, y'know, put it in a public place? Sure, in a suite we rented above a parking lot . . ."

Day follows day.

Claim-staking by means of a new bill or a proposal where something turns up in the public domain is the way to legislative empire; others follow on naturally. The National Science Foundation authorization is about to expire? Well, why not attempt to establish some kind of special Subcommittee on Science within Labor and Public Welfare, Senator Yarborough permitting, and then go for a bigger appropriation for the following year, and then . . .

Whereas Gifford tended to be schoolmasterly sometimes, the much admired square-cut legislative aide James Flug, who runs his key Administrative Practices and Procedures Committee, cuts his otherwise precise phrases adrift, slurs into that Brooklyn drawl when what he is thinking about is enough ahead of whatever he is actually saying. Virtually from the day he came over from helping out Ramsey Clark at Justice, Flug has been at Ted Kennedy's elbow around the Washington and Massachusetts hearing rooms. His *Hofjude*, watching up so placidly from underneath his blue-black slab of hair, those leaden hazel eyes adrift and half-alive inside the deep office pallors of his face. Then, in an instant, above a kind of bulb-lipped pinch of mouth, thoughtful, a glaze of very very sensual pleasure crosses into them as Flug picks out the testimony, the blank exchanges, something he immediately prints very large on a legal block for Kennedy to lip-read a moment later against the next witness's commotion. There is a kind of shrugging incontestable Hebraic self-confidence about James Flug as regards matters of the intellect; this Edward Kennedy recognizes, trusts, understands exactly how to utilize.

Trusting anybody that much, for Kennedy especially, takes a peculiar courage. Roles evolve; as early as 1967 Flug had a way of handling the alarums and excursions around the Kennedy office that carried over into his head-scratching innovations later on when he became Chief Counsel of Kennedy's broadly investigative Subcommittee on Administrative Practices and Procedures (ADPRAC).

Flug tends a firehouse telephone. "At the very least there ought to be a dialogue between you and [Wayne] Morse about your rights, that you have your Miranda rights, your immediate presentment rights," he opened one morning after listening for a long moment utterly without expression. Flug had been tracing for me the stages of an earlier Cloakroom struggle when his continually ringing telephone had rung another time. "I can get somebody over at Justice to write it for you." He recurred to December of 1967; the avuncular General Hershey had bestirred himself enough to call a conference and again suggest that draft boards draft campus war protesters.

"Our guy," as many of the staffers often referred to Kennedy, appeared on the Senate floor that afternoon to deliver a draft excoriating Hershey for persecuting free speech; just then Flug was on loan roughing out an appropriate response for "Their guy," Robert Kennedy, with Peter Edelman, one of the New York senator's legislative aides. It was a pounceable moment; both Kennedys pounced, if from characteristic directions. On TV that night an interviewer noted that Congressman Moss had asked that Hershey resign; did Edward Kennedy agree? Just then Kennedy had moved away neatly by pointing out that the man was not the issue, the effect of the draft on the people was the issue . . . Month by month, still keeping his reservations to himself, Ted Kennedy's doubts about U.S. involvement in the war in Vietnam had been deepening since his whirlwind visit to the region in 1965 stirred up his horror at the millions of refugees the conflict was producing.

The great strategy-book performance of Kennedy at his wiliest and Jim Flug at his most pinpoint-brilliant had occurred during the spring-to-fall 1967 redistricting battle. Voting rights—who gets to vote, and how these votes are counted—had become a running source of conflict between Edward Kennedy and Everett Dirksen; Kennedy scored the mortal touché this time. Kennedy had been absorbed since law school in the evolution of all those legal dodges that collectively resulted in the loss of franchise for many American citizens. Countermaneuvering by Kennedy in 1965, when Dirksen was pushing his Senate resolution to invalidate the Supreme Court's insistence on the application of the one-man-one-vote principle to intrastate reapportionment, had won him a good deal of respect among the colleagues and driven Everett Dirksen to attempt a much more arduous state-legislature-by-state-legislature amendment attempt; Dirksen's bloodthirsty single-mindedness in l'affaire Morrissey probably owed more than Dirksen would have admitted to Kennedy's dexterity in kicking the bejesus out of the prospects of his franchise initiative.

Reapportionment's twin issue, at the federal level, was redistricting: The last comprehensive updating of the districts had taken place in 1909; for twenty years Emanuel Celler, Chairman of the House Judiciary Committee, had been squeezing the leadership for guidelines that squared with the current census results.

One version of Celler's latest proposals had made it across the floor of the House and died in the Senate Judiciary Committee in 1965, plucked so raw that even H.R. 2508's once-enthusiastic sponsor Manny Celler admitted to reporters that it amounted to a "can of worms," a paternal embarrassment.

All this was timid enough; as soon as the House passed H.R. 2508 lopsidedly on April 27 and sent it to the Senate, James O. Eastland shooed it at once into an ad hoc subcommittee of the Judiciary Committee chaired by Sam J. Ervin of North Carolina. No hearings were scheduled.

There was an air of furtive dispatch about the May 15 agenda item that caught the careful eye of Jimmy Flug in Kennedy's office. Kennedy himself was headed north on one of his chronic bouts of Massachusetts politicking when Congressman John Conyers of Michigan, who had already led what little fight there was over the measure in the House Judiciary Committee and on the floor of the House, called Kennedy's office to try to stir some resistance to H.R. 2508 on the Senate side, and was surprised, in view of Massachusetts' own redistricting squabble, to find himself listened to.

A black politician who owed his own seat to Detroit's 1964 redistricting, the shrewd, hard-working shrewd Conyers had seen very quickly through a "reform" measure that at best deferred meaningful redistricting five full years and left it largely to the paranoid imaginations of rural state legislatures to redraw district boundaries. Kennedy, contacted under way, hurried back. A reporter close to the situation insists that Kennedy "didn't quite get it" and would have preferred to let the whole thing ride until he had the time to work source material through.

"Senator, you've just got to raise an objection to this thing in the Judiciary Committee and force them to hold the thing over another week," Flug insisted; a formal balk like this among the colleagues is a serious business, not lightly undertaken: Kennedy agreed with Flug to lodge the necessary protest. If Flug couldn't substantiate his objections, though, he'd better look out.

On May 23, before that full-committee meeting Kennedy had demanded, he offered the Kennedy amendment. This eliminated the 35 percent population leeway among districts, reducing it to 10 percent as of 1968, and removed the reference to state determination of standards of compactness. The Judiciary Committee rejected the amendment 10-5, although Dodd, Hart, Tydings, and Bayh stood with Kennedy, and the minority released a report on its objections, specifying that H.R. 2508 as written was inadequately discussed, unclear, liable to be found unconstitutional, and in its compactness provision "an invitation to gerrymander with impunity," certain to result in "unjustifiable inequities" and likely to result in "massive litigation and delay."

The most infectious of the arguments and the best of the phrasing came directly from Kennedy's own floor speech of May 25, which opened with a nice flourish of Edwardian diplomacy—"As I pointed out to the members of the Senate Judiciary Committee the other day, four of their states have been in the leadership in this progress. In Mississippi, the home of our chairman, the legislature redistricted last year . . ."

As shrewd as ever about timing into the calendar delays, Ted hooked in his brother Robert and saw to it that a tingle of alarm went out along that magnetic grid of Kennedy associations. Staff people called in reporters and editorial writers and gave them reprints of Kennedy's speeches and a prechewed analysis of the differences between H.R. 2508 raw and H.R. 2508 Kennedy-amended.

After Kennedy's May 25 speech, and to his surprise, Tennessee Republican freshman Howard H. Baker, Everett Dirksen's son-in-law, called Kennedy's office and announced that he agreed with Kennedy's amendment and was willing to help. Working the Republican side, Baker was able to convince a good many moderates and even a few conservatives that not only was the reform democratic—it was also likely to lead to a net gain in Republicans elected to the House, especially in the South, where the existing abuses were helping the pattern of one-party courthouse dictatorships to survive.

By the time Manny Celler's featherless little contribution came onto the Senate floor for voting, it was no longer the sort of "administrative" or "political" offering that would have otherwise arrived unnoticed. Flug and the rest of the staff had overstuffed The Bag over the Memorial Day political tour Kennedy had already scheduled and followed up with everything related; when Kennedy got back, Flug recalls, "I was snowed. I spent several nights at his house going over the questions and answers. He was tremendously well prepared. Probably more than we were. Probably more than anybody else in the Senate."

The voting itself occurred two mornings later. Eighty-three senators were lured onto the floor. Mansfield fed back a bit of time for Baker and Kennedy to pitch for votes and answer last-second worries.

"The vote started," Flug remembers, "and it was very hard to tell. Then votes started coming in one by one. Senators kept walking in, they kept walking over to him. He had spent the time between establishing a live quorum and the vote buttonholing people, still explaining his position on the issue. I had lost count. I was running around getting the question marks over to the senator. Then we noticed the people on the floor looking up and smiling. The first thing we knew the vote was forty-four to thirty-nine."

The Kennedy amendment stood. "It had been an effort by the Republicans, the Southerners, the old men around here who wanted to slip something through for their forces in the House," Flug says. "The senator used all the devices, techniques, apparatus of the old men who specialize in finishing a bill off in subcommittee or conference. He knows the other senators, what they need, how they think. There was never that break in momentum which, say, a request from the Parliamentarian or the presiding officer can involve, that changing of the atmosphere. By blocking H.R. 2508 he kept the legislation off the Court's back, let them continue modernizing the political units, got them into the gerrrymandering field. We think," Flug has a cryptic smile, "it worked out nicely."

A lovely spoiling operation, this redistricting fight. By the late sixties time and normal membership attrition had left Kennedy well up on the list of senators on the Labor and Public Welfare Committee, a ranking member of the Health Subcommittee and the Education Sub-committee, and chairman himself of the Subcommittee on Aging. There are a lot of old people; more people over sixty-five vote than people under thirty, and they are very alert—perhaps because they have more leisure to think about their interests—about where their best interests lie. Something about the very old obviously touched Kennedy—plucked at his bemusement at the absurdity of things altogether. Besides, there was unoccupied political ground here, and pretty soon he was the one to chair the extension of the Older Americans Act, managing it through the Senate 88-0 and steering it adroitly around a conference by negotiating with his opposite numbers in the House. Then he arranged to hold hearings on another proposal, the Senior Service Corps, which led to an appearance of an assortment of old hillbilly jug players called the Fiddlers and the Stompers so animated that saturnine, embittered old Senator McClellan put on a funny hat and danced.

Into problems of the aging now, Kennedy found one hand washing the other. He noted a shortage of trained people to care for the elderly, tacked an amendment onto an HEW appropriation bill to fund a six-month study, which led him to an unexplored body of information, of experts, to testify at some future hearing that in turn led to a bill of his own to remedy the situation. The elderly were turning into Edward Kennedy's national constituency.

One quiet breakthrough Kennedy managed in 1966 led to the kind of comparison with his brother that stirred in Edward very ambivalent emotions. Lyndon Johnson's ramshackle Economic Opportunities Act, the "Poverty Program," was up for extensive amending that year. Both Kennedys served on Labor and Public Welfare; Edward added about $125 million–worth of amendments and saw nearly half of them through all the floor fights and conference wrangles to eventual funding; Robert sponsored $350 million–worth of amendments of which passed only the $29 million "special impact" allowances for job training and economic development—and that in good part through the cooperation of Javits. What helped so many of Edward Kennedy's recommendations was, as always, attention to legal detail and a projection of administrative follow-through.

Typical was Kennedy's proposal for a national network of neighborhood health centers, clinics, where poor people could get at least rudimentary medical services without dragging across some deteriorating urban sprawl to a remote university outpatient department. Somewhere in Kennedy's head lurked the memory of the 1965 riots in Watts, ignited by the sass two patrolmen reported from a desperate Negro husband with a wife in labor.

In 1966, moving around Boston with Dave Burke (himself the son of a policeman) soaking up the life of plain people, Kennedy came upon the efforts of Doctors Jack Geiger and Court Gibson at Columbia Point in black Roxbury to bring quality medical help, with a small grant from the OEO and the cooperation of Tufts Medical School, to a community four bus rides and 90 cents from the nearest public facility. It interested him. He convened the Tufts group and Joe English and Li Bamberger of the OEO. At the Ritz in Boston they chewed over the rough draft of an amendment the legislative office of the Senate had pulled together and returned to the Poverty Subcommittee of Labor and Public Welfare with a very specific plan for forty such clinics nationally, each with regular consulting hours and a dentist on Tuesday and an eye doctor on Thursday. The recommendation was detailed, left room for student involvement in a fellowship program, and was—for what it offered—an excellent legislative buy. Both houses looked it over, pinched it scarcely at all—a testimony to the thoroughness of its sponsor—and bought. Over the decades to come these community health centers would increase to more than 1,200 and become a mainstay of what little public medicine was out there in America.

By 1967 our massive and deteriorating involvement in Vietnam was laying its shadow across everything else that mattered. Ted Kennedy's 1965 junket to Vietnam to have a look at the horrific, compounding refugee problem had tipped him off to the underlying hopelessness of our adventure in Southeast Asia in human terms. The Tet Offensive, three years later, underlined our military desperation. Both brothers were beginning to feel the effects even in relatively small matters. Asking questions around college campuses, Ted Kennedy kept encountering the indignation of young people over the draft; here was an issue overdue, Kennedy couldn't help realizing that, and throughout 1967, starting with a January speech at the National Press Club and a bill filed in the form of a joint resolution, he recommended higher standards of fairness, predictability—a lottery in some form, presumably—and the use of the service as an instrument of social betterment, deferments for trade apprentices as well as graduate students, some consideration of social justice.

The problem was, insurmountably, that the masterly Richard Russell owned the Senate Armed Services Committee, Kennedy wasn't on it, and the Armed Services Committee made draft policy. Bellying up politely, Kennedy got Russell's permission to chair some hearings of his own inside Labor and Public Welfare on the "civilian effects of the draft," testified as to his findings before both the House and Senate Armed Services Committees, and influenced the Senate bill importantly. The House bill was antediluvian. In House-Senate conference, smiling as usual toward Kennedy whenever he saw him, Dick Russell gallantly gave away virtually every reformist provision Kennedy had intrigued to include.

Kennedy fell back to his reserves, pulled in his experts, from Charles Fried to Adam Yarmolinsky, solicited supporting executive-department letters from Cyrus Vance, Ramsey Clark, Jack Vaughn, and Sargent Shriver, activated the American Civil Liberties Union, and threatened a personal ten-hour inquisition of the conference report's proponents.

Russell had long before stopped smiling; throaty references to "our men who are injured in the battlefield" sounded in the chamber; the critical vote on Kennedy's reform amendment to the draft went against him 23–72. He had helped sharpen the public malaise over draft policy, prodded the Defense Department to greater efforts to reeducate its prey, even pushed the Supreme Court toward its subsequent broadened definitions of conscientious objection and prepared the way for the Nixon administration's mild draft reform efforts a few years later. The findings of the president's own commission squared nicely with Kennedy's. But the Army needed boys, now, and when the plans for perpetuating that meat grinder for the underprivileged came across his desk. Lyndon Johnson autographed their lower right corner, unhesitatingly:

"The senator knew he was going to lose on the draft," Dave Burke remarks. "And he hates to lose." Hated it, but—this the younger brother part—was able to live with it. Recognized it as the essence of legislative life—you lost on an issue until you won on it. Ted Kennedy in 1967 was still a man with Hubert Humphrey's picture on his inner office wall.

3. Bobby

Edward Kennedy lived with it; for Bobby it was obviously harder. Until he became a presidential candidate himself—and so inescapably had to set out formal issue positions of his own—Robert Kennedy seemed frequently to regard the government (and the executive branch especially) as if the whole thing constituted the institutional remains of his brother the president's intentions, his unburied ideological body. "It happened that I was at a dinner party at Roger Mudd's house," the mordant Jimmy Doyle remembers, "at the time Mudd had just finished making a documentary about Bobby. He was there himself, in his usual overworked tired bad mood, trying to be pleasant company, but without much success. Sarge Shriver was there, and Senator Fred Harris and Mrs. Harris, who is a Native American, and Bobby was talking to her about his trips through Mississippi and Oklahoma and the poverty on the Indian reservations. He really did have a thing for Indians.

"I made the comment that the VISTA kids working with Indians and Okies were doing a helluva lot more than the Peace Corps kids. I felt the Peace Corps was in the doldrums, and I suppose I was trying to compliment Missus Harris, who worked with VISTA." It must have been dangerous conversational terrain anyhow; Shriver had developed the Peace Corps, then moved on to oversee VISTA as a subsidiary of the Office of Economic Opportunity, and at that time was increasingly non grata among the Kennedy brothers because of his willingness to continue on at high appointive posts in the Johnson administration.

"Then—right away—" Doyle remembers, "Bobby and I got into a big argument. He was insulted. He asked me to back up my statement. I said I didn't have much experience, but that I recently talked with a Peace Corpsman back from Tanzania, who told me the kids got sick of it after six months or so. The boy said that it was a nice experience, but he wished he hadn't signed up for two years.

"Bob said he'd been to Tanzania and that wasn't the impression he had.

We started to talk about South America. I said I had more experience there, my brother is a priest in a mission to Bolivia, and I knew of the failures of the Alliance, and I didn't think more American Catholic projects were what South America needed.

"And things started getting heated. He brought up a book review of de Toledano's *RFK: The Man Who Would Be President*, in which I had said there was a gold mine for a Conservative Murray Kempton, especially the stuff about the Joe McCarthy period and the Hoffa pursuit. Bob wanted to know what he was supposed to do about Hoffa. I said, the attorney general of the United States has more to do than pursue one guy. By then Mudd was serving brandy, but neither of us would get up. We got a little loud, in fact, and finally Mary McGrory came over and started citing William Butler Yeats at us to break it up."

Those obsessively sore hackles of Robert Kennedy's were getting raised with regularity around Washington those frustrated middle years. Everything hurt, everything was reminiscent. "You guys sure know how to go where the shooting is," a longtime idea man of both Kennedys, having spotted a *Daily News* lead about a refugee camp Ted had just visited coming under Viet Cong bombardment, blurted to Bob in a New York taxicab; for the rest of the ride Robert Kennedy was utterly out of touch, gazed without sight across the midtown avenues. Ted Kennedy had blowup photographs of the president, taken during merry weekends at Hyannis Port, around his recreation room for his own children to grow up with. "Bobby couldn't have stood that," an intimate remarks.

Constituent courtesies did not come naturally. Melody Miller, who broke in as an intern in Robert Kennedy's office, remembers how Bob would handshake his way down a line of perhaps a dozen New Yorkers visiting their senator's offices. "Nice to see you; nice to see you; nice to see you," Bob would intone in that flat, rather sterile delivery of his, rarely looking up. Ted had a personal aside for every visitor.

Bobby did try. At one point an aide brought the grizzled mystic poet Allen Ginsberg in to meet Bobby. Ginsberg sat down and responded to the politician's greeting with his mantra—uuummmm, uuummmm, uuummmmm—and before very long left. "I'm not sure I got too much of that," Robert Kennedy conceded.

It hurt to remember, yet somehow it was a betrayal to forget. As Lyndon Johnson, moving beyond the wariness of his takeover, began to replace the administrators and shift, little by little, the emphases and priorities, and even some of the policies and purposes around his government, Robert Kennedy began to show many of the resentments and agonies of self-control typical of an ex-husband watching the once-wife he still loves changing herself to suit another man. At home to his ultimate impulses in the executive branch, Robert Kennedy attempted to turn his back on that.

Intragovernmental relations were another thing entirely for his fast-maturing kid brother. Traceable even to his freshman months in Washington, Edward Kennedy had put himself to exceptional pains to keep a coherent and emotionally unsnarled pattern of contacts not only to the president himself but to the invaluable sprawled resources of the executive departments. His aides, drawn largely from the other end of Pennsylvania Avenue, had been assiduous about checking through the adequacy of the funding and administration of any of his projects once it had finally been signed into law.

If one of the president's experts didn't seem to care for one of Ted Kennedy's proposals, Ted had a way of telephoning or showing up himself to try to head off an unfavorable report, changing the wording, perhaps, or arranging one of those quiet "trade-offs" of his. Himself the chief legislative mover behind the Teacher Corps idea, he pocketed the IOU and muffled his annoyance when the White House co-opted the political profits.

"Throughout the Johnson administration," says Robert Wood, Kennedy's onetime college teacher—who had been in and out of government since the early fifties, served as first Undersecretary, then, briefly, Secretary of the newly established Department of Housing and Urban Development, and was a stalwart of the reformist Massachusetts Democratic Advisory Council— "Ted continued his self-appointed responsibility as consultant with me about [Massachusetts] party affairs. He was very scrupulous about separating that from our relationship as senator and Undersecretary." Kennedy's office was regularly in touch with HUD to make inquiry in behalf of constituents, ask after the status of projects, consult about legislation. "I dealt with him as I would any other senator," Wood says. "It was a comfortable relationship."

However, "as tension between the president and Robert Kennedy grew there came to be a . . . a second element in our relationship. Robert Kennedy presented major housing legislation, and he asked me to comment on it privately. We did, but Robert Kennedy chose to take the advice of his young advisers. And of course [Secretary] Weaver and I had to blast him. Ted was unaffected. He made a very good statement at my confirmation as Secretary. One night at the—Club, Teddy and I saw each other, and waved, and he said, 'We'll talk after the election.' It was hard for both of us after Robert Kennedy announced his campaign."

Accumulated impatience was clogging exchanges on both sides of the aisle.

"He had his muscle as attorney general," Duff Reed, at the time administrative assistant to Kentucky's moderate Republican Senator Thruston Morton, remarked to me of Bobby in 1967, "but in the Senate he's a ninety-eight-pound weakling. In the Senate you can sway, not swat. He's been less effective than he might have been. If Teddy offered an amendment and Morton even partially agreed he would be much more likely to go along than if Bobby offered it."

The tonsorially irreproachable Morton was equally straightforward. "There are little things, like the fact that Ted Kennedy goes to the barbershop more than Robert Kennedy, who looks like a damned beatnik. It's—" Morton hesitated and plunged, "today, the last week of the session, we all want to get finished and go home, and we have to get the Social Security Bill through, and Bobby insists on pushing through that measure of his involving aid to dependent children. Now Mills in the House will kill the whole thing, and we'll all be on the spot. And everything gets delayed. It embarrasses the colleagues. It appears to me sometimes as if Bobby jumps in right away on something that has big publicity value." The astute Meg Greenfield, writing about the brothers Kennedy in 1966, mentioned Bob Kennedy's mountain of amendments, "most of which simply sank from sight," and concluded, "what resentment this sort of thing provokes among Robert Kennedy's colleagues tends to be exacerbated by an overeager staff that has regularly interpreted his least achievement to the press as a coup, a personal triumph over the system."

The system, the old game. Nineteen sixty-six, and already this hissing. "I realized only later," Peter Edelman, Bob Kennedy's legislative assistant and resident Young Turk, confessed as much to himself as to me when everything was done, "that he [Robert Kennedy] didn't have much confidence in us, Adam [Walinsky] and me. He depended on people he knew. But they were leaving, and he had to start out with a whole new cast of characters."

Whether Robert Kennedy trusted them yet, he felt their existence, took in their emotions across those sensibilities of his that were so exposed at times that his looking away, appearing to turn off, signified that he could really bear very little more. A man with Robert Kennedy's moral intensity and gifts for analysis, who had been disinfecting corners of the government since the tax prosecution of Attorney General J. Howard McGrath in 1952, had smoldered with doubts long enough about justice in institutional America.

He had the time to catch up; procedurally, the Senate was excruciating. "I'd rather see him in the executive branch," said Joe Dolan, his administrative assistant, who had worked with his boss in both the 1960 campaign and the

Justice Department. "This thing has its frustrations, disappointments you don't get there. You do what you want, how you want to do it. In racial situations, etc., you make the book. I always have thought that with the Kennedys they moved in campaigns, they have no reluctance to be innovators. Innovation in the Senate is usually confined to the substance, not to the way the legislation is passed. You can't get your name on bills until you've been around eighteen years . . ."

"RFK started out in the Senate, apart from a tremendous interest in education, with no clear sense of which way he was going," Peter Edelman remembers; interest came fast—within weeks of taking his place he made his maiden speech on nuclear proliferation—but very often his interests blew in and out. Certainly there were effective moments, fortuitous ideas annealed onto the processing legislation beneath the heat and influence of Kennedy's personality.

In a sudden early move that left the articulate Javits nonplussed, a Kennedy amendment added Appalachian-program money for thirteen upstate New York counties. He attached the quality control features to the 1965 Elementary and Secondary School Education Act. Shoved hard by Jack Conway, Walter Reuther's man in Washington and one of the few representatives of "the system" from whom Kennedy could expect lobby help and unequivocal political support, he got overdue debate started on increased Social Security assistance. There were possibilities opening like "Margo's Bill," which offered special benefits to the mentally retarded dependents of Armed Forces personnel, and a bit of legislation that got VISTA and Teachers' Corps people into prisons to teach. There was some satisfaction in these—very often things Adam spotted, things he caught sight of a little at Justice. But the big panacea-blueprinting Robert Kennedy bills—the Social Security Bill, the welfare reform proposals, the housing-tax incentive master plan—these stagnated.

Stagnated, in a paradoxical way, owing to their sterile laboratory-of-the-mind origins. Their need for rubbing against and taking into themselves the contagions of the political process itself, antibodies from the corrupt old System. The ideas were good ideas: timely, scrupulously drafted, and presented in floor speeches burped of the usual senatorial gases and with a stripped power appropriate to the intensity of their logic.

Many opened issues up, from policy assaults on our misbegotten Vietnam approaches to cigarette advertising—the sort of broadsides that stirred his political brother Edward to send a page around with a note that read, "I'm not leaving, because I'm afraid to go outside." A hesitation reflecting his boss's own hurt mood comes into Peter Edelman's recollection of the way

Senator McClellan (Bob Kennedy's affectionate mentor throughout the later fifties during the Racket Committee days, but embittered with him, indeed with virtually everything ten years later) quietly put together an intercommittee power play that stole Kennedy's own drug-rehabilitation proposals and turned them over to McClellan's personal Subcommittee on Crime. That shocked; Teddy experienced fewer such surprises.

Touchy as he was, the sense of being chronically rebuffed by the Senate regulars had to affect Robert Kennedy's movements in the Senate. Robert was never one to preoccupy himself with the flow of minor constituent problems of the type that put Teddy on the telephone to the head of the Cranberry Growers' Association the night after a premature frost on the bogs to offer to try for Small Business Administration money or, perhaps, arrange to sell cranberries to the Army; for Bobby, cranberries were hard to think about when the Pakistani ambassador had been waiting three-quarters of an hour already beneath the Lincoln Center poster. More and more, as successive projects flowered and died for him, Robert Kennedy began to operate his Senate office as a kind of shadowy little government-unto-himself.

While accepting $7 million of federal special-impact funds, he depended primarily on his own matchless contacts and organizing talents to create and operate the gigantic Bedford-Stuyvesant Public Corporations. His trips to Poland and South Africa and Latin America and England and France were more like state visits than fact-finding operations; the press—and a furious Lyndon Johnson—treated his confidential talks with Etienne Manac'h of the French Foreign Ministry as an exchange of peace feelers between two independent diplomatic entities. Kennedy's indignant investigations of ghettos or braceros or reservation squalor drew more television attention than presidential commission findings.

Helping out other Democrats in 1966, as a Kennedy aide remembers it, Robert Kennedy moved around the country beneath "a fantastic public relations panoply. Bobby had a chartered 727 filled with speechwriters, advance men, the whole thing, very elaborately set up." A reporter recalls motorcades in which the candidate whom Bobby had flown out to help would have been exiled to an unobtrusive rear car; Bob would be up front, waving that stiff crowd-compelling wave of his. Ted, on the other hand, normally took a commercial plane out, often alone, expected his hosts to send a car to the airport, and stayed around to shake the last hand at the unavoidable $100-a-plate banquet. Reelected colleagues remembered.

The difference between the brothers' approaches translated into the most incidental gestures. It happened that I spent the afternoon of December 12, 1967—the date the hapless General Hershey flannelmouthed his way into trouble with his reiterated recommendations about drafting troublemakers—mostly hanging around the Senate press gallery. It was a typical floor session. The place was deserted most of the time, what continuity there was provided largely by the presence, in his frontal leather chair, of Arizona's eighty-nine-year-old Carl Hayden, his brittle-looking triangular ears semi-cocked toward whatever noise anybody was making and both withered hands holding tight to the chair arms. Pages frolicked around the steps of the dais.

I happened to look up the moment Robert Kennedy of New York pushed through the Cloakroom doors and started across the worn Oriental runner along the back. There was a wariness about his amble somewhere between that of the smallest boy in dancing class and a wolverine half-blind with daylight—he lifted his Prince Valiant head to sniff at the moment, restraightening his necktie as he went.

Bobby had been scouting prior to putting in his stint as President pro Tem of the Senate; a few minutes later he reappeared with two intimidating-looking tomes beneath his arm, plucked his long nose thoughtfully, put glasses on, and read, presiding. Humpty Dumpty Karl Mundt of South Dakota, allotted time for a budget message, lisped his unwillingness to see the legislators "function as a bunch of peaceniks, a bunch of draft-dodgers in the war on waste," suggested that a lawmaker should practice what he preached, and was of the opinion that what was sauce for the goose was sauce for the gander. Robert Kennedy read. Spessard Holland came in now, requested and received time, and fell into a colloquy that required him to remind one of the distinguished colleagues that, not having been a lawyer, there were things he might not realize that he, Holland, having been a lawyer and then a judge, did.

Robert Kennedy looked up and frowned; Carl Hayden raised himself vertebra by vertebra and—grasping the rim of a desk on each side of the aisle with each successive step—hobbled out.

Edward Kennedy entered. He took his place with the ease of a man in the periodical room of his club, leafed through the newspaper with a docile countenance, his face—especially as I was seeing him, from the press gallery—foreshortened and accordingly accentuating the tendency to a blotchy pulpiness above the jawline and that resigned pout, eyes rolled a little upward, so that a lot of eye white shows, his Oh Lord look, the dutiful fat boy reconciled to the punishment appointed. Hubert Humphrey appeared;

Ted Kennedy, alive instantly, stood and grinned and came right over to converse in hearty whispers with the vice president, who beamed up and gripped firmly both of Kennedy's shoulders.

Ted Kennedy had requested time to pursue this matter of what the Vietnam War had been doing to the civilians in the area; his presentation was subdued, a matter pretty much of suggestively arrayed statistics, delivered in a low pleasant voice that began to thicken with feeling when he referred to the hundreds of wounded South Vietnamese that lay in sheds, corridors, on floors, sometimes even in open countrysides awaiting surgery that, except in emergency cases, might be delayed a year. "The brain-child's talkin'," one potbellied gallery usher said to another as I left for an appointment. "Wanna listen?"

I got back briefly the following morning. Edward Kennedy—changed into a gray figured suit—was listening to the last few paragraphs of an inspired indictment Senator Fulbright was just finishing of America's world role and the military-industrial complex. The colleagues were scattered. There was some discussion; Kennedy himself stood introducing his draft amendment and broke it off to remark that it "struck him as very curious that some of our friends who are most determined to protect the rights of our states nationally are also most determined to project themselves into the lives of other peoples," a remark he deleted later from the Congressional Record. Joe Kennedy might have been whispering in his ear.

National fatigue with the war in Vietnam was settling in; it happened that Robert Kennedy had been a leading hawk when the problems in Vietnam deepened during his brother's presidency, and was especially gung ho about sending over the sixteen thousand shock troops the Diem government requested to protect the helicopter-borne Rangers the Kennedy administration had dispatched initially. The million North Vietnamese Roman Catholics the U.S. Navy had injected into South Vietnam after Dienbienphu were rousing the local Buddhists to organize the Viet Cong.

The discussion moved bit by bit into an exchange between Edward Kennedy and the persistent Jacob Javits about General Hershey's recalcitrance. "I simply cannot understand," Javits insisted, "why this has not aroused greater protest in the country."

"I understand," Kennedy said, "that the Justice Department has given instructions to General Hershey as to due process, and now it appears that, as the result of an action brought by the National Student Association, the Attorney General will have to defend General Hershey."

"Doesn't that show an inconsistency, an anomaly?" Javits wondered.

". . . I believe we are in a preposterous situation. General Hershey has, using this saving clause, gone right back to his October 26 letter," Kennedy said, suggesting that the problem for the draft-eligible person is to find out what, exactly, affects his status.

"The president is the man to do it, and we might just as well say so and have it understood," thrusted Javits.

Kennedy deflected. "I shall write General Hershey today and request that he supply me with a list of the men who have been reclassified . . ." He himself already had an amendment to the Selective Service Act to redefine the word "delinquent," since "we cannot permit the draft laws to be used as a club to forestall the free exercise of constitutional rights . . ." Edward Kennedy was well under way into helping set up an incremental process which, by cutting back middle-class exemptions, pressured the well-born, too, to present *their* sons for the meat grinder in Vietnam. Once the terms changed, quite quickly the incursion wasn't worth it.

"Move in for the kill. I'm behind you," as Robert Kennedy once opened a note he sent his brother on the floor. "Way behind."

Cannonball

1. *The Hamlet Phase*

Notebooking aboard the Ruthless Cannonball, Robert Kennedy's 1968 campaign train in Indiana, was future-looking and incessant, judging by the memoir details that began to turn up six or eight months afterwards. By then the doggerel Robert Kennedy's retinue of close-in press people had written in Indiana was no longer just a parody of "The Wabash Cannonball," a theme song of ironic camaraderie. That Kennedy should have battered through his last campaign with such determination to keep so absurd and brutal a rendezvous on the greasy Hotel Ambassador corridor floor seemed . . . unacceptable, to steal one of Bob Kennedy's overcharged understatements, too much for even the dourest of reporters: Accounts of the Ruthless Cannonball's last run in service get extremely bumpy sometimes. Grief and redress dictate. Robert becomes the total focus; members of the Kennedy organization who produced this political water-to-wine miracle come across largely as names.

One name that tends to get cited voluminously in everybody's index but brushed over very quickly in the text itself—one of a large group at a meeting, an emissary at a critical moment, on the telephone from South Dakota as the miseries set in after the Oregon loss—is the forever arriving and departing Edward Kennedy. Insistently reporter-shy still, Edward Kennedy prefers this; the result is that here, as usual, his involvement tends to be misappraised, downgraded. "Robert regarded his younger brother as having a brilliant political instinct and trusted it above all others," Gwirtzman and Bill Vanden

Heuvel, who ought to know, state flatly. Anybody willing to connect up, one after the next, the spot assignments Ted Kennedy caught once his brother announced can get some sense of the scope and character of his talents. Turned around, the multiplicity of Ted's assignments implies the skills Bob Kennedy, congenital realist that he was, understood he himself didn't have.

The opinion is prevalent among the longstanding Kennedy people that the posthumous memoirs about Robert Kennedy have shown a misleading tendency to overstate his observed drift toward radical—i.e., antiestablishmentarian, anti-institutional—positions. Still, allowing for the ingrained familial skepticism about the Vested Interests and Bob Kennedy's long, disgusted early look into corruption and criminal handholding between the Respectables and the Mob, the necessity for several months of deal-doing with hundreds and hundreds of florid men with much more highly developed appetites than senses of smell—the prospect of mounting a traditional run for the Democratic presidential nomination—was clearly less than enchanting to Robert F. Kennedy that winter-spring of 1968.

Bobby himself, when Jack was canvassing Joe's acquaintances for contributions in 1960, had caught the ticket for Carlos Marcello, kingpin of the New Orleans Mob, and bit back the humiliation consequent to being turned down because Marcello, not too long before a target of Bob's Rackets Committee, was already pledged to Lyndon and Nixon. As attorney general, Bobby got his own back by kidnapping Marcello and dumping him off in Guatemala.

"I remember when I first began to travel with Bob," says Fred Dutton, John Kennedy's old Assistant for Congressional Affairs, abruptly processed that year into a confidant and scheduler and traveling companion for Robert, "if he met somebody he needed, somebody important, and he didn't happen to like 'em, he'd—he'd turn off. Like that, off. I was shocked." Teddy didn't turn off.

The inverse of all this, of course, was Robert Kennedy's increasingly deep—and politically suicidal—emotional involvement with the system's victims, the poor, the excluded, the unwhite. By 1968 comments he recognized as politically reckless but simply couldn't seem to help bubbled out of him. His remark that, if he hadn't been born rich, he would probably be a revolutionary—this got around, scared people.

On tour with the Poverty Subcommittee of Labor and Public Welfare in the Mississippi Delta in April of 1967, as Peter Edelman reconstructs it, Kennedy and his staff found themselves wandering the beaten dirt roads between shacks while naked black children with bellies swollen with malnutrition and sores that would not heal drew back in fright as the dignitaries bore down on them. Edelman remembers going alone with Robert Kennedy into a shanty in which a one-and-a-half-year-old child, its legs so weak it couldn't stand, was "just sort of shmushing around in some rice on a plate. The senator got down on his hands and knees and tried to get some response."

"After he got back," Melody Miller, Robert Kennedy's volunteer receptionist at the time, would recollect, "he closed the door to his office for several days and I heard him pacing back and forth, back and forth . . ."

Never the most obliging of colleagues, it was getting harder and harder for Robert Kennedy—given the crossruff of the deeply analytical and the intense and narrowly emotional that powered his intellect—to think in terms of working something out agreeable all around with Senator Eastland or Senator Stennis, of going along so as to be getting along. He was beginning to show the deepest doubts about where, exactly, they all of them were intending to get to so agreeably and briskly.

Something else that was already pulsating like a toxin throughout the bloodstream of the big recumbent Kennedy Organization was the fact that in any definable way it wasn't an Organization at all but rather an amalgamation of individuals animated by motives ranging from idealism to dreams of old power reacquired, and that the organization was, close-up, unbossable. The decades since a Kennedy political operation amounted to Jack at rallies and Kenny and Larry running around the state and plenty of bookkeeping backup from Park Avenue, Inc., with the financier stepping in to throw Mark Dalton onto the street or pitch a tantrum about an ultraliberal ad or sweet-talk support out of an anonymous party boss—since those simple bloodletting days everything had shifted. Camelot had intervened.

From absolute dynasty the Kennedy undertaking had evolved during the Johnson years into a kind of running board of directors conclave: the Old Boys were out there in commercial and political America building operations of their own—O'Brien was Postmaster General, Sorensen was august among the partners at Weiss Rifkind, Kenny had a flourishing educational testing business, which he ran between paroxysms of craving for the Massachusetts governor's mansion. And by now, of course, nothing happened without the benediction of the recent administration dignitaries—McNamara, Goodwin, Averell Harriman, and the rest.

The assortment of old friends and onetime Kennedy administration figures who got together for late-evening parties at Steve Smith's place or lunched, heads bent toward each other a little, at Sans Souci—most of these quick-witted and irreverent functionaries pitched in when Bobby made his belated decision to run. As traditionally with the Kennedys, responsibility was easily given and advice was freely sought. But the consequence, the success or failure from following the course recommended was very carefully watched; an adviser's reputation took on or gave up weight almost hour by hour. Better, often, to reserve one's opinion than try to live down a blunder of judgment.

This technique worked well enough into events as long as there remained a central figure resolute enough, sure enough of himself, to divine the necessary course of action and sort things out. The missile crisis remained for Bob Kennedy the model triumph for the collective decision-making process. But when the situation became ambiguous—or when the central personality hesitates, unsure of himself, seeing the evils and risks inherent in whatever he does—then the drag in every direction by so many strongly disagreeing sanctified personalities could pull virtually every decision to pieces, paralyze action, sacrifice the moment of initiative forever. "My problem is that I don't have anybody to do for me what I did for my brother," Robert Kennedy was heard to lament as his primary campaign started to shave the ditch. Nobody can contest a myth. The surviving brothers were increasingly helpless before the authority of the imagined past.

At least in 1967–68 the dilemma was pragmatic, out there at political arm's length. Suspicions that there was going to be at least the possibility of alternate choices of action developed as early as the summer of 1967. The Congressional elections of 1966 had turned out extraordinarily poorly for the Democrats, a number of the key prestige holdovers from the Kennedy administration—McGeorge Bundy, Goodwin, Robert McNamara—either had already left their posts in the Johnson government or were being shove-eased out. The war in Vietnam had long before turned into one of those funhouse rides during which the light at the end of the tunnel turns again and again into an oncoming locomotive. The American public was looking queasier and queasier and *queasier*.

Once a prominent hawk, Bob Kennedy now hated the conduct of the war enough to disavow publicly, in his March 2, 1967 speech on the Senate floor advocating a bombing halt and an opening of negotiations with the North Vietnamese, any suspicion of loyalty to the Johnsonian approaches. Still, people whose judgment and character he still regarded highly—Maxwell Taylor, Walt Rostow, Averell Harriman—continued to support Lyndon. The political danger persisted that the flash of light around the next bend might indeed signal the exit from this misbegotten bloodbath, a turn of events which would leave Bob Kennedy and his advisers sidetracked by history while a triumphantly reelected Lyndon Johnson beamed, vindicated, the man who carried through the intentions of John F. Kennedy in Asia.

Beginning with the October 1967 meeting in Pierre Salinger's suite at the Regency, and carrying through the overlapping December 10 talks over lunch at Bill Vanden Heuvel's house in Manhattan, Kennedy intimates gathered to hash through their preliminary assessments. Between these two meetings Eugene McCarthy had announced his candidacy, on November 30, and Bob Kennedy's opinion of McCarthy, whom he regarded as vain, ineffective, and lazy, was such that the largest apprehension at first about the McCarthy candidacy was that it would turn into such a debacle that the entire peace movement—and Bob Kennedy's impact in particular—would be vitiated by McCarthy's desultory performance.

Awakened, the Kennedy people reconsidered. The wisdom that came out of these preliminary meetings led to soundings in important places nationally, the deliberate effort to get Kennedy friends into 1968 convention delegations, the reservation of hotel space in Chicago, and a quiet November 1967 poll in New Hampshire that showed Bob Kennedy ahead of Gene McCarthy but well behind Lyndon Johnson in that advance-warning little state.

By November the spectrum of advice among the regulars was better defined. Along with his legislative assistants Edelman and Walinsky, who were pointedly omitted from these early sessions of primarily political appraisal, Dick Goodwin—whose judgments were as highly valued, prickly, and independent as ever—and Arthur Schlesinger both were outspoken as to their conviction that Bob should announce his candidacy as early as possible and start organizing: They thought they heard the ice of traditional politics cracking. The terse Kenny O'Donnell tended more month by month to agree with them; Dutton was less sure; Vanden Heuvel, Sorensen, and Teddy Kennedy all obviously felt—and continued to feel—that the idea of Bob's candidacy in 1968 was politically misbegotten, unrealistic, liable to abort his career entirely.

Most of whatever Ted Kennedy knew about presidential politicking he had learned from his brother Robert; it was as if, throughout that torturous long 1968 winter of equivocation and reappraisal, Bob Kennedy, in his near-panic at finding himself unable to decide, was again and again to find himself turning with confused emotions to a rational and professionally detached version of his earlier self in his skeptical younger brother. Ted Kennedy's own ultimate motives remain, as always, a little ambivalent finally, perhaps even to himself: Without really intending it, his actor's impulse to devil's-advocate his brother's decision, force him to granulate it very fine before committing himself irreversibly, very probably contributed in its way to Bob Kennedy's anguish of indetermination.

"There were three or four occasions during the period of the fall of 1967 when Bob and I talked about it to some extent," Ted Kennedy would later relate to me. "We went to Sun Valley for Christmas, and I thought by the time I left from there for Vietnam that I could be reasonably sure he wasn't going to run. After being gone for two weeks I landed on the West Coast and talked to him by phone, and I found that the subject had been opened again . . ." Kennedy cites his brother's disillusionment at the Johnson war policy and the slighting of the Kerner Report as contributory, but beneath the politics one picks up the implication: The piranha around his office were gnawing again at Bob Kennedy's political common sense.

"My feeling," Ted recalled, "was that the real issue was the question of the extent to which he'd be able actually to change policies. That was the test that should be applied, and I think it appeared very primary to me that the issue wouldn't be the war issue but the personality issue, the apparent search for power by Robert Kennedy, which would awaken many of the apparently latent feelings among some people . . . The opportunity for bringing about new kinds of directions, new departures, appeared to be elsewhere."

Kennedy sighed. "When I came back from Vietnam I was completely a-decisional; I didn't recommend or suggest when I talked to him about it—I felt strongly that it was something that was growing within him. I didn't attempt to influence him. I felt the best service I could provide was to bring to bear on the decision various views, not get into it myself——."

Still, the slippage between what Bob Kennedy wanted to do and what Ted Kennedy felt it was politically coherent to do had started; the ordinary Kennedy interval between the two brothers opened, widened, week to week. "Teddy doesn't think I ought to run," Bob kept observing unhappily to his various advisers; it amounted to the most uncomfortable stone in the shoe of his miserable decision. Their communication was becoming less and less direct: Several times Bob arranged for men they both trusted to sit down with Ted and explain things.

"You know it's his instinct to go," Ted, the faithful Burke in tow, responded to Dick Goodwin in February at a quiet dinner in Boston at the Charles. "And"—hopefully—"he always does best when he follows his instinct." Dick Goodwin asked Edward what John Kennedy would have done under the circumstances. "He'd have advised against it. But he'd have done it himself," Ted came back, straining to believe that too. Fred Dutton, whose mission Edward

Kennedy surmised before he had seated himself, received a curt, "I know he's going to run. Now the thing to do is make some sense of it."

Making sense came hard.

The reminiscences of Bob's junior advisers drum away with charges that Ted Kennedy and "all those old John F. Kennedy guys" simply couldn't drag their worn-out, backward-looking attitudes beyond what passed still for the "conventional political wisdom." Admitted; what this kind of allegation avoids—what it would finally have taken a back-to-the-wall Robert Kennedy in Chicago to demonstrate—is whether the rules in Larry O'Brien's venerable book of tactics still obtained by 1968. Ted Kennedy's reservations went well beyond observing over cigars that no eligible modern president who wanted it had ever been denied his party's renomination. Beyond the shared apprehension that a well-founded peace candidate would tear away just enough votes in November to cost the Democrats the White House.

Typically, Edward Kennedy saw the decision as a very large problem composed of innumerable picayune maneuverings, of playing up to the right faction in a ward feud, of perverse personalities to be won over somehow and monies to be coaxed out of the still-dubious Steve Smith and enticing a small delegation beyond unit-rule thinking on the second ballot—as ever Teddy Kennedy was haunted by the imagination of the practical, how. This remained a finite thing, political America, an entity he had been getting to know working the territory for his brothers, Masonic lodge by Arizona vestry, just as he had comprehended Massachusetts in 1962. He had learned to come away from each fund raiser, each three-block motorcade, with a sense of the situation *in that place*, impression enough to consolidate as a stickpin to push into his mental map of the nation. Until the entire country was dense enough with stickpins he trusted, so that in 1968 he was already capable of stepping away, and studying the pattern, and considering the impatient Bobby, and asking himself the unavoidable *how*. And saying: No. Not now, not yet.

"Teddy didn't believe you should use up what capital you had on a moral issue," Dun Gifford said simply; it wasn't so much that the issue was the wrong one as that, politically speaking, in America the moral approach was broadly ineffective. "Why is it that my slant on Vietnam"—stopping the bombing—"goes right by people but Teddy's"—the expensive dislocations resulting from the refugee problem, and, after Ted's January 1968 return, the endemic governmental corruption—"gets so much attention?" Bob asked an old friend that winter. It seems never to have struck him that to the Milwaukee patriot bomb-dropping was traditional, but the way those devious little bastards in Saigon were tucking "my money" away in Swiss banks was thought-provoking, exasperating. It occurred to Edward.

Like the immediate question of whose son got sucked into the draft, the issues that Edward Kennedy was raising affected Americans at home, their children, their pocketbooks. Every well-advised politician in America realized after Tet in 1968 the war had to be foreclosed: It was turning into an expensive and disappointing geopolitical experiment. That didn't mean that the public at large was ready for the solutions of the overemotional middle Kennedy brother, senselessly ranting to the blacks and Chicanos, who had already been quoted as stating publicly that he favored sending blood to the North Vietnamese and pushing Communists into a South Vietnamese coalition government.

The backdrop issues aside, intraparty breakage in Massachusetts alone was enough to touch off sharp ripplings of alarm inside a names-and-numbers specialist like Ted. Where was this treacherous departure from settled policy supposed to take all of them? Who were their allies here, the blabbermouths and wailers of the peace movement, irrational blacks, yearning for their indefinable revolution, aggrieved kids, dedicated Johnson-dumpers? Too volatile, too likely to blow out the substitute walls of the coalition at any time and leave Robert Kennedy's political insides dotted across the landscape of institutional America.

Jimmy Flug, who would be left behind to tend the Senate for both Kennedy brothers once Bob declared, still remembers the politics. The ramshackle piece of legislation entitled The Omnibus Crime Control and Safe Streets Act of 1968 was moving through the drafting process at Judiciary while Ted and Bob were barnstorming through the primaries. To accommodate the fears of old-guard reactionaries like James Eastland and John McClellan and Sam Ervin, the bill "had a lot of crap in it, including wiretapping," Flug saw, although it did mandate "something very important, The National Institute of Justice." One afternoon while Flug was hanging around the Cloakroom waiting for Ted to call in, the vote on the Crime Bill was announced.

"What's your recommendation on the Crime Bill?" Ted wanted to know immediately.

"I said, 'Well, if I were a senator I would vote against it,'" Flug said.

"Jim, you're not a senator. *I'm* the senator. I don't care what you would do. Give me your recommendation about what *I* should do."

"That was an important point," Flug admits. "And I probably recommended that he vote for it. And he probably did."

Whichever way you jumped, you lost somebody. "I'm the only candidate who ever united business, labor, liberals, Southerners, bosses, and intellectuals," Robert Kennedy himself noted. "They're all against me." Who better to frame the nightmare than the experienced Bobby, shuddering to imagine the August convention in Chicago presided over with a heavy gavel by a chairman of Mayor Daley's selection and policed by Lyndon's National Committee operatives watching to be sure they knew which way the floor cables all ran, the passes all double-monitored, the galleries packed with construction workers, and George Meany and Joe Rauh at opposite ends of the corridors to grab wavering delegates and pull them back inside solidly behind Lyndon.

"Bobby's therapy is going to cost the family eight million dollars," Ted Kennedy reportedly told one intimate, gloomily; Teddy was now forced to admit, at least to himself, that his brother's predicament was as much psychological as political. The war was terrible, but stopping it was an issue, perhaps the last issue—to which he could authentically give himself. Bob Kennedy's heart for life and politics was visibly giving out. "I don't believe he can keep this carnival of his going another four years," one agile Washington aide had told me in 1967 when 1972 came up; most likely Bob agreed.

There was an exhaustion of morale to worry about here, a disturbing tendency toward sieges of blankness and wildness. As if his brother's anxieties were not enough of a liberated high-tension wire crackling and snapping on its own in a dangerously conductive political atmosphere, Ted Kennedy was beginning to notice sparks suggestive, to him at least, of an uncommon energy—equally stripped of a decent conservative insulation—coming off the beginnings of the McCarthy campaign. Languid Gene, all spite and whimsicality until that time, a man whose sense of himself seemed to require that he try to appear as if he had just come up from unimaginably turgid intellectual depths, very slow and blinking in the face of the light and his voice always sounding as if he were just getting over a cold.

"No one in Washington respects that man," Robert Kennedy had muttered to Sorensen in 1964, shutting off all speculation that—should McCarthy indeed come up the vice-presidential choice of the ever-coy Lyndon Johnson—it might be a party-unifying move were Bob to nominate the Minnesotan. Bob Kennedy's distaste for the man owed as much to his perception of McCarthy's own cold annoyance at being summoned in 1956 to receive an "audience" with John Kennedy. Jack's vice-presidential prospects glimmered as his suspicion of McCarthy's motives when—very much the ambitious freshman senator eager before his Majority Leader Lyndon—McCarthy delivered the clever, sentimentally gripping speech nominating

Adlai Stevenson in Los Angeles that gave the downcast John Kennedy crowd the shudders.

Since 1960 Eugene McCarthy had taken on the moves of a basking shark in the pools of the Senate, a loner and a feeder on the minute organisms of a generalized liberalism. Furthermore, not much of a worker and, clearly, straining under very little urgency about attempting much: contemptuous of his colleagues, as often as not, snide, yet whispered about as being suspiciously into debt with Important Interests. In 1964, in a watershed vote, McCarthy voted to retain the 27.5 percent oil depletion allowance and ran for president "as a penance for all I've done for Bob Kerr and Lyndon and Russell Long." McCarthy, whose most casual asides so very often cut deeper into bone than other people's thrusts, tossed that one off half-seriously to a bureau chief who was himself enough of an Irishman and a Catholic to understand the extent of the spiritual peril in which the senator viewed himself. McCarthy was . . . willful, undependable.

Edward Kennedy's read on McCarthy corresponded with his brother's. "Gene!" Ted Kennedy, a little out of breath, had opened right up a few years earlier upon discovering the man he was after sitting over his food in the Senate dining room; it was 1965, and Kennedy's poll-tax amendment was coming to a vote imminently.

"I'm having my lunch," Eugene McCarthy said.

"But Gene, the vote is going on, now, in the chamber——."

"Ted"—McCarthy seemed to be chewing, if possible, even slower than before—"I'm-eating-my-lunch." McCarthy wandered up a little later on, thought it over a moment, cast his vote: against the Kennedy Amendment.

"I'm not a great Kennedy watcher," Gene McCarthy told me once. "I'm beginning to think the Kennedys watch me much more than I watch them." In November of 1967, when McCarthy announced his candidacy formally, Edward Kennedy was in Geneva at the annual refugee conference; when he got the news he telephoned his party chairman in Massachusetts, Lester Hyman, and hinted around to the effect that it might be useful if he would . . . perhaps . . . look into what sort of thing McCarthy had in mind . . .

Hyman, a cheerful plunger, telephoned McCarthy and invited him to lunch. "I was surprised," Hyman still remembers. "All he would talk about was LBJ, how McCarthy was a possibility as vice president on the ticket in 1964 but Johnson had really wanted Humphrey on the ticket with him, and he, Gene, had sensed that and sent the president a wire underscoring his own support for Humphrey, but before he could release it Johnson had telephoned urgently to insist that McCarthy not release the wire but instead come to Atlantic City and be sure to bring his family . . ." McCarthy had; in fact the whole performance amounted, after all, to one more presidential ruse expressly devised to keep Hubert dancing on his back legs and whinnying a few hours longer.

Among the Minnesota crowd Eugene and Abigail went to intimate parties with, the incident got a lot of humorous play; after a while McCarthy's friends stopped mentioning it. Word spread around Washington that what had happened was embittering Gene, souring him. Pride wounded, fed the encroaching suspicion that for all his early self-assurance and poise and power of intellect, other men—simpler men, like the shrewd but superficial president, the awkward artificially tutored Kennedy brothers—were going to realize in the end what he, McCarthy, intuitively claimed all along. Something in the once docile McCarthy was becoming murderous. Ted Kennedy, who now sniffed something going sharply bad, suspected that Eugene McCarthy was going to be a very dangerous man to have in the vicinity of even a little blood in the political water.

Ted Kennedy could not miss the way Eugene McCarthy handled himself as early as November–December of 1967, his contempt for the geniality normal to a politician in territory not his own. The Chairman of the Democratic State Committee and therefore, ipso facto, Edward Kennedy's personal choice to run the Massachusetts party, was Lester Hyman, who had come into the job when Gerard Doherty, essentially a terse, knuckle-busting technician, finally gave it up.

After years of exposure to Doherty's mudflat personality, dealing with Hyman was like a stroll through steaming hanging gardens. Lester is a tall swarthy rather epicurean man whose close-set black warm eyes look glued to his distinguished nose. Careful about his tailoring, he has a way of dwelling affectionately on vowel sounds that produced in Kennedy headquarters a barrage of anti-Semitic hate notes from denizens of Chelsea and South Boston walk-ups heartsick to think that the party of Jim Curley and Onions Burke had been placed by a fellow Irishman in the hands of this reincarnated Disraeli.

Ted Kennedy delegated Lester to help figure Gene McCarthy out, and Lester kept at it throughout the campaign. Typical of Lester's puzzled efforts was his backgrounding and briefing session with the indifferent candidate when McCarthy appeared in Boston to address a rally at the Fenway late in the spring. McCarthy had the liberal Commonwealth's first-ballot strength locked up, by default; Hyman had done him the courtesy of scheduling a private introduction to all seventy-two actual delegates, men and women of various personal views, many dedicated Kennedy organization people who had worked for Jack throughout the fifties. The Kennedy cousins Joe Gargan and Bob Fitzgerald were among the slate members, Hyman took care to impress on Gene: If he wanted to hold these people through successive convention ballots McCarthy would be well advised to consider what he said.

Confronted by his pledged slate, McCarthy was curt, flip, and calculatedly brutal. Rather than answer specific questions he referred his delegates to earlier policy statements and speeches, dismissed the blacks wholesale as one segment where "Bobby has the market cornered," and responded, when asked what kind of president he had it in mind to be, that he admired the tenure of Harry Truman, observing gratuitously that "JFK did nothing." Gargan and Fitzgerald in particular, Hyman noticed, were "turning blue."

The bombardment from President Johnson had started, of course, many months before that. Whenever he could lure his state chairmen to Washington, Lyndon seemed to make a particular point of drawing his leader in Massachusetts aside, frowning earnestly as he hung one swollen Western hand on the tailored drape of Lester's shoulder and proposing—hoarse with sincerity—that he, Lester, try to imagine how he would handle things if he had six divisions of our best American boys to worry about in a war six thousand miles from the mainland and he were confronted with a choice between continuing to support the bombing—which Robert Kennedy, never referred to directly, now opposed—or not bombing and letting our boys get killed. "I was out every night talking up LBJ's points," Hyman remembers.

Breaking his glance fretfully out of the corner into which he had already been boxed by the jittery Lyndon Johnson, Lester was having trouble following the maneuvers Eugene McCarthy was attempting among Hyman's own hodgepodge of Massachusetts regulars. The breakaway point politically was March 5, 1968, the final date on which a presidential candidate was permitted to file intent and run in the binding April 30 Massachusetts presidential primary.

As early as November 30, 1967, McCarthy and Edward Kennedy had gotten together and touched on Gene's prospects in the Bay State. Ted Kennedy's own feelings about the Vietnam War, McCarthy's pinning issue, were openly much closer to Gene's than to the locked-in Johnson's. An accommodation came out of the meeting, vaguely—characteristically vaguely—phrased but well understood, as far as Edward Kennedy was concerned, according to the terms of which McCarthy would stay out of the primary in Massachusetts in return for Ted Kennedy's hard assurance that the Massachusetts delegation that turned up in Chicago would arrive aflutter with bona fide doves.

Whatever he finally decided, McCarthy agreed not to get involved politically in Massachusetts without further discussions with Ted.

By the time Robert Kennedy got around to conferring with him in December, the desultory McCarthy was feeling pressure to take the whole thing at least half as seriously as did his backers. Having hinted at his own readiness to help the ineffable McCarthy out, Bob Kennedy assured the would-be peace candidate that he would be very well advised to bypass Massachusetts (where a private Kennedy poll showed McCarthy's support was decidedly greater than Robert Kennedy's own) and turn and engage with the Johnson administration in New Hampshire (where another private Kennedy poll suggested that McCarthy was likely to catch up with political obliteration early).

At the beginning of December, a conglomeration of would-be activists met at the Chicago meeting of the New Politics Committee and voted on a resolution supporting the president and his war policy, 45–3. Edward Kennedy had wandered in late, followed the voting, and got cornered by a radio interviewer as he was trying to work his way out unnoticed. Did he agree with the hawkish resolution? the reporter asked. "I don't agree with the language; however I can live with it," Kennedy replied

Almost until the moment he announced, Bob Kennedy hadn't actively repudiated the possibility of some ultimate re-re-examination after which he might openly forgo any serious prospect of getting into the race. Ted, who perceived his brother's incapacitating ambivalence, started being overcareful.

Pratfalls resulted. On Friday, March 8, five days before McCarthy's epochal success in the New Hampshire primary, Bob charged his brother with conveying to the campaigning McCarthy personally word of his, Bob's, final *final* intention probably to enter the primaries once New Hampshire was over. Ted looked around the Senate Office Building, didn't find McCarthy, and simply made no further effort to carry Bob's message. Ted obviously felt that tipping McCarthy off now and letting the guileful Gene use the information to his own advantage wasn't worth the cheap insurance having warned the forerunning peace candidate might provide. Deeper than that, Ted hated the whole idea of Bobby's candidacy.

When Bob, who had been in California picking over a slate of potential Kennedy delegates with Jesse Unruh, returned to Hickory Hill on Saturday and discovered that nothing about his impending candidacy had been leaked to either McCarthy or the papers, he first telephoned Arthur Schlesinger—who begged off—and then asked Ted to send the message via Dick Goodwin, by now an obsessive opponent of the war and at that moment himself in New Hampshire pulling together a brilliant publicity campaign for McCarthy.

First Ted, then Bob checking on Ted, telephoned Goodwin and asked him to inform McCarthy—the phrase is sharp in Goodwin's memory—that Bob "hadn't foreclosed the involvement, definitely." It struck the lawyer part of the astute Goodwin's mind that he had better be careful to keep his role as carefully defined as possible, in view of his awkward position as the adviser to the principals in both camps: He agreed only to convey the message as an exact quote from Bob to Gene, as something he had been tasked to tell McCarthy. When Robert Kennedy reached him he agreed, Goodwin remembers, "if grumpily"; it was evident to Goodwin, too, that Bob still hadn't really made up his mind.

Real authority, decision, was everywhere and nowhere. "I wish there was somebody who could do for me what I did for my brother" was turning into a mantra, something Bobby would repeatedly mumble to reporters in the midst of the frenzy of successive primaries. Much of the confusion came out of the fact that there was nobody at that point to do for Bob what his brother and, more important, his father—and this would pertain to the very largest matters—had actually done for themselves: decided. By March of 1968 Ted Kennedy obviously saw what his older brother, well advised or not, needed and did not seem quite able to do. Ted was enough of a technician to realize how important every day, every hour, from then on was likely to become; Bobby's anxious uncharacteristic late straw-grasping was demoralizing them both.

What put Bob into it, of course, was McCarthy's incredible 42 percent showing in the New Hampshire Democratic primary. "How do you think I could have done?" Bob Kennedy asked Goodwin by telephone that night. When Goodwin guessed that he could have picked up at least 60 percent of New Hampshire's Democrats, Robert "hadn't liked it"; he hadn't liked Gene's offhand remark, on hearing Bob Kennedy's own highly publicized blundering election-day admission that he was "actively reconsidering the possibilities . . . ," that in McCarthy's opinion the race was "a little bit crowded now"; least of all had he appreciated McCarthy's offer, in a terse private meeting in Ted's office when McCarthy got to Washington, to serve as president only one term and leave the field to Robert after that. The candidacy of the Minnesota senator—who, one way or the other, would have to be squeezed out of the race quite early if Kennedy himself were to have much of a chance—had opened by giving McCarthy such an infusion of power and confidence that Bob felt lightheaded just thinking about it.

The New Hampshire primary fell on Tuesday, March 12. Bob, if he did run, wanted to announce no later than March 15, so as to remain eligible for the Nebraska primary. He spent the week plotting hapless strategies designed to leach the authenticity out of McCarthy's crusade. One hope was the Peace Commission idea (originally the brainchild of Mayor Daley, and now very actively pushed by Theodore Sorensen), which was supposed to result in the selection by Johnson of a commission of moderates to study the prosecution of the war with an eye to foreclosing it.

Lyndon Johnson himself evidently sent out enough mixed signals on the proposal to encourage Sorensen, at least. On March 13 Robert Kennedy asked Ted Kennedy to call the new Secretary of Defense and onetime Kennedy lawyer Clark Clifford and arrange a meeting to select a panel empowered to recommend a face-saving political strategy—delay Bob's entry—and vaporize Gene McCarthy's one meaningful public issue and very likely his candidacy.

Ted called Clifford but—again that dangerous slippage—while he arranged a meeting, did not, to Clifford's recollection, make clear what Bobby in fact had in mind. "I think Teddy thought the Peace Commission idea was absurd," Fred Dutton commented subsequently; Lyndon Johnson, who saw it as tantamount to admitting his own ineptness at handling the war, did too. The president's response was "instantaneous and very clear": No. Bobby's transparent machinations were making Ted jumpy; at one of those innumerable unhappy conclaves, this one in Steve Smith's New York apartment the night of March 13, Ted, watching Bob's appearance on the Cronkite show, broke out: "What the hell's the point of holding this meeting when he's already made up his mind!"

Robert Kennedy had one more idea. The night of March 15, Friday, with the historic Senate Caucus Room reserved for the Saturday announcement, Bob arranged for Ted to fly to Green Bay, Wisconsin, with Dick Goodwin and Blair Clark to propose to the campaigning McCarthy that, rather than sap each other in a series of transcontinental political spoiling operations, the two peace candidates divide up the pre-California primaries in the hope of demonstrating so much popular support that Johnson would be forced to retire; then, in the significant California and New York primaries, the two could battle it out directly.

The germ of the proposal, Goodwin remembers, came from McCarthy strategist Curt Gans. When the three arrived at the Holiday Inn in snowy Green Bay, Clark and Goodwin briefed Gene first; then McCarthy received Ted. McCarthy insisted on keeping his wife, Abigail, and his daughter Mary in the room, too—a sure sign in political circles that turkey was not to be talked—and whenever Ted, in his multi-syllabic roundabout way, got anywhere near the matter he had been traveling half the night to broach, the outrage in Missus McCarthy's tone was so unmistakable that Teddy didn't bother.

A group of John F. Kennedy people had stayed over at Hickory Hill that night; when Ted's return plane landed he woke up Bill Vanden Heuvel, who had been sleeping on a couch in the downstairs library, then went upstairs and informed Arthur Schlesinger Jr. that "Abigail turned it down." At breakfast that morning Schlesinger, who felt very strongly that for Bob to jump in so soon after McCarthy's upset would reinvigorate the *ruthless* charges, had started to advise at least a short further delay when Ted cut him off with an uncharacteristic curtness.

"No, Bob's mind is made up. Let's have no more discussion. Let's not weaken his confidence."

2. *Indiana*

Born far too late, the 1968 Kennedy campaign wobbled off in every direction simultaneously. Confusions emerged immediately in that strange mix of political apologia and statement of intent Bob Kennedy delivered before the assembled Washington press in the Senate Caucus Room: "At stake is not simply the leadership of our party and even our country, it is our right to the moral leadership of this planet . . ." Ted Sorensen had written it for Bob, to the predictable fury of Walinsky and Edelman, whose plain-spoken text Sorensen had loaded to waddling with those portentous balanced late-Roman locutions of his, burnished prose effulgent with geopolitical moral strictures. Compelled at the last second to contest the airy ripostes of Eugene McCarthy, Bob Kennedy now lumbered onstage in chain mail.

This much, at least, the Kennedys caught onto early. Except for a couple of presidential press-conference statements, Sorensen spent the campaign working on scenarios around the Washington headquarters while other people wrote the speeches and did the on-the-spot scheduling for what amounted to a series of independent state primary blitzes.

Sorensen is frank about the essential quandary: "No agreement was ever reached on titles for Ted Kennedy, Steve Smith, Larry O'Brien, Ken O'Donnell, Fred Dutton, or me, nor were functions and lines of authority ever clearly drawn. This was partly because we were all too rushed and partly because of some sensitive personality problems that the candidate was too

busy to settle, although he had foreseen some of them in his talk that first
night with Ted, Steve, and me."

With democracy this rampant at the top, somebody had to emerge as
more than equal. Edward Kennedy, partly because he was a linear Kennedy,
shrugged once and took his cudgel up as primus inter pares. "Let's see," he
observed, bemused a little as the insiders settled down at separate tables for
the first session of many with their loose-leaf notebooks full of the addresses
and telephone numbers, "there's California over there, there's New York over
there. That leaves forty-eight for me."

Edward Kennedy's assignment had been to deal with the "non-primary"
states; in fact, he was expected to climb into anything anyplace and do whatever he saw that needed his skills in particular. Lester Hyman remembers
standing around the bedroom of Edward Kennedy's narrow little townhouse
on Charles River Square watching Teddy slide the drawer linings from under
his shirts to letter up, in his uneven printed scrawl WELCOME BOBBY to give
to people along the South Boston Saint Patrick's Day parade route. Outside,
jammed in between the curb and the frozen pachysandra, Ted Kennedy's car
had become too cold to start. "The vaunted Kennedy machine rides again,"
Ted muttered against the fallaway of the starter whining.

In the general backup of overdue decisions now flooding the strategy-
room floor, Ted Kennedy, at least, was loose enough yet to edge toward some
kind of resolution. The day Bob announced, Gerard Doherty in Boston had
called to leave word with Dave Burke that he was available to help; the following Tuesday Ted returned his call.

"We're thinking of Indiana," Ted allowed after a quick cordiality or two.
"Do you——" Kennedy hesitated. Doherty had barely started up his law practice, besides which he was as knobby as anybody around with those boils of
raw Boston-Irish self-doubt that signaled: Approach me gingerly. "Do you .
. . do you think you have somebody you could send out for us . . . ?"

As long as that was the way Ted was going to go about the thing, Gerard
Doherty did know somebody. It took him about a day and a half to cover his
pending law business; on Thursday afternoon he climbed onto the shuttle
to Washington. Staff people around the 20th and L Street headquarters had
already pulled together material that sorted out Indiana's newly enacted pre-
primary regulations, the toughest of which required each of the prospective
candidates to submit fifty-five hundred sound, authenticatable signatures,
five hundred to a Congressional district, by the March 28 deadline.

Along with the flat scowl from behind those thin-rimmed tortoiseshell
eyeglasses, the most intimidating thing to politicians about Gerry Doherty

is his ability, undistracted by sentiment, to count. By 1968 Doherty's reputation across Massachusetts was that of a born Cassandra, one whose practice it was to read a poll, talk to a few of the guys around, glance down a row or two of figures, and, all but invariably, recommend against. It took Gerard Doherty just seventy-two hours once he reached Indianapolis to pull together and spring his signature drive on Indiana Governor Branigin's unsuspecting organization.

Gerry returned with a high sense of exhilaration. Ted, who knew his own dour organizer well, looked encouraged throughout the day-long in-and-out meeting, presided over by Ted Sorensen and Steve Smith. Smith especially was full of questions, especially aware, perhaps, of what kind of money was involved in moving into a state this big and pumping it up overnight. Indiana was to involve a paid organization that mounted up to four hundred people; when the final audits were in, the expenses to the Kennedy offices, Park Avenue, Inc. were projected as high as $3 million.

Ted Kennedy's original estimate that this campaign was going to cost the Kennedy family $8 million was already starting to look way too low. Furthermore, as I detailed in *Bobby and J. Edgar*, the more than $10 million that the Ambassador had quietly extorted from his career-long cronies in the underworld to stake Jack in 1960 was not going to kick in at any point to help underwrite the detested Bobby.

By that time Pierre Salinger had come out and held a few political hands around the state, smoked a number of cigars, and was back in Washington unconvinced; the Kennedys tried a quick, secret poll, too quick and too secret to produce anything anybody was willing to rely on. Discussion continued. "On and off, there were a lot of people there," Doherty remembers. "I'm sure I was the only one in the room who felt he could carry Indiana. Then one time Teddy came into the room, and I think he figured that since I had given up all this time he had to be for me." Doherty and Robert Kennedy flew out to Indianapolis together; Bob was still wary, chronically observing to Doherty that, now that he was running for president himself, he had to pick and choose. He worried about how badly John Kennedy had done against Nixon in Indiana in 1960. An excited crowd of eight thousand people met them in Indianapolis. Ted Kennedy was installed already, operating out of a hotel suite in the Sheraton Lincoln; Bobby met him there. Well? the candidate presumptive wondered without quite voicing it across the Kennedy interval; his kid brother looked at him. "Yeah, go."

In the end, Fred Dutton remembers, it came back down to Bob and Ted. Nobody there admits it, exactly, but the ensuing five weeks devoted to rendering up Indiana politically was a trans-Kennedy hogpile from which fingers and built-up shoes and pieces of ear belonging to some very expensive-to-retain heads kept flying out as real authority changed hands. The primary communiqué had passed from Bob to Ted on March 28: Your man sucked us into Indiana; you get operational responsibility.

Whatever tentative strategic dovetailing there had been on March 28 came completely apart at the joints on March 31 when Lyndon Johnson, at the conclusion of his epoch-ending, cut-back-the-bombing speech, allowed as to how he had thought the whole thing over and decided that he was not—repeat, not—going to allow his name to be put into nomination for another term as president by his beloved Democratic Party in August in Chicago. Bill Vanden Heuvel, who was with Robert Kennedy when the president stepped down, remembers that Bob alone among the astonished and euphoric group of intimates at the New York Kennedy apartment at 870 United Nations Plaza realized "how much tougher the race was going to be with the great moral issue gone."

Later that evening Vanden Heuvel reached Ted Kennedy, who had been eating dinner in Indianapolis when the president aired his decision. He, too, Vanden Heuvel discovered a few minutes later, regarded Johnson's withdrawal as a setback; he spent that evening and much of the day following on the telephone to the Western party leaders he did so well with like Senator Howard Cannon of Nevada and Governors William Guy of North Dakota and Warren Hearnes of Missouri in the hope of forcing early commitments; "he, too, found," Vanden Heuvel notes, "a reluctance . . ."

Humphrey was already on the telephone himself, as indeed was Eugene McCarthy. There seeme to be an uncommunicated early consensus around the country that Humphrey, deservedly popular with the professionals, was very likely to wind up the Democratic nominee.

The morning after Johnson pulled out, Ted Kennedy telephoned Gordon Saint Angelo, the powerful Chairman of the Democratic Party in Indiana, and arranged a private meeting in Chicago for later in the day. Indiana's crusty Governor Roger Branigin had himself announced for the race two weeks earlier—nudged from the right by Humphrey, who promised $130,000 of the party's Washington campaign budget. Indiana's Senator Birch Bayh (who was identified generally as a liberal and a Kennedy sympathizer and regarded McCarthy's effort as misbegotten, mischievous, and completely without serious prospects) offered Branigin his core cadre of home professionals. Most unsettling of all, Branigin was pushed from the middle by the ambidextrous Saint Angelo, who presided over a rich party treasury.

The week before, during Gerry Doherty's signature drive, Saint Angelo had remarked with concern to Ted Kennedy that he just might have the 5,500 legally required signatures Doherty was assembling declared invalid as fast as they came in, a suggestion to which the practical Doherty produced a well-thought-through counter-suggestion: "Just tell him that if he monkeys around with the signatures, you'll break him in two."

According to the plot outline of the 1968 Kennedy effort, Indiana was to lance once and for all the professional hesitancies about Robert Kennedy's general appeal the way the 1960 West Virginia primary had opened things up for Jack: It was to be the showpiece blockade and glad occupation of heartland America's Bigot Country. West Virginia was well remembered from those spring weeks of Bob's own early blooding to politics, when he had himself been, in the then-desperate Hubert Humphrey's cry, a "young, emotional, juvenile," self-important among the stripped-out hills and shantytowns of West Virginia with "a little black bag and a checkbook" to endow the treasuries of each hillbilly courthouse machine. Unfortunately, as Gerry Doherty said, "When the Indiana guys saw us coming they invariably pulled their shades down."

"The Kennnedys are terrible organizers," Arthur Schlesinger would tell me over the years, "but they are brilliant improvisers." Indiana proved that out. It also tested whatever Edward Kennedy knew or hoped he knew about election engineering. "What are you doing?" an old friend asked Ted, watching him scrounging among the file cabinets, checking things off lists between telephone calls in the dumpy downtown headquarters above the daily upheaval of "Tara Invaded" downstairs in the decrepit movie theater that was playing and replaying *Gone With The Wind*. Dave Burke was intercepting troublemakers to face down with his studied phony gravity; Jim Flug was in the back, thinking. "I'm doing the political organization work," Edward Kennedy muttered. "It's terrible work but it's the most important. Bobby is the star, Bobby makes the speeches."

"The Indiana primary changed the balances completely between Bobby and Ted," Jimmy Doyle observed not very long after: The lifelong Kennedy undercurrent of seething jocularity, the older-to-younger fond half-abusive teasing that wore at things whenever the two were together altered now day by day. The Bob who liked to pinch-rub Ted's lapels before the colleagues and remark on the "good goods" he was wearing, or note that Teddy had come out ahead of time and was "subverting my campaign"—that Bob was losing self-assurance fast and being replaced by the genuinely underdog candidate who was worried, and unsure, and worried about being so unsure, and needing his brother's help so badly and was well aware that that, too, would have to be paid for, transacted in a final way on the Kennedy prestige exchange.

If Ted and his guy Doherty were running the Indiana thing, then power would unavoidably have to be parceled out to Teddy's people too. "There had been no general planning prior to Bob's announcement," Dave Burke says. "After Bobby announced we started to meet every afternoon with the media people. First problems were the most rudimentary, the basic. Space. How many phones? Who sits where? Who can make contractual obligations, who can be reached in this state, in that state? Time was so short that if these three staffs were ever to meld it had to be quickly, on short notice. That's how it was: If you want to bitch, out! We said, who wants the contract on X? I do. OK, you've got it, if you need scream time, call. You've got three weeks. Friction melted away after Indiana."

That April in Indiana the first thing they both made sure to clear up with Bob was Doherty's sole franchise. "There were certain people I didn't want in the state," Doherty remembers. "I picked 90 percent of the organization people myself, brought them in from Massachusetts. I said to Ted, 'Look, do you want me to work at this thing or do you want me to hold hands with the spies?' That was my price. He understood." Doherty's skin was thin; he wanted that much well recognized to start with: When Bob Kennedy's rough, seasoned coordinator of advance planning, Jerry Bruno, called into the head-quarters as peeved as hell that nobody had met his plane in Indianapolis, Doherty got on the line for long enough to suggest that since he didn't seem well enough oriented to find his way in from the airport, his prospects of leading the candidate around the state were poor: Why didn't he just get on the next plane East? Bruno made it on his own.

Other nuncios appeared. Lawrence F. O'Brien—confessor to the politics of two presidents by then and probably capable of exacting loyalty from a three-pound river rock—gave Lyndon Johnson his notice the day after the March 31 speech and turned up by the middle of April in Indiana to plump for Bobby. Indiana already promised an enormously expensive media campaign. The break the Kennedys got early in April was the arrival—shambling, unkempt and banjo-eyed as ever—of that brilliant, unpredictable freelance of language and publicity Richard Goodwin. Fervently opposed to our involvement in Vietnam, Goodwin had been hustling for Gene McCarthy.

By April 10, when he arrived in Indianapolis, Goodwin's feelings and status in the Kennedy organization had become "increasingly complicated." "I told Bobby a long time before that that if he ran he ought to hire a penthouse apartment for all of us old JFK people," Goodwin observes, coming up with each inspired phrase half-muffled as if what he is saying were pulled out of a disheveled bed of ideas on which nobody had changed the sheets for months and months, "and stick us all up there, and load the place up with whiskey and food and cigars, and once a day we'd get together and write a long telegram full of marvelous strategy ideas. And then what he ought to do is accept the telegram every day and throw it into the wastebasket without ever bothering to open it. And let his own young, hungry kids give him advice. They knew him, and they knew what he really wanted."

Whatever he himself advised, Goodwin felt he had to offer Bob Kennedy his services as soon as he could reasonably explain himself once Kennedy announced. Goodwin had joined Eugene McCarthy's effort early enough to put together the masterly publicity that was instrumental in McCarthy's amazing performance in New Hampshire—a deed that, along with its perpetrator, Robert Kennedy had viewed with mixed emotions, referring to Goodwin as "his nibs" and refusing to speak to him for some weeks. Goodwin stayed with McCarthy, whom he found, finally, unapproachable, through the Wisconsin primary; when Bobby announced and Gene asked him to continue, Goodwin protested that he couldn't "play a key role in a campaign the real object of which has to be to destroy the political career of a friend of mine."

"Isn't that the point, though?" the mordant McCarthy wondered.

"Yes. That's why I'm leaving."

Biting back his anger out of respect for Goodwin's unrivaled talents as an analyst, publicist, and position man, Bob Kennedy gave Dick an unusually free hand. "We just went ahead and produced. Ran up bills. Lots of bills." Before long, sixteen television stations across barren Hoosierland were studding their viewing hours with spots produced by Goodwin and John Frankenheimer and Charles Guggenheim: Moments on the campaign trail, student questioners, answered sweetly, reasonably, by a trustworthy Bobby, newly clippered and awfully concerned about problems the folks in the heartland had never realized Bob had ever bothered himself much with.

This barbered version of the zealot *The Indianapolis Star* liked to equate with Savonarola was quite willing to identify himself to such businessmen's groups as the Civitan Club of Vincennes as "part of an administration in which private enterprise and the people were freed of the cycles of boom and bust . . . ," during which the "profits of corporations after taxes rose . . . almost 40 percent . . ." As the onetime "chief law enforcement officer of the United States," he advocated decentralization, policies to "bring the cost of living under control," and business "enlisted as an ally of private progress." He rejected the notion that the federal government was to decide "where a school was to be located" and advocated strengthening "our police departments so they know how to cope with riots."

After a national swing Bob was back in Indiana to finish up April with ten days of grinding old-time whistle-stop campaigning. Grimacing through the murderous schedule of union halls and supermarkets and fieldhouse rallies, depot speeches from the five-car "Wabash Cannonball" along the legended Peru-Wabash-Huntington-Fort Wayne route: The prevailing mood was of jokes, noise, fatigue, and the suspicion whenever the overstocked brain cleared an instant that time was being wasted. Time was running out.

Having entered the race as a peace-and-stop-the-bombing-and-negotiate-with-Hanoi candidate, Bob had watched Lyndon Johnson pack his central issues up and take them overboard with himself into retirement. Robert Kennedy was, more and more, half despite himself, developing subjects and approaches mostly documented by his brother Edward, principally draft reform, a revised national health policy, a fair set of income tax provisions. A primary RFK proposal, utilizing a revised tax incentive program to persuade big business to revitalize the ghettos, went nowhere.

The Ukrainians in Saint Michael's Hall and the blacks along their bottle-strewn side streets and a horde of happy half-drunken Polacks wolfing kielbasa on Dyngus Day might keep the proletarian pandemonium rising, claw cufflinks out of the candidate's sleeves and chip his tooth in their eagerness to get close. But Robert Kennedy was no more able to unite them, "bridge" their animosities, than any other politician. When the votes were counted Kennedy would, for example, have lost 59 of the 70 white precincts in Gary. Indiana was 65 percent white-collar, white-faced, white-protective citizens who had been reading their *Indianapolis Star* every day and paled with alarm at what its publisher kept suggesting about the way "The Kennedys" had arrived in force to butcher their beloved values. "Maybe it's just not my time," Robert Kennedy sighed the day before the polls opened. "But I've learned something from Indiana. The country is changing . . ." Changing, certainly, but by then, as Ted well recognized, much more slowly than Robert F. Kennedy.

On April 4, long before his Indiana campaign reached running speed, Bob Kennedy got word that Martin Luther King had been gunned down in Memphis. His responses, pure and very natural to him, tell a lot about the way Robert Kennedy now conceived of himself. He acted, in essence, neither as merely a United States senator nor even a case-hardened friend of the

King family's—let alone as a man just then undertaking to make himself the next President of the United States. Apprehending with a precision perhaps no other white American did that the news alone would prove pyrotechnic across the ghettos of America from Roxbury to Watts, he immediately took upon himself the role of the sole legitimate and trusted white man to the nation's blacks. He quieted a mob in Indianapolis, telephoned Coretta to comfort her and make the necessary arrangements to return Martin's body to Atlanta in a Kennedy-chartered plane, put himself in touch with his sphinx-like onetime Civil Rights Department head Burke Marshall and sent him out ahead of himself to damp things down in Memphis. Rushing back to Washington he negotiated on his own authority with a representation of the Negro leadership, then personally visited the ghettos to reassure and quiet the mob.

Decrying the threat of violence in the streets, Robert Kennedy pointed up ". . . another kind of violence . . . slower but just as deadly, destructive as the shot or the bomb in the night. This is the violence of institutions: indifference and inaction and slow decay. This is the violence that afflicts the poor, that poisons relations between men because their skin has different colors. This is a slow destruction of a child by hunger, and schools without books and homes without heat in the winter.

"This is the weakening of a man's spirits by denying him the chance to stand as a father and as a man among other men." Bob Kennedy was speaking for the rising minority which he, while still in exile, already led.

Once Bob returned to Indiana, rattling through the hustings with the messages of good cheer and change to security actuaries and poultry farmers who didn't like his looks to start with, his voice, high and oily normally, rasped. Good Bobby howled, and Bad Bobby howled, and the May 7 primary day wasn't looking any more promising because of it. "I didn't relate to Robert Kennedy," Doherty says, neither sad nor happy about that, recalling it as one more thing he was forced to deal with as red-hot became white-hot. "I stayed with Teddy. Bobby used to get nervous, he'd get hold of Ted and work on him: 'Are you sure Doherty knows what he's doing?' Ted would reassure him; then, as soon as he got a chance, he'd call and ask me, 'Are you sure you know what you're doing, Gerry?' Then I'd call my guys, David Harrison and the people I brought in, and I'd ask, 'Are you guys sure you know what you're doing . . . ?' But Ted stood up to it, kept the harpies and sharpies off my back, Dolan, Bruno . . .

"And, through the whole thing, Teddy held my hand. I don't know how, exactly, but he senses, he senses things like—the right room to use with people he wants to influence, which of the approaches, how long to talk. He was a good campaign manager. If there was one single guy who understood it best it was Ted. Steve could tell you what had to be done, but Ted had a sort of political split vision, he was the campaigner/strategist. He knew how to meld the two of them. Then he got very concerned when Larry O'Brien came in and went to work; he worried that after all the heavy lifting I'd done in the early days that . . . that nobody should come along and say to me, 'OK, kid, screw.' This human thing."

Finally, closer to the deadline edge than any of them had cared to get, hard political experience told. The outside coordinators the headquarters could depend on surfaced; the absence of organization regulars made it easier to train and monitor the enthusiasts they got. The emphasis shifted from converting people to isolating Kennedy's natural constituency and getting it to the polling places. Bob, calming, came back with impressions about what went and what didn't, returned to the headquarters excited at the response he was getting talking about extended Medicare and Aid for Older Americans; one imagines his younger brother smiling quietly.

"Bob went into that thing in Indiana way over to the left on the race and poverty issues," Fred Dutton observes, "Ted was one of those who tried to get him to the middle of the road. To moderate his position. He knew exactly what we were getting into, probably because people talked to him; his acceptance in the Senate, in organized labor, was so much greater than Bob's."

"You mean I got more votes than Ted?" a reporter recalls Bob having answered, hearing the results of a desultory Massachusetts write-in campaign, unhappy at the way the Massachusetts delegation had slipped away by default to Eugene McCarthy. "That's a fantastic showing," the reliable Ethel was quick to say; Ted tried to gesture the reporter off as unobtrusively as he could.

Bob won Indiana by 42 percent to McCarthy's 27 percent to Branigan's 30 percent. What vote there was in Indiana for Bob, all of them recognized, they had isolated and cornered; it was a technician's triumph. Technique, and a lot of Kennedy money.

"Election night I got a call to come over to Bob's suite at the Airport Motel," Doherty says in conclusion. "I didn't go. I stayed with my own people. At 10 PM I got a panicky call: Bob wanted me to come out, and to bring along anybody I chose to be with, anybody I wanted with me. All of us went. I'm sure this was at Teddy's insistence."

3. *The Primaries*

But Ted's responsibility now, free finally of Indiana, was for the most part to show up at the closed party primaries and conventions in the big sloppy-rich delegate-heavy industrial states. He went prepared to do a favor and accept a favor, work his effulgent back-room personality to break down out of those delegations of professionals as many convention votes as might prove detachable for Bob. This was a service everyone involved understood Ted was as naturally well-fitted to perform as Bobby was not.

May remained difficult. It was Edward Kennedy's well-tutored inclination to prepare carefully each situation he got himself into; he retained his deep conservative suspicion of any strategy predicated on the implied political violences of threat and bluff, of stampeding delegates by intimidating them. Promoted everywhere by Lyndon Johnson, Hubert Humphrey's candidacy fell across the closed Democratic caucuses in industrial America with the inevitability of night. With David Burke in tow, Ted Kennedy turned up among the political pros in Pennsylvania, and Ohio, and Illinois, and sounded the leadership out. Nobody much liked Bobby, David Burke told me afterward, and the consensus for Hubert was so one-sided that he plainly had a clear majority of the delegates by the middle of May. Bob's cause was hopeless.

John Kennedy's primary campaign in 1960 had itself been a raid. But the days were over when an annoyed Jack Kennedy could call out a Wisconsin newspaper publisher, label him a "cheap, bigoted son of a bitch" so loud the astounded Jackie could hear it all through a door and be astonished further to see the two men emerge a few minutes later, shaking hands and chatting quietly and smiling. The electorate was searching for calmer waters, and there was a feeling among Democratic politicians that Bob Kennedy was a man of too much plume and dynamism to take the people into anything like that. Ted felt it early, unmistakably, in Massachusetts. "I'm coming out for Bobby," Lester Hyman, who had been agonizing over his own decision after pointedly not returning David Burke's call, declared at once when he met Ted at the airport a few days after Bob Kennedy announced.

"Why do that?" Edward Kennedy wanted to know. "You're up for state chairman in May. Why not wait, keep quiet . . . ? If you're reelected, then you can help us."

After Indiana, stupefied as Bob obviously was still by the wind-down after two straight weeks of barnstorming, aides began to notice the way his mood kept verging on inertia and depression whenever his attention wavered. "I think I blew it," he had murmured to Bill Vanden Heuvel the night Goodwin telephoned the New Hampshire results to him. By early May Robert Kennedy was finally taking in the fact that Eugene McCarthy, although refusing to get up at five in the morning to shake hands at factory gates, rarely poking into ghettos—this cold slowly smiling unapproachable man with his air of cosmic unconcern simply was not going to accommodate Bobby by sidetracking himself. McCarthy's sense of entitlement was turning out to be the equal of Robert Kennedy's own. The "A students" were working the neighborhoods of the country door-to-door in the hope of dumping Bobby. Suddenly Bob felt old.

As the Humphrey campaign solidified quietly, Ted Kennedy, honcho, chief strategist, and front man for the non–primary states, was in and out. He put himself through twenty-four-hour days during which the closest thing to sleep was to doze an hour after being briefed in a jet to Huron, South Dakota, or Erie, Pennsylvania; dinner was three bites and one swallow of whiskey and ginger ale at each of several testimonial dinners, a reception, and a midnight conference. Teddy's overriding theme everywhere was Bobby, the only Real Winner; his devil, whenever he found it, was the unit rule, that bylaw of so many conventions that required the whole of a delegation to go the way of its majority.

There was a spattering of successes. In Iowa—where the carefully organized Kennedy campaign could exert its influence on a series of open caucuses that began at the grass-roots precinct level and remained accessible—Bobby wound up with 28 of the 45 votes. In South Dakota, a corner of the West Ted liked especially because of his appreciation of the way, when his little plane landed on grass, Indian chiefs on ponies waited alongside the landing strip to welcome him, territory he thought of as belonging to the "people with very big hands," Ted—with the organizing help of Pat Lucey of Wisconsin and Dave Harrison, Doherty's man—was able to run off a beautiful little delegate slam, all 26 delegates from Hubert Humphrey's birth state, hopeful magic to phone in on the open line to Bob, who, having just been dumped in Oregon, was very worried he was going to be upset, and plainly needed whatever juju he could inhale to finish strong enough in California.

Teddy worked the warm little Western delegations, where he had goodwill left over from 1960; in a series of pinpoint appeals he flew into Arizona on the eve of the state convention and worked it through one evening reception for five hundred and into the following morning, one-on-one with the delegates, and left for Albuquerque in mid-morning, where he concentrated on pushing for second-ballot strength.

"If it were you, Teddy," Wayne Owens, along to help, remembers old party hands saying over and over; then back to Tucson to pry out five sure votes; then Salt Lake City and another reception for the delegates, where gracious but stubborn efforts were made to chivvy out of a delegation that had agreed to keep among its options enough commitments here and there to open the entire group up. Back and forth, in and out; in Vermont, with Doherty there to assist Governor Hoff in loosening things, Ted worked the count up to seven to Humphrey's ten to McCarthy's five—useful but not . . . not enough, a back-drag, if anything: Maine had meanwhile gone for Humphrey 20-7, Connecticut refused to commit itself, the Kennedys' own New England wasn't working out, coming around properly . . .

Teddy, on airplanes and off airplanes all May like a sagebrush veterinarian hoping to survive a season of hoof-and-mouth-disease scares, found Kennedy allies-presumptive and leaders loyal a decade before succumbing to the nationwide plague of Humphreyism in heart-stopping numbers. Nothing was to be assumed. Delegations like that of New Jersey, regarded even by the careful Kenny O'Donnell as sure in early April, were gone over, Hubert's, before that wet month ended. The critical benevolence of the labor unions, almost every single local, seemed to slide day by day away from Bob toward the labor-tested Humphrey. The gigantic iceberg of George Meany's AFL-CIO went early; the Teamsters were beyond hope; agonizingly, to Bob in particular, even Cesar Chavez at first refused to make an unequivocal commitment. Walter Reuther was holding back, ominously, mindful, as Hubert H. Humphrey was not shy at all about reminding one of the many caucuses meeting among the suites and committee rooms of Michigan's Cobo Hall, that Hubert H. Humphrey had been the man at the point of outermost progress for working people for twenty years in America. The Peace Corps had been Hubert H. Humphrey's idea, and the important poverty legislation, and the notion of a ban on nuclear proliferation, and Medicare. And who, after all, had been the one to contrive to shame the Democrats into inserting the first of the civil-rights planks ever in the platform in 1948 . . . ?

"That doesn't help Bobby," an agitated Lester Hyman complained to Leonard Woodcock when Woodcock toted up Humphrey's accomplishments.

"We're all delegates. Some are for McCarthy, some are for Bobby, and some are for Humphrey. When Mr. Reuther makes up his mind"—Woodcock's hand, fingers spread, closed into an expressive fist. So Reuther was not, after all, finally, to be depended upon: Fewer seemed reliable each hour; cave-ins were impending.

"It seemed to me we were always getting to groups just after either Harris or Gronouski had obviously convinced them," Dave Burke remembers. A desperation was infiltrating the geniality. "I know you've just been addressed by a fine ambassador to Poland," Ted would open to a group of delegates. "We liked him; in fact my brother appointed him postmaster general. Fred Harris is a very good friend of mine. I notice that when they learned we were here they sent so many able people in to help the vice president out . . . we must be doing something right . . ."

It was a rock-breaking operation; Ted had known that, at least, well enough beforehand. "The major question was what the United Auto Workers were going to do," he himself recalled to me. "They were very much split. A strong segment was sympathetic to Bobby. The old element had its allegiances to Hubert, but there was a newer politics group quite active for us.

"You were permitted to go around, of course, but you knew in advance they elected about 60 percent of their committee members two years in advance, and there was going to be very little decided by the germinating impact of the candidate . . ."

Or the candidate's brother. Meanwhile, the floors stayed cement; Ted's back hurt. "I don't like that sonofabitch of a brother of yours," Hyman recalls more than one delegate venturing, soused enough to work his way over to Ted and show "The Kennedys" what kind of a man he was, "but I'd vote for you." "The way he could laugh that off!" Hyman says now, shaking his head, recollecting the way the grin would freeze a second or two longer than meant anything, the hinges inside his heavy jaw would compress and release themselves, compress and release themselves, clenching and reclenching. Ted would pull his attention off carefully, pick up on the next face pressing nearer. "Why do people hate my brother so?" an exhausted Ted Kennedy was to wonder aloud to Lester, flying out of Detroit. It was a conundrum he was much too tired to consider just then.

The Michigan delegate preferences broke down into 40 votes for RFK, 47 for Humphrey, 2 for Eugene McCarthy, and 7 undecided. It was an honorable showing. But honor—to the Kennedys, at least—had always seemed flavorless except as a garnishment to victory.

Even allowing for Edward Kennedy's knack for blinking away the uncomfortable, there had to be, as May ended, a deeper and deeper reddening of embarrassment to his normally high-colored face as he listened to his own voice offering the familiar litany underscoring Bob's status as the "only Democrat who can win in November," when, during the previous ten days, both Humphrey and McCarthy had caught the chronically out-of-kilter Kennedy campaign with two perfectly placed mortar blasts. The Oregon setback was one, of course; the other was the Pennsylvania debacle.

"We had a very difficult time in Pennsylvania," Ted himself admitted to me. "A very difficult time. The state is Joe Barr [the Mayor of Pittsburgh], Mayor Tate [of Philadelphia], and the steelworkers. Three influential figures who amount to the Democratic operation there. All three were strong for Hubert."

Depending on this, the Humphrey planners had organized the state committee to arrange a "special meeting" for May 25 that was intended to demonstrate Humphrey's strength to leaders in other large industrial states and pile delegates on the accelerating Humphrey bandwagon. On April 19 Pennsylvania had voted in a presidential primary in which the only name on the Democratic ballot, Eugene McCarthy's, received 428,259 votes to 65,000 for Robert Kennedy and 73,000 for Humphrey-Johnson.

It was an unpromising background; the Kennedy brothers had not improved their prospects by first snubbing the cantankerous Mayor James Tate in 1968 when he had asked for campaign help—which the obliging vice president had hurried in to tender. On April 1, two weeks after Tate had publicly called Kennedy a "wise guy" for getting into the race, Robert Kennedy appeared with him at a fund-raising dinner and made himself label the hard-handed old wire puller "one of the greatest mayors in the United States," adding, "from time to time I'm going to look down at Mayor Tate to see if he is smiling." Tate was well aware that the Kennedys had been looking down on him for years, and he had never been smiling.

On May 25, in Harrisburg, Ted Kennedy wasn't smiling very much. "We went to their convention," he remembered, "and spoke up there, and we thought we made some inroads. They weren't very significant, as things turned out: At a subsequent meeting of the state central committee, Humphrey was strongly endorsed. The only leader we had was Billy Green, the Congressman [and second-generation boss, son of Bill Green the financier, who had supported Jack]. There was a profile in courage there. He was the only leader of significance to support Bob, rather an interesting sidelight . . ." Teddy trailed off.

Pennsylvania turned out to be, once the Humphrey strategy became clear, a real hand-to-hand Kennedy shock troops assault. Kenny O'Donnell and Paul Kirk landed on the union people hard, and Ted Kennedy and Dave Burke went through the entire political handbook of gentler approaches, and because there were so many to keep straight they brought in Dun Gifford— who as Ted's man, had moved over within the Washington headquarters from

working on the financial breakdowns to become operating head, within Dave
Hackett's overall responsibility, of the intelligence operation, the "boiler
room," for the non-primary states.

The "boiler-room" operation was responsible by 1968 for sophisticated
intelligence gathering and general coordination. It had evolved out of the
1952 back-room clearing house, little more than a bullpen of Kelly Girls on
telephones making sure the Kennedy Secretaries had plenty of bumper stickers. In 1968, the girls in the boiler room were the functioning day-to-day
brain stem and central nervous system for the entire rushed, frantic, bewilderingly overlapped effort. Isolated nearly to quarantine in their remote
windowless back room of the Washington headquarters, each girl with her
assigned states taped to the wall in front of her, they fed exact information
into and relayed discoveries back from the advancing people out ahead of
Bobby's Road Show, as they referred to it. They passed through the remark of
a labor leader here, an officeholder fired a day before and resentful elsewhere:
whatever held up, whatever might help later.

"These were unusual girls," Joey Gargan, who himself ran a lot of the
advance for Bob's campaign, said later. "Picked to do their jobs. Clear minds,
integrity, courage, willing to devote long hours of thankless service to the
most sensitive, difficult job, everything to be kept confidential . . . They knew
all our secrets. Girls who had, basically, to have no personal lives, no personal problems. After Bobby's death, you know, many of those girls worked
what amounted to seventy-four hours straight without sleep, without food,
virtually." Gargan paused but couldn't help himself; Chappaquiddick had
intervened, and under my questioning the anguish over Mary Jo Kopechne
had returned: "Hardly the group of girls anybody would pick for a weekend
of . . . of dalliance!"

In Harrisburg, as later in California, the count of delegates and com-
plexity of the information to be sorted and appraised and fed at the correct
moment to the principals complicated everything so much that Dun Gifford
arrived to filter the last-second sorting-out. Holed up in a Harrisburg hotel,
Dun, backed up by the boiler room, fed notes to Ted indicating who among
the delegates were the sixteen influential ones, made sure each got at least
a telephone call from the candidate's brother before the "special meeting"
convened. The ritual dance in Pennsylvania was accordingly timetabled and
informed precisely to the final cross-wrist handshake and the expenditure of
the last nicely calculated leap of personal charm, and was—very disappoint-
edly but not really unexpected, at least to Ted—very much a failure.

The day after the "special meeting" in Harrisburg Ted Kennedy and Steve

Smith met in a restaurant in Portland, Oregon, for one of their glummer meals together. "The beginning of the campaign was awfully confused," Arthur Schlesinger has said. "Sorensen, O'Donnell, and Ted Kennedy argued a lot, I remember. Titles: Wasn't one of them the campaign director, another the campaign manager?—I'm not sure I can tell you how they worked it out, finally." By May 26 nobody was lobbying for Field Marshal anymore. The thing was doomed. All the Kennedy money, as Steve Smith couldn't help admitting, wasn't going to make a lot of difference. By then Kennedy's safety men were fanning out up and down Oregon and California hoping to lay a hand on crazylegs Eugene McCarthy.

Instead of showing the good grace and political realism to resign from the effort after Indiana and turn his enthusiasts over to the expectant Robert Kennedy, McCarthy announced that Indiana hadn't shown much; the "direct confrontation" would come in Nebraska. Former Lieutenant Governor Phil Sorensen and Jim Green had started early, recruited the regular Democratic organization in Nebraska, and mounted a powerful statewide effort that won Bob 51.5 percent of the ballots cast and the preponderance of the delegates vs. McCarthy's very respectable 31 percent. McCarthy—nonchalant as ever about his earlier statements—then chose largely to ignore what he anticipated in Nebraska and let Bobby burn himself out running up a showing none of the professionals were likely to care one way or the other about.

Eugene McCarthy sent ahead the money and proven organizers that bypassing Nebraska released to Oregon and California to tighten up the local efforts out West. The primaries in the Far West have been exhaustively written about. Oregon was to be the funhouse mirror for the surviving Kennedys; two days before the balloting Ted Kennedy and Steve Smith, looking over the campaign there, knew well enough what Bob had probably to expect by then. The sustaining explanations for the loss remained that Oregon amounted, in Bob Kennedy's words, to "one giant suburb," freer than anywhere else, in Eugene McCarthy's words, of "the less intelligent and less well-educated voters" who made up the natural Kennedy following.

At home in Oregon the McCarthy organizers had turned out his kind of constituents in sufficient numbers with an effective academically based cadre of peace activists determined to break the string of primary victories Robert Kennedy needed to keep his candidacy "viable," as he was clumsy enough to put it himself, one unguarded moment, into the microphone of the San Francisco Press Club. The demographic analysis Bob Kennedy and Eugene McCarthy shared assumes that the proper Kennedy constituency is coexistent with the ethnically unassimilated and culturally disinherited, the eternal "Gladys," with the rings of fat around the ankles, who was so thunderstruck to touch the Ambassador's hand so many years earlier.

Only by daring always, and winning always, would any Kennedy retain his authenticity, which put the obligation expressly on the people of Oregon either to select Bobby or destroy him as an option. Robert Kennedy started acting like the child who "threatened to hold his breath unless the people of Oregon voted for him." As late in the campaign as his evening television remarks on May 14, primary day in Nebraska, he was still publicly hopeful that he and McCarthy could "perhaps work together . . . in Oregon and California," an offer much like the proposal the walrus and the carpenter made to the oysters. Whatever Eugene McCarthy wanted in 1968, it certainly wasn't to become Robert Kennedy's lunch.

His misery-wrinkled little hawk's face folding into itself more deeply hour by hour, his tone becoming an urgent rasp, Robert Kennedy was confusing the way the world had to be for him with the way it was. Once he had lost in Oregon the gritty final snapshots emerged in which Bob Kennedy was snarling at his key aides about their guitar playing and half-trotting away from the Eugene McCarthy he was dodging in debate at the Portland zoo.

The unreality was everywhere. "Who was running Oregon?" the plain-spoken Gifford repeats aloud. "That was the problem: We never did find out. That's why we lost the goddamn thing." When Congresswoman Edith Green, who had successfully run Jack Kennedy's primary campaign against favorite son Wayne Morse, took the unusual step—unusual for anybody on the Hill, at least—of volunteering early to run things for him in Oregon, Bob, touched, accepted, and gave the often fierce and extremely prerogative-conscious lady legislator complete veto rights.

The Kennedys woke up slowly and very reluctantly to what wasn't happening; by mid-May, when Oregon in its turn loomed as the appointed testing ground and anteroom to the major shakedown expected in California, the Kennedys' chance to recover balance had come and gone. The polls looked ominous. Mrs. Green, who had put together for Bob, as of April 28, a head-quarters consisting of two desks and three people, was fiercely jealous of the more experienced Kennedy campaign hands like Herbert Schmertz, and replaced him with Barrett Prettyman, a Green confidant, who was utterly unable to get it together. For all the belated influx of Kennedy talent—Larry O'Brien, Steve Smith, Joe Dolan, John Nolan, John Douglas, a wrecking crew McCarthy lost little time characterizing as vintage hoods repositioned in pine-scented Oregon but redolent of the ground-out cigars of the "old politics"—

very few new ideas occurred to the tiring Kennedy regulars that bitter final week.

Teddy, who was on the telephone constantly, appeared to good effect before labor groups that wouldn't have tolerated Bobby, but nothing was going to warm the key leaders up; there were no "people" to appeal to. The whole state exhibited a dismaying paucity of ghettos. "We hit Oregon like running right into a brick wall," David Burke says.

Mrs. Green hung on. She had been, irreducibly, Somebody Jack Trusted, a loyalist early aboard; Bob backed her up. She advised him not to debate McCarthy, which hurt him; she delivered a rousing stump speech in the face of election-night projections that indicated—correctly—that she was not going even to carry her own district for Bob. Until the moment he climbed on that final airplane for California, Bob let Edith Green influence very heavily the issues, the media techniques, and the appearance schedule around the state. Bob lost, 38.8 percent to McCarthy's 44.7 percent, with the Johnson write-in at a little over 12 and Humphrey at 4. It was the first loss in a contested election for a Kennedy.

Edith Green had the last word until the end. It proved, as John Kennedy once said of Bob as a boy, that he had "either a lot of guts or no common sense at all." How John or Joe Kennedy would have handled the loyal but obstructive Congresswoman isn't hard to imagine. Either way, Eugene McCarthy mopped up.

4. Los Angeles

Oregon had been low-budgeted; one of the mid-March arguments in favor of letting Mrs. Green run the state was the fact that she was something of a bargain; California was likely to be expensive, and the auditors at Park Avenue, Inc., were counting the pennies wherever they could. In the end, to save some face within the situation, Oregon did cost money; California was expensive too, although there as well the hope was to scale the expenditures down, staff up Jesse Unruh's personal following, and try to keep away from an escalating media war with either Humphrey or McCarthy.

A low-budget strategy like this presumed the ability to deliver his state of "Big Daddy" Jesse Unruh himself, Speaker and Great Horned Owl of the California Assembly—three hundred pounds at one time of beak and political talon, inside a mountain of plumage so soft as to approach noiselessness as it made a welcome rich meal of this union chieftain or that nouveau riche savings-and-loan speculator.

April had already ended before the planners at 20th and L realized that the Democratic Party in California was approaching plague conditions as far as they were concerned. McCarthy's uncanny "furry people," the legions of collegiate field mice with their psychedelic headquarters slogans and block parties and wee-hours bouts of solicitation in prosperous neighborhoods, had already overrun much of the state. Trapped Unruh and his young sleek aides, with their answers for everything, in their belfries in Sacramento and Los Angeles and left them all sitting blinking wisely, full of outdated knowledge, and far too little money raised on their own, and not enough coming from S. Smith and Company. They were out of touch. On May 1 Steve Smith moved full time into the Los Angeles headquarters, Goodwin was installed to conjure up his coruscating slogans with Frankenheimer, and—at Ted Kennedy's repeated urging—Charles Guggenheim arrived. Within a matter of days the sweet nauseating media-blanket of the political fumigator had started to slow the merry McCarthy people down.

The Park Avenue, Inc. wing, hoped to pressure Unruh into funding the California campaign with donations from politically itchy local figures like Louis Warschaw and Howard Ahmanson. But it had realized too late that the habitual Western backers either were afraid of U.S. Treasury interference, still loyal to (or scared of) the administration, or—where liberal sentiment was genuine—skimmed early and effectively by Martin Stone of the McCarthy campaign. Steve Smith arrived with a corrective checkbook, but the tenor of the individual background noises, some on and a great many off the record, suggests that there was a . . . a reluctance to part with the millions of dollars it was evidently going to take to even things up in California: Apart from the working real estate ventures Steve presided over normally, notably the Chicago Merchandise Mart, most of the money available was income directly from the trusts of the individual brothers and sisters. Where were the hoods of yesteryear?

The Kennedy brothers and sisters tithed for Bobby, finally, although there was reportedly a good deal of unfiltered grumbling. California seemed limitless, although it had by now been discovered by the heirs that the Kennedy holdings were not. Such staples as the Bobby buttons turned up much later than would have done much good; as in Indiana volunteers were in short enough supply so that most workers actually had to be paid, unlike the idealistic McCarthyites. Rolling, the McCarthy organizers hit on devices like arranging for Gene to do free radio interviews everywhere he went; the penetration of these all over a state of freeway commuters was instantaneous and effective and maddening to the Kennedy accountants with their heavy schedule of expensive TV spots.

At the same time Robert Kennedy, obviously prompted more and more by psychological necessity than political common sense, was conducting a campaign heavily scheduled with motorcades and speeches to California blacks and Mexican-Americans. "These are my people," he yelled over his shoulder as he hung three-quarters out of an open car while adulatory mobs pulled whatever came off away; his exchanges now approached rapturous demagoguery. "What," he would yell, feigning disbelief, "Senator McCarthy hasn't been here?"

"No . . . o!"

"Doesn't he care for you?"

"No . . . o!"

"And doesn't Vice President Humphrey care?"

"No . . . o!"

This may have been calories to Bobby's famished ego just then—he was campaigning so hard he passed out with exhaustion at least once those final days—but it was thick across the tongues of machinist union members and small businessmen watching the tube after a hot day working a lathe or tending a counter. The last few weeks Unruh and Smith and John Siegenthaler got together what there was of organized support for Bobby. California has rigid statutes protecting civil service people so there were very few state employees to help, but Unruh's own staff kept chucking away. Organized labor remained skeptical; the few union officials, like Tom Consiglio, who wanted to work for Bob, felt George Meany's hard disapproval.

The morning of Bob Kennedy's highly touted "debate" with Eugene McCarthy in San Francisco Bob scratched a breakfast with six hundred labor leaders from all over California, an event it had taken a prodigy of persuasion by Kennedy's few labor supporters in the state, Paul Shrade of the UAW in particular, to arrange. Instead, Kennedy locked himself up for briefing sessions with Burke Marshall, Edelman, Mankiewicz, Dutton, Unruh, Sorensen, Schlesinger, Milton Gwirtzman—many of the same people who helped John Kennedy get ready for Nixon. Then he went out handshaking on Fisherman's Wharf. Reports of what Bob was doing—and canceling—reached Ted Kennedy in South Dakota; Teddy said nothing but shook his head, expressively. That night McCarthy and Kennedy exchanged powder-puff punches on ABC television; six hundred union leaders remained miffed.

Three days after that Bob Kennedy won the California preferential primary 1,472,166 to Gene's 1,322,608, with 80,286 for Tom Lynch, the administration stand-in; again, Eugene McCarthy had shaved Bob close enough as the professionals read results to steal his impact. The brutal primary in New York awaited him thirteen days later.

But before that Sirhan Sirhan had caught Robert Kennedy handshaking his way along the steamtables of the Hotel Ambassador kitchen—observing one last Kennedy ritual, happy to have the chance, hopeful—and ostensibly murdered him. Decades later, evidence would leak in the declassified Los Angeles coroner's report on the homicide that Sirhan had in effect mounted a distraction: Extreme powder burns at the base of Bobby's neck indicated the involvement of a pro, a button man.

Whichever way it happened, Robert Kennedy was dead.

This was an outcome people close to Robert Kennedy had worried about all along. Jacqueline Kennedy, who had drawn ever closer to her attentive brother-in-law over the five years since Jack's death and kept Bob's picture by her bed, had repeatedly warned intimates that Bob was taking too many chances, that he, too, was going to get himself shot. Ted kept his premonitions to himself, but the undertow of dread and resignation that anybody who knew him well could not mistake continued to churn beneath his gregarious personality.

Some suggestion, at least, of the pain and fatalism starting to haunt Teddy more every day came through at the final Mass for Bobby. "My brother," Edward Kennedy intoned, the hocks of his jaws above his deaconlike cutaway blotchy from too many nights without sleep by the time he spoke at the Saint Patrick's Cathedral funeral—he was struggling to steer his swollen baritone around the catches of his sobs—"my brother need not be idealized or enlarged in death beyond what he was in life, to be remembered simply as a good and decent man, who saw wrong and tried to right it, saw suffering and tried to heal it, saw war and tried to stop it."

Then, familiar—"Some men see things as they are and say 'Why?' I dream things that never were and say 'Why not?'"

The phrasing owed most of its falls, as it frequently did, to Gwirtzman, but the judgment of Robert that informed it was the one his younger brother had come to little by little over years. Robert Kennedy vs. America. America, institutional America, beloved and mysterious enemy for generations by June of 1968. The implacable presence, which had already provoked such an array of family personalities, from the wheedling graces of Honey Fitz to the raw emphatic power of the Ambassador.

Until, refining itself with suffering, it eventuated in the coercive poise of the boyish president himself. But Robert Kennedy, irradiated after 1963 by grief and loss: Robert Kennedy had mutated. Sometimes, pressured, he fell back on the simplified reflexes that allowed him to tap Martin Luther King's telephone or threaten the suburbanites of the nation with "10,000 black people" swarming into their gated Orange Counties. When Robert Kennedy died he was moving beyond the appetite for simple power the way the financier, decades earlier, moved beyond the fascination with mere accumulated money. Their suspicions that he was passing out of their control had made Bob Kennedy harder and harder to understand among the ordinary power brokers. The Mob, which had come to hate this most implacable of the Kennedy brothers, was not going to take another chance.

Robert Kennedy's "Why not?" buzzes right out of the lexicon of the ordinary like a hornet and endangers our fat national neck. Well before the early June evening he died Robert Kennedy had already moved, existentially, far beyond the help of politics. "Why did they do that, why did they have to do that?" the inconsolable Larry O'Brien kept sobbing as Bob Kennedy's funeral train jounced alongside tenement wetwash toward Arlington. "Couldn't they see? Couldn't they see? He didn't have a chance!"

CHAPTER IX

Two Summers

1. Recovery

While Robert Kennedy lay dying on the Hotel Ambassador's greasy pass-through corridor floor, Ted Kennedy and David Burke, in hopes of a breather, had just gotten into their suite at the Hotel Fairmount in San Francisco after standing in for Bob at the inevitable victory rally for the North California volunteers. Kennedy eased his back into a chair and turned on the hotel room television set; there was such confusion on the picture tube that neither of them was sure whether or not he had the network coverage of Los Angeles. Moments later it was clear enough that they were watching Los Angeles, and that Robert Kennedy had been critically wounded.

"We better get down there" was all Burke remembers Edward Kennedy having said for the next several hours. Burke called a local congressman's office, and, minutes later, an air force jet fighter rushed Burke, Edward Kennedy, John Siegenthaler, and Bob Fitzgerald to Los Angeles, where a helicopter lifted Kennedy directly to the central receiving hospital. "I can't let go," Ted Kennedy told Dun Gifford. "We have a job to do. If I let go Ethel will let go, and my mother will let go, and all my sisters . . ." He didn't; throughout the twenty-four-hour vigil at the nearby Hospital of the Good Samaritan he didn't let go.

On the presidential jet East, a newsman remembers how, sitting up with the coffin, Ted Kennedy seemed more angry than bereaved. "I'm going to show them," Kennedy had said, repeatedly. "I'm going to show them what they've done, what Bobby meant to this country, what they lost." He held onto himself through the unloading of the coffin, through another night of sitting up in the bare cathedral waiting for the funeral, through the eulogy and the slow procession out and another hearse ride and the miles of train-riding toward the gravesite at Arlington, a final motorcade, the lugging of the casket up the slope of hillside, the draping of it with an American flag, lowering it. Then Edward dragged himself back to the family limousines with everybody else. After that Ted Kennedy was rarely to be detected around Washington throughout the remainder of the summer——.

So that Edward Kennedy's response to the death of Bobby at first had been . . . anger, a thick primary emotion that left no space at all for either political calculations or worries about getting killed himself. The public Edward Kennedy (his lips a line, his movements heavy-weighted but noble, stately) played handsomely his appropriate public part; the man inside cherished like an anesthetic the density of his rage. "Don't close headquarters yet—Teddy's fighting mad," one Kennedy careerist reportedly exhorted another on the funeral train.

Rage wore off too; that couldn't be helped; day by day as the Cape Cod summer started, sensation began again. Two realities took meaning: Life would continue now, but Bobby wouldn't. Within the family itself, among the brother and sisters, there were many respects in which Bobby's death was already being felt more sharply and poignantly than the loss of the more aloof president. Bob Kennedy could be a chider, a ragger, one to glower and mutter hastily whenever he disapproved. But those quirks, too, were side effects of Robert Kennedy's persisting state of pure nervous energy restlessly expending itself, his need to determine inside himself what was wrong and what was needed, and—because he himself itched with self-consciousness so much of the time—his sensitivity to the unhappiness of others.

Virtually since he had been a teenager, Bob had taken his position as the one to come up with a word of reassurance, an observation they could live with emotionally. With Joe cut off he had assumed the leadership; his was the final word; he could condemn and spell out the rules for the rest of them, and nevertheless he was quick to forgive, he found it within himself to understand without condemning when a badly conceived marriage finally fell apart. Like his father as a younger man, Bobby could apparently read minds, and was surprisingly patient and willing to help because of that. He sensed immediately, like shadows across faces, any suppressed disagreement, disapproval from advisers he trusted. Brusque and relentless among outsiders, he was very patient with people he loved. "When we were boys," Joe Gargan muses, "he spent so much time with Teddy. Working on his sailing but, more than that, to . . . to tell him. Be disciplined. Be courageous. Meet every challenge with what ability you have. Be prepared for whatever opportunity may come your way. Bob was . . . he was an awfully good person."

Bob Kennedy—a good person, trustworthy as far as the older people were concerned when it came to grasping and promulgating the much-articulated familial values, good reflexive judgment, a boy who didn't mind being as stubborn as hell about the enforcement part whenever what he knew was right was involved. Hard-shelled at times; that was protection too. The instant the assassin's bullet struck it was finished, leaving Edward Kennedy to inherit a limelight he would never again be able to avoid.

Edward Kennedy hurried into hiding. Robert Kennedy, bereaved, had intuitively tightened, glazed; Edward Kennedy now began the terrible drawn-out maneuvers intended to exorcise his grief by abstracting it, depersonalizing it somehow. He returned that summer terribly set back, sought out the places and friends and escapades that had relaxed and satisfied him during the more carefree years of his boyhood and schooling. Among the children he had always been particularly devoted to his father, the one to accompany the old man in his wheelchair to a World Series game or give up all hope of sleep for a night to drive down and join the obviously grateful tremulous financier for breakfast: Now he stayed very close.

Joe Kennedy wept, terribly upset. Ted made sure to be in and out throughout the next few weeks, appeared on a June 15 telecast standing with his mother above his father's wheelchair to thank the nation for its notes of condolence . . .

If a man keeps something inside himself simple for years enough, he will most probably one day come upon a recognition of his personal metaphor: The sea was Edward Kennedy's. As traces of grief and apprehension about what was going to be expected now seeped into his thoughts those midsummer days, Kennedy's most immediate impulse was to escape the overinhabited land and spend more and more of his time upon the water claiming a peace for himself from the long simplified periods of the ocean. Early mornings in which the sun slices over the deck and into the eyes like a fire sheet before his schooner the *Mya* is properly out of the harbor, the murder undertow barely to be felt, not quite a vibration, something to ripple a little the surface across the rim of a daybreak teacup. Long periods, space and time in which to lose whatever mentality is festering, hold irrevocable decisions off until the relief of night.

It became a summer of broken voyages. There were a great many easy little day trips to places like Nantucket with Joan and the kids and dogs to drop in for lunch on such friends as Dun Gifford and Pebbles. Much sailing of the *Victura* in meets and regattas, usually with the ever-accessible Joe Gargan to crew, many trophies and the quiet satisfaction for Ted in finding that the youngsters in the family now took with excitement to learning how to handle the boat in competition: He went so far that summer as to request of the Wianno people the privilege of substituting two boys—he had young John and his own son Teddy in mind—for a man during certain of the races; the Wianno governors sympathized, but refused.

With durable old friends Ted organized long memory-heavy cruises up the rocks along the Maine coast, the tour Bobby had loved, putting in after a day with darkness falling at Gene Tunney's island or stopping early for cocktails and dinners with fond associates like Tom Watson or Douglas Dillon— entertainments during which everybody tried extra hard, Ted's flushing face again bridling the way it used to with his deep chortle of appreciative laughter. He would seem to the others watching him quite . . . quite normal, getting over it fast, almost all right again. But the next day on the *Mya* that old glassy-eyed set look would harden onto him, and he—normally quiet enough upon the water—wouldn't say very much hour by hour, steered silently, allowing the shoreline to pass through him, let its long chain of boulders and foam and swamp grass scrub some of the poisons out of his recuperating spirit. Back at the Compound he had started to keep to himself more than he ever before had, walked the beaches and dunes incessantly, usually alone: The seascape watercolors he had again begun to do now took on a revealing concentration, the great masses driven and dramatic, skies gray to bursting beneath which pitiful sailboats pushed in a line to their moorings beyond the bar of a breakwater.

Enormous hesitations were backpressuring. "It's inaccurate to say he was drunk most of the time," a confidant of the summer commented afterwards. "It's also inaccurate to say he wasn't drunk at all." There was a pause, an exceedingly thoughtful pause. "He never drank on the boat, though——." Among the gentry around Hyannis Port, watching always for something with salt on its tail whenever it concerned the Kennedys, rumors and sly little barroom stories were circulating in regard to what "they" were up to this summer.

"He was a basket case," one summer resident insists, recounting the incident in a local restaurant during which Ted Kennedy, Joe Gargan, and ten or twelve Green Berets barged in and talked the proprietor into staying open, having already drunk ferociously enough to have reached the stage where they were smashing their glasses against walls with the pledge "No one shall drink from this glass again," and finally—tongues among the townspeople fluttered when this got around—settling down to eat a dinner which waiters from another restaurant had suddenly, to the astonishment of the manager— burst in to set before the Kennedy party.

That part even Joe Gargan admits; he himself had ordered the steaks hours earlier and forgotten about it: "You know me," Gargan laughs, "the perfect advance man." The food had ultimately turned up at Squaw Island and then the Compound itself in search of its purchasers, who had long before lost interest in watching the Green Berets rope up and scale the Ambassador's gables and peaks and plummet off, after which the party had moved on to a round or two of drinks at the home of Kennedy's neighbor, Jack Fallon. "The Green Beret colonel was Teddy's kind of guy," Gargan reminisces happily. "Twelve drops behind enemy lines. But that's really all there was to that, if you want to know the truth. I imagine the fellow in the restaurant was so annoyed about the food he must have exaggerated the rest of the incident."

The incident unfolds like a vignette from the older, the Smilin' Ed era of Ted Kennedy's dying boyhood. The kind of fun outgrown during those last prepolitical months in the DA's office, when he had kept the columnists titillated at Washington weekend parties by shoving thoughtful New Frontiersmen into the Hickory Hill swimming pool.

Now, with Bobby gone, there wasn't anybody in the family Ted could be sure he would have to confront. He was pointedly unamused at the disclosure of such frolicking as the picture that made the media rounds of himself and Joe III caping yearling bulls in early July when the senator flew over to drop his nephew off for a summer in Spain.

Without Bobby there was nobody to wonder sharply what was worthwhile about the kind of details a very playful journalist had not hesitated to include (in a November 1968 shocker in *Life*) about the Kennedy-Onassis marriage dealing with an unnoticed brief vacation cruise aboard Onassis's yacht the *Christina* the previous August in which the then Jackie Kennedy and her brother-in-law the surviving senator had participated. An Athenian bouzouki band entertained; Ted Kennedy had spent the evening—astride, perhaps, one of those barstools his gamy little host had arranged to have covered with the gently tanned leather from one whale testicle—working on the ouzo in company with a "laughing cowboy from Texas" and "two pretty girls, one blond 'with cerulean eyes,'" as a surreptitious reporter pretending to manage the band observed, and the other "dark and with one leg in a cast." Publicly noted, but—like the observation that through the whole of that politically eventful summer this sitting senior senator from Massachusetts had barely stopped by to look over the mail in his office in Washington, D.C.—downplayed, pretty much ignored.

For throughout that summer and autumn and winter Edward Kennedy was the beneficiary of an unconscious judgment the morbidly trend-sensitive editorial-room arbiters of the media had evidently agreed upon: This survivor among the Kennedy boys was obviously going to be turned by the role he had inherited into the kind of copy they would have to have, and he was therefore to be covered with a degree of selectivity—not to say finickiness—not otherwise very often granted a leader events had projected into a role of such magnitude.

And so for more than a year after Bob Kennedy died Edward Kennedy could expect most-favored-celebrity treatment. One had only to talk privately at the time with shirtsleeve bureau reporters—who complained constantly that Kennedy, often through Dick Drayne, his press aide, had dealt blandly, abruptly, evasively, often cavalierly with them (ducking interviews, not getting information back when promised)—then glance through the appreciative and determinedly compassionate pieces they wrote, to find oneself puzzling over the disparities. There was the dutiful, scrupulously briefed, precocious child of the Senate. Then—usually outside Washington—there was Ted on the loose. Swollen, boisterous, indulging every festering appetite. The outlaw playboy JFK had occasionally cautioned. The rampant Minotaur.

"What was unspoken between me and my friends was my reason for excess," Kennedy would confess with great precision in his posthumous memoir. "It was all part of my desire to escape, to keep moving, to avoid painful memories. And so I lived this string of years in the present tense, not despondently, because that is not my nature, but certainly with a sense of the void."

The assassinated Senator Robert Kennedy and the assassinated President John Kennedy were, overall, as unalike as a ferret and a lawn peacock. For all their dissimilarities, they shared one indispensable public skill: Both understood the press. The press is an information scavenger. Reporters are conditioned to nip at whatever they glimpse, hopeful of any morsel substantive enough to smuggle to a city editor. Newspaper reporters especially, as Norman Mailer notes, live with the tapeworm of blue-collar origins. The astute politician, alive to this, makes very sure the reporter's designated place on the buses and airplanes of some upcoming event is secure, the drinks are discreetly bought beforehand, the newsman gets his chance for a "color" interview while seated next to the Important Personality.

Both John Kennedy and Bob Kennedy, realizing all this early, worked the press avidly. As early as the Rackets Committee hearing days, one seasoned newsman remembers getting a furious telephone call from Sorensen on behalf of John Kennedy and a delighted call from Robert Kennedy regarding the same piece extolling Bob's cross-examination vis-á-vis his brother. Both older Kennedys obviously liked many press and media people enough to cultivate social friendships with them, seek them out, key to their responses. The older Kennedy boys—whatever the editors or publishers preferred— tended to get a very forgiving press.

Ted Kennedy inherited what appeared for a long while to be a puncture-proof mantle of favorable coverage. While John and Bob were alive, Teddy's instinct was to step back and away from publicity of any kind that would infringe on, shadow in any way, what they were doing. Interviewing Ted Kennedy tended to yield notebook material that was consistently empty, above-the-battle, not really awfully useful to the reporter hunting for color, or some sort of insight breakthrough, or perhaps vital dirt beneath the day's events. Most reporters very clearly seemed to Kennedy much too superficially informed to bother about; easier to be agreeable and noncommittal than begin at the beginning.

Besides, he himself had always gotten rather a good press, a sympathetic press, especially in the contemporary glossy magazine pieces, full of vapid copy testifying to what a likable chap he was, watchful paragraphs tastefully appreciative of Joan's legs and Ted's own firm young patrician hand at the tiller of the *Victura*. Coverage like this suited Kennedy, suited his back-room modes of operation. There were certainly no press people he thought of genuinely as friends: He actually didn't need any, obviously couldn't imagine the political utility of risking his complicated privacy to gain a better awareness of what the unpredictable nonentities of the working press were into now. Bob died; Ted suddenly discovered himself, week by week, thrust into the frontal role. Yet still—greatest paradox of all—the more Ted continued to duck away from publicity the more euphoric it continued to become; Kennedy's approach grew loftier yet.

The Eumenides awaited.

2. Temptation

Edward Kennedy might personally be floundering through some sort of Cape Cod seawater cure, but as the various old-style, cut-and-try Democratic tacticians began to realize how far this summer had already deepened into its pre-convention doldrums, his was the name they were all of a sudden most tempted to insert into their shifting convention calculations. Martyrdom lends enchantment; it now appeared that, even among the professionals who had feared Robert's inclinations most, the infernal Kennedys were going to be harder to survive without than come to some modus vivendi with.

Money raisers in both camps missed Robert in particular: Such a frenetic little bugbear, he and his hope of a power grab had been able to rouse shivers and simpers of distaste among the salon philanthropists of the peace movement—while, on the party's other extreme, Bobby could be depended on to make the labor bosses and their special-interest patrons gag and contribute to alternate candidates. But with Robert Kennedy out, so much of the emotional pressure inside the party had leaked away: Eugene McCarthy and the peace effort already flapped lifeless in the political winds, a remnant, and the Humphrey first-ballot nomination was so utterly assured that any contribution to Hubert seemed gratuitous, a waste. The money stopped coming; the momentum which, it was hoped, would carry them all beyond the convention was guttering fast.

The threat from Nixon and the Republicans, meanwhile, had started to take on veracity. Successive Harris Polls that summer suggested that Ted Kennedy on the Democratic ticket could add five million votes to the party's November showing, turn a two-point tossup into an eight-point landslide. The punctilio of overtures to Ted began.

The realization that he was to be the one toward whom the heavy final vector of such a tumultuous winter and spring was going to swing at last came very slowly to the preoccupied Kennedy. The mathematics the planners kept pushing might very well be unarguable; the turmoil of his feelings swamped all mathematics. The political chores Ted Kennedy found it within himself to do were concerned mostly with picking up after Bobby. He got together, on the second of July, for chowder at his house on Squaw Island— with apparatchiks from the Bobby camp ranging from Robert McNamara and Arthur Schlesinger and John Glenn and Dick Goodwin to Burke Marshall and Fred Dutton and Peter Edelman—to pick over ideas that might lead to a "living memorial" to Robert; the conversation eventuated in the Robert Kennedy Memorial Foundation, a grant program for slum youngsters with a knack for leadership. Many people among Ted's huge acquaintanceship had written condolences; most got a replica of the funeral card with a few words scrawled at the bottom by Edward Kennedy personally.

At the urging of Dave Hackett and his cousin Joey, always one to fret, Kennedy tried to show some gratitude to the girls who held up so uncomplainingly throughout their months in the boiler room at 20th and L. The idea of such a gesture had occurred to Gargan before Bob died—Angie Novello, Bob's very protective personal secretary, had scotched the notion the previous summer. Now Joe Gargan invited all of them for a 1968 midsummer week-end at the Cape, arranged for them to stay at various summer homes around the Compound—Cricket Keough, Esther Newburgh, and Suzy Tannenbaum stayed over at the Gargan place; Carol Paolozzi and Mary Jo Kopechne spent the nights at the Shriver home. It was still hard for Ted to be around people he associated with Bob and didn't know awfully well himself, so Gargan took the lot of them aboard the *Mya* for a sail to Nantucket and a reunion cookout with the Giffords. Ted and Joan Kennedy arranged and played host at a cocktail party for them at his Squaw Island house. The girls—without exception bright, plucky, forthrightly plain-looking, and unattached—appreciated the seaside break, the weekend of political joking around and reminiscences in the midst of what was otherwise largely a slow, hot summer of D.C. job-hunting.

All this was quietly done, en famille, not much more really than intermittent whispers that barely interrupted the remedial seaside days; the conversation inland was already much much louder. Other voices, tremolo excitement-pitched wheedling voices and suspicious voices croaking up the aridness of cigar-baked tracheas, idealistic voices and the heavy slow emphatic voices of self-made political middlemen who may not know much, kid, but one thing they know is how to figure—the voices Bobby hated had started to follow his younger brother like the murmurs of ghosts as he sought what respite he could in soothing and rocking Hyannis Port.

Warning hunches came early. "We had lunch in New York a couple of weeks after Bobby's funeral," Bill Vanden Heuvel recounts, "and I mentioned that it seemed to me that it wouldn't be too long before things settled down and a lot of people started thinking, and there was going to be pressure on Ted to make himself available for the Democratic ticket. He seemed sur-prised at that, very surprised at that. Then, as events worked out, Teddy and I were sailing on the *Mya*—not really that many weeks afterwards. Perhaps it was August? Early August? We were at anchor for the night, I remember it was off Maine, terribly foggy, and we were signaled somehow that there was a very important call for Teddy, he had to get to a telephone. So we untied the dinghy and rowed ourselves ashore.

"There was this little pay phone in a booth among the rocks, and Ted used that. It turned out to be Mayor Daley—it wasn't the first time Daley had called, and it certainly wasn't the last: They wanted Ted on the ticket. The implication was that the brokers had decided that Hubert wasn't going to win all by himself, that with Ted on either the bottom or the top of the ticket they probably could—they didn't make that awfully clear, I gathered—and what was his thinking?

"Ted was quiet, he kept very much to himself whenever I saw him," Vanden Heuvel continues. "He kept asking—mostly to himself, but aloud at times. 'What was it all about?' It was not the fatalism of Bob; it was a much larger fatalism. He kept wondering, Was it worth all this? He has a great desire to live, takes a great joy out of life. And he had begun to realize the danger, the fear, that he was going to be the next."

"They'll say he was off fooling around on a boat when they needed him," one impatient booster muttered. "They won't forget." "They" were already gabbling, flocking and quacking ceaselessly at statehouse dinners and after rallies and in clubhouse basement rooms: With a momentary shudder of dignity regained, Mike DiSalle had already, by July 14, appointed himself gander-in-charge of sounding the loudest sounds anywhere in behalf of Ted. The week after that, at the National Governors' Conference, in Cincinnati, Kennedy in absentia was ear-high in unsolicited endearments. Mayor Daley, sly mischief, dropped hints like anvils about a "draft." Governors Hughes of New Jersey, McNair of South Carolina, and McKeithen of Louisiana, as well as Lieutenant Governor Shapiro of Illinois, exposed a variety of shades of sympathy for the idea—most quite worried already as preliminary polls showed how badly the national ticket was in need of something fresh and strong enough to lug their floundering state tickets over in November.

Leaders from all over the country kept pulling aside the ubiquitous Humphrey to emphasize what a colossal asset this most likable among the Kennedy boys could prove to him; Humphrey worked up a breathlessness of his own as he reassured the regulars that Teddy was "young," "capable," "a good senator," and, needless to say, could expect to find himself welcomed very warmly onto any ticket headed by Hubert Horatio Humphrey. Kennedy's Washington office issued his public response on July 26: The honor was sincerely appreciated, but "for me, this year, it is impossible . . . I will not be able to accept the Vice-Presidential nomination . . ."

Chronic reassurances that his differences with the Kennedy servitors were in no way "as wide as they have led themselves to believe" became a Humphrey staple that summer along with those three-fingered little elbow lifts of his as Hubert worked the Democratic conclaves. In fact, the front-runner was inclined to pull away as inconspicuously—as gingerly—as possible from the notion of any Kennedy candidacy; the way the Ohio and Illinois bosses kept putting off committing their delegations until just before the convention was worrying the keyed-up South Dakota druggist's son awfully.

His memories hurt. His 1960 embroilment with John Kennedy left him moaning. It had been Bob Kennedy's expectation, looking beyond the late-June New York primary, to "chase Hubert's ass all over the country," anticipating that if the voluble but weak Humphrey were attacked relentlessly enough he'd—in Dick Goodwin's reminiscence—"finally fall apart." Humphrey had been apprehensive enough about Bob; the prospect of taking his chances that a volatile and nostalgic convention might not turn a Hubert Humphrey–Edward Kennedy ticket upside down looked uninviting to the loquacious vice president.

When Hubert and Ted Kennedy did get together for that private little "visit like neighbors" that Humphrey was promoting, the vice president was more interested in ascertaining whether he could rest comfortably, satisfied that Kennedy would not in any way open himself to being dark-horsed onto the top of the ticket than in pushing Ted to reconsider his statement of unavailability.

Again, as was so often the case with Edward Kennedy, the very high-minded earnestness and resonance of his delivery blurred what he meant, exactly, perhaps even to Kennedy himself. Ted had clearly hoped to allay the worst of Humphrey's fears; at the same time—Kennedy's summer-long political delirium was obviously passing—he was going to keep viable the possibility of his intervention in some capacity, at some point in the campaign, as a soft threat with which to nudge the Johnson-intimidated candidate-presumptive leftwards.

Deceptively brisk in public, Hubert coddled his recurrent doubts. Then, on August 21, days before the Democratic Convention was to commence in Chicago, Edward Kennedy appeared before a luncheon of the Worcester, Massachusetts, Chamber of Commerce to make a nationally televised speech that was touted beforehand as his first true public hoisting of the Kennedys' "fallen standard." "There is no safety in hiding," he intoned, "not for me nor any of us here today." He began by deploring the way the young and poor have felt impelled to defy the very basis of our system, while alluding to the "hope" of a "new politics of citizen participation."

But Vietnam was his subject: He mounted his critique of the administration's approaches sensibly, in terms patriotic businessmen who read their realities out of ledger pages were likely to grasp. Two hundred thousand American casualties so far, a hundred billion of our tax dollars, "the resources that were to have fulfilled the promise of American life"—gone.

Kennedy's own proposals were careful and specific: End the bombing in the north unconditionally, cut back personnel and operations in the south, negotiate with Hanoi for removal of all foreign forces, allocate special aid to the Saigon regime so that it "will not promptly collapse on our departure." No talk here of any coalition government, blood for the North Vietnamese, ousting the corrupt and repressive Thieu and Ky, cutting losses, eviscerating the CIA. Rather, the war in Vietnam had been an unwise corporative investment. It now appeared well advised to create a separate entity there, ease our investment funds out, allow it to slide—retaining face, image was very important—into receivership: practical problems, practical solutions, practical men would understand.

The Worcester speech was a technician's triumph; emotionally, it had come a little prematurely. "When I started to work with Ted he was all politics," David Burke told me late in 1970. "Now he's all issues." If there was an exact historical moment during which the crossover occurred it had to be during the fallen-standard speech, as adept a political job as anybody could imagine, the sort of synthesis a group of the "advisers" had proposed to Ted as early as the second of July.

After a summer during which he had, without apology, largely avoided Washington, Kennedy turned up in his Senate offices early that third week in August. "He seemed fine," Burke says. "On the Vietnam speech we had a lot of differences. We settled. It was a matter of one guy trying to get his position in before another." Then, hours before the speech was scheduled for delivery, the Russians had invaded Czechoslovakia, an event Kennedy noted barely in the address but which shook him privately, recalled the extent to which the Cold War presuppositions endured.

"After the speech he was drained," Burke remembers, thinking back to the long drive back to Hyannis Port with Jimmy Breslin. "The ice got thicker and thicker." Breslin had been a friend, something of a tour jester at times with Bob; Ted was sunk into an afterwash of realization of what being the spokesman meant, what being Bob meant. One could hire sonorous phrases forever, piece out enviable compromises, but what help was that really going to be if the goddamned country—Ted's country—Ted's worry now—expired? His mood stayed depressed, flat. "A display of emotion is a weakness to an Irishman," Burke notes, cutting it off. "There was no handwringing."

The estimable Hubert perused the fallen-standard speech and felt his resolute old campaigner's rictus of a smile wilt steadily. August had already provided one long culminating tremor of vice-presidential effort at self-control anyhow. Lyndon Johnson, abusive of the uncomplaining Humphrey during the headiest of periods, was by this time raving through his menopausal final weeks of uncontested party dominance, drumming away off the record to reporters about his expectations of an instant summit with the Russians. It would deliver peace in Vietnam, bagged, to his terrified heir as a nomination present, while visiting upon his would-be successor that cowman's touch that caponized—dressing him down before newsmen as a weak man who "cries too much," looked and talked "like he belongs to the past," and was so soft about the war in Vietnam as, in Theodore White's words, to "stretch the patriotism of John Connally."

The front-runner was well aware that Johnson was quite capable at any time during or even after the convention of plucking him raw and smothering him at leisure. Johnson's hold on the regulars all over the country, and the needed 527 delegates from the South especially, was firm, and on the convention machinery it was so rigid that Humphrey's own son-in-law was to have to get up early and stand in line every morning for gallery seats for the Humphrey family.

The measurement that counted, at least from the skittish Humphrey's standpoint, was establishing the exact distance that was not so far from the ravening Lyndon Johnson as to estrange him nor—this leaders and counselors from all across the great liberal center of the party coalition had been chorusing all summer—so close as to have to backpack the gutshot political remains of the discredited president through the long campaign months that could lead otherwise to victory. Humphrey had jarred the regular Democratic machine early in the convention by letting it be known that he personally had nothing against modifying the unit rule—through which the Old Guard had long maintained control—and prohibiting it in 1972.

The meat-cleaver issue here, as before and after that year in the streets, was how to proceed in Southeast Asia. Hubert Humphrey started there, straining to forestall trouble with his earnest if misleading August 17 New York speech that hard-pedaled the similarities between his views and the late Robert Kennedy's. He tried very quickly to link up a concatenation of aides and sympathizers that ran from David Ginsburg through the receptive Ted Sorensen to the truly war-hating Kenneth O'Donnell. The Democratic Platform Committee that started to meet in Washington on August 19 was presided over by Hale Boggs, very much the president's man, and included, among its 110 members, as many as forty "doves." Whatever chance they had was blanketed by the news of the Czechoslovakian invasion, and Lyndon Johnson's timely off-the-record Armageddon clankings, to which the gnomic Eugene McCarthy added his discordant fife notes by dismissing the travesty as "not a major crisis." Revulsion set many moderates recoiling toward a much harder position.

Many of the onetime Bobby people, who had interspersed among the candidates—the adaptable Goodwin back in place as Eugene McCarthy's ideologue and O'Donnell, Dutton, Sorensen, and John Gilligan divided among the others—flared through a long session of drafts and redrafts that eventuated, on the night of Friday, August 23, in the splinter "peace plank." The plank was offered seriously, their most conciliatory gesture; foreseeing a platform committee setback, it started by ignoring such Johnsonian bugaboos as mention of a civil war while urging a "swift conclusion," encouraging our "South Vietnamese allies to negotiate a political reconciliation with the National Liberation Front looking toward a government which is broadly representative," "an unconditional" bombing halt, and a staged mutual withdrawal.

Lyndon wasn't having any. Contemptuously, he had waved away even the milder "majority" plank proposals. The vice president was well aware by now that the peace coalition was going to take its proposals to the floor. And all this portending just days after—perilous coincidence to Hubert's dyspepsia-prone stomach—the stunned Edward Kennedy had emerged without warning from his summer incommunicado to deliver, with heavy intent, a speech that line for line, proposal for proposal, very nearly duplicated the peace insurgents' manifesto.

As if the peace-plank provocations were not enough to keep Humphrey grumping in his suite at the Conrad Hilton, fussily emptying ashtrays, there were well-substantiated reports of the premature Friday appearance in Chicago of Steve Smith, Kennedy ramrod since Jack got serious. Smith turned up again on Sunday morning. He was a member of the New York delegation, certainly, but why the rush of telephone calls and visits that started within minutes of the moment he checked into his suite at the nearby Standard Club? Humphrey was well aware of Smith's professed distaste for the idea of any Edward Kennedy candidacy in 1968; he had been quoted reliably about that on the burial trainride, during which he reportedly threatened to dissociate himself in public from anything that opportunistic. Ted, traumatized, had seemed most uncongenial to the idea, having refused any personal appearance in the Convention City and insisting that the people on his senatorial staff keep away.

Then, disconcertingly, Smith had reappeared. Within minutes, it seemed, rumors galvanized the Humphrey people about Smith meetings with Jesse Unruh and Dick Daley and Mike DiSalle of Ohio (who by Sunday night had set up an openly Draft Kennedy office in his suite at the Sherman House) and (via the enterprising Goodwin) an allegedly receptive Eugene McCarthy.

Throughout Sunday and into Monday the longtime Kennedy sympathizers and aides who were also delegates, inside the Massachusetts, New York, and California groups especially, appeared to be soliciting some count as to how many delegates would look with favor upon an Edward Kennedy presidential nomination; the network journalists, led by Sander Vanocur, news-starved in the information lull, were reporting this dramatic turn minutely.

That endless Sunday Humphrey discovered that the critical Southern delegation leaders, fuming still at what they regarded as Hubert's sellout of the unit rule at just the time they were expecting serious challenges from black alternative delegations, might just shop around for a more understanding candidate. Lyndon was reportedly venomous.

A very worried Hubert Humphrey recognized that he was going to have to take a political reading here that had better not miss reality by much. Within the Convention City halls two spectres loomed entwined: the supercharged floor vote pledging him to choose between the administration's "war" plank or the administration-repudiating "peace" plank; the fast-consolidating movement to replace Humphrey with Edward Moore Kennedy. The threats were interinvolved, that Humphrey sensed, but to make the correct move astutely enough to survive not only the convention but also the November election, Humphrey had to understand how.

Was the overnight Kennedy candidacy a feint by the peace-obsessed factions of the party, utilizing the desperation about the loss of the White House apparent among machine regulars, to bluff Humphrey into accepting the peace plank? Cut himself free from Johnson, run, in effect, against his own administration? Or was the peace plank itself a ghost platform for an Edward Kennedy candidacy that he, Humphrey, by casting away from the derelict president and supporting, might legitimize? And so perhaps assist in his own presidential decapitation?

Or was the dupe here Edward Kennedy? Was he in danger of being skewered upon his brothers' fallen standard and trotted out ahead of the most unlikely reformist-machine alliance since Boss Tweed feathered political nests? The Edward Kennedy candidacy might be the sole way left to circumvent debacle with Humphrey, as Richard Goodwin and Richard Daley together—a pair of Oriental minds fit for negotiation—appear both to have concluded. But what about their stunned pre-candidate in fantasy Hyannis Port?

By now the tactical situation, the convention and its alluring combinations, had started to . . . to fascinate Kennedy; he was himself evidently beginning to eye that opium pipe of a coup that mesmerized both Goodwin and Daley. "It all started really at Ted's house in Washington the previous Friday, when he authorized Smith to go out there," a Kennedy adviser admits. Smith went, saw Daley, threw the newsmen who found out about the visit off for a couple of hours by vowing that the talk was "about quite another matter" from any political coalition behind his brother-in-law, and returned to Hyannis Port ostensibly with nothing to reveal: nothing.

Except that of course the Kennedys' senior dragoman had not descended upon rebellious Chicago a meaningful two days before the voting wholly to present himself. That is—political deaf-and-dumb being mostly timing gestures—Smith would never have selected that schedule unless delegated by the newly ascended Leader of All the Kennedys to appear before Illinois' primal satrap and entertain the possibility of some kind of Kennedy involvement with the 1968 ticket. Smith presented it low, close to the political ground where that snout-like but famously mobile nose of Chicago's kingmaker of a mayor was rumored to take in suggestive odors soonest.

Daley had been mulling the thing over for at least a week. Ever since the delegates had started to converge, His Honor had been bumping over and over into weeping industrial delegation leaders ill at the prospect of having to get behind the impending Humphrey nomination. The liabilities promised cramps in advance: the funding dried up, the indigestible war to support, a ticket so weak local officeholders were doomed, lucrative federal appointments gone once the White House got away from them. The possibilities were threatening enough to disturb a coarse man, and Chicago's omnivorous mayor was actually—one needed to know where to prod—morbidly sensitive.

As early as he could put his call through Saturday morning, Richard Daley got Edward Kennedy on the line in Hyannis Port. Daley's great strengths had never depended on verbal finesse; his voice on the telephone sounded strangled as he attempted not to push too hard. He'd been moving around a lot. He'd been talking to a lot of leaders in the Party. Pennsylvania leaders. Ohio leaders. The thing about it was, Humphrey was in trouble, and Teddy ought to be a candidate, he ought to come to Chicago, he ought to offer the party people a sign, a real sign, that he was available in case there happened to be, y'know, a draft?

Welllll—Kennedy was letting his voice just hang there like a background

tone, thin all the urgency out of the mayor's proposals—of course that was
impossible, he wasn't going out. But Steve was going out the next day, Sunday; Steve would be in touch.

Steve Smith returned to Chicago Sunday; within minutes of noon he had
the impatient Daley on one of his telephones. Daley had his move worked
out: "The boys," Daley now proposed, "might decide to hold off for forty-
eight hours." This was boss bravado with an unanticipated fillip. Daley had
been personally uneasy about the party and about the elections longer than
virtually anybody else. He had resisted early blandishments from Bobby and
late approaches from Hubert, who had wanted to push him into a spring
preferential caucusing of Illinois' 118 delegates. Daley had been nursing
vagrant hopes of some kind of a Lyndon Johnson restoration throughout
the summer.

Now, by holding off his own state's caucus for an unprecedented two full
days into the convention itself, he was deliberately fomenting an uneasiness
about Hubert that was virtually certain, given the plague conditions that
would prevail, to result in a day at least of "softness" and groping toward
some stronger-seeming candidate. And indeed, the moment word of Daley's
well-calculated delay was out, California was reported ready for a Kennedy
candidacy, and New York, and a third of that key Pennsylvania delegation
Ted had attempted to churn for Bobby; the bluff if enigmatic mayor seemed
able to deliver.

The quintessential danger was that Richard Daley's intent hadn't changed
since July: He wanted Ted lured into the open, dragging duty-to-the-
Democratic Party and duty-to-Bob, to manacle onto the bottom of the ticket.
Unhappy vice-president material, surety for five million extra votes.

Whatever its scale and suddenness, Dick Daley's forty-eight hours had
to break down like any other political problem: Compile accurate information; isolate the options; choose. Information. "I was at the Conrad Hilton,"
Fred Dutton would muse, "and Steve called me. I went over to his place. His
mood was complicated, cautious, but he was beginning to think the situation was not bad." They came and went all Sunday and Monday. "Steve was
extremely specific," Lester Hyman notes. "We were in no way to give encouragement, just find out what his real strength was. We—I think there were
ten of us altogether. Bob Fitzgerald, Tunney, myself—went around. If asked,
we said he was not a candidate. We went all night. You've got to remember
that the peace plank was pending, and almost everybody was getting angry
with Humphrey because he wouldn't compromise over that. So I started to
get calls from everybody on whether Ted would consider. I would say no,

but they kept coming. Those Michigan people, they were after me all night long. Then Curt Gans, McCarthy's guy. We kept saying no no no. But we kept counting. By Tuesday morning Steve added it all up and Ted had at least twelve hundred votes firm."

Twelve hundred, Hyman reports; by other accounts, Steve Smith's included, the total topped out at 1,400, enough; for Kennedy himself, watching the birdlike Smith peck delegate commitments like scraps out of the teeth of Mayor Daley's crocodilian convention, the risk remained that, the moment he showed himself, the great agape jaws of Daley's two-day entrapment period would slap shut and separate the political Kennedy from the protective reticence that had preserved him so far. Above all he did not want to be cornered into accepting the vice-presidential nomination. Intentions were serious enough by the weekend to require David Hackett—Bob's intimate, the head Kennedy intelligence technician since 1960, the man who perfected the system that required three reliable sources to have passed word along to the appropriate boiler-room people before the Kennedys would confirm a delegate commitment. Hackett was abruptly jerked from his seaside vacation, flown to Chicago, and provided with clerical help and lines enough to the convention floor from the appointed Merchandise Mart hideaway.

Kennedy himself kept cross-checking, interpreting, penetrating Steve's cautious accounting with probes of his own. "There's a big movement on," the ebullient Jesse Unruh blared back on the telephone to GHQ Hyannis Port; Ted, remembering well how Unruh's unfounded assurances had suckered Bobby into the race the winter before, blasted him: "I don't care about a big movement. What are the facts?"

"He was obviously wary," insists Fred Dutton, one of Kennedy's relays. "Trying to get multiple readings, trying not to get sucked in." As the timetable ran out the numbers were firm; only the politicians were treacherous. There were 2,622 delegates qualified to vote, so that it took 1,312 to snag the nomination. Daley's alluring grace period ran out, presumably, sometime late Tuesday; the floor fight over the Vietnam plank might be expected to occur Tuesday night or Wednesday; the presidential balloting commenced shortly after that.

Smith pulled Daley out of the scheduled Sunday Illinois caucus to pass along Kennedy's thoughts on hearing Daley's delayed offer. He, Kennedy, intended in no way to organize a movement of delegates toward his own alleged candidacy but would go so far as to let Daley know that he was likely to respond to a "genuine draft." A "genuine draft": The notion that Kennedy could defer the public admission of his own availability until after the majority of the delegates had already gone on record for him was preposterous; still, there was no murmuring among the professionals when public-address speakers all over the Convention City carried the announcement of disavowal from Edward Kennedy to Mike DiSalle. The professionals contemplated Kennedy's wish unflustered: It wasn't that Kennedy was going to be forever reluctant; he simply wasn't willing to succumb to comeback-hungry Mike.

The hand that was eliciting goose pimples as it approached beneath the convention's notoriously thin political covers was that of the whimsical— the murderously whimsical—Eugene McCarthy. Coy Gene appears to have given the first public notice as to the direction his attentions were wandering to the untiring Goodwin, whom McCarthy drew aside just after his staff had finished its last Monday-morning strategy session to ask, offhandedly, "What about this Teddy thing?" The two had alluded to a Kennedy involvement before, but McCarthy's tone had something in it now to set the suggestible Goodwin's heart hammering; Goodwin hurried to assure McCarthy that in his judgment Edward Kennedy was most unlikely to let himself be pulled into a fracas that would splinter the peace delegations. But McCarthy had something else in mind—all of them now faced their last pre-convention moment, and whatever the penitential glories of the spring and summer, politics was getting urgent. "Well," McCarthy continued slowly, summoning up unsuspected reserves of tolerance, "we ought to do it together. After all, experience isn't really important in a president. Character and judgment are the real thing. Of course he's young, but those fellows in the revolution were young—Jefferson and Hamilton."

Not one more word was necessary; three times that Monday alone Smith and Goodwin exchanged telephone calls over the course of which Goodwin attempted to allay the most pernicious Kennedy worries. Ted remembered the way McCarthy had jackknifed on his promise not to announce for the Massachusetts preferential primary without at least a nod to him. Smith projected a situation in which McCarthy, having lured Edward Kennedy into plain view with private commitments, might find himself seized by one of those whims of his and trade his Kennedy advocacy away to a Humphrey frightened enough to soften on Vietnam and take Gene McCarthy along as vice-presidential nominee. Enough confidence—in Goodwin, if not in McCarthy—had developed by Tuesday morning for McCarthy and Smith to schedule a meeting in Goodwin's room at the Hilton for four-thirty that afternoon.

Reporters swarmed; both Smith and McCarthy knew that the fact of the meeting itself could never be kept quiet long: It meant to everybody that

Ted was prepared to edge a half-step closer. Within a few months each of the principals had issued a sort of White Paper of his own about what went on. Goodwin wrote for himself in *Look*; Peter Maas's piece in *New York* magazine amounted to Smith talking; McCarthy granted an interview to *The Boston Globe*. All agree that Steve Smith protected himself immediately by insisting early that Ted Kennedy was in no respects yet to be conidered a formal candidate; that McCarthy realized by now—stated openly—that he himself couldn't make it; that Kennedy's views about Vietnam were the closest of anybody in the running to McCarthy's own; and that, while McCarthy would like to see his own name placed in nomination and even, if "possible" (as Goodwin wrote) "have a run on the first ballot," he would indicate beforehand that it "would be perfunctory" (Maas), and remove himself at the proper time, and "urge my people to support Teddy." *Time* was subsequently to refer to "tears of gratitude" in Smith's eyes at the moment McCarthy told him "While I'm doing this for Teddy, I could never have done it for Bobby."

Maas subsequently observed, quoting Smith, "Somebody mistook it for all the spit in them." A substantiated report the next day described Smith's fury at discovering that somebody in the McCarthy group had leaked word to a CBS newsman that Smith had spent two hours with Gene pleading for McCarthy's backing.

Smith may have been angry in overheated Chicago; in Hyannis Port Edward Kennedy stayed cool enough. What counted with him now was not so much what McCarthy had said as what he hadn't. Gene had rather delicately refused, as Smith divulged afterwards, to nominate Kennedy, and so to provide that classical gesture of reconciliation the divided party required.

"Teddy had the best chance of carrying," McCarthy told me later. "Even the threat of his nomination put the pressure on Hubert to accept the compromise on the peace plank. What we agreed on there came close to what he said in the Worcester speech." Underneath everything, as McCarthy added, he considered the Kennedys overfinanced amateurs, a rich man's sons, who were unequipped for real power. They aspired to the reputation of hardened professionals, athletes. He himself was tough enough for the real world: The Kennedys were softball players, but McCarthy had played semipro baseball.

By then, throughout the Democratic Party, Gene McCarthy was being reviled as essentially a spoiler. Even the disgruntled Daley, who grumbled to Smith that "Jack Kennedy knew how to count and Robert Kennedy knew how to count, and your young man had better learn quick," shrugged off word of the McCarthy offer with a curse.

Squeezing Hubert; it seemed to be everybody's nasty hankering those dog days in Chicago: to work a hand into at least one of the trouser pockets of the already-goosey Politician of Joy as the crisis of floor debate on the party's Vietnam position approached, effective to steer him a little bit at best—or, if absolutely required, grab deep enough to deliver him yelping and bounding. Good gamesmanship amounted to utilizing the threat of a convention-breaking rival to move the wavering Humphrey toward one or the other commitment. Superb gamesmanship—a level of play the deceptive mayor imagined himself up to—required utilizing the pacific Kennedy to frighten Humphrey into staying put.

The elements were historically enormous, beyond personality or party for perhaps the first time since 1860: Great careers, lifetime reputations, now depended for their justification on what the Democrats in assembly now swallowed. Eugene McCarthy's integrity, Hubert Humphrey's liberalism, Lyndon Johnson's explanation to posterity for all the bloodletting, Robert Kennedy's human judgment—these were among the larger indigestibles the vote on this single issue threatened to reconstitute.

Mobs felt it in the streets, mobs bellowed against it in the galleries, and telephones kept ringing and people kept answering and Mayor Daley's Convention City was like a great stomach terribly roiled and raving to upchuck in one unspeakable overflow everything it had stood for since 1932—the idealism and reform, the coatholders in dented hats sucking after patronage and Harry Hopkins's ulcerated dream of equality and fat men under freight platforms making sweetheart deals. Addled old Robert Frost forgetting his own ceremonial poem in the confusion of snowflakes and limousines and personal helicopter service and John F. Kennedy accepting a clump of high-denomination bills in a rubber band in cash on the street from a Republican who didn't want a fuss made and didn't get one, not even a smile worth remembering . . .

Everything . . . passed; by dinnertime Tuesday Hubert was his recognizable peckish self again. As stabilizing as anything else was Humphrey's belated discovery that Edward Kennedy's hand in his pocket was attached ultimately to Edward M. Kennedy. "I didn't call it [the draft effort] off as strongly until Tuesday, because those who were involved in the minority plank felt that my being involved might help their position," Kennedy later told me directly.

Lester Hyman, who had telephoned Ted to lay before him his conviction that Steve's vote counters really had put together enough delegates to grab Teddy the nomination, would record the answer he got in Newsweek forty years later: "I asked him whether he believed us when we said we really had the votes for him. He replied that he did. Then why, I asked, would he not make himself available as a candidate? 'For two reasons,' he replied. 'First, the delegates would be doing it out of sympathy for Bobby . . .' And second, 'because I am not yet ready to be president of the United States.'"

This Hubert evidently sensed. To Humphrey that meant that Kennedy, too, was probably bluffing. Doves like George McGovern had already announced themselves prepared to move over to Kennedy, but Kennedy's own staff still wasn't around, Daley was jollier suddenly minute by minute, and the persistent telephoning from Hyannis Port seemed concerned mostly with reversing the platform stand of such Humphrey sympathizers as Massachusetts's hawkish Maurice Donahue.

Kennedy was stopped; bluffs and threats were being everywhere discounted. Lyndon Johnson, clearly unwilling to let this spreading Teddy talk take on much more life, turned Marvin Watson loose on the Southern governors still clucking about the unit-rule sellout; residual talk of defection by delegates from Alabama and Missouri guttered. A reinvigorated Humphrey now played the politics of the situation without a worry, backed the hawk war plank to its one-sided Wednesday success confident that Edward Kennedy in Hyannis Port would not stir.

By then Kennedy couldn't. Smith's audience with Eugene McCarthy lasted perhaps ten minutes; as soon as that was over Smith checked in with Kennedy in Hyannis Port; by four forty-five Daley, steaming, called Ted to flog his listless dark horse one final unavailing time. "The delegates in Chicago were like a collection of condemned men," Arthur Schlesinger explained later. "When the talk of Teddy's candidacy started I talked to him two or three times. I thought he simply couldn't do it that way, he wanted to go if he ever went on his own record, not on something related to his brothers." Yet there were so many . . . considerations, complications, factors that one had an obligation to review . . .

"On the one hand," Kennedy himself would try to explain to me himself, parsing his feelings retroactively, "here would appear to be, if it were able to be worked out, the opportunity to carry out in the most effective way possible the things Bobby had lived and died for. This was the makeweight on one side. On the other side was the complete real loss of spirit in terms of willingness to run. I just didn't have the stomach for that. I didn't feel I was personally equipped for the race; I thought it was much too great a burden to place on my family at that time. People would be considering the candidacy for entirely the wrong reasons . . . Was there ever a time I ever seriously thought of making the race? No."

Still . . . "We're going to have to climb many many mountains before we're going to have the vote totals that we have tonight," Vanden Heuvel, who was managing the peace-plank strategy along with Goodwin, called Hyannis Port to exclaim. "I found it especially difficult when people called from the floor," Dave Burke remembers. "They were in despair. You try to devise a way of answering people who say, 'I just talked to X in the Y delegation, and you can have 'em if you want 'em.' Then they'd get sore." There is prima facie evidence of serious intent simply in the fact that Gwirtzman and Burke were there, in Hyannis Port, backstopping Teddy, both flown up unexpectedly over the weekend; it is also germane that Kennedy kept these two well away from himself: Enough was plucking at him without having to confront Burke's obvious moral horror at the entire project.

"Milty and I were opposed to even giving it a moment's thought," Burke says. "Ted clowned with us throughout the whole thing. He'd call, clowning around, say—you know—'Why not?' Or 'OK, I'll write my acceptance speech myself.' The next day," Burke let his breath out slowly simply thinking about Monday night, "the next day it was clear it never really entered his mind."

The convention slept crapulous Tuesday; Ted Kennedy was still its dream of innocence. It awoke Wednesday disheveled and perhaps a little bit loathsome to itself, sticky with its mood of unwanted decision-making. But by then its traditional appetites were returning.

Kennedy's crisis was behind him too. He hadn't trusted Daley, he certainly hadn't trusted Eugene McCarthy, and apparently he hadn't trusted himself much either. "This was Bobby's year," he confided to a friend, and at breakfast time Wednesday morning Kennedy called Humphrey in Daley's suite to repudiate any attempt to challenge him. The Vietnam peace plank was busted just after 4 PM. Edwin Muskie of Maine, a moderate, picked up the vice-presidential nomination. Vanden Heuvel, furious, had threatened to nominate LBJ so that the puppet-master himself would get his chance to dance beneath the strings; the Humphrey backers' counterthreat of an embarrassing late Edward Kennedy nomination stymied that. By now the convention floor was strewn with smuggled-in Bobby stickers; four hundred Draft Kennedy posters were belatedly printed and up; everything was over. "Teddy called me when the time came," Dutton recalls. "He was Bob Kennedy's cold gray eyes and JFK's detachment. The decision was totally his."

3. The Whip

"I think one reason Ted pulled back in Chicago at the point he did," Lester Hyman conjectured later, "was that he felt he had given Hubert Humphrey his word, and in the end he wouldn't really do anything to hurt Humphrey, whom he genuinely likes. Also—this was not expressed, but was clear enough—he was still in a state of shock. I spent one full day two weeks after the convention with Ted in Hyannis Port. He would be doing fine; then he would stop, stare out the window. Ted didn't do that.

"Something else surprised me that day: Ted seemed to be the only professional politician I talked to who was sanguine about Humphrey's chances at that point. He said, 'We are really going to try and help him. I want one man close to me who understands campaigning nationally to go with Ed Muskie and help with his speechwriting. Will you do it?' I went, and of course Muskie did very well, really arrived during those eight weeks. The day after the election I got a call from Ted. 'Lestah,' he said immediately. 'What did you do, create a monstah?' He still needles me about it. 'You are going to be seated next to a very good friend of yours,' he said the other day when we were talking over a fund raiser. 'Do you remember Senator Muskie of Maine . . . ?'"

But neither buoyancy before the election nor playfulness later could gloss over Kennedy's suspicions that his own presidential feint had in fact helped sucker Hubert into that untenable Vietnam stance. Gauged either by the thinness of the street crowds the Humphrey appearances were drawing or the indifference of the traditional heavy contributors, Hubert's presidential campaign foundered. Few cared. Humphrey's onetime protégé Eugene McCarthy, after a period of spiritual rejuvenation on the French Riviera, busied himself covering the World Series for *Life*. Johnson, still eying Hubert narrowly, withheld National Committee funds. Conservatives considered Nixon.

On September 10, during a Chicopee rally for Kennedy's Massachusetts ally Representative Edward Boland, Kennedy bestowed formal endorsement on the Humphrey-Muskie push. It was Kennedy's first forthright indication to the national party that his political appetite was improving; nine days after that, at a colossal Boston street rally for Humphrey Kennedy himself arranged, he subjected it to revolutionary politics.

By noon a crowd of twenty thousand was trapped beneath the department store facades at the junction of serpentine Washington and Summer streets. Neither politician was concentrating much; Kennedy and Humphrey both seemed to be mumbling something incomprehensible, hugging each other forlornly in public in the hope of reconciling in their sleep. Kennedy opened with the sort of maidenly little one-liner he normally relied on Dick Drayne to confect for him. "Some time ago the vice president came to Massachusetts, and he and I were involved in opposite sides of a bitter and most important struggle. But we were victorious—the Boston Red Sox beat the Minnesota Twins."

Hundreds of deeply involved college students and antiwar activists froze; if tone were money, Kennedy had bankrupted himself. He continued, "If there is any lesson to be learned from 1968, it is that there is no room for anarchy, there is no room for violence," and touted up the Democratic nominee as a fighting liberal who opposed a Republican already announced as intending to hold up ratification of the nuclear nonproliferation treaty. By now the crowd leaders had given up on Kennedy, cries of "Shame on Teddy!" and "Dump the Hump!" and "Sellout!" spread. Kennedy forced through, blundered into his declaration that, though this was an "uphill battle . . . I remember another one in West Virginia, when a candidate was significantly behind in the polls . . ." It was the first time anybody could remember a Kennedy being widely booed in Massachusetts.

The ructions of the autumn dispersed; inside Kennedy the ferment of loss and responsibilities was, little by little, beginning to breed an intimation of the sort of role he might play now. That fall was a weary entr'acte, so much time shredded into chores, fund raisers for Bobby's $3.2 million debt, spots for occasional liberals. A week could disappear into errands for Ethel: advising concerned Milton officials to give the impudent but academically busted Joe III a "good swift kick in the ass," standing over Ethel herself as she was delivered of Rory, her eleventh, by Caesarean, Ted's face mask spattered by the incision. Kennedy had nearly passed out, but within minutes he was so rapt and involved he was giving the obstetrician suggestions.

Living "day to day," he mused his future together decade by decade. What Kennedy decides is clearest usually from results, what he does. The important move Kennedy made next, piecing out tactics as he went along just before the 91st Congress opened, was the maneuver his breathless staffers were subsequently to refer to as the "Whip Fight." Grabbing the Assistant Majority Leader's job from Russell Long was, in fact, very much a fight, a ravine battle between two warlords, for each of whom a loss meant bloodletting. Nothing clarifies Kennedy's political refinement and the psychological economy of his best work more than the realization that, by the time the results were public—ninety minutes after the critical Senate caucus convened—most news reports agreed in treating it as somewhat of an . . . an inevitability, a bestowal, as if a lot of Ted Kennedy's affectionate colleagues had chipped in privately to procure him something he'd appreciate.

As if Ted had just . . . happened to like the idea. Taken to the notion sitting restlessly in his Sun Valley suite waiting for his misrouted ski boots so he could join Joan and Ethel and John Tunney and Andy Williams on Baldy Mountain. Then, between calls to the baggage depots, a few quick season's greetings to some of the colleagues, pretty soon an idea was germinating: Why not think about rounding up support for Assistant Majority Leader himself . . . ?

The ruminations that started Kennedy telephoning began with his sense of the vulnerability of the party's existing Assistant Majority Leader, Russell Long, the Gentleman from Louisiana. Long—whose demagogue father, Huey, "The Kingfish," and mother, Rose, had both served briefly in the U.S. Senate—had come into the Upper Body in 1948; he'd arrived at thirty, as with Kennedy, as early as the Constitution allowed. By 1965, when Humphrey ascended to the vice presidency, Long, an affable man still subject to an occasional populist flourish, went after the Assistant Majority Leader's job. Long was armpit-high in seniority already, and he was prepared—blatantly prepared, no apologies—to dispense the favors accrued seniority made possible: vouchers on possible oil lobby funds for upcoming campaigns, logrolling commitments, even the begrudged presentation of John C. Calhoun's own desk to South Carolina's Olin Johnson. Long contrived his victory on the second caucus ballot.

A lot of the Long family money was still being churned into existence by a corporate descendant of Huey's own Win-Or-Lose Oil Company. Enticingly enough, by 1965 Long was ranking majority member of the arterial Senate Finance Committee, shortly to become its powerful chairman, and thus in a perfect position to see after the senior lobbyists for the insurance as well as the oil and natural gas industries.

Among the more moderate colleagues, a number of whom might otherwise have hesitated, permitting Russell Long his honorific simply didn't seem worth getting aroused about. The politically wary Lyndon Johnson was unwilling to leave the indispensable comptroller functions previously discharged by the Whip in some befuddled colleague's hands. Johnson pipelined them to Bobby Baker (who, as Assistant to the Majority Leader, was a salaried employee completely at the Majority Leader's behest) as his ambulatory clearinghouse in charge of keeping track of who was where, whose bills were being held up or pushed in which subcommittee, who wasn't needed at which juncture of the debate for a roll call, whom—given his viewpoint on an issue—it might be unpolitic to alert when a relevant bill came onto the floor.

This left the Whip's role largely in helping plan the flow of legislation and standing in on the floor for the Majority Leader or Secretary to the Majority—i.e., avid little Bobby Byrd. The residual Whip job thus tended to tie a member down without involving him in the favor-trading that is of the essence of Cloakroom influence. Hubert Humphrey had given some content to the post primarily because of his tirelessness about buttonholing colleagues in behalf of bills he favored: His rank thus allowed him something of a peripatetic Cloakroom forum.

By 1968 Long had backslid, turned into something of an embarrassment to his dignified colleagues. A sullen self-importance replaced the refreshing bumptiousness with which Long had once endeared himself, at least to reporters, by responding to earlier charges of having spread oil money around with a playful "Shucks, that's the name of the game." "At least Ted Kennedy never drank on the Senate Floor," a colleague and a Southerner observed to me once the 1968 contest was over. "Long he . . . he reeled in sometimes. His friends finally had to vote against him."

What made Long vulnerable just then was the concern about Nixon. Corrupt old plains Democrats whose careers had started with forgotten agrarian revolts and privileged ward Democrats who began as union organizers realized overnight that some of the institutional luxuries nobody cared about under Eisenhower and Kennedy and Johnson (such as retaining leaders of the sluggishness of Russell Long on the party's books as "Whip") were henceforth prohibitive. The Democratic Majority Leader, the prim and leathery Mike Mansfield, while unimpeachable and trusted everywhere and certain to retain his post, was far too diffident and mannerly to scheme and drive and deliver against a seasoned politician reascendant as president. Except for Mansfield, Southerners filled all the leadership posts, with most of Long's responsibilities as Whip discharged by that forever scurrying popinjay Bobby Byrd of West Virginia.

"Christmas was the first time I had a chance to . . . think about other things," Kennedy said later. After Friday, December 27, Ted did his thinking between telephone calls. Kennedy's tone throughout that primary round remained cautionary. First responses sounded mixed: Joe Tydings and Birch Bayh encouraged Kennedy; older liberals such as Scoop Jackson, Philip Hart, and John Pastore seemed perplexed as to why Kennedy should want so confining a post. Hart had himself just been through an effort to promote an interest in the leadership situation for Muskie. Fearful of Ted Kennedy's premature lead in the internal polls and much better known after his vice-presidential run, Muskie announced that his intention at the moment was to travel and speak widely and "try and stimulate discussion and constructive programs with respect to the problems of the country . . . . Well, now," he conceded bluntly, "to be tied down in Washington would limit my opportunities to do that."

Locked up, tied down, confined—buffeted by so much publicity, Kennedy was attracted by the well-fortified privacy of a leadership cove: gregarious yet full of respect, everybody's kid brother still—the Assistant Leader of the Majority. He would be addressing issues not merely as the senator from Massachusetts or the conceivable 1972 nominee of the party. It would be his responsibility as the Democrats' second-ranking organizer to confront every important question: The U.S. Senate would become his academy. The ambiguity of such a role shimmered beckoningly.

Kennedy persevered. Sunday night he alerted the surprised David Burke in Virginia with instructions to check around among the staffers and try to locate as many as possible among the fifty-seven vacationing Democratic members. By that time Kennedy had telephoned his ostensible rival, Muskie, to push him to try for the leadership. Once Muskie refused, Kennedy ventured, after a careful pause, that . . . perhaps . . . he just might . . . might himself consider running. Muskie's support secured, Kennedy immediately solicited Humphrey's benevolent encouragement and the promise of telephone calls. Kennedy now pushed beyond his immediate wing among the liberals, enlisted the tentative approval of less predictable powers like Albert Gore and Abraham Ribicoff.

About to commit himself, Kennedy hurried, before second thoughts set in, to secure—if not the support, at least the sympathetic neutrality—of his powerful elders. Mansfield, while prevented by his own post from canvassing personally, soon had his activist staff helping the Kennedy regulars. Warren Magnuson, as Chairman of the potent Commerce Committee, was willing to announce his influential backing and work on his fellow members early enough to offset the patronage enticements a surprised and rattled Long was in a position to distribute.

Kennedy's first great breakthroughs were the responses of Richard Russell, dean of the Senate—a family acquaintance since Joe Kennedy's knock-about political days and about to take over the chairmanship of the key Appropriations Committee—and John Stennis, about to replace *him* at the top of Armed Services. Neither grandee, of course, cared to risk word leaking out of his personally having voted against Long, but each was so annoyed with Long's recent antics that both indicated, in Russell's words, that key Southern leaders would not be "putting any roadblocks" in the way of Kennedy's election. Kennedy's strategy of position was, with this support, likely to carry. He had assured himself of the noninterference of the aging Southern leaders at the time when, their numbers thinning, they were otherwise intriguing to frustrate liberal aspirants; they were not above maneuvering to protect their collective clout by shifting from Armed Services to the liberal-threatened Judiciary Committee the serviceable Robert Byrd—who a number of them openly felt should himself have the Whip's job, having discharged most of its remaining duties for years.

Courtesy required that Kennedy at some point inform Russell Long himself: Kennedy reached Long personally by telephone in the midst of a planning session at his McLean, Virginia, house Monday. Kennedy returned from the telephone shaking his head: Out of the fifty or so senators he had talked to during the previous three days, it now appeared that nobody had tipped Long off in Baton Rouge.

One colleague Kennedy hadn't involved earlier than he needed to was Eugene McCarthy. "There was no time for personal contacts," Kennedy told a reporter from *Time* once he had ensconced himself. "The telephone is not very satisfactory, but it was the only way. I suppose," the senator seemed unsure, "I suppose some other calls were made. But the people who made them did so on their own." Innocence goes quickly, and by 1969 Kennedy was solicitous of his. Yet in all probability Kennedy's claim is accurate: The important pressuring efforts, the hoard of presented chits, the cascade of Kennedy-pleading calls almost every colleague got, were instigated pretty much spontaneously. "Just as the Kennedys are a clan," the penetrating Dutton remarks, "there is a clannishness about the people who gather with them. The Harrimans and Gilpatricks and Watsons. What holds it all together isn't really loyalty so much as common interest, contagion, excitement." Dutton nails it down: The Kennedys didn't solicit your help exactly. You entered their community, assumed your appropriate distance: At the appointed moment, the spark leaped.

By Thursday afternoon McCarthy had suggested that Ted stop by his office for a couple of minutes. By then McCarthy was a man undergoing political electrocution on the installment plan. It is a question whether Kennedy hadn't troubled Gene because he presupposed his enmity, or whether (given McCarthy's availability to oil money and Long's role as paymaster) he regarded the Minnesotan as pocketed in advance, or whether he hoped to spotlight Long's fall so as to disabuse some of McCarthy's more gullible backers—whichever, Kennedy appeared in McCarthy's apselike sanctorum detached.

McCarthy didn't disappoint. "I don't know," he observed, offhandedly. "I haven't got anything against Russell Long. I don't see any reason to strike out against him over something this unimportant." McCarthy had refused Muskie in December; he saw no consistency in supporting a Kennedy challenge now. (Weeks afterward McCarthy was to give a magazine interview in which he characterized his Finance Committee Chairman Long—who had stood up on the Senate floor to applaud Chicago's police for having clubbed in the skulls of McCarthy's chief supporters—as "about as liberal on most issues as anybody in the Senate.") Then, in a gesture of philosophical stunting certain to produce giggles of vertigo among leading McCarthyites (many of whom had been cabling and writing and calling him urgently all week in Kennedy's behalf, Kenneth Galbraith to Joe Duffey to Steve Cohen to Bill O'Dwyer), McCarthy explained that installing Kennedy as Whip would amount to a cruel deception of the liberal community, substituting the appearance of reform for the substance.

Those overworked Kennedy constituent lists had, of course, been in day-and-night use all week. Kennedy was actively promising to make the Whip's job "important to the nation, the Senate and the party"; sympathizers were threatening holdouts with a 1972 embargo on endorsements. Question marks like Joseph Montoya of New Mexico, a moderate who, like his senior colleague Clinton Anderson, worked hard at keeping things agreeable with Southeastern oil interests, found, after evading a commitment to Kennedy directly, that leaders inside his own state organization like County Chairman Bill Bayatt, George Gonzalaz, and Ed Guthierez were on the telephone unexpectedly, perturbed to have heard somehow of Montoya's hesitation.

University people kept calling; Montoya, up for reelection in 1970, needed the Mexican-American community en bloc. I. W. Abel, impressed increasingly by Edward Kennedy, called key people himself. The Connecticut Democrats caucused and telephoned both Ribicoff and Dodd to underline their preference for Kennedy. Fulbright, expected to send an open proxy, now returned hurriedly from Europe for the secret paper ballot.

Individuals were torn. Long bustled around to remind colleagues like Vance Hartke and Gaylord Nelson and Ralph Yarborough of favors past, agreed in a moment of desperation to trade Nelson his own place on a coveted select committee for a promised vote. Nelson, chewed by auto lobbyists, privately assured Kennedy of his vote if he truly needed it. On Thursday the influential Border Stater Albert Gore hustled the moderates by publicly avowing his intention to vote for Kennedy; on countercue four prominent oilmen from Oklahoma telephoned Fred Harris to urge him to stand by Long.

"I had Kennedy outgunned in the Senate, but he had me outgunned in the country," a surprised-looking Russell Long, exuding sportsmanship, announced to the press immediately after the caucus adjourned, following it up with his recommendation that "Mr. Nixon should be very careful and watch himself for the future . . ." The surprise was mostly for the cameras: By the time the Democrats caucused, Long's important guns had been long since spiked, and he was certainly veteran enough to know it beforehand.

Denied the austere sponsoring authority of either Stennis or Russell, Long had to depend for his seconding speeches on the ineffective Spessard Holland and Allen Ellender, chairman of the Agricultural Committee and a onetime hometown lieutenant to The Kingfish himself. En caucus Ellender supplemented his reputation for international gaffes by rounding into an overblown attack on Kennedy as, at once, an interloper and a child to the Senior Body's subtle ways: Smirks started to spread across wrinkled faces.

The word was long since out that, as far as the leading Southerners were concerned, anybody could vote for Kennedy with impunity. Preliminary adjustments had been made all across the Cloakroom; for example, Magnuson had helped arrange matters so that Spong of Virginia, a committee favorite of his, could accept Kennedy without worrying about reprisals from the dying Byrd machine; Richard Russell himself made it clear to his protégé, Daniel Inouye, that he had no objections to the Hawaiian's preference for Kennedy. Muskie and Jackson both spoke warmly in Kennedy's behalf; Kennedy slid into power, 31–26.

"I do not view this in any way as a personal victory," Kennedy was to insist into the push of notebooks and microphones minutes after the caucus ended. What carried his challenge, he observed, were "the winds of change, so evident in 1968, which expressed themselves in the Senate, which, as the center of Democratic opposition now," would have to gather its force and reassert itself as an "active, creative, aggressive institution."

"Confident" that Ed Muskie could have become Assistant Majority Leader had he so chosen, the newly anointed Whip waved off the allegation that his leadership role would give him a "power base" for 1972: "I do not believe it has implications of that kind," Kennedy ventured, adding, "It is an extremely time-consuming job which will give me responsibilities in the Senate and will keep me there. There'll be more demands on my time that will require my presence on the Senate floor. This job will restrict the opportunity to travel."

Then, grinning, "Of course I can always visit with my colleagues here on the floor." Prodded, Kennedy confessed that "I haven't got a legislative program as such" and continued, "We're interested in more public participation in regulatory agency decisions. Poor people need a voice in these decisions that so affect their lives . . . These are many of the programs Robert Kennedy was interested in . . ."

Kennedy's observations skip through the public mind, as usual, with nowhere a phrase catching. He has prepared the achievement for six premonitory years. Dropped in—alone among the colleagues—on Thomas Dodd to say a word about how sorry he is *personally* to have to vote for the censure motion. Staggered out (or dumped his drink covertly into the wastebasket: So often there are two versions of Kennedy stories just as there are two versions of Kennedy) after bourbon in the morning with Eastland. Smoothed over feelings Bobby riled so often and now finds himself banking politically the guilt so many of the members find themselves contending with subsequent to Bob's assassination. Cashes in among the regulars for his August forbearance in taking the nomination while—among the insurgents—picking up due bills for having gotten involved at all. The moment is tricky but his: Everything Kennedy says now is even flatter, more guarded and anti-personal than usual, emphatic while stressing that there be no gloating over Long, that he personally represents no more than the embodiment of a quickened liberal impulse.

"The [Whip] job has acquired some significance," Russell Long observed: significance, not importance. It remained "washing the sweatshirts" in McCarthy's verbal shrug. But Edward Kennedy has been washing sweatshirts most of his life: If, during the next four years, he could beg off a Jefferson-Jackson Day dinner in Omaha or bypass a *Meet the Press* without finding himself stoned as a renegade, well . . .

"He felt that he had done all right in debate but had not played a large enough part in the legislative scenario," one aide observes. As Assistant Majority Leader Kennedy might hope that—allowing for the disinclination of the taciturn Mansfield to discipline to partisan advantage (not to mention Mansfield's lacks as a non-lawyer and the rumors of his 1970 retirement)—perhaps finesse enough as the Whip might lead one into a role as . . . as Chief Scenarist? Becoming the Leader himself? Interviewed a few weeks afterward he was already divulging his hopes of "invigorating" the progressives in the Democratic caucus, who had allowed the Democratic Policy Committee to reduce its role "over the past eight years" to regulating the flow of legislation to the floor rather than, in Kennedy's words, "fill the function that was originally conceived for it—that is, to formulate ways and means of enacting the party platform into law."

While disclaiming, the morning of his election, any "legislative program as such," Kennedy volunteered immediately, "We're interested in the regulatory agency decisions." He followed that in, appearing before Judiciary Chairman James O. Eastland to request, with every backbencher politesse, the Chairmanship of Judiciary's Subcommittee on Administrative Practices and Procedures. The Subcommittee Chairman throughout the sixties had been Edward Long of Missouri, who, nudged by his abrasive Chief Counsel Bud Finsterwald, had busied the Subcommittee primarily with efforts to impugn the integrity of various administrative departments—the approach that in 1963 forced Edward Kennedy himself to resign from ADPRAC.

Throughout the previous few sessions Edward Long seemed to have given his Subcommittee over completely to scratching up testimony to discredit the Justice Department brief on Bobby's primary bête noir, Jimmy Hoffa. Long's constituency back home finally understood his preoccupation when evidence was compiled that the same St. Louis attorney, Morris Shenker, who had shipped Long $160,000 in "forwarding fees," represented Hoffa.

The Democrats in Missouri dumped Long in the 1968 primary; as the 91st Congress opened, therefore, the Administrative Practices and Procedure Chairmanship lay vacant. Despite its bland-sounding, bureaucracy-invoking designation, control of ADPRAC conferred on its chairman in effect a hunting licence to investigate and publicize whatever looked controversial all across the government. Normally, of course, the ranking Democrat on the Subcommittee would have grabbed off this potentially headline-attracting post: Kennedy had not been serving at all on the Subcommittee, so tact was indispensable.

Eastland—unwilling to turn down a youngster who still might just get to be president any minute—soon ascertained that the three surviving Democrats on the Subcommittee, Hart, Bayh, and Quentin Burdick, appeared forewarned and amenable. Ted picked up the chairmanship and installed Jim Flug—excessively shrewd, unflappable, a rare liberal gut-fighter—as Chief Counsel. Then Kennedy began his initial Subcommittee meeting, on March 27, by reading into the record the mandate of Administrative Practices and Procedures. As authorized under the Legislative Reorganization Act of 1946, the Subcommittee was empowered "to make a full and complete study and investigation of the administrative practices and procedures within the departments and agencies of the United States, in the exercise of their rulemaking, licensing, investigatory, law enforcement and adjudicatory functions . . ." To a fine-print-reading workaholic like Edward Kennedy a mandate like this was beyond exhilarating. While the Democrats occupied the White House, no sane Democratic lawmaker could be expected fully to exploit this virtually limitless investigative capacity. Nineteen sixty-nine was different. Richard Nixon's puffy young administration, between yawns, woke up to discover itself subjected to a disconcertingly familiar pair of half-hooded Democratic eyes.

4. *Law and Order*

Nobody around the White House noticed that the freckled Kennedy hand inside the surgical glove was trembling too. Among people who knew Kennedy well, there was already concern at his volatility that winter of 1968–69: swollen with aggressiveness at times, all-consuming; then, without warning, drained by the old hesitations—a tendency to bolt, reverse himself, cautiously find his way back to a less grandiose mood.

Privacy got harder and harder. "The Boss is hiding out in the Whip's chambers," his aides around the Old Senate Office Building joked; that became a pregnable refuge too. "He thought it would free him substantially, so he could speak as Whip, but it hasn't worked," David Burke conceded within a couple of months. "He is now, still, more than ever, Ted Kennedy." At a New York dinner Kennedy claimed ruefully to have consulted Ed Muskie beforehand and been urged to try for the post in order to get himself "close to the leadership"; Kennedy was close already: locked in.

"As near as I can tell, this job consists of what we find to do," Kennedy had advised Wayne Owens, the hollow-cheeked young Utah lawyer with the permanent seminarian's pallor he invited over from Senator Moss's staff to manage the Whip's office. Mansfield was evidently going to continue exercising the leadership prerogatives; Bobby Byrd would protect his chores. It had been Kennedy's hope that, between the sinew of Mansfield and the errand-running of Byrd, he himself might convene a kind of ideological party caucus, attempt to "Whip the majority," as Burke proposed, "in terms of issues, not telephone calls."

By means of the biweekly sessions of the Democratic Policy Committee, which shortly included ten chosen Democrats as well as the leadership, Kennedy attempted to coordinate tactics and help ramify support for favored legislation. The generation of senior Southerners that had been running the Senate, while still cagey and arrogant enough to bypass Birch Bayh as chairman of the potent Appropriations Committee, was dying off. To help offset the conservatives' superior manipulative skill and coordination, Kennedy instituted special study sessions for new senators with the Parliamentarian, promulgated a weekly Whip's Letter to inform the members of upcoming legislation, set up a tape-centered communications network to which each colleague could, at the touch of a button in the Whip's office, be alerted and pick up and listen to proceedings relayed from the floor.

The result was to upgrade the resources and effectuality among the liberal Senators, who so often found their preferences in committee buried upside down or amended into oblivion. The Policy Committee gave Kennedy a rostrum from which to pitch for trade-offs. Typical of his best effort was his success at persuading Mansfield, the Policy Committee, and ultimately reformers of both parties to hold hostage the presidential request on the business tax credit and the extension of the surtax until the Nixon administration agreed to specific reforms.

Good work, every bit of it, subtle and overdue, but harder and harder to accomplish for anyone of such political heft as Edward Kennedy. For all his gradualist hopes, Kennedy was everywhere regarded as president-in-waiting. To worried advisers in the executive branch—to many within his own legislative Democratic Party—he was already oversized, unmistakably the next president. "Teddy's got it locked up . . ." Muskie told Stewart Alsop in March. "There's the money, and the mystique, and Teddy's an able, charming guy too. When everybody begins saying this early it's going to be Teddy—why, it's going to be Teddy, almost sure to be." It was a role nobody could possibly underplay: Ted's whisper tore the national eardrum.

This had to affect Kennedy: It showed up in committee work first. "At first," recalled Ralph Yarborough of Texas, who sat on the Labor and Public Welfare Committee from 1959 on and so could compare the work of all three brothers Kennedy, "when Edward Kennedy first came on the Committee he seemed not only young, but his activities, his questioning, were not really up to that of JFK and Robert Kennedy. They seemed far superior at that time. Then, in the middle sixties, as he sat on the Committee a while, he began to improve. His questions grew sharper, very sharp; he seemed to develop the Kennedy ability to pack a great deal into one question. Then, after Robert Kennedy was assassinated, his development seemed to me"—Yarborough had become Committee Chairman by that time—"considerably accelerated, almost phenomenal. But he still wasn't like Bob, who would pull a quip that would get a laugh at the expense of another senator. The delays were so abrasive to Bob; his mind always seemed out beyond the narrow confines of the

committee room, the floor—he wanted to solve the problem, jump ahead
to the solution."

Yet as the weather warmed up in 1969, the colleagues couldn't help
remarking in Ted at least a little of Bobby, Bobby with the gloves on, maybe,
but more impatient, with less and less padding all the time. "He's far more
decisive," David Burke decided in June, starting off with enthusiasm enough
but trailing away a bit as he went on, shaded a little by afterthoughts. "All
the people he usually relies on for small decisions. You make the best case
you can—he does what he wants. That's different. Cesar Chavez wants him
to come to California. We all say no, couldn't possibly, no security. I spent
the whole day reiterating the argument. He called me up at five-fifteen. The
plane left at six. Or Memphis. The Martin Luther King funeral anniversary.
You go to Memphis, you may not go home. Bricks. Teargas." Burke undoes
and refastens the second button on his vest. "He goes."

The gleam in Kennedy's eye that reflects the inflation of power is unfamiliar and obviously a little bit anguishing to David Burke, devoted background
figure and enthusiastic family man, not at all sure he is going to like being
second man on the presidential bobsled as he watches his boss polishing up
the runners. "He has a sense of his new role," Burke says, in explanation.
"There's no one else in the structure above him."

Way up but obviously feeling a little bit . . . precarious. His first time out
as ringleader of the liberals, rounding up opposition to Walter Hickel as Secretary of the Interior, Kennedy requested that Hickel meet with him privately
before Hickel's televised Interior Committee appearance. Hickel had joined
the oil lobby in opposing the "Free Trade" port off the coast of Maine; the
afternoon Hickel's appointment came onto the floor for a vote Kennedy was
watching, ponderous but evidently very nervous as he wiped his palm back
and forth across his mouth, picked absently at his eye, his ear, massaged his
chest under his coat, flicked the end of his nose.

Other liberals came and went, slipped into the chair next to him, whispered. In repose Kennedy's big round head looked refined and fissured with
pain. "We have now come to a time for the Senate to advise and consent on
the nomination of Walter Hickel as Secretary of the Interior," the president
pro tem intoned. When his turn came Kennedy rounded his lips, almost
tonelessly: No. Hickel carried anyway. Kennedy's back hurt; as he left the
Cloakroom his massive high forehead was whitened with pain and he walked
very slowly, with as little movement as possible of the knees.

In committee work the responsibility was indeed making him very sharp,
but at times it was making him testy too. "He has a remarkable ability to press

his point without arousing the opposition," one colleague had remarked just after the Whip face-off. "The South, for example, loves him. And he's not buying their respect through surrender. Birch Bayh and Phil Hart say he's the toughest member on Judiciary." By April Kennedy had started leaving bruises, personalizing in ways he never had before.

The showcase hearings before Kennedy's Subcommittee on Administrative Practices and Procedures, on March 27 and 28, were an inquiry into illegal race patterns in the hiring practices of government contractors. They moved very quickly into the effort by Kennedy to substantiate, as he himself put it at the opening of the second session, his clear suspicions that "The new government places a low priority on the vindication of civil rights, that seemingly minor procedural changes mask basic shifts in the government's determination to eliminate segregation and discrimination."

The colloquy that made headlines the first day was that between Clifford Alexander, the urbane but highly charged young black Chairman of the Equal Employment Opportunity Commission, and Everett McKinley Dirksen, the ranking Republican on the Subcommittee. Like the Cowardly Lion who had just gotten Courage, Dirksen was in a noticeable sweat at the time to prove his fortitude to his new—and not awfully interested—president. His strategy was alternately to bait Alexander into libertarian outbursts and lure him unsuspecting into agreeing that he would indeed be "competent to utilize" an authority that would "abolish the Compliance Board" and put the "functions" of going after the great corporations "in your shop." Kennedy just as deftly slipped in to lead Alexander back from the brink with his observation that "It seems to me that it would put an extraordinary burden upon your agency to have you monitor every kind of federal contract in every federal department unless we are going to change dramatically your whole mission. And I think there are ways of strengthening your particular office . . . to permit you to do the job better."

Unable to get near enough to Alexander for long enough to distort his testimony, Dirksen finally roared: ". . . Why, there are people walking around Washington every day who are harassed one way or another by this operation. And I am advised by one Corporation that they have spent a million dollars just to go to hearings . . . So what I am getting at is this harassment business, like your carnival hearing out in Los Angeles . . ."

The exchange continued a few minutes more; suddenly Kennedy broke in: "Mr. Alexander, I just want to say that I hope no one has been threatened in here this morning because they have been trying to do the job they are expected to do . . ." Kennedy concluded by commending Alexander for "the kind of demeanor this morning which is the clearest indication to me and to those who are here from the press that you did conduct a judicious hearing, and that you are a reasonable man, and that there was not any carnival out in Los Angeles."

Mr. Alexander: "Thank you, sir."

Senator Dirksen: "Well, Mr. Alexander, I listened with interest to the sermonizing of my colleague. I am about as humble a person as ever set foot in shoe leather. I would not hurt a fly. I would not even hurt him."

Senator Kennedy: "Is this the carnival?"

Senator Dirksen: "This is the carnival."

The next day Kennedy took on David Packard, the new Deputy Secretary of Defense, over the awarding of Department of Defense contracts to the Dan River, Stevens, and Burlington textile mills without the companies' having submitted an acceptable written plan of compliance (after years of fruitless exchanges) with federal standards of job equality. Perhaps as ominous as anything else to Kennedy was Packard's naive display of locker-room optimism. ". . . did you outline even orally the same kinds of goals, the same kinds of objectives, which appear in any of the written compliance plans, which had been agreed to under the existing regulations?" Kennedy's sarcasm carried among its undertones an exasperation with so many generations of gentlemen, so many understandings that never quite came to anything, all the way back to the mudflats of East Boston and County Wexford.

As 1969 budded Edward Kennedy was discovering, as Robert Kennedy so frustratingly discovered, that the mantle of the anti-president tethered him. Richard Nixon was much much freer to move in and out of developing events, frame the public's reactions, preempt and coopt whatever he liked. So many of the Nixon programs the first few years amounted to hastily modeled replicas, quick cheap versions of federal programs that had been alive and spreading—often wastefully, sometimes badly administered—during the John Kennedy and Robert Kennedy and Lyndon Johnson years. Meanwhile the OEO and the public health programs and the legal services for the poor and pioneering titles by the ream were all being made more "efficient," shrunken.

Politically speaking, nothing was truly secure. After years of presiding, glum but persistent, over the Senate's bad conscience about draft procedures, Kennedy had the mixed pleasure of discovering one surprised May morning that the president had indeed directed, as Kennedy had urged for years, that eligible youngsters be selected by lottery. Kennedy endorsed the Nixon decision warmly, if a little bit puzzled, then came to discover that the day-by-day effect of the new procedures was about the same as the worst of the old procedures. Kennedy's heretofore inflammatory proposals to open diplomatic and cultural contacts with the Communist Chinese shortly became an administration initiative. Richard Nixon pronounced himself a champion of sweeping tax reform—too sweeping to affect anybody important, as things transpired; Kennedy, who had already begun shredding the tax laws all over the carpets of the Senate, watched that issue reduced to a confetti of reformist rhetoric and packed off to the White House beyond partisan eyes.

As the administration's pseudo-reforms spread, Kennedy found himself—perhaps with more invective than was comfortable—denouncing the "vested interests." He reactivated his years-old enmity with the powerful gun lobby by organizing the counter-lobby, the Emerging Committee for Gun Control, headed by John Glenn. He helped push Title IV, which prohibited the sale of mail-order handguns to nondealers, into the 1968 Crime Bill. Kennedy introduced a bill to curb the power of the privately owned public utilities. By March 5 he was denouncing them for racist hiring practices. He strafed the Council of Economic Advisors and the Department of the Interior for unwarranted price rises in the oil and natural gas industries, and suggested that he himself had reason to believe that, had the president objected, the prices would have been rolled back fast.

Yet the winter ended, and spring became summer, and Edward Kennedy, who aspired to the leadership of all the Democrats, was tongue-tied and evasive when it came to the great virulent domestic issue of that year, "law and order." Pundits quickly noticed that, among our squeamish citizenry, "law and order" was code for beating back the blacks in the cities. The attempt was already under way when Richard Nixon became president to delete from our code of laws the traditional protections against unwarrranted invasions of privacy, improper search and seizure, arbitrary arrest, and detention without trial—as well as the freedom publicly to express unpopular opinions without fear of punishment, the definition and assurance of which altogether constitute the central achievement of English Common Law and United States constitutional history. Kennedy wasn't touching that.

While openly attempting to vitiate and forestall the decade's well-advanced legal and procedural efforts in behalf of civil rights, the administration made it its public priority to identify and punish resistance among the noisy minority—a bedful of uncongenial public enemies that ran from collegiate antiwar activists to Cosa Nostra hangers-on, and included newsmen unwilling to disclose their sources, "neo-isolationists" and Weathermen. The trial of the Chicago Seven suggested what was going to happen when determined lawyers enforced laws of questionable constitutionality.

Edward Kennedy's own performance during this building crisis, especially during the half-year throughout which he functioned as the rallying personality of the Democrats, is not at all heartening. John Kennedy once noted that the hottest place in hell is reserved for the man who knows what is right and shirks it. Throughout the spring of 1968, when the Omnibus Safe Streets Act was pinched into shape among the subcommittees of Judiciary, Edward Kennedy—who had otherwise been slated to handle the liberal counter-maneuvering—was on the road for Bobby.

The day the Senate considered Title II (that pie in the face Sam Ervin and John McClellan and James O. Eastland lofted toward the Warren Court by attempting legislatively to nullify the central *Miranda* and *Escobedo* decisions, which dragged the nation's constabulary beyond the rubber-hose era by requiring the police to inform an ignorant suspect of his rights and avail an accused poor man of a lawyer), Jim Flug prevailed upon Kennedy to fly back from Oregon. Kennedy delivered a speech that challenged his colleagues to consider "whether we have found some substitute for due process of law, for the assistance of counsel, for the accusatory rather than the inquisitory system of justice, for the great writ of habeas corpus, and, finally, for the Supreme Court as final arbiter of law and guarantor of justice . . . They are threatened because some Americans have panicked about crime and want scapegoats to flay and panaceas to grasp at."

It was as succinct and devastating a statement as anybody made. One of the panic-stricken a few weeks later, when the entire Omnibus Bill came up for a vote, was clearly Kennedy himself: Reassuring himself because his own recommended Institute of Law Enforcement and Criminal Justice was included, Kennedy and a surprisingly flaccid Flug concluded that it would be politic to go along. It was that day of pandemonium in Harrisburg, Pennsylvania. Kennedy was traveling, but his office announced that, had he been in D.C., he would have voted for Nixon's bill.

That decision recorded, Kennedy was in no position to rally the liberals as the New Order began to apply this enabling legislation and lobby a suppliant Congress for more. As that Republican spring loosened political earth, odors wafted. En route to "revenue sharing," the Nixon administration was generous around state capitols with the "block grant" money, no strings or

controls. With it excitable rurally controlled local governments could procure police officers to roam the empty countryside, heavily armored vehicles
to quell uneasiness in the slums, and live rounds for such as the National
Guard volunteers who pacified Kent State. Tapping and bugging were widespread, even encouraged: The relevant Title III of the Safe Streets Act permitted officials at almost every level, once they themselves had decreed that
an emergency existed, forty-eight hours of unrestricted wiretapping and
bugging rights; only then did they have to think about requesting a judge's
warrant.

Critical months passed before the Supreme Court began to snip away at
these recently arrogated powers. Nixon Attorney General John Mitchell's
first response, upon being asked how his Justice Department would differ
from Ramsey Clark's, was to suggest that he intended to make proper use of
electrical and electronic surveillance in national security cases; Clark, went
the implication, had been incompetent and derelict.

On January 23, 1970, the new administration, still hampered annoyingly
by the Constitution, would push through the Senate its Organized Crime
Bill, an acid bath that ate away one whole side of the Fifth Amendment's
protection against self-incrimination, permitted a grand jury to put away
reluctant witnesses for as long as three years without trial, set a five-year
cutoff date on a witness's right to challenge illegally obtained evidence, let
the court determine what from a body of evidence the accused may see, and
permitted a judge to impose a thirty-year sentence on anyone convicted of a
felony if he were determined to be, in a special hearing, a "dangerous special
offender," the grounds for which included his having engaged in "a pattern
of conduct which . . . constituted a substantial source of his income, and in
which he manifested special skill or expertise."

Nineteen seventy was an election year; the public hysteria persisted. Mike
Mansfield, who voted for the Organized Crime Bill, noted, in virtually the
same gently sad aside the Safe Streets Act had provoked, ". . . sometimes I
wish I were a lawyer. At other times I am very glad that I never entered that
profession." Kennedy, who had entered that profession, and had resisted the
worst provisos of the legislation in Committee, would vote for the Organized
Crime Bill too.

By then Edward Kennedy was badly compromised. The spring of 1969,
with the administration's "preventive detention" and "no-knock" police
break-ins entering the code-word subglossary, the resistance Edward Kennedy could have formed around himself might very well have changed
our political history. Perhaps it was his own sense of the backswitching

ambiguities of civil liberties, which—like the war—shifted modalities with the changing fortunes of the Kennedys themselves.

Crime in the Streets had begun, as much as anywhere, as an effective Bobby-the-Crimebuster issue in Illinois. "Do you know a lot of these people think Bobby is more of a law-and-order man than I am!" Richard Nixon had exclaimed to an aide in Oregon, locking onto the issue at once and toning his presidency to that. Civil liberties had never been Robert Kennedy's most heartfelt concern; he had been the attorney general, after all, who petitioned the Congress for wider wiretapping rights.

Watchful lest Edward Kennedy (who had shown a clear understanding of the niceties and a tendency to champion dissent) attempt to turn the issue around before the administration could marshal its defenses, selected "leaks" began to work their way the spring of 1969 into Department of Justice news releases. After some heavy references injected into the Houston hearing of Cassius Clay's draft appeal, Clyde Tolson, the Deputy Director of the FBI, exploited the occasion of an anti-Bureau column by Carl Rowan on the matter of Robert Kennedy's having tapped the telephones of Martin Luther King.

Robert Kennedy, questioned about the matter during the California primary, had not exactly denied the charge. Now—the week of June 16, 1969—it had evidently been decided to make clear to whomever it might concern that the FBI had a signed memo from Robert F. Kennedy initiating the tapping. By that time Jim Flug was presiding as the Chief Counsel of the Administrative Practices and Procedures Subcommittee. The news—and the politically pernicious implications—stopped him immediately: Within minutes he was clearing and coordinating all memories of the matter and the press statements of anybody involved at the time—Courtney Evans (Bob's man in the FBI), Burke Marshall, Ramsey Clark.

As Lyndon Johnson's attorney general, Nicholas Katzenbach was out beyond the magnetic grid of the totally dependable. What he could be expected to say would have to be fitted somehow into what the rest of them released. Various Bobbys were quickly projected: the overworked Bobby who signed that sort of thing without reading everything too carefully, the Bobby who was plagued to exasperation by J. Edgar Hoover's constant requests to tap King's phone and gave in to prove to Hoover that King was not an agent of the Communist Conspiracy, the post-assassination Bobby who was so blocked by loss he was not really able to follow what was going on, didn't really know . . .

All explanations surfaced; the incident proved unimportant, died

overnight. But perhaps it had its desired effect; except for an oblique reference in a college graduation-day speech or two, a rather listless comment
now and then on the Senate floor, Edward Kennedy let the Crime-in-the-
Streets issue alone.

The front Kennedy did decide to open that spring of his Anti-Presidency, the
policy underbelly he thought he perceived, involved funding the administration's carryover anti-ballistic-missile proposals. As the first president of the
emerging Era of Negotiation, Richard Nixon was now determined to negotiate from "force," which, in technological 1969, read "sufficiency." As recently
as 1968, when the item was newly requested by a still-reluctant McNamara,
the vote to deploy the thin "Sentinel" network of anti-ballistic missiles
around fourteen to twenty selected communities had carried by 52–34 against
the concerted opposition of Philip Hart and John Sherman Cooper. A year
later the Department of Defense, which had already started to bulldoze exurban scrubland in Libertyville, Illinois; Seattle, Washington; and Reading,
Massachusetts, returned to Congress with its request for $5.5 billion more.
    . . . Letters, a trickle at first, then a disorganized torrent, began to arrive at
the offices of congressmen and senators. Philip Hart had already assembled
forty-plus probable votes against the funding by the end of January 1969.
Suddenly, on February 2, entering the debate behind a whiff of buckshot,
Kennedy released to the press the text of a letter he had just sent over to
Secretary of Defense Melvin Laird, in which he ticked off his own objections
to the projected Sentinel project. Kennedy found it technologically dubious,
likely to undermine the ongoing attempt to negotiate an arms limitation with
the Soviets, certain to expose huge population centers to the risk of accidental wipeout, costly beyond projections, and a distortion of federal funding
priorities. He recommended a "freeze" pending what he understood was "an
intensive review of the Sentinel system . . . you and your associates are presently carrying out . . ." Edward Kennedy was taking the issue over.
    Or was he really—did he intend anything like that? Because, once you get
behind the thing, this Armageddon with the military-industrial complex had
started, a matter of days before, as no more than a . . . a letter, another initiative somebody around the office had thrown at him. They had been tossing
proposals around behind closed doors for years, and the Boss had thought it
over and liked it, the gentry in Reading would remember. Ted had told Dun
Gifford to run around a little and try and figure out, Gifford remembers,
"whether there was a Senate peg to hang it on. I talked with Goodwin, and
Abe Chayes at Harvard, and then I stopped over at the Pentagon and talked

to General Mayo, General Starburg's deputy, and a few people in the Army Corps of Engineers in Massachusetts. And then I suggested to the Senator on a Friday that he write a letter to Laird suggesting that work on the two sites where it had begun be stopped pending the Pentagon's review rights.

"He read the letter and said, 'Doesn't this same logic apply to stopping the whole Sentinel program?' We came back and I redrafted the letter, made it longer, and delivered it to Laird and put it out as a release on Sunday. Then he sort of waffled around with it. Then on Monday Mendel Rivers in the House stated that his committee would not approve proceeding in Chicago and Seattle. On Wednesday Laird announced that all Sentinel construction would now stop. He claimed his decision preceded the Kennedy letter. It was a fantastic victory. But what to do next?"

But within weeks "spokesmen" in the Pentagon were letting it be known that the Sentinel program was vital, issuing their "reappraisals." "Senator Kennedy looked up one day after looking the new Department of Defense justifications over," Gifford remembers, "and said, 'Jesus Christ, this stuff isn't a review at all.'" So Kennedy himself decided to institute his own review, authorizing a kind of Commission Report from the Anti-Administration on this vital concern. On February 19 he announced that he had asked Jerome Wiesner of MIT and Abraham Chayes of Harvard to prepare a "dispassion-ate, inclusive, and exhaustive" review, a "non-Pentagon" report that he had already arranged to have presented to the relevant House and Senate com-mittees; John Stennis of Armed Services had already agreed by the time the Kennedy announcement appeared. By March 6 Kennedy's brain trust had taken on experts from George Rathjens, a onetime systems analyst for the Department of Defense, to the Kremlinologist Marshall Shulman, to Arthur Goldberg; its impact threatened to eclipse the Pentagon's own rushed late study of the matter.

Meanwhile, Kennedy's own staff kept churning the issue around the Hill: a network of staffmen from the office of Senators Hart, Gore, Cooper, Kennedy, Bayh, Brooke, Javits, Mansfield, and Nelson met regularly, exchanged mate-rial, and tried to keep all their bosses working in concert. By March 9 an AP poll had shown that fifty-seven Senators were willing to announce themselves ready to oppose the administration on Sentinel in May. The anti-Pentagon report had become a four-hundred-page book with twenty-two contributors.

The Kennedy group was already putting together its own nationwide lobbying and pressuring apparatus; Kennedy himself was constantly on the phone to influential friends all over the country helping set up a bipar-tisan committee to coordinate and popularize and surface the opposition.

Russell Long, who hurt enough a month after he lost the Whip job to put out a newsletter to his constituents explaining the loss, referred to "the fact that the Kennedy family has developed an extremely strong nation-wide organization which has the very best of contacts with the press of the nation, with those who own and control the television media and with the various university groups, as well as strong representation in every State Democratic organization in the United States.

"The connections of the Kennedy organization are so vast and reach into so many places in business, commerce, labor and religion that one could write several volumes about it and still leave a great deal unsaid," Long concluded, ascribing the loss of eleven Whip votes to depredations from this octopus. Long's tone was inflated, but his assessment was justifiable. As March opened, wavering congressmen and senators were feeling the protracted attentions of important local constituencies they didn't really know they had, now consciously focused on them and how they were going to work and vote regarding the ABM controversy.

Then, on March 14, following the ritual convocation of the resuscitated National Security Council, President Nixon announced that he had, indeed, decided to stand by his earlier conclusions and deploy the defensive missiles, let there be no mistaking that. But on close study he had decided that rather than deploy the double-punching Spartan-Sprint complexes among the suburbs around the two or three dozen cities they had initially been supposed to protect, he was now planning to concentrate on two sites, Malstrom Air Force Base, in Montana, and Grand Forks Air Force Base, in North Dakota, there to ward off attack on the Minuteman installations, not to protect people, against a recently revealed Soviet "first strike" capability, not an accident or a Chinese suicide attack, and with the name of Safeguard now, not Sentinel, according to a timetable of deployment that would vary according to the international situation.

Except for those details, he was not reneging one inch.

The liberals, who "want you to jump out the window for them on every issue that comes along," as a Kennedy aide quoted his boss at the time, still weren't satisfied, regarded themselves as outmaneuvered; Kennedy himself muttered about "shifting sands." But Nixon had played the politics of the crisis with adroitness, trading substance for shadow, selling out, as usual, at a small but pocketable political profit. Within hours both Stennis and Rivers had announced for the revised Nixon plan and both Mansfield and House Speaker John McCormack expected enough of the moderates to side with the president to assure him of his necessary summer funding. Insisting at the time that he "felt it would be an uphill fight, but I feel it can be won," Kennedy was not, as the debate over whether to institute the program dragged through the congressional spring, acting much like anybody preoccupied with being first over the top.

The issue was "in trouble," he confessed to a key aide. "He thinks it's lost anyway," the aide confessed to me. "Because the president can lay off the issue, work it around any way he chooses, authorize it directly or withhold funds while the disarmament talks look promising." It happened that Harper and Row was about to publish a bound version of his Commission Report in opposition to the Sentinel, and Kennedy was working on the introduction. His best hope for the moment was avoiding a Kennedy-Nixon face-off over the issue, which would inescapably invite defection among sympathetic Republicans. He released his introduction finally, wearily, because he felt the book had assumed an importance that threatened the issue itself.

Everything threatened something now: Everything was suddenly so unbecomingly personal. He hated that usually; sometimes it produced trade-offs, provided momentary relief. When headlines detailing the slaughter and starvation in Biafra became too gruesome for Kennedy's nights to tolerate he was able to persuade Richard Nixon, nudging him during the interminable leadership conferences, to follow up Lyndon Johnson's sale of eight C-97 cargo planes to the relief agencies (Kennedy's idea too) with money and the appointment of a special coordinator for Biafran relief. Vietnam was dragging on, and Kennedy blew up over administration reports of an American "victory" after ten bloody assaults that cost sixty dead GIs and three hundred wounded in capturing Ap Bia, "Hamburger Hill." "Senseless and irresponsible," Kennedy boomed on the Senate floor, "American boys are too valuable to be sacrificed for a false sense of military pride . . . The assault on 'Hamburger Hill' is only symptomatic of a mentality and a policy that requires immediate attention."

"It hit everybody awfully hard," Dave Burke remembers. "They were all reeling around holding their stomachs. Henry Kissinger got the charts out looking just like Walt Rostow . . . Teddy needed that sometimes. I remember the way he came off the floor after a savage exchange with Strom Thurmond. I was angry, that's a pissing contest with a skunk. But not him. He was clapping his hands. 'Well, I got my exercise today.' He'll never find his old X on that floor in there . . ."

Enormous and vulnerable, testy, then incomprehensibly meek—Kennedy that winter and spring was a power monstrosity, a blimp of glands, able to overturn the president one morning and reduced to a stomach-churning backbencher an hour later by the arch of one of Richard Brevart Russell's eyebrows. The politician stumbled; the human being stumbled, desperately at times——.

5. Alaska

More perilous than anything else was muddling among the effects of Bobby. In mid-April, acceding "reluctantly" to Senator Yarborough's request that he himself take over Bob's Special Subcommittee on Indian Education, Edward Kennedy directed a Senate group comprising himself, Walter Mondale, and Republicans George Murphy, Henry Bellmon, and William Saxbe on a three-day tundra-hopping investigation of the shacks and squalid sod hutches of Alaska's 55,000 Indians, Eskimos, and Aleuts. Nearly a month earlier the staff director of the Subcommittee, Adrian Parmenter, had worked up a forty-three-page memorandum proposing that the staffers shape photographic and TV coverage around the "native poverty contrasted with the affluence of government institutions" so as to emphasize that the treatment of the natives was "a rather striking example of colonialistic and discriminating behavior." The touring was accordingly rugged, 3,600 miles punctuated whenever the party's three little C-130s bounced down onto northern rivers to let its caravan of legislators and staffers and newsmen wade through thigh-high Arctic snow in search of diseased villagers and forgotten Stone Age corners of the North like Tuluksak and Nunapitchuk.

For a day and a half the Republican members kept quiet; then, seething over with claims of being elbowed aside by the Subcommittee staffers, furious with the "stage-managed scenario" that "was turning [the trip] into a kind of Roman circus," as George Murphy of California flared out, he, Bellmon and—more quietly—William Saxbe deserted the investigation. Alaska's own Republican Senator Ted Stevens, not a Subcommittee member, and Representative Howard Pollock stayed on.

The administration was undisguisedly hoping to degrade the whole investigation by politicizing it to help forestall a buildup of voter pressure for Eskimo anti-poverty and educational expenditures; Kennedy himself had just contrived to reverse an administration fund cutoff inside the Senate Select Committee on Hunger. As the budget trimmers saw it, the whole poverty issue was taking on an unwelcome persistence.

The expedition simply could not help looking, to White House strategists, too much like the icecap version of Bobby's travels in darkest Delta

Mississippi—the squalor sought out, the cameras, the heir apparent discovering the inevitable pathetic aboriginal child wasting away bravely, wordlessly, in a corner (this time of pneumonia, not pellagra), the furious establishmentarian charges of opportunism . . . Exciting, perhaps, satisfying for sure to the ham in Ted, but hard, harder minute by minute, because as the tour became so intensely politicized the chance to accomplish anything substantial receded and the opportunity for hurtful blunders was everywhere. Every question had to be read as gesture, every gesture was threatening.

As the strain tightened, in one of the C-130s, writer Brock Brower, listening to Kennedy patch into his thoughts, his justification to himself for being there, doing this, watched him withdraw, "an inch at a time," in anticipation and with a heavy telltale sigh of concession, the silver hip flask that had been Bobby's, and taste. "First time I've used it," Kennedy told Brower, needing badly to make that clear. He had tried most of the other strategies already by that time, the raffishness, the playfulness, the fond exaggerations, but the world, the self, was getting harder and harder to outsmart.

"Look Look Look Sylvia Sylvia Sylvia," he exclaimed to Time Inc.'s Sylvia Wright during one after-supper walk. "Stars! Stars! First one to find the northern lights gets a beer." The exuberance that the few people who knew him well recognized as verging on hysteria was taking over. At Arctic Village—north of the Arctic Circle, beyond the Yukon River—by a fluke, the remnant of the party found itself cut off for a few hours on a patch of permafrost so remote that, perhaps for the first time in his life, Kennedy felt himself utterly out of touch with the entire world. Snowmobiles whizzed across the pack, a crazy couple who obviously had no idea who—or what—Ted Kennedy represented contemplated him without interest. He was ecstatic.

But returning hop by hop to civilization, the ever-heavier atmosphere bore down on Kennedy hourly. Still loosened up enough to search himself, working steadily on the booze, he recurred to that paradigm of all human existence from which had emerged all pain, all possibilities: his family. He talked about his father, his brother Joe, examined himself against Joe, dead, and Bobby, dead. "They're going to shoot my ass off the way they shot Bobby's," he kept insisting.

He was exhausted, deadeyed by the time his entourage of staffers and media people filed aboard a commercial jet in Fairbanks. Except for one small family, the Kennedy group, which had held up the flight for more than an hour, was alone in a large compartment. Most newsmen drink, and many are devoted to drinking, but that night Kennedy shocked the most case-hardened. "He started whackin' the bottle in Fairbanks," one of them remembers. "He'd had nothing to eat, and it was drink drink drink drink drink, no sleep at all. He was all over the place, weavin' up the aisle, chanting Es-ki-mow Pow-er, pelting one of his guys with pillows, y'know, 'C'mon, wake up, you're not supposed to sleep on these goddamned trips!' There was this poor hapless family, I remember, in the seats in front of where he wound up standing, the baby was trying to sleep on the plane seat, and one of the aides brought Kennedy some very hot coffee, and he took it, and it just hung there in his hand, scalding hot, wavering, over the sleeping kid's face, until a couple of us got up and went over and eased him back down into his seat. His staff guys—Drayne—did what they could, but what the hell——."

"Ted was celebrating the fact that he had escaped for a few days from David Burke," another observer says simply. "Burke is, after all, a cop's son, but Dick Drayne simply couldn't control Teddy when trouble was coming."

Kennedy kept at it on the last leg of the flight, from Seattle to Dulles Airport in Washington. A sizable crowd, fronted by Joan and the three Kennedy children, was waiting for him. "We started to get ourselves together," a newsman remembers. "I looked out and everybody was there all right, the TV cameras, the whole world. I left behind Kennedy, and he did look awful, his eyes were like oysters on the half-shell. Joan saw and her jaw dropped four feet. I remember thinking, That's all for you, buddy. Then little Patrick rushed over to him, and Kennedy picked the little boy up and kissed him, and Patrick's head blocked off the cameras, and Kennedy was home free. The kid stole the show."

It was a revealing incident, although the pre-Chappaquiddick press, as usual, buried it. Ted Kennedy had never been particularly guarded during his less discreet moments, but there had been about his performance on that long plane ride home an intensity of desperation, of abandon, that upset everyone there: Limited-distribution memos circulated, especially inside the editorial offices of the magazines. The most celebrated of these became the one John Lindsay of Newsweek's Washington office pulled together. Lindsay had himself quite recently overcome a torturous drinking problem, he had ultimately come greatly to respect Robert Kennedy, and he had seen enough of Edward Kennedy over the winter to pick up constant signals of deep-seated emotional disruption: a tendency to stop in mid-sentence, shift moods inexplicably, break into unexpected tears, turn up boisterous with a few early "pops" at public events.

Kennedy, Lindsay concluded, was slipping out of control, careening toward some unavoidable crackup. Kennedy's driving, always wild (as JFK's had notoriously been), was frightening even to his closest staffers, who fended the subject off in tight half-humorous asides. He had a tendency at times to lose himself in conversation, look back laughing over his shoulder while at the wheel, pay little attention to where he was going so that he was forever threading back onto main routes. The temptation in April among senior editorial people was to ignore such reportorial observations, dismiss them as out of proportion. But they lay ticking in files throughout the late spring and early summer. By the middle of the session that spring a number of Kennedy's colleagues, too, were well aware of all this, concerned about it: Ed Muskie, speaking with typical frankness off the record, conceded the '72 nomination to Kennedy, except that—shaking his head gravely—the way Ted had recently been drinking at times, and driving at times . . .

Inside the circuit of Kennedy intimates, that magnetic grid of associates and accumulated trustees of the compiled Kennedy legacy, the general discouragement with Ted Kennedy's off-hours antics was quickly becoming, if anything, more prevalent and heavily emphasized than among the following press. Few among the advisers had much occasion to pay a lot of close attention, against the buzz and stress of their own reflexive chivvying for position in New York or Washington, to the slow accession to influence and gathering cumulative legislative effect Kennedy had managed, shunning publicity as he worked, inside the Senate.

Individuals among them, in touch with Kennedy about particular problems, discovered him unexpectedly well versed, less year by year the playboy knockabout they remembered bouncing around Hyannis Port. As early as 1963 Dick Goodwin, representing the White House's interest in the Northeast Airlines route controversy, found himself dealing with Kennedy: "He really impressed me. He knew all the details. You don't pick up that kind of knowledge out of the air." "I think he knew more about the draft than anybody in the Senate, including Stennis," Burke Marshall, who headed the Presidential Commission on Draft Policy, noted later.

But these were rare, accidental contacts. Among the more sophisticated, Kennedy was evoking skepticism by the extent of his obsession with working through every issue personally, developing his own staff specialists rather than depend on the academic liaison that kept Harvard experts like Archibald Cox forever at John Kennedy's elbow during the later fifties. How insecure *was* he? Yet when, as during the ABM jockeying, Kennedy did go outside for prestigious advice and help, there were staff rumblings.

What many among the palace guard, the retainers, did see, toward midnight around the big Smith apartment across from the Metropolitan Museum, or at the Cape, or after the outsiders left Ted's sprawling estate in

McLean, was the same hulking hilarious buffoon, the inimitable lifetime kid brother still playing it for laughs, full of Irish drinking songs and blue-eyed pratfall charms, who had tickled his brother the president with his renditions of "Hooray for Hollywood" twenty years earlier. It was a role Ted Kennedy still cherished in a way, and detested in a way, but—especially when walled in by the Bobby people and the JFK people—could not seem to help continuing to play.

This hurt him: Among the old friends and campaign specialists who were hurried into Chicago that weekend of political playmaking that virtually assured Kennedy a first-ballot sweep, several were privately so dubious about his competence for such a position as president, and relieved when he backed away, that they themselves began to respect him genuinely for the first time when he refused the nomination.

Habitually, like most lifetime pluggers, Kennedy arranged to get to bed by ten-thirty or eleven except when The Bag was too full; when he stayed up later, put-on artist that he was still, he avoided showing how much the lower back hurt him. The old sense of competitive tension toward his brother's legatees, as toward his brothers, his depression at their loss, was likely to tighten in him enough to start the drinking. Several drinks normally did it; congenitally receptive to people, buoyed simply by feeling them around himself, it actually took very little to tempt him into hilarity. To Kennedy insiders—many of whom were not Catholic, not Irish, but rather carried with themselves the skepticism toward the overuse of alcohol bred into serious Calvinists and Jews—to them heavy drinking was not so much a good man's weakness, as the Irish adage had it, as a weak man's goodness.

Neither Robert nor John Kennedy, faithful to the old financier's dread of liquor, normally drank very much, and so it was especially horrifying to the loyalists to see the surviving Kennedy brother, in whom a number of them in their own ambivalent questing hearts were already starting to reside some hope of a belated restoration, easing into what a number regarded as a psychological dependency on drink. The fresh-faced lad, giddy with a high-ball at twenty, now presented himself as a thickening lout approaching forty, dangerous and unpredictable at times, the Minotaur erupting from the labyrinth. "A computah?" one Massachusetts intimate of John and Bobby's replied on being told about Kennedy's knack for absorbing and interrelating information. "Well, maybe that's what we need now in the presidency. A computah, a computah with alcohol in all its circuits."

The insiders were also alarmed that Joan Kennedy should show every sign—while still sweet, frank, considerate, and unworldly as ever—of alcohol problems of her own. Uncertainty, loneliness, recurrent rumors too specific to ignore linking Ted with glamorous women everywhere he went, no privacy at all, what with the dotting of hardened security men in the resented blue suits that seemed to infiltrate their pastel dreams—it all seemed to be trapping them both, worsening, each sick about the other and sicker for that.

"Do you know what it's like to have your wife frightened all the time?" Kennedy demanded suddenly of an AP reporter on another of those airplane rides that spring that shook his feelings loose. "I'm not afraid to die. I'm too young to die." Literally until the day he passed away, through divorce proceedings and legal maneuvering to keep Joan and her lawyers away from the family assets and backpage squibs in the papers that noted that Joan had been picked up again, too smashed to find her way back to her apartment— Kennedy continued to ransack his soul for some way to accommodate Joan. "We thought we were in love," he observed sadly in his memoirs; even after he remarried, Ted made sure that his despondent first wife got an invitation to holiday events that included their children.

But Joan was increasingly desolate, and so was he. He hid it as well as he could, and so did she, but within the disciplining requirements of the Kennedy family the pressures kept backing up, Joan developed an intermittent tic in her cheek. "People criticize Jackie for going her own way where the Kennedys are concerned," she told a reporter, "but this family can be overwhelming. For years I went along with everything they said because I didn't dare to do otherwise, but now I speak up and say what I think and it seems to work out better for everyone."

Joan had revealed herself in 1964 as too effective a campaigner to waste— she had worked hard for Bob in Indiana in 1968, gone back to tour for Birch Bayh that fall, accommodated herself to the separations, the private trips to Paris, the refreshments and polite evasions wealth permits to anxiety. Nothing helped enough: Joan—fresh-faced and cheerily uninterested in liquor at all at Manhattanville—had proceeded from smilingly refusing any to enjoying a drink now and again to—as the sixties thickened—needing a drink badly at times, too badly. Even social drinking mixed poorly with Joan's imperishable naivete. "No, I have to wear this, I promised a photographer from *Women's Wear Daily* he could photograph me in this," she told a hostess who offered her a change of clothes one afternoon at a party during which she had spilled coffee down her front.

Nothing was dependable, the children felt it—the susceptible little Teddy was obsessed all day with the idea that he could never see his father again, so that his father broke off whatever he was doing to call him up and calm him down, reassure him toward nightfall. Ted and Joan: They were the couple on the wedding cake eleven years afterward, the sugar gone rotten, the vegetable-dyed bow tie drooping and the lace of the wedding veil withering back into carbon. If alcohol helped, alcohol would have to.

Throughout all of which Kennedy advisers watched. "If you get drunk regularly in public with various important personalities," one of them ventured privately, thoughtfully, of Ted, "there has to be an element of self-humiliation present, doesn't there?" It was a question worth asking about a man who was generally regarded that spring as very probably the oncoming President of the United States.

6. Gargan's Party

Then, toward midnight of July 18, 1969, Edward Kennedy's scraped-up knockaround 1967 Oldsmobile 88 flipped off the Dike Bridge into the black surging tidal estuary of Poucha Pond: There erupted that splash heard 'round the world. The incident was wholly a fluke and inevitable, absurd and tragic, overreported and misunderstood hours after it happened and now. It is no psychodramatization to insist that, in the midst of that weeks-long nightmare, a great deal died for Edward Kennedy: the deteriorated leavings of Camelot; the dependencies Bobby was able, somehow, to impose still; the deep confusions every time Kennedy met the unblinking eyes of his paralyzed old father, for whom all this was about to prove the ultimate shock too many. This crisis was live or die. "I think," Arthur Schlesinger said to me more than a year afterward, "that with Chappaquiddick the iron went into Edward Kennedy's soul."

To Kennedy himself, the horrors of Chappaquiddick—not only the terror and frenzy and disorientation of the accident and the panic-stricken night, but every bit as much the shock and irresolution throughout the week that led to Kennedy's hapless television address amounted to more than he could bring himself to accept. "In a sense Chappaquiddick had to be the materialization of all Teddy Kennedy's worst dreams," observed Dick Goodwin, who arrived to help within hours of the moment Kennedy finally turned himself in at the Edgartown police station.

And in fact it would be hard to imagine a humiliation or a degradation, personal or political, the crisis would not in some way involve before it had played its scourging process out. Sickened and constantly anxious himself by now at the merest apprehension of violence, Kennedy's own poor judgment had resulted in the death of somebody who, after working devotedly over years for Bob, had remained a supporter. Someone it was cardinal that he help and protect.

Avowedly realistic, he had proved unable in crisis to separate what he knew had happened from what he preferred to fantasize had not. After an adult lifetime of attempting to establish his own career in his own way, he had been so rattled and unsure of himself that he had on reflex turned over the responsibility, the vital decision-making, to men who had been no better than secondary figures, support staff to his brothers. Then he had allowed them to grill him skeptically, openly dubious, as if he were an unreliable schoolboy, then override him, act in a way his own political instincts told him was ill-advised, suicidal. Throughout all of which the hated press of the world was packed outside as many as eight hundred strong and all but licking the grass and bark and fence posts for blood and rumors.

Yet who could have started with any inkling, from the office-clambake/bugs-biting/*Gasoline Alley* frame of the thing, that overnight it was going to turn into something like that, Wagnerian, The Fall of the House of Kennedy? Out of a . . . a gesture, something so . . . so desultory, so mundane. Out of this unpromising several hours of Kennedy's sailing weekend devoted to sanctifying for the help their memories of the efforts so far, evoking whatever was sentimentally of use.

It started with Joey Gargan, willing eager hapless Joey busy playing out his role, his "lot in life," as he liked to refer to it sometimes after enough drinks, in the hope that you would really understand what almost-Kennedyhood meant. If anybody was the prod that weekend, it had to be—he was himself the first to make the point—Gargan. Joe had presumed that the traditional long regatta weekend at Edgartown would present the perfect format within which to combine a soupçon of Kennedy sociability toward his sidekicks during the grueling Massachusetts campaigns of the sixties—Ray LaRosa, Charlie Tretter, Paul Markham—with an effort to show some gratitude to the boiler-room girls Gargan had gotten to know in the spring of 1968 bouncing in and out of the 20th and L Street headquarters between advancing sessions for Bobby around the primary circuit.

The get-together on the Cape the previous summer had seemed to leave the girls well rested and most appreciative of the hospitality. They might be pressed into service soon enough if Ted actually made his move in 1972. Joey was most persuasive in making the case for having them all up.

Among the brusque driving aides who slammed Bobby's late hard effort together, Gargan's contributions had not been taken especially seriously by the political pros compared with, say, the assertive genius of the advancing showman Jerry Bruno. Around the boiler room, however, the overworked girls, pressed constantly to keep straight the massive influx of information, examine it and feed it back to the "road show" of the peripatetic Robert Kennedy, appreciated Gargan's unvarying solicitude of them, his reliable good-humored concern. When the time came, in the judgment of the senior Kennedy strategists, to slow down, phase out such time-consuming gestures to this assortment of able, hard-working women, Gargan himself proved reluctant.

Fixated on the "six married men—six secretaries—inaccessible Cottage—slept overnight" formula which the pulps started within hours to feed their readers, few press people and almost nobody in the alerted and suspicious public seems then or afterward to have caught on very clearly to who, actually, was who that uncomfortable night on Chappaquiddick Island. "If the Kennedys had intended to stage an orgy I'm sure they would have gone after a higher standard of excellence," one insider remarks. This struck the girls themselves: "If that's what people thought they should have circulated pictures of ourselves with our clothes off," one laughed afterward to her lawyer.

In fact, within the Kennedy operations, many of the girls were formidable. "People brought *them* coffee," a Kennedy staffer says simply, epitomizing the boiler-room girls' status. Cautiously picked for discretion, brains, loyalty, humor under strain, and the ability to stay ahead of a fluctuating set of intelligence estimates, the girls were accorded wide freedom to act, negotiate and close deals at times in the name of the candidate, travel when necessary, even, at times, get involved and share judgments in situations of which they themselves in many ways had the most working knowledge.

Mary Jo Kopechne was among the most highly regarded among them. Borrowed originally from Senator George Smathers's staff—Smathers had loved to roister with John Kennedy during his easygoing early Senate years—Mary Jo had roomed for a time with Bobby Baker's notorious squeeze, Carol Tyler. Mary Jo had filled in around Hickory Hill, helping with the children and giving one whole night to typing Bob's breakaway Vietnam speech. She traveled in his behalf—they knew each other well enough to have Kennedy style "in" jokes, banked, like so many Kennedy jokes, off such drolleries of personality as those of a prominent Louisiana politico whose silk suits and shirts and alligator shoes left both of them giggling. She was supposedly serious about a man in the State Department.

Writing over Robert Kennedy's name, she once encouraged the idea of a woman who requested that a small island in Long Island Sound the Army was abandoning be made available to the mentally retarded; Bob, who had approved other plans, was forever afterward asking her whether she had given any islands away that morning. Her value to Robert Kennedy was such that she did not merely type his announcement of candidacy that long night at Hickory Hill, she was consulted by him and Sorensen as to its particular phrasings. She was the sort of girl who seemed always to be there, while seldom particularly noticeable. During the 1968 campaign she was the key Washington contact in charge of keeping track—every map and pin in place behind those windowless walls—of everything in critical Indiana and Pennsylvania, as well as Kentucky and the District of Columbia.

What remains one of the lesser mysteries of that unlikely social event is precisely what Mary Jo and three of the other girls thought when they ultimately did pull into Edgartown on Thursday, checked into the Katama Shores Motel, and had their escorted tour of the facilities their energetic advance man Joey had arranged for them over the projected four days and three nights of their regatta weekend. Chappaquiddick Island's Lawrence Cottage, which Joe had originally taken for his own family until his mother-in-law got sick, was to serve as beach house, bathhouse, and undisturbed rallying point.

"What a dump!" the forthright Crimmins, no habitue of chateaux himself, reportedly breathed on first ambling around the premises. There was nothing particularly objectionable about the place: It was just plain, a meatcutter's hideaway with knotty pine paneling all over the walls, chintz, maple-stained rockers and plenty of auction-room daybeds.

Homely, Christ, but serviceable. And not only the appurtenances, the Lawrence Cottage and Kennedy's weathered black Oldsmobile and the collapsible "cookout" Joey Gargan carted over to thaw out his supermarket frozen-hard sausage hors d'oeuvres, but—how to avoid this?—the people, the dramatis personae. So that the weekend came off—not pennants flying, not regatta glamor and Tom Collinses out on the fieldstone veranda of the yacht club but . . . work, reminiscences of work, like that time they waited in the car so long before pulling up, timed perfectly, as the candidate waved and touched and grin-grinned one last time before sliding into the front seat while Crimmins eased into the jam of people, children slap-slap-slapping the windshield while old Jack accelerates slowly, bounces somebody's knee out of the way before Bobby turns, really furious for once, and says *Goddammit Jack, I don't care if we are five minutes late, don't do that——*.

Which eventuated in Crimmins's getting sour once the group settled in because they brought this up, sixty-three and a bachelor, and his kidneys as unreliable as hell and because Gargan couldn't get enough reservations at the Shiretown he has four straight nights to look forward to in that godforsaken shit-hole of a cottage . . .

On Chappaquiddick Crimmins was the first to arrive, having driven Kennedy's Oldsmobile down Wednesday, its trunk foresightedly loaded with three half-gallons of vodka, four fifths of scotch, two bottles of rum, and a couple of cases of beer in cans, all bought right in South Boston before departing. Jack got into one of the rum bottles that first night in the loneliness of the Lawrence Cottage (dank brackish place) that he disliked on sight. By Thursday Ray LaRosa, forty-one, compact, taciturn, onetime fireman, now a "Civil Defense Adviser" willing to put in his turn at escort and equerry service for Joey, had arrived with his maroon Mercury, which Joey decided to keep on the Edgartown side of the cut so as to save the automobile ferrying fees. LaRosa had been working the security and advance for Joe; he was an old pal of the late Eddie Moss; he and Crimmins were expected to double up and help with the chores, the picking-up. Neither Crimmins nor LaRosa knew most of the boiler-room girls, especially, except, in passing, Mary Ellen and Nance Lyons, both originally Massachusetts natives. But even there it was hard to mistake a . . . a class difference, to put a finger on it, frankly, to go along with the steep age differential.

The Lyonses were aggressive, bright—Mary Ellen is, in the words of a 1968 Democratic National Committee citation, "a woman doer," who intended shortly to go after a law degree; like Mary Jo and Esther Newburgh, who was already an administrative assistant at the Urban Institute, who would soon move in at a high level into the Goldberg gubernatorial campaign and from there into the Muskie pre-campaign and on to a major career as a literary agent. The Lyonses and the rest of the onetime boiler-room girls were aggressive, of solid middle-class origins, intellectually a bit high-assed, frankly ambitious.

The only one among the younger men invited who fit, was on a comparable plane, made sense beyond the numerical pairing off, was malleable Charlie Tretter, constitutionally full of smiles, who, having worked in the Washington office and on the road for Bob in '68, knew most of the girls beforehand and—although himself a lawyer and an executive of the New England Regional Commission—still did a lot of the driving and errand running for Ted Kennedy around Massachusetts when Crimmins could not slide away from his putative job as investigator for the office of the district attorney of Suffolk County, Ted's old employer.

Among up-to-the-minute Boston-based State House tipsters, the shocker on the guest list of Joey Gargan's breathlessly organized beach party would inevitably be Gargan's onetime Georgetown Prep schoolmate Paul F. Markham. By July of 1969 Paul Markham had, unlike the rest of the Gargan collection, already reached a mid-career checkpoint from which he could now begin to think of himself as really arriving. Gargan had certainly helped; still, any professional rise that owes what Markham's did to a gently nurtured association with so powerful a group as the Kennedy family must also owe a lot of its success to a combination of real ability and assured tact—why else would the Kennedys, after all, go out of their way for anyone? Teddy, who had been noted early in his political life for his unusual—for a Kennedy— lack of vindictiveness and his generosity to his friends, appreciated it particularly when not too many favors were expected and competence enough was demonstrated.

By such standards Paul Markham had always looked trustworthy. Well buttoned up but legalistically imaginative enough about the work he did even when he labored with Joe in the tort factory at Badger, Parrish, where the two refreshed their schoolboy friendship, Markham had subsequently worked out well on the staff of the Small Business Administration, come on after Bobby appointed him an Assistant U.S. Attorney General from Massachusetts in 1963, serving along with Joe Gargan, and stayed with the office after Joey quit to help Ted in 1964.

In 1967, when his predecessor gave up the post to accept a judgeship, on Ted Kennedy's strong recommendation Lyndon Johnson appointed Paul to the top federal prosecutor's job in the Commonwealth, U.S. Attorney. Widely regarded in legal circles until that time as an "underachiever," the tall diffident attorney proved a surprising success; under his management a federal team reversed a state-court ruling and requalified the testimony of Joseph Barbarosa that ultimately put away, on a charge of conspiring to murder, Raymond Patriarcha, alleged to be the Cosa Nostra chieftain for New England. With the administration change in January, Markham had resigned his job the April before the cookout at Chappaquiddick.

Among politicians in Massachusetts, payoff-prone and favor-seeking as so many always were and continue to be, Markham's kind of rung-by-rung ascension took savvy. Filling in on one of the interminable touch games, he separated his shoulder at the Compound in 1966. He crewed in races for Ted. He knew Ted Kennedy well enough, off and on, but Joey remained his contact; to talk to Markham after Chappaquiddick you cleared the interview with Gargan.

Approached with the usual jocularity by Gargan a few weeks before the

Edgartown Regatta weekend that summer, Paul had readily agreed. Surely, he'd come along and fill the party out if that was what Joey wanted. But doubts hung; Markham was obviously torn. "The girls that were there, Christ, I didn't even know any of them, they were there as a nice gesture—" Markham later explained to me, hollow-cheeked by then, hollow-voiced, living with what was left of his mangled lawyer's reputation. How could he explain; who would really believe what happened?

After sailing over in the *Victura* that Thursday with Gargan and a kid, Howie Hall, in a preliminary race, Markham had banged up his leg and lost his chance to share in the glamour of crewing for Ted. He'd had to give up his bed at the Shiretown when Ted came, and now looked forward to two nights in the camp on Chappaquiddick Island listening to Crimmins grumble nonstop. After that he'd drifted through two aimless uncomfortable days, offended Esther Newburgh by inadvertently brushing her leg when several of the revelers attempted to get some sleep on the porch, then found himself consigned for the rest of the night to the back of Gargan's rented car.

Markham's world crashed when he found himself obliged to watch helplessly while a deeply shocked Kennedy gave senseless orders that he, Markham, would later be vilified for obeying. He started that weekend fair-haired, at thirty-eight a personage; three miserable days later he was all but busted, utterly reduced, singled out nationally beneath the gigantic klieg light of the scandal as Joey Gargan's Gargan——.

On Friday at one-thirty in the afternoon Kennedy's charter from Boston set down on the Martha's Vineyard inland airstrip. "I knew," Kennedy acknowledged wearily afterward, "that the girls were up there, that we were going to get together, that there was a cottage someplace. I hadn't troubled myself as to the details . . ." Congressman Tip O'Neill, Kennedy's seatmate on the shuttle to Boston, remembers his Massachusetts colleague as "tired as hell." After a feverish spring the hectic midsummer session was already coming in like a sirocco with its searing ABM showdown imminent as well as, to counter the administration's hold-the-line efforts, Kennedy's own Democratic inflation alert, a passing brainstorm Jim Flug was already pulling together, already contacting Arthur Okun and Walter Heller to help challenge the Nixon experts' figures total-by-interpretation.

Self-driven and overworked, Kennedy was now, in the view of one reporter who saw him in mid-July, "utterly uptight, wholly preoccupied," pushing, worried, tense. What Kennedy needed badly and knew he needed badly was rest, a few weeks offstage, free and remote from whispering and demanding Washington. Throughout the middle sixties the Edgartown Regatta weekend had often been lovingly organized as something of a blowoff, genuinely a party; by 1969 all that looked complicated. Now, normally willing to help keep the morale of the "little people" high, Kennedy had been lackluster at best about this idea of Joey's, about once more hosting a "time" for the half-dozen girls or so who worked so hard for Bobby.

Certainly he'd made a considerable effort earlier: In January, when Dun Gifford and Dave Hackett had gotten together and given a party for the boiler-room group, Teddy had made it a special point to come by and liven up the proceedings for as long as he could manage to stay. "The drill that night, the joke," Hackett remembers, "was that we invited two eligible guys for each of the girls. There wasn't any hanky-panky at all, and no permanent relationships came out of the evening, but everyone who was there agrees that it was one of those great times, really memorable."

In late spring the girls had given a party of their own at Andy Vitali's apartment for everybody who worked with Bob; Ted hadn't been able to stop by, the party went flat, and Nance Lyons, who worked in his Senate office, had chided him because he had never made it over. Kennedy regretted that; when Gargan broached his idea for the Edgartown Regatta get-together it seemed a reasonable idea on the telephone; that Friday a long evening of making an effort with the girls had started to look like work. Arriving on the island an hour before the race started Ted reportedly took Gargan aside and claimed unusual fatigue, wondered in his oblique way whether . . . then, seeing how much having him around meant to Joey, agreed finally to stay and pitch in as co-host for at least a couple of hours during the mid-evening.

The point is—Kennedy did go: more precisely, stayed around and fraternized, if that was supposed to help Joey drag his entertainment for the girls through the shank of that interminable evening, torturous as it proved soon enough to be, assailed every moment by memories and mosquitoes. Ted Kennedy had gotten his first brief look at the cottage Joe had leased for their convenience hours before he had the chance to drop his bag at the Shiretown; out-of-sorts from mid-Atlantic grime and travel fatigue he had asked Crimmins, who met his charter by prearrangement, whether he might possibly get in a quick dip in the ocean before the afternoon's race started.

Jack was grumbling still (half under his breath) about the way having to chauffeur the girls around was ruining his vacation, they took so long to dress, they disappeared into the Edgartown boutiques instead of moving the day right along. Meanwhile Crimmins had hurried his employer out to the water, across the car ferry, over Main Street, out to the Lawrence Cottage to put a suit on and halfway back quickly to bounce down the margin of the macadam onto the gravel-spitting Dike Road, over the bridge and across to the lonely deserted East Beach for the quick plunge into the midday breakers. It was Kennedy's first look at the setup Joey had organized: By two-thirty he was back in Edgartown Harbor wading out to the mooring of the *Victura* with Joe Gargan and Howie Hall in time for the delayed start of the regatta competition.

By seven or so Kennedy was back in the Lawrence Cottage, having raced, done disappointingly—ninth—enjoyed the first sip or two of beer for the day on board and perhaps half a can with Ross Richards, winner of the first leg of the race, and then directed Crimmins to take him back across in time to savor a badly needed hot tub in peace before the others arrived. Soaking his torn back, Kennedy asked Crimmins to please prepare him a rum and Coca-Cola, the first of two highballs he worked on throughout the remainder of the evening.

All afternoon Paul Markham had been drifting back and forth between the cottage, the Yacht Club, the Edgartown Wharf, East Beach; at seven-thirty he and Tretter and Gargan returned to the cottage for the evening. Kennedy was up and dressed in fresh wash pants, a polo shirt, and the back brace, red and revived-looking after his tub, and intent on giving Jack Crimmins mock hell because it appeared to Kennedy that Jack had, during the two nights he had been solacing himself with the rum supply, punished it immoderately: "Gee, Jack, who has been drinking all the rum?" the senator repeatedly wanted to know. "There is hardly any left, you didn't leave me any rum." Crimmins, a veteran of Kennedy's pinprick ragging, went stolidly about getting himself neatly dressed. Everybody was relaxed; after a couple of minutes of piling on Kennedy and Gargan about their unimpressive performance over the race course that afternoon, Paul Markham and Kennedy started to talk seriously about the political utility of Kennedy's new Whip situation.

At eight-fifteen precisely—Gargan had worked the logistics out meticulously—Joey picked up the girls and Ray LaRosa in the white rented Valiant on the Chappaquiddick side of the cut and brought them along to the cottage. Most of the girls had been swimming late in the morning and, throughout the late afternoon, watched the Kennedy group race from a boat Joe had chartered for them. They arrived now in an easygoing cluster, just up in their Edgartown motel rooms from naps and out of showers, several of them dazed a little after their unaccustomed hours in the sun, expecting—what, an evening of political gossip? Some dancing, perhaps, singing. It was becoming twilight.

Joe was already superbusy, straining, perspiring at the temples to remain as methodical as possible, threatened for all his abstractive fussiness by an oncoming twit. There is a wonderful couple of pages in the subsequent inquest testimony during which Gargan manages to nonplus even the skeptical and cantankerous Judge James Boyle by paralyzing the questioning as he keeps returning to the cooking details, insists on going into his every effort to position the "cookout" in the patchy lawn on a spot where he could watch it from the kitchen window, start the charcoal, turn the unreliable old cottage oven up to exactly the necessary temperature—450 degrees—and leave the frozen cheese and sausage hors d'oeuvres in there for just long enough—twelve minutes—before solemnly wondering whether several of the girls would mind passing them around to the others. The exchange reflects Gargan's Good-Soldier-Schweik-like willingness to tell absolutely everything.

This provides the ironic tingle: The Power of the Kennedys is about to be upended in less than three hours, and what Joey Gargan remembers most clearly is how long to leave the crimped foil slab of the hors d'oeuvres from the Edgartown beach grocer baking in exactly how hot an oven. Gargan, already legendary for his ultrathin buttermilk pancakes, is sweating away out there behind the little low pass-over divider on which the informal bar, three huge vodka gallon bottles and scotch and a bowl of chips or whatever those are, are available to everybody, and Ted is making the newcomers their first round of drinks, and outside it is getting dusky.

Inside it is getting hot; Charlie Tretter, who is in and out all evening and accordingly remembers the evening in slices, in alternately deepening moods, remembers the pre-prandial segment as if it were clipped in without the sound from some vintage Our Gang Comedy: Joey, his back to everybody at the oven, working "like a Trojan," the girls and their drinks, conversation, trouble with conversation, single ticklish beads of perspiration sliding down the furrows of backs just under where light summer bras hooked . . .

Tretter had run over to Edgartown once for cigarettes and ice and Coke; when Joey discovered that grilling the two-inch steaks in shifts meant it was going to be a while before everybody was fed, Tretter and little Cricket Keough—a pal from Bob's campaign—borrowed the keys to Kennedy's Oldsmobile from Crimmins and went after a radio at the Shiretown in Edgartown. When they got back Cricket left her psychedelic-flowered purse in the Oldsmobile.

The cottage was really hot, full of sultry seaside air the descending night had trapped; it was better outside but the saltwater mosquitoes swarmed beneath the pine trees; a slice of moon was out for an hour or so. Tretter, accommodating instinctively but as spunky as ever with his soft held-in pageboy frivolities, returned to a rich, even a melancholy scene. "The mood was kind of mixed," as he later recalled. "I don't think Teddy was really—I don't know, being together like that . . . I remember listening to the girls, the long string of reminiscences I myself wasn't really privy to, anecdotes, stories that came out of the Bobby campaign. What I'm getting at is, I worked for the senator for a long time, and I think I know him pretty well, well enough to realize that he was—he was not exuberant. He was not having a helluva good time."

They ate, steak, slowly, in shifts. "There were getting to be long lapses in the evening, people were standing up and Kennedy was working hard at being a good host," Tretter noted. "If there was a girl not saying much he would try and draw her out. It was just that the conversation, what was said— Bobby. He was a presence."

By shortly after eleven, Crimmins, tiring fast and starting to worry about what kind of a night's sleep he was supposed to get there, was already suggesting with perhaps a little bit of pepper in his tone that everybody who was going to go back had better think about going back. Joe Gargan, falling back to that put-upon, drawn-out archness that betokens another effort of patience with Jack when he is becoming a trial, reassured the girls that it wasn't that late yet, he had discussed the matter personally with the ferryboat operator and there was a strong possibility of the boat remaining in service until I AM, although that would entail an extra charge. Crimmins, not mollified, suggested that somebody drive over and give the ferryman twenty bucks to make sure that he would stick around.

At that point, despairing inside, Kennedy attempted to move the reveries away from the '68 campaign and announced that "Charlie Tretter is now going to give one of his great Boston-pol speeches." Tretter tried, stood on a chair and went through one of his Jim Curley/Honey Fitz routines: The utterly grounded mood of the moment wouldn't tolerate that. "People kept shouting, 'Siddown, siddown,'" Tretter would reflect. "I remember behind me seeing Joey, still working away like a one-armed paperhanger."

"As parties go," Kennedy himself confessed to me not long afterward, "it was dull." They sang; a few couples danced a little. "It was just . . . just something to give one the chance to talk with those people. As I remember," Kennedy continued, haltingly, "I looked at my watch. I said it was late, eleven-fifteen, eleven-thirty. I'd been talking with her [Mary Jo Kopechne]. She said she was ready to go." An acute sunburn on her back after watching the sailing all afternoon was making Mary Jo miserable. Ted himself was increasingly depressed from all these reminiscences about Bobby. Kennedy, from out on the patchy little cottage lawn, summoned the obviously overfatigued Jack Crimmins, and informed Crimmins he would be driving himself back to the ferry slip, that he would be taking Miss Kopechne, that she wasn't feeling very well, was bothered a little by the sun on the beach that day.

The two disappeared in the humid dark and a moment later the Oldsmobile started, pulled away; the rest of the party, inside or out, stood talking, laughing there a while, desultorily. The moon was down already; it was a little cooler outside; inside, everybody was still too hot actually to notice much.

Poucha Pond, the eternally surging tidal estuary into which Kennedy's Oldsmobile pitched head-over just before the hump of the Dike Bridge threw up its off-kilter back—the pond was itself a contrivance, a dead-ended, manmade catchwater permitted by the formation of a thin long ocean-nibbled pikehook of dunes and Atlantic littoral. The surface of the pond, always moving in and out of the encroaching marsh grass, looks wind-stippled and black even in wide-open daylight.

By his own admission Kennedy had been traveling approximately twenty miles an hour after he left the main road and inadvertently kept going straight onto dirt where the road turned left. The dirt road descended gently; Kennedy saw the bridge in the headlights but reacted too slowly once he realized that the bridge itself was about to dogleg to the left and stamped the brakes with whatever reflex kicked in. He remembered the vehicle lifting into air; the next thing he remembered was Mary Jo pummeling him; his eyes opening he remembered gulping air, the awareness of being upside down with water pouring in, in the darkness on the two of them, the unsuccessful struggle to get the door open and feeling for the window and then a sense of blacking out.

The emotion he later reported to friends was aghastness, incredulity that such a thing could be happening to him again; with that there was a premonition of release as seawater flooded his lungs, of composure: He would die now. ". . . then somehow I can remember coming up to the last energy of just pushing, pressing, and coming up to the surface."

Kennedy's memory of everything after the Oldsmobile's front tire left the bridge's shallow rub rail and started to bounce out over the fallaway was broken, incomplete, and was to remain incomplete and confused for the next few days. The report of Kennedy's local doctor, Robert Watt, details the medical findings: Thrown against the inside of the car Kennedy had suffered "a half-inch abrasion and hematoma over the right mastoid, a contusion of the vertex, spasm of the posterior cervical musculature and . . . tenderness . . . of the lumbar area . . ." He had "a big spongy swelling" at the top of his head, consistent with the very large hematoma pressing on his brain; X-ray studies confirmed the cervical strain. Watt notes, "a temporary loss of consciousness and retrograde amnesia," and continues, "Impairment of judgment and confused behavior are symptoms consistent with an injury of the character sustained by the patient."

Swept out and away by the very intense trapped tide, Kennedy found some kind of muddy footing and sloughed back toward the Oldsmobile's submerged weak headlights. Belching, wheezing, coughing, he was tiring fast; he claims to have surface-dived seven or eight times in the hope of pulling the girl out too; head throbbing, neck aching, he exhausted himself, and floated and crawled out to the strand, spent, and lay resting on the grass. By then, Kennedy estimates, a half-hour to forty-five minutes had passed. He had enough breath back to begin to stumble up Dike Road, unaware of lights to the extent that in the moonless blackness he strained to make out the foliage along the margins of the road itself as he stumbled toward the hardtop.

Approximately fifteen minutes later he arrived at the Lawrence Cottage. It was after midnight by now; Kennedy spotted Ray LaRosa catching a breather on the cottage steps, told him, "Get me Joe." Gargan appeared; Kennedy told him, ". . . better get Paul, too." Gargan walked back and told LaRosa to summon Paul Markham. Orders and responses moved reliably up and down the lifetime pecking order. Markham appeared. "'There has been a terrible accident,'" Kennedy testified having told Markham. "'We have got to go,' and we took off down the road, the Main Road there." Markham's memory of the exchange is slightly—but meaningfully—different. "'There has been an accident,'" he was to claim Kennedy said to him. "'Mary Jo was with me down at the bridge,' and let's go." They went, Gargan driving, fast. Nobody asked which bridge.

If there was one hope of a moment during which the situation might still be salvaged, it had to be precisely this one, when Edward Kennedy, half off his hinges with shock already, settled into the back seat of Gargan's rented Valiant and started issuing rescue orders. But among the three of them, whatever the crisis, who was about to violate the drill of a lifetime?

What survived in neither the police report nor the twelve depleting hours afterward was the terrible fatigue-poisoned overexhilarated stress all three felt. Flooring it up Main Street, spattering back pebbles along the corrugated Dike Road, the crazy certainty dawned that unbelievable luck had to reward unbelievable nerve. A lot of this trembles back into Gargan's syntax as he later recalls having parked and angled the Valiant so as to shine its lights at the barely submerged tires-up Oldsmobile. "Well," Gargan says, "I looked down and I saw this car. The car was completely underwater . . . Paul Markham at that time started down toward the water. I said, 'Paul, don't go in that car, Paul, without taking your clothes off,' and so Paul came back."

The command levels held: Gargan instructed Markham. "At that time I was at the right front fender by the right front wheel. I took my clothes off, including my underwear. I was stark naked. Paul Markham took his clothes off." The precision of Gargan's recollection seems uncanny, indelible; at one point he was actually able to force himself back into the vehicle and "then began to lose naturally my breath at one point and I tried to get out. I couldn't get out. I was stuck, and I was stuck because I was sideways, which is, to tell you the truth, stupid, and I finally realized what the problem was and I turned myself this way (indicating) and pushed myself out and came to the top of the water." This is prime Gargan, as incontrovertible as Holden Caulfield at his most unguarded and confessional. Watching and making suggestions from the bank Edward Kennedy oversaw this final effort; when this had failed, leaving Gargan all scraped and the wavering Markham dripping in his underwear, it was a little after one in the morning. All three tottered back into the Valiant and proceeded, wearily now, in the direction of the ferry slip.

Barely 1 AM at the latest by this time, but second thoughts and a palpable uncertainty about what actually did happen were beginning to batter both Markham and Gargan. More accurately, perhaps, than anybody else around, Gargan understands and can fit even a performance like this into the makeup of his huge senatorial firehorse of a cousin. Both accomplices that night were later to testify that Kennedy had told them, that mineshaft of a predawn morning, that he had simply missed the turn with Mary Jo and jounced at twenty miles an hour up the gravel and off the bridge.

Kennedy himself, respectfully cornered several times by District Attorney Edmund Dinis and more openly by a dubious Judge Boyle on this question exactly, kept picking it up each time wherever it looked most harmless. "At what point, Mr. Kennedy," District Attorney Dinis would later ask him, "did you realize that you were driving on a dirt road?" Kennedy: "Just sometime when I was—I don't remember any specific time . . ." Dinis: "Did you realize at that moment that you were not heading for the ferry?" Kennedy: "At the moment I went off the bridge, I certainly did."

Even Kennedy's morning-after police report, while indicating that the senator was headed ultimately toward the ferry landing, was unfamiliar with the road and went straight where he might normally have been expected to turn left, never in fact states explicitly that he had left the macadamized road unintentionally. It was a point that was later to annoy and bother the people in Bobby's brain trust who wanted the truth, goddamit, so they could make up their own minds about what the whole affair meant. "The unsatisfactory thing was the continued suggestion that he was heading for the ferry landing," one of them complained to me privately. "I gather he was heading for the beach." Then, hopefully, "That doesn't seem to me the most sinister thing in the world . . ."

A matter of weeks after the incident itself, submitting to a private interview on the details—eyes tormented, wringing an invisible handkerchief until his knuckles whitened—Kennedy again ducked a query as to this matter exactly, insisting only that there was a "reasonable explanation" why the two took that wrong turn at eleven-thirty or so. Certainly, as a lifelong intimate of Kennedy's, Joe Gargan knew, immediately, without anything direct ever having to be said, what sort of "reasonable explanation" Kennedy might have elaborated if he could have summoned the spiritual energy and believed anybody would understand.

Even out there, at Joey's remote little cookout, the walls had started to close in on Teddy, even there, there had been "too many blue suits," as he tended to murmur, too many Secret Service men, friends, self-consciously, security-watchful friends, aides, choking memories of Bobby—he had had to escape and go someplace and pick up a larger rhythm. That summer the yearning for solitude was coming over him prodigiously at times, like a spell. His breakaway mood, tipped off very often by a display of his exhilarated leprechaun humor, that momentary mock roguishness. Very often this ushered in an interlude of very rapid seduction and release with some accommodating woman at hand. The exhilaration of the bestial, transmogrification into the Minotaur.

The road turned; one envisions Kennedy swinging the wheel right, hard. Mary Jo, who knew him slightly, would presumably have known Bobby intimately enough to sense Kennedy's mood. Two bumpy minutes later the daughter of the closed-mouthed Mrs. Malm, who kept the house overlooking the bridge, reading herself to sleep underneath an open window, looked up and heard a car, "going fairly fast," headed in the direction of the Dike.

"I knew Mary Jo, yes," Kennedy later said, slowly. "She was very bright, lively, personable, loyal. Intelligent, highly intelligent. I'd gone to the party the Hacketts gave for the girls in January, and I think . . . I think that was the only other time other than during the campaign I'd talked really with Mary Jo." He had seen her innumerable times, of course, taking dictation from Ethel, job hunting around Gifford's desk in his own office, working with

Wendell Pigman at Bobby's—yet she had, as a newsman later commented, not unkindly, "the face nobody remembered"; the most "political" and astute of anybody in the boiler room, she lacked . . . lacked . . . Everybody knew, although nobody was about to say, of course. The First Communion–style picture of Mary Jo that went out over the wires in time for the Sunday edition was a kind of reverse shocker to everybody, with the mascara airbrushed in and even a soft inviting gleam to the eyes.

In truth she had been, as her twenty-eighth year ended, pastier and tougher, intimidating in a quiet way, certainly not at all a girl of the sort Ted Kennedy, with his reported availability to pushovers wooable on the telephone with his Mister Moo-ah routines, was likely to think he had much hope of dragging behind a dune and out in time for the midnight ferry. Still, depression can prove an insidious aphrodisiac.

"One of the great ironies of the situation," one Kennedy stalwart concedes, "was that a man whose shadow reputation was of a great swordsman was caught in a situation where he was not . . . was not in any way attempting to . . . attempting to——."

All this, unsaid, Joe Gargan of course sensed immediately. "Senator Kennedy," Gargan later related freely, "was very emotional, extremely upset, very disturbed, and he was using this expression which I have heard before, but he was using it particularly that night. 'Can you believe it, Joe, can you believe it, I don't believe it, I don't believe this could happen, I just can't believe it . . .'" That this should be happening to a *Kennedy*! The family reading on the universe—as his generation had been pressured to interpret it—allowed for constant risk but only permitted successful outcomes. Calming for the moment, Kennedy had told Gargan that "he was going down the road, the dirt road headed towards I don't know what. He suddenly saw the bridge in front of him and that was it."

Gargan and Markham, disbalanced by the plague of angry editorials dubbing them the Laurel and Hardy of the Kennedy debacle, were both to persist in claims that they had, indeed, pointed out to Kennedy that somebody must report the accident, and immediately. But nobody moved. The two were seized by the predicament, in essence, that paralyzed not only Joey and Paul at Poucha Pond and at the approach to the ferry slip, but also the lead figures who gathered throughout the following week in Hyannis Port, men who had damped down an incipient civil war and intercontinental missile exchanges: Certainly everybody saw where the dangers were and grasped, in large, what needed to be done, but nobody was prepared to act instead of, without express permission from, the principal, Edward Kennedy, and risk his own reputation on the success of the consequences. That got to be too much responsibility.

The decision hung: Kennedy again broke down, nearly sobbing, insisting, "This couldn't have happened. I don't know how it happened." More critical minutes passed. "OK," Kennedy demanded finally, "take me back to the ferry." But back at the ferry slip no course of action emerged of itself either. Gargan again insisted that the accident be reported and recommended to Kennedy that he call Dave Burke, his administrative assistant, who could alert the family at Hyannis Port, and Burke Marshall, "the best lawyer I know," who could frame advice before reporting the accident to the Edgartown police.

Sitting in the Valiant, looking out over the lights of the harbor five hundred feet away, the three were steps away from a telephone pay station, one of the few in Edgartown, the same phone to which Gargan would lead Kennedy back to call and finally reach David Burke seven hours later. But nobody used the telephone then, and Gargan's testimony makes evident enough why. Competent lawyers in open daylight, the three were functioning now in response to tribal loyalties. Kennedy, although upset and confused, remained Kennedy, chief by accession, grantee to power. As Joe Gargan himself broke down the requirements, his cousin's first accountability was to his family, to prepare them as well as he was able, then to himself. It happened that the surviving familial nutbuster, Steve Smith, had dropped out for several weeks and was believed to be incommunicado with unknown companions on the islands of Majorca and Ibiza off eastern Spain. This left Burke Marshall as the possible operative Shaman, the human being in whom, by unconscious agreement, Robert Kennedy's soul might be said to abide. Robert Kennedy, who all their lives had been the central wizard in any familial crisis, had singled Marshall out of all men as having "the best judgment of anybody I know." Then, all primary obligations met, Kennedy must report the accident.

Edward Kennedy's own assessment was similar, except that, as chieftain, he began to be racked, as soon as he could pull together enough of whatever was still working in his mind to consider the practical, by premonitions of his fearful responsibility to the family of the poor drowned girl. Driving to the ferry slip, he remembers, "a lot of different thoughts came into my mind at that time about how I was really going to be able to call Mrs. Kopechne at some time in the middle of the night to tell her that her daughter was drowned, to be able to call my own mother and my own father, relate to them, my wife, and I even—even though I knew that Mary Jo Kopechne was dead and believed firmly that she was in the back of that car I willed that she remained alive.

"As we drove down that road I was almost looking out the front window and windows trying to see her walking down that road. I related this to Gargan and Markham and they said they understood this feeling, but it was necessary to report it."

It is as if, blown over by the dementia of this nightmare, there has come upended the entire tangle of Kennedy's preconscious root system. Fears, cravings, utterly unrealistic expectations of himself, exorbitant demands on Society—within his clot-addled brain a deep-seated confusion prevailed between what was actually happening and what he could tolerate. The insecure, overworked adult who had now been given to understand that he was a sure thing to become the next Great Leader of the Free World was contending with the suppressed anxieties of the eight-year-old child (as he was to confess to me decades afterward) who dreaded that he, too, would prove unworthy of the father, like the lobotomized Rosemary, and disappear as well.

Every vulnerability played into those bewildering hours: his distaste for abrupt decisions, his paralysis at the onset of deadly violence, his habit of offloading the nitty-gritty in a crisis on professional flunkies and slipping personally out from under, his compounding awareness of defeat at having again been incapable of saving somebody who had served the higher purposes of the Kennedys. His sanity worn thinner and thinner by overwork, by worry, by too much unwanted responsibility: Whatever he had drunk that evening no doubt helped tip into his worn-out system a perilous toxicity.

The concussion Kennedy absorbed that night, with its unavoidable hemorrhaging and lesions, was more than enough, too much. While he was himself, subsequently, to refer to shock and panic, whatever was left of his inbred self-esteem worked to prevent him from admitting to himself that he, too, pushed brutally enough, could in fact lose control. Better guilty than crazy, better demonic than helpless.

Almost from the moment the scandal broke publicly the Kennedys were accused of everything from buying judges to suborning witnesses in order to avoid disastrous legal charges. In fact, one of the most vexing struggles his friends and relatives and lawyers had with Ted was to keep him from attempting to present himself as guilty of a great deal more than the facts and the law allowed. A man whose primary fixation, after having involved himself in the death of an associate, is how he will be able to bring himself to face the parents of the victim has been knocked out of touch for the moment: Feudal emotions were in control.

The struggle to drag Kennedy back into the present throughout the next week or so is an understated but persistent theme among the memories of the advisers. Steve Smith would epitomize what *his* mission was. "He's back, he's working, he's doing fine, he stayed in the same business. What else do you want to know?" Considering the possibilities at the time, that was obviously quite enough for Steve.

The back-and-forth among Gargan, Markham, and Kennedy continued, directionless and without decisions, until the three had parked just short of the ferry slip. They had passed several houses, their lights still on, where they might have phoned the incident in and summoned the police and perhaps a rescue team. Nobody cared to take the initiative, not without Ted's consent. With that, as Gargan stated to the court, "The Senator said to me, to both of us basically, 'All right, all right, I will take care of it, you go back, don't upset the girls, don't get them involved; I will take care of it.'" He climbed out of the back seat, took three steps, dove off the pier and started to swim across the cut toward Martha's Vineyard. The two retainers stood there, watching Kennedy until he was halfway across, then resettled themselves into their shared front seat and drove slowly back to the cottage, suffered second thoughts, swung around and drove back to the ferry slip just in case . . . By then Kennedy was invisible out there someplace upon the water, safe on the opposite shore—at least both accomplices certainly hoped he was.

" 'Bail out, pretend you weren't there, don't disturb the girls, I'll take care of this, it's my scene,'" a close friend of Markham's reports Paul as having quoted Kennedy at the ferry slip. The irrational guilt surged; only unalloyed self-sacrifice could wash it away. "Markham, Gargan," a knockabout ally of Edward Kennedy's through a decade of Massachusetts skirmishes snorts, projecting that pierside turn aloud to himself. "The relationship with those two in one sense is not good. They would never fight with him. I'm sure he came on like gangbusters. Both of them are basically honorable kinds of guys, courteous, and he was probably screeching and screaming . . ." Attempting to confront the blast of it, each of the implicated bystanders recoiled.

Any excuse served. After all, as Kennedy's confidants in the matter, Paul Markham and Gargan were not merely old friends vacationing together now but, functionally speaking, Kennedy's lawyers; as responsible officers of the court, whatever he told them they could only reveal after being granted his express permission. As late as midmorning Saturday, when the shocked and disheveled pair were able finally to nudge Kennedy into alerting his Washington office and nerve himself up enough to file a police report, Kennedy was to persist in this confused charitability of his.

"I don't want you people put in the middle of this thing," he reiterated to Markham. "I'm not going to involve you. As far as you know, you didn't know anything about the accident that night." So Kennedy's accident report left that unhidable second round out. Unexplained time lapses appeared in the rendition of events; press doubts poured into the crisis like bacteria.

With Gargan and Markham snaked away by LaRosa, what party was left inside and around the Lawrence Cottage seemed to drift even more irrecoverably into doldrums. Crimmins had gone to bed in disgust, and the remaining girls and LaRosa, having gradually given up the expectation of getting across to Edgartown now that both cars were nowhere around, started to kill time by taking aimless walks up and down the Main Street highway in hopes of running into Joey somewhere. Not long before 2 AM, Nance Lyons, greeting a car that slowed down with *Shove off, buddy, we're not pickups,* was surprised to discover that it wasn't Joey Gargan at all but—as she was to learn much much later—that most agreeable sharp-eyed Deputy Sheriff Christopher Look, who had a few minutes before surprised a stopped, dark Massachusetts car with three forms in it, a license plate that started with an *L* and had the number *1* toward the beginning and at the end, like Kennedy's—and which, when Look climbed out of his own vehicle and hailed it, backed off and rumbled down unlit Dike Road.

Charlie Tretter and Cricket Keough tried another direction, came back after a while to look in on what appeared to be an empty cottage, both cars still gone, which to the suggestible Tretter looked like a possible joke by LaRosa on him, since he himself, a habitual latecomer, had been delayed and had snarled LaRosa up when LaRosa met them all Thursday coming off the ferry from Woods Hole. Tretter and Cricket wandered hopefully toward the ferry slip; when they got back the group was already settled in at Gargan's suggestion on what beds and studio couches there were. Tretter and the long-suffering little Cricket lay out for the night on the floor near the screen door, beside the nervous, tossing Joe Gargan.

Speculation among the girls about the disappearance of Joe and Paul centered on the notion that the senator's car had gotten stuck in sand, something that had recently bedeviled somebody several of them knew; neither Gargan nor Markham, after they returned at close to two in the morning, disabused them of that idea. The two were unmistakably bushed and tense with their knowledge of something.

Markham, slumping with fatigue against Esther Newburgh's susceptible leg, was told sharply to remove his weight, at once: Markham explained that he was tired, exhausted, and that even if he were at liberty to tell her, she really would not believe what happened. Nobody followed that up. Gargan himself claimed afterward that he himself never did try to explain away their absence to anybody at the cottage that night, but Mary Ellen Lyons later testified that he had told her that the senator swam across to Edgartown, that he and Paul jumped after him, and that Mary Jo had herself taken Kennedy's car over on the last ferry. Nobody pursued it: By then everybody was tired, fractious, wishing grumpily that he or she had made it back to a comfortable bed at the Katama or the Shiretown, envying Mary Jo.

Joseph Gargan slept fitfully, moaning and rolling again and again against the uncomfortable Tretter in his sleep. Paul Markham moved around all night, relocating successively from the daybed to a chair to an attempt at sleep just before morning in the back seat of the Valiant.

Edward Kennedy slept very little either. Traumatized by the accident, Kennedy had very nearly been drowned again swimming across the five-hundred-foot cut; halfway over the tide grabbed him and dragged him toward the Edgartown light and the undertow began to suck him down irresistibly when the tide apparently turned; there was the momentary smooth equalization of forces through which he churned in slow empty mechanical exhaustion to pull himself up the piers of the wharf and shamble, shoeless, his pants and polo shirt plucked half off his body so that his brace was exposed, into the dying chaos of the first regatta night in Edgartown. Legs gone, Kennedy stumbled up a side street, half-collapsed against a tree for strength, and finally made it into the Shiretown Inn and up the stairs. Shaking with chill, he stripped, his headache throbbing, neck torn, back half out, desolated, confused.

An enormous noise was around him, in him; hand over hand and dizzy he pulled on dry pants and a shirt, descended the stairs outside, and, after mentioning the noise, asked the person hovering just beyond the balcony floodlight whether he had an idea what time it was: Kennedy remembered being told: two-thirty. He climbed the steps another time. Tossing, pacing around the room, he was unable to budge his shattered emotions from their fixated need to believe that Joe and Paul were going to come and pick him up in the morning, the sun would be up, and it would be a new morning and they would tell him that Mary Jo was still alive, that the thing had not really happened and that he would be spared the terrifying responsibility of telephoning Mrs. Kopechne to tell her that he had acted so unwisely as somehow to have destroyed one of his own, his charges.

"... I just couldn't gain the strength within me, the moral strength to call Mrs. Kopechne at two o'clock in the morning and tell her her daughter was dead," Kennedy said later. This stopped Kennedy again and again. It was too much; for days it was to remain too much.

Not long after the tragedy, Kennedy told me as much as he could remember about his own behavior. I had brought up the accident while going into the political fallout of the catastrophe in the Whip's office. Once he understood that I wanted him to deal directly with the accident, he suggested that we meet for breakfast in his townhouse at Charles River Square the following week. There were too many ears cocked in Washington.

A lot of his confusion came from his uncertainty about what had actually occurred. Kennedy told me that he remembered waking up a few hours after he reached his room from a fitful, dream-tossed sleep and made his way downstairs and asked the innkeeper, who was half-asleep in the office, whether he had heard of a car's going off a bridge on Chappaquiddick. Kennedy claimed that he himself wasn't sure whether the entire horrible incident had actually happened or whether he might have dreamed it. The innkeeper hadn't heard about anything like that. Kennedy trudged back upstairs and tried to sleep a few more hours.

Several calls Kennedy placed that chaotic night were to Helga Wagner. A svelte young Austrian ski racer, all-around sportswoman, and jewelry designer who had migrated as early as 1963, at eighteen, to Palm Beach, Helga, along with her sister Margaret, quickly found her way into the vacation coterie that was forming around the Kennedys and the Smiths. Helga and her sister, whose husband had just been killed in a plane crash, were staying with the golfer Chris Dunphey and were invited the day Helga arrived in America to attend a dinner party at the house of Colonel Paul, which Jack Kennedy rented for vacation getaways.

With Ted Kennedy's marriage disintegrating, the affectionate yet worldly Helga had begun what would develop into a decade-plus-long affair with the troubled senator. For many years to come this canny, soigné Central European beauty, with her marvelous head of leonine streaked-blonde hair and sparkling blue eyes, offered the overstressed young senator a place to catch his breath, a sailing companion, relief from the round-the-clock expectations of his surviving and demanding family and the clamor of the colleagues. Close friends of the period would characterize Helga as the love of Ted Kennedy's life.

Investigators have puzzled over why Kennedy called *her* in his frazzled condition. Over the course of a long exploratory conversation recently Helga was finally able to talk to me about what went on. Were the calls personal? "No, no," she exclaimed in her lovely Tyrolean patois, "Actually, he wanted to get in touch with his sister, Jean, and *wenn* I had the phone number, and he did not tell me *anything* about the accident. I have no idea.

"And we just talked, and he was kind of . . . I had a feeling he was a bit— how shall I say?—absent-minded, he wasn't what he usually was." Hours after the Oldsmobile crashed to the ocean's floor, blood from the hematoma forming on Kennedy's brain was starting to contort his reactions.

In fact, the information the increasingly confused Kennedy was really after was the whereabouts of Jean's husband, Steve Smith, who had disappeared for a time with his flame of the moment to Majorca. Helga maintains that she wasn't able to help locate Steve; Jean probably couldn't either. With Bobby dead, Ted Kennedy's entire instinct was to claw out in hopes of shifting the responsibility for dealing with this catastrophe to the surviving surrogate for his father, the tough-minded little brother-in-law who ran the Kennedy money out of a suite in the Pan Am Building. Decades of offloading crisis, of turning over serious trouble to a lawyer or an accountant or a flunky or—in old Joe's case—a reliable gangster when that was what it took, had kicked in again for Teddy. Efface what happened; blot it out. Cash in the required papal indulgences. As Kennedy's quasi-amnesiac condition deepened, every impulse cried escape.

Five hours after he had haltingly addressed the Shiretown innkeeper, Russell Peachey, Senator Edward M. Kennedy, groomed neatly and freshly dressed in slacks and a pair of immaculate topsiders, encountered Ross Richards on Water Street adjacent to the Shiretown; the two sailors repaired to the exposed courtyard landing their rooms in the Mayberry House Annex shared, and fell into a quarter of an hour or so of small talk about the Friday racing. Saturday looked promising. Stanley Moore dropped by; Mrs. Richards came out of their entry to join the conversation at ten minutes before eight. To Richards and his wife, at least, Kennedy seemed as ever.

In fact, Kennedy had met Richards after unsuccessfully attempting to telephone Steve Smith's office at seven-thirty to try to reach Burke Marshall. Ted looked cheery, was not evidencing at all the gritted amiability of the politician but—operating with a politician's reflexes to select from among the refractions of his splintered consciousness—was apparently able to convince even himself with a persona that effaced completely the experiences of the night.

At eight Paul Markman and Joe Gargan, damp-looking and woebedraggled, ascended the outside staircase. Kennedy had inadvertently locked himself out of his room; Gargan fetched the key. Kennedy regretted good-humoredly that he wasn't free to have breakfast with the Richardses but suggested that he might just possibly be able to join their party a little later on.

There are circumstances under which nobody rational is serene, and the moment Paul Markham started to mount the Shiretown courtyard steps and glimpsed that picture of equanimity—Kennedy sitting there quietly, making empty conversation—"It was obvious to me at that time that nothing had been done . . . There was no commotion. There was no . . . he was just seated there at the table." Markham and Gargan moved Kennedy into his room like a pair of bouncers and closed the door.

"I didn't report it," Kennedy said.

Aghast, Markham pulled out of Kennedy his tumbled memories of swimming across, of his night just sitting on the hotel room bed. "'It just was a nightmare,'" Markham reports Kennedy as having said. "'I was not even sure it happened.'" And again he described the car, the rolling off the bridge, the lungs full of seawater. Part of Kennedy's mental process had obviously snagged there, then. At that moment Charlie Tretter, who had come back with Gargan and Markham and had stopped by his cabin to shower and put on fresh clothes, appeared at the landing and looked in the window and, thinking he saw in the movement of Kennedy's head a gesture inviting him in, breezed through the door and received a slow deadly half-mad look from Kennedy he had never before seen, meaningful as a slap: Tretter left.

Steered now by Markham and Gargan (who subsequently, with his advance man's smugness about the logistics of things, his secret quiet pride in minutiae, was to insist to the district attorney, "You have to remember that I have been coming here and racing for thirty years and one thing you can't get in an Edgartown weekend, Mr. Dinis, is a telephone. I know all the telephones on this island well and . . . I wanted a place where the senator could talk privately . . ."), Kennedy was ferried back to the Chappaquiddick side to "that little thing that looks like an MTA station with a phone in it just beside the driveoff." Steve Ewing, the ferryboat urchin who helped dock and undock the raftlike *On Time*, remembers Kennedy's manner as easygoing still, untroubled. While Markham and Gargan waited, tensely, Kennedy slipped into the pay station and was able this time to put himself in touch with David Burke in Arlington, Virginia.

Kennedy roughed in the situation for Burke, told him to try to notify Marshall, to go to the Old Senate Office Building office, and to prepare himself for a deluge of telephone calls. Perhaps more than anything that happened to him that epic morning-after, listening to David Burke's urgent, even feverish basso, with its home inflections of reverberant ethical force, started truly to ground Kennedy, began to awaken in the inoperative part of Kennedy's mind a tickle of cognizance that this thing had indeed happened, it was there forever now.

Burke recognized at once the extent of the dislocation his employer now suffered. Throughout the rest of that Saturday Burke telephoned the people he himself felt they would need, groped cautiously for some kind of grip they could establish on things. By early evening, leaving Dick Drayne to kibitz and hold down the Washington press as well as he could, Burke caught the shuttle to Boston. A newsman knowledgeable enough to know who David was slid into the adjoining seat.

"All I saw was a couple of things that were moving on the wire," the reporter opened gingerly. "It wasn't working, hanging together at all. Don't you think you should make some kind of . . . of full disclosure soon?"

"No," Burke said. "I don't think we're going to do that. The senator is not in very good shape; I'm going to go up there, and maybe sit under a tree with him, and then we'll have to see."

With Burke, as ever, reality began: Kennedy emerged from the pay station badly shaken up, undisguisedly stricken.

By that time the Edgartown Fire Department scuba diver, John Farrar, had slid the corpse of Mary Jo Kopechne out of Kennedy's upside-down Oldsmobile. She was in almost perfect physical condition, "as if she had just come from a party," dressed in a white blouse and blue slacks, sandals, and her come-open chain belt. Rigor mortis had set in, and her hands were rigidly clawed, purportedly from holding herself so as to keep her face as long as she could in the trapped air of the rear footwell. Farrar recovered Cricket Keough's purse, too. Word of the accident had worked its way back to the Chappaquiddick ferry slip by that time. Dick Hewitt, the On Time's skipper for the Saturday morning shift, was back before Kennedy got off the phone to Washington. He told Markham that the car that had come off Dike Bridge had been identified as Senator Kennedy's. "I asked him if he was aware of the accident, and he said, yes, we just heard about it." Then Hewitt took all three of them back to the wharf at Edgartown.

When Kennedy hurried up the Edgartown cobblestones to turn himself in to Police Chief Dominick Arena, Markham went along; Gargan, on Kennedy's suggestion, drove out to the Katama Shores to break the news to the others. The episode as Gargan appears to have edited it for the girls featured a distraught Edward Kennedy appearing outside the Lawrence Cottage, summoning Markham and himself, and demanding, without another word, that the two of them "get me to Edgartown." The moment the three reached the ferry slip the senator allegedly dove off: Gargan and Markham jumped in after him (a heroic they both were to disavow before Judge Boyle) but couldn't overtake Kennedy and returned, disconsolate and worried, to the shoreline. Gargan also informed this group that Mary Jo was now, it would appear, dead; this caused "tremendous emotional breakdown" among the affected girls. When the open grief subsided a little Gargan returned to Edgartown, browsing events at the station house in his eyebrow-arching way, ready again—forever ready—to help anybody who needed it now.

Chief Arena was a big fleshy shoulder-grabbing Itlo whose range of day-to-day police experience until that berserk Saturday morning—he himself was forthright enough about admitting it—was pretty largely of the sort that required an officer to prod dangerous-looking snapping turtles deeper into the nearby marshes and shoo marauding basset hounds back under picket fences before they grubbed up too many planter pansies. Until the implacable working press drove the unhappy cop onto a schedule of tranquilizers, Dominick Arena's prevailing manner was bowling-league easygoing; he kept his police procedures informal too. Once Arena had radio-telephoned the registration number of the Oldsmobile his men were starting to winch up out of Poucha Pond to headquarters and received the news that the car belonged to Senator Edward M. Kennedy, Arena radioed the stationhouse back with the intention of telling the desk officer to go find Kennedy himself. It was approaching ten o'clock; Kennedy was there already.

The two played a cagey little round of Twenty Questions over the cruiser radio:

Arena: "I am sorry, I have some bad news: Your car was in an accident over here and the young lady is dead."
Kennedy: "I know."
Arena: "Can you tell me was there anybody else in the car?"
Kennedy: "Yes."
Arena: "Are they in the water?"
Kennedy: "No."

Arena: "Can I talk to you?"

Kennedy: "Yes."

Arena: "Would you like to talk to me?"

But Kennedy distinctly preferred to explain things at the Edgartown stationhouse. When Arena got back he told Kennedy he was sorry about what happened; Kennedy was direct: "Yes, I know, I was the driver." Arena accepted the information, glumly. "What would you like for me to do?" Kennedy reportedly said. "We must both do what is right or we will both be criticized for it."

Reminded of that, Arena requested a statement; Kennedy preferred to write that out, so Arena conducted him to the selectmen's office down the hall, where he and Markham—with Markham block-printing it out—produced Kennedy's original version of what had happened. Before he attempted that, though, Kennedy telephoned the Kopechne parents and, sobbing heavily, finally made clear to them that their daughter Mary Jo had died in an accident.

Arena, in the meanwhile, returned to the Dike Bridge vicinity to make sure the Oldsmobile got onto the bank and that the curiosity-seekers flooding the area were not creating a traffic problem. He returned to the station at eleven, received Kennedy's report, found it hard to read and had a secretary type it up in duplicate and later claimed to have thrown the original away.

There were enough police details to keep Kennedy around Edgartown for the next five hours: He telephoned his Washington office repeatedly, attempting to be sure of background information Arena had requested. He asked David Burke to locate his driver's license, which was reportedly discovered in the glove compartment of his McLean car. Mostly, he was trying to get ready for whatever in God's name was going to happen now.

At a quarter to three, two policemen transported Kennedy, Gargan, and Markham to the Martha's Vineyard airport to catch a charter to Hyannis Port. Kennedy was in the front seat. *Oh, my God, what has happened*, one of them reports Ted as having mumbled, over and over. *What's happened?*

"There was," the inspector remembers, "no direct conversation."

In November of 1969—sere changeover month of central Atlantic spraystorms, through most of which the old Ambassador lay utterly depleted finally, dying—Edward Kennedy attempted a painting of the Compound envisioned from the oceanside. The canvas is elemental, black greens and rich blue plumage of clouds that look as if squeezed onto the canvas directly and thinned and brush driven into rough configuration there. Everything really central gets a stroke or two: the shoreline of faceted dangerous protectively enclosing boulders; the slime-lapped old dock with its splitting piles; the *Victura* at mooring; above the sloped irregular playing-field lawns towers the big house in all its Victorian-Colonial deformity, cropping out its gables and porches. There is a suggestion of rooftops; the shaggy horizon is broken only by the towers of the Saint Francis Xavier Church. "This place is so much a part of all the Kennedys," Edward scrawled below a copy of the work he sent to me.

Not that the resounding old institution survives only in memory. The environs are there, rooms a stranger could walk around in and pictures of dead men's faces in silver frames atop the grand piano. It is a museum for complicated emotions mostly, an entrapment for memory, an inviolable place, within which nobody will ever be shot through the temples or mangled in an airplane no matter what, no matter how. Whatever happens, one can depend on escape and security here. This is the cradle, the undoer, the never-never land.

The moment his charter set down at Barnstable Airport that summer Saturday, Edward Kennedy was driven home. Kennedy circuits had been alive for six hours now with this unaccountable but galvanizing news. "The Boss drove off a bridge on Martha's Vineyard and one of Bobby's secretaries got killed," Dave Burke called the D.C. office to inform Kennedy's press man Dick Drayne, who was granting a magazine reporter one of his shrugged-through, hinting-around interviews behind his balustrade of piled yellow clips.

"Anything happen?" the reporter asked; Drayne looked perplexed.

"No—no, nothing, really," Drayne assured the interviewer. "I sat there all through that morning waiting for the roof to fall in," Drayne later conceded to me. "The story was on the wires, about a former Kennedy secretary getting drowned. I knew what they didn't, that he was driving the car. It was unbelievable. People poured in here, and I could only give them what was already public." Burke got to the office; Kennedy kept calling in from the Edgartown police station, four or five times. "I could tell he was very upset, very depressed, but he could still come up with answers," Drayne said.

Kennedy's focus remained the Kopechnes. The assassination of Martin Luther King seemed to offer some kind of precedent within the Kennedy experience; after consulting with the senator, Burke dispatched the smooth-talking Bill Vanden Heuvel to the Kopechne home in Berkeley Heights, New Jersey, to try to help things there. The reception astonished Vanden Heuvel: Mrs. Kopechne met him with "Thank God the senator is all right. It would be terrible if something happened to him." Burke reached Dun Gifford at his vacation house on Nantucket Island at half past ten: Burke, then Kennedy (whom Gifford called back to corroborate his instructions), told Gifford to island-hop as soon as he could to Edgartown and help identify Mary Jo's corpse, and see to it that the remains were removed to whichever funeral home the Kopechnes selected.

By the time Gifford arrived, the County Associate Medical Examiner, Dr. Donald Mills, had gone over the body quickly at pondside, diagnosed death by drowning—the characteristic bloody foam coughed up by drowning victims had stained Mary Jo's collar and the back of her blouse—determined to his own satisfaction that there had been no indication of any kind of foul play, no bruises or fractures, nothing to suggest the need for an autopsy.

Mills so informed the office of District Attorney Dinis, who had left that decision to Mills, and turned the body over routinely to Eugene Frieh, the area mortician. Frieh and an assistant washed away the brine, drew off a blood sample which, when tested, indicated the equivalency of .09 percent alcohol in her system, perhaps three drinks' worth, examined the corpse closely enough themselves to be sure that there was no noticeable bruise on it except a slight abrasion of a knuckle of the left hand, and went ahead and embalmed it.

Even before Gifford arrived the mortician had received a telephone call from John Kielty of the Kielty Funeral Home in Plymouth, Pennsylvania, who claimed to have been authorized by Mrs. Kopechne to see that the body was returned to Plymouth as soon as possible for burial. Dun got there in time to observe the last of the preparations—having remembered Mary Jo in life closely enough to help the assistant mortician choose a tint for the cheeks, hand-carried the death certificate over for Dr. Mills to sign the next day, and accompanied Mary Jo's body to New Bedford, where he and the body changed to a larger plane and lifted off directly for Pennsylvania.

By that time the newspaper editorialists, hungry for detail and increasingly skeptical, were wondering in print why no autopsy had been performed so far. Tabloids designated Gifford "The Body Snatcher." Two parish priests materialized almost immediately at the Kopechnes' door to advise the family: "Mary Jo is with God. She is at rest. Don't disturb her." The Kopechnes agreed. By then the Kennedy women, Ethel and Joan in particular, had telephoned condolences and were moving in to help however they could. Kennedy himself reportedly presented $90,904 of his own to the Kopechne family, which was followed up with $50,000 from his insurance company.

Later in the morning that skullbreaking Saturday, David Burke had finally located the legendary Burke Marshall in Waltham, Massachusetts, working on the records at the Kennedy archives. Edward Kennedy was subsequently to refer to Marshall as "one of the dearest and oldest friends that I have." If, in his way, Marshall was, the emotion arrived secondhand through Bobby. There are certain unmistakable rare faces and unforgettable voices one takes in, almost immediately, as much too worldly-sad to corrupt: Marshall had one each, his look gone honorably at fifty to chiseled corners and leathery pouches; a compassionate, almost tear-threatened voice within which every word is patient, solemn, carefully measured first, then bitten one final time before release. "I told him I'd come down there and help wherever I could as his friend and attorney," Marshall remembered; he arrived at the Compound between one and two, preceding the returned Kennedy.

With Marshall's arrival, control slipped irrecoverably out of Kennedy's tremulous hands. Importing Burke Marshall to deal with a motor vehicle code violation was tantamount to whipping frosting with the great screw propeller of the *Queen Elizabeth*; Marshall had entered knowing that he was the anointed manager of as sure a losing—more probably, as disastrous—a crisis as the Kennedys had ever experienced. Burke Marshall was heavy legal equipment. He had made his name originally as a standout antitrust lawyer in Washington, accepted Bobby's offer to come into the Justice Department as the Assistant U.S. Attorney General in charge of Civil Rights, and—having turned down the deanship of the Yale Law School for the time being—had taken employment as the General Counsel and Vice President of IBM. In his attaché case he brought along a note from Lyndon Johnson that maintained that "in thirty-three years of service with the Federal Government," the president had "never known a person who rendered a better quality of public service." Very few of Bob Kennedy's favorites gleaned recommendations like that from JFK's volcanic successor; Marshall was to embellish his medals for tact by his marvelously adroit dealing with the King family and the black community when Martin Luther King died.

Even to this legendary defuser of blockbusters, Edward Kennedy's Chappaquiddick predicament appeared to offer very few safe places into which to pry. "When I talked at first to Ted after he was back in Hyannis Port he was so upset he didn't . . . the question really was where to begin," Marshall would remember. "I advised him to have a medical examination. He truly did not know whether he might have had a medical problem. He was obviously disoriented, but he appeared coherent. Then, after I was with him for a while I came to the conclusion he had a blockage, that a lot of his mind wasn't accepting yet what was happening to him. He told me he had been convinced,

somehow, that Mary Jo Kopechne got out, got away. I don't think he shook
that idea off for a while. The Kennedys have a way of seeming fine, going
forward without interruption under stress—I remember them all at the time
of Bobby's funeral—but inside a great deal is blocked off. That night, in that
situation, I think Ted Kennedy might very well have functioned so that the
people with him, particularly if they weren't strong-minded people, would
think that he knew exactly what he was doing."

Marshall's corner-turning earliest decision was to try to keep Kennedy
from risking any further kind of public explanation until, at the very earliest,
he had stood trial on whatever charges Chief Arena decided to press. Leaving
the scene of an accident was the probable offense, but there were much more
serious possibilities: driving to endanger, or even, quite possibly, manslaughter. Kennedy's condition varied hour by hour. At times throughout that week
he talked of abandoning everything, leaving politics: The people closest to
him found him inconsolable one moment, virtually normal an hour afterwards. The danger was great of his breaking down badly at a press conference, presenting himself as hopeless. "The reason I thought he should not
make a statement to the press," Marshall would acknowledge to me, "was
that I did not know enough about his legal situation. A lawyer's instinct with
his friends and clients is to shut up. Politically," Marshall mused, "it was a
bad thing, I suppose . . ."

Largely innocent of the gritty workings of either the Massachusetts Criminal Code or the congenital backstabbing of Commonwealth politics, Marshall started to telephone some of the Kennedys' more workaday lawyerly
contacts to confirm the details. Personal feelings were inevitably bruised.
"I don't think I should have slashed my wrists or anything," says one Boston retainer who put in his years for Ted and found himself left out of this
cataclysmic turn of things. Marshall refused to take in the Massachusetts
lawyer's reading of the relevant ordinances: "I told him, just so you know.
The statute's been changed. He wasn't taking it in: I had already checked the
whole island out; within twenty minutes, I knew that X who was involved
had a drinking problem, the judge was likely to react this way . . . We had the
whole book on the guy. And I wasn't . . . I couldn't . . . Here they had a guy
at the controls who just did not know the factual situation."

Nitpickers from the press were already arriving by the hundreds: They
were already out there by nightfall, already sore in the arches and angry, pacing the elm-lined residential streets, beyond the police rope-off, peeping over
Hyannis Port picket fences.

Part-time Kennedy advisers swarmed into town; one, hurrying down from

Boston, urged the managers to "tell 'em anything; tell 'em the senator ate franks and beans for supper for Chrissake——." Noncommunication thickened; trying to second-guess reporters at a run-through press conference, the sometime aide was increasingly depressed by the string of no-comments the crisis-handlers demanded.

Another avatar of the desperately missed Bobby, Dick Goodwin, the man Bob had respected most, if grudgingly at times, for his reliable apprehension of the oncoming public mood, had already been buckled into the crisis in case a statement had to be readied quickly. Perhaps earlier than anybody there, Goodwin was attentive to the thunder of newsmen outside shifting from foot to foot, waiting, calling their city desks and raging editors, again with nothing; again, no report. The delay was insupportable; still, as the very largest decisions hovered, Goodwin saw, Kennedy was "obviously panicky still, obviously really shaken up, and yet nobody else was really willing to make the kind of serious decisions a situation of this sort required. We had there a great, headless, talented monster. Nobody could decide what to do.

"So, finally, by the middle of the week they transformed it into a political problem, which they could deal with. I left after the third day; by then they were trying to say something and still avoid the connotation of immorality— the old Irish-Catholic fear of ever suggesting that you were screwing anybody outside of marriage. Drink and sex acquired a disproportionate size." Goodwin had already prepared a comprehensive description, low-keyed, based on the facts he had been told, with as many loopholes covered as possible, which he recommended affixing to the police report and so making available to the ravening press indirectly.

Kennedy remained paralyzed. "Never would have happened if Bobby was there," Lyndon Johnson had snorted in Johnson City on viewing the first reports of the incident; Ted Kennedy, in his heart, was fully aware of that. Old Kennedy hands like McNamara, angry for the legacy, were demanding, pique showing, to hear the entire truth. As he came to himself slowly Ted was being reduced: more the baby brother again hour by hour, the confidence he needed shaken by the dubious Camelotians who were catechizing him unremittingly and concluding that he came up short.

"The week afterwards I remember as a time of great and searching speculation over the incidents surrounding the whole tragedy," Kennedy told me during the aftermath of the crisis. "I didn't want to set up any kind of discussion with the funeral coming up, the grief of the family . . . many cross streams, people coming up and saying you ought to go to press conferences, my own feeling about the circumstances. It was just a very . . . I don't know how you'd describe the period other than as a great . . . great——. What seemed important one hour seemed unimportant a second hour, enormously difficult and complex . . ."

Typically, Kennedy's own later assessment of the predicament remains likely to stand up as the most reasoned, the most sensitive and yet, uncannily, the most de-emotionalized around. "By the time I got back to the Cape and saw Ted—it was Sunday night or Monday, I can't remember which—he was in a state of mind I'd never quite seen him in before, down but determined," Dun Gifford said. "He wanted to make a statement, go to court and get the whole goddamned thing settled right then." Yet, as Kennedy himself admitted, hours later he would be racked, indecisive, sobbing on the telephone again to the Kopechnes or shrugging off all friendship to walk by the wasted beach alone. His hellzapoppin' college friend Claude Hooten flew in from Paris to buck him up; it helped, slightly.

By Tuesday, when the regulars—Ethel, Lem Billings, Dave Hackett, Joan, Dun, and Bill Vanden Heuvel—rallied with Kennedy himself to the Kopechne funeral at Saint Vincent's in Plymouth, Pennsylvania, the terrible drear again descended. Leaving through the gamut of newsmen, all pulp above his neck brace, a bleached and guilty and vulnerable-looking ghost of his normal boisterous public presence, Kennedy mumbled a promise to make a full statement as soon as possible.

By the time the charter dropped them all off at Hyannis Port Steve Smith was back from Majorca and installed; Marshall, who had a sick father and a vacationing family of his own to resettle, had waited until Smith was back before dropping out for the rest of the week. With Steve Smith's appearance Ted Kennedy's primary impulse, which was to go to the public directly and risk whatever legal upshots developed, got stifled, immediately and powerfully.

Smith was an extraordinary personality—he had the capacity to move into almost any situation with an abbreviated quick deadliness, so fast that it would take a Bobby resuscitated to have any hope of standing up to his murderous gifts of decision and execution. Smith and his operatives out of the Pan Am Building at 200 Park Avenue had the New York self-assurance of back-room specialists responsible for the *real* money and media control.

Throughout all the recent campaigns the hard-driving, chain-smoking Smith was involved from the first projections until the last nonplussed local hotel owner—backing away from bargaining sessions throughout which Smith's brutal representatives like Paul Corbin kept slicing successively the cents-to-the-dollar settlement the Kennedys would consider—got his disheartening note from Smith's office suggesting that the hotelier should perhaps have come to terms earlier. The Kennedys' Massachusetts handlers stayed bitter over the arrogance of the New York bookkeepers. One of the few family matters Ted Kennedy's Washington staff ever heard him mutter about was his brother-in-law's tight-fistedness. There was something confusing about being billed universally as the Leader Of All The Kennedys and still having to be careful as a truant schoolboy about overspending pocket money——.

Now, well into what was perhaps the prickliest crisis in the history of the family, Steve was taking over without even bothering to ask, just as he had taken over, calmed the crowds, helped cut through most of the immediate chaos while Bobby was dying in Los Angeles. Moving at once, he decided which lawyers should supplement Edgartown attorney Richard McCarron up to and beyond handling the leaving-the-scene charge for which Ted was already scheduled to appear in court a week later, on Monday.

Goodwin left; McNamara arrived, greeted, with the high humor typical of the advisers behind closed doors, with: Well, here comes the genius who put together the Bay of Pigs and the war in Vietnam. Let's see what he can accomplish with this one. Sorensen appeared, full already of brooding reproach for what Ted Kennedy's mischief was going to do to Jack's legacy.

They were all vulnerable, and Smith was overstimulated. "Our prime concern was whether or not the guy survived the thing," he exploded when I pushed him later, "whether he rode out the still possible charge of manslaughter. You've got to remember that half the press of the world was standing outside in the street. Those guys acted like it was the Five P.M. Express, Christ, there were telephones all over the goddamn place. If this weren't a public man, in fact if this had been anybody but Edward Kennedy, we wouldn't have gotten the attention. Then when Dinis decided on an inquest, an imprecise process devoted primarily to train accidents that hadn't been used in Massachusetts since—I don't know, never—that was the toughest decision, not to go to the inquest under Judge Boyle's general ground rules, according to which it would have been treated on a small country island, a local judge hearing the burden of those rather serious questions . . . Under those ground rules, in a circus atmosphere——."

The crisis dilated; the reporters were roaming Martha's Vineyard, Chappaquiddick Island, Hyannis Port like starved wolves whose stomachs, growling, were audible through all the boxwood, behind all the police barricades. John Farrar, the flip, brisk diver who pulled Mary Jo's body out, was granting interviews freely in the stockroom of the Turf and Tackle, volunteered his opinions: Mary Jo had suffocated, not drowned; the Oldsmobile trunk was still dry when the car was finally dragged up; Mary Jo's position as found suggested that she had been after the last trapped air; the undertaker allegedly admitted her lungs had barely a cupful of water in them. If only Farrar had been summoned in time.

Deputy Christopher Look's story came out, his assurances that he had seen, just before 1 AM, three people in a black car with the L-pattern license back up and turn down Dike Road. Russell Peachey remembered his two-thirty exchange with Kennedy at the Shiretown. A nation of Hercule Poirots was busy with every fresh edition now: new evidence the news-starved scavengers were surfacing as they waited, old impatiences with Ted darkening into open indictment as all of them waited begging something from the Compound, a tidbit, a statement.

By midweek *Newsweek* roared to press with the cover story that toxified Edward Kennedy's euphoric publicity once and for all, inserting early in the piece the claim that Kennedy's "closest associates" had been "powerfully concerned with his indulgent drinking habits, his daredevil driving, and his ever-ready eye for a pretty face." *Newsweek* reporter John Lindsay had not written the piece himself, but the information came immediately from his spring memorandum, laughed off at the time but now the buried mine that the resettling of Edward Kennedy's reputation had detonated beneath the Duchy of rocking Hyannis Port. The family—Steve Smith and Ethel in particular—started furious and remained furious. Ted was being *crucified*.

Perhaps the least upset about the publicity as such, with its inescapable political damages, was Edward Kennedy himself. Shock had given way to remorse by then, and remorse to a realism and stoic resolve about the whole thing that was making it more and more possible, as each hour passed, for Kennedy to take his own crisis over for himself. He asked that his trial date be moved up, held as soon as possible. He decided, against the advice of Judge Clark of Brockton and his son, lawyers regarded as the best motor-vehicle-accident men in Massachusetts, to plead, simply, guilty to leaving the scene. In fact, by contacting Gargan and Markham and apprising them of the situation he had discharged his essential legal obligation; the lawyers and advisers, the shrewd and inventive Edward Hanify especially, felt they could successfully plead nolo contendere. Edward Kennedy himself decided the matter. Hating the idea of dragging the affair out further, he wanted to plead guilty and take whatever punishment Judge Boyle of the Edgartown District Court decided on then. A very detailed inquest, with five volumes of testimony, dragged through the fall and produced its verdict the following

January. Boyle, fatherly once he heard it all, noted that Kennedy had already "suffered beyond any sentence this court can impose," and sentenced him to two months in jail—suspended.

Once the initial shock wore off Kennedy also felt, deeply, the need to make some sort of public statement before the tabloids inflamed this thing beyond recovery. After securing the agreement of the newly returned Burke Marshall he called Dick Drayne the morning of Friday, the twenty-fifth of July, and told him to set up some kind of format within which he could make a short statement to the people of Massachusetts; both men were well aware that the substance, at least, of whatever he said would certainly be carried nationwide.

Kennedy himself determined the burden of the statement; the tone, with its taint of an abandoned grandeur, owed much of its phrasing to Theodore Sorensen. "Who am I to question the judgment of somebody my brother relied on so closely as he did on Sorensen?" one participant remembers Kennedy having consoled himself. Dave Burke contributed. The low-rent solicitation of support from Massachusetts voters—joked away afterward as the Jim Curley, or send-in-your-boxtops touch—was requested by Kennedy himself and crafted by Milton Gwirtzman.

Kennedy bombed. "Almost anything he could have said would have been better than what did happen," the outspoken Goodwin later remarked. "He did the worst thing he could have—he Nixonized the situation." I was myself at the Yachtsman, the press headquarters in Hyannis Port, when Kennedy's fifteen-minute address was aired live; a minute or two into the speech the mood of the room—especially among people who admired the Kennedys— curdled utterly. "Teddy needed some people, needed them in terms of numbers," Gerry Doherty said later; Kennedy's sense of the situation was not really there yet, his absolute political pitch, and touch after touch throughout the speech demonstrated that.

As a document, the statement covered the major facts adequately; the problem was tonal, the ever-ready rolling references to the Kennedy curse, to the greats of Massachusetts history, the suggestion of his "moral" guilt— as opposed (implicit nobility) to his legal guilt for leaving the accident, his "indefensible" conduct that night, the stentorian gobbledygook about courage, what one must do, what past courage cannot provide, the soul-searching about whether he would stay in public life—the whole thing played as a collage of phony-noble rags, a throat-catching tuba serenade of poseur rhetoric so obviously calculated to melt down any survivors among those suet-ankled ladies on whom the Kennedys could rely when all else failed.

As a device it worked all right; as a device it turned the stomachs of alert people all over the country. "He was like a baby, he was just like a baby, kicking his feet and holding his breath until people will say they've forgiven him," hectic little Sylvia Wright of *Life*, still crushed at breakfast the next morning, mourned again and again. Many years later, attempting to deal with the accident in his autobiography, Kennedy again attempted to turn the whole thing around, to join the posse: As for "Mary Jo Kopechne and me. We had no romantic relationship whatsoever. Yet I understood that my reputation was such that many people would seize on the circumstances to attack Mary Jo's character." Much of his maneuvering throughout the catastrophe was to protect *Mary Jo!*

Kennedy realized the extent of the damage only soon enough; Sorensen withdrew, still saddened and dismayed. He deleted most of the references to Ted Kennedy's bright promise from his new book, *The Kennedy Legacy*, already in bound galleys, and made it clear enough during several subsequent television interviews that, to his mind, this kid brother just . . . didn't . . . have it. Kennedy, on his side, had found something out about battening on leftover reputations. Several of the same associates who had felt betrayed for almost a year because Kennedy moved away from the Democratic nomination were retroactively incensed now that he should ever have entertained the notion. He himself emerged from the crisis saddened, shaken terribly at times but shorn of many obligations to the past, of an intimidated baby brother's obeisance before other men, other moods and eras. Lighter, identified much more fully to himself, he returned grimly to the Senate early in August, prepared to rebuild.

The present started.

CHAPTER X

Human Size

1. The Crawl Back

"Tell me, do you actually think," Ted Kennedy demanded searchingly of one friend just after the Senate reconvened in September, "do you think, if some of them, people, the colleagues invite me, and I go to speak in their campaigns will it be . . . will it be . . . is it so that they can fill the tables with people who really want to pay to come for a look at the, at the freak?"

"I didn't say anything," Kennedy's luncheon partner remembers having remarked, "but I thought—you always were a freak, don't you understand that? As a Kennedy, especially after Jack died. Now for the first time they're going to see you as a person, as one more legislator, good, bad, weak at times, able at times . . ."

Kennedy underwent the bends on surfacing in Washington. "Come here, right back where you belong," boomed the paternal Mansfield on spotting Ted in the Cloakroom, there, kind of waiting around for somebody, timid for once about pushing through that cloakroom door all by himself, needing to hear Mansfield's often-reiterated litany about how he was a "better senator than anybody else in the family"; Humphrey had already pleaded with this "remarkable public servant" not to step down; Senator Fred Harris, the Democratic National Chairman, rang with his conviction that Kennedy's decision to return and defend his seat in 1970 was "good for the country, for Massachusetts, for the Senate and the Democratic Party."

Generous intentions; dying falls; Kennedy himself knew better. "Can you imagine how it feels, walking down these corridors, and the tourists are staring at me? And I know what they're thinking," he confided, weeks after his return. "I know what they're thinking. Can you imagine that, if I had in fact done what they think, done what they think . . . that I could hurt the Senate, that I would be here?" No fornication; not drunk; Kennedy would swear to it, raise his right hand without realizing it like a witness in the box, over and over, to individuals who mattered. "It hurt him," one aide admitted. "These guys are all traders of power, legal prestige, moxie, and when it becomes obvious that you are no longer a presidential candidate you lose a lot. I don't think they liked him any less. They just needed him less."

Kennedy's was to be a historical seizure of political morning-mouth: no more the handground salts of power with which the Democratic Party's cooks had been fattening up this sleek boss persona. The seasonings of ambition to accompany the Filipino cigarillos and monogrammed shirts and cautiously stroked-through Cloakroom bargains that by now connoted Kennedy's personal style. Kennedy had not really understood who—or what—he was to all these people until the funk of his political extinction was afloat upon the air. After Chappaquiddick he was not nearly so appetizing; they were not nearly so interested.

The Senior Senator from Massachusetts Edward Kennedy who had returned to his front-row seat in the well of the Senate in September, sat through the pumped-up welcomes and decent Republican silences, was a phenomenon skeletonized. He appeared reduced literally, the heft of a grieving power-intoxicated year and a half metabolized off his bones those weeks of groping around the Cape, his eyes (all hooded brash appraisal less than a month before, now red-flagged, downcast, then sliding up to query with open anxiety the eyes of everybody he met) demanding: What are you thinking? What do you think of me now?

By mid-September, succumbing a little to the desperate hilarity of his staff as Burke and Drayne spun off their absurdist one-liners while quietly telephoning in the Boss's absence to try to find out which veterans' group still wanted him as a speaker, would Congressman X feel better if Senator Kennedy were to defer his motorcade appearance until after next November—Kennedy did not brighten so much as resign himself. "Remember when people used to ask me for my autograph?" he wondered to one aide as they left an elevator three weeks after his return. He laughed as much as he could about the little old lady who waddled up to him on the street in Boston and, pulling his sad head down to her own, whispered, "You know you can trust me, Teddy. I voted for your brother. Now, what really happened that night on Chappaquiddick Island?" He was absorbing it, day by day, even incorporating it into the necessary abrasive teasing he took to favorite staff members. When he soon fell, within a pollster's strongly admired category group, from 85 percent to 45 percent, he remarked to Wayne Owens, "Can you imagine how much trouble you'd be in if you'd caused that drop in my popularity?" *You'd* be in; Kennedy was characteristically working himself away from the thing, turning reality inside out.

It kept closing in. "The anxiety, the sadness—it comes on in waves still," Burke remarked in November. "His defenses keep breaking down. Work, that's the only real defense for him, he's working terribly hard again, too hard maybe. But it seems to help."

"I'm trying not to think about it," Kennedy said, straightforwardly, to one friend. "I really think I did all I could have, given the situation, my condition . . . all anybody else could have done." Anybody else, yes, but all a *Kennedy* could hold himself accountable for? He limited his liability now to human bankruptcies, common standards: The mania of a lifetime was passing. The best you can, the Ambassador had urged, and after that, the hell with it. "Whenever he was around here he was like . . . like a god. Now he's . . . he's just another man," one colleague snapped. Matt Storin, who interviewed Kennedy often for *The Boston Globe*, found him, once the immediate aftershock of Chappaquiddick had dissipated itself, a lot looser than before the incident. Between nightmare and breakdown, Fate had intervened.

Regulars on his staff, hoping not to watch too closely, were impressed and surprised. "He was the best I've ever seen him in cross-examination," Jim Flug said of his boss's performance during the September Administrative Practices and Procedures hearings into the Federal Trade Commission. One of Kennedy's witnesses, FTC Chairman Paul Dixon, presuming, evidently, that Kennedy had been too badly weakened to worry about, felt Kennedy's well-wrought and relentless questions pinning him into unwelcome corners throughout his testimony. Dixon, stunned, suggested that other subcommittee members were laughing at Kennedy's persistence. "Now, to whom are you referring?" Kennedy demanded, annoyed enough by then at a Dixon slur of Ralph Nader. "I don't see anybody here laughing. I don't think anybody here would do that. Is it all right if they smile? Can we smile? Would that just be OK?"

Reacting before the full Judiciary Committee to Supreme Court nominee Clement Haynsworth's claim that Robert Kennedy had once cleared him of all conflict of interest, Kennedy interrupted to deny that: The onetime attorney general had alleged only that Haynsworth had committed no criminal acts; furthermore, Kennedy added, Haynsworth was not a "contemporary man." That helped give character to a gathering hesitation; while reticent about signing either the Bayh or Hart opinions, Kennedy stayed very close to the strategy sessions among the liberals. Flug, who attended nearly all of them, helped feed the press whatever was needed to slow down the floor vote for which the conservatives pressed; then, once doubts about Haynsworth were so endemic that even the Republican leadership was publicly dubious, Kennedy helped force a quick vote before the administration and thinning publicity worked to palliate the objections. Haynsworth was rejected.

Strategists in the administration, after their exultation at the way the accident at Chappaquiddick appeared to have vitiated the morale of the Democrats in the Senate, were puzzled, startled. "You must be pleased," one Washington lawyer, long a friend of Ted's, opened upon encountering a Nixon staffer, "about the president's trip to Europe."

"Yeah," the staffer said, "but the Kennedy thing was all over the front pages."

"Can I tell you something in the strictest of confidence?" the lawyer said.

"Sure, what?"

"We planned it that way."

"For one split second he looked at me," the lawyer recollected. "Then he said, 'really?' and then he did a double-take about that and tried to laugh the whole idea off."

Better days; worse days; what Kennedy as politician regretted most as he picked up on pending legislation was the marked falloff in his immediate voltage, the extent to which the worldwide shock had scorched across that network of secondary-influence circuitry the Kennedys depended on. This Kennedy saw virtually from the day he got back. On August 5, gone down to Washington to deliver his anchorman's five-page floor speech against funding the Safeguard missile system—a summation the sympathetic Phil Hart called "a hallmark of his entire distinguished career in the Senate"—Kennedy sat unsmilingly at his leadership desk while the key liberal amendment failed 50–51. Nevertheless, the Pentagon's long and potentially disastrous "blank check" era was finally coming to its end. The following day the Senate pushed through a rigorous congressional "auditing" requirement for most subsequent strategic allocations. Still, as the culmination of half a year of entrenched liberal pick-and-shovel work, the fact that the Safeguard continued to be funded was a setback. Had Kennedy returned to operate at the top of his influence, free to squeeze, promise, telephone important constituents, counter-lobby throughout those last few critical hours, the final vote might very possibly have swung against the administration. Chappaquiddick's larger costs accumulated.

In public, at least, the senator continued to show as much of the old pugnacity as he could muster. Privately, his performance was becoming at times unpredictable, patchy, erratic. Amending when the chances came, as one did when Kennedy made sure the renewal of the student-loan program was written to push private banks to help the youngsters of non-customers. Fighting, unsuccessfully, such retrogressive steps as the Bennett Amendment, which rescinded federal supervision of the sale of much handgun ammunition—a measure the still-smarting Russell Long had contrived to stuff covertly into the routine extension of the Interest Equalization Tax Act—Kennedy kept hemstitching wherever he could.

Wary as ever about secondary consequences, Kennedy tacked onto the 1969 Federal Coal Mine Health and Safety Act a proviso prohibiting recriminations against miners who registered complaints to the authorities. After bearing down heavily on the government late in September by initiating hearings before Administrative Practices and Procedures on draft reform, Kennedy cornered a reluctant Mendel Rivers and persuaded him to conduct counterhearings of his own. The administration, now that the draft's longstanding abuses were even further forced into public attention, asked for and got a Congressional revision of the 1967 act to again allow a lottery.

By now Kennedy was well aware that a general lottery, if the academic and professional exemption pattern were not reformed along with it, was likely to leave the process more discriminatory than before. Kennedy recognized the administration's espoused goal of an all-professional force as a bid to buy up a mercenary army from among the poor and "insulate from the horrors of war middle- and upper-class Americans who might lead the protest against senseless foreign adventures." Very skeptical at this turn of the administration's "remedial" legislation, Kennedy accepted a November 5, 1969, face-off with Kingman Brewster, president of Yale, who had been informed that Kennedy was in a position to block the Nixon lottery proposals. Brewster, backed by a large solid constituency of middle-class young people, put enough of a public blast on Kennedy to force him to back off and let the Nixon proposal through. As his price for succumbing to Brewster and Stennis, Kennedy extracted a promise that the conservatives would help reform the exemption pattern in 1971.

Kennedy swallowed hard on the civil-liberties issue too. "The D.C. Crime Bill sneaked through here the other day," Flug admitted, with a resigned moue, in December. "It was our fault. They shouldn't be able to run stuff in like that under the noses of the liberals on the Committee, especially after we—the Boss and Hart together—had fought it in Committee and collaborated on the amendments that took care of the most obnoxious things in it, particularly in limiting those no-knock searches to felonies. That got accepted in part, and a third was included in the language of the report. But it wasn't enough, it was a ninety-eight-page bill and he wasn't . . . we weren't . . . He told me the next day, 'Gee, we really should have done something.'" That hottest place in hell reddened menacingly.

While losing a brilliantly argued floor assault on Senators Hruska and McClellan over the administration's proposals to limit a defendant's rights to demand evidence illegally procured against himself—during which Kennedy questioned which "conspirators," exactly, that legalistic cow-catcher of a Title X in the Organized Crime Bill was expected to clear out of the Justice Department's path—he pinpointed the issue exactly: "If we cannot enumerate the kinds of criminal activities that make up organized crime, then I do not think we further the cause of justice by enacting a statute so all-encompassing that we pick up groups we never intended to pick up." Nevertheless, Kennedy voted with the heavy majority in favor of the final legislation.

2. Chappaquiddick Redux

Edward Kennedy labored among the colleagues, frowned above his hands at his own uneven concentration as 1969 became 1970; over the same months those overstimulated townspeople of Edgartown now constituted themselves a sort of salt-water Yankee chorus. Each time the investigation opened up in headlines again, fresh interviews quoted in the conservative *New Bedford Standard Times* continued to blister Edward Kennedy's post-Chappaquiddick reputation. The misleading and indecisive management of the crisis during its first few hours and days had aroused a kind of intense international prurience. Kennedy's Saturday-morning police report had omitted Markham and Gargan's complicity; his television presentation had overloaded and emotionalized what was in fact a reasonably complete presentation of the events themselves, although by-passing the question of that missed turn entirely.

After that initial bewildered week, when nobody in significant authority in Massachusetts seemed to be prepared to investigate properly, the operatic District Attorney for the Southern District of Massachusetts, Edmund Dinis, strode onstage with that personal gusto that lacked only the background flutter of a velvet cape and on July 31, 1969, made known his determination that, in view of the continuing uncertainties, he had himself requested that the Massachusetts Superior Court authorize an investigation into the Kopechne death by means of the loose, non-accusatory form of an inquest. With this initial public letter to Massachusetts's Supreme Court Justice Joseph Tauro began half a year of investigation perilous to the names and careers of both Edward Kennedy and Edmund Dinis himself. On January 5, 1970—six months after the accident, when the publicity was finally dying down and Edward Kennedy was beginning to find his balance in the Senate again—the inquest in Edgartown rolled back into view like a bloated corpse.

To outsiders, Dinis's public letter seemed appropriate to his manner, one more bravado gesture. The DA was popular enough, very much a bachelor, practiced, voluble, mavericky at times with smooth hard-to-predict movements. Dinis' trim curly hair had begun to gray becomingly at forty-four. There was the large richly paneled office in the Dinis Building in New Bedford out of which he had openly conducted, throughout his public career, a most lucrative insurance and law practice, overseen by portraits of Churchill, Lincoln, FDR, James Michael Curley and (in reverential mezzotint) a blow-up of the house political prodigy, Edmund Dinis.

Dinis had done nicely enough for himself; he made his quota of blunders too. In 1962, unsurprisingly, Edmund Dinis had persisted in supporting Eddie McCormack's futile bid for the Democratic nomination; it was to Edward Kennedy's long memory of this that Dinis preferred to ascribe the popular senator's standoffishness toward him just before the state elections in 1968, after Dinis had again snagged the Democratic nomination for Congressman from the Tenth District and was running against the Republican Margaret Heckler. The fact was that the forever watchful senator had been—behind closed committee-room doors—warned away because an investigation in depth was pending into Dinis' alleged practice of soliciting insurance business beneath his Office of the District Attorney letterhead.

For all Dinis's personal flash, his impulse from the morning the Kennedy scandal broke had clearly been to hope that somebody either closer to or farther from the scene of the misfortune—the Edgartown Special Prosecutor Walter Steele, perhaps, or possibly a remote figure like Attorney General Quinn—might wring out of the witnesses what, precisely, had transpired that humid Chappaquiddick evening. Nobody else moved either. Meanwhile, *The New York Times* labeled Kennedy's own explanation a "partially irrelevant and totally unsatisfactory ex parte account," and his guilty plea that same day a cheap device that "forestalled any further questioning in court."

"The press kept giving the whole thing a more and more macabre turn," Dinis said to me subsequently. "Then we had those idiot professors like Packard at Stanford and Belli, a notorious legal scavenger, volunteering their opinions. The whole thing turned into a Roman Circus . . . ."

Whatever hope the Edgartown authorities themselves had of running down the facts had already been frustrated by the quiet if impeccably executed general evacuation the Kennedy aides had arranged; within hours the embalmed remains of Mary Jo Kopechne had departed the island, the Lawrence Cottage was picked over meticulously and so well scrubbed that later clue-seekers were reduced to scrounging through the island dump in hopes of locating empty whiskey bottles; every one of the cookout participants appeared to have been whisked away.

Everything seemed withheld, from a file copy of Kennedy's credit card calls that night and morning at the New England AT&T offices to agreement as to which lawyers were now empowered to speak for the absent senator. The daily announcement from besieged Hyannis Port remained predictable: "There is no decision. There is no statement." When Edgartown's assistant medical examiner Donald Mills, floundering among political upshots, had radio-telephoned the district attorney's office from Poucha Pondside to back himself up as to whether an autopsy was indicated here, Dinis himself unavailable. If Mills himself was satisfied that there had been no indication of foul play consequent to an on-the-spot examination of the dead girl, there was presumably no real need to enlarge suspicions by actually conducting an autopsy.

"This is just an automobile case," Dinis reportedly told Arena directly that morning. "You handle it." So that Dinis's first impulse had clearly been to ease the burden of the decision back onto the deputy coroner; Mills was himself to proclaim to whichever reporters would listen during the weeks following that the guiding judgment was the district attorney's. The word was already all over the Island that young Vineyard Haven pharmacist Leslie Leland, foreman of the then-sitting 1969–70 Grand Jury, was concerned increasingly with the delay in settling the dust Chappaquiddick had raised, and was drafting a letter to the Massachusetts Attorney General's office querying him as to the procedures involved in himself initiating a Grand Jury probe.

Bombarded, Edmund Dinis abruptly executed his overdue turnabout. On July 31 his office in New Bedford made available to the press a copy of the letter he had that day dispatched to Massachusetts Chief Justice Tauro in which he had proposed, respectfully, that Tauro order an inquest into the events of July 18–19 and that the proceedings be removed from Judge Boyle's chambers and convened before a judge of the Superior Court, and that this special inquiry take place as soon as possible. Tauro decided no. Cornered publicly, Dinis now sought and obtained a court order for an inquest to determine if the girl's death "may have resulted from the act of negligence of a person or persons other than the deceased."

The announcement of the impending inquest landed on the Kennedy camp like a monsoon. By ordering up an inquest, as opposed to a Grand Jury investigation, Dinis had originally hoped to avoid any "inference of criminality." This could be more quietly accomplished, Dinis had reasoned, away from the prejudices of rich, provincial Edgartown, still dominated by summering Bull Republicans who had disliked the sight of the willful, pushy Kennedy family for generations. Their forebears had thrown young Joe Junior and Jack into jail one sloppy evening in the thirties and more recently denied the vacationing Senator Edward access to the Yacht Club restaurant for lack of a necktie. Should this inquiry of his get away from him, become an inquisitorial stakeburning, Dinis' heavily Democratic South Shore constituency of Portuguese fishermen and Italian factory workers, well known as sympathetic to Edward Kennedy, was likely to turn on Dinis and pull him apart politically.

Judge James Boyle, involved in this clumsy situation whether he liked it or not, wasted no time whatsoever before overturning everything. Distinguished wattles stiffening with decision, the judge made it clear within a day or two that he had perused what material he was able to come upon as regards the nature of an inquest, thought about it, and was now prepared to propose his ground rules. "This is not a trial. There is no defendant. No person has been accused of a crime." Therefore, there was to be no right of cross-examination by a witness' lawyer, no right of objection, anything—technical information, rumor, malicious gossip—was admissible and likely to be explored at the judge's leisure.

To Kennedy's claque of advisers and lawyers, such procedure sounded fit for a tar-and-feathering party. Judge Boyle was rumored to be irked at the slippery way Kennedy, after pleading guilty in his court the Friday morning after the accident, seemed to have hedged his plea on television later in the day. The inquest form, little altered since it originated in twelfth-century England to let a coroner gather evidence prior to the moment the King's Justice arrived, was now an anachronistic proceeding altogether in Massachusetts.

So lawyers wrangled. What alarmed the Kennedy retainers most immediately was the threat of still another searing wave of unpredictable publicity. Frantic, Joan miscarried. Kennedy's defense attorneys Edward B. Hanify and his assistants pleaded with Judge Boyle to bar the press from the inquest sessions; Boyle, taking thought briefly, said no.

The advisers congratulated themselves quietly for having by-passed that horror for the moment. Not that they always helped a lot. On the *David Frost Show*, the strenuous Sorensen had blurted on about "how hard [it was] for me to suspend my own moral judgments," and pointedly recalled having been "insistent that whatever he [Kennedy] said to the public it not contain misstatements of fact," and characterized Kennedy's actions as "indefensible," and "so clear an indication of his action under pressure at this time in his life."

Kennedy personally had argued heatedly for letting the inquest take place and permitting whatever might happen to happen. Much of the fall was taken up with Dinis's request for an exhumation and autopsy. On October 20–21 there was convened a formal hearing in Pennsylvania. An assortment of experts on legal forensic medicine testified (quietly, disagreeing at times) about what sort of evidence an autopsy might yield, in agreement largely that the "cobweb" of blood on Mary Jo's collar and back suggested that she had lived some time before being asphyxiated and drowned in the overturned car. The Massachusetts police chemist John McHugh testified that routine subsequent tests of Mary Jo's slacks had showed no trace of the presence of seminal fluid, a matter of great interest to Kennedy's following in the tabloids.

Dinis himself testified that he had finally ordered an autopsy on July 20 at 10 AM, only to be told—incorrectly—that the "Kennedy people" had removed Mary Jo's embalmed remains a half-hour earlier. District Judge Boyle then scheduled the inquest itself: it was to be convened on January 5, closed to the press, in blizzard-ragged mid-winter Edgartown.

The inquest itself proved largely inconsequential. An assortment of townspeople appeared to answer questions about a recurrent rumor that an unauthorized airplane had landed and taken off from the Martha's Vineyard airport between 2 AM and 4 AM the night of the drowning. The diver, John Farrar, testified that Mary Jo had died of asphyxiation once the air bubble in Kennedy's Oldsmobile was used up. He could have saved her had he been summoned in time. Doctor Robert Watt, who had examined the senator shortly after the accident, described the "big, spongy" hematoma the X-ray had revealed lodged against Kennedy's brain.

After two days, having been strongly advised by Dinis that no further charges were indicated against Kennedy, Leslie Leland, the foreman of the Grand Jury, announced at ten-fifty on April 7 that "I have no presentments."

"Does the Grand Jury have any presentments?" the presiding Superior Court Judge Wilfred Paquet cracked out. "And stand up."

Leland arose very slowly on wobbly knees. "The Grand Jury has no presentments."

I caught up with Dinis pouring down a quiet beer inside the briny gallery of the ferryboat to the mainland. He was ebullient that the affair was finished, finally, as far as he was concerned. "The papers, everybody that said I was after Kennedy. They were reading my mind again. When somebody reads my mind it gets my ass."

When, after a dispute with the stenographers, the transcript of the inquest was finally released, Kennedy probably had second thoughts about holding the wide-open inquest Boyle originally demanded. After reviewing the testimony, the persistent old man had concluded in his summation that Kennedy had had no expectation of returning to Edgartown the night of July 18, that he had deliberately turned right on Dike Road, and, having admitted to twenty-miles-an-hour en route to the bridge, was ipso facto guilty of operating his motor vehicle "negligently," and so contributing to Mary Jo's death. "That was the hook Boyle intended to hang him by," Dinis later confided.

Charges had been left to Dinis; Dinis had decided privately not to press any. In fact, whenever counseling Leland's Grand Jury, Dinis tended to shrug the whole effort off, kept Boyle's clear suggestion that Kennedy had been driving recklessly to himself, shrugged off all further investigation efforts as "Mickey-Mouse," and—worldly sadness pervading his tone—advised the Grand Jury that he himself had "batted his head against this for a long time already," and what could anybody else do now? Edward B. Hanify's defense had proved impregnable.

There were a number of discrepancies which escaped notice. Kennedy had been without his driver's license that night, as an enterprising reporter who lucked into Kennedy's license in Virginia and submitted it to salinity tests established. The telephone company representative who testified at the inquest produced records that did not even include all the calls Kennedy and his aides admitted having charged to his credit card, let alone the hours on the telephone others were to allege he spent that miserable July night. One of Kennedy's aides through much of the seventies, Rick Burke, cites seventeen calls Kennedy placed from his room at the Shiretown, several to Helga Wagner.

Such skeptical reporters as Arthur Egan of the reactionary *Manchester Union Leader* bruited about the information that the ubiquitous Hanify was a director of the New England Telephone Company and so might very well have been helpful in masking the telephone records. Hanify himself had, in a 1960 lawsuit, defended Judge Paquet when he changed his mind and ameliorated his own sentence on a pair of bookies.

Perhaps Dinis's career in politics had already been mangled enough; in November of 1970, campaigning again for district attorney, he lost by 15,000 votes. "She died and I got defeated," New Bedford's boldest orator mused later. "The Press! They take you for a Nantucket Sleighride. You know what that is. Once they put the harpoon into you you've had it. You go where it makes you go, even to the bottom. And that is where I went. You're perhaps a little wiser"—even Dinis's self-criticisms are grandiose—"but much much sadder."

3. Strategizing Defense

Scorched among the colleagues much of the time, scorched around the Massachusetts court system for nearly a year, scorched fiercely and repeatedly in the press—as winter and spring came Kennedy could tell a lot about what and who he was now from where the blisters were forming. It may have been too, as Joey Gargan had long expected, that when the Ambassador gave up and died, finally something essential in Edward Kennedy was free to proceed, at last, into the public domain. Again, as with Jack and Bobby, Edward Kennedy had been the messenger delegated to break the bad news. The despairing Ambassador appeared to shrink into his wheelchair, jaw slumping, his mummified face emptied of expression: This last, most reckless and unpromising among the sons of Joseph P. Kennedy had managed to liquidate his own political prospects. From then on, 81, the dispirited founding father would refuse nourishment. "The core of his extended family kept watch at his bedside in the final hours," Kennedy himself later wrote. ". . . my mother, Ann Gargan, Pat, Eunice and Sargent Shriver, Jean and Steve Smith, Jackie, Ethel, Joan, and myself," reportedly taking shifts in sleeping bags on the floor or under blankets in a rocking chair. "I wondered whether I had shortened my father's life from the shock I had visited on him . . . The pain of that burden was almost unbearable."

But personality is as ineluctable as longing; Kennedy seemed to be hardening—one saw it happen virtually week by week now—into his mature identity, his adult alignment. Indications appeared every day. Kennedy began to depart, more and more, from that sweetly tutored niceness he nurtured around the colleagues; newspeople began to look at each other when the senator came back in public to questions in a language bereft of those empty, circuitous phrasings that sounded more like transliterations out of industrial Latin than spoken American.

"Wouldn't it be possible to produce a Democratic Agnew?" I remember hearing one eager college girl, disturbed by the widely heralded impact of the slasher vice president, ask Kennedy at a university forum the spring of 1970.

"I certainly hope not," Kennedy replied, downing *that*. Poked, inevitably, about the dim, remote, unlikely chance that he might yet conceivably upset Muskie and take the Democratic nomination, Kennedy observed—prescient, there seemed no danger at the time at all: "These days I just wish I could get Bobby Byrd to stop putting so much heat on my ass." Kennedy grinned; then, reddening, "I accept your nomination." Then, cornered by a question, he waltzed professionally around it by telling a fine story, full of the sound effects he loves to include in his stories, of the day a lively looking little girl with a $50--a-day heroin habit appeared before the Senate's Juvenile Delinquency Subcommittee and confessed—"and the cameras are going whirr whirr whirr—" that she supported her addiction by selling herself.

"'What, you sell yourself!'" her aging senatorial inquisitor asked. "'When did you do it last?'"

"'Oh, last night.'"

"'And you take the money and buy *drugs* with it!'"

"Whirr whirr whirr whirr. 'Senator,' the girl says, 'you shouldn't knock something you haven't tried.' The questioning then passed to me. I don't think I've ever said 'No questions' so quickly."

The hitherto private Edward Kennedy was testing its first public offering. So much protective baby fat had disappeared so suddenly. It was as if Kennedy's fully awakened appetite for raw power was at him more consumingly day by day now, while—paradoxically, deteriorating poll result by slighted amendment, unreturned telephone call by committee membership denied— he felt his political clout ebbing too fast to reorganize his life around time and seniority.

Like Bobby his last few years, Ted already has a sense that time might be running out. He *must* become the agent of change! Who else will tear out of America its most diseased organs? The abashedness is gone that provoked Kennedy in an early 1969 private meeting with his genial but distant Massachusetts Republican colleague Ed Brooke: so many mumbled indirections and hints as to what he was actually after that Brooke had to send a staffer to a Kennedy staff member afterward to determine—and acquiesce

good-humoredly to—whatever it was that his senior Commonwealth colleague actually wanted. It turned out to be the reinstatement of five of his
longstanding twenty-one postmaster appointments.

So Kennedy had become blunter. While careful enough about protecting
the legislative reserves he identified as his—refugees, health, science policy,
his Special Committee on the Aging, the draft, minorities—Kennedy was
roving wider, moving into position to dominate areas in which he had earlier
been, at best, interested.

He injected himself and the Subcommittee into the volatile issue of air
safety through a series of hearings dealing with the effectiveness of the Federal Aeronautics Administration. After an autumn of exchanges with experts
and drop-in visits to clinics and hospitals, Kennedy had made new headlines
with his televised December 19, 1969, Lowell Lecture at Boston University
proposing that "consumers of health," everybody, stage a "national effort—a
revolution—that will stimulate action by Congress and produce a more equi-
table health system." Still limping a little five years after so many agonizing
months in the Stryker frame, Edward Kennedy was confronting what would
quickly become his signature issue. Dying, in July of 2009 he would refer
to health care as "the cause of my life," which "goes to the heart of my belief
in a just society." Before long Kennedy would turn himself into the world's
greatest expert on the subject.

This would have to mean, Kennedy made clear that winter, a vast
government-coordinated and -administered health-insurance program,
measures that in combination would constitute something close to what the
medical lobby, shivering, referred to as "socialized medicine." HEW recoiled;
Elliot Richardson, already anchoring the Nixon administration as the Secretary of Health, Education and Welfare, counterproposed a patchwork that
Kennedy was to dismiss as more of the familiar "poorhouse" medicine the
Republicans had been coming up with since Harry Truman first had the
effrontery to speak of universal coverage. Kennedy also suggested a massive
federal effort to overcome cancer; the administration backed away from the
idea, then re-presented it as its own.

The Democratic Majority Leader had left to Kennedy the heavy lifting
involved in linking tax reform to the surtax extension. With the Kopechne
drowning having immobilized his Whip for the moment, Mansfield found that
liberal control of the issue was starting to wobble. But during the weeks just
before the Christmas recess Kennedy seemed to have recovered enough trac-
tion to close in on tax revision again, this time with a late flurry of amendments

proposing a progressive tax on undervalued charitable donations and a base levy of up to fifteen percent on anybody's tax-free declaration.

Such reforms jeopardized those largely unnoticed relief valves in the tax code on which the genteel rich had come to depend to ease their obligations to the IRS. Having proposed to rip some of the juiciest of tax breaks out of institutional America, Kennedy was starting to estrange establishment dignitaries who up until that point had tended to go along with his progressive initiatives, municipal leaders and the heads of educational institutions especially. By then Russell Long and the fiscal conservatives on his Finance Committee were yowling tirelessly.

Kennedy then endangered the digestion of the entrenched further with his amendment to allow individuals a $25 income-tax credit for political contributions, a device calculated to free legislators of their obligations to lobbyists and self-interested political philanthropists. As if Russell Long and his oil-lobby boosters were not unhappy enough with Kennedy's impudent little nips by that time, in a deadly bland floor speech on December 8, 1969, Kennedy inserted into the *Congressional Record* an "illustrative listing" of those corporations for whom one or another sort of selective tax relief had been quietly provided within the hermetic Finance Committee itself. Kennedy went to elaborate pains—his cuteness here was widely and not altogether favorably remarked—to single out the Western Massachusetts Electric Company, which had been permitted to alter its accounting procedures to reduce its tax liability.

Then Kennedy ran down the rest of a list notably heavy-laden with defense contractors and, especially, oil producing and pipeline companies. By that time Russell Long was hopping all over the chamber. Kennedy's popularity among subscribers to *The Oil and Gas Journal* dropped further when, after pestering Secretary of the Interior Hickel regularly, he took advantage of what Jim Flug called his "wild-card jurisdiction" as Chairman of Administrative Practices and Procedures to gadfly White House Counselor Shultz, director of the Office of Management and Budget, and George Lincoln of the Office of Emergency Preparedness into liberalizing import tariffs out of fear of what could prove to be a most unsettling round of Senate hearings on the subject of industry-wide monopolistic practices.

That election autumn of 1970, with gas prices rising steeply in New England, the Kennedy office initiated a series of telephone calls that disclosed that there was plenty of gas still stored around the region if only one knew how to talk to the local executives; gas prices promptly fell. This was the sort of situation the Federal Power Commission had been advised to look into; to make sure it looked far enough Kennedy proposed that Congress underwrite a Public Counsel Corporation, to represent the public itself in all deliberations of the various Federal regulatory agencies.

While few of Kennedy's turn-of-the-year proposals got far for the moment, his knack for drawing publicity and his technique of pecking away at situations the interests felt were none of the public's business were starting to look serious. This fellow wasn't merely a liberal, or even a radical at heart. He was a populist. He threatened the system. Even these initiatory snaps of Kennedy's had a way finally of eliciting attention, of depositing the very guts of an issue all over the national pavement.

As winter deepened, Kennedy's knack for taking over and winning outright when it came to the more sizable issues was apparent again, his gifts for legislative kick-the-can. When promising legislation made it into committee, the senator appeared to be no more than a barely interested bystander, strolling somewhere in the vicinity of a seemingly shapeless tangle of proposals and testimony by experts and inexplicit platform promises and bills going noplace. Then, abruptly, while Kennedy still took some care to hide whatever fierce gleam had begun to enlighten those canted predator eyes, he had a way of ambling a step or so closer to have a look and—without much of a sign to anybody—pulling back one polished black Oxford to deliver a kick of such dumbfounding sheer impact to the entire snarled issue that proponents and experts, colleagues and lobbyists and presidential aides and judges of the federal court were immediately to be seen running in every direction at once, hollering, exhorting one another, fuming, like fire ants behind a tractor. The issue now became Kennedy's.

Procuring eighteen-year-olds the vote by statute, like Kennedy's 1965 overnight raid on the regional poll tax, owed much to Kennedy's timing while playing against the vicissitudes of the legislative calendar and his close to uncanny guesswork about how much of an extra burden the surrounding legislation would tolerate. Matters in the Senate, by early in the spring of 1970, had so worked out that hearings were ongoing over what would normally seem two unrelated batches of lawmaking. Birch Bayh's subcommittee considering a constitutional amendment to enfranchise eighteen-year-olds had convened; at the same time Sam Ervin and his Subcommittee on Constitutional Rights were looking into the extension of the expiring 1965 Voting Rights Act. Broadly speaking, sentiment inside the Nixon administration was known to be unsympathetic to both. Youngsters, the political dopesters there concluded, were much more likely to support the more libertarian Democrats. While floundering early, the quietly espoused Southern Strategy—the conservative administration's not overly discreet wink to its peckerwood constituency—articulated a discreet effort to nullify legislation that had already created a sizable black electorate to threaten the Confederacy.

Aware of Kennedy's persistent interest in franchise enlargement, Carey Parker, Dun Gifford's replacement as legislative assistant, had started in, virtually on arrival, working up a ghost brief for Kennedy to demonstrate that, since 1966, the Supreme Court had been showing itself to be much more latitudinarian as regards all general attempts to regulate and standardize regional franchise prerequisites. As the Court stood, Parker was convinced, it would go along with a simple act of Congress that lowered the voting age in all elections to eighteen.

Parker had quite recently served as a clerk to Justice Potter Stewart and remained sensitive to the mind of the post-Warren court; Kennedy listened. Why not—Kennedy's thinking immediately sought out a political dynamic— why not attempt to fasten the eighteen-year-old-vote provision onto the Voting Rights Extension Bill and throw the Nixon administration on the defensive? Each measure was certain to be heavily backpressured by its black or its youthful constituency; the entire package, Kennedy hoped, would bulk too large in the headlines to dispatch with a furtive veto.

It was a bold enough idea; Kennedy followed it in boldly. His broadly distributed memorandum lit up the debate in flashes of scholarship and controversy. Falling back, as ever, on authoritative support, Kennedy drew moderate professors Archibald Cox and Paul Freund into the fight by demonstrating that such a method seemed constitutional to them; Parker produced a signed supporting opinion in a law-review article from one, a few sentences in a commencement speech by the other. The language of the amendment Kennedy now proposed was lifted directly from Bobby's 1965 rider that enfranchised New York's Puerto Ricans; for Puerto Ricans Kennedy substituted eighteen-to-twenty-one-year-old citizens.

Real trouble was anticipated on the House of Representatives side; Manny Celler, Chairman of the Judiciary Committee, reportedly disliked the idea. Such longtime ideological Kennedy allies as Clarence Mitchell and Joe Rauh of the Civil-Rights Lobby, a lot more anxious at this point to see the Voting Rights Act extended than voting privileges extended to kids, were skeptical enough to sap liberal enthusiasm in hearings. Reliable civil-rights proponents such as Phil Hart and Hugh Scott, concerned at the way the House had already shown signs of wanting to weaken its version of the voting-rights extension, were apprehensive that Kennedy's unexpected add-ons would sink the legislation completely. It looked like the poll-tax embroilment all over again.

The colleague who first took in what such an electorate shift would mean to American politics was Majority Leader Mansfield; he and Warren Magnuson of Washington, where a similar effort was under way within the state legislature, got together in early March, intercepted the Voting Rights Bill before it could disappear into Jim Eastland's hip pocket, and—while Kennedy was in Ireland to deliver the Edmund Burke lecture—tacked on the eighteen-year-old-vote rider. When Kennedy returned he discovered that his two-headed monster had already been passed in the Senate; with powers like Mansfield and Magnuson pushing, the bill was given precedence in the legislative calendar and zipped through the Upper Body by the middle of the month.

The salient danger now was that the Mansfield-Magnuson-Kennedy amendment would get stripped off in Celler's Judiciary Committee or compromised out of existence in a late House-Senate Conference. Professorial envoys from the White House were very very earnest around the House of Representatives as they argued to convince key people that so radical a measure so unprepared for was likely to bolix up voting procedures for at least the next two elections while the legislation ground through the agonies of judicial review; Kennedy solicited opposing letters from thirty legal scholars.

Reawakening old Jawn McCormack, Kennedy persuaded him to draw fellow veteran Manny Celler aside and reflect upon the way the times themselves had changed. It was a young person's world more and more, and a true leader needed to know how to update his position gracefully . . . To back up the Speaker's avuncular persuasions, the Kennedy staff was scrambling all over the Hill to organize a bipartisan cadre of pro-amendment Congressmen, nine Republicans and seven junior Democrats within the House Judiciary Committee alone. A telling memorandum went around the House too; isolated, cajoled by his Speaker and threatened by a broad-scale revolt within his own committee, bombarded by press attention suddenly, Manny Celler caved in. The civil-rights lobby, recognizing that the entire package was now going to be voted up or down, shifted its viewpoint and helped.

The House voted the Senate bill through unmolested on June 17. Nixon, with an unhappy aside to the effect that the youth provision was likely to prove unconstitutional, signed the bill into law five days later.

There was every expectation of a quick court test: Anticipating that, Kennedy suggested on the Senate floor and before the Democratic Policy

Committee that the Senate itself retain a lawyer to defend the amendment. When Republicans Scott and Griffin indicated that they felt such a move would reflect insultingly on the competence of the Justice Department, Kennedy as an individual accepted the offer of the Youth Franchise Coalition, an amalgam of youth groups, to appear as an amicus curiae, a friend of the court, to plead their case before the D.C. district judges. He appeared in mid-September; the decision went 3–0 to Kennedy's presentation, which formed the heart of the brief the Supreme Court soon heard, after which it agreed to the legitimacy of the Mansfield-Kennedy amendment. After that, the amendment to extend the franchise to eighteen-year-olds in state and local elections flowed through the needed thirty-eight state legislatures in less than a year; the expense and trouble of keeping double voter regulation lists hurried it on its way. A new—politically, a revolutionary—bloc of millions of young voters now filtered onto American voting rolls.

4. Carswell

One element that made the strategy behind the Voting Rights Act extension outrageous around the Nixon camp was the way it seemed to be basket-woven into the opposition to the administration's selection for that still-available Supreme Court seat, the Gentleman Judge from Florida, George Harrold Carswell. Getting involved in stopping Carswell seemed, so far as Kennedy could tell at first, quite likely to inflame the Republicans around Judiciary, annoy the president, and leave Kennedy himself muddied up consequent to one more unavoidable liberal defeat. G. Harrold Carswell was never going to mature into another Frankfurter—that even his boosters admitted—but he came over on initial perusal as smart enough to have avoided conflict-of-interest mix-ups and blatant misrepresentations of his own career. The Tallahassee jurist appeared to be a light-footed small-town bar-association-style table-hopper with a photogenic family, reserved enough to get along nicely among his peers on the District Bench and—since 1968—the Fifth Circuit Court of Appeals. Carswell's neckties were neat-figured; he looked a man in the eye.

G. Harrold Carswell on the bench was also—the civil-rights mavens around Washington had tagged him, belatedly, about the time he made it onto the Fifth Circuit—choleric and backward-looking. Carswell had been a judge since 1953; he had an extraordinarily high reversal rate, and civil-rights lawyers complained that he was intemperate and abusive to the extent of having given a couple of them the runaround when they requested their habeas corpus rights. The problem was that—presupposing the way newspapers play information—all this was likely to get very little inflammatory publicity. What the liberals needed was to come upon dramatizable evidence of malfeasance, some germ-ridden sliver of scandal which, protected until its moment, might yet be squeezed into sight beneath the television cameras.

The strategy that recommended itself, even before senatorial opposition started to coalesce, was somehow to slow the proceedings both in Judiciary and on the floor for long enough to give the civil-rights researchers and lawyers their opportunity to dig. As legislative affairs timed in that winter, dragging back on the Carswell nomination played beautifully into the larger intentions of Kennedy and Mansfield; by refusing to permit debate on Carswell until the voting-rights/youth enfranchisement legislation could be whisked across the floor of the chamber, Carswell became a hostage to guarantee the voting-rights extension.

Between January 27 and February 3, 1970, when the full Judiciary Committee held hearings on the Carswell nomination, the opposition among the Committee liberals, although evident enough, appeared token. Carswell had himself disavowed a flamingly segregationist 1948 speech; he seemed to explain away his involvement in 1956 in the reincorporation of what had been a Jacksonville public golf course as a private segregated club.

Kennedy, during the early questioning, concentrated on Carswell's background, his associations in private practice, and—this had been at the center of the Haynsworth turndown—the possibility of his having heard cases involving ex-clients once he was on the bench. Kennedy then requested that Carswell provide the committee a list of cases in which he had sat that involved former clients; the Republican Whip, Robert Griffin, broke in to call that a "ridiculous request," a "fishing expedition." Kennedy, angered but containing it, indicated that he had something very exact in mind by referring to Carswell's involvement in *Bonwanno v. Seaboard Airline Railroad Company.*

If Kennedy was angry—and stayed angry after the hearing, holding on to that quiet brawler undertone people who knew him well saw was more and more out in the open lately—it may have been because Griffin *was* onto him. Kennedy had been fishing. The administration people had let it be bruited around town that they blamed Kennedy for having dragged out the Haynsworth approval; Kennedy wanted no more Justice Department scalphunters after him than necessary with reelection coming up. He was feeling heat from civil-rights lobbyists skeptical after Kennedy had voted for what they regarded as repressive organized crime legislation and now seemed to be backing away from a confrontation over the reactionary Carswell.

The insurgent Chief Counsel of Kennedy's "wild card" Subcommittee on Administrative Practices and Procedures, Jimmy Flug, kept after his boss. Within one year of Kennedy's Chairmanship of Administrative Practices, he and Flug had turned that frantic clutter of offices into one of the primary junction boxes of the institutional reform that was electrifying the Capitol. "No fair, I will not let you bug J. Edgar Hoover's office," Kennedy had inscribed a picture to Flug when he set him up as his Chief Counsel in 1969; for all his shoulder-shrugging Jewish warmth, Flug, who served during his early twenties as Ramsey Clark's Executive Assistant, was no doubt capable of proposing that.

Flug's telephones were going all day with calls from his following among newspapermen, Nader lawyers, civil-rights groups, other senators' aides, out-of-office politicians, secretaries looking for work . . . Jim was jumpy already at the quality of the Nixon appointments to federal benches Low and High; Carswell, he concluded early, was likely to turn into an irreversible disaster.

Flug had been working on Kennedy before Carswell appeared. Marian Wright Edelman, the brilliant young black lawyer who was the director of the Washington Research Project, had already mobilized her troupe of incensed Florida attorneys, assistants Richard Seymour and Larry Sellers, and a television reporter, Ed Roeder, to help piece Carswell's dossier together. Roeder had uncovered the 1948 speech; Seymour found out about the Jacksonville Country Club endorsement and showed copies of the papers to the ADA's Joe Rauh and to Jimmy Flug; after that Flug was in daily touch with the Tallahassee people.

By the time of the Judiciary hearings, Flug thought he had a strong lead stemming from the fact that Carswell was a close personal friend of Edward Ball's, a duPont relative who was a tremendous financial power in Florida. Ball had been a client of Carswell's law firm and an antitrust hearing involving duPont proceeded before Carswell's court. Flug's jerry-built investigative team and Eastland's Judiciary Committee staffers proceeded to play a wonderful little round of keep-away with the eight huge crates of papers relating to the case that were discovered in the Federal Records Center in Georgia; when Flug finally reacquired the documents he recruited a bunch of George Washington University Law School volunteers to try to discover the sort of improper judicial favoritism for which Kennedy had ostensibly been "fishing" on January 27.

By then, virtually whether Kennedy liked it or not, Flug wasn't doing anything except conspiring to stop Carswell. Once Birch Bayh and Ed Brooke took over the formal management of the opposition, Flug's job got simpler;

he could feed through whatever he knew via liberal conduits on Judiciary—Bayh, Tydings, Kennedy and Hart. Flug produced a detailed strategy memo underlining Carswell's weaknesses—even Florida's ex-Governor LeRoy Collins was put off privately—that started "I smell blood."

Flug watched the breaks appear. Thurmond blundered and so helped delay the process of getting the nomination voted through Judiciary. Flug proposed a Monday morning meeting of the Senate aides to discuss Carswell and thirty arrived. On February 20 the four key aides, led by Flug, put together the Judiciary Committee Minority Report; the thing was overdone, full of unprovable allegations and "purple prose, mostly mine," Flug admits; all four Judiciary liberals were angry, and Kennedy himself was forced to spend an hour on the phone going over the draft line by line. Kennedy's anti-Carswell floor speech was among the toughest.

By the time the Voting Rights Act passed, on March 13, the prestigious Judge Tuttle of the Fifth Circuit Court had rescinded his support of Carswell; Roman Hruska was so badly shaken that he wandered off the Senate floor and told a reporter, "There are a lot of mediocre judges and people and lawyers" who were "entitled to a little representation . . ." As Carswell backers reeled, Flug encouraged a television reporter to check with the eminent jurist Minor Wisdom, another Fifth Circuit colleague, who admitted, "I stand with Tuttle"; Flug promoted full coverage.

Inevitably, somebody wondered how Kennedy, after backing a judge like Morrissey for the bench, dared to oppose Carswell. Kennedy—well aware since Morrissey of the quicksand that threatened a weak man's passage—agreed cheerily; yes, he had himself intended to bring that up: Remember how he had withdrawn the nomination when heavy opposition surfaced? Then—late but usable, that germy little sliver the anti-Carswell people had been hoping for all along—on March 26 *The Washington Post* ran a front-page story in which it alleged that on January 26, the night before he presented his vague struggling-to-remember-the-whole-dim-episode performance as the Judiciary Committee hearings opened, Carswell had recounted the Jacksonville golf course incident in some detail to Charles Horsky and Norman Ramsey of the American Bar Association.

Flug immediately got Kennedy to request documentation from Horsky—who, under Flug's guidance, drafted a memo indicating that Ramsey had shown photostats of the relevant documentation to Carswell. By April 6, several days after Bayh had foxed the White House's Bryce Harlow and Richard Kleindienst with a deft little parliamentary screen pass involving the recommittal of Carswell's nomination to Judiciary, the final floor vote occurred: Carswell got stomped, 51–45. Kennedy looked pleased enough; the normally imperturbable Flug, standing in the back of the chamber, was reportedly "laughing and weeping at the same time."

That winter of 1970 Kennedy had sustained himself. "I'm not interested in the box score," he protested to Bill Honan in May. "I think there are times when certain issues have to be raised and confronted. Like a lot of basic civil-liberties questions. I'm going to continue to raise these issues because I believe I'm fulfilling a responsibility to the Senate, my own beliefs, and to my state by doing so. There are those who may say you've lost some impact, but in the long run if you continue to raise the issues you believe in your colleagues will think more of you."

In private conversation Kennedy appeared to feel the institutional death-grips loosening. Other times he seemed to suffer from a sort of projected historical despair; he identified the clichéd violence of youngsters in the streets, with their "same old procedures, writing on the same old cardboards with detachable handles," with the violence on which "I am an authority . . . . All it brings is pain and suffering. And there is no place for that in our society." Would the traumas of his life "just go on and on and on?" Kennedy wondered to an aide; would he and his world move beyond this somehow?

Kennedy's most profound views, whatever he had been able to intellectualize so far, appeared in his largely overlooked speech of March 3, 1970, at Trinity College, Dublin. "I worked weeks on that speech," he complained privately, "and all the papers could find to write about was the way some Irish Maoists banged their placards against the windshield of the car—" Drafted in collaboration with David Burke, Kennedy's address drew its dramatic vitality from a characterization of the eighteenth-century English political thinker Edmund Burke, a statesman who, as Kennedy perceived him, reflected uncannily one contemporary American senator's apprehension of himself.

"At first glance," he began, "the public career of Edmund Burke seems laced with inconsistencies. He was dedicated to the established order and institutions of his time, yet was sympathetic to the demands and complaints of the colonies that formed my nation. He was devoted to the wisdom of the past, yet he was a leader in reforming the basic structures of government. He was an intensely pragmatic realist who heeded the facts of political life when proposing policies, yet he was dominated by powerful moral values and the hopes which flow from such values.

"Still Edmund Burke was not an inconsistent man. Rather he reflected the inconsistency of society itself. What appeared to be Burke's conflicts of views and temperament were, in reality, the product of his unwavering human skepticism, the great gift of your experience to Western political thought, and to my own country in particular.

"Edmund Burke was a complex man and he was a moderate man. His moderation did not consist in automatically taking the middle position between left and right, radical and reactionary, one extreme and the other. He was a moderate, not because he lacked passion or conviction, but because he combined an acute sense of human limitation with a deep reverence for the moral values essential to human liberation. To him a lifetime of thought and action consumed by the slow labor of improving the human condition was more valuable than all the rhetoric of destruction and impossible visions. He was not in the market of human and political affairs for the windfall or the notoriety that history soon buries under its chronicle of real achievements."

Kennedy then moved out into unexpected depths of historical judgment. "Over the last few years of decline in the civil-rights momentum the voice of the moderate man was not clear. Though many such men remained, many others left the field. The attention of some was diverted by war. In the heat of the struggle some were afraid to speak out against the excesses of the extremes, and many leaders upon whom we depended, both black and white, were lost to violence. Whatever the cause, the tide has shifted in America away from progress and equity."

Late in the speech, Kennedy again warned, unfashionably, of a counter-danger the networks picked up and used to epitomize the speech:

"The young have their own harsh rhetoric, they often consider the com-promise position to be a 'sell-out,' and their ability to be disruptive and take to the street—no longer an ability in question—is now becoming a mechani-cal act. The result is less and less effectiveness. And as one who shares many of their hopes and aspirations for the future, I feel constrained to warn that history is a harsh judge of those so caught up with revolution that they forget reformation."

Kennedy's concluding vision approached the apocalyptic: "So I fear that the present reactions—the words 'law and order,' the trials and jailings, the public statements and name-calling by men in high places—are only the touch of a giant. Aimless and frivolous acts will turn the millions of citi-zens, whose fears spring from shared anxieties, frustrations and discontents, against progress and reform. Some argue that intolerance and violence are justified because modern society is violent and intolerant. Even if that were true, the argument is purest demagoguery. The objective of the discontented should not be revenge, but change. The only question for the serious man is whether these acts are effective tools of liberating change. They are not effective. They are not moral. And thus the use of violent acts is self-indulgent and, worse, the unwitting instrument of those who seek to impose oppression from the right."

Prophetic, Kennedy's voice echoes back now from beyond events.

5. Reelection

"Each day in the nation's capital is lived for the sole purpose of getting to the next," Kennedy intoned on June 12, 1970, acknowledging renomination by his Massachusetts party in convention. "Gone is the vision we knew so well! Gone is faith in America." Election summer gloominess; such a portliness of rhetoric that it takes the torrential perspiration bulging out of Kennedy's peaky temples to certify his outrage, lend a little sincerity——.

The perspiration is genuine; Kennedy is already moving, earlier even than ever before and very very powerfully into the lacerating process of getting himself reelected in Massachusetts. The mentality of Richard Nixon overhangs the nation. The horror and disillusionment Kennedy can feel every day with barely a year having passed since the global humiliation of Chappaquiddick means that he will have to subject himself to an excrutiating campaign, with important Republican money available to challenge his seat.

And along with the anticipated sixth-year grind Kennedy now needs to sate . . . renewed hungers, an appetite for justification become uncontrollable again. And because Kennedy feels this the regulars too are carried into this nightmare year-long effort, following where they can and dropping off when they have to throughout those terrible battering early-morning to early-morning days he puts everybody through, week after week after week

Massachusetts has always been love/hate for the Kennedys: It shows whenever the professionals inside the state Democratic Party attempt a nice clean zinger nobody will find out about later. Ever since 1967, when the legislature one-sidedly upended the proposal to relocate the MTA subway-car barns out in Dorchester so the Kennedy library would have a proper site near Harvard, Kennedy has alternately fidgeted and exploded among the retainers about that. When, shortly after Chappaquiddick, Massachusetts House Speaker Barkley spoke up publicly about a vote of confidence for Ted, early soundings led to the idea's being quietly dropped.

Knives wait. Little by little Kennedy's earlier ideological involvement in Massachusetts politics, his dutiful attendance at Democratic Advisory Council meetings, his willingness to absorb the political damages involved in backing up Mayor Kevin White against Louise Day Hicks, espousing busing, lending a little support and a few dollars to one or another of the Democrats involved in the party's ritual saber-dance preceding the fratricidal gubernatorial primaries—whatever hopes Kennedy had had for such an involvement are pretty well exhausted now: By 1970 Kennedy is roundabout when it comes to favors beyond an exhortation at a fund-raising drink-'em-up, and Kennedy expects few special favors for himself.

So that throughout 1970 Kennedy is back in Massachusetts early and often, ragged, starving emotionally, stripped of illusions, very experienced, and showing a compulsiveness about everything up to and including the 1 AM headquarters sweep-out. On October 26, a typical campaigning day as the roadshow matured, a couple of cars led by Kennedy and his new midnight Chevrolet, the redoubtable blank-looking Crimmins at the wheel—it was too early for Crimmins even to scowl at six in the morning—swung by the press pickup point on the Tremont Street side of the Parker House. By 1970 I had done this enough to anticipate how keyed-up all of them were going to be: six o'clock promptly, kicking off a day chockablock with twenty-three speeches, inspections, layovers, high-school rallies, fund-raising receptions, projects, Portuguese-American Club addresses, not to mention . . . Et cetera, and everything so tight that five minutes lost at the start of things could mean a day throughout which the normal pressures were carried out like shock waves and compressed by mid-morning into panic. Kennedy's motherly Mongol-eyed press aide Dick Drayne, his modish hyacinth ringlets too greasy to gunk clean this late in the reelection stretch, was already too high-strung even to attempt one of his soggier wisecracks . . .

October 26 was typical of any day back in the Massachusetts precincts; by seven-fifteen Kennedy in his dirty raincoat and ripple-sole shoes was out among 'em in the Somerville city yards, attempting early-morning charm with a handful of Greater Boston garbagemen, lolling around the big orange compounding trucks: "Just wanted to say a word. Everybody ready for a speech? No speech [grin-grin]. Whenever I get to see some aah . . . working people I remember the day my primary opponent in 1962 McCormack kept telling people I hadn't worked a day in my life, and then this big fellow comes up and asks . . . haven't worked a day in your life? . . . haven't missed a thing . . . just wanted you to know we're interested in all the help you can give us . . ." And after that the rest interspersed with *nice to see yas* and *thanks-a-lot* while making one's way briskly beyond the warm vegetative stink of garbage and the cold stench of motor oil in crumbling cement . . .

After which it's back to the cars, *Quick! In!* and on to the Somerville Police Station.

Kennedy reviews the boys in blue, their traditional embossed brass buttons lustrous, and mentions the amendment he had within the last week been able to slip into the Law Enforcement Assistance Act to provide for federally paid police life insurance; then on to the firehouse. That summer Kennedy had remarked in a speech—showing up his new relish for delivering a knucklebuster now and then wherever it lands—that the party should not allow its "love affair with campus youth" to "build a barrier between the party and the young hard hats"; Kennedy is obviously not going to encourage any such barriers on *his* home territory.

By 8:05 the candidate was marching himself back and forth along the ramp of the Sullivan Square subway station, at-large handshaking, the limp still discernible as he listed into the Sun Spot Diner to grab hands still crumby with English muffins and tell startled middle-aged file clerks how nice it was to see them again; there was the inevitable kiddo secretary with the inevitable red crinkle-finished wet-vinyl raincoat cherishing the freshly shaken hand she pledged to her girlfriend never to wash again . . .

By that time Kennedy was halfway back to the cars to rush over to the stage of the Father Matignon High School to ask the squirming teenies, his ponderous jocularity intact, "Did you beat Austin Prep?" before telling them all about his work with the Youth Coalition groups on the eighteen-year-old voting legislation. Unlike Jack with his bladed stabbing gestures, Kennedy carved his meaning out in little flapping scooping motions of his left hand—"This nation has a sense of com*mit*ment"—took his invariable poll on Vietnam policy and marijuana legislation, solicited adolescent views.

Maybe if they legalize it the kids wunt want to take it know what I mean? a kid says. *Since it wunt be any fun.*

But what if research shows it is no more dangerous than alcohol? Kennedy wonders, bringing up the Organized Crime Bill study; however he tries, Kennedy can't help patronizing them, springboarding: "Dave has his finger on the number-one problem in the state—we've got the highest unemployment rate since 1958, the highest interest rate since the Civil War . . ."

Kennedy knows he must get on with it; the nuns in the outside seats are looking sharper-and sharper-eyed; after ten minutes a lot of the girls looked menstrual-tense and many of the boys were hunched up and half-wrapped around their distracted mind-wandering hard-ons . . .

The stops tick off: a Project for the Aged—"My mother's out campaigning;

she's too young to retire," along with the "Who remembers my grandfather the Mayor?" routines, attempted against the embarrassed slosh of dentures sticky and uncomfortable whenever sugar from the crullers or candy-dits on butter cookies wash in behind and need to be sucked at. Then the big crusher-team factory at Somerville High, with tough looks coming back as Kennedy announces that he thinks "the young people today are the most hopeful and interested generation in the history of our country," more questions above a buzz of student displeasure—*She's probably a radical, I never wooda went up there*—and on and out and dropping in on the local weekly newspaper's offices, the VFW post—push health care, a drop-by to visit the Somerville fire chief in the hospital, then a wash-up and a quick lunch at the home of the Democratic ex-mayor, superrich crabmeat salad, oily enough to lubricate the bearings of even the most hyperthyroid political day, while Kennedy laughs with his hostess over the way his kids used to come see Dad in the hospital to ride around on the Stryker frame——.

The day goes on, an address to local businessmen—little resonance, as expected—harping on the abuses of the Big Oil Interests, another high school, the North Cambridge Catholic High School, back into the car——.

Afternoon: the reaches of the telephone company, a day-care center: "Do you like bunnies?" Kennedy asks a child fake-napping on her pallet. "*I like bunnies.*" To the black leadership Kennedy details the movement in Congress away from permitting real citizen participation, the effort to kill the Murphy Amendment, to rewrite an appropriations bill on the floor; his listeners, choked with slogans, looked glazed at the detail. Whenever something substantial comes into the exchanges Kennedy's insipid learned routines evaporate, the private energy and outrage spill over: "The FBI's hands are tied? I don't know where they're tied—they've got extensive wiretapping and they're wiretapping us to death. Typical of this administration's attitude. Cut back on people. Cut back on OEO, cut back on the Milk Program. Everybody pays so much attention to Spiro Agnew, but this is where it's at. And we're going to give 'em HELL." Kennedy all but needed to restrain a whoop.

The afternoon wore on; a Neighborhood House—lots of Afros, sassy bread-and-roses mothers, noise. Before the amassed research and consulting PhDs of Arthur D. Little, Inc., Kennedy pressed his successful defense of the National Science Foundation appropriation; under expert questioning he impressed experts in their own fields by his computer-like facility for differentiating and bringing back detail as regarded housing appropriations at every legislative stage, mismanagement of the economy, crime statistics, the administration's abandonment of the Narcotics Rehabilitation Act. He defended his unpopular refusal to cosponsor or vote for the Equal Rights Amendment, the purposes of which he felt could be better served by Title VII of the 1964 Civil Rights Act and the dangers of which—industrial exploitation of women—he felt outweighed the merits.

As often throughout this campaign, even during his town-meeting format, during which he roamed groups with a microphone, addressing each question brought up head-on, even during his unanticipated face-off debate when he encountered his Republican opponent, Si Spaulding, at Bridgewater—Kennedy's newly aggressive mood, the impatience along with the wealth of facts startled people. Before each stop he glanced through a staff memo on the concerns he would probably have to answer; once there, he left that in the car and fielded and developed answers in every direction.

Leaving Arthur D. Little, Kennedy was still up, stimulated. "Jesus, Jack," Kennedy said as Crimmins sideswiped a baffle en route back to the turnpike, "thaaat's what we needed. I just lost anybody I convinced." But he was exhilarated, boyish. That day Paul Samuelson had just received the Nobel Prize; the economist's response over the car radio, during which he suggested that Congress should get the Medal of Honor for having thwarted the administration's disastrous expenditure cuts, provoked Kennedy: "See, see, he must have been listening to what I just said!" When a Beechcraft full of American generals was downed in southern Russia Kennedy wondered, "What the hell those generals were doing around there in the first place."

Rich political blood was raising Kennedy's color again; after a stopover at his Charles River Square house during which Kennedy took the necessary tub and emerged, his face red and his hair beaver-sleek to eat beans and steak while wrangling people on the telephone, he left again to exhort the faithful over smoked clams at a restaurant rally, aroused the Cambridge Portuguese-American Club, stopped by a Greek Orthodox church reception and plugged away for liberal Congressmen and the hospitalized Mayor White at a huge Political Club screamfest.

Rushing through a toll station to hold to schedule, Crimmins, hanging on grimly, bumped the Chevrolet over an eighteen-inch separator and down again; Kennedy's molars nearly flattened his tongue. "Jesus, Jack," he opened up, "here we've just begun to relax, get the day behind us a little, and now this——."

Paul Kirk, Kennedy's young political assistant and currently a key Massachusetts operative, helped out a little: "You just give the kid a steak——."

"Yeah, Jack," Kennedy decided, "you drive better hungry."

An hour after that, on toward midnight, Kennedy was back at the Tremont

Street campaign quarters, a warren of cheap plywood and egg-crate fluorescent lights, wandering around in shirtsleeves making sure for himself the operation was solid.

"Jaack! Jaack!" Kennedy bellowed over the dividers the moment his driver disappeared for a breather. There was a pause. "Yah?"

"Why can't you sound a little friendlier?"

That day was another in a series planned throughout 1970 to reintroduce the state to their put-upon senior senator, to demonstrate to millions of voters that he was still utterly theirs. To underscore his absolute commitment to continue in public service, his insistence that he was already beyond the fallout from Chappaquiddick, Kennedy made a point of dragging along that fellow-symbol of his abiding humiliation, his only-human cousin Joey Gargan.

I had watched that exercise in redemption played out one unforgettable spring afternoon a few months earlier, marching with the Kennedys in the 1970 Saint Patrick's Day Parade, an event that Ted Kennedy skipped the March after Bobby was shot. A foot parader is one long beautiful slow-moving target, after all, but Ted Kennedy had insisted on marching, proof of the expiation process.

A very nervous Joe Gargan, marching through the street mobs next to his cousin, had overseen the route and the safety procedures. One imperative was always to keep the principal moving; as the parade surged and choked against the embankments of windy Southie (while children with complexions like root-cellar potatoes hung out half-broken three-decker windows or slithered in to grab Joan Kennedy, set-faced beneath her green velvet hair bow, and try to stick their IT'S A GREAT DAY FOR THE IRISH buttons into her thigh through her coat), just short of the reviewing stand for the Gold Star Mothers and the Benjamin Dean School and DiMaggio Brothers Cleaners and Fahey Drugs—everything stopped. The cops outriding the rear on their snarling bikes were squeezed back by the surging mob; the brass band rounded a brick corner someplace ahead and flatted with distance. A teenager with a blazer across the back of which was sewn, in script, ST. KEVIN'S EMERALD GEMS seemed to have fought through to Ted and Joan too late for Gargan to spin him around; a heavy woman in a cloth coat appeared to collar the boy: Ted Kennedy noticed her camera.

"Would you like a picture with me?" Kennedy yelled to the badly flustered mother. The heavy woman nodded, stunned for a second with self-conscious pleasure.

"We're behind schedule, Ted, if you want to know the truth," Gargan gasped out.

"My cousin would be glad to take our picture," Kennedy insisted; Gargan's eyes, uncontrollably, canvassed the surrounding high broken tenement windows for rifle barrels, looked a little wild behind his glasses. He accepted the camera, fumbled a moment to locate the viewfinder——.

"Get back, Joe, back," the senator insisted. "Get both of us." A tot in a slouch hat with a huge bouquet of green carnations broke away from a man in an Erin-go-bragh boater and squirmed between two Secret Service men's legs and hurtled into Joan.

"Get us quick, Joe, quick, get us quickly," Ted Kennedy urged his cousin. "Come on now, quick, Joe, get an extra pop, make sure something comes out——." The mass of the crowd behind toppled the Kennedy party forward; Gargan's long black overcoated arm with the camera in its hand trailed backwards and fed the camera beyond the nonplussed woman's grasp; the elbow of Gargan's opposite arm was already levering an old cheek mostly purpled with whiskey-blooms out and around the path of his cousin to bob, lost forever, into the afterflow of bodies. Ted Kennedy and Joan Kennedy were back in step with the drumbeats again.

The neighborhood was largely black; the authorities let the school out immediately as Kennedy finished; the street overflowed with kids who jam it, climb up on the hood of the big Chevrolet sedan into which the Kennedys have now taken refuge for a few minutes before they rejoin the parade and bang the windshield and reach in the driver's-side window.

Jack Crimmins, upset, worried about the schedule, found Kennedy's arm hanging there in front of his eyes to touch some fingertips. "Hey," Crimmins blows up at Kennedy, "watch it, Mac! I'm drivin'."

Crimmins almost drove into somebody's thigh; Kennedy blasted Crimmins; the Jack and Teddy show was under way. A teenager grabbed the roof's drain edge and hung on; the Chevrolet dragged him a few feet before he skipped off.

"Ha ha ha, the kid's got some courage," Kennedy said.

"Hey, kid," Crimmins yelled out, "for Chrissake go home." He turned. "That's the worst thing in the world, lettin' them outa school. Should keep them after." A long-haired lad, bumper left, stood unbudgeable: Drive over me! "Look at this guy on your left," Crimmins erupted. "The world's nutty. I'll get nutty too."

"You know, Jack," Kennedy explained sweetly; too sweetly. "You're doing this to try and get kids interested in the system. They go home, they tell their mother and dad—."

"They'll be tellin' a judge, one of 'em gets hurt."

The approach the Kennedy political mechanics had decided on the year before had been to push Kennedy out there, let him show himself everywhere, stamp out the notion that he had been "hiding"; after some occasional early foot-shuffling Kennedy had found that he could do that, in fact needed to do that. By mid-campaign, typically, after a day of making the rounds according to the demands of Barbara Souliotis's airless schedule around the state, Kennedy was usually back to close up the Tremont Street headquarters himself.

"Nobody really knows what is going on at this point except Teddy Kennedy," Burke divulged by the fall of 1970. I dropped by myself one night close to the end; nothing out of the ordinary had been happening recently: A couple of bomb threats growled in over the telephone; a swarm of hip kids had attempted to occupy the headquarters and start the Revolution in behalf of Freedom until Dave Burke, a little embarrassed at his own sophistry, prevailed by assuring them that they were curtailing his liberty, go home to bed; the starry-eyed but inexperienced Congressional candidate Father Drinan had hemmed and hawed on television about whether he was for Ted Kennedy, until a Kennedy organizer terrorized him by suggesting that Kennedy's feelings were hurt and, worse, neither funds nor endorsement were going to be forthcoming until Drinan's enthusiasm returned . . .

Seasoned Kennedy organizers—Gerry Doherty and Ted's giddy behemoth of a Boston office manager, Jim King, along with Eddie Martin—were pitching. The Washington staff philosophers hid upstairs, there was the usual determined voter registration drive. One element was conspicuous by its absence: The comptroller functions, long overseen by Park Agency operatives, "the hired guns" dropping in with very pointed suggestions, passed effectively to Kennedy Headquarters in Boston . . .

Steve Smith himself, near apoplexy with the Goldberg gubernatorial effort, tried to get up every ten days to review the spending. The approximately $700,000 needed this time had all been raised at loyalist fund raisers, outside family coffers completely, unique perhaps in Kennedy political history. There was no mushroom of financial scandal this time as there had been in 1962, when both a *Boston Globe* reporter and a Boston University political scientist, Murray Levin, suggested that the Kennedys had circumvented new Massachusetts fund-disclosure laws by funneling expenditures through the Dowd advertising agency. A commendable straightforwardness was possible this time because Kennedy's Republican opponent, Josiah Spaulding, a nicely bred politely spoken near-Brahmin, differed with Kennedy on relatively little. Spaulding had attracted very little national Republican money once it was clear to the White House that such favored "killer candidates" as the Volpe Administration's ex-commissioner John McCarthy and cartoonist Al Capp would not be involved.

Edward Kennedy was reelected, finally, by a well-shook-down 58 percent majority, a half-million-voter bulge. He absorbed more "blanks" than usual on the Democratic ticket; he delivered his acceptance speech wet-combed under Parker House ballroom lights. Joan and several of the sisters and Ethel and Lem Billings were there to celebrate, hear Kennedy josh Joe Kennedy III for recruiting so many volunteers, all girls. The family group repaired to a suite in the hotel. There Kennedy watched the Western returns coming in. Kennedy was buoyant; when Roman Hruska nearly lost he got excited. "I just wrote my story," a privileged newsman ribbed Kennedy a little. "I said this was the beginning of your campaign for president in 1972." "This god-damned ----," Kennedy, very expansive now, expostulated. "Always trying to shove me out in front where I can get shot."

"Okay, I'll go out and look for somebody else."

"Welllll——." Kennedy's look was sidelong. "Check with me before you do *that*."

6. Ambush

Ambition wakes up sullen. "Read this!" *The Washington Star*'s mordant Jimmy Doyle stage-whispered to me one afternoon while both of us dawdled in the Senate's rococo press lobby. He pushed over the *Congressional Record* for the previous afternoon, the first Monday back that began the 91st Congress's frustrating eulogy-clogged rump session. Deliberations in the chamber closed jarringly.

"Mr. BYRD of West Virginia: Mr. President, if there be no further business to come before the Senate——."

Kennedy cut him off: "Mr. President, if there be no further business to come before the Senate, I move, in accordance with the previous order, and, pursuant to Senate Resolution 481, as a further mark of respect for General Charles de Gaulle, former President of France, that the Senate now adjourn."

Members involuntarily looked up, bristled: Those two are at it again. Something is intended that goes a long way beyond an admonitory little hip-check in there to remind the overeager Secretary to the Democratic Conference

that the Assistant Majority Leader has now returned to his appropriate station; that plonk about de Gaulle was heavy-laden. There may have been a
sharpened brusqueness to the way Kennedy brought it off this time, but
Kennedy's open pique with Byrd started early enough: "Sometimes I can't
even make a routine motion," the ambitious West Virginian had recently
complained to a friend. "This has been going on for two years. I just have to
sit there and take it."

Robert Carlyle Byrd's leadership drives constitute some danger to Kennedy, of course, but the more sensitive colleagues long ago picked up on
Kennedy's well-reciprocated deeper distaste for the ways of the ultraserious
dry-mouthed ulcer-prone busybody who turned what was once no more than
an honorific—Party Secretary—into a still petty but incredibly pervasive
instrumentality. Perhaps the mature Byrd bears rather a disquieting simi-
larity to something about the aspiring Edward M. Kennedy himself; perhaps
Kennedy finds Byrd especially offputting in his own more luxuriant early
middle age; however it is, a kind of species hatred has broken out here that
neither man can handle very well.

Where Byrd is concerned Kennedy is as full of snappish exasperation as
a puppy mastiff who sniffs a daring little mole moving around his territory
somewhere, in and out, watching, nibbling whenever he is away. In Bobby
Byrd's opinion, of course, it is the newcomer Kennedy who is the interloper;
he feels quite outspokenly—and few around the Upper Body would quarrel
with this—that, having been Secretary to the Conference during the last half
of the Whipdom of the desultory Long, as well as the first two years of the
absentee Kennedy's, "I've been doing the work all along. The only difference
is, I would have the title."

So that a poisonous little closet conflict of imperatives has long been in
the making behind closed Caucus Room doors; with both men convincingly
reelected in November there had developed a sort of circling and coun-
tercircling for position as the 91st Congress shuffled through its expiring
weeks.

For Bobby Byrd, however artfully he contrived to keep Kennedy himself
at loose nervous ends by ducking reporters, indicating whenever he got the
chance that he had "no plans insofar as the organization of the Senate is concerned," that if he did not seek the Whip position he very definitely intended
to run for Party Secretary again—however confusing Byrd's incessant tactical scurrying looked, there was a sort of deadly Snopesian directness about
Byrd's leadership hopes that Edward Kennedy himself now obviously lacked:
Byrd longed to improve himself.

Kennedy—this was especially clear to anybody who knew him well enough to fathom his ambiguities that season—Kennedy was not that convinced anymore. "I'll be there while the other fellows are running around the country," he noted as 1970 closed. There was a hollowness. His manifold responsibilities as Whip too often amounted to housekeeping, clerical chores, and cut too deeply into the time he needed for important issues. Sometimes responsibilities got neglected. Byrd, darting in and out all day, *was* concerning himself with a lot of the details.

"I've thought about retirement, sure," Kennedy himself shocked Bill Honan of *The New York Times* by conceding in May. "And I've made up my mind that if my effectiveness is not there, if my effectiveness has been compromised, I won't stay in public life." Axioms were openly crumbling; corollaries drifted. "It's still a shitty job," concluded the deceptively somnolent aide who administered the Assistant Majority Leader's offices for Teddy, Wayne Owens. "It's prevented him from getting out in front on the gut issues. This bothered him, and he's been going at it maybe two-thirds of the way. He went after the post because he thought it would be a way to do things, rather than sit and trade favors. He's just not a Hubert H. Humphrey, who used the authority to go ask individual senators to vote with him on particular issues. At one point last summer he thought about giving it up, but then he realized he didn't want to lose his place in the Steering and Policy Committees."

Restive anyhow, Kennedy had returned to the Senate after the months of campaigning. The exhilaration of control, absolute single-minded mastery of his own campaign, bedrock footing every minute—by November it had changed him enough, simplified him enough—so that the last lingering recurrent ache of the Chappaquiddick accident appeared to have burned out of his bones finally. The Senate as he reaccustomed himself to its ticklish little protocols and its prevailing air of grandiose self-approval seemed to have altered too. The maudlin-eyed preoccupied mumbling figure of a year before had disappeared into this surprising new self-assurance that—some of the senior people disliked seeing this happen—was more than a little reminiscent of the intermittent hubris of Bobby's last years.

The months of campaigning appeared to have aroused Ted Kennedy's temperament unhealthily: He seemed to want to bring back to Washington his habit throughout the campaign of flaring out at "The Interests," and in embarrassing detail. "You have that contract to build destroyers going to Litton Industries in Mississippi despite the fact that one of the principal stockholders, _____, was one of the fund raisers . . ." "I'm not interested in spending your money on supersonic airplanes to speed the Jet Set to Paris in half the time"—a lot of exaggerated rhetoric was finding its way into Kennedy's attitude and voting patterns.

Already piqued with Kennedy for the bites he had taken out of the oil lobby, and conferring the vote on eighteen-year-old punks, and torpedoing Carswell, conservative Southern Democrats continued to question his suitability for the leadership. More moderate Democrats were starting to bristle at his implausible lauding of the "courage" of the Nixon administration—which *was* generating remedial legislation—for proposing the family assistance program and sticking to it, a theme he carried over to the Senate floor, rising to lambast his Republican colleagues for not supporting their own administration. Since Chappaquiddick a lot of the kid-brother deference the colleagues had so appreciated seemed to have disappeared in Kennedy.

Haymakers landed everywhere. When the president authorized a raiding party into the North Vietnamese POW camps Kennedy was quick to "admire their courage," but "deplore the policy that permitted them to go." He dispatched John Nolan, a Bobby confidant and onetime Justice Department lawyer, to Paris to receive a list of American prisoners from the Hanoi regime; Senator Fulbright, at least, had alerted the State Department before releasing his. In Europe to attend a NATO conference the second week of November, Kennedy had abraded the sensitivities of the London tabloid *The People* by allegedly dancing until five in the morning with the former King Umberto's daughter Maria Pia.

It all looked enough like the pattern of calculated shadow-government diplomacy Bob Kennedy had fallen into when the presidential bug bit him to spark rumors that the White House again regarded Ted as the likely 1972 Democratic candidate. That Jim Flug was quietly advising key liberals and labor leaders not to commit any open support for Muskie, that the unexpected number of Kennedy faithful the 1970 elections had swept into office—Pat Lucey, John Gilligan, John Tunney, Milton Schaap—were to provide key cadre to assure a 1972 Kennedy-coalition nomination for Teddy.

Like a risen Bobby, Edward Kennedy's rhetoric was assuming an energy, even a heedlessness at times, that suggested that the audience he sought was waiting well beyond the floor and committee rooms of the Senate itself: colleagues felt he was exploiting them to secure a forum. When Nixon took advantage of the Christmas recess to pocket veto the $225 million medical education bill, Kennedy labeled the procedure itself unconstitutional, a "promiscuous use of the pocket veto" that constituted a threat to the prerogatives of Congress, and himself threatened an amendment to clear the infraction up. He hailed the December 21 Supreme Court acceptance of the law permitting eighteen-year-olds to vote in federal elections as a decision that "solidly affirms" the authority of Congress to "enforce the majestic guarantees of the Fourteenth Amendment" and immediately put in a joint resolution proposal to secure the disallowed right of the young to vote in state and local contests.

No opportunity looked too far-fetched; when Kennedy unexpectedly pushed onto the floor the controversial 1970 Consumer Protection Act, Minority Whip Griffin protested barely in time; Majority Leader Mansfield found himself apologizing for his deputy's dubious judgment: ". . . interested Senators were not consulted. It should not have been done."

This was not the first time since Edward Kennedy showed signs of getting his breath back after Chappaquiddick that his sinewy Majority Leader sucked thoughtfully on the stem of his pipe and wondered privately what in hell he might expect now. Conversely, Kennedy assistants were clearly peeved at the way the Majority Leader, without a word in advance to his Assistant, had "grabbed" Kennedy's youth-franchise idea—language, constitutional briefing background, legislative tactics, everything—while Kennedy was in Ireland and shoved it through the Senate to his own credit; Mansfield, for his part, was known to feel that by adding Kennedy's name to the bill and acknowledging his contribution Ted got what recognition he deserved.

A decent cordiality survived that, of course. Kennedy remained publicly delighted to give the Mansfield Lecture at the University of Montana. Nobody's umbrage was chillier at word of House Minority Leader Gerald Ford's put-down of Mansfield for ineffectuality during the post-session. But there was a hesitancy. In a private letter shortly before the session ended Mansfield, while noting that Kennedy was, now that he had finally finished campaigning, "applying himself very diligently to his duties on the floor," characterized his deputy as regarded style and effectiveness as "in between both his brothers," although certainly "more of a Senate man than both." Meanwhile, Kennedy seemed to want to extend the drifting rump session of the Senate indefinitely. With that deceptively mild asperity of his, Mansfield observed that it looked as if the meetings were going to go on until January 3.

With the caucus voting for the Whip post coming up in January, one of the Kennedy staffers argued that "Much as he [Mansfield] liked people to do stooge work, his sense of substance would have precluded putting Bobby Byrd in position to become Majority Leader someday." Another agreed, though remarking Mansfield's obvious relish at the way he could "plug Byrd in with the wave of a hand." But what was clearly happening was that Mansfield was not letting it be known that he would be personally aggrieved should his most recent deputy get dumped.

This freed lesser men all up and down the aisles to vote in caucus whichever way they themselves preferred. Such a senatorial dreadnought as Washington's Warren Magnuson, a major sponsor of Kennedy in 1968, who had expected to support him again, was dismayed that Kennedy had proved so implacable and worked with such persistence in the rump session against the continued funding of the SST, with all that meant to Seattle; "Scoop" Jackson was equally sorrowful.

"It's subtle," Jim Flug remarked afterward. "How much does Boeing have to say to Lockheed?" Stuart Symington, a powerful Kennedy friend in 1968, refused angrily to say how he had voted during the January 21 caucus, as did another of the longstanding Kennedy backers, Abraham Ribicoff. Foreign Affairs Chairman Fulbright would not comment either. Kennedy's 1969 accession to the leadership was about to be replayed—backward. The liberal powers—primary, then secondary—were independently closing their hands.

While the Areopagi frowned stonily, the more accessible younger colleagues were slipping out their unattributed reservations about Kennedy. Referring to Mansfield as a "very inflexible, impersonal" leader uninterested in tipping off a fellow in the ranks when one of his bills was near the top of the calendar, one liberal confessed that he had grown dependent on Bobby Byrd to keep track of things like that in time to alert him. "He's built it on courtesy. That's why he's popular. I call Bob Byrd for everything and everybody else does too. The only reason I would vote for Kennedy is his liberal leanings." Afterward, a liberal who claimed he himself voted for Kennedy was blunter: "Bob Byrd would do even the smallest chores for senators. Ted Kennedy didn't do a damn thing for anybody." A switcher carried it the rest of the way. "[Kennedy] really is aloof and superior. Kennedy was absent a lot and when he was here he didn't see himself as helping or acting as an errand boy. Bobby Byrd was proud to be an errand boy."

Rumor had it that not all of the errands the morose little West Virginia Secretary to the Democratic Conference was willing to run remained as unexceptionable as pairing two opposed candidates sneaked off for the weekend, or remembering to drop one of the committee chairman an anniversary note. A lot of what hasn't yet been strip-mined out of West Virginia remains coal country, and much of what coal is left is owned and mined by the major petroleum interests. Both before and after the leadership elections, the Washington lobbyist for the American Petroleum Institute, Perry Woofter, Byrd's

own onetime administrative assistant, was all over the Senate office buildings, first soliciting, then thanking, sympathetic members.

The unforgiving Russell Long was seen high, happy, and bubbling glad
predictions at a Washington party the night of January 20. From his seat
on the key Appropriations Committee, Bobby Byrd had long been one to
understand a fellow senator's needs and help meet them; himself secure
in West Virginia—he was reelected in 1970, after an abbreviated campaign
punctuated with his preacherly mountaineering harangues, by an inarguable
77 percent—Byrd dropped jaws all around the Democratic Conference by
cutting up the whole of his $18,000 allotment from the Senatorial Campaign
Committee among more endangered colleagues like Frank Moss, Quentin
Burdick, Vance Hartke, and Gale McGee, all wavering, all out there somewhere to his political left. "Ideologically, Bobby is in the Stone Age," one of
his supporting colleagues admitted happily; a reconstituted Ku Klux Klan
Kleagle, while more or less a Great Society fellow traveler during the Johnson years, Byrd had of late been reliable on the reactionary side of virtually
every legislative watershed—for Haynsworth and Carswell, supporting ABM,
against key civil-rights legislation; as Chairman of the D.C. Appropriations
Subcommittee he regularly beetled his brow and scourged welfare mothers
around Washington for "immorality." "I can't believe"—one of the most
perceptive aides around the Hill had drawled to me in November—"that a
predominantly liberal Democratic caucus . . . is going to elect as its Whip . . .
a guy who is generally regarded as probably the worst racist in the Senate." This was apparently a faulty reading even that early: By early January
1971, a lopsided majority of the Senate's predominantly liberal Democrats
were clearly prepared to favor Byrd as their second leader over Edward M.
Kennedy.

A year and a half since Chappaquiddick, and so many of the liberal colleagues seemed to be just standing there all of a sudden, the colossal wave
of fellow-feeling lost, and so much damage—Yarborough gone, Gore gone,
Harris on the run—and what, really, had any of them to show for supporting this offspring of Camelot? And why? This survivor among the Kennedys
having now himself altered so bewilderingly, the smooth-featured long-jawed
ex-jock who sir'ed hell out of everybody except maybe the pages around the
Chamber is . . . displaced. Barely recognizable as the heavyset prematurely
middle-aged Senior Senator from Massachusetts with the impenetrable
expression, the dark mane razor-cut to the nape now, like a good Italian
hairdresser's, and everything about his face now corrupted into such complicated rich French curves . . .

While part of Kennedy's mind obviously preferred to regard any challenge by the likes of that bustling onetime garbage picker and night-school graduate Robert Carlyle Byrd as something he himself shouldn't care to dignify, another corner of Kennedy's great political sensitivity kept jerking out alarms. He confronted the danger spottily, stumblingly: For all the hillbilly stomper exclamations and the doggerel and the fulsomeness to the others and the overused shoeshine rag Byrd allegedly kept tucked in an inside pocket, the Secretary not only knew how to count but habitually remained a lap ahead.

Whenever floor procedure was involved, Kennedy sensed the dangers. In November he startled the leadership of both parties by requesting of the top Republicans that, since Senate protocol required that their people direct procedural inquiries to the highest ranking Democratic leader on the floor, they restrain any questions unless Mansfield or he himself were available. Minority Leader Hugh Scott of Pennsylvania was seen to elevate his eyebrows at so clumsy and unprecedented a suggestion from one for whose judgment he had acquired some regard. Scott presented Kennedy his answer with rounded mouth: No.

Colleagues exchange amused looks at the way Byrd kept circling the chamber, a little scrawny fellow with George-Raft-dapper hair and a pursy mouth, jealous whenever Mansfield was in attendance in his front leadership bench, waiting for Mansfield to leave so he could drop into it to help his most esteemed Leader out. Soon Kennedy was counter-circling. Off the floor, Robert Byrd was forever phoning to hold a plane for a delayed colleague, then dictating a little note thanking the man for the privilege of serving him, then slipping into that bench next to the overloaded Mansfield to reschedule the time of a vote for a colleague too long at lunch with an important constituent.

As the youngest of nine, Kennedy was more than familiar with the ins and outs of kowtowing. One minute Byrd was tweaking Kennedy with an on-the-run press interview during which he claimed that he wouldn't run against Kennedy unless he had the votes. But he has reason to believe he has the votes should he so choose . . . Above ground, Kennedy tried to bluff and retaliate in his own way, allowing the story to be planted that, should Byrd contest with him and lose, he would undoubtedly supplant Byrd from his beloved sinecure as Secretary to the Democratic Conference. Perhaps with Ernest Hollings.

As the caucus vote grew closer, Kennedy was very hesitant to bring down a lot of artillary from outside. Nobody had forgotten the sharp secondary problems among the colleagues in 1969 after his belated arm-twisting threatened

to cost the oil boys their tax breaks and so stirred up heavy political contributors and normally left-wing influentials, especially in the West. Seats
were lost. He remained very hesitant to try to find out how effective his onetime loyalists in academia and Big Labor and the marginally liberal Rocky
Mountain money-raisers might prove to be unless he absolutely had to.

Furthermore, checking around, Kennedy early concluded—and stuck with
his conclusion—that his return as Whip was not that endangered. "It didn't
look as if it was going to be any kind of a problem in November, and it didn't
look like a problem the day of the vote," Dave Burke still insists. "No matter
what the papers said. He had done the same things he had done in '69. We
knew he had three or four votes more than enough to win. I walked the halls
with him. He was just as tough, wise, cynical . . . He started a month or so
early with the follow-up calls——." Still, Dick Drayne remembers, "Going
into it he had misgivings. There were a few people he counted on who were
not returning our calls, a bad sign." With liberal stalwarts like Yarborough
and Gore purged by expertly inserted oil money and Agnew bombast, their
replacements were harder to assess. Adlai Stevenson III kept his own counsel; Bentsen of Texas was reportedly quite conservative; Lawton Chiles of
Florida, unpromisingly, claimed the Whip's job should go to a technician,
not an ideological man.

This resonated to the common growl that Kennedy was trying to install
himself up as the liberal's philosopher-in-chief: When you wanted your pants
pressed, philosophy would not tell you where the crease should go. Fred Harris was still getting shoved by the oil interests; Marvin Watson—who had
held onto his five-star hatchet-man rank by moving across the Power Structure from the Johnson White House to become Senior Sandbagger for the
oil and gas lobby—was quite definite about his feeling that if Harris intended
to stay in the Senate he had better be prepared to turn himself around on
this one.

Old scars ached once it was widely realized that the political weather
looked ready for a change. Alaska's Mike Gravel, judged to have supported
Long in the 1969 Whip fight, believed himself to have been shouldered
humiliatingly aside during the subsequent Kennedy tour of his own state
and denied his preferred appointment to the Commerce Committee.

Nixon staffers were repeatedly outraged at the way, no matter how firmly
discretion was urged, material discussed at the White House leadership meetings seemed to seep through into press reports within a couple of hours.
Kennedy was assumed to be the leak, and there was a very outspoken Nixon
preference that Kennedy be replaced by Bobby Byrd, whose pedestrian style,

cultural bias, and certified closed-mouthedness were much more sympathetic to the White House inner circle. Byrd was also looked upon as a more reliable source of early-warning information about what was in ferment among the Democratic Senate staffs: The White House counselors were finally becoming aware of what their sublime ignorance about Congressional tactical work had cost them during the Haynsworth and Carswell debacles. Favors and promises moved eagerly now in steady arbitrage up and down Pennsylvania Avenue.

Arrangements, very nearly too subtle to enunciate, took shape. Harrison Williams of New Jersey, a presumptive Kennedy supporter in 1969 who had recommitted himself earlier, avoided all telephone calls from the Kennedy offices the last three days before the January 21 caucus; word drifted around the Hill of a conversation between Williams and Jennings Randolph, Byrd's West Virginia colleague and patron, as a result of which Randolph resigned his ranking position on Labor and Public Welfare and Williams moved up to the coveted Chairmanship.

Kennedy was "rejected as Whip," in the published judgment of Washington's ubiquitous Warren Rogers, "primarily because he incautiously believed that Sens. Quentin N. Burdick of North Dakota, Thomas J. McIntyre of New Hampshire, Stuart Symington of Missouri and Harrison A. Williams Jr. of New Jersey would keep their word and vote for him." Other defector lists vary slightly; Rogers's remains as serviceable as anybody's.

The surprise was the extent to which Edward Kennedy misled himself. Having received an unsolicited tender of support from such a shaggy, eminent Bourbon Southerner as Mississippi's Allen Ellender, Ted turned it down. He presupposed his moderate and liberal support was solid; he consequently saw no reason to humiliate Byrd to that extent. There is sound reason to believe that even Big Jim Eastland was preparing himself to vote for Kennedy; Bobby Byrd's damnable pushiness and his way of bouncing up with those sharp little distracting squeaks about supposed infractions of parliamentary procedure were rankling some of the more courtly Senior Chairmen. Kennedy appears never to have doubted that he could depend on the necessary twenty-eight votes he had to have; when, at 10:30 AM, the ballots were counted and Byrd had won 31–24, Kennedy was dumbfounded. Byrd, evasive in his dry way until virtually the hour the caucus convened, was scrupulous not to announce until he had the ballot of the prestigious, dying Richard Brevart Russell—"counted his key votes with a stethoscope," one cynic observed—and even Byrd seems to have had no idea where those extra three supporters came from: Several—political assassination is properly an impulsive act—had misspelled Byrd's name. "Once I pick the liberal buckshot out of my behind, I'll be over to help pull the liberal daggers out of your back," Morris Udall telephoned Kennedy afterwards.

Kennedy personally had very little stomach for combing down the list in search of treacheries. A couple of old-time friends who dropped by to console him in his Senate offices found his mood as close to raffish and relieved as angry. One of them proposed a Senate motion to make him a refugee-for-a-day. "At least in Vietnam you knew which direction the bullets were coming from," Kennedy laughed, or tried to, observing that "the best thing we got out of the Whip job was the day we got it"; by that time twenty-eight of the colleagues had telephoned to inform him that they had definitely voted for him. In time Kennedy would assure Robert Byrd that disencumbering himself of the Whip responsibilities had been the best move he could have made. Years and years later, when word of Ted Kennedy's terminal illness reached the Senate floor, ailing old Bobby Byrd wept openly.

Kennedy had been reassessed; he had been reassessing; it would require a discipline more exact than politics to determine which reappraisal came first. Whichever, this loss probably wiped away the last of Kennedy's self-imposed apprenticeship. After venturing, with strained gameness, that "if you don't know how to lose you don't deserve to win," Kennedy observed, just after the caucus, in response to a question about whether he thought the other presidential contenders had gotten together against him, that he "would like to think those who supported me thought I could do the job, and those who supported Senator Byrd thought he could do it." There was the familiar beyondness; now, he explained patiently, he expected "to devote more of my energies to more of the issues, the national health insurance, and reform of the draft."

Joe Kennedy was dead. Robert Kennedy was dead. David Burke was leaving. Kennedy would be overworked but free.

There were dragons enough.

BOOK TWO

I don't think there's any point in being Irish if you don't
think the world is going to break your heart eventually.

DANIEL P. MOYNIHAN, 1963
(*Time*, March 16, 1970)

Still bewildered by the Chappaquiddick accident, set down hard by his colleagues during the Whip vote, fatherless, missing Bobby and about to lose the irreplaceable David Burke—for Edward Kennedy 1970 was turning into the year he would have to re-create himself or give it up. I caught some inkling of what he himself had in mind after quite a frank exchange one morning in his Boston residence at Charles River Square. Once we had talked everything through, Edward Kennedy hoisted himself out of his chair to accompany me to the street.

Just off the vestibule he pulled up to direct my attention to a framed letter by Daniel Webster, which he took a moment to read aloud. Webster was a hero of Kennedy's, an opinionated yet in the end incorruptible advocate for Massachusetts in both the U.S. House of Representatives and the U.S. Senate for thirty-seven years, punctuated by stretches as Secretary of State as well as an abortive campaign as Whig candidate for U.S. president.

I had been sounding Kennedy out in the hope of ascertaining where he was headed next. He had lost his clout as Whip, yet within the Senate Kennedy was starting to pull in around himself an ever-augmented following, colleagues inclined to regard Kennedy—nobody else prepared more carefully, cast a wider net—as the emerging champion of the antiwar Left. The lunatic Right simmered; Kennedy remained worried, as he would confess freely to a friend, that he was about to "get my ass blown off."

Tough as things got at times, what impressed me even in those days was Kennedy's extraordinary detachment, the way he was able to keep his predicament in context. I suspect he gave himself away to a certain extent with his admiration for Webster. Daniel Webster had staying power. He had an impact on the civilization of his time. An unremitting old toper in private life, his preoccupation was not in the end with his reputation or his personal fortune but rather the prospects of the divided Republic. No setback could scuttle him. He defined an age.

Bludgeoned incessantly by controversy, Webster could maintain himself.

So could Edward Kennedy. Kennedy had taken punishment, much of it self-inflicted. He remained very slow to define himself beyond the context of his background. Chappaquiddick very nearly destroyed him. Kennedy's marriage was tortured, and much of the time his children were palpably upset and frightened. I thought he fed on myth too much of the time. He remained a prisoner of the imagined past.

While Kennedy as an acquaintance had always seemed well disposed, the access I'd gotten as a journalist had varied according to his circumstances at the time we talked. When things were upbeat, and he was universally lionized, he could be difficult to corner. My way of alluding in print to the fault lines and rough spots of Kennedy's character understandably made him skittish. Undoubtedly touchiest of all, a number of the loyalists he depended on had turned into friends of mine. Yet I'd been dedicated to many of the same ideals he had over the years, and emphasized his contributions. And so when everything was collapsing, Kennedy tended to open up his schedule for me.

One of Kennedy's talents—unique among the politicians I've dealt with—was his capacity to step back even during the worst of disasters and contemplate the entire scene, particularly his own ineptitude, with mordant detachment. This came through again and again in correspondence we had over the years. Pre-publication magazine excerpts from *The Education of Edward Kennedy*, for example, had highlighted his hectic and increasingly alcoholic behavior the spring leading into the Chappaquiddick episode. Kennedy's mercurial press aide, Dick Drayne, had run me down by telephone in Vail after one piece appeared to chew my head off personally. The staff was roiled up, yet again.

Kennedy himself stayed out of it. Then, once the biography was published in 1972, he wrote me in another connection, and added toward the end of the note that he hadn't "had the chance to read your book from one end to the other, but have glanced at some of the chapters, especially the references to Jack Crimmins." Outspoken old Jack Crimmins had remained Kennedy's driver around Boston at that time, and my vignettes of Ted giving Crimmins that patented Kennedy needle to relieve the exhaustion of some overscheduled day of campaigning obviously tickled Kennedy: He chose to reformulate my work—and tease me—by treating it as Edward Kennedy's existence as perceived from Jack Crimmins's perspective. Kennedy abused and babied Crimmins mercilessly. It was to spare this snarky, choleric street Irishman the chore of chauffeuring the senator and Mary Jo Kopechne to the ferry landing at Chappaquiddick after Jack had had too much to drink that Kennedy had taken the fateful wheel himself.

Even before Bobby died, Ted Kennedy was losing himself in contemplation of the intricacies of the Senate. He'd started to explore power, its usages, its seductiveness. Like alcohol or revelry, work could very often protect you from your thoughts. Unlike his two brothers, who in the end had taken the government by storm, Edward Kennedy had grasped that it was possible to build influence out in a place like the Senate in such a way that in the end one became impregnable. One became a power center, a kind of counterpart to the presidency itself.

This could take decades, of course, but Kennedy was comfortable with decades. And more than that, he had the temperament for such a grind. He was the only man in public life I knew who routinely referred to himself as a "politician," with all the cigar smoke and obnoxious deal-making a term like that has come to exude. The Senate is a small world, ninety-nine colleagues at a time, hundreds over the years, and generation by generation Kennedy would expend his charm on virtually every one. He could be irascible sometimes, with a weakness for demagoguing issues, but there has been nobody else out there since Lyndon Johnson to match Kennedy's talent for sizing people up and capitalizing on the particulars.

Along with tactical skill, Kennedy had taken on gravity enough to force through his convictions. He'd never been much put off at being called a liberal, and battled for three decades to prevent the society from becoming a trough for the interests. Yet at the same time Kennedy saw right away that on a day-to-day basis even a James Eastland or a Strom Thurmond or a Dan Quayle wasn't ideologically monolithic; there would be sentiments or points of honor or even a glimmer of patriotism through which to lure them into camp. Kennedy's aptitude for coalition-building convulsed successive White House staffs. Democratic and Republican presidents alike discovered the success of their administrations was coming to depend on Edward Kennedy's willingness to bring his friends along. Even when he lost, he tended to recast the presumptions of the debate and open the way for victories later on.

Taking on so many assignments, across such an unequaled spectrum, Kennedy continued to overlap the constituencies which looked to him for expertise and support. They ran in time from the traditional voiceless minorities and labor union functionaries to biomedical programmers and flight controllers and CEOs in emerging technologies and big-city prosecuting attorneys and movie stars and immigrants (documented and otherwise) and active and retired senior military and Archbishop Desmond Tutu and New Bedford fishermen just in from the Grand Banks. Endlessly curious, irresistibly involved, Edward Kennedy would peruse our life down to the finest human particular.

In 1972 I imagined I'd told Kennedy's story. It had barely opened.

CHAPTER I

The Comeback

1. Confession

It was the worst of times, again. It required the scandal-ridden summer of 1991 to drag him to the podium, throughout which the pounding by the media only seemed to scale up in ferocity, and chits were expended to quash a censure hearing, and he himself sat stony and ineffectual above the Clarence Thomas proceedings. Even his ex-wife, Joan, broke back into the headlines by losing her Massachusetts driver's license after one too many citations for rolling around fried.

"I am painfully aware that the criticism directed at me in recent months involves far more than honest disagreement with my positions," Edward Kennedy intoned before a handpicked audience at the Kennedy School that October, "or the usual criticism from the far right. I recognize my own shortcomings—the faults in the conduct of my private life. I realize that I alone am responsible for them, and I alone must confront them."

Insiders could have told you two things about Edward Kennedy by 1991. He was a parliamentary genius—before he was finished Kennedy had introduced an estimated 2,500 bills and seen 550 enacted into law. Three hundred bore his name, and hundreds and hundreds in addition carried his unique fingerprints. Kennedy himself, virtually single-handed at times, had killed off innumerable reactionary proposals and knocked down any number of obnoxious federal appointments.

Yet at the same time he was, as *The New York Times* saw fit to acknowledge the day after he died, "a Rabelaisian figure . . . a melancholy character who persevered . . . while living the heedless private life of a playboy and a rake for many of his years . . . a man of unbridled appetite . . ."

Not to overplay the drinking. By 1991 dissipation had been boiling away beneath the surface of his career for more than three decades. The humiliations of Chappaquiddick had momentarily given Kennedy pause. But out of those terrible months had come the revelation that he was politically indestructible—the worst had happened, the girl had drowned, after which he had run away, and a year later the voters of Massachusetts had returned Kennedy to the Senate by a lopsided majority. For Ted the game appeared to be rigged by God so that public accomplishment nullified private indulgence.

Inherently a superstitious man, Kennedy concluded that he had a deal with fate. As the seventies opened the traditional restraints had fallen away. Joe Kennedy, the all-powerful father from whom a glance of disapproval was usually more than enough, expired in 1969. Bobby was long gone. David Burke withdrew into commercial New York. Joan, full of the desperate hope that relocating away from Kennedy's maddening evasiveness and the constant chorus of rumors about her husband's philandering might help her overcome *her* drinking, was in and out of the McLean estate for years and finally took a little flat by herself in Boston in 1978, ostensibly to study the piano.

For two decades Kennedy had pounded away in the Senate during daylight hours and all but run amok in private. And then in 1991 the stars and moon had fallen on Edward Kennedy again. Pushing sixty, Kennedy was again taking a pounding from the tabloids, confronting his outraged, disappointed public. Only confession on a transcontinental scale was likely to shrive away so many sins.

That October of 1991 in Cambridge it was as if, en tableau, hovering over the fifty-nine-year-old Edward Kennedy, just beyond the television lights, images of the Easter recess were still floating. Kennedy at the Au Bar, slumped above a table in the corner with his unstable son Patrick and his nephew Willy Smith at three in the morning Easter Sunday, absorbing whiskey and holding court to a procession of divorcées and barflies half his age. Returned to the Palm Beach mansion, drifting in his nightshirt like an enormous moth across the gloom toward Patrick and one of the women they had enticed back to the ancestral Kennedy hideaway La Guerida, then hanging there above the pair in the shadowy ground-floor sitting room until Patrick's date—unable later to remember precisely whether she had anything on at the time—felt so "weirded out" that she had given it up and fled.

And wound up resting in his bedroom, finally, and purportedly unable

18. ABOVE LEFT: Challenges of 1965. Cane "Temporary" and David Burke. **19.** ABOVE RIGHT: Judge Francis X. Morrissey. **20.** BELOW: Colleagues, 1965. Senators Thomas Kuchel, Phillip Hart, Edward Kennedy, Mike Mansfield, Everett Dirksen, Jacob Javits.

21. LEFT: The bridge, July 19, 1969.
22. BELOW: The boiler-room girls. Left to right: Rosemary Keough, Mary Ellen Lyons, Nance Lyons, Susan Tannenbaum, Esther Newburg.

23. Edmund Dinis indulges press.

24. ABOVE: July 25, 1969. Confronting a sea of troubles, with Steve Smith at the helm, after pleading guilty to leaving the scene. **25. BELOW:** 1970. Plugging back. Left to right: Subcommittee witness Ralph Nader, Jim Flug, Dick Drayne, Kennedy.

26. LEFT: Saint Patrick's Day, 1970. Kennedy's celebrated appeal to women almost finishes him, while Joan (middle) and Cousin Joey Gargan (to Joan's left) look on in horror. 27. BELOW: 1968. Scrambling in another presidential primary, this time for Bobby.

28. Getting the boilerplate right with Carey Parker, the legislative assistant legendary around Capitol Hill as "The 101st Senator."

29. ABOVE: Willy Smith, Steve's son and Ted's companion on the 1991 Easter weekend in Palm Beach that almost obliterated Kennedy politically—again. 30. BELOW: Edward Kennedy—whose determination to bull through the Senate sanctions on South Africa collapsed apartheid—introduces Nelson and Winnie Mandela to his son Patrick.

31. ABOVE: For decades a vital player in the shadow diplomacy that brought down the Soviet Union, Kennedy accompanied by Jackie Onassis welcome Gorbachev's Foreign Minister Eduard Shevardnadze to the United States in 1992. **32.** BELOW: Kennedy with the unflappable Melody Miller, the press aide who defused forty years of Kennedy family crises.

33. RIGHT: One hearing too many, with water bottle.
34. BELOW: At the JFK Library in 2001: Gerald Ford accepts the Profiles in Courage Award from Caroline Kennedy while Uncle Teddy beams.

35. Mitt Romney, the hard-charging Mormon dynast who very nearly cost Kennedy his seat in 1994.

36. ABOVE: Looking better—Kennedy with his brainy, dynamic new bride Victoria Reggie.
37. BELOW: March 23, 2010. President Barack Obama, overseen by the Democratic power structure, with Vicki Kennedy grinning with satisfaction above his right elbow, signs the Universal Health Care Act, which would constitute Edward Kennedy's most significant legacy.

to hear or respond to the terrified screams for help Patricia Bowman, Willy Smith's acquisition, claimed *she* had sounded all across the lawns from the gritty beach where Smith was alleged to be assaulting her by then, horsing off her panties and grinding up flotsam and debris into her underparts in his determination to get-this-over-with . . .

Images of America's nobility. News of the incident had spread within hours, with never any hope it could be contained to the supermarket rags or burned out as incidental news, buried in the mainstream press. Like anything that related to Edward Kennedy, as the nineties opened, the atmosphere was richly overloaded. A decade of midlife bachelorhood had not been generous to Kennedy, he acted it and looked it, and well before Willy Smith's adventure brought down the firestorm even the nonpartisan "lifestyle" magazines were conditioning a receptive public.

In February of 1990, more than a year ahead of the Palm Beach incident, the late Michael Kelly took aim and epitomized his subject in GQ as a "Senator Bedfellow figure, an aging Irish boyo clutching a bottle and diddling a blonde." Kelly would remain particularly unsparing wherever it came to Kennedy's appearance: "Up close, the face is a shock. The skin has gone from red roses to gin blossoms. The tracery of burst capillaries shines faintly through the scaly scarlet patches that cover the bloated, mottled cheeks." In no hurry, Kelly works his way down the topography of Kennedy's face—the bulbous nose, the corrugated forehead, the Chiclet teeth. "The eyes have yellowed too, and they are so bloodshot, it looks as if he's been weeping."

At fifty-seven, Kennedy struck Kelly as primarily a "'husk,' dried up and hollowed out," uncertain in his gait, fluttery, living out a perpetual morning after, staggering through his "autumn years." Was anyone genuinely surprised the night the Palm Beach incident torched whatever was left of Ted Kennedy's reputation?

Kennedy had been left for dead before, of course. Once footage from the 1991 Easter weekend started to unroll, no one in the media could help but summon up details from another vacation weekend, in July almost twenty-two years earlier, when Edward Kennedy's Oldsmobile had skidded off the Dike Bridge at Chappaquiddick Island. Then, too, the press had literally laid siege, reporters by the hundreds, standing around in clumps outside the hedges of the sprawling estate of Joseph P. Kennedy in Hyannis Port.

It all seemed hallucinated to me, even at the time. One year before that, a matter of months after Bobby was gunned down, Edward Kennedy had very nearly found himself conscripted as the Democratic candidate for president in Chicago. The votes, evidently, were there. In place of the tall, halting figure in the neck brace with the buffaloed look on his handsome stricken face being conducted in and out of cars headed for preliminary proceedings in the Edgartown courtroom, this might by then have been a thirty-seven-year-old American president. Political fortunes come about on a dime in America, but this was stunning.

What reporters generally missed—what I missed sometimes over the course of the stomach-churning cycles of Kennedy's career—was that his importance did not depend, in the last analysis, on his momentary popularity with the press, or the accidents of his episodic personal life, or his drinking, or even his repute among the colleagues. Kennedy's career was buoyed up early and late by the depth of his political commitment. Ordinary people picked that up, they responded to that. They weren't angels either.

So in the end Edward Kennedy's mission would remain so immediate to him no tragedy, no scandal had yet been able to drag him permanently off course. Neither Jack nor Bobby was ever quite able to ground a political identity in bedrock this unshakable. The decades of sporadic adolescent shenanigans that would have—in fact, have always—plowed under the reputation and crippled the performance of lesser politicians had left Kennedy viable. Commitment kept coming through. Ted Kennedy was larger than his appetites.

This had a lot to do, I determined over time, with his intense if multilayered involvement with his family. Not merely the individuals, but more than that the ethos, the legend of what the Kennedys were and what they were supposed to be. For Jack and even Bobby—and certainly for the manipulative Ambassador Joe—the glorification of the Kennedys had been by way of public relations hype, something of a tool, a highly saleable myth they merchandised into power and votes.

For Ted, ultimately, Camelot opened around him, a kind of glorious if intimidating confinement. His sense of responsibility for keeping this gigantic illusion intact haunted him; it kept him deeply frightened that if he let the family's expectations down he would be crushed, humiliated, destroyed. His astute son Teddy emphasized shortly after his father died that he "wasn't a perfect human being," that a great deal of his underlying frenzy stemmed from his efforts to somehow get out ahead of what Ted himself called "the darkness" because "he believed in redemption, atonement."

As Kennedy himself would confide to me during one astonishing interview, even as a child he became very apprehensive that if he didn't accomplish what the family expected—i.e., what Joseph P. Kennedy expected—he might be cast out, disappear. In *Bobby and J. Edgar* I tried to explore the origins of all these fears in chapters like "Gangster Values." Good works, public service—everything amounted to compensation, expiation. The so-called Kennedy mystique remained a distillation of painfully noble purposes, a vision so demanding that for years his inability to flesh out its possibilities had almost a stunting effect on Ted, it kept him drinking and testing his duende on woman after woman, it retarded the evolution of his personality by decades.

I had been repeatedly struck during the first years of my exchanges with Kennedy by how often and reflexively he referred to his "superior brothers"— what they had thought about this issue or that, how what he was proposing that season advanced the concerns of the late president or the fallen senator. For years this came over as artificial to me—an attempt to legitimize himself in the context of their efforts. I suspected at times that even Kennedy's weakness—the random, hectic tomcatting, his propensity for noisy strident moralizing from the podium—amounted to a kind of homage to the pair who left their big, clownish kid brother behind. Acting all this out had a way of telling on Kennedy. Both Chappaquiddick and the Palm Beach incident came out of too many months of mourning for a family member, too acute an awareness of what was lost once and for all.

He was often reminded of his unworthiness. The day Ted finally delivered his maiden speech on the Senate floor, Senator Philip Hart happened to stop by Attorney General Robert Kennedy's office, where he congratulated Bobby on Ted's eloquent presentation. "Teddy gave a good speech?" Bobby reportedly snapped. "I suppose it's possible. Who do you imagine wrote it for him?" I got the same response from Bobby not long afterwards.

With somebody of less devotion, resentment might have surfaced. Kennedy himself soldiered on, preoccupied with who his family had been, what they had done for him. He remained the last-born, the foundling whose justification for being would be to redeem the heritage.

Soon after the Chappaquiddick episode, in the fall of 1969, once Kennedy was back in the Senate, I went to sound him out in the ornate recesses of the Whip's chambers. We dealt with legislation at hand, his health, finally—I proceeded very tentatively here—questions that still needed answering about the accident itself. On that subject he responded in a measured way, gravely, the sadness coming through although he appeared relatively self-possessed. Then (I was preparing to leave) I offered my condolences on the death of his father. Kennedy looked at me; his voice broke; tears sprang into his eyes and started down his cheeks. He still stood prepared to deal with his own troubles, but even the mention of the old buccaneer wobbling paralyzed in his wheelchair stirred up too much, it left Kennedy helpless.

2. *Love and Death*

Even Chappaquiddick had not been enough to convince the Nixon White House that Ted was down. "This is quite a day on another front too!" Richard Nixon exulted as the news from Edgartown blanked out the moon landing in 1969. "It'll be hard to hush this one up." Nixon's staff investigator John Caulfield quickly dispatched a heavy-duty, off-the-books operative, Anthony Ulasewicz, to prowl Martha's Vineyard, and months later the two set up a love nest in Manhattan in a fruitless attempt to ensnare one of the "boiler-room girls" who attended the fateful cookout. The following winter Caulfield personally tailed Kennedy throughout a stopover in Hawaii, in the hope of catching him out in a compromised situation. By then Kennedy's sapping tactics in opposition to the war were once again bleeding the Nixon administration.

Kennedy felt pressure building. War-horses among the Democrats remained steamed at Kennedy for ducking away from the nomination in 1968, convinced that he might have retained the White House and spared them years of frustration and powerlessness. He hadn't been ready, Ted kept attempting to explain to anyone who would listen. It wasn't that easy.

It really had taken all Kennedy had to push through the 1970 campaign in Massachusetts, greeting commuters outside subway landings while rounds of testimony thrown off by the protracted inquest into the death of Mary Jo Kopechne kept landing across his campaign like artillery fire. The press remained merciless. "You see this?" Kennedy had demanded, presenting me with that morning's tabloid photo of himself trailed by a perky Italian socialite at Charles de Gaulle's funeral the morning I stopped by Kennedy's house on Charles River Square in Boston to pose a few belated questions of my own regarding the accident. "I not only wasn't involved with this woman," Kennedy had exploded. "So far as I know I never clapped eyes on her before or since." In time, with investigation, it developed that Charles Colson at the White House had circulated the photo as part of an undercover program to discredit the recovering senator.

With two brothers shot, it seemed so inescapable at the time that there was some nut out there, up for the hat trick. Kennedy felt that, every conscious minute. That March of 1970, while I was marching with the senator's party in the Saint Patrick's Day parade through downtown Lawrence, some wag set off a cannon cracker; Kennedy's smile froze immediately, I saw his legs buckle and his entire body flinch as he fought the impulse to flatten himself against the asphalt. I remember how ashen he went, how clouded his eyes looked until he recovered himself.

Yet within a few hours he was again marching, this time in South Boston. "This is mission impossible," one of his security handlers muttered as we attempted to press along the close streets, a mob for several miles overflowing against the ropes, cheering, heckling. Joan Kennedy was too terrified to speak. What police there were attempted to peruse the upper windows of street after street of three-deckers in hopes of spotting the glint of a rifle barrel in time. Halfway through the march a heavyset woman lurched free of the crowd and grabbed Kennedy from the back, hooking up her mammoth doughy forearm and trapping Kennedy around the neck. Somebody in our party immediately fell on her and pried her off; Kennedy gasped for breath, his back in spasm.

"Why'dja do that?" the big woman roared. "Hey, whataya, secret soivuce?"

The parade moved ahead.

"Even more than Jack or Bobby, Teddy has an amazing ability to sustain himself," a reporter who'd followed all three around remarked at the time. He recalled the newspaper editor in Madison who was giving them fits all through the Wisconsin primary. "Jack felt he had to confront this guy and demand at least a semblance of fairness. They talked a while, and Jack wasn't getting anywhere, and finally he said, 'Well, write what you want, you vicious anti-Catholic sonofabitch.'

"And the publisher said, 'Yeah, well, up your ass.'

"My point being, Teddy would have handled it with a little more finesse. On the professional level, Ted never forgets that tomorrow will undoubtedly arrive. Privately, of course, he's still a player-arounder in almost a childish sense. He drives too fast, and if he's got some girl he likes he'll show her off to people—you know, laugh, giggle, splash around in the pool. Like a little boy, somebody to fool around with."

Those were the days when a politician had a private life, left out of news columns by unwritten journalist agreement. Kennedy liked women, everybody acknowledged that, not least the heir apparent. This was a feature his friends ascribed to natural warmth, stimulated by a lot of booze and the availability of girls. It was an aspect of politics, lagniappe, a sort of droit de seigneur that went with ownership of the electorate. Just as a medieval nobleman might drop off his horse at the sight of some lively peasant girl's well-turned haunch among the harvest sheaves, and refresh his loins beneath a noonday sun, so Kennedy had few inhibitions about declaring his interests, then promptly following up. No coercion was involved, nor even much seduction given the customary tight scheduling. He'd been like that at least since adolescence.

All through the sixties in Washington everybody heard the stories. Midlevel State Department officers from New Delhi to Panama City came back with tales of Teddy on senatorial junkets, rousting some poor attaché out of bed at two in the morning to lead him on a crawl among the livelier bordellos. Out West to address a convention, according to another story, the senator picked up a showgirl in Las Vegas toward the end of the evening and settled down afterwards in the bedroom of a suite. A local deputy sheriff stood guard outside all night; early the next morning—Kennedy had a plane to catch—the nervous lawman knocked on the bedroom door, waited, then eased inside and tapped the tangle of flesh beneath the sheet on an exposed shoulder. Kennedy reportedly came to, rolled naked and muzzy out onto his feet, and hit the deputy so hard he dislocated his jaw.

A display like that was noteworthy, but rare. Kennedy appreciated fun. He would remain devoted to more durable mistresses like Helga Wagner, but on the many occasions he found himself out on the road, chairing hearings or campaigning for sympathetic Democrats he resorted to a classical little black book. Every once in a while—in Aspen, on Manhattan's Upper East Side, around San Francisco, here and there in Georgetown—I would run into good-looking, been-around socialite types who saw no reason not to divulge that they were on Kennedy's list.

The story they told tended to be the same. Kennedy would pull into town, they would get a call: Any chance of availability toward the end of the afternoon? Boisterous and attentive, the senator might show up at four and post one of his aides outside the door to remind him that he had to give an address downtown at seven. The two would repair to the lady's bedroom, where Kennedy would perform. Emotionally, the exchange was about as meaningful as a handshake, except messier. The aide would knock on the door in plenty of time for Kennedy to wash up and tug on his back brace and pull himself together prior to his upcoming speech, and his host would be left with a sense of having met her responsibilities. Flowers often followed.

This sort of interlude fell under the rubric of recreation. Kennedy needed to break loose from time to time to shake off the endless overscheduled days in the Senate, the exertion of patience as one hour droned into the next. Dedication was the game; Kennedy played it. "Bobby never really wanted any committee chairmanships, or subcommittee chairmanships," Frank Mankiewicz once observed. For Bob the Senate had remained a way station. Ted aspired to power there, craved responsibility, and almost always took and made the most of whatever he could get and endured with unflagging good humor the endless extra work.

As early as his committee counsel days for Joe McCarthy, Bobby had had a way of boring in on witnesses, rattling loose their inlays. Ted at his most self-righteous and scathing kept open the possibility of redemption. Typical was a grilling I heard him subject an official to at Logan Airport in Boston in 1970 vis-á-vis the facility's antiquated air control system.

After much close questioning, the official ventured hopefully that he would "say the system was safe part of the time."

"What part of the time?" Kennedy wanted to know. "Is it going to be safe when I fly back to Washington tomorrow?"

"Well," the official proposed, "give me your flight number."

Kennedy couldn't help grinning. Bobby might have blown up.

It did not help to lose his post as Assistant Majority Leader—Whip— to Robert Byrd. After 1971 Ted Kennedy would concentrate on spreading himself as widely as possible among as many important committees as he could entice into taking him—Justice, Health/Education/and Welfare, and even, by the Reagan years (this came as a surprise) Armed Services. Before long he presided over the biggest—more than one hundred, meticulously selected, a number on salaries he himself paid—and by common agreement the best staff around the Congress. Many of his senior people would move on to senior positions all over the federal government, all independent of routine Democratic Party pecking order protocol.

Like his father and brothers, to back his regulars up Kennedy cultivated a private clientele of outside experts and advisers. He would not again find himself beholden only to the liberals, or hesitate to build his alliances where opportunity offered itself, across the entire ideological spectrum. All this would demand a prodigious amount of work. But Kennedy was a prodigious worker.

Between the open political vendettas brought on by the sputtering war and the mass disillusion with politics in the wake of Watergate, little in the way of idealism was to survive the Nixon-dominated seventies. Remedial impulses in both parties gave way under Republican administrations to concessions to well-heeled special interest groups and political action committees as campaigns turned increasingly expensive in the age of television. By then Kennedy's spectrum of issues was largely in place—immigration, the franchise, tax equity, fairer antitrust implementation, minorities, women's concerns, health—and didn't evolve much from year to year.

Not that Kennedy lost his appetite for legislative breakthroughs, or genuinely minded flirting with the interests from time to time to corner a little advantage. A bill to deregulate the airlines worked out along with a measure to deregulate trucking, and reminded Kennedy how much more gratifying the whole process seemed to get once he and big business were sliding along in the same direction. "He even taught me some of life's harder lessons," Kennedy's son Teddy would declare at his father's funeral Mass, "such as how to like Republicans." Too often these seductive departures left the Congress pregnant with second-rate legislation.

Another promising arena for bipartisan success was law enforcement. The uproar in the streets was terrifying genteel society. The war in Vietnam was eating the country alive, it was the era of Black Power and the Yippies and the Weatherpeople. War protesters staged a raid on the FBI office in Media, Pennsylvania, and distributed documents dealing with the Bureau's abuses of personal privacy. I remember sitting in a basement bar knocking them back with Joey Gargan in 1970 when word came down that some group had blown the façade off a Chase Manhattan Bank. Gargan hid his face in his hands. Left and right, individuals with serious assets were starting to panic.

Accordingly, Law and Order was now writ very bold on the Nixon administration's flag. Early in the seventies Kennedy joined with John McClellan in proposing to turn the Brown Commission's recommendations into a remodeled federal criminal code. To leave his mark Kennedy hired as his legislative assistant in 1975 an owlish former Assistant U.S. attorney for the Southern District of New York, still seething over abuses of the federal court system by the criminal community. "When I came down here to work for Kennedy," Ken Feinberg insisted to me, "I told him: 'I'm a liberal and I'm in favor of housing and all that but as for crime, Senator—crime can't wait!'" Kennedy agreed. "I think he found that he'd always been uncomfortable with his stance on criminal justice," Feinberg soon concluded. "Jim Flug and those people set the senator back on this stuff. Since when have the Kennedys been so permissive in the civil liberties field? Besides"—Feinberg hesitated—"there was a tremendous vacuum opening politically on the right. Hruska was retiring, McClellan was retiring . . ."

The initial draft, S-1, caught birdshot from so many academic blinds its sponsors pulled back. The successor bill, S-1437, aroused libertarians like Vern Countryman of Harvard Law because of stringency of sentencing, the abolition of parole, and the effort to introduce into the legislation a vague, new category of trespass Countryman called "inchoate crimes," largely conspiratorial intention. Countryman, like the American Civil Liberties Union, felt this was likely to place "outrageously severe limitations" on individual rights to assemble, organize, obtain governmental information, disobey public servants.

It was probably a measure of Kennedy's desperation after Chappaquiddick that he was willing to champion this sort of jackboot legislation and placate a paranoidal president who intended to obliterate *him* politically. Never especially tuned in when it came to civil liberties, enthusiastically pulling every stop, Kennedy rolled S-1437 through, 72–15, with support that stretched from Gaylord Nelson to Sam Hayakawa, with Strom Thurmond helping lead the charge. Fortunately, this abomination failed of approval in the House of Representatives, unlike Kennedy's equally controversial reform of federal wiretapping procedures, which now required warrants from a judge but permitted the invasion of conversations which "may" be "harmful to the United States" or against the law. Politically, this blank-check payoff to the right required a sop, so Kennedy pushed through LEAA grants to local police departments.

CHAPTER 11

Finishing Nixon

1. Remaining Alive

The presence of Richard Nixon in the White House felt unsettling, inappropriate to Edward Kennedy. It was as if fate had turned everything upside down, reversed history and repudiated Jack. Morbidly sensitive at all times, Nixon himself was quick to perceive in the fledgling senator the reincarnation of all those irrestible Kennedy claims, already gathering to roll over the White House and nullify his own stumbling presidency. Nixon was well aware that Ted might very easily have lucked into his party's nomination in 1968 and ridden an overnight wave of sentiment into the White House.

By 1970 Nixon's 1972 reelection was preoccupying the White House operatives. Throughout much of the Democratic Party an Edward Kennedy candidacy was regarded as a foregone conclusion. The astuteness with which Kennedy and his staff around the Administrative Practices and Procedures Subcommittee, presided over by the merciless Jimmy Flug, had bled white the nominations first of Haynesworth, then Carswell, suggested that this youngest Kennedy brother was a lot more than bonhomie and a famous name. Nixon authorized H. R. Haldeman to keep those footpads he had sent out to spook Kennedy after Chappaquiddick, Jack Caulfield and Tony Ulasewicz, busy on Kennedy's trail. After all, they had followed him to Hawaii and supposedly furnished a Manhattan apartment in "Chicago whorehouse" style in hopes of luring dupes from the Chappaquiddick cookout crowd and winkling out the dirt.

As the June 14, 2010, declassification of FBI records ponited up, this was the era when right-wing screwballs around the country were murmuring about pulling off the hat trick, blowing away the last of the Kennedy brothers. Kennedy's blonde young receptionist of the period, Melody Miller, ultimately slowed down so many mental cases that the Capitol Police made her an honorary member and the Secret Service awarded her their official necktie. Death threats poured in by mail; few ever got to Kennedy, who handled his underlying apprehension well. But it was always there.

Melody's years of fronting Kennedy's offices were punctuated by potentially lethal flare-ups. One caller sounded ominous enough to Melody to induce her to signal the office chief of staff, who called in the FBI. For forty-five minutes the ever more wrung-out Melody chatted up the seething caller while Bureau technicians traced the call and closed in on the perpetrator.

"Normally I didn't call the police on many of the mentally ill people because I could talk them down," Miller explained to me later on. "They just needed to be listened to. I basically just ran a mental health clinic in the reception room."

Occasionally things got out of hand. One heavyset black woman kept turning up intent on cornering Kennedy about an inner-city project she had in mind, and with every visit she was louder and more abusive. On the woman's third visit she got so worked up that Melody murmured the code to summon the Capitol Police into an intercom—"The books are ready in 431"—and slipped away for a moment to lock the door to the administrative offices behind her.

Abruptly, flanked by "two gold badges," one a captain, the woman bolted through the intervening door before Melody could throw the lock and into Kennedy's office, where he was being briefed. Everybody was "screaming and yelling" Melody would remember, and she herself leapt on the woman, so that "we ended up in a pile on the floor," with the two cops stomping up behind.

"The senator was absolutely magnificent," Melody would recall. "He got up from behind his desk and he starts to talk in a very soft voice—everybody else is still yelling—so that everybody had to be quiet to hear him. And that immediately lowered the volume. Then he got Bob Bates, an African-American on the staff, to sit down with her. Bob said it was like trying to deal with feathers . . ."

The threat hung over Kennedy, palpable, for decades. Whenever there was any kind of warning, a couple of plainclothesmen moved in and sat for weeks in Kennedy's office reception area. Outside his house at McLean the Fairfax County Police often kept cruisers parked, ostentatiously. Twice lunatics got inside Kennedy's house, while another crept into Kennedy's McLean bedroom suite and was caught hiding under the bed, waiting. Kennedy routinely wore a Kevlar vest when speaking before any good-sized crowd.

An assassin almost cornered Kennedy in his Massachusetts headquarters in Boston, and Kennedy stayed away from that poorly protected suite from then on. Superficially he was poised; underneath he was spooked. Senators who attended Everett Dirksen's funeral with Ted came back to relate that, toward the end of the ceremony, a twenty-one-gun salute was scheduled for the fallen Republican hero. Nobody had alerted Ted; by the second report he was in the process of diving into the grave when a couple of the colleagues grabbed him.

2. Cross-purposes

With Ted Kennedy calling more of the plays every season as his political moxie started to return, many Nixonian initiatives got stymied. The Democrats were jubilant, but in later years a number of the participants would entertain second thoughts. Nixon had taken power as Dwight Eisenhower's heir, the spokesman for a Republican Party that regarded itself as a progressive force. This was a simpler world, before the government-wide ossification brought on by the "military-industrial complex" whose lobbyists would seethe en masse through the halls of Congress.

It must be faced: During Richard Nixon's tenure as president a surprising amount of overdue remedial legislation, unfinished during the final year of Lyndon Johnson's truncated presidency, worked its way through both houses and got signed into law. Already preoccupied with medical care, having managed a 1966 bill that established the first thirty poverty health centers, Kennedy—as the Chairman after 1970 of the Senate Health Committee—suffered no qualms about enlisting Nixon's support behind the scenes to help authorize the National Cancer Institute. As chairman of the Health Subcommittee, Kennedy oversaw the drafting of the boilerplate that got the bill approved and looked on cheerfully when—this Nixon demanded through the auspices of Bobby's old braintruster, banker Benno Schmidt—Republican Pete Dominick's name went on the legislation; Kennedy was almost always willing to trade off credit for substance. But Kennedy did intend ultimately to own this issue, and over many years considerations of turf sometimes blanked out considerations of principle.

One bad mistake Kennedy himself was willing to admit to in later years was his opposition to the Republican president's overall proposals on health care. Nixon had intended "to bring comprehensive, high quality health care within the reach of all Americans" by mandating that all employers offer health insurance while requiring the states to "approve specific plans, oversee rates, ensure adequate disclosure, require an annual audit and take other appropriate measures," to cover the uninsured. Initially, while dubious about any measure that might turn into a windfall for the insurance companies, Kennedy agreed to examine Nixon's proposals as a place to start. But the leadership of the unions, the CIO and the United Auto Workers especially, opposed the White House initiatives because they were looking for better terms later on, at least for their own memberships. As the spectre of Watergate loomed, Kennedy stepped back and Nixon's proposals vaporized. The leadership of the industrial unions had now begun their disastrous flirtation with this last of the Kennedy brothers, whose presidency they could smell coming out of the future. Responding, Kennedy himself had started to avoid any potentially compromising collaboration with the increasingly troubled Nixon White House.

3. Abortion

His preoccupation with health inevitably left Kennedy immersed in "women's issues," especially with feminists and freedom-of-choice advocates hardening into a powerful, sometimes suicide-prone lobby inside the liberal coalition. Over many Congresses, Kennedy pushed through a great deal of legislation high on the agenda of the women's movement—laws to protect the privacy of medical records, government subsidized care for HIV sufferers, a program to underwrite the lying-in expenses of indigent expectant mothers which ultimately covered 8.7 million. It didn't take very many years before he had to come to terms with abortion.

For the primary spokesman for America's most headline-hungry Roman-Catholic family, whose First Communion had been overseen by the Pope, to present himself as a champion of abortion rights in the Senate invited stupefying risks. Running against Sy Spaulding in 1970 in Massachusetts Kennedy had repudiated "abortion on demand," solving "the world's population problem" by aborting the browns and the blacks, "the kids in mental hospitals, they're parasites on the environment . . . old people in institutions . . ." In 1971 he had written in a letter: "While the deep concern of a woman bearing an unwanted child merits consideration and sympathy, it is my personal feeling that the legalization of abortion on demand is not in accordance with the value which our civilization places on human life . . . Wanted or unwanted, I believe that human life, even in its earliest stages, has certain rights which must be recognized—the right to be born, the right to love, the right to grow old." This generation must ". . . fulfill its responsibility to its children from the very moment of conception."

Two years later *Roe v. Wade* lifted state restrictions on abortion. The majority had spoken. By then Kennedy's fragile marriage was crumbling and a divorce seemed inevitable. In coming years Kennedy would himself propose the Freedom of Choice Act and speak against the Hyde Amendment, which limited Medicaid funding for abortion. He supported gay rights laws. Melody Miller remembers sitting in on an early discussion between Kennedy and his long-term medical adviser, Dr. Larry Horowitz. "The issue was economic discrimination," Melody maintains. "State laws differed, and what it amounted to was that poor women couldn't just jump on a plane and go to a legal clinic in New York or Puerto Rico. They had to deal with makeshifts, coat hanger abortions and blood poisoning and the rest of it. So they were dying in a disproportionate way . . ."

Inside his own family, Kennedy's reversal went down hard. "I recall the frustration of his sister Eunice with his position," David Burke says. "He really liked Eunice a great deal. But when that issue was coming up, and the phone would ring, and it was Eunice, he would say to me: 'Why don't you pick it up?' She wouldn't take no for an answer."

Kennedy held the line. His ringing condemnation of "Robert Bork's America" in 1987 as "a land in which women would be forced into back alley abortions" probably altered the ground rules for Supreme Court nominations permanently. Even the clinical bestialities attendant to partial-birth abortions never made him reconsider.

At Kennedy's death one Catholic-Action spokesman put out a release headlined "Pro-Abortion, Pro-Sodomite Ted Kennedy's Roman-Catholic Funeral Mass *SCANDALIZES* Pro-Life, Pro-Marriage *Catholic* Group." As the senator was dying, Barack Obama presented the pope with a letter from Kennedy which asserted that ". . . though I have fallen short through human failings I've never failed to believe and respect the fundamental teachings of my faith."

Pope Benedict did not respond.

4. The New Nixon

During at least his first several years in office, the powdered, stumbling apparition his enemies liked to refer to as Tricky Dick was a lot less in evidence than after his reelection. Nixon brought back from California his personable, moderate political adviser Robert Finch, the ex–Lieutenant Governor of California, and installed him as his original Secretary of Health, Education and Welfare. Patrick Moynihan, originally a freethinking, iconoclastic Harvard professor who had held important subcabinet posts in the Kennedy and Johnson administrations, was invited to set up the Urban Affairs Council, to deal with hot potatoes like hard-core poverty and enforced busing. Kennedy—who was taking a battering from local rabble-rousers like Louise Day Hicks on the busing issue—was glad to watch this conservative administration interpose itself between himself and the angry tomato-throwing townie mobs gathering around Boston's city hall.

A lot got done. The Environmental Protection Agency was established in 1970 to deal with air and water pollution, noise, and radiation. It instituted the Superfund. The same year, with Kennedy's support, the Occupational Safety and Health Administration was authorized to monitor workplace conditions. The RICO Act—the first really effective legislation to bring organized crime in America under control, germinated in the Robert Kennedy Justice Department and babied through the Congress by one of Bobby's hard-edged protégés, G. Robert Blakey—finally gave law enforcement the means to run down the bosses and put them away. In time its twin, the Witness Protection Program, provided squealers a place to hide.

From Kennedy's point of view a lot of this was undermining, like Disraeli's strategies to dish the Whigs. When Nixon mandated affirmative action in employment and ended the dual-school system in the South, even many liberals were inclined to give the "New Nixon" a shot. The draw-down of American soldiers in Vietnam aroused Kennedy's scorn: "It is Asian, now, fighting Asian, and they do it for purposes more than their own." This made no sense; it was the wail of an incipient demagogue panicked about losing his issue. Only Nixon's breathtaking decision to listen to Henry Kissinger and convene a summit conference in Bejing in 1971 seemed to quell Kennedy's resentment for long enough to elicit a public statement. "Rarely, I think, has the action of any president so captured the imagination and support of the American people . . ." Nixon could fool you. It was many years since the China Lobby met.

But after 1972, during which the McGovern effort—Ted's brother-in-law, after all, had served as the sacrificial Democratic vice-presidential candidate—brought down the worst defeat for the party in a generation, Kennedy's resentment hardened. Recognizing the enormous Republican advantage with fund raisers, Kennedy steered through Congress the first bipartisan campaign finance overhaul legislation in 1972 and followed it up in 1973 with a law limiting campaign contributions and providing for public financing for presidential elections.

Working majorities were going to get harder to corner. The Democrats had lost every state but Massachusetts, and here he was confronted by a twitchy president obsessed with catching Ted "in the sack" with some errant bimbo. The Nixon years had not proven particularly fruitful for Kennedy, although he had managed to push through Meals on Wheels and the Title IX prohibition of discrimination against women in educational institutions, the matrix of women's sport programs nationwide.

The contretemps with Nixon, the months of plotting which had to culminate with one of them belly-up, felt unnatural to anybody as conciliatory as Ted. When you destroyed the president you scorched out the presidency, a job he was allegedly next in line to inherit. Kennedy was well aware of how lucky he had been that Caulfield and Ulasewicz kept showing up in the wrong place at the wrong time. But who could mistake Nixon's irrational determination to eliminate this last, most effective of the brothers?

How safe was too safe, especially with the Nixon administration monitoring every move? Days after George Wallace got shot in 1972, Kennedy requested Secret Service protection at home, then called it off when he sensed that he had himself become the target of unstinting surveillance— an intuition, as the Nixon tapes would suggest, he was well advised to credit. By then violence contorted every possibility. Once Arthur Bremer laid a couple of paralyzing slugs into George Wallace that May of 1972, Nixon's first response, according to the Oval Office tapes, was to bark: "Can we pin it on Teddy?" Fortunately for both politicians, nothing came of any of it.

Going through Kennedy's 2009 memoir, *True Compass*, Kennedy's legendary Administrative Practices and Procedures honcho Jimmy Flug told me recently, even *he* encountered details he had never known, "like the fact that the Nixon people had somebody asking questions at the press conference a few days after Chappaquiddick." To counterattack became a matter of self-preservation. "I saw a Nixon tape I hadn't seen the other day, just after Kennedy asked for Secret Service protection," Flug remarked, "And Nixon says, 'Oh, this is going to be wonderful, now we'll know everything he does.' And Haldeman says, 'Yeah, I know just the guy for the job, he worked for the Secret Service, we were very nice to him and he knows he's in our debt, and he came over to me the other day and said, if there's anything I can do for you, you've got it. If you want me to be on this Secret Service detail, that's fine. If you want me to kill somebody, I'll kill somebody." Flug chuckled. "This is the kind of people they had in their coven."

Kennedy's first real shot at the administration had come at the end of February in 1972, when Drew Pearson's successor, Jack Anderson, started to publish columns which quoted an internal IT&T memo written by the company's ditzy lobbyist Dita Beard. It specified that Justice Department Deputy Attorney General Richard Kleindienst, in line to replace the compromised John Mitchell, had agreed to drop an antitrust investigation of the conglomerate in return for an unreported $400,000 to underwrite the upcoming Republican convention in San Diego.

Kennedy requested that Sam Ervin, as chair of the Constitutional Rights Subcommittee, reopen hearings into IT&T; when, as Kennedy had anticipated, the cagey Ervin came back in a memo suggesting that *Kennedy* would be in a better position to mount the brief, touchy investigation, Kennedy held out for subpoena powers and turned Flug loose.

Archibald Cox's astute aide for Public Affairs, the fast-moving newsman James Doyle, would characterize Flug as a "bright, abrasive onetime Justice Department lawyer under Katzenbach," as whose confidential assistant he had served after clerking at the U.S. Court of Appeals who "had been in the thick of every Senate Judiciary Committee fight since then." Once Gerald Ford squelched all talk of an investigation in the House, Flug began to explore his theory that the same ferrets who had burgled the office of Dr. Lewis Fielding, Daniel Ellsberg's psychiatrist, were probably behind a series of events which would eventuate in Watergate.

Kennedy brought Flug along when, in late March of 1972, he led a bipartisan delegation to the Rocky Mountain Osteopathic Hospital to confront Dita, whom Kennedy himself describes as "a crusty, fast-talking woman in her early fifties who sprayed jumbled thoughts in salty language at us as she alternately sucked on cigarettes and gulped from her oxygen mask."

Dita was unnerved. Days earlier she had received a terrifying visit from Plumber mastermind E. Howard Hunt, decked out in a bizarre red wig and croaking through a voice-altering device and intent on intimidating the unpredictable lobbyist into renouncing her memo. But Dita broke down under Kennedy's questioning. Nixon, alarmed, suggested to Chuck Colson that he instigate a raft of telegrams to Kennedy demanding, "Isn't one woman on your hands enough?"

Determined on promotion, Richard Kleindienst abruptly demanded *further* hearings to clear his name. "Kennedy thought Kleindienst was crazy to want to reopen the hearings, they had just been reported out," Flug notes. "The result was twenty-two days of additional hearings. Every day led us to something new. It was a total can of worms. Haldeman found out that *Hunt* was involved, and went to Dita Beard's hospital room . . ."

Dita Beard's revelations hurt. Even Republicans understood about money changing hands. One recurrent charge that had long chafed Nixon—first surfaced by Drew Pearson in 1960 but picked up around the media as the Nixon presidency started to feed on itself—was the alleged "payoff" Nixon's brother Donald had taken from the billionaire Howard Hughes. This $205,000 was supposedly borrowed from the notorious Hughes to expand the family grocery store in Whittier, California. The squeamish president's flesh crawled at the rumor that "Nixonburgers" would be introduced.

Any involvement with the tall, elusive Hughes, with his sinister mustache and his well-established Mob connections, was liable to damage Nixon, badly. A lawsuit in January of 1971 surfaced a Hughes gift to Richard Nixon himself of $195,000 shortly after the loss in 1960, which H. R. Haldeman decided to categorize as a "belated campaign contribution." Advised daily by Murray Clotiner, for years the ranking underworld attorney in California, Nixon decided that the best way to neutralize any potentially ruinous political upshots was to gather evidence of the *Democrats'* susceptibility to handouts from the calculating billionaire airman.

As it happened, the well-worn Kennedy strategist and campaign organizer Lawrence O'Brien had recently been elected chairman of the Democratic National Committee. O'Brien had done well-paid consulting work for Hughes. Now he would be managing the Party's affairs out of a suite at the Watergate. If documents could be obtained linking big money from Hughes to the Democrats, Nixon would have something to counter with in case the Hughes payoffs were to erupt during the pending election.

But they needed those documents. This would be an ideal project for a small cohort of mostly ex-CIA personnel which Chuck Colson had put together as an adjunct of The Committee to Reelect the President under Donald Segretti to "plug leaks" like that of the Pentagon Papers around the government, "the Plumbers." It was to be led by the versatile and unscrupulous ex-Agency stalwart E. Howard Hunt.

Throughout 1971 the war in Vietnam was dragging on unbearably; all plans to wind things down, offload on the Vietnamese this compounding mess, continued to fall apart. Nixon's response, attempting to obliterate the North Vietnamese supply routes through Cambodia, "the Christmas bombings," produced nothing but bad press. By then Edward Kennedy had emerged as among the most outspoken critics of the war, expanding his assaults on administration policy from refugee affairs to strategy. The spectacle of our first Quaker president laying waste to hundreds of miles of jungle stirred Kennedy's familiar response of bitter humor. The president, he announced at the black-tie Gridiron Dinner in March of 1971, had missed the annual get-together with the press because he was lurking in Key Biscayne "at the local Bijou watching *Patton* for the forty-third time."

Kennedy had begun compiling his own thick clipping file on the Beard–IT&T–Hughes entanglement. Nixon was clearly panicking. When a May demonstration at the Capitol led to "field arrests" by Attorney General John Mitchell, Kennedy authorized his subcommittee to get into the legalities.

Reacting, Colson told Hunt to find—or concoct—evidence that JFK was party to the murder of President Ngo Dinh Diem of South Vietnam. The pious Roman Catholic Diem had been the occasional houseguest of Joseph P. Kennedy in Hyannis Port, and there was suspicion among the Nixon advisers that—after going along with Cardinal Spellman and boosting Diem into power and precipitating a civil war with the Buddist majority in Vietnam—the Kennedy White House had lost its nerve and authorized Diem's assassination. Proof was lacking, so Hunt came up with a doctored cable reedited by means of a razor blade and a Xerox machine which disappeared once the editors of *Life* insisted on photographing the bogus document.

By this point the White House was starting to hobgoblinize Larry O'Brien. "Should this Kennedy mafia-dominated intelligence gun-for-hire be turned against us in '72, we would, indeed, have a dangerous and formidable foe," a memorandum from Jack Caulfied warned. That this hard-working if plodding details man for the Kennedys since the fifties might appear diabolically clever to *anybody* would have dumbfounded old Joe. But the Oval Office panicked: When O'Brien hammered away at the illegal $400,000 from ITT, anger began to compound. Word ultimately came down from Colson via G. Gordon Liddy that the time had come to bug the Watergate headquarters of Democratic Chairman Lawrence O'Brien.

The Plumbers went in twice. The second time, on June 17, 1972, they got caught. By then George McGovern, running hard on a peace platform, had the Democratic nomination sewn up. Edward Kennedy was being widely discussed as a very strong vice-presidential prospect, possibly strong enough to allow the Democrats to dump the president.

In truth, Kennedy wasn't interested in the vice-presidential nomination, but he was very interested in cooling out this crowd in the White House that wouldn't leave him alone. When Gerald Ford made sure the House Banking

Committee ignored Watergate too, Kennedy attempted to involve Justiciary but attempted to keep his own head down. "Teddy Kennedy decided that this was the sort of thing he should investigate *personally*" Nixon would mutter afterward. From then on Kennedy staffers—read Ad-Prac Chief Counsel Flug and Joe Kennedy's cold-eyed ex-FBI bookkeeper, Carmine Bellino—went through every piece of paper generated by Nixon's reelection committee and traded whatever looked promising with Woodward and Bernstein of *The Washington Post*.

"I know the people around Nixon," Kennedy conceded to Bernstein. "They're thugs."

The White House wriggled. Robert Dole, reading from a speech drafted by White House aide Pat Buchanan, termed *Washington Post* editor Ben Bradlee "an old Kennedy coat holder." Even after Nixon got reelected overwhelmingly in 1972, too much was already out there for the administration to circumvent. As the new session of Congress convened, heavily Democratic, Kennedy pressed for full-scale Senate hearings into the facts behind the Watergate break-ins.

Reelected, Nixon attempted to insulate the Oval Office. Threatened with heavy sentences by Judge John Sirica, the Watergate burglars had begun to crack. One, James McCord, confessed to finding himself under "political pressure" to remain silent. Hoping to cut his losses and distance himself, Nixon attempted to arrange for "hush money" for the burglars and fired H. R. Haldeman and John Ehrlichman. To demonstrate his honorable intent, Nixon nominated as his attorney general to replace the compromised Kleindienst the immaculate Elliot Richardson, who had already served him as Secretary of Health, Education and Welfare and (briefly) Defense.

At this point Edward Kennedy intervened again. As a prospective Democratic nominee in 1976, Majority Leader Mansfield decided, Kennedy was to be left off the special committee which was to investigate Watergate. Nixon wasn't about to relent. "White House tapes of February, 1973 revealed Nixon and his counsel John Dean discussing the new Ervin committee and how they might spin it as merely a front for me and my own pernicious vendetta against the president," Kennedy observes in his memoirs.

Perhaps there were grounds. "When Richardson was nominated, Kennedy told him he could not be confirmed unless he had a special prosecutor mandate that was acceptable to us," Flug recently emphasized to me. Kennedy's standing among his colleagues was such that Richardson evidently felt forced to comply. "Nixon's experience with Richardson as a cabinet member must have inclined him to believe that he could do business with him as attorney general," Flug concluded. "That he would be able to control anybody, that he was the boss. He needed somebody who was squeaky clean."

The special prosecutor they agreed upon was Archibald Cox, on whom was to be conferred unlimited money and unlimited power to grant immunity and to indict. To get himself confirmed, Flug remembers, "Kennedy insisted that Elliot agree not to fire Cox—because he knew that sooner or later it was going to come to that—unless Cox violated 'extraordinary proprieties.' And of course that language was virtually written in Kennedy's office, with Kennedy and Richardson sitting down and going over the wording of the mandate. I believe that Elliot came to believe that Kennedy had done him a favor, but I'm not sure he believed it before the fact . . ."

A lifelong Democrat who had served as solicitor general under John Kennedy, Cox staffed up with attorneys who had worked for Jack, Bobby, and Ted. Cox went to work on the Watergate ringleaders. It didn't take long before the many hours of incriminating Oval Office tapes Nixon had been recording to help document his memoirs got subpoenaed. The young White House lawyer John Dean started talking. Nixon was implicated, over and over. Cornered, Nixon fired first Richardson, then his deputy William Ruckelshaus, when they both refused to oust Cox. Finally Nixon's solicitor general, Robert Bork, stepped in and threw Cox out.

With this "Saturday Night Massacre" Nixon had essentially rendered himself defenseless. Under the abiding Kennedy ally, Speaker Tip O'Neill, impeachment proceedings began in the House. Nixon had already replaced his vice president and belated protégé, the word-monger Spiro Agnew, when proof materialized that Agnew had solicited kickbacks wholesale while governor of Maryland. The compliant Gerald Ford replaced Agnew. By the summer it was a question for Nixon either of leaving or getting thrown out. On August 9, 1974, Richard Nixon resigned.

5. Family Life

With domestic pressures building, Kennedy attempted to escape politics as usual and jump into an international format, breakouts with a tendency to echo the legacies of his brothers. At Aristotle Onassis's death, in 1973, Kennedy traveled to Skorpios with his sister-in-law and took over the several years of legal battles that produced a $26 million settlement for JFK's widow. While Jackie, according to Gore Vidal, "lived up to their encyclopedic prenuptial agreement," the bitter Onassis had attempted to renege. "Finally Christina was told that if she didn't pay off Jackie, no Onassis ship could ever again dock in an American port." Hardball: Joe Kennedy would have nodded from beyond the grave.

Once Watergate receded, Kennedy accepted an invitation from the leadership in the Kremlin to bring his family and enter into arms control talks in Moscow in April of 1974. Attempting to replicate JFK's success in ending atmospheric detonations, Kennedy pushed for a total ban on nuclear testing. He succeeded in presenting Joan's plea to General Secretary Brezhnev to let the great Soviet cellist Mstislav Rostropovich emigrate to the West, a concession he replicated four years later at another Soviet arms-control exchange by springing the vociferous Jewish refusenik Anatoly Shcharansky. Like Bobby, Ted managed a lot of leverage on successive administrations of both parties by privately opening very productive Cold War back-channels.

These occasional, well publicized bursts of marital solidarity fooled nobody around Washington. While Ted and Joan remained married until 1981, they lived their lives increasingly apart. Contemporaries attempted to make allowances. Even during Kennedy's funeral Mass the media commentators tended to let it go with a sidelong reference to the great man's "personal demons." Teddy Jr., in what was certainly the outstanding eulogy of that torturous morning, identified himself as bearing "a name it hasn't always been easy to live with . . ."

As George Smathers remarked, John Kennedy's two great obsessions were sex and death. If you were frightened enough, taking chances and sexual abandon were life-affirming, two ways of warding off oblivion for the moment. Sex was a release, "the little death," as the French say. Teddy Junior obviously understood that. "He was a lover of everything French—cheese, wine, women," Kennedy's son remembered fondly. He was who he was.

During periods of great stress the restraints tended to lift. Rick Burke, a stiff, pallid Catholic youngster Kennedy had recruited out of the mailroom and broken in as his personal driver and factotum, would write of wandering through a sizeable engagement party Kennedy was tossing at his McLean estate in October of 1973 for his charming and supremely efficient personal secretary, Angelique Voutselas. Angelique was of Greek origin, and so a Greek band with a provocative female vocalist was on hand to entertain the crowd. In the kitchen, Kennedy personally was mixing daiquiris in the blender. Joan was already blotto, her pancake makeup running; she jerked away repeatedly from her embarrassed husband as he begged, "C'mon, Joansie. Pull yourself together . . ."

Finally giving it up, Kennedy had flagged down a couple of retainers and growled: "Get her out of here." The two servants dragged Mrs. Kennedy away and locked her in her room. A few hours later, after the party broke up, Burke made his way back into the sprawling house to check out details. One of the double doors to the library was ajar, and Burke "caught my breath as I saw the Senator on the floor of the library, lying atop the sexy Greek singer."

Joan Kennedy drank; Ted felt responsible and drank too much out of desperation; then Ted acted up and Joan fled to Boston or Paris to lose herself in the discotheque life where paparazzi would catch her in a see-through dress and sell their more revealing prints to the American tabloids. Joan had developed herself into a concert-level pianist. She was a member of the National Symphony Orchestra and performed as a soloist for the Boston Pops, but alchohol had come to blot everything else out. She was sneaking bottles into her rooms and locking herself in; one regular remembers having Joan sidle up to him at a gathering at McLean and attempt to charm him into smuggling a water glass full of vodka to her in hopes that Ted wouldn't notice.

The children were increasingly upset; Kara ran away repeatedly; little Patrick's asthma became more acute and his father got tagged with giving him the steroid injections which permitted him to breathe. Joan's alchoholism remained awkward for both Ted and Joan to confront, especially since Kennedy himself was drinking heavily and running around quite openly and experimenting with everybody and everything. Rick Burke records having opened a small cardboard box that came in the mail which contained a couple of hundred yellow capsules of amyl nitrate—poppers. Kennedy had taken to snapping open a capsule under his nose when his energy level was low or during sex to capitalize on the rush.

Psychologically, Ted and Joan were drowning together. License, guilt and excess had tangled around them both like chains.

How reckless things got was exemplified by one of the incidents in Rick Burke's memoir. By previous arrangement, one March afternoon a couple of svelte, good-natured starfuckers from Florida in skimpy sundresses showed up at the Kennedy offices, and Burke was delegated by the Boss to take them out to dinner. Kennedy had several political receptions to attend: first things first. Toward eleven o'clock Kennedy joined the trio in McLean, where the two couples gathered around a coffee table while one of the women prepared four lines of coke—she was Ted's connection—which they took turns snorting with a rolled-up hundred-dollar bill before decamping in pairs to their respective beds.

Like Jack before him, Teddy was playing around in California. Once, leaving Kennedy's Capitol Hill office, I ran into Jack Nicholson just arriving. I knew Jack through other connections, and this was an era when he was reported to be cruising virtually full time on grass. We all talked briefly about mutual acquaintances, but I exited quickly. Jack and Ted obviously had a heavy schedule.

Properly oiled, Kennedy could get playful to the point of heart-stopping. On the Society-divorcée circuit stories were making the rounds about Ted Kennedy with his pants off, chasing some intended conquest around the sitting room while snuffling up a handful of cocaine to keep it up long enough to remain functional.

In Kennedy's defense, this was the moment in our social history when cocaine was America's drug du jour. What ambitious hostess on Manhattan's Upper East Side did not lay in a bowl of the magic powder to liven up the late-night proceedings? George W. Bush was giving his father fits . . .

Still—risky behavior; perhaps not the smartest way to cope with stress, especially with Nixon's bloodhounds camped out in the shrubbery and Teddy Jr.'s anguish permeating his overworked father's emotions. By 1973 I had published my first biography of the senator and was researching a new work about the Mellon family. When I was around Washington, at Kennedy's insistence, I always made it a point to stop by his offices and compare notes. One day I looked in and found him uncharacteristically downcast, preoccupied. We talked a little politics; suddenly Kennedy burst out, his face reddening and a hand trembling with the effort to hang onto himself as he pitched out his nasty little Davidoff cigar and scrounged it into an ashtray. "You know, Burton, I understand that there are perhaps fifty children in the United States with this thing. And I've got one."

Ted wagged his great, shaggy leonine head. A biopsy on a lump just below the knee had recently revealed a chondrosarcoma, an aggressive cancer of the cartiledge, on his son Teddy's left leg. The leg would have to come off. Months of grueling radiation and chemotherapy would determine whether there was any hope of a cure. I thought that Kennedy looked awful. The best tailors couldn't hide the spreading paunch, his overstuffed, bulbous look. His face was puffy, the hooded eyes bulging, bloodshot.

At that point, dethroning Nixon wasn't nearly so significant

6. Changing the Guard

Gerald Ford's short presidency served as a kind of interregnum; Ford's best-remembered initiative was to pardon Nixon. Golf took up a lot of the president's time. With Henry Kissinger still flicking the controls, the discreet evacuation of whatever American troops were left in Vietnam continued. The last stage degenerated into a rout, with helicopters lifting disheveled diplomats and anybody else who was willing to cling to the skids off the roof of the embassy in Saigon.

Democratic regulars around Washington were excited briefly by the restoration in 1976 under Jimmy Carter. To most of the suits around Washington, Carter amounted to a letdown. He remained several decades ahead of his time when it came to the environment, and the sight of his tidy little person in a tight sweater in the White House might have roused the rural types, but to the D.C. establishment Carter still looked like a peanut farmer. Iran slid into the hands of the Ayatollahs; the economy fell apart. Interest rates jumped but employment collapsed. Jimmy Carter was not about to attempt to project American power or undertake expensive programs to prime the pump. His prescription was simple: Turn down the thermostat and everything will be all right.

By 1978 Kennedy's disquiet with Jimmy Carter was building; pressure started rising overnight across the Democratic Party for Kennedy to bump Carter out in 1980. The big-government veterans around Washington had had enough. Kennedy's constituency was shifting; his allegiance to the Law and Order fanatics like Ken Feinberg had started to waver, but the trick remained to placate his more conservative colleagues on both sides of the aisle while appearing to keep the faith with the Old Liberal factions in the Party, in particular the black leaders and the labor leaders.

Allowing for the country's mood, all those hairsplitting civil libertarians in the universities looked like unchecked baggage. Under Kenneth Feinberg's tutelage the criminal code's third version, S-1722, emerged half as thick as either of its predecessors, the federal jurisdiction narrowed instead of widened, with lots of excisions in areas that bothered Professor Countryman. "The ACLU performed a valuable service to that legislation," Feinberg's replacement as legislative assistant, the brilliant, acerbic Carey Parker, observed. "They flagged ten or fifteen issues they cared about. We left them out."

Nevertheless, by spring of 1979 Kennedy's initial flirtation with the troll-ridden right had largely run its course; Kennedy brother-in-law and campaign strategist Steve Smith was reportedly telephoning his people around the country advising them to preserve their options. Kennedy was returning to orthodoxy. This was again the spokesman for the "underrepresented," Kennedy of the liberals, the chair by 1979 of the Justiciary Committee, grizzling at the temples with two fingers curled to mask the susceptible mouth as a lifetime of subcommittee proceedings rolled on beneath those flattering lights. Inspired staff appointments came and went, including Harvard Law School professor Stephen Breyer (ultimately headed toward the Supreme Court) to work on deregulation along with the bright-eyed and enterprising NAACP activist Ron Brown, who opened up new possibilities for Kennedy around D.C. after dark.

Immovable on the entitlement side, Kennedy had continued throughout the previous decade to manifest enough political courage to defend forced busing in Boston, support the ERA, countenance abortion on demand, close down the war in Vietnam, push through the first formal investigation of the burglary at the Watergate, then promote Archibald Cox as special Watergate prosecutor, in the spirit of a prankster insinuating a pit bull into a tank of alley cats.

Openly attacking Jimmy Carter released long-pent energies. "The staff now feels that Kennedy is riding the crest of a wave, that he is immune," said one employee after things got interesting. Office life, as ever, was rough and tumble.

"There is tremendous internal staff competition," remarked one member. "He promotes internal intrigue, he relishes playing one of us off against another to get the most good work out of us. If something goes wrong he'll say, 'Jesus, what's wrong, why haven't you straightened that goddamned thing out?' We do it because the rewards, the recognition, are tremendous." Others around the Hill tended to regard Kennedy's people as bright, but abrasive and pushy. "Kennedy would say, 'Good, that's the only way to get anything done around this fucking place,'" observed one of them. Kennedy himself functioned, now that his staff was largely a generation younger than himself, with a hardy paternalism—a demanding father, much like his own, also well worth listening to. "He'll look at anything, but when it comes to the legislative realities, he'll decide," an aide noted. "He likes to work at home with key people at night. No phone. That's where he educates us."

In and out myself, I began to develop misgivings about how this change of the guard was working out. On assignment covering Kennedy for *The Washingtonian* during the later seventies, it seemed to me a number of the staff replacements weren't anything like up to their counterparts during the sixties. His administrative aide—the volatile Rick Burke had been moved up into the top slot—combined the lightness of touch, the quick responses, and the metabolic resilience necessary to work for somebody like Kennedy, who never had hesitated to jerk any employee out of bed at three in the morning to take a memo. But Rick Burke remained a factotum, a kind of spineless concierge Kennedy had raised up to facilitate his indulgences, in no way the sidekick to grab the tiller when the boat was about to capsize.

The fact was, *this* Burke had nowhere near the inborn authority, the gravitas, of the irreplaceable David Burke. David Burke had been a peer—where issues, morality, and public affairs were involved he had amounted to Ted's guru—and so when David Burke moved on to a spectacular career that included the presidency of CBS News and chairmanship of the Dreyfus Corporation, Edward Kennedy was bereft. In a great many ways Burke had functioned as the young senator's alter ego, the spokesman for his better angels, the man he battened off intellectually and spiritually and habitually overworked. A lifelong insomniac, Kennedy tended to give up on sleep during the early hours of the morning and drive over to Burke's home and let himself into the dark house and watch the dawn come up. "I'm just getting used to the idea that I can now be certain that I will come down my staircase to prepare breakfast and not find Edward Kennedy sitting in a living room chair, waiting for my husband to appear," Burke's delightful wife Trixie confided to me over dinner shortly after the family moved to White Plains. Harnessed to Kennedy expectations, employees deserved no private existence, partly because Kennedy didn't.

One afternoon, just as the Christmas recess of 1974–75 ended, I stopped by and Kennedy invited me to join him as he walked over to the floor of the Senate to answer a roll call. Young Teddy had recently lost his leg to cancer, and there was still very little hope. We took the shuttle car that runs the tunnel between the Senate office buildings and the Capitol. Inside the elevator were Senators Lowell Weicker and George McGovern and the explosive, hard-bitten Strom Thurmond, whose puckered old pate was stippled just then with the liver-colored dots of his very recent hair transplant.

"Senator," Thurmond said, and with obvious sincerity, "Ah was awful sorry to hear about your boy. Ah know what that can do to a kid. Ah got a chile, know what Ah mean? Last summer he got this terrible dah-a-ree-a."

Kennedy nodded, saying nothing. The big muscles at the hinge of his jaw started cording. "It was awful," Thurmond said. "Your boy ever get dah-a-ree-a, Senator?"

"He—"

"Well, that's what mah son got himself. And it lasted a lot of the summer, too. So Ah know what you're goin' through."

Kennedy didn't say anything.

That winter, and for the next eighteen months, Kennedy and his son took on a kind of ritual agony which may have affected them both as deeply as anything in their lives. Every three weeks, first in Children's Hospital in Boston, then later in Washington, they underwent a weekend alone together, throughout most of which the thirteen-year-old Teddy was in and out of paroxysms of intense nausea from intravenous ingestion of an extremely powerful but toxic methotrexate compound, which researchers felt offered what hope there was. This was not great. Ted slept in a nearby chair so he would be at hand to administer the antidote by injection. "It's all very much like picking up coffee grounds with a sponge," Kennedy lamented to me. "You can scrape and scrape. But unless you get every last cell there's no point." The drug cost more than $2,000 per treatment, a figure Kennedy himself would later bring up in hearings to underline the final medical resorts open to the rich but denied everybody else.

In Washington, between injections, Kennedy spent what time he could encouraging his son. "It was very rough," he said soon afterward. "Very, very rough. He's a courageous boy, but it is very tough, the whole thing. Starting with the process of telling a child that he is about to lose a leg." The fact that Teddy did survive and appears to have managed a cure still seems a dispensation. "The silver streak in that grim and difficult time is that it has formed a bond between him and me that has just been . . . extraordinary. I can't tell whether it would have been so or not otherwise."

This livened Kennedy up, and he was quickly launched on a description of how his son subsequently learned to ski with one leg—twenty yards and fall the first day, fifty yards the next. At his father's funeral Mass, Teddy elaborated on how, soon after the amputation, Ted bullied and cajoled his despairing son into dragging the family Flexible Flyer up the snowy Hyannis Port driveway inch by inch so the suddenly exhilarated boy could ride down grinning on Ted's back. If you wanted it badly enough, anything was possible. "Having measured up to that particular process I find in Teddy a great sense of assurance, of self-worth," Kennedy said. "He is a very sensitive boy, but in an upbeat way. He takes a lot of time with people; he's very interested. He's personable. At least I find him that way."

Kennedy still called home most days to assure his children that nobody had killed him yet. The youngest child, Patrick, was far enough gone with asthma to sleep in an iron lung much of the time, and often carried inhalation equipment. The eldest, Kara, was reportedly terrified of "catching" her brother's cancer, and—encouraged by one of the many household employees who were forever hiring on and resigning—ameliorated the strain with grass and hash. There was a period during which she ran away repeatedly, sometimes to one of the county-run "safe homes," where somebody would telephone the senator, who then would arrive, red-faced and furious with the local authorities, to pick Kara up. "Teddy's illness was such a traumatic event," Kennedy admits with reference to Kara. "The center, the attention went entirely to him."

Inside the walls, far from the conviction the Ambassador had attempted to inculcate that his descendents were unique, natural winners, superachievers, Ted's children couldn't help but conclude that the worst was in store, that they would have to all but burn themselves out to make it through. "My father taught me that even the most profound losses are survivable," Teddy Jr. would recall at his father's funeral Mass. Working on his sailing with Ted, Teddy mused about the evenings on which "we'd be out late, and the family dinner would be getting cold, and we'd still be out there practicing our jibs and our spinnaker sets. And my father would say, 'Teddy, you see, most of the other sailors are smarter and more talented than we are, but the reason we are going to win is because we are going to work harder.' And he wasn't just talking about sailing."

And as for Joan? "She spent a lot of time with Teddy," Kennedy said, very quietly. "She felt better during that period." Joan noted this also. "I remember about four and a half years ago when my son Teddy had his leg amputated, I didn't take a drink. I was in okay shape while he was in the hospital. I was the mother by the bedside. But as soon as he was well and back in school, I just collapsed. I needed some relief from having to be so damn brave all the time."

This quotation is directly from Joan Braden's long interview with Joan Kennedy in the August 1978 *McCall's*. That Joan might speak—might now be permitted to speak—so publicly of matters which, while alluded to often enough these days even in the respectable press, had never been commented on officially, does suggest a wholesale and deliberate emptying of emotional attics. Something had to change.

Acquaintances saw this coming. One, a longstanding journalist friend of the Kennedy family's, remembers stopping at Kennedy's house in Hyannis Port to talk and have a drink. As he was leaving, Kennedy suggested that the visitor hadn't had a chance yet to say hello to Joan, and led him around to the back of the house; Joan lay crumpled up, passed out in the back seat of one of the Kennedy cars. "She was a rag mop," the friend observes. "I've seen drunks often enough, but what I was looking at there was the result of a two- or three-day bender. I think Kennedy just wanted me to see what he was up against. If something got printed, he was prepared for that."

The most poignant of Joan Kennedy's remarks concerned her failure to discuss her terrifying alcohol problem with her husband: "I tried to talk about it but I was embarrassed and Ted was embarrassed about it." This lasted a decade at least. "The Irish can do that with great distinction," says one old-timer, who knows the Kennedys well. "They just part slowly, and nobody can talk about it. Divorce is unthinkable; nobody can say it. The shorthand system takes over. 'I'm going out with the boys' or 'I'm going on a political trip.' And she can't say 'You're going out to get laid' or something. And then it's over; it ends without a shot being fired."

Blame must be laid in part on the accumulated effects of overwork, of overscheduling, on the "stresses"—an important word to Joan those days—that piled up when experts crowded in so often at dinnertime, and aides stayed over, and hour after hour the conversation revolved around technical details or matters of legislative strategy—in which Joan manifested, at best, a dutiful passing interest. As Joan blanked out, or put in time at sanitariums like Silver Hill, Kennedy himself took over, showed up at junior high assemblies and squeezed in sledding afternoons and interludes of kickball with the youngsters. Joan became an onlooker; the beauty in the photographs around their houses had come to differ so markedly from the sad, swollen, preoccupied forty-year-old that visitors felt haunted. In the summer of 1977 Joan joined Alcoholics Anonymous and took the pledge, and shortly after that she moved permanently to Boston and started working toward a degree in music at Lesley graduate school, with the announced intention of teaching. She gradually stopped drinking. For the time being.

"People ask whether newspaper stories about Ted and girls hurt my feelings," Joan told Braden. "Of course they hurt my feelings. They went to the core of my self-esteem." There is a nakedness to this no rationalizations can cover.

The fact is, Kennedy had been on the prowl all along. The day Ted married Joan, Jack Kennedy had advised his kid brother that marriage did not mean he had to abandon the ladies, and there is no evidence that Ted ever did. "The senator would like to take you home tonight," Bo Burlingham quotes Richard Goodwin, secondhand, approaching a recalcitrant young female journalist at a Cambridge party, soon after the senator had bestowed on her a "very intense, very meaningful stare." She reportedly declined, but not everybody would. Pimping for the senator was expected of certain employees.

What sometimes ruffled Kennedy is how much people built this into.

"Where'd you get that, *Human Events*?" Kennedy snarled over television some years ago when one of the panelists alluded to the senator's publicized conquests. Some wag took pictures of Ted's legs protruding from under a table at The Brasserie, a restaurant with private upstairs rooms, and sold the photos to a tabloid. Who or what was under the senator was hard to make out. When a celebrated companion flew East and actually presented herself at the Old Senate Office Building, Kennedy cued an assistant with one meaningful sideways gesture of the eyes the moment his visitor turned away: Get her out of here! This was, after all, Kennedy's place of business. Not very long afterward a friend of some years' standing went after Kennedy about all the notoriety the relationship involved. The senator appeared perplexed. "What difference does it make? I'm not in love with her," he responded at once. So much about life had become warding off collapse.

CHAPTER III

The Brass Ring

1. Premonitions

In September of 1978 I came by Kennedy's hideaway office just off the dome of the Capitol to interview him for a magazine piece. I well remember watching him slump there, squirming to get comfortable, while against the small of his aching back he worked the fingers of one trembling hand to adjust just right the warmth of his heating pad. Its bright, obvious cord trailed alongside the sprawl of a trouser leg and into an outlet someplace behind his battered, buttoned love seat. There was a stack of file folders piled up next to him, from which his Benjamin Franklin glasses kept threatening to slide each time he reached out to gesture with his fingertips. Kennedy would be forty-seven in February, on George Washington's birthday, and accordingly had been alive longer than any of his brothers. Primogeniture had reversed itself and left him senior to them all.

The back hurt; the senator kept boosting himself gingerly to offset the pain. His weight was up just then; each exertion produced bulges. The alarm buzzer sounded, signaling a vote, and Kennedy made use of the delay the noise required by dredging up the remains of a cigar; his mottled brick jowls worked heavily to reignite it. Those hooded eyes—heavily veined—strayed back into focus. I forgot between visits how supernaturally large Kennedy's face invariably looked to me.

Suddenly the buzzer stopped; I attempted another question; Kennedy's honeyed explanation continued. There was, as always, a tendency to leave himself out of his commentary, to sidestep personal involvement. "I suppose at different times in the political experience that you have conflicts, and you learn soon that those you oppose one day you are going to work very closely with on another. Otherwise your effectiveness around here is very limited," he remarked, with reference to Bobby Byrd, whom he had recently again assured that losing the Whip post was probably the greatest break he'd had. Or—regarding Carter—"We've got some . . . uh . . . areas of difference." But mostly the answers are responsive and satisfying—sharp, complete, overlaying point after point with background and precision. We discussed the crime bill, the health bill, the snares and gratifications involved with working alongside the Carter administration.

In fact, as soon as Carter became a feasible candidate in 1976 there had been bull-of-the-herd exchanges. As early as May that year Kennedy had pointedly refused to meet with the front-runner in Washington, then lambasted Carter for appearing "indefinite and imprecise" on critical issues, to which the Georgian responded—precise on this point—"I don't have to kiss his ass." Then Carter got elected; in Washington, Kennedy's broad shadow fell across a disheartening amount of government business. Carter's kiss planted early would soon look cheap at the price.

Their rivalry kept surfacing over health insurance. More than any other, this was Kennedy's touchstone. As chairman since 1971 of the forerunner of the Subcommittee on Health and Scientific Research of the Human Resources Committee, Kennedy had decided years before that anything short of comprehensive, mandatory national coverage couldn't meet public needs. Slogging through the primaries, Jimmy Carter had kept his own thoughts on the subject largely to himself until his candidacy looked serious. Then—after meetings with labor, whose support he'd require—Carter went so far as to propose that: "rates for institutional care and physician services should be set in advance, prospectively."

After Carter became president his interest in health insurance dampened. Kennedy brooded all spring, and then on May 17, 1977, before the United Auto Workers in Los Angeles, he stressed that "health reform" was already in danger of becoming the "missing promise" of the new administration. The shock registered instantly; the next day, also before the Auto Workers, President Carter declared that he intended to have the administration's bill ready before the end of 1978.

Throughout the previous autumn Kennedy had been collaborating very closely with Douglas Fraser, president of the United Auto Workers, who, like other labor leaders, regarded health with close to single-issue intensity. Fraser brought new energy to Walter Reuther's Committee for National

Health Insurance, which enlisted the groups in America Kennedy referred to as "underrepresented elements"—old people, clerics, farmers, nurses, minorities. With Hubert Humphrey dead, Kennedy became the spokesman in Congress for millions of bypassed citizens. Such coalitions are under-financed, temporary, and fragile, but it was Kennedy's perception that this could hold together—and pick up legislative majorities—if he and Carter could agree on language in time.

There were personnel problems: Kennedy respected Stuart Eizenstat, who represented the White House, but he was badly put off by lackadaisical Georgia staffers. "Ted is so tough on staff, he just doesn't tolerate sloppy staff work," said one observer. "I think he thinks Carter has some awful chowder-heads around." Negotiations made slow headway; a date of Friday, July 28, was set to announce the details; unexpectedly, on July 18, Eizenstat dropped in on Kennedy's health staff director, Dr. Larry Horowitz, to leave a draft of what the administration expected.

Kennedy and his people were dumbfounded. They'd gone along with the administration's $20 billion–a–year initial projection, a skeletal bureaucracy, a continuing role for private insurers. They'd conceded a maximum of discretion on the executive side in implementing stages of the program—a two-year start-up period, with benefits phased in through 1983, 1985, 1987. Now Carter reserved for the president a sequence of "trigger devices" to abort any phase of the program should factors in the economy make health spending undesirable. This arbitrary a procedure was unthinkable to Fraser. "The next morning Kennedy went in and saw Carter to urge that they stick together on the issue," Horowitz said. "Carter wouldn't budge."

Kennedy braced for confrontation. Just before the administration was scheduled to release its bill, Kennedy telephoned HEW Secretary Joe Califano to alert the secretary that he had decided to convene his own press conference on July 28, and that he expected to attack the Carter plan. Perhaps Califano might present the administration's ideas first. The alarmed president summoned Kennedy in hopes of compromise. Too late: Kennedy seized the headlines, flanked on the podium by an array of church, farm, and labor leaders headed by George Meany.

The president was guilty, Kennedy proclaimed, of a "failure of leadership," which now threatened to "make our efforts more difficult in the future." He and his subcommittee would proceed with hearings on their own. As for the Carter proposal? "The groups of elderly and the labor unions are still for our plan," Kennedy told a reporter after a few days. "The Senate Finance

Committee is supporting a bill limited to catastrophic illness, but as for Carter, I don't know who's supporting his bill."

"I don't myself question the motives of the president," Kennedy explained to me soon afterward. "I think he felt that he would be able to set in motion a series of bills whose outcome would be the same as ours. My own sense was—after sixteen years in the Senate—that the House and the Senate would pass the easiest part of this bill, and leave it." The inflated red face looked melancholy, pouting. "Our feeling, of course, is that health care is a right. If this is conditioned on a set of circumstances, that really isn't a right at all."

In December of 1978, visiting Memphis, the aroused Massachusetts senator was far enough along to share his alarms and excursions with delegates to Carter's handpicked Democratic National Conference. One palm stretched reassuringly above the expectant crowd, Kennedy harangued this sea of organization regulars for "policy that cuts spending to the bone in areas like jobs and health," while promoting "greater fat and waste through inflationary spending for defense." The tumult was dumbfounding. "We went down there just to fire a shot across the bow," one Kennedy aide admitted. "We did not expect the depth and intensity of the reaction."

Carter reacted clumsily. The Massachusetts senator's "special aura of appreciation," he told a press conference, owed much to the "position of his family in our nation and in our party." This cut to Kennedy's self-esteem. This was becoming personal.

2. Foreign Affairs

Edward Kennedy could marshal the talents of a staff that approached one hundred top people once he became Judiciary chairman. "If it's on the table, eat it!" Ted often quoted his father to me. Now he moved without apology into areas of statecraft with little or nothing to do with legitimate committee assignments. Let Carter draw his own conclusions.

Take foreign policy. Shortly before we talked that September of 1978 Kennedy had appeared in Russia to attend a United Nations health conference and to converse at extraordinary length with Soviet General Secretary Brezhnev. This offstage baby summit, not Kennedy's first, was leisurely but effective: The senator was concerned, he said, in putting over "one senator's views" to ease the after-effects of the Carter State Department's blundering reformulation of the all-but-complete SALT II agreements. This might be particularly useful now, Kennedy felt, since Carter hadn't bothered to take anybody in Congress with him to Vienna. Kennedy's involvement was predicated on "private assurances" by his hosts that the show trial of International Harvester representative Francis Jay Crawford for currency violations wouldn't embarrass this visitor. Before Kennedy left Moscow Crawford had been let go and eighteen dissident Jewish families were permitted to emigrate.

Within the Senate itself Kennedy had operated solidly to the left of Carter on shifting international problem areas. Kennedy amendments on Chile and Argentina terminated resupply of military equipment to their governments on grounds of gross violations of human rights. "He was a major player," one insider observes, "throughout the crises in Nicaragua and the Dominican Republic."

Kennedy's readiness to shadow—and bypass—the administration became apparent over China. China was Kennedy's issue—he proposed some measure of relations with the People's Republic as early as 1967, and stood by enthusiastically when Kissinger approached the mainland. Carter neglected China; in January of 1978 Kennedy took his family to Peking, met Deng Xiao-Ping, and returned to prod the administration.

On December 15, abruptly, Carter announced the establishment of regular diplomatic relations with the People's Republic, along with his decision to allow the mutual defense treaty with Taiwan to lapse. The whirlwind was anticipated: The vestigial China Lobby peeped, and Barry Goldwater immediately threatened to sue the president for infringing on Senate prerogatives.

On January 25, 1979, presiding over a quiet dinner for eighteen that was overlooked by the press, Kennedy invited to his home in McLean a delegation of mainland Chinese led by the new Chinese ambassador, His Excellency Chai Tse-min. Also present were Assistant Secretary of State Richard Holbrooke, Ambassador Woodcock, a member of the National Security Council, and senators Culver, Cranston, Glenn, Percy, Bentsen, and Bayh. Sometime during the evening, obviously by prearrangement, Foreign Relations member Percy sounded out the ambassador from China on a proposed Kennedy-Cranston Resolution, the gist of which was manifestly the proviso "Whereas the United States recognizes that an armed attack directed against Taiwan would represent a danger to the stability and peace of the area." Should aggression occur, the resolution proceeded, "The President is directed to inform the Congress promptly."

With a historic wink, Chai Tse-min indicated that he foresaw no problem, since "Whatever comes out must be consistent with normalization."

Sponsored by colleagues ranging from McGovern to Hayakawa, the Taiwan Relations Act went on the books in March, welcomed, Kennedy China expert Jan Kalicki noted, "by the Chinese on both sides of the Taiwan Strait."

The president wasn't impressed. "The so-called Kennedy-Cranston resolution," he indicated, was a diplomatic redundancy. At about this period Carter's attorney general, Griffin Bell, highlighted White House sentiment. "The president . . . asked me the other day if I thought Senator Kennedy would accept an appointment to the Supreme Court. I replied that I did not believe he would want to give up being co-president."

Kennedy had been coy, comparatively, second-guessing the administration about Taiwan. Regarding energy policy, over which he plastered Carter's decision-making all spring, Kennedy opened up freely. As chairman of the Joint Economic Committee's Subcommittee on Energy as well as a primary mover on Judiciary inside the watchdog Subcommittee on Antitrust, Monopoly and Business Rights, the Massachusetts senior senator was as knowledgeable as anybody at either end of Pennsylvania Avenue concerning oil and the corporations.

Kennedy's complaint was twofold. With time and politics, Kennedy banged away, Carter and his Department of Energy turned all the way around on commitments central to Carter's support in 1976. Carter had pledged to oppose deregulation of old oil and natural gas not under existing contracts, to prohibit horizontal energy monopolies, to expedite a strategic petroleum reserve, to downplay atomic reactors. Administration policy had worked toward precisely the opposite ends in virtually every case, compounding treachery with blunders like pouring 92 million barrels of oil into salt domes without providing for equipment to pump it out, ignoring enormous refinery profits that flouted Carter's announced guidelines, "bungling" gas negotiations with Mexico. To conservation—by 1979 a Kennedy keystone—Carter rendered "lip service."

In April of 1979 the president announced his decision to deregulate domestic oil reserves in phases through 1981. This move was unconditional, Carter admitted, although he was hoping for some kind of industry quid pro quo. Kennedy erupted publicly. The petroleum industry, he charged at once, had "intimidated the Administration into throwing in the towel without even entering the ring on the issue of price decontrol. And second, it has also intimidated the Administration into submitting a token windfall tax that is no more than a transparent fig leaf over the vast new profits the industry will reap."

"Baloney," Carter responded.

Kennedy's willingness to rubber-stamp Jimmy Carter's presidency was reaching historically low levels.

3. The Tempters

On May 2, 1979, just leaving the White House after a Law Day ceremony, Kennedy brushed off reporters who wondered whether Carter's recent decisions affected Kennedy's own prospects. "I've indicated that I expect the president to be a candidate," he muttered in passing.

"Does that mean Kennedy would not seek the presidency?"

"I can use my own words as well as yours or anybody else's," the Massachusetts senator snapped.

Could this be happening? "How can I run for the presidency, for God's sake?" Kennedy asked one intimate in 1974. "I'd have to do it with my back to the wall, and these days there isn't even a wall behind me anymore." He'd meant his immediate family; now relations were stabilizing. There were emotional considerations. "Right!" he told an acquaintance who remarked, on a transcontinental coach flight as 1978 was ending, that if he ever did become president he'd get a proper seat on Air Force One. "Planes. Airplanes and the telephones—that's just what Bobby used to say, those are the two great benefits of the presidency." He'd rearranged to stretch his back a little. "Otherwise, you can have the goddamned job," Edward Kennedy said.

By 1979 a well-positioned Democrat summed up: "All spring and summer people were coming to Senator Kennedy, people he had known for a long time, and they were saying: This administration is dangerous. It has no goals, it has no policies, it has no juices, it has no organization, it has no consistent positions, it has no leaders. It acts out of confusion, out of desperation, out of panic, it acts out of short-run political and legislative goals induced by a very fleeting set of tactics. It set itself up into positions where it is totally vulnerable to the opposite of what it started out to get in the first place, and then it calls getting the opposite of what it started out to get as somehow a victory." In short, utter chaos.

Other voices Kennedy heard reflected career concerns. In 1980 an extraordinary number of Democratic senators—twenty-four—many liberal, came up for election, an exposure that threatened the party with minority status for the first time since 1952. "There was a great deal of talk at the time that the Democrats would lose the Senate," Carey Parker recalled in 1979.

Kennedy's balding, circumspect legislative assistant then took this one step closer to a hint: "A lot of committee chairmen were nervous."

According to one senator who expected a fight to retain his seat in 1980, "various labor people were going around," who "came to me, to urge the people that were up in '80 to urge Ted to run." The energetic Al Barkan, head bouncer for the AFL-CIO's Committee on Political Education, pops up in several conversations; one source very close to Kennedy maintains that anti-Carter feeling among the major union chieftains was running so strong at this point that the message Kennedy got was "Prepare to move now, or forget about us in 1984." The endorsement by William Winpisinger of the Machinists was primarily the testing edge. Auto Workers, Graphic Artists, Government Employees got ready.

Kennedy heard all this, daily, spreading. Reverberations reached the White House; the gizzardy little president reacted. He red-penciled Kennedy's recommendation that Archibald Cox go onto the Court of Appeals, potentially a costly veto to inflict on a Judiciary Committee chairman when 152 federal judgeships, a full third, were up for appointment. In June of 1979 the president himself enunciated the White House position on the subject. "If Kennedy runs," he told a delegation of badly startled congressmen, "I'll whip his ass."

"I always knew the White House would stand behind me," Kennedy responded, "but I didn't realize how close they would be." This broke him up. Then—allowing himself one step—"If I were to run, which I don't intend to, I would hope to win."

This perception of himself as critic—on occasion, with veto powers—of ongoing presidential policy Edward Kennedy came by naturally. Virtually from the day he intervened to sweet-talk William Randolph Hearst into conceding the vital California delegation to Franklin Roosevelt in 1932, the founder Joseph P. Kennedy had arrogated for himself at the very least a consulting role in White House decision-making. By 1937 Joseph Kennedy's influence over contemporary Democratic isolationists was so great, the authoritative Ted Morgan concludes, that "FDR . . . sent Joe Kennedy to London, wanting him out of the country rather than lending his talents to the conservative wing of the party." By 1940 Joe was divulging to intimates like Arthur Krock that Roosevelt had privately knuckled under and pledged to support him as a presidential candidate in 1944 if he got behind FDR's unprecedented third term. With Joe ambition died hard, and then was offloaded onto his boys.

To become the president came down as part of the legacy. What *kind* of president had evolved. Jack had been cool, moderate, skittish at the prospect that anybody might tag him as a liberal. Virtually from the moment Edward Kennedy decided to go for his brother's old seat in the Senate he had been unabashed about announcing his own fixed political position. "I'm a liberal," he told reporters who tried to pin him down. And that was that, forever— pinned down. A lifetime as anchor man at the far end of the Kennedy lineup couldn't help but condition his development as a freshman senator. He'd been a toy, the butt of too many jokes.

Well aware of himself as something of an afterthought in this clan of quick-witted opportunists, Kennedy sensed the countervailing strength of consistency, the long-range payoff that might come with taking a solid ideological position, defining for himself a role durable enough to outlast the headlines of a season. Compared with his older brothers, with their Gold Coast digs at Harvard and their valets and their Long Island/Café Society circle of friends, Ted—and to some extent Bobby—interacted with a plainer America. Ted served in the military as a PFC, at Harvard he volunteered at a settlement house, he married the daughter of an advertising executive, not the heiress to the seedy nobility of the Bouviers and the Auchinclosses.

Campaigning, Kennedy attempted to shake every hand in the Commonwealth. Ted understood exactly what the day was like for the laborer gutting fish on the wharfs, the mill worker terrified because he just lost his job and there is no insurance now to deal with his wife's stomach cancer. Kennedy could never forget for long his own anguishing hospitalization after the plane crash and Teddy Jr.'s ordeal when he lost his leg. Awful however you lived it, but what if they hadn't been wealthy enough to pay for the most advanced treatment . . . ? Liberalism—populism—would come quite naturally to Edward Kennedy. He understood what animated Lyndon Johnson perfectly.

Bobby had fewer compunctions. "Am I still interested in getting Jimmy Hoffa?" I heard him snap once in 1968, all viscous gutturals, to one old friend at a noisy family skiing weekend shortly before he declared himself. Some retainer was passing around those inedible tuna sandwiches the Kennedys appear to favor. "Why would I worry about him when I've got Lyndon to work on?"

Given the family tradition, this was nothing new, challenging the White House. The problem for Ted was bucking a president from his own party. By 1979 Edward Kennedy had come to accept the notion without a lot of enthusiasm, activated in good part by his perception that Jimmy Carter was selling liberals out, and partly by a panic spreading among the party wheel horses around the country, with whom Teddy had always gotten along, that Carter was collapsing in the polls, he couldn't win reelection, he'd take the party down with him. That, and perhaps a reverb in Kennedy's genetic memory to remind him that a run at the Oval Office was expected of him before he died.

When had he decided to go? Only Ted could have answered that. David Burke once confided to me that when Teddy wanted advice from somebody he really trusted he found a quiet place, and locked the door, and talked to himself.

People closest to Kennedy agree that he let his presidential decision drift until the summer recess of 1979, but it was there by September. By that time Jimmy Carter's slide looked irrecoverable, too steep to make an issue out of splitting the party. His public approval rate hit 19 percent. The draft-Kennedy movements were already picking up steam. Carter's down-from-the-mountain shakeup, which cost the strongest of the cabinet members' jobs, looked beyond desperation, at least to Kennedy. "He was especially annoyed at the way they booted Joe Califano," one close aide stressed. "The senator felt that Califano was an able and competent Cabinet officer, into some very good things. They needed a scapegoat, somebody to blame, and there was reason to believe that Califano's anti-smoking policies had alienated the powers-that-be in North Carolina, which the White House thought it needed for reelection. So they fired Joe. The senator felt that was not the way to run a government."

Phases of his thinking could easily be plotted. By early spring, responding to *Boston Globe* veteran Robert Healy, the senator did concede that if and when Carter decided to relinquish a second term, he himself would have to think "terribly seriously" about what to do. This ignited the wires. Such bits in political code became commoner and commoner. Kennedy let in reporters that summer and talked about Chappaquiddick.

Kennedy's back was manageable; an ulcer had healed, and there was no concern now after a skin cancer excision from his nose. He'd gotten his weight down, finally. Kara, and now Teddy, were enrolled in college in Connecticut. "I saw him the day after the August recess," divulged one colleague, who had asked Kennedy whether he might attend a 1980 fund raiser in his state. "He said, 'Well, I'll do anything I can. But let's wait until things sort out a bit.' That, to me, was the first concrete indication. Then, you know, Rose gave her blessing, and Joan gave hers, and after that it was The Week That Was. Every day there was some new revelation."

Ultimately Kennedy explained himself. "My father always said," he again regaled one doubter, "'If it's on the table, eat it.'" He scheduled his announcement of candidacy for November 7, as soon as political decency allowed after the October 20 opening of the Kennedy Library. Jimmy Carter was expected to give the dedicatory speech.

Carter had an undertaker's touch, reporters wrote afterward, but hadn't the president demonstrated a lot more style at that than all those grabby Kennedys combined? The way he twitted Teddy by quoting Jack at him about waiting his turn? Punchy! The box score opened: one Carter, zilch to the challenger. Onlookers were already screaming for an early knockdown.

More insidious—and more damaging—was the nationwide fallout from the CBS documentary *Teddy*, written and reported by Roger Mudd. Mudd had operated on the fringes of the Hickory Hill circle. The hour was culled from the network's recent coverage of the senator; its tone and movement came out of clips that Mudd had selected after several long interviews, one on September 29, 1979, at Hyannis Port, to which the senator had agreed before he decided to run.

Mudd set Kennedy up. Mudd—whose career was troubled at that point—had been a friend of Bobby's, so Ted consented to the interview on the understanding that this would be a preliminary sounding-out, softballs. No need to see the questions in advance. As the tape rolled, Kennedy found that half of the airtime directly involved Chappaquiddick; the montage of shots of the bridge and the overturned Oldsmobile alternated with questions he'd answered again and again over the preceding decade, unrevealing and self-protective. Kennedy dodged and weaved. Frustrated and coldly angry, Mudd concluded that "It is now obvious that Kennedy and his advisers plan to volunteer nothing more on Chappaquiddick, or make any attempt to clear away the lingering contradictions."

He had already upset Kennedy by referring to Kennedy's marriage as one that existed "only on selected occasions," to which the senator responded, badly thrown off: "Well, I think that . . . it's a . . . it's had some difficult times, but I think we have . . . we, I think have been able to make some very good progress and it's . . . I would say that it's . . . delighted to share the time and the relationship that we, that we do share." Although admitting that Kennedy was indeed a "first-class senator," Mudd explained that away by characterizing him as a "captive of his bushy-tailed staff," and demonstrated this dependence with a sequence showing Kennedy greeting a congressman by his first name a moment after an aide whispered a name into the senator's ear. Mudd bored away openly at Kennedy's reputation as a skirt chaser, and dealt with Joan's alcohol problem, to which the shaken Kennedy himself referred. Asked why he wanted to be president, Kennedy maundered in every direction, painfully self-conscious about attacking the powers that be.

4. The Challenger

With Kennedy scheduled to announce his candidacy on November 7, 1979, CBS broadcast the documentary early, on Sunday night, November 4, opposite *Jaws*. Late in October, according to a close Kennedy aide, the network "released the transcript"—with all Kennedy's emotional staggerings rendered on the page—"to the White House, who gave it to the reporters three days before it ran. It reads a lot worse than it looks." The first round of columns taking off on Kennedy was based on these; Kennedy's initial drop registered.

The image of Kennedy to emerge from Mudd's documentary overwhelmed the journalistic community. A disgusted Jimmy Breslin proposed that Kennedy start out by establishing: "I'm no good and I can prove it." Much of this translated into compromised political results. Florida's premature "preferential convention" opted one-sidedly for the president. A Democratic National Committee straw poll favored Carter over Jerry Brown or Kennedy. An uncommonly seductive president showed up in Chicago and only Steve Smith's last-minute appeal to political decency turned Chicago mayor Jane Byrne (anchored still by the Merchandise Mart, the Kennedys *owned* Chicago) around in time.

Liberals who could count—Rick Stearns from the McGovern operation, the recent Kennedy press aide Robert Shrum and Eddie Martin (both Kennedy staffers lent to Carter as speechwriters in 1976, and promptly disillusioned), Jim Flug, Peter Edelman from Bobby's old retinue—joined Kennedy almost immediately. Before November was finished Ted Kennedy was rolling across the hustings to demand that his party help him "end twelve years of Republican rule and put a real Democrat in the White House." Meanwhile—quietly—Kennedy hardened on defense issues.

There were dangerous ifs.

If nobody blasted Kennedy.

If Joan remained stable.

So far she'd responded. When President Carter spoke at the JFK library dedication in October of 1979 Joan certainly seemed merry enough, her hair like straw before that prevailing Dorchester wind. The television batteries picked up on Joan plucking for a moment at Jimmy Carter's sleeve, giggling at an aside, while on her other flank her husband waited set-lipped. Local reporters noted that Joan had apparently forgotten her wedding ring some-place in the apartment.

Yet several weeks afterward, summoned to the rostrum at Faneuil Hall to second her husband's candidacy, she looked a masterpiece of overnight political restoration. Tailored perfectly in violet, doe-eyed again and aglow with makeup, her hair two spun-gold fronds to frame that vulnerable sensi-tive chin. "I look forward very, very enthusiastically to my husband being a candidate," Joan opened. Her quavering voice guttered; she clutched the rostrum. "Soon," she resumed shortly, "I will be talking with members of the press and at that time I hope to answer all of your questions that you might have on your minds today." Behind Joan, unremarked, little Patrick wept quietly.

Public life and private. The year before, struggling to explain all this at least to himself, Kennedy observed to me in rather a humbled tone, "The more I discover about other people's personal lives the more I see that every house-hold has . . . problems, in one form or another. People do the best they can."

It came to this: the politics of compassion. "I suspect people feel a lot of that," one veteran Washingtonian remarked at the time. "They pick it up just looking at Kennedy and listening to his voice—the vibrating warmth, even the garbage side. I have a feeling that's part of the reason for his tremendous strength in the polls. Their lives are shambles, and they know he's taken his share. He's a known quantity, familiar, and they can sense that like all great leaders he identifies with them."

The euphoria around Kennedy persisted almost until the day he announced his candidacy. Then and now analysts trace the first true crack in the cam-paign to the airing of Kennedy's interview with Roger Mudd. There would be charges that Mudd deliberately blindsided Kennedy, that Mudd remained affected in some obscure way by memories of Mary Jo Kopechne, that by exploiting a merciless pattern of editing and intercutting he intended to dem-onstrate to his peers that despite his membership in Ethel Kennedy's entou-rage he had kept himself unbeholden to Ted. But even Kennedy's intimates were startled at the way the senator stumbled and temporized throughout, unnerved by personal questions and unable to explain with any coher-ence his own motives in seeking the presidency. "It was like, I want to be president because the sea is so deep and the sky is so blue," Mudd observed afterward.

Rocked by the Mudd interview, Kennedy formalized his candidacy late in

November of 1979 and launched into barnstorming. Early weeks were head-long, strenuous, as if he expected to wrap it up in one furious round. Kennedy would later confess that he had spent much too much time attempting to decide whether he wanted to run, and not nearly enough establishing how. Yet frequently his manner seemed desultory and uncertain between bursts of rhetoric, as if he found himself shoved out onto the stage and suddenly seemed puzzled about what people expected. Whenever crowds responded listlessly he attempted to harangue them to life.

Quite often he lost track. "Roll up your sleeves and your mother and your fathers," he implored one audience in November. A week later, just as the hostage crisis was breaking in Teheran, the fatigued campaigner favored a late-evening radio interviewer with his opinion of the deposed Shah: "The Shah had the reins of power and ran one of the most violent regimes in the history of mankind—in the form of terrorism and the basic and fundamental violations of human rights, in the most cruel circumstances, to his own people . . ." Why admit the Shah, "with his umpteen billions of dollars that he's stolen from Iran and, at the same time, say to Hispanics who are here legally that they have to wait nine years to bring their wife and children to this country?"

This was a response that stunned the establishment, Republican and Democrat equally. Reza Pahlevi had carried water for American policymakers in the Middle East since World War II ended, the CIA manipulated him back into power in 1953. He may have been a sonovabitch, as FDR once phrased it, but he was *our* sonovabitch. Even at hillbilly levels much of the electorate understood that the Shah had been our catspaw, a ruler we subsidized in return for permission to bulldoze into place the SAC bases and install the all-powerful CIA apparat through which we were able to maintain control of the oil bonanza all across the region. To have let that slip away under an American president too uncoordinated to rescue our hostages from our own embassy was tragic; to defend the ragheads who had dispossessed our puppet was unforgiveable.

Shortly afterward Kennedy press spokesman Tom Southwick confessed to "ayatollah dreams," during which his boss wrote Khomeini: "'Greetings, I will give my blood for you!'" Kennedy had responded honestly, and in politics that is almost always a mistake.

"Ted Kennedy is the worst politician I've ever seen in my life at saying nothing," Bob Shrum says—Shrum means by this the worst at suppressing his opinions—and when he censored himself his delivery got so stilted audiences clawed toward the exits. As the crutial weeks went on, Kennedy alternated between bumbling around the issues and blurting what he really thought. Too often his impulses violated the public mood. Days after Jimmy Carter responded to the Soviet Union's invasion of Afghanistan with a grain embargo against Moscow, Kennedy denounced it as "unworkable and unfair" to the American farmer. The American *farmer*? Again, Jimmy Carter had gauged the popular current, while Kennedy was swept away. Kennedy's polls slipped—slowly those early weeks, and then in what David Broder characterized as a "dizzying downward spiral."

"What's wrong? I'm not going to list the things that are wrong—everything is wrong," one "hollow-eyed senior strategist" admitted to me at the time; fourteen years later, another adviser who has been close to Kennedy for decades admits there were good reasons for such a dramatic turn. "Kennedy had been drafted by the power structure of the Democratic Party. At that point we were doing the homework we should have done in April, May, June. These people were appalled that we couldn't run a good campaign." Chappaquiddick details resurfaced. Figures who had been allied to the Kennedys for several political generations—Abe Ribicoff, Averell Harriman, ultimately John Glenn, and even, in the end, Kennedy's football teammate and sailing partner John Culver—sidled over to back the president. Big Labor defected wholesale.

In the Iowa caucuses, where crowds seemed responsive, Kennedy lost 2–1. By then, Kennedy's advisers admit, the president, impregnable in the Rose Garden, was strategizing the hostage crisis perfectly. As the year played out, it won Carter the nomination and cost him the election.

One immediate consequence was that the money dried up. A campaign that had begun with the leasing of a jet quickly turned hand-to-mouth. Steve Smith and the Kennedy bookkeepers in the Pan Am Building wanted Teddy to succeed, but they were immovable when it came to risking any more family capital, which was melting away fast without the financier to bring in the long shots. Both Jack and Bobby ran fortified by Steve Smith's heavy checkbook, but now a consensus had been reached that Ted would have to generate anything he needed on his own. Cash was an increasing problem: Joe Kennedy's children were long conditioned to be spenders—I remember well sitting in his outer office while the Kennedys' feisty little brother-in-law reamed out Pat Lawford for charging to the family accounts an exorbitantly expensive fur coat.

One minor consequence of all this was that I got a call in early January of 1980 inquiring as to whether I might have room in our vast warren of a converted boardinghouse in New Hampshire to put up four key women from

Kennedy's D.C. office during the weeks leading to the crucial New Hampshire primary. It was all right with us. Our children were small at that time, and they were a little bit nonplussed when the Kennedy delegation, led by Joanna Reagan and Connie Lambert, turned up that mid-winter in a rented car and took over their bunk rooms on the third floor. The campaign's all-business quartet skidded out of our icy driveway very early every morning to attempt to put together a credible primary inside the labyrinth of plywood partitions at the Manchester storefront.

I remember looking in at Manchester one frigid evening. The banks of telephones had finally stopped ringing, the horde of student volunteers, many up for the duration from Massachusetts, were turning in whatever flyers were left over and headed toward the bars. By then a big, pink, plump fellow just out of his teens, Teddy Kennedy Jr., seemed to be directing traffic. I asked for his father; Teddy gestured a little grandly toward the back. Sure enough, the Minotaur was occupying himself in the depths of the labyrinth: His sleeves rolled up and an expression of great concentration on his face, the would-be candidate was shuffling along manning a push broom, herding a sizeable pile of debris ahead of him toward the stragglers by the entrance.

Kennedy lost New Hampshire, overwhelmingly. Early in the campaign, after Ted got slaughtered in Iowa, Jimmy Flug had called me for ideas, and I roughed in a number of talking points I thought might help, which immediately seemed to fortify the stump speech Kennedy tried out at Georgetown and ultimately brought in the big eastern industrial states—Pennsylvania, New York, then California—which began to drift into his column. But this wasn't nearly enough, or soon enough. The candidate had reached a point at which, struggling to avoid gaffes, he spoke so slowly that there were jokes about a defective teleprompter. This was a Kennedy campaign, columnists wrote, without a Kennedy. The struggle to present himself as a consensus candidate increasingly left him tongue-tied. Kennedy's ulcer started bleeding again. Reporters dubbed his entourage "The Bozo Zone."

By February a lot of the fault-finding devolved on Stephen Smith. Smith had assumed by right the managerial role in Ted's campaign. To hired-gun veterans of the McGovern drive in '72 like Carl Wagner and Rick Stearns, the chain-smoking Kennedy brother-in-law came over as too well-dressed, too sure of himself, and innocent of oncoming technology. Up-to-date methods could get expensive. Smith declined to designate a single media adviser for months, and continued to press, according to one bystander, "outdated, anachronistic ideas on polling, on advertising, on how television works." A

consultant brought in late, Joe Napolitan, subsequently told Smith his initial round of ads was "an embarrassment, probably the worst television ever
produced for a presidential candidate in American history."

Smith was a serious Catholic himself, and Kennedy's women's-right-to-
choose stand in the face of the rising abortion issue left him uncharacteristically irresolute, paralyzed about how to handle zealots picketing clinics
around the country. The problem was melding three generations of Kennedy
advisers into something that worked. "More than anything else Steve had a
strong desire to protect Kennedy," Bob Shrum would tell me shortly afterwards. "Between Iowa and the convention he was primarily concerned that
Kennedy not be damaged more than he already had been. But at the beginning, when everybody thought he was going to win and millions of people
were jumping on the ship, there might be twenty-eight people in the room
and everybody would have a vote." Consensus was virtually impossible.

Ted's recent acquisitions presented a whole new generation of advisers.
Smith played it straight and tried to give everybody a hearing, but he was
brusque and quick-tempered much of the time, and remained a hard sell.
"I joined the campaign in November," Shrum says, "and somebody told me
that Steve and I started to get along in world-record time. I started to get
along with him in March, four months into things, once we were working
together on media for New York." Sixties veterans like Ted Sorenson and
Dick Goodwin were in and out.

For family reasons, replacing Steve was out of the question. By April,
one insider divulged to a reporter, "Teddy just doesn't give Steve authority
to make all the decisions and he keeps things back. He plays him off the
boards a bit." The friction was heating up between the field operation and
the headquarters, with more power gravitating every week to the relentless
Paul Kirk, backed up by Larry Horowitz and Tony Podesta and Joe Crangle,
while Bob Shrum and Carey Parker stuck with the candidate and traded off
the speechwriting.

"It was never quite clear who was really in charge of the campaign," Jim
Flug acknowledged decades afterward. "For whatever reason it didn't quite
gel, and as the money problems got worse that limited the amount of advertising you could do, and a lot of staff disappeared, and so it ended up—the
results showed it. Paul Kirk would later ascribe the chaos to their "abrupt
start," which precluded the "anticipatory shopping or interviewing of people
who just might get such a thing together . . . It was in part the accident of
timing. The first couple of attempts weren't satisfactory." They continued to
reinvent the machine even as it ran away. Kennedy himself juggled twenty-

hour days on the stump with stolen moments to edit his own speeches, horse-trade with primary state managers, sneak calls in to squeeze fresh cash from supporters.

After the autumn mudslide Smith was emphatically disinclined to deplete the family assets further to maintain the trappings of a juggernaut. The chartered United Airlines 727 had given way to a much smaller aircraft, which survivors still characterize as a "zoo," with everybody pitching fresh approaches while the polls plummeted. Reporters—their editors increasingly snappish because the Kennedy campaign billed twice as much as counterparts in either party—attempted to justify the costs by worming favors and divulgences out of Kennedy's malleable office manager, the ever-permissive Rick Burke.

Everybody aboard still alludes, in Shrum's words, to the candidate's "resilience and good temper, the way he dealt with all of us and mostly with himself under conditions under which most people would have buckled." Emerging from an interview with *The New York Times* editorial board during which Kennedy discovered that biographical information supplied by Shrum and Carey Parker was largely inaccurate, their boss had eased back into the tucks of his limousine to remark, "Listen, I will thank you two to let me make my own mistakes. As you may have noticed, I'm outstanding at that."

The eighteen- and nineteen-hour days precluded the usual highballs, although Kennedy, revved up and impatient as ever with delays and frustrations, let down during breaks by eating too much. The roly-poly Shrum remembers how he and his boss could "devour a two-pound cheese fairly quickly, given the right circumstances." Shrum recalls grazing nonstop throughout one fourteen-hour plane ride on an Air New England charter, which they had rented to save money without anticipating refueling stops in Charleston, South Carolina, and Indianapolis en route to an appearance in Kansas City. "As we were coming in the pilot couldn't find the airport, and Denny Shaw and Larry Horowitz and I stood crowded in the front of the plane trying to locate it on a road map."

Another factor to reckon with was the senator's unpredictable wife Joan, back on the tour primarily at her own instigation. Spotted around the boondocks wearing "a loud plaid suit, a purple blouse, and eye shadow to match," Joan presented herself as a "very sophisticated lady," who had already met Mr. Brezhnev and the leaders of China, "all these things Mrs. Carter has not done yet." She rationalized the fact that she had lived alone in Boston the last two years as full of advantages. Left behind in McLean with Patrick, Ted had grown much closer to his son. If Ted did win, she expected to join him in the White House. Her relocation had facilitated "my journey back to health." "One of the side effects of her unnerving speeches," Mary McGrory wrote, "was that some people who did not like her husband liked him less after hearing her troubles. 'It's been therapy for her,' grumped a Kennedy supporter. 'But how does it help him?'"

The pounding he took as he went along seemed somehow to loosen Ted up more than it undid him. He was assimilating fast. On January 28 he gave the speech at Georgetown that dragged the props in under his campaign, belatedly responding in the process to Roger Mudd's costly question as to why he was running for the office. "I believe we must not permit the dream of social progress to be shattered by those whose premises have failed," he summed it up toward the close. "We cannot permit the Democratic party to remain captive to those who have been so confused about its ideals."

He had already laced into the newly propounded "Carter Doctrine," which, with its open commitment to military intervention in the Persian Gulf, "offers defense contractors a bright future of expansion and profit." Fifty years of American blundering was anticipated in this one charge. Kennedy preferred to start with obligations both ways between the United States and the Gulf powers, bartering military support for oil stability. He blamed President Carter directly for having let the Shah into the United States for treatment and thereby precipitating the hostage crisis. Rather than reenacting draft registration, Kennedy called for gas rationing, along with wage and price controls to bring the rampant inflation down. "I want to be the president who at last closes tax loopholes and tames monopoly . . . halts the loss of rural land to giant conglomerates . . . brings national health insurance to safeguard every family from the fear of bankruptcy due to illness." It was a platform thirty years ahead of its time.

One idea man at the center of Kennedy's campaign sensed another dynamic. "Once it became apparent in the polling data that all these nice calculations about whether you should or you shouldn't come out for price controls and the rest weren't going to affect the outcome one way or the other, you might as well just throw everything at it because you weren't at a point where it was even worth calculating risks anymore. So he just went and did that: The Georgetown speech was just the classic liberal speech." There wasn't any need, Kennedy felt, to propitiate the Democratic right. "Now he had found his voice, and he could talk the way he was used to talking. And people saw that it was authentic.

"But beyond that—and I wouldn't want this attributed to me—I have a personal hypothesis that he lacked confidence in his ability to be president, and one of the reasons why his performance improved so drastically was in inverse relationship to how much he thought he had a chance to be president. The less he thought he could win the better a candidate he was. Although members of his family thought his fear of being shot was his biggest fear . . ."

Spring brought victories. Underfunded all the way, Kennedy won in New York, in Pennsylvania, in Connecticut and Rhode Island and in New Jersey and finally in California. This was a surprising showing, but it was never enough. Furthermore, as one of Kennedy's handlers admitted afterward, "There are always in the second stage of the primaries a lot of people, party professionals, who just want to slow down the front-runner for reasons of their own. So he benefited from the people who had decided to renominate Carter but weren't just going to hand it to him."

Kennedy continued to close, but Carter had the delegates. By the end of June the wheel horses of the party were starting to drop by to urge Ted to let it go. He was damaging Carter. Instead, Kennedy pushed the Judiciary Committee to probe Billy Carter's dealings with the Libyan government. He challenged the president to release his delegates and open the convention up. Bob Shrum and Jimmy Flug especially continued to feast on dreams, and Kennedy sometimes speculated as to what might happen if the delegates succumbed en masse to the right chemistry, at the right moment.

On fumes of glory, several generations of Kennedyites coasted into Manhattan in August. Money was so short that Ted and Joan lived out of a suite they shared with Bob Shrum and Carey Parker. Flug, who had been troubleshooting the campaign from Iowa to Maryland, had been installed as press secretary by Paul Kirk after Pennsylvania. At the convention itself "We had no budget whatsoever," Flug remembers. "The delegate operation had whatever money there was. So I was in charge of setting up the press operation. Installing lines is very expensive, especially in New York. We had a press room in the hotel, and a press room in the garden. I did not pay for one phone. I had a bank of pay phones in each place. The press people we liked we gave the incoming numbers for the pay phones."

It wasn't over yet. Even after the rules committee cut off all hope of releasing committed delegates, Kennedy people kept ratcheting the platform steadily to the left. Ted had brought in the tough-minded Harold Ickes Jr. to supervise convention tactics, and quickly prevailed on planks that incorporated a $12 billion jobs program and the guarantee of a job for every American, reproductive freedom, and the withholding of party support from

candidates who waffled on the Equal Rights Amendment. Carter managers
held fast against comprehensive health insurance and mandatory wage and
price controls.

Kennedy's speech lifted all the boats. Insisting at the outset that he was
there "not to argue as a candidate, but to affirm a cause," Kennedy was
emotionally repositioning himself to confront a Ronald Reagan presidency.
"The great adventure which our opponents offer is a voyage into the past,"
he offered. "Progress is our heritage, not theirs." In uncanny anticipation
of the transcontinental pepper grinder through which Reagonomics would
feed the wage earners of the nation, Kennedy noted that "The poor may be
out of political fashion, but they are not without human needs. The middle
class may be angry, but they have not lost the dream that all Americans can
advance together . . . Let us pledge that we will never misuse unemployment,
high interest rates, and human misery as false weapons against inflation . . .
The tax cut of our Republican opponents takes the name of tax reform in
vain. It is a wonderfully Republican idea that would redistribute income in
the wrong direction . . .

"For me," Kennedy concluded, "a few hours ago, this campaign came to
an end. For all those whose cares have been our concern, the work goes on,
the cause endures, the hope still lives, and the dream shall never die."

Kennedy campaigned for Carter, if without much relish, and even that little was purchased, according to a bitter vignette in Hamilton Jordan's memoirs, with discretionary Carter funds extracted behind closed doors by Steve
Smith to defray Kennedy's campaign bills. Reagan prevailed. Joan returned
to Boston, and after an interval there was a quiet divorce in 1981.

CHAPTER IV

The Politics of
Counterinsurgency

1. Linebacker

A decade now opened during which—except for the quadrennial speculation as to whether he would run again—Kennedy's name came up a lot less
frequently in the respectable press, although the tabloids remained devoted.
There was a suspicion that he was sinking bit by bit, preoccupied with booze
and bimbettes. Kennedy was roaming widely, but somehow the opinion-
makers remained oblivious to the fact that most of the working year, days
and many nights, Kennedy was already engaging the Reagan administration,
often all but single-handed.

"Goddamn it," Bob Shrum said in the aftermath, "whatever criticism
people have of this guy, just remember that in the early eighties, when everybody else was running for cover, he absolutely refused to. He stood up on
stuff that was very tough to stand up on." This required for Kennedy the
rethinking of alliances, the restructuring of issues frequently. He had lost
his presidential bid, but he was moving now to formulate around himself
something close to a shadow government.

The reversal of political tides that installed Ronald Reagan washed irreplaceable Democrats out. The House held, but many of the ablest among
the younger, more liberal senators lost, so that the Senate itself passed over
to the Republicans. George McGovern fell, along with Warren Magnuson

and Birch Bayh and Frank Church and even John Culver. These were the stalwarts who tended to stand with Kennedy, his basis for power. Howard Baker moved up to Majority Leader, then, tapped as Chief of Staff by the White House, relinquished to Robert Dole. "That's one thing about being Leader," Dole promptly acknowledged in his velvet snarl. "I don't have to let Ted Kennedy run the place."

On Labor and Human Resources, guardian of the "entitlements," Kennedy was now subject to the chairmanship of Utah conservative Orrin Hatch. "My leader," he told the press, reportedly "exploding with laughter." Kennedy emerged as Ranking Minority Member, seven Democrats versus nine Republicans. He could anticipate that little he proposed would make it out of committee.

The door blocked, Kennedy rattled the windows. Of nine committee Republicans, two tended to side with the Democrats on human services questions: education-minded Robert Stafford of Vermont and Connecticut's Lowell Weicker, by then an established maverick. Tom Rollins, who ran Kennedy's staff on the labor committee through much of the eighties, remembers the afternoon when Weicker was speechifying directly in the teeth of White House policy, while Robert Dole stood nearby, glaring. "I know what you guys are thinking," Weicker broke off to tell Dole. "You'd like to trade me for a Democrat and two draft picks."

"Forget the draft picks," Dole muttered.

While acknowledging that there was little the Democrats could do to forestall the $23 billion in cuts to social programs the Reagan administration demanded, Kennedy concentrated on keeping the programs themselves alive. Since 1933, Democratic presidents had lobbied to weave into the books what commentators would come to refer to as the "social safety net." Starting with the Social Security and minimum wage legislation and labor union provisions enacted under the New Deal, and expanded in the rush of Lyndon Johnson's New Frontier to provide for Medicare and Medicaid as well as the breakthrough civil- and voting-rights requirements, these sweeping and bitterly contested protections and entitlements altered profoundly the relationship between voters and their government.

Wide-ranging, costly, and replete with millions of patronage jobs and opportunities for limitless pork-barrel trade-offs, this infrastructure of welfare remained a glory to the Left and a compounding stomachache of increasing taxes and overlapping federal regulation to the traditional Right. To politicians of every persuasion, it looked like money and influence. Among the cabinet posts, the ever-expanding Department of Health and Human

Services disposed of a far bigger budget than any other bureaucracy, dwarfing even the Pentagon. Its counterpart in the Senate, the Committee on Labor and Human Resources, was well positioned to authorize and direct these colossal nationwide expenditures.

So it was not a complete surprise when Edward Kennedy decided prior to the 1980 elections to relinquish the leadership of the prestigious Judiciary Committee in return for the chairmanship of Labor and Human Resources. In any fruitful year most of the big-ticket legislation working its way through Congress would now come directly beneath his hand. He and his sharp-eyed staffers could tinker with, define the terms, where necessary recut provisions before they became subject to the politicizing give-and-take of routine committee debate. He could quietly scuttle anything obnoxious. Whatever got reported out, made it onto the Senate floor and came up for voting—he'd leave his fingerprints on that. When finally the House version came along, and senators had to be selected for the conference so that a reconciled bill might emerge for the president's signature, senatorial usage would mandate that the Chairman—or the Ranking Minority Member—retain the privilege of challenging such delegates as the Majority Leader selected.

Although denied the chairmanship in 1980 by the unexpected loss of the Senate to a Republican majority, as Ranking Minority Member Kennedy quickly proved himself maddeningly dangerous and inventive. With help from Stafford and Weicker Kennedy preserved a range of services, from school-lunch subsidies to the $25,000 family-income limit for students applying for college loans. He maneuvered to keep Title I education funds out of block grants to the states, resisted cuts in Social Security, made sure the low-income fuel assistance program continued, fought off the termination of the services of the Comprehensive Employment and Training Act (CETA). On the Senate floor he prevailed over Hatch's effort to gut legal assistance to the poor, which survived with two-thirds of its allocation after a 74–26 vote.

"After the '80 campaign," Kennedy recalled to me a decade later, "even before the inauguration, it was very, very clear to me that the focus and attention of the Reagan presidency was to undermine the basic construct of the human-services programs, which I had always thought were not to be sort of a handout but a hand up." To slow down this wrecking crew, Kennedy made his alliances where he found them.

For example, as the ranking Democrat on Labor and Human Resources, Kennedy managed to enlist a newly elected conservative from Indiana, Dan Quayle, in pushing through the Job Training Partnership Act, which appealed to susceptible Republicans as a replacement for CETA. Funded at $3.9 billion, it created a mechanism through which private industry groups and local officials would provide one million job slots and train 2–3 million new workers a year.

The bill got through, Kennedy remembered, but Quayle was "basically stiffed by the White House, which urged other Republicans not to attend quorums and conference committees. Even after it passed, they weren't going to have a signing ceremony for him." Nevertheless, it had passed. Kennedy had now demonstrated that—especially when he graciously allowed some gullible Republican to take the credit for the breakthrough—he could continue to infiltrate into the social structure the laws he wanted passed irrespective of who controlled the Congress or even the White House. Over his five decades Kennedy collaborated with (read: had his way with), among others, Republicans Hugh Scott on campaign finance, Strom Thurmond on crime, John Danforth on civil rights, Judd Gregg, John Boehner and Michael Enzi on education, and Jacob Javits, Nancy Kassebaum, and—spectacularly—Orrin Hatch on health.

Not that it wasn't shoveling against the tide, those grueling Reagan years. "I mean, you're talking about an administration that opposed the extension of the Voting Rights Act," Kennedy summed it up for me with a toss of his mane.

Subparagraph by subparagraph, Kennedy and what diehards he could convince managed to deflect or at worst slow down the bulldozing of half a century of social engineering. This was depressing work, Rollins remembers, a matter of slapping a hold on whatever the administration "was pushing, of never passing anything by unanimous consent and forcing Republican trade-offs to keep any proposal alive." Rollins cites one "ugly, bruising" interlude during which Kennedy and his staff spent four days in a hearing room to block the appointment of the conservative lawyer Jeff Zuckerman as general counsel of the Equal Employment Opportunity Commission when Clarence Thomas was chairman. On day three the questioning got so rough Zuckerman sobbed, and in the end he went down.

Since "hearings" could not be authorized without a committee majority, Kennedy found that he could attract press and force public attention by reinventing the hearing under another rubric. This he would call the "forum." Once witnesses were alerted, Kennedy booked the Senate caucus room and excoriated the administration over the hypocrisies behind "constructive engagement" in South Africa or nation-building in Central America. This alternative format added nuclear winter to the national nightmare after the

Soviet scientist Yevgeniy Velikhov and the American writer and astronomer Carl Sagan testified that a nuclear exchange could blanket the stratosphere with dust and deny the planet enough sunlight for life to survive.

Within months of the inauguration Kennedy had argued against administration proposals to strip $749 billion from corporate and personal taxes through 1986. This "tree ripe with the richest plums for the wealthiest individuals and corporations" would produce "only bitter fruit for workers and middle class," Kennedy prophesied. What sort of monetary policy was this under which "Gulf and Mobil can borrow over $5 billion each in a single two-day period, but a working family cannot obtain a home mortgage even at the fantastic rate of 19 percent?" If "Ronald Reagan does not know the facts about how this recession began, then Ed Meese ought to wake him up and tell him!"

Aghast at the "jellybean economics" catching hold across Reagan-era America, Kennedy drove an amendment through which directed the administration to "take appropriate action on a voluntary basis to encourage banking or other financial institutions to exercise voluntary restraints in extending credit for the purpose of unproductive large-scale corporative takeovers." Nineteen eighty-one wasn't finished, and Kennedy was already projecting the decade's catastrophic banking failures, its looming deficit calamities.

In 1982, ignoring the traditional limitation of two major committee appointments per senator, Kennedy persuaded his Republican colleagues to grant him a seat on the Armed Services Committee to add to Justice and Labor and Human Resources. Kennedy prepared to comment on—and involve himself in—a wide array of defense and foreign policy questions. "He doesn't steal credit," observed James Wieghart, the respected former D.C. bureau chief of the *New York Daily News* who handled the press for Kennedy for a time. "He just absorbs it." Kennedy was already criticizing the projected $180 billion arms buildup, the resurrection of the "discredited and extravagant B-1 bomber," additional nuclear aircraft carriers. With Armed Services credentials he continued to attack the B-1 as a "supersonic Edsel in the sky," the MX as a "missile without a mission." As for Star Wars: "We must reject the preposterous notion of a lone ranger in the sky, firing silver laser bullets and shooting missiles out of the hands of Soviet outlaws."

Kennedy spoke against the administration's dispatch of fifty-four military advisers to support the repression in El Salvador. As Reagan's first term was winding to an end, Kennedy was vociferous in his attacks against U.S. military involvement throughout Central America. His success in cutting back $21 million in aid to the Contras along with $62 million to El Salvador was telling enough by March of 1984 to alarm Rob Simmons, the CIA retiree who looked after the majority's interests as staff director for the Senate Select Committee on Intelligence. As for the CIA itself? As early as 1978 Kennedy had himself authored the Foreign Intelligence Surveillance Act, which created special courts to monitor U.S. intelligence agency surveillance. By the Reagan years I was putting together my book about the early decades of the Agency, *The Old Boys*, and Kennedy would call me from time to time to try and find out what my conflicted spooks over in Langley were up to.

The Agency's covert mining of Managua harbor had surfaced in the press that week, Barry Goldwater was outraged ("I've pulled [CIA Director Bill] Casey's nuts out of the fire on so many occasions," Goldwater exclaimed to Simmons, "I feel like such a fool"), and Simmons was especially concerned because "Teddy Kennedy was going to attack the funding" on the Senate floor. On April 19, by a vote of 84 to 12, Kennedy marshaled a resolution through the Republican-controlled Senate that recommended a ban on the use of U.S. funds to mine Nicaraguan waters, "a first step," Kennedy specified, "to halt President Reagan's secret war in Nicaragua." "It was the first debate on the floor of the Senate on U.S. policy in Central America," his national security assistant Greg Craig recalled for me, "and it would not have happened if Ted Kennedy had not single-handedly involved himself."

This, along with Massachusetts Representative Boland's amendments in the House, helped move along the excruciating process that led to cease-fires throughout the region. Closer senatorial attention would culminate in the Iran-Contra scandals. Despite himself, Barry Goldwater was impressed. He professed to be horrified ("Oh, my God, here we go again") when Kennedy first wangled his way into Armed Services, but the Massachusetts senator's attentiveness as chair of the Tactical Warfare Subcommittee to the feelings and requirements of the senior brass forced Goldwater to admit that "you are a valuable member of the committee . . . Frankly, you have the kind of attitude that we need."

Next, Kennedy landed on the Manpower Subcommittee as the ranking Democrat, which gave him a lot of input as to the distribution of perhaps $85 billion a year of defense money. Kennedy recut his schedule to visit U.S. military installations around the world, from troop ships of the Southern command headed for equatorial waters to Lockheed's experimental "skunkworks" in California, and became a champion of enlisted troops especially. Kennedy spoke for the Marine Corps, and defended the Osprey helicopter. He gave his attention to concerns like spousal employment on bases, day care, health and education availability, and pay levels—counterparts to the issues on which he was himself expert after years on the Labor Committee. "He did the nitty-gritty work," Greg Craig emphasizes. "Not high profile. You weren't going to run for president doing that stuff."

His Armed Services involvement made him a lot more credible once he began to critique the ever-swelling Reagan budget. Kennedy swung his influence behind the enhancement of conventional forces, cruise missile technology, stealth aircraft, the missile submarine armada, perfected command and control systems. Echoing JFK's nonproliferation concerns, Ted became the Senate's foremost spokesman for negotiating a bilateral nuclear freeze. He now saw clearly the connection between U.S. support for ruling elites around the world and the emergence of revolutionary challenges. "Instead of cutting off food stamps to our own people," Kennedy implored Democrats at their midterm convention in 1982, "let us cut back the feast of military aid to fatten dictatorships around the world." It wouldn't be long before old friends like Panamanian businessman Gabriel Lewis would alert Kennedy to the back-alley corruption and abuses by administration favorite Manuel Noriega, Panama's increasingly controversial strongman.

Kennedy swamped Republican businessman Ray Shamie for reelection in Massachusetts in 1982, and there were stirrings toward a 1984 presidential effort. When Kennedy and Fritz Mondale both showed up at a breakfast rally in Iowa in October 1982 Kennedy ventured that "Some people have even written in the newspaper that we're out here forming political organizations for the future.

"Well, let me tell you, Vice President Mondale and I don't like to read those stories. He doesn't like to read 'em about me, and I don't like to read 'em about him." Privately, Kennedy couldn't help cultivating dreams.

Before the end of that year Kennedy had already withdrawn, emphasizing in his statement that it was "very soon" to expect his children to go through such an experience again, especially since "the decision that Joan and I have made about our marriage has been painful for our children as well as ourselves." His children had been "very sophisticated" in maintaining their opposition and put the stress on all he could accomplish by persevering in the Senate.

Not that he was ready quite yet to give up twitting the possibility. His New Year's wishes, Kennedy suggested early in 1983, were "Jobs, a nuclear freeze, and Patrick changes his mind."

For all that, as early as 1985 Kennedy took himself out of consideration for the 1988 presidential race; the decision "much increased my effectiveness in the Senate," he later maintained. He cited in particular the way this decision helped "build a coalition here in favor of sanctions against South Africa . . . My stepping back helped us override a presidential veto of the sanctions," he recalled to me. As for the trade-offs? "When you're a presidential contender, you always get more attention around here but less credibility. When you're not, you get more credibility but less attention. That's always been the classic commentary."

Regrets about abandoning his presidential aspirations? "I always felt that was more in perceptions than what I was actually doin' around here," Kennedy threw out, and changed the subject.

Truthfully, Kennedy was always relieved enough to have his Massachusetts reelection tucked away. The process invariably looked a lot more automatic to outsiders than it did to Kennedy. In 1988 he topped the hit list of Terry Dolan's National Conservative Political Action Committee (NCPAC), and there were those around Washington who felt that bumping Ted Kennedy would do the right more good than enthroning Ronald Reagan. NCPAC's promotional literature projected Kennedy as Jabba the Hutt, a vast, heartless monster of collectivistic appetites intent on slurping down, alive and wriggling, the plethora of tax breaks and trust fund incomes and offshore opportunities on which the propertied classes continued to batten.

Worse, shortly after his 1980 primary defeat, Kennedy started up his own political action committee, The Fund for a Democratic Majority, and it was shortly raising upward of $500,000 a year, intended for selected senatorial candidates. This meant to alarmists on the right that, along with his overloaded domestic agenda and an increasingly grating tendency to mouth off on defense policy, Kennedy commanded a war chest. He could pick favorites and skew election results anywhere he chose. The right was frantic as Kennedy's PAC showed little compunction about hobgoblinizing *them*, a technique on which reactionaries all across America had come to feel they had a patent. Kennedy had booted the presidency, but with a staff which again approached one hundred he amounted to a one-man government in exile.

Virtually every White House initiative had to allow for Kennedy's demonstrated genius at laying parliamentary roadblocks or enlisting public opinion to quash the unacceptable. His talent for "marking up" a piece of legislation behind closed doors—in committee or subcommittee, in conference with House members once bills were passed—resulted again and again in legislation that fell far short of what Reagan's business-oriented advisers had hoped to pressure from Congress. Under Kennedy's untiring guardianship, the reformist agenda propounded originally by FDR survived the Reagan era.

2. Private Life

Among well-washed Republicans Kennedy all but blotted out the sun. Even his person threatened. Kennedy's weight, for example, went up and down by fifty or sixty pounds according to his appetites of the season or whichever election was pending. Mike Barnicle of *The Boston Globe*, an admirer all along of Kennedy's outsider militancy in the face of the "pious whores" in both parties, devoted one hilarious column to the senator's expanding corpus. "You know where he stands," Barnicle wrote in 1984. "There's a dent in the ground." Barnicle insisted that Ted sent out for "wider laurels to rest on," and that—unkindest of all—"When the Republicans talk about cutting the fat out of the budget, Kennedy takes it personally."

Periodically, Kennedy undertook a diet of "chocolate glop," forewent the extensive catered lunch—complete with a plate-wide, inch-thick slice of prime rib and a bottle of choice bordeaux and potatoes au gratin and a large salad with chunky blue-cheese dressing and a giant wedge of apple pie with ice cream—which eased his midday schedule. One noon, while I was interviewing Teddy in his office and he was dispatching this epic spread, he looked up unexpectedly and asked whether I had had lunch.

"Not yet," I commented, busy filling my notebook.

"I'll order you something. A sandwich?"

"A *sandwich?*" I suggested he let it go.

His charming, ever-protective office spokeswoman Melody Miller had by then been promoted to deputy press secretary and handled the innumerable media squeakers involving the Kennedy family while maintaining a sharp watch over Kennedy's privacy. She insisted that as a discipline Kennedy laid off the booze entirely between the first of the year and his birthday, February 22. Defenders blamed a weakness for ice cream—especially the extra-rich butter-brickle-style treat he allowed himself, often a couple of quarts at a time, toward nightfall—for the senator's girth. But Kennedy himself, braced by a posse of reporters, waved all that away one afternoon to confess, freely, "It's the sauce, boys," before lurching toward another committee room.

How bad was Kennedy's drinking? At times, under stress, his hands trembled badly, purportedly a familial problem. Blotches disfigured the swell of his cheeks, while along his nose, where reconstructive surgery had left a kind of polyp to replace a basal cell skin cancer, there remained a dense permanent shine. Kennedy's thick, wavy hair now seemed to be silvering overnight.

A story was making the rounds that Kennedy was tippling all day, so that by afternoon he couldn't make a quorum call. Such rumors remained precisely wrong: As a point of pride Kennedy habitually turned away any serious drinking so long as the Senate was in session. When deliberations ground on through the end of the afternoon or into the evening, and all the hours of standing and hoisting himself in and out of chairs had tightened his back to the point of spasm, it made him irritable with the effort to suppress the pain and harder than ever on the overworked staff that scrambled to meet his demands. "I wish this god damned thing would end," an aide remembers overhearing Kennedy mutter. "I need a vodka."

Away from the colleagues, Kennedy continued to drink. He would refer at times to never soaking up more than his "limit," but his limit turned out to be quite a lot. One newsman I knew sat in the next seat from Ted throughout a flight to Europe: He called for one whiskey after the next from the flight attendant, the first drink well before the aircraft left the ground, and consumed at least a fifth before the plane got down.

By then he was showing it. It started early. I remember once, during Kennedy's 1970 post-Chappaquiddick campaign for the Senate, tagging along for dinner in Kennedy's Charles River Square apartment in Boston. The air all day had been unbreathable with stress and recrimination. Kennedy himself prepared the meal, one shoulder hunched up to cradle the telephone over which he was giving instructions to some aide in Washington, one hand stirring the string beans on the stove while the other gripped the tumbler of bad rye he was pouring down straight, refill after refill. Occasionally Kennedy interrupted the call to top off my glass. It had been a long, wearing day on the streets, and Ted was binge drinking to recover his animus.

Especially for a legislator who styled himself a champion of women's rights, Kennedy's rampages after hours kept Georgetown in delectable shock. He worked the rallies and conventions unabashedly. Although he was scrupulous about insulating policy people, regulars around the office sometimes found themselves on discreet assignments unrelated to any law. One stalwart was delegated each Christmastime to pick up identical silk scarves for good sports throughout the Republic on whom the senator periodically dropped in unannounced. Others found themselves bird-dogging a live prospect across a crowded reception, under orders to recommend a drink in the back of the senator's limousine, or even—there were verified claims—perhaps a line of coke.

Kennedy was regularly spotted at Manhattan singles bars. Like JFK's, Ted's hands were subject to roaming quite widely, under tablecloths and between the seats on commercial flights. One friend of mine, a well-known portrait photographer who had been hired to take Ted's picture while he was weekending with his mother in Palm Beach, found herself countermanding Ted's order to the butler to drop her overnight luggage off in his suite. She would be leaving immediately after the shoot. Enough gossip got around to keep the matrons of Georgetown uneasy, many fearful that Kennedy might lumber in and plant himself alongside one of their daughters.

Intermittently—sometimes simultaneously—Kennedy would find himself involved in a serious and deeply felt affair, like his very confidential long-term involvement with the Austrian/Palm-Beach jewelry designer Helga Wagner, whose other admirers included Prince Charles. An October, 1979 tell-all issue of *Time* refers to "dalliances" with socialites Amanda Burden and D.C. social-ite Paige Lee Hufty, an extended fling with the Olympic skier Suzy Chaffee, and even an interlude with the wife of the Canadian Prime Minister, fast-moving Margaret Trudeau.

3. Working Both Sides

Nevertheless—pace *National Enquirer*—it remained a fact that Kennedy spent most evenings alone, settled in at McLean to sip on a weak scotch while marking up the bales of paperwork the members of his various com-mittee staffs competed to stuff into his notorious portmanteau, The Bag. Something of an insomniac, Kennedy tended to work late and get up early to sit over breakfast with aides or imported experts before driving to Capi-tol Hill to take on his appointment schedule. He habitually worked two full shifts, offloading everything he could onto his army of staffers so he could confine himself to whatever specifically required a senator. Kennedy flirted with exhaustion a lot of the time. Underneath, he was acutely lonely.

By announcing before he needed to that he would not go after the Dem-ocratic nomination in 1984, Kennedy made it easier to keep his distance from both wings of the party. In important particulars, conventional liber-alism wasn't working. Even before 1980, for example, Kennedy's views had hardened as to what might produce effective law enforcement in America. He would work closely with Strom Thurmond to produce a crime control bill with bail reform, harsher sentencing, and even preventive detention, the prospects of which particularly horrified the American Civil Liberties Union.

There were complaints then—there would be many more later—that Kennedy was so interested in leaving his imprimatur on certain bills that he was selling out his principles to effect some compromise. Kennedy would repeatedly have to defend a number of these accommodations with the conservatives. The argument his office generally put out was that Kennedy got more for the liberals than he gave up, so the emerging legislation was a net plus. Sometimes that was true. After an unusually tough exchange with Thurmond during a Labor Committee embroilment, Kennedy supposedly joined the crusty South Carolinian for the walk to a Judiciary Committee meeting. "C'mon Strom," he reportedly reassured the old man, slapping a hand over his shoulder, "let's go upstairs and I'll give you a few judges."

Once Reagan was reelected, Kennedy delivered a landmark speech at Hofstra University in which he proclaimed that Democrats cannot "cede to the other side issues like economic growth and America's standing in the world." There was "a difference between being a party that cares about labor and being a labor party . . . a party that cares about women and being a women's party. We can and we must be a party that cares about minorities without becoming a minority party. We are citizens first and constituencies second." To hard-core liberals, this sounded a lot like a concession speech.

In short order Kennedy hosted Ronald Reagan at a fund raiser at the Kennedy Center and endorsed the line-item veto to bring the budget under control. While continuing to maintain that supply-side economics "should have been left on the back of the cocktail napkin on which it was first worked out ten years ago," Kennedy broke with many of the Democrats to back the Gramm-Rudman-Hollings Act, which mandated deficit reductions no matter which federal programs had to feel the knife. He called the budget process "a shambles," and admitted that "Congress is not only not part of the solution, it is definitely part of the problem."

All this was further and further from tax and spend. "You know, I liked you a lot better before I moved to the right," Kennedy chided Orrin Hatch after Orrin landed him a good one in debate. The prim Utah conservative couldn't help but respond at times to Kennedy's great heart and parliamentary legerdemain. He viewed Kennedy's antics around town as ripe for upgrading. "I admire him so much," Hatch conceded as early as 1982. "I'm just going to send the Mormon missionaries to him to straighten out the rest of his life." Ted agreed that it might be time. Kennedy was about to hornswoggle Labor and Human Resources into submitting an overall domestic budget $8 billion above the administration's request as well as doubling the Pell Grant money to underwrite college tuitions.

Kennedy had already discovered that Hatch's conservative imprimatur lent just enough convincing spin to legislation to give it a solid chance, and he kept looking for opportunities to support his chairman. The pair teamed up to ram through a questionable bill to permit U.S. pharmaceutical companies to sell their product abroad before it cleared American testing requirements (biotechnology was booming in Massachusetts). They kicked up AIDS funding together, cosponsored bills on mental health and the privacy of medical records, Alzheimer's research and religious freedom, joined efforts to deal with welfare dependency and a law to ban the use of lie detectors by private employers.

"He's knocked a lot of rough edges off me," Hatch conceded, "and for that I'm grateful. Also, he's a first-class legislator, and whenever we work together I think we can accomplish just about anything." Some people think a bill with both their names on it, Hatch joked, "means one of us hasn't read it." Reactions around the Senate were far less infatuated. "I'm gettin' damned tired of votin' on all that Kennedy-Hatch legislation goin' through," Jesse Helms was overheard to remark.

In 1986 the Democrats recaptured the Senate. Nine of the eleven incoming freshman Democrats got money and campaign guidance from Kennedy's Fund for a Democratic Majority. Kennedy again assumed the chairmanship of Labor and Human Resources. "When we took the Senate back he was transformed, a new man," Tom Rollins recollects. "He worked like an animal. He called me immediately and brought us up to Hyannis Port. We could not overpaper him. Nobody ever wrote a memo he thought was too long. Everything came back with his handwriting all over it. Until then what we had mostly been doing was trying to stop legislation the administration wanted, throwing as much sand in the machinery as possible.

"From then on we had a program, timetables, he managed that operation very tightly." A lot of Kennedy legislation now made it out of committee; much passed the Senate. Of this, a good deal couldn't survive the conference proceedings, and whatever got that far was likely to confront a White House veto. But important hearings, vital drafting and the accumulation of support among the colleagues prepared the way for a great deal of success once Reagan stepped down.

Kennedy's popularity on both sides of the aisle was now an enduring catalyst. "If you want to find Ted Kennedy," suggested his regular drinking buddy Christopher Dodd of Connecticut, "listen for the laughter." A close aide remarks that once freshman colleagues recognized that Kennedy was not a "raving liberal lefty they tended to gravitate to him, they found his hearty Irishness attractive, compared with the standard blow-dried Republicans."

As good a case in point as any would be Kennedy's jostling, affectionate relationship with Alan Simpson, the hard-right Wyoming conservative

Republican. Simpson came to Washington in 1978, like other provincial lawyers hellbent on forestalling the giveaway socialism Kennedy supposedly represented. What Simpson quickly came to marvel over was the extent to which Kennedy would immerse himself in any issue he took on. The Senate's notorious lion of the left would attack on every front to get whatever he wanted, but once he had committed himself, given his word to accept a compromise or an amendment or an earmark intended to protect his adversary's flank at home during the next election—that was it. Ted's word was good enough, always.

A number of their better-publicized scuffles blew up while they were attempting to reformulate the immigration laws. Simpson's longtime adviser Dick Day has remarked that the politics of immigration is "compounded out of equal parts emotion, racism, guilt, and fear"; immigrants are not a factor in Wyoming, so Simpson was less than overjoyed to find himself drafted onto a presidential commission with Kennedy to recut immigration policy.

After 1980 Simpson chaired the immigration subcommittee within the Justice Committee, with Kennedy as ranking Democrat. Together, they pieced out the 1987 Simpson-Mazolli Act (illegal immigration), along with the 1990 Kennedy-Simpson Act (legal immigration). Much amounted to a redrafting of legislation Kennedy himself had authored twenty-two years earlier. Immigration quotas based on duplicating the existing pattern of national origin were to be replaced by priorities for immigrants with family already in the United States and/or professional skills in short supply here. The numbers to be admitted were opened up. With American birthrates falling, whatever outraged nativists thought, these modifications undoubtedly saved large segments of the economy and rejuvenated our technology as we emerged into the computer age.

Jerry Tinker, who directed the immigration shop for Kennedy, remembered the pair during quorum calls. "They had totally opposite senses of humor," Tinker observes. "Simpson's material tended to be Western, anecdotal, 'very rich' in flavor. Kennedy is more of a mime, a storyteller. At quiet moments Simpson would sidle over in his lanky way, and kind of lean toward Kennedy, and say, 'Ted, have you heard this one?' Then he would tell some ribald classic and Kennedy with his Irish laughter would bring the rafters down. I remember once Bobby Byrd, who is something of a stickler for decorum, came over and tried to hush them up."

For some years Kennedy and Simpson enjoyed a weekly few minutes of adversarial debate on a radio show called "Face-Off" on the Mutual Broadcasting System, with each carping away according to partisan dogma. This kind of ritual may satisfy the true believers, but it is a long way from life around the Cloakroom of the Senate.

Not everything was reconcilable. After 1981, with White House encouragement, the largely Republican-appointed Supreme Court was trimming back civil-rights interpretation. When, in 1982, the landmark Voting Rights Act of 1965 was slated to expire, the word came out of the Justice Department that it was the administration's preference that the law not be renewed. Kennedy moved in vigorously, brought Republican Majority Leader Robert Dole around an inch at a time, and in the end rallied a coalition which pushed the renewal through, with provisions to override a Supreme Court decision that otherwise would have undercut it.

In 1984 the Supreme Court in the Grove City Case had ruled that Title 6 of the 1964 Education Act, which prohibited the federal government from funding educational institutions which discriminated by race, applied only to that program in the institution which discriminated, not to the institution overall. Kennedy promptly orchestrated passage of the Civil Rights Restoration Act to reaffirm the law's intent and got it enacted over a presidential veto. Supported by Republican moderates, Kennedy installed some teeth in the Fair Housing Amendments Acts of 1988, a reworking of the 1968 law which the Reaganites in the White House now proposed to undermine. Here too Kennedy eased Robert Dole away from the administration until Dole wound up supporting the upgrade.

No matter what, health care remained a front-burner issue for Kennedy, and when, in 1988, there seemed to be an opportunity to push through both houses a bill mandating total coverage for the elderly through federal catastrophic illness insurance, Kennedy popped up early as its primary champion in the Senate. The bill passed, Reagan signed it, and once the wealthiest 40 percent of the elderly realized that *they* were now expected to pay a heavy surcharge on their Medicare premiums the roar rising out of the suburbs terrified politicians across the country. A mob of well-heeled seniors chased the heavyset originator of the bill in the House, Dan Rosenkowski, all over a middle-western parking lot and Kennedy backed off, fast. The act was repealed in 1990.

Still, with a Democratic majority in the Senate, on most issues Kennedy could drive the legislative calendar. Again conniving with Dole, who was himself crippled fighting during World War II, Kennedy directed the passage of the Americans with Disabilities Act in 1990, working out the details with John Sununu and Attorney General Thornburgh. Republicans could not resist him.

The Supreme Court was still pecking away at civil-rights legislation, especially where it impacted employment discrimination. The head of Kennedy's staff at the Justice Committee, Jeff Blattner, now found his boss "energetic, focused, and relentless," dug in and determined enough to break a Republican filibuster with a cloture vote, "and in the end he prevailed." Under mounting bipartisan pressure from moderates like John Danforth of Missouri, George H.W. Bush did not veto the renewal of the Civil Rights Act in 1990–91.

4. Bork

Without question Kennedy's bloodiest and most gratifying battle throughout the Reagan years was the confirmation donnybrook over the Supreme Court nomination of Robert Bork. With his Silenus goatee and bulging, impudent eyes, Robert Bork came over as a disheveled escapee from some subterranean think tank. Bork had the résumé—law professor at Yale, important government posts, the federal bench—and at the outset nobody expected a tussle. But Kennedy hadn't forgotten that it was Bork, as solicitor general, who contravened the agreement Kennedy himself had originally negotiated with the Nixon White House and—after Elliot Richardson and William Ruckleshaus refused—fired Watergate special prosecutor Archibald Cox in a belated effort to salvage the ruined Nixon presidency.

Kennedy set his staff to digging, and what they unearthed confirmed his misgivings. On the day in 1987 that Reagan formally nominated Bork, Kennedy was thoroughly primed. "Robert Bork's America," he prophesied in a floor speech, "is a land in which women would be forced into back-alley abortions, blacks would sit at segregated lunch counters, rogue police could break down citizen's doors in midnight raids, schoolchildren could not be taught about evolution, writers and artists could be censored at the whim of government and the doors of the federal courts would be shut on the fingers of millions of citizens . . ."

Crafted by Carey Parker, this speech roused overnight apprehension on the Left, and anger and resentment across the Right. Longtime Kennedy adviser Charles Fried felt that so virulent an attack on the nominee was unwarranted and was quite likely to radicalize the two parties and invite a level of invective which might stymie future high-court nominations. The language was undoubtedly overdrawn, but behind each charge Kennedy's researchers had something. In fact the strategy governing the speech, Jeff Blattner would concede, "was to alert the Senate and the country immediately to the enormous issues at stake and, in effect, to freeze senators who might otherwise have made some comment favorable to the nomination without being fully informed about Judge Bork's record and views."

Bork's opinions on central issues—voting rights, women's rights (especially *Roe v. Wade*), and restrictive covenants—while in some cases expressed many years earlier—"were not consonant with the constitution and equal justice under law." Kennedy mobilized his interest-group networks nationwide and talked with a number of swing senators of both parties. He coordinated closely with committee chairman Joe Biden, as well as with Allen Cranston and Howard Metzenbaum. He got Joe Lowery of the Southern Christian Leadership Conference to whip up black preachers across the country.

"There wasn't any deal-making," Blattner insisted. "It was just flat-out political combat, no quarter given or taken, no horse-trading or logrolling." Robert Bork himself, increasingly indignant and unappealing, went on too long beneath the committee lights, and frequently in the wrong direction. Under Kennedy's uncompromising stage management the pressure built session by session and in the end Bork lost, and resoundingly.

In later years conservative legal scholars would look back and claim that it was Kennedy's brutal strafing of Robert Bork—emphasizing not only what he had done but what he might do—that polarized the Supreme Court and prevented from then on the sort of consensus that had permitted the selection of essentially moderate, comparatively nonpartisan jurists for the highest bench. From Kennedy's point of view the stakes were too high, the threat of a rollback of civil rights too urgent.

5. Abroad

Miffed after losing Bork, managers around the White House were touchy about Kennedy's propensity to interfere with, personalize, situations overseas. He sent an adventure-loving staff man, Gare Smith, to trouble spots from Western Sahara to the backlands of Burma to dodge bullets and meet with pro-democracy activists and bring back dispassionate appraisals. A series of "forums" Kennedy convened on violence in Central America brought to Washington's attention a number of witnesses from the region, including several Miskito Indian spokesmen. Their culture was already being decimated by raids from the Sandinista army. When Daniel Ortega came to the U.N., Kennedy set up a secret six-hour meeting between the Indian leader Brooklyn Riviera and Ortega which led to a deal according to which the CIA was forced to stop instigating the Indians to attack the Sandinista regulars.

Like Tip O'Neill in the House, Kennedy had been maneuvering behind
the scenes to hose down the low-grade war between the Sandinistas and the
Contras, the leadership of which was interested mostly in smuggling drugs
into the United States with help from the administration and skimming the
funds the administration's secret Iran-Contra deals were spinning off. Under
Kennedy's heavy gaze, Ortega backed off, and the aboriginal Miskitos soon
recovered a measure of security and sovereignty in their homelands on the
Atlantic coast.

Kennedy tried to heal the breach in El Salvador by lining up enough votes
around the Senate to cut military support for the conservative government
in half while establishing a close personal friendship with José Napolean
Duarte, the gutsy Christian Democrat who represented the Salvadorans'
sole alternative to the death-squad politics of Roberto d'Aubuisson. Duarte
was a regular dinner guest in McLean on his periodic trips to Washington,
and when the embattled Salvadoran president showed up at Walter Reed for
cancer treatments Kennedy made it a point to visit him at his bedside. "In
hospital situations, where he's meeting people, touching people, there's no
one like him," Greg Craig would notice. "He doesn't intrude. He's gentle.
But he's there."

By 1987, once Panama began unraveling, Kennedy was watching closely.
Most of the businessmen in Panama's reformist Civic Crusade were contacts
of long standing, and Kennedy was quick, as charges of maladministration
and drug-running began to surface against Manuel Noriega, to put forward
legislation that led to economic sanctions against the Noriega government
as well as empowering a fact-finding group. Republican senators like Jesse
Helms and Alphonse D'Amato were particularly incensed with Noriega and
Kennedy swiftly harnessed their irritation to keep the Senate, Craig recalls,
"way out ahead of the administration."

Yet when the Bush administration launched Operation Just Cause in
December of 1989 Kennedy denounced the incursion. "The feel-good
invasion of Panama does not feel so good anymore," he announced, finding "nothing in the public record that justifies the invasion." He feared "the
outcry against the invasion" had "significantly boosted the prospects of the
Sandinistas in the Nicaraguan elections that will take place next month."

Here, as with Desert Storm two years afterward, Kennedy made clear
his inherited dislike of military intervention. Better to try and compel real
reform from within than reshuffle the principals. Greg Craig didn't agree
in either situation, but advisers must advise, not decide. Kennedy preferred
letting sanctions run their course.

6. Bishop Tutu

Kennedy felt the successes of sanctions in Poland and South Africa pointed up their effectiveness. South Africa in particular—there, Kennedy had a vested emotional interest. In October of 1984, when something fast approaching a race war was rising in the Transvaal, Kennedy had a lunch with Episco-pal Archbishop Desmond Tutu and Alan Boesak, both revered black leaders then attempting to create the multiracial United Democratic Front. Kennedy asked what he could do to help. Visit South Africa, they suggested.

A few weeks later Tutu won the Nobel Peace Prize. The trip was delayed for over a year. "I had always been somewhat reluctant to go down there," Kennedy confessed to me, "because I thought my brother Bob's trip [in June of 1966] had been such a powerful visit, with so much substance and symbol-ism, sort of like a bell that was continuing to ring. I didn't want to interfere with the chimes. But they were very persuasive."

Kennedy's trip in January of 1985 was exhausting and dangerous. His arrival in South Africa was greeted by a demonstration of angry blacks, foot soldiers for the militant anti-white radicals of AZAPO abetted by the white South African police. Ignoring the government's advice, Kennedy passed the night in Tutu's modest bungalow in Soweto. He was reportedly the first white to sleep in the tortured township. "Staying there, sleeping in the bed, seeing the Nobel Prize right next to the bed . . ." Recalling it all for me, Kennedy had to chuckle, hollowly. "He had the choir of his church come over. They sang songs. Soft songs. To put me to sleep. They just sang in the living room. I knew he was as tired as I was. He said: 'You'll sleep, I'll show you how to sleep.' You know, at first you say, 'My God, there's singing out there.' But you know, it sort of rocks you to sleep . . ."

Kennedy got back determined to highlight the problem. He gave a dinner party to which he invited the chairman of the Foreign Relations Commit-tee, Richard Lugar, along with Nancy Kassebaum, the chair of the Subcom-mittee on African affairs. Also at the table were the respected ex-president of Australia Malcolm Fraser and the former Nigerian president Obassanjo. Their inquiry and recommendations regarding South Africa would supply the blueprint for the Kennedy-Weicker bill. Committee by committee, for-mally and informally, the Kennedy-Weicker "tag-team" worked colleagues on both sides of the aisle and in the end drove through a bill that initially cut off investment in South Africa until the repression was lifted. He and his independent-minded Republican colleague Lowell Weiker had brought down such a firestorm of recrimination over the white oppression in South Africa and the persecution of Nelson Mandela that even consciences on the right were stirred, to the annoyance of the trade-minded Reagan administration.

Later on, once Mandela was finally out of prison and elected President of South Africa, he was smuggled into Kennedy's offices on his first official trip to Washington to express his gratitude personally. Characteristically, Kennedy shunned any press coverage but arranged to have the black members of his staff slip in after hours to meet a legend they never expected to confront.

Working colleagues from both parties, Weicker and Kennedy wormed through the South Africa sanction bill after two years to face the predictable Reagan veto, which the Senate overruled by eleven votes. South Africa would evolve.

Kennedy inherited the prerogative—at least, he assumed he did—to pursue an independent foreign policy vis-à-vis the Soviet Union. "My brothers had a relationship with Dobrynin which went back with them, and went back with me . . . I started to visit the Soviet Union in 1974." There was a long meeting then and in 1978 with Brezhnev. Each time Kennedy traveled to Moscow, conditions of his visit were negotiated in advance—so many refuseniks to receive exit visas, so much time on radio or television. "I remember one speech at the University of Moscow, where they said I could talk to the whole school. But then they gave me a very small hall. They had those kinds of little dances."

Everything changed when Gorbachev took over in 1985. Kennedy found the new General Secretary "robust, expansive, responsive to questions. Challenging, self-confident—certainly an entirely different kind of Soviet leader than we'd met at other times." He'd known Foreign Secretary Eduard Shevardnadze since 1978. Furthermore, as a member of the Senate Arms Control Delegation, Kennedy sat in on meetings two or three times a year with Soviet experts like V. V. Alexandrov and Velikhov. The Russians remained alarmed at the prospect of a "Nuclear Winter" in the event of an atomic exchange. Even after he formally left the senator's employ, Kennedy's key health aide during the later seventies, Dr. Larry Horowitz, went back and forth to keep himself abreast of the debate at meetings, there were early forums, and over the Reagan years Kennedy's office began to function for the Soviets as a back-channel to American politics.

When, toward the end of Reagan's second term, the Soviets thought seriously about scrapping their intermediate-range ballistic missiles, they went to Kennedy first, who got the word to the administration's senior arms negotiator, Max Kampelman. Kennedy and his experts sat in on a number of the exchanges and when the Intermediate-Range Nuclear Forces missile treaty was signed, in 1988, Secretary of State George Shultz acknowledged the senator's contribution. After skirmishing with William Casey and Bob Gates of the CIA for most of the decade over the question of whether a thaw was really possible with the Soviets, Shultz secretly appreciated the extent to which the ice-breakers Kennedy kept dispatching had prepared the way to glasnost.

By 1990 *Pravda* was headlining the greeting Soviet President Gorbachev had extended to his "old friend, Edward Kennedy." The senator was in Moscow to plead for Soviet restraint in Lithuania and underline to the Russians that the United States was not very likely to negotiate away its command of the seas. Yet at the same time Kennedy was interested in exploring with the Soviets ways to verify the location of underwater nuclear weaponry. Kennedy hoped to bring back something with which to cajole the Bush administration into dealing with sea power during the ongoing disarmament negotiations.

As with domestic matters, Kennedy kept his experts and intermediaries probing whatever opportunities he spotted, stocking him with background information and sounding out every possibility. As a situation ripened—in Central America, in South Africa and China, in the Soviet Union—Kennedy would intervene personally, prodding both Congress and often enough a sluggish administration into formulations and results. All this was normally a responsibility of the president. But Kennedy saw nothing in the Constitution to prevent him from helping the president along.

CHAPTER V

Bush I

1. Catch-up

The administration sometimes welcomed a hand from Kennedy, especially on the sly. Still, once he got reelected in Massachusetts and returned to the Senate in 1988, Kennedy had picked up so much legislative momentum, along with an enhanced majority, that key Republicans started looking at each other. "Behind the scenes we've become good friends," Orrin Hatch told one reporter. "But I've found he's tough in the clinches." To another reporter Hatch confessed that, in a fight over principle, Kennedy "will murder you, he'll roll right over you . . . He'll trample you in the ground and then he'll grind his heel in you." Still, Orrin couldn't help liking Ted.

On issues such as the bill prohibiting plant closings without advance notice to workers and freedom of choice Kennedy was streamrolling the debate, and not in a direction even indulgent Republicans were pleased to go. "You can talk to Ted, you can reason with him, you can bargain with him," New Hampshire's hard-nosed Warren Rudman conceded. "Sure he's an inflexible liberal—if he's got the votes. If he doesn't, he'll deal. He's a pragmatist, he's damned effective. He's a force to be reckoned with."

Nick Littlefield came on as staff director of Kennedy's Labor Committee, and virtually by the day things started to open up. The Bush administration "holds office but doesn't know what to do with it" Kennedy said in March of 1989. He was thinking aloud. Here was a vacuum to be filled. Two years later the 101st Congress turned out to have been the most productive generator of remedial social legislation since Lyndon Johnson's heyday. Of sixty-three proposals put forward by the Senate's Democratic Policy Committee, fifty-seven became law, with half, twenty-eight, originating in Kennedy's renamed Health, Education, Labor and Pensions Committee. They included the 1990 Child Care Act and the National and Community Services Act and expanded Head Start, the vast, groundbreaking Americans with Disabilities Act, the McKinney Homeless Assistance Act, the Perkins Vocational Education Program, the Excellence in Math and Science Act, the National Health Service Corps, the Ryan White AIDS Care Act, and on and on down to the raising of the minimum wage and the reauthorization of the National Endowment Act without the "content restrictions" for which the likes of Jesse Helms were fulminating.

After 1990, pummeled worse every month by Republican ideologues and worried about reelection, Bush began to bring down a series of vetoes on innovations like the Family Leave Bill and even the reauthorization of the Kennedy-initiated National Institutes of Health, while marshaling Senate Republicans to block the elementary and secondary school reform proposals and the Striker Replacement Bill. These ideas were suspended for the moment, but they were out there now in public debate and they would all soon become, as Littlefield notes, "major themes of the Clinton campaign" and help Clinton "focus attention on the do-nothing quality of the Bush administration in the domestic area."

2. Beyond Bimbo Limbo

Perhaps it was accidental that, just as Edward Kennedy was taking on unimagined legislative velocity, another fusillade of books and articles came in, concentrated on his private life. Most wounding—and thorough—was undoubtedly that notorious Michael Kelly piece in GQ in February of 1990. Kelly presented an album of relentlessly candid shots of an uncouth and bibulous fraternity roustabout, the sort of "Regency rake" prefigured in Hogarth. This rude, besotted figure came through as devoted mostly to sport with nubile lobbyists under restaurant tables or toppled across some enthusiast in the well of a speedboat off Saint-Tropez.

Many of the liveliest stories featured horseplay with Chris Dodd. There was the time the two well-lubricated bachelor senators supposedly grabbed up the woman who was serving them for a terrifying round of "waitress toss," or dueled with gladiolus stalks, or executed the Mexican hat dance on pictures of themselves they plucked from café walls. Another account finds Dodd, naked alongside a pair of fellow nudettes, sneaking across the back lawn at McLean to rap on Kennedy's window, flaunting a bottle of champagne and demanding a Jacuzzi, totally astonishing Kennedy's bed partner of the evening.

Christopher Dodd had replaced to a certain extent the accommodating Joey Gargan, who during the earlier decades invariably cleared his schedule for a spree with cousin Ted. But life got bumpier for the ingenuous Gargan, he disliked Kennedy's stand on abortion, and after he contributed to Leo Damore's rakeover of Chappaquiddick (*Senatorial Privilege*, 1988) the cousins would keep their distance. The news break in Damore's book, purportedly based on Gargan's confession, alleged that Ted had tried to pressure Joey into filing a false accident report, according to which Joey was at the wheel of the Oldsmobile. Gargan never went public with the charge directly, and, although a right-wing publisher did print the book in 1988, the allegation served finally to further degrade everyone involved.

Although Kennedy was undoubtedly available for action, and did lapse sometimes into "binge drinking," everybody around him insists that more and more Kennedy's free moments centered on relationships with "substantive, fortyish women." His taste still ran to long-stemmed blondes, in most cases accomplished, sweet-tempered ladies he took quite seriously for a season or two and courted with such energy that they were dazzled and permanently intrigued. A number would remain friends and turn up at McLean with the trophy husbands they had acquired.

Throughout much of the seventies Helga Wagner remained primus inter pares, the warm, reassuring stopover on whose devotion Kennedy could count. They sailed the Caribbean together. "Well, we were very good friends, let's put it that way," she remembers now. "He was a very, very special person. He cheered everybody up, he was always doing things for others. I came from Austria; you never met anybody like that over there.

"So wonderful and decent. He was very—how shall I say—emotional? He quoted poems all the time, wrote notes all the time. And the *energy* he had!" As for the . . . indulgences? "I never thought he was an alcoholic," Helga would maintain. "I have to tell you, he had gone through so much. Once you have lost two siblings . . . I thought the worst of all was when his son had a leg taken off . . . And then the fact that he was always in pain. I often wonder, when you have to take so many painkillers all the time, what does that do to you?

"He handled it very, very well."

The list would run over the course of the eighties from Countess Lana Campbell to Susan St. James to singer Claudia Cummings to Terry

Muilenberg and, toward the end, Dragana Lickle, with aesthetes like Lacey Neuhaus Dorn presiding at intimate dinner parties at McLean attended by a few select couples; Tennessee Senator Jim Sasser and his wife were regulars. Kennedy dated an earnest senior aide from the HELP Committee for a time, and there was one extravagantly endowed flight attendant who disappeared with Kennedy on getaways over several seasons, a playful, good-natured counterpoint throughout a number of relationships.

Important romances soon took on a moonlight-and-roses quality, but inevitably the moment came when commitment loomed. Kennedy would pull shy and break things off. "I just couldn't bear to try again at marriage and have everything come apart on me again," he told a close friend.

One day in 1987 Kennedy invited Bob Shrum to dinner. "I went out there thinking it would be the usual thing," Shrum recalls. "There would be seven or eight people, and we'd have dinner, and sit around and talk afterwards.

"But there were just the two of us. We had this long dinner, and I couldn't figure out what the heck was going on. And afterwards he said, 'Let's go in the library and have a drink.'

"So we did. And then he looked at me suddenly and he said, 'I think you ought to get married.' I had been going out for some time at that point with Mary Louise. 'You've fallen in love,' Ted told me. 'I can tell. All your friends can tell. It would be very good for you. It's a wonderful thing to find someone.'

"Kennedy is not a person who ever indulges in couch conversation, and I was so taken aback that I could hardly speak. He meant it, clearly, and I almost found it wistful. Because what he was saying, at least to me, was that he wished he could find the same thing. My wife and I sometimes joke that Ted Kennedy was our marriage counselor."

So there were contradictory tensions, the frustrations of too much bachelorhood. Accordingly, once in a while, Kennedy tended to pull the cork and let the demons erupt. Too many blue suits sometimes, too many months straight of standing with his arms out while security people strapped on the Kevlar vest or aides writhed as Kennedy's perspiring driver jerked in and out of traffic to overtake the last shuttle departing National. Alcohol made him real to himself for a couple of hours, and that was frequently enough.

They'd deal with breakage afterward. Kennedy's press aide Melody Miller, who had watched one damage control prodigy after another since Chappaquiddick, laughs about the evening she boosted Kennedy into his overcoat the night before a recess with the reminder, "Now, remember about telephoto lenses. They come this long, and they can pick things up for miles." A muzzy, widely distributed shot of a naked, radically overweight Kennedy sprawled on top of a long-suffering companion in a boat somewhere in the Mediterranean had recently hit the tabloids.

It requires Melody's tact—along with her years in service—to carry that off. References to Kennedy's indulgences could chill the air, bring on the snittiness nobody liked to deal with. "If that's what we're going to talk about," Kennedy gibed David Burke, generations of advisers ago by then, one afternoon when Burke had the temerity to refer to one of Kennedy's wilder weekends, "why don't I lie down here on the couch? How much do you get for your services, doctor? Is it still $75 an hour?" Ted Kennedy reportedly cut off John Culver for four years for lecturing him about alcoholism.

Most staff members saw little or nothing of Kennedy when he was out and roistering. But mention his smoking days, and many still wrinkle their noses. As early as the sixties, Kennedy liked to puff on a little Filipino cigar when riding in a car or after a meal. Then, toward the end of the seventies, he took a liking to big, heavy Davidoffs, imported from Geneva. Alan Simpson, who hated the dry, acrid smoke, silently bore with Kennedy for several weeks when they were drafting the new immigration laws. One day Kennedy arrived, cigar in hand.

"Ted," Simpson told him, "you can bring anyone, or anything, or any idea into this office. But you can't bring that cigar."

By the later eighties Steve Smith was dying of lung cancer. The role of Smith inside that generation of Kennedys could take a while to explain. He had a function among his in-laws that kept him involved as crisis manager and controller extraordinaire, mother hen and trigger-tempered martinet. I remember a few months before Bobby died, standing next to him at the bottom of a slalom course in New Hampshire watching Smith carve smooth, economical turns, another order of athlete from the ragtag of Kennedys slamming between the flags. "He could still miss a gate!" Bobby turned to me and all but hissed, between a curse and a prayer.

But Smith hadn't missed. He rarely missed. Several times I visited him in the warren of offices in the Pan Am Building from which he tracked the investments of Joseph P. Kennedy, Inc. He seemed quite accessible—he confided in me on one occasion as to his own smothered political ambitions, forever kept on hold as one after the other of the brothers went on to push for higher office. He could be devastatingly testy—I asked him once why it took him so long to make his way back to Cape Cod from Majorca, where he was vacationing, the week after Chappaquiddick; I feared for several bitter seconds that he intended to fly straight over his desk and rip open my throat.

Throughout Smith's tenure the Joseph P. Kennedy holdings had tended to bog down in real estate, especially the Merchandise Marts. But lucky or otherwise, Smith continued to carry authority tempered with responsibility. He remained uncharacteristically indulgent with timorous, dedicated Lem Billings, Jack's roommate-for-life and for many years a fixture around the Pan Am suite. Capital preservation remained primary. When Ted's presidential move floundered, who else but Steve could reach in and turn his water off?

So that the news that Steve had terminal lung cancer sent a paralyzing frisson through the Kennedy family. For Ted in particular this feisty brother-in-law had become like a surviving brother. The two were close enough to accommodate almost anything in each other, but one day—Steve was terribly weakened—he beckoned Kennedy closer. The senator had already developed an ominous, rasping cough. "Teddy," he all but whispered, "you should stop smoking."

When Kennedy next visited Smith in his hospital bed he was largely comatose. Kennedy wanted to tell him that the family had decided to name the new wing of the Kennedy Library after Steve, but he would never be certain Smith understood. Telling me all this, Kennedy's voice had deserted him and I thought he was going to fall apart completely. In November of 1989 Kennedy introduced an anti-smoking bill. He regretted that he had started smoking cigars, he testified. Now he would try and stop. He did stop, and before long his hack abated.

Steve's death in 1990 left Kennedy more bereft than ever. Mourners at Steve's funeral watched Kennedy unable to deliver the eulogy. To one Kennedy veteran it was like watching Ted crumpled in the washroom in Los Angeles the night Bobby died. He seemed utterly frozen with pain, lost, almost catatonic.

Playing into Kennedy's anguish just then was probably the realization that now he alone would have to contend with the uncontrollable descendents of his siblings. The Kennedy publicity machine tends to pump up Ted's role as a kind of surrogate father as one by one his brothers, then his brothers-in-law died or dropped off and he was forced to take increasing responsibility for the several dozen nieces and nephews emerging into adolescence. Kennedy's own three children were sick, but in the end all three were salvageable. Bob's kids, the boys especially, ran wild even while both parents were around. In rented condominiums the boys would tear out the fixtures and stave in the sheetrock walls. In *The Kennedys* Peter Collier and David Horowitz have detailed the boys' hair-raising flirtations with heavy recreational drugs—bland, always-serviceable Lem Billings seems to have functioned as their companion and occasional connection—and Robert Jr. wound up with a heroin addiction while the talented David came apart completely and expired alone in a motel in Palm Beach. The Lawfords were a chronic problem. The younger generation regarded—and disregarded—Uncle Teddy with amused affection and referred to him as "Le Grand Fromage," the big cheese.

Whatever they thought of him, Ted was always there. When Jacqueline Kennedy divorced Aristotle Onassis, Kennedy had negotiated the $20-plus million settlement, to which Jackie's companion later in life, Maurice Templesman, added a zero with his priceless investment advice. Rumors surfaced about Ted and Jacqueline, but people who knew them both well invariably discount any such allegation. "She was his adored brother's wife, and he put her on a pedestal," one maintains. "He was her guardian and whenever she was to present herself at a public event—which she hated—he insisted on going over all the details beforehand himself."

A secret chain-smoker, Jacqueline endured serious bouts of depression, in the midst of which her brother-in-law made it a point to appear and cheer her up. I happened to be campaigning with Kennedy in Massachusetts in 1994 a few weeks after Jackie died and he was still musing over how startled he had been to be summoned to his sister-in-law's bedside for last rites.

3. Palm Beach

More, certainly, than alcohol, it's important to factor in Steve Smith's death to comprehend properly the "Palm Beach incident," the publicity extravaganza and ordeal by innuendo that threatened for some months to extinguish Kennedy's career. Especially with Bobby gone, Smith had amounted to a stand-in for Old Joe, the managerial presence who made the rest possible. I would hear various renditions of the episode at Steve's funeral when Ted, attempting the oration, had seized up again and again and ultimately gave it up and staggered down the aisle unable even to nod to the other mourners, "his jaw going back and forth in the effort not to break down completely. He was in as bad shape as I've ever seen him," a family intimate concedes. Like the Chappaquiddick cookout, Good Friday that fateful Easter weekend of 1991 at Palm Beach started out as a deferred wake, the chance to come to terms with the anguish of another bitter loss.

"And we were visiting in the patio after dinner," Kennedy himself would testify months afterward, "and the conversation was a very emotional conversation, a very difficult one. Brought back a lot of very special memories to me, particularly with the loss of Steve, who really was a brother to me and to the other members of the family. And I found at the end of that conversation that I was not able to think about sleeping. It was a very draining conversation . . . So we left that place, and we went to, out. We went to Au Bar's. I wish I'd gone for a long walk on the beach instead."

Florida changes the lighting. La Guerida, the crumbling Kennedy vacation compound on North Ocean Boulevard, had serviced four generations of off-duty family at that point. This was the tile-roofed Mizner hacienda Joe picked up at Depression prices to accommodate the vacation needs of Jimmy Roosevelt and Clare and Henry Luce and Winston Churchill and J. Edgar Hoover (along with Clyde Tolson) and Murray—"the Camel"—Humphreys, senior strategy man for the Chicago Outfit, and, of course, the ever-appreciative Cardinal Spellman. Joe had his stroke on a golf course near this house. Robert Kennedy's son David had overdosed in a motel nearby on a visit to his grandmother. Here, in a deck chair on the back lawn, Jack Kennedy marked up the galleys of *Profiles in Courage* while his back mended in 1957, with Teddy on hand for entertainment. JFK picked his cabinet members here, and the night he died some of his tony Republican neighbors reportedly celebrated his assassination at "many large parties," toasting Lee Harvey Oswald and embracing this turn of events as "wonderful news."

So Palm Beach remained at once a temptation and a bed of thorns. Kennedy himself once told me that nobody in his generation had ever dared just drop in at La Guerida; this was a facility Joe reserved for himself, a getaway estate where he could sunbathe naked in the bullpen by the pool, while his secretary of the moment slathered him with coconut oil.

By 1991, with Rose too enfeebled to bear up through the plane trip south anymore, groups of her descendants booked time at the increasingly neglected old fortress for weekends and holidays; this helped keep vacation costs reasonable. Ever since the fifties the holdings of the Kennedys have remained surprisingly stagnant, much of their assessed value—the figure usually released runs in the $200 million range—tied up for years around Chicago, with second and third mortgages draining off disposable cash flow. Kennedy's personal income in 1972 had been released to the newspapers and totaled $385,995, enough to get by on but certainly not enough to put him among even the wealthier colleagues in the Senate. Subsequently, a series of poorly timed speculations by a New York hedge fund strategist had bitten even deeper into capital. Joe's children might still indulge themselves with a lavish hand, but even during Steve Smith's tenure the grandchildren were on notice.

Palm Beach was also a venue for discharging more intimate family responsibilities. From time to time her keepers would convey the lobotomized Rosemary from the desolate and now—except for her—deserted Catholic boarding school in Wisconsin where she has been grumbling through her decades so she could spend a couple of days in the sun with whichever of the siblings could make it down. Well into her seventies now, Rosemary liked to take a drink. But drinking made her morose, depression seemed to trigger some subcategory of Tourette's syndrome, and as she wandered off muttering four-letter imprecations Rosemary's brother and sisters were left to shrug their shoulders and regard one another.

Thus, Palm Beach for the Kennedys remained beset with phantoms. Ted and his younger son Patrick arrived that Easter of 1991 at the invitation of his widowed sister Jean, who had assembled a floating party of perhaps ten including her grown children Willy and Amanda and the retired FBI agent and JFK bodyguard William Barry and his son. The agenda was free-form. The seniors would talk, mostly, which gave the younger people opportunity to group off and experiment with the nightlife.

Palm Beach at night has maintained its reputation through much of the century—a string of watering holes where exhausted money meets avid, heartless climbers. Too agitated to think about sleeping after hours of reminiscences, Edward Kennedy had "noticed both Patrick and my nephew Will go by the glass windows which are just adjacent to the patio" of the Palm Beach estate, "and I opened the door and called for Will and Patrick and they answered. And I asked them whether they wanted to go out—I needed to talk to Patrick or to William—and they said yes they would."

Summoned by the patriarch, the younger men accompanied Ted to the hotspot of the season just then, Au Bar, on Royal Poinciana Way. It has been said that Kennedy was like a shark who presses on day and night to keep from drowning in a sea of memories. But it is also still true that he appreciated a party. As *Boston Globe* reporter Jack Farrell discovered reading pretrial depositions, the evening in question "was not the first night that week the boys—including Ted—had gone to Au Bar and picked up girls and brought them home."

There remains some confusion about the chronology here—Willy Smith's sister Amanda would claim that he picked her up along with some friends at another boite, Lulu's, at two that morning—but there is no question that during the early hours Kennedy and his party settled in around an Au Bar table. Already confronting tax troubles, the club was written up locally as "a Eurotrash kind of place." In business since November, its opening night turnout had included, according to *The Palm Beach Post*, "royalty, a few nonviolent felons, gigolos (one reportedly has his chest hair dyed), society princesses, plus Senator Ted Kennedy (he'll spend Christmas in Hawaii) and a less noticed Senator Christopher Dodd."

That early Saturday morning before Easter Kennedy and his party sat quietly, overshadowed by the return of Ivana Trump, in town for the polo matches. Patrick—who overcame a severe cocaine problem by spending a summer during the mid-eighties in Spofford Hall, the drug-and-alcohol-rehabilitation center outside Keene, New Hampshire—was careful to confine himself to a couple of ginger ales. As with Teddy Jr., controlled substances could turn into a threat. Later, as a U.S. congressman from Rhode Island, Patrick sometimes edgewalked the subject. When Lincoln Chafee replaced John Chafee in a Rhode Island Senate seat, Patrick cracked that "Now when I hear someone talk about a Rhode Island politician whose father was a senator and got to Washington on his family name, used cocaine and wasn't very smart, I know there's only a 50-50 chance it's me."

A tall, low-keyed, susceptible youngster with scrupulously parted auburn hair and the eyes of a frightened witness, still subject to perilous asthma attacks, Patrick had lived on at home in McLean when his mother relocated to Boston, and he and his father had become particularly close and mutually accepting. Kennedy campaigned when Patrick ran for the Rhode Island legislature in 1988 ("What a comedown!" the senator had exclaimed to a bystander. "Eight years ago I was a presidential contender, and here I am pushing doorbells in Providence"), and stood by apprehensively while his son had a tumor removed from his spine.

"He's my life," Patrick told one interviewer, explaining why he was founding his own political career. He "wanted to follow in my father's footsteps, but leave my own tracks behind." His father had always "asked my opinion on issues he was working on. That's how I was able to cope with the fact that his work was very intrusive in our lives. I could accept it without being resentful."

People drift into conversation easily at a singles club, and not very long after his party arrived Patrick found himself bantering with a local woman named Anne Mercer, who quickly moved over to attach herself to the Kennedy party accompanied by her friend, the twenty-nine-year-old divorcee Patricia Bowman. The mood was withdrawn among the Kennedys, not to say depressed. "Patrick looked like he was having a terrible time," Anne would note afterward, "and I said to him, jokingly, 'you look like you're having a great time,' and Senator Kennedy said to me, 'Who are you to say anything?'"

Throughout Kennedy's adult life, periodically, the need seems to have become urgent for a few hours of societal bottom-feeding. Rose Kennedy had suffered because the nice people of Boston never invited her over, and Jack Kennedy quipped that even after he left the presidency he still wouldn't be eligible for Boston's better clubs.

Ted Kennedy carried his bruises, and from time to time they showed. "I suppose you're finding them a lot more . . . more interesting than we ever were," he opened up one night when I ran into him in the lobby of the Sheraton Ritz. He meant the Mellon family, the subject of my current book. Ted's face was flushed with whiskey and the exertion of addressing a conference room of Catholic priests; Kennedy had rolled out into the lobby of the Ritz-Carlton, spotted me, and thrown his arms around me and lifted me off the floor. Robert Squires, the political publicist with whom I had just finished dinner, immediately stage-whispered: "Hersh, a show of force like this is not necessary."

Descendants of the Mellons obviously had a certain authenticity in Ted's eyes compared with the Kennedys, whose claim to aristocracy—even royalty—originated for the most part in some press agent's trunk of special effects. On occasion this could produce an awkwardness with Ted around peers, a sense of compounding social strain. He needed the relief at times of luxuriating among commoner people, of harvesting the devotion of the sort of cast-offs and upmarket Lumpen which tended to congregate in bideawees like Au Bar while the world was sleeping. Yet exposure risked rejection sometimes, the disappointments of lèse-majesté. When one went slumming, the least one might count on was a few moments of unalloyed adoration.

Around three, his back aching and his feelings bruised, Edward Kennedy, accompanied by Patrick and somebody Patrick had attracted, a waitress named Michele Cassone, decided to abandon the overcrowded club and head back to La Guerida. Willy Smith by then was dancing with Patricia Bowman, and they would return separately.

Once she got back to the mansion Cassone remembers having sat on an esplanade above the crashing of the surf and talking. They discussed "big families and scuba diving," she revealed afterward, although most of the time "it was Senator Kennedy holding court." At one point a tall, naked woman with slicked-back hair stalked through the shadows along the sand and into the ocean.

Not long after that the young people excused themselves. A couple of minutes before four, Michele Cassone would recall, while she and Patrick were "cuddling" in one of the downstairs rooms, Patrick's father appeared in what was apparently his nightshirt. He was "just there with a weird look on his face," Michele insisted. "I was weirded out."

"I'm out of here," Michele Cassone proclaimed. Patrick walked her to her car. "Does your father embarrass you?" Michele demanded of Patrick. It was a moonlit, semitropical night on which Kennedy obviously felt haunted, and out of date. Meanwhile, on a nearby stage, Patricia Bowman and William Kennedy Smith were playing out the pas de deux that ultimately lit up a hundred million television screens.

Patrick Kennedy would allude to having run into Patricia Bowman while she was in and out of the mansion a few times, before Anne Mercer appeared to drive her home. Patricia had unnerved Willy, who expressed his relief that he had "pulled out" in time and conveyed to Patrick his apprehension that she was the sort of person who "comes to your house, who is insisting on finding out whether he is a Kennedy or not." She was "sort of a fatal attraction," Patrick concluded on his own. "This girl is really whacked out." Patricia had left once, driven away, but then "in no time the woman reappears in the house. My heart skipped a beat when I saw her standing in the doorway."

Patrick's intuitions were proved out early the following afternoon, when Patricia Bowman filed rape charges. Originally Bowman ostensibly asserted to Detective Christine Rigolo that Senator Kennedy had watched Smith assault her; she then withdrew the claim, which would be discounted afterward by investigators as a "clerical error."

Within a day the story leaked. When Palm Beach police turned up at the mansion on Sunday most of the Kennedys were at Saint Edward's Roman Catholic Church for the Easter Mass, after which they repaired to a nearby restaurant for Bloody Marys and lunch. At that point William Barry seems to have left the impression with the officers who came by La Guerida that William Smith and Edward Kennedy were already on their way to Washington, while Ted Kennedy himself, informed that the charge was "sexual battery," claimed that he had "no idea" who the plaintiff was, and supposedly did not make the connection to rape but rather assumed that the police were primarily concerned with a number of objets d'art which Patricia Bowman had ostensibly carted off—a sizable urn, a notepad, and several small pictures. Patricia Bowman would insist that she had taken these objects to prove that she had visited the mansion; apologists for the Kennedys would bruit it about that the entire scenario was concocted to cover a theft.

Nevertheless, the family did not waste time before hiring a sharp local attorney and onetime drug prosecutor, Mark Schnapp, and instigating a counterattack. Private detectives stepped in to investigate the alleged victim's background. Patricia Bowman's stepfather, Michael G. O'Neil, turned out to be the former chairman of General Tire and Rubber, and he would make it plain right away that he was rich and infuriated enough to take the Kennedys on wholesale. This could become very hard to contain.

"Within three or four days" investigators on the Kennedy payroll had assembled "a picture of Patricia Bowman as somebody who used cocaine, ran around with cocaine dealers, had abortions, split up with the father of her child—that sort of thing," one reporter on the scene remembers. And they were not making it difficult for the press to share all that. By April 14 *The New York Times* had joined *The Boston Herald* and CBS News in naming the alleged rape victim, until then a taboo in establishment journalism. The feature in the *Times* dwelt on Patricia's "wild streak," her seventeen driving tickets, her penchant for "fun with the ne'er-do-wells of cafe society." The Great Gray Lady was rocking with the tabloids.

It is a cliché of American political reportage that the public has no memory. But these days the media do, and it is murderous if selective. Rumor gets legitimized fast, and one evening's whisper turns into the morning's banner headline in *The New York Times*, frequently above the fold.

This is a process the astute *Boston Globe* feature writer John Aloysius Farrell has dubbed the "tabloidization of mainstream journalism." His editors in Boston got Farrell down to Florida the late March weekend in 1991 when the rape charges surfaced with instructions to determine as fast as possible whether Kennedy himself was implicated. Farrell quickly satisfied himself that the senator would not be charged. "What I didn't anticipate," Farrell says now, "was that this would turn into a sort of huge chapter in the war between the sexes. . . That it would be seen in Boston as a test of whether the *Globe* was finally going to cover the Kennedys hard, and that it would open this whole chapter of his private life which had only been vaguely hinted at if even mentioned in the *Globe* for thirty years."

"The whole thing turned into a media free-for-all," Farrell concludes. "This is the first instance that I can remember where the reporting in the supermarket tabloids made it to the newspaper tabloids and spilled through the wire services into the mainstream press so quickly. Kennedy's people were as shocked as I was."

Whichever angle you took, the tone and proportions of the imbroglio, this projection of privilege on a romp, brought down an unremitting press barrage. In Massachusetts in particular even the loyalists were irate. *The Boston Globe*'s streetwise columnist Mike Barnicle, who over the decades so often had spoken up for Kennedy, had finally had enough: "Kennedy stated he was simply enjoying a 'traditional Easter weekend,' which makes you wonder what these people do to celebrate something like Father's Day. Wear towels and run after girls, the younger Kennedy men rounding up the handsome women and allowing the 59-year-old Teddy to cut one out of the crowd?"

"Surrounded by sycophants," Barnicle wound it up, "Edward Kennedy thinks his name and title are license to do whatever he wants, and apparently the only voice he hears in that dark, lonely time before danger calls is the drink saying: 'Go ahead. You can get away with anything.'" The Minotaur was out there, naked, running before the spearpoints of the press.

Halfway through his indictment the astute Barnicle ventured a prognostication guaranteed to stop hearts across Capitol Hill. More of Kennedy's "core constituency disappears with each day's obituaries," Mike observed, and "next time out, if he indeed runs again, he will positively be beaten by any credible candidate with the money to wage a decent campaign."

It wouldn't be long before poll results vindicated Barnicle. The following July a Boston Herald-WCVB survey cited 62 percent of its respondents as of the opinion that Kennedy should not run for reelection in 1994. By 2 to 1 those replying to the pollster felt Kennedy misled Palm Beach authorities. Some 55 percent characterized Kennedy's job performance as fair to poor. Governor William Weld would beat Kennedy in a statewide election 59–34. Nearly half who answered would admit that they were less likely to vote for Kennedy in the wake of "his drinking and his actions in Palm Beach."

Around Boston and the District a number of the people Ted Kennedy had worked with and depended on his entire adult life were bracing themselves, unhappily, to walk away. "We'd like to see him recover enough to finish out his term with a little dignity and retire," one told me; another, with whom the senator had always conferred in any emergency, reported that this time he simply hadn't heard anything. Nor had he inquired. There really wasn't much to say.

The magazine press now fell to conducting a succession of autopsies in print of Kennedy's character. *Time* referred to the perception of Ted as a "Palm Beach boozer, lout and tabloid grotesque . . ." *Newsweek* termed him "the living symbol of the family flaws." Hearsay and invective of an unexampled ferocity promptly found its way into the staidest publication; even the Chappaquiddick publicity, disastrous as it was, had been confined pretty largely to speculation about the accident.

A manuscript that Putnam intended to bring out was going around New York in galleys. This was the exposé in which Rick Burke, Kennedy's office manager toward the end of the seventies and through his run at the Democratic nomination, presented his ex-boss as drug-soaked and uncontrollable much of the time, popping vials of amyl nitrate or snorting cocaine while grabbing after anything presentable. Certain of Kennedy's women Burke took the poetic licence of presenting in "composite" form; in fact, after close chronological examination, contemporaries in Kennedy's offices attributed a number of Burke's details to the hallucinatory transports that landed him in a mental hospital after shooting out the windshield of his own car and demanding police protection against alleged assassins. But a number of details checked out. After business reverses Burke needed money badly. Before publication Putnam scrubbed the book, which ultimately did appear as *The Senator* in 1992, published by St. Martin's.

Charges from Burke's book started leaking, first into the tabloids and presently into the more accountable press. Such representations were hard to deflect in the face of the prevailing lava flow. Kennedy conceded to a reporter that he would "have to be a little more attentive to behavior," but insisted that he had "never felt that I have a [drinking] problem."

A Senate Ethics Committee inquiry into Kennedy's actions as conduct which reflected badly on the Senate was lodged in June and dismissed after a week. In October Kennedy won the Claude Pepper Distinguished Service Award from his colleagues, and even nippy Minority Leader Robert Dole, while conceding his "disagreement with Ted on most of the public policy issues of the day," allowed as how he had "never doubted for a minute his commitment to help the elderly, the ill, and those Americans who have been on the outside looking in for far too long." This registered as something between an endorsement and a eulogy.

The decades of personal involvement for which Kennedy was legendary around the Senate probably saved him. Word had quickly circulated that when the insurgent young Chairman of the Judiciary Committee, Joe Biden, whom Kennedy had gone out of his way to mentor from the day of his arrival, developed brain aneurysms and had to spend a season recuperating, unable to read, at home in Wilmington, Kennedy had repeatedly taken the train out on Friday afternoons and verbally filled Biden in on the week's deliberations. Most colleagues on both sides of the aisle had stories to tell of similar kindnesses, telephone calls from Ted that saved awkward situations or congratulations on an anniversary or a word or two that offered a tip to salvage some legislative effort, not always liberal. He would be hard to dislodge.

Kennedy's adult children stood by and tried to help, each in his own way. Teddy, who had just graduated from the Yale School of Forestry, now enrolled himself publicly in the drug and alcohol program at the Institute of Living at Hartford. He took his father aside and leveled with him about the drinking. "In my family and among my friends," he told a reporter, "I've seen what happens when people don't address the problem." *Which* people he did not need to specify. "I realized that nothing could be right when that part was wrong."

Kennedy bit his lip and attempted to face up. "I recognize my own short-comings," he now came forward and confessed to a hand-picked audience of the faithful at the Kennedy Center at Harvard on October 25, "the faults in the conduct of my private life. I realize that I alone am responsible for them, and I am the one who must confront them." This hadn't come easily. Only Kennedy could comprehend the pressure building month by month, and what it took to lift it sometimes.

4. *Rosemary*

Time spent in Palm Beach invariably brought Rosemary to mind. One discussion I had with Kennedy late in the nineties started Kennedy musing about how it was that health had turned into such a leitmotiv throughout his entire senatorial career. Touching on the litany of illness that had plagued his family, Kennedy seemed to drift without my leading him particularly into subjects more painful and searching by far than anything he'd ever been willing to talk to me about before. Buried resentments and anxieties came through in ways I couldn't have imagined in earlier years, when mention of the others invariably provoked a reflexive low bow toward all those Easter Island Heads. He could now confront, apparently, a great deal.

"Well, as a young child," Kennedy had begun, "I saw the way my older sister Rosemary had, you know, mental retardation. There was concern for her. But I also saw at that time what a loving and wonderful person she was, and how she was in so many ways, uh, almost gentler and tenderer and more loving even than other brothers and sisters . . . I knew even as a younger person about the challenges that she faced . . . And that probably made a subtle and not-so-subtle impression on me as a child who grew up in that family, and a consciousness just about some of the mysteries, you know, in terms of health care."

Rosemary. Of all the setbacks, her ordeal came earliest and somehow remained most poignant. She had, after all, lived on. Rose Kennedy herself would call Rosemary's life "the first of the tragedies that were to befall us," and more was implied than that nature had crossed Rosemary's wires. The regret went very deep, beyond the stressful, competitive regimen that helped upset Rosemary, even beyond the botched prefrontal lobotomy behind the mother's back that left Rosemary to serve out the later decades of her long, angry life in St. Coletta's convent school in Jefferson, Wisconsin.

The question has arisen as to how limited Rosemary was, what role she found for herself inside that busy, ambition-ridden household. Rose Kennedy's personal assistant, Barbara Gibson, has published several fully coherent diary entries Rosemary wrote while traveling with her sister Eunice at twenty. Barbara Gibson herself concludes that, while apparently dyslexic, Rosemary was able to operate comfortably near the bottom of the normal range and that a procedure as radical as a lobotomy was in no way indicated. Family acquaintances who knew Rosemary as a child insist she was mildly retarded even then. Jack's Choate roommate, Lem Billings, would characterize her to me as in later adolescence sexually frustrated and frantic at times, with an increasing tendency to lash out at all the clamor and competition around herself.

As Edward Kennedy had underscored in our discussion, Rosemary was uniquely affectionate and understanding of the others. Barbara Gibson suggests that Rosemary's unexpected lobotomy, followed by her abrupt disappearance from the family circle, left the nine-year-old Teddy particularly confused and apprehensive, "never letting himself become too close to anyone, carrying anger, fear, and guilt trapped inside his troubled heart . . . The message was clear. Disobey Joe and Rose Kennedy and you will cease to exist."

Since we had come so close, I ventured to ask Ted what he had thought when Rosemary disappeared so unexpectedly and so permanently. "I thought," he had answered glumly, "that I had better do what Dad wanted or the same thing could happen to me."

This cuts very deep into Kennedy's most closely guarded apprehensions, the cravings that drove him and the fears he needed to anesthetize. I am reminded of a passage in his autobiography. While Ted was still a rambunctious thirteen-year-old his father had put his choices to him. "You can have a serious life or a nonserious life, Teddy. I'll still love you whichever choice you make. But if you decide to have a nonserious life, I won't have much time for you. You make up your own mind. There are too many children who are doing things here that are interesting for me to do much with you."

". . . *won't have much time for you.*" This was a profound threat. Kennedy's mother was increasingly withheld, emotionally unavailable. It was the father who inspired this emerging baby brother, dandled him on his lap and read him the funny papers, moved him, dealt with his screwups and validated his future. To find oneself excluded from the Ambassador's presence amounted to oblivion. There were several ways to disappear.

5. Recovery

One price Kennedy's notoriety exacted became evident that fall of 1991 during the Clarence Thomas/Anita Hill hearings. Millions who had depended on Kennedy to nail down the social consequences, to pose the puncturing question, now watched him brooding through the rounds of inquiry with little to contribute. He looked painfully detached a lot of the time and occasionally downright sheepish. Each time he did speak up he risked another round of digs by the pundits, of wholesale tabloid abuse. "Are we an old boys' club," he broke out once in defense of Anita Hill, "insensitive at best, and perhaps something worse? Will we strain to concoct any excuse? To impose any burden? To tolerate any insubstantial attack on a woman in order to rationalize a vote for this nomination?" But this resonated oddly, falling across a public which attributed to the senator negligence, at the very least, in the face of rape.

Kennedy weighed in another time to point out how "the vanishing views of Judge Thomas have become a major issue in these hearings," and added that Thomas's American Bar Association ratings were lower than those of Robert Bork, of Harold Carswell, of Clement Haynsworth. This reminded the cognoscenti that all three nominees had been denied Supreme Court seats through Kennedy's intervention. Kennedy's staff director on Judiciary, Jeff Blattner, later insisted that Kennedy was never intended to play a central role in the Thomas hearings.

Since 1988, while Joe Biden was recovering and Ted took over again as Chairman of the Judiciary Committee, Biden and Kennedy had collaborated with an extraordinary mutual sensitivity. There was an understanding early that Democratic Senators Patrick Leahy of Vermont and Howell Heflin of Alabama would lead the questioning of Thomas, while Hatch of Utah and Arlen Specter of Pennsylvania would defend the nomination. Just then Kennedy's energies were absorbed with jockeying the Civil Rights Bill of 1991 through the Senate. The help of Jack Danforth of Missouri was critical; Danforth was Thomas's primary Senate sponsor.

Relegated to the back benches, Kennedy and his staff were admittedly a stroke or two behind in establishing how spotty Thomas's record was, how retrograde his opinions. Reliable allies in vital civil-rights groups, especially the NAACP, tended to hang back rather than oppose early a fellow African-American, especially one the administration's "pinpoint strategy" was promoting hard as a battler from impoverished circumstances whose story of personal success must inspire and reassure.

Before Thomas started juking, repudiating the tangled and reactionary phrasemaking that represented his contribution to legal literature, many of the senators had already come forward with support. "In hindsight," Blattner admits, "the lack of an effort on the part of opponents to make Judge Thomas's record and views clear early on proved to seriously undermine the ultimate effort to defeat his nomination." By then the supercharged sexual vaudeville over Thomas's alleged overtures to Anita Hill left everybody in sight shuffling toward the Cloakroom.

Could Kennedy, unencumbered, have upended Clarence Thomas? "I'm convinced he could have," says Jimmy Flug, whose reputation for extricating the Senate from a series of rotten Supreme Court choices goes back to dumping Harold Carswell. "Without the Palm Beach problem." Had they been free to crank up earlier, to enlist their constituencies. Thomas got in, narrowly, but over the following months Warren Rudman would repudiate his own vote on public television, and David Boren has expressed regrets, and Wyche Fowler was reportedly back-pedaling. If Kennedy had indeed limited himself to a walk on the beach that fateful Easter weekend we might have been spared the prospect of a series of disastrous Supreme Court decisions which brought us Clarence Thomas's America.

In December of 1991 the fever broke. Called to the witness stand at the rape trial of William Smith in West Palm Beach, Kennedy seemed forthcoming, calm, senatorial. The widely broadcast proceedings had permitted enough of the sensationalist detritus to settle to convince the broad public that Kennedy's involvement was unintended, peripheral. On December 11 a jury found William Smith innocent. An expertly mounted defense by his attorney, Roy Black, along with Smith's heartfelt and frequently embarrassing depiction of a series of sticky exchanges on the night beach, replete with partial ejaculations, half-healed bruises, incomplete tumescence, and too much or not enough sand in Patricia Bowman's panties ultimately convinced the jurors that what had happened was in all likelihood consensual. Smith's uncle gained back a measure of innocence by association.

If anything, Kennedy staffers agree, their boss seemed steadier than usual throughout the long ordeal. "Even during the rape trial, which must have been rock bottom," Dave Nexon says, "he still had the same zest, worked the same hours . . ."

By 1991 the White House was blockading a lot of legislation. Under pressure from Republican moderates, Bush finally signed the Civil Rights Act of 1991 as well as the pioneering National Service proposal and the reauthorized Higher Education Act. But mossbacks and heavy campaign contributors around the country were now "beating up on Bush," remembers Kennedy's staff director on the Labor Committee, Nick Littlefield, and Bush staff director John Sununu had just observed that "As far as I'm concerned, Congress can go home." There ensued a string of presidential vetoes that included the Family Leave bill, the Striker Replacement Bill, the Elementary and Secondary School Reform Act (which Kennedy had shepherded through the Senate 92-6), and out to the reauthorization of the National Institute of Health.

6. *Vicki*

One development which sustained Kennedy was a new romance. Sloe-eyed and chestnut-haired, Victoria Reggie was frank, sprightly, and comparatively young at thirty-eight. But she was different on impact from the maturing starlets and D.C. socialites whom Kennedy had been squiring in public for decades. She was patently authentic, an unabashed free spirit. Victoria's grandparents on both sides were immigrants from Beirut, Maronite Christians who settled into the small-town life of Crowley, Louisiana, and pulled a heavy oar in the local Catholic church while easing their children into business and politics. Victoria's mother, Doris, was an heiress to the Bunny Bread baking fortune. There was a warmth here, a sense of belonging, which could not help but appeal to Kennedy just then, living day to day once more as a national pariah.

Furthermore, Victoria's father, Judge Edmund Reggie, was an influential wheeler-dealer lawyer and close associate of the controversial governor Edwin Edwards. Reggie caught the eye of the younger Kennedys before they amounted to anything on the national level, at the 1956 convention which nominated Adlai Stevenson. Jack Kennedy was mounting his unsuccessful eleventh-hour effort to grab the vice-presidential slot from Estes Kefauver. Himself a delegate from Louisiana, the judge took immediately to Jack and Bobby, warmed by their "great Boston accents," Victoria relates, "as well as the fact that neither of them wore BrylCreem in their hair." When Russell Long disappeared for a few hours to find a drink, Reggie lined the delegation up behind John Kennedy.

For Victoria, like Ted, a lot of the fascination is in the all-too-human

details. By 1960 Judge Reggie was managing a big section of the Deep South
for the Kennedys, and remained a powerful local retainer in 1968 and again
in 1980. Kennedy found himself drawn to this spirited, tight-knit family, and
particularly the judge, who was already fending off by 1982 what amounted
to eleven federal indictments for fraud and mismanagement in a scramble
to salvage his collapsing savings and loan holdings. Throughout a decade
of battering in the courts Edmund Reggie remained beautifully turned out,
solid behind Kennedy interests, and devoted but never obsequious. Reggie
called Ted "The Commander" "because he's always ordering everybody else
around all the time," and Kennedy just took it and chuckled and showed up
regularly for more. The Reggies maintained a summer house on Nantucket,
and Kennedy liked to sail over and visit them there.

For decades Kennedy barely noticed Victoria. She grew up happy in Crowley, one of the six Reggie children, a superstar in the local parochial school
who developed so fast that her mother still thinks of her as getting "out of
a chair in five or six different parts at a time." Graduating Phi Beta Kappa
from Sophie Newcomb College, she was president of her sorority. At Tulane
Law School she made the law review and graduated summa cum laude
before deserting this paradise of Cajun burgers and catfish platters to put in
a stint of clerking in the U.S. Seventh Circuit Court of Appeals in Chicago.
She met her first husband—Grier Raclin, a low-keyed telecommunications
attorney—with whom she had two children and moved to D.C. The marriage
came apart and they were divorced in 1990.

Meanwhile, Victoria had become a partner in the Washington firm of
Keck, Mahin and Cate. Her specialty was banking, particularly loan restructuring and workout. One colleague would characterize her as "charismatic
and hard-driving," and popular with her clients. She developed a reputation
for settlement negotiations during which no prisoners were taken, a memory
for details it took her spontaneity and brio to keep from intimidating her
contemporaries.

A colleague at Keck, Mahin who was also a familiar of Kennedy's, Peter
Edelman, opens other possibilities: "She's smart, she's very funny, and you
know how much he values being able to laugh. She's kind of outrageous in
a wonderful way, very earthy. He's fortunate to have found her." In Victoria
the fussy, demanding, daylight side of Kennedy's personality was met with
a ripple of the Dionysian.

Throughout Kennedy's occasional visits to the Reggies "We saw each
other but then we didn't see each other," Victoria comments. Then, in June
of 1991, Vicki gave a fortieth-anniversary party for her parents in D.C. at her

house on Woodley Park. Edmund invited The Commander, who showed up without a date. "I teased him about that," Victoria remembers, "and I guess the rest is history."

"Ted was a very nice, polite, dedicated suitor. Very very sweet and very considerate," Victoria says. "He always called me the day after a date to tell me he had a very nice time." Roses arrived by truckload. Victoria was working hard, she had natural hesitations, and it was important to her to spend as much time with her children as she could, so most evenings that summer she and Kennedy and Caroline, six, and Curran, nine, got together at Woodley Park. Victoria usually cooked—crawfish étouffée and grape leaves and tabouli are specialties—after which Kennedy was likely to slide down onto the floor with Caroline and help her with her coloring books.

Publicity from the Palm Beach affair was still lighting up the media but "we were in a very insulated situation," Victoria recalled to me. "It wasn't like the topic of dinner table conversation. We were just two people getting to know each other." Throughout the Smith trial Kennedy called her every day. "She was his solace away from the storm," one friend says. "It gave him confidence that she would be there during hard times." She helped draft his fateful mea culpa speech.

When Kennedy finally decided to propose he braced himself and telephoned a few old friends, starting with John Tunney and John Culver. They were so unabashedly pleased—none of the usual needling, nothing but warmth and congratulations—that Kennedy followed up with calls to a few others and in the end reached dozens of people, including a string of one-time girlfriends and, by the end, Joan. Everybody wished him well. It was a job getting Kennedy off the telephone that afternoon. He could feel resurrection breaking like the dawn.

Kennedy popped the question at the opera, Victoria remembers, and "I was very happy that he asked me." She knew that Kennedy was "a person who had been dating a great deal," as her father put it, she'd seen enough herself to conclude that his drinking wasn't going to pose a problem, and she was deeply in love. She understood Kennedy thoroughly. Any time he threatened to throw his weight around Vicki did not hesitate to tweak him about whether he really hadn't married her to get his poll results up. This was a marriage of passion between equals, the only arrangement possible for someone who insisted cheerfully that "I have lived my life in terms of the empowerment of women."

Not that this inhibited Victoria from taking on touchier, more traditional assignments. With reelection in 1994 coming up, Vicki organized a reception in Boston for Ted for 1,200 influential New England women, importing five Democratic senators to demonstrate that Kennedy was holding his own in Washington. She put together a Western-style barbecue when Teddy Jr. married Katherine Anne Gershman in October of 1993. To form some bond with Joan—who had been up and down—Victoria reportedly telephoned her and asked for advice about piano lessons for Caroline. Kennedy routinely included Victoria in staff-run strategy sessions.

Merely talking about Ted would light up Victoria's impudent hazel eyes, thrust forward her strong Levantine chin and nose. "Really, life's wonderful," Victoria Kennedy was willing to sum it up. "We laugh a lot, we definitely laugh a lot. I think I'm the luckiest woman on earth."

In Boston, Cardinal Bernard Law continued to block Kennedy's appeal for an annulment of his marriage to Joan. But with or without the church, Kennedy went ahead and married Vicki in a small, private ceremony in July of 1992. By then Bill Clinton had long since locked up the Democratic nomination.

In a short biography of Kennedy, journalist Edward Klein expands on the effect Kennedy's remarriage had on the rest of the family: "From the beginning, all three of Ted's kids were opposed to the marriage, and they let their father know how they felt." Ted had refused to consider a prenuptial agreement, and this meant, Klein quotes a family lawyer. "'His kids are furious because Vicki is going to get everything,'" an estate Klein estimates at $30 million.

Kennedy's many nephews and nieces, especially Bobby's headstrong brood, were especially outraged as their permissive guardian, Le Grand Fromage, came under the direction of this soigné but definite second wife, who knew what she wanted. At his memorial service Caroline Kennedy would allude to her huge, darling uncle, at whose easygoing establishment "the best laughs and the best cookies" were always to be found. The carte blanche era was over. Even in Hyannis Port, where, traditionally, anything went, Vicki had directed that NO TRESPASSING signs close off the beach to passersby, and when a horde of Bobby's grandchildren showed up to trash—again—the swimming pool, they were turned away squalling. Victoria might have "saved my life," as Kennedy kept protesting, but not everybody was enchanted with the byproducts of salvation.

CHAPTER VI

Back From the Dead

1. Clinton

The relationship between Bill Clinton and Edward Kennedy had taken some months to come to a boil. Still wary about styling himself too far to the left, even in Massachusetts, Clinton skirted joint campaign appearances with the senator. The two men "don't really have a relationship," one Clinton aide told the press. Clinton was famously proud of the widely distributed photograph of himself as a Boy's Nation junior delegate shaking JFK's hand on a trip to Washington. Ted Kennedy had made it a point to telephone Clinton in Little Rock to congratulate—or console—him after each gubernatorial election, and Clinton would reciprocate by helping Kennedy's staff pull together background material implicating Robert Bork, a professor of Clinton's at Yale Law School.

But as a cofounder and chairman of the centrist Democratic Leadership Council, Clinton ducked too open an association with this Moloch of progressivism whom Republicans delighted in caricaturing as out to empty everybody's pocket into the public trough. Such perceptions of Kennedy were ludicrously out of date—had never meant very much—and behind the scenes Kennedy helped where he could to promote Clinton's candidacy. Kennedy strategists, from Paul Tully and Bill Carrick to Rick Stearns and Ron Brown, signed on with Clinton, along with office specialists like Kennedy's foreign-policy aide Nancy Soderberg. But relations remained arms-length.

What brought the two politicians together in the end was the exploding health issue. The off-year Senate triumph in 1991 in Pennsylvania of longtime

Kennedy spear carrier Harris Wofford flagged health abuses across America. What Kennedy managed, over decades of concern, was largely to pinpoint the emerging inequities in the medical delivery system and suggest new solutions. Kennedy initiatives dating back to the end of the sixties had underscored the maldistribution of health care nationwide, the inappropriateness that we, the richest Western nation, should remain the only major industrialized society without universal health coverage. After all, disagreements with the Carter administration over both the urgency and the timing of health reform had more than anything else inveigled Kennedy into running in 1980.

Along with his West Virginia colleague Jay Rockefeller and California's Henry Waxman in the House, Kennedy kept the drumbeat going throughout the Reagan years—his bills would range from attacks on the administration for starving out research to demands for limits on overbilling by hospitals and doctors to defenses of "family planning options" to bipartisan resolutions to bring the "37 million uncovered Americans into the health care system" by way of state and employer mandates.

This last proposal surfaced in 1996. Kennedy had long since given up on looking to the federal government—the "single payer"—and acknowledged that the best chances of passage lay in propitiating the insurance interests. Between his opposition to the disclosure provisions of the administration's AIDS package as an "invitation to drive the epidemic underground and encourage its spread" and year after year of scattered hearings to point up such suppressed outrages as the prevalence of leukemia at nuclear reactor sites, Kennedy kept the spotlight moving. He pressed for Lifecare, nursing facilities for the deteriorating elderly. He fought for the right of health care workers to bring up abortion during family planning sessions.

More than anything else, Kennedy recognized that irresponsible policymaking in the insurance industry was compounding the panic. In April of 1992 Kennedy spelled it out before the Health Insurance Association of America: "Your private sector role has unquestionably made the crisis worse," he leveled at them. "The message sent out by too many of your member companies is unmistakably clear: Don't insure anyone unless you think they won't get sick. And if you make a mistake, do your best to walk away from it. Do all you can to stop Congress from acting . . ." Kennedy was already defining, in detail, what Barack Obama would have to confront a decade and a half later.

What Kennedy laid before Hillary Clinton and her task force in 1993 was literally decades of spadework, numberless hearings and staff studies and libraries full of expert testimony already subjected to analysis and ready to translate into legislation. "The senator decided early on to cooperate as closely with the president as he could," emphasized Dave Nexon, Kennedy's health staff director. "He likes Clinton, they're on the same wavelength. The administration invited our Hill staff to come in and cooperate, and after a while we had ten people involved, everybody, including the fellows. I personally spent 90 percent of my time down there. Hillary is phenomenal . . ."

It wasn't really a stretch for either Kennedy or Clinton, who quickly embroidered on their older brother/kid brother material. "Kennedy has been reinventing government, reexamining traditional liberal positions for a long time," one senior in both camps suggests. "There isn't any sense of 'Gee, I should have been there.' Look at all those people having their prima donna ways—Sam Nunn, David Boren, Dave McCurdy. You know, there are aspects of the Clinton proposals Kennedy is not so pleased with, especially the public health side of the legislation—what happens to low-income people, chronically ill children, mental health. You'll see him press his points in some way— from the inside. He understands that the president and Hillary see the whole playing field, the pressures and counter-pressures . . ."

Grateful, Bill Clinton had shown a flattering receptivity to the Kennedys during White House functions. Jean Smith—cooling down after a reportedly quite bitter go-around with her kid brother coming out of the Palm Beach crunch—would go on to Ireland as U.S. ambassador. Curtsies continued both ways.

There had been awkward moments as well during the appointments process. Kennedy was obviously nonplussed at the way the White House bumped ailing Circuit Court Justice Stephen Breyer, once a Kennedy aide and the prime mover behind airline and truck deregulation, from a Supreme Court nomination in June of 1993 after hauling him out of a hospital bed while Kennedy was trading chits with senators Dole and Hatch to lock Breyer in. Kennedy claimed to sympathize with these "tough, close decisions," by the president, but added, dejectedly, "He's a friend. Steve's a friend, so I can understand his disappointment."

Clinton, rarely dropping a beat, made it a point to address a Kennedy fund raiser in Massachusetts later in the month. "Every effort to bring the American people together across that which divides us," the president asserted, "every effort has the imprint of Ted Kennedy." Clinton ticked off Kennedy's accomplishments merely in the previous twelve months. In his turn, Kennedy proclaimed that "We have waited for this president for twelve long years. We in Massachusetts are going to stump for the president's economic program, for his health program, and we are going to get him reelected."

Kennedy meant that. He functioned as the floor manager of Clinton's National Service plan, which cleared the Senate 54–40. He worked a complicated double-shuffle on Pennsylvania's Arlen Specter and his law-and-order Republicans that drove through the prohibition against blockading abortion clinic entrances without jeopardizing strikers' rights. A bear for decades on women's issues, Kennedy had years earlier pushed through a support subsidy for poor pregnant women which assisted 8.7 million in getting proper care throughout their deliveries. He sponsored a bill to let the federal government—not banks—finance student loans, saving undergraduates many millions.

Wherever the battle was thickest, Clinton's first year, Kennedy was most likely to show up early. When Clinton returned to Boston to help open the Stephen E. Smith Center at the Kennedy Library, Congressman Joe Kennedy II came out publicly for NAFTA and grabbed his uncle's shoulder: "Are you listening to this?" Ted, fearful of his labor support, broke into a grin and turned his tie around like a hangman's noose. But in the end he took a breath and voted with Clinton on the North American Free Trade Agreement.

As month after month throughout 1993 the Clinton administration's health bill foundered, Kennedy pushed his own collateral proposals through the Health, Education, Labor and Pensions Committee (HELP), which he chaired, an effort to salvage as much as possible and impart to the issue recovered momentum. Simultaneously, Kennedy jacked up federal support—from $34 to $65 billion—for medical education and teaching hospitals, a major industry in Massachusetts. Here was a program Hillary had initially proposed to cut; Bill Clinton personally reversed the administration's position, concedes one insider, "to avoid having surgery performed on his bill in Teddy's committee." One hand still washed the other, even among friends.

Successes were racking up; nevertheless—this must be said—there was a suspicion among hard-core liberals that Kennedy was trimming his principles more week by week to propitiate Clinton's Democratic Leadership corner-cutters. That in his desperation to escape the enduring Palm Beach fallout he would consent to anything to get his name on bills. Although in the end, testifying at the Smith trial in December of 1991, Kennedy came through as measured, statesmanlike, tangential to the scandal, the public would remain divided over the verdict of innocence. The shadow was ominously slow to pass. "Republicans at the time told me that there was this sort of feeling that Kennedy could be had," notes one close observer. Concessions to Strom Thurmond on the Crime Bill still left civil libertarians upset.

Kennedy still liked to maintain that "We are citizens first and constituencies second." Such positions were noble enough, but now they tended to soften Kennedy's edges. There was a suspicion building that Ted was losing his ideological fire. Others across the spectrum—Sam Nunn, Daniel Moynihan, Howard Metzenbaum—whatever the range of their beliefs, still seemed to stand for something throughout the Party. Like his NAFTA waffling, Kennedy's flexibility on the health issue—the same issue that provoked him into challenging Jimmy Carter for bringing forward a set of proposals a lot more substantive than anything Bill Clinton was likely to sign—raised hackles in labor halls. By then it hadn't gone unnoticed that, of the $9.2 million Kennedy's discontinued Fund for a Democratic Majority had raised over the previous decade, less than a million was ever paid out directly to underwrite other Democrats. Most onlookers would concede that Ted had all but single-handedly staved much of the Reagan Revolution off. But that was then. Was there anything left?

A fund raiser in June of 1993 produced $500,000 in reelection money for Kennedy, cash he would need. Perceived as vulnerable after the Palm Beach publicity bloodbath, there was a compounding list of potential Republican challengers to Kennedy, led off by Governor William Weld and ex-Secretary of Transportation Andrew Card and—a rising threat—George Romney's son Mitt. A *Boston Globe* poll that spring pegged the Massachusetts voters at 41 percent favorable to Kennedy, 40 percent unfavorable. Kennedy let it be known, according to the *Globe*, that he "hoped people sense what his marriage last July has meant to him." He made sure to find himself widely quoted that his remarriage had "saved his life." Meanwhile, the federal government was winding up a decade of litigation against Kennedy's new father-in-law. In September Judge Edmund Reggie would plead nolo contendere to a misapplication of funds charge and subject himself to 120 days of home detention, three years of probation, and a $30,000 fine.

Nevertheless, public wrath was lifting: Redemption was in the wind. Kennedy's mastery of pork-barreling had generated a range of federal subsidies to the financially hard-pressed Commonwealth, from billions to construct the Central Artery tunnel (the Big Dig) and clean up Boston Harbor to $29 million for the Center for Photonomics Research at Boston University, which Kennedy tucked into a 1991 defense appropriations bill along with timely intervention to salvage a huge Martin Marietta plant. Even the humblest constituent could depend on a quick response from the Kennedy offices in Boston and D.C.

The afternoon the Clintons visited Jackie Onassis on Martha's Vineyard in 1993, Kennedy waited until he had the president out on the water before pitching not only his own ideas about health but also the urgency of awarding a new Department of Defense accounting facility to troubled nearby Southbridge.

With reelection coming up, politics reverts. Between legislative sessions and into the winter of 1994, Kennedy had been pounding through Massachusetts. Campaigning remains a grind—"The fun goes out of it, you end up in sweaty hotel rooms seeing nothing but one television crew after another," Kennedy warned his nephew Joe in 1986—but Ted could still find ways to liven up the afternoons. Rolling up to a mob of construction workers while canvassing the Commonwealth late in 1993, Kennedy's office manager Paul Donovan divulged, the senator cranked a window down and shouted across the havoc: "Listen, you fellows, go take the rest of the day off. Tell 'em the senator said it was OK."

That Kennedy was emerging from the pall became clear from the press reception of Joe McGinniss's long-dreaded biography of the senator, *The Last Brother*. The book was exceedingly tough on Kennedy, and spiked with insupportable supposition. But at its richest moments McGinniss's study did indeed project a fascinating rendition of the Kennedys as a "Dysfunctional Poster Family," in Ellen Goodman's words, alternately driven and self-indulgent, and in the end recklessly self-destructive.

What made the book most notable was the extent to which the reviewing organs savaged it. It was as if the same opinion-makers who two years earlier simply could not dig up enough with which to foul Kennedy's reputation now colluded to sanctify the remains. The roast was over.

It was as if the nation as well as the Congress finally understood that, blow-offs and all, Kennedy was ultimately irreplaceable. Wounds healed. Kennedy made a point of stepping back when his press nemesis Rupert Murdoch bought the bankrupt *New York Post*, and before long even Murdoch's *Boston Herald* had to admit that Kennedy was in fact Massachusetts's outstanding advocate in Congress. By October of 1993 Kennedy's "admiration level" had crept up to 58 percent. The crisis seemed manageable.

2. Mitt

In politics too often admiration doesn't guarantee electability. By mid-spring of 1994, with reelection in Massachusetts coming up, the needles of prognosis were jumping in their seismographs. Much more than money was already involved. "Tell me," one gruff old loyalist from JFK's aging entourage demanded of me without warning over dinner. "Would you say that in

Teddy's case there are enough brain cells left, for Christ's sake, to get him through a real campaign? He'd have to debate Mitt Romney.

"There are a lot of people in Massachusetts—and these are people who really don't have anything against Teddy, they think he's done the job. But at the same time they haven't forgotten Palm Beach, and I think a helluva lot of them feel that it's gotten to be—you know—gold watch time."

A few weeks earlier, a *Boston Globe* poll had concluded that while 60 percent of the electorate still regarded Kennedy favorably, only 38 percent felt that he merited another term, while 62 percent felt that it was time for somebody else. A mainstay for Kennedy Democrats for decades, new ownership and a shakeup on the *Globe*'s editorial page left even *its* support in question. The crust was thin suddenly; beneath everything oblivion boiled.

At that stage George Romney's telegenic son Mitt was rounding into favor as the Republican nominee. Kennedy himself still tended to dismiss the increasingly serious challenge, resorting to his familiar dictum that he intended to campaign for his established principles, not against any particular individual. This meant he still regarded himself as comfortably ahead.

Nevertheless, he had been packing his weekends with extra days of campaigning around the Commonwealth. One Monday toward the end of June I arranged to join Kennedy's party. It had been sultry all weekend on the Cape, miasmal, but during the previous few hours the heat wave across New England had taken a turn. Although the sun was out a breeze was up, and windows in the van were open. "My God, what weather!" Kennedy exclaimed while the van pulled out, twisting against his safety belt on the passenger side to confront the middle seats. He tipped his Orange Slice up, straight out of the can. "Those guys back there, they know what they're doin'," Kennedy announced. "They do it well, there's really a sense of pride."

We were just pulling away from an hour at the GE jet-engine plant at Lynn, a classic campaign stopover, divided between buttering up the executives and joshing and hand-shaking the senator's jovial way along the echoing plant floor. For all the computer-driven lathes from Cincinnati Milacron and display tables decked out with mirror-finish turbine discs, there persisted a reliable nineteenth-century stolidity to the place. Heavy machinery grinding away made normal conversation impossible; the smell of cutting oil off mountains of scrolled-steel shavings flattened out the stale trapped air.

"In all the time I've been on the Armed Services Committee," Kennedy had been careful to reassure the management during his short address, "no matter where the frames come from, the engines are GE—Lynn." Behind him, mounted like a trophy, a prototype jet engine gleamed, dominant throughout the industry.

What sticks with Kennedy, reminiscing in the van, is what lives tending those huge gray machines have amounted to, what people's prospects are. "Did you hear that union rep telling me that they can produce a casting in there right now in one day that used to take them sixteen days?" Kennedy wonders, at large. "It's mind-boggling. They have an incentive system—that's what this guy was tellin' us—they get the bonuses. The corporate guys just sort of stand there writing this stuff down . . ."

Industrial America was coming around. "I remember in '68," Edward Kennedy laughs, "they had these tanning factories up here on the North Shore. The parts would come in from Australia. Big wood barrels, filled with hides and acid. So many things you can't remember, but this I can remember as if it were yesterday.

"I'd gone through on two different occasions. They gave you these big rubber overshoes to put on, because otherwise the acid would eat the threads in your shoes. So, the second time I didn't put the overshoes on, and the next morning the soles of my shoes peeled right off. Like Band-Aids. Because the acid sits this thick on the floor of the place, and here these people are right in it all day, and they are touchin' it, and bending over and scratchin' themselves . . . And I noticed their teeth—all cavities, and comin' out of their mouths at every angle. It wasn't long after that that I got a ten-million-dollar fluoridation bill through—after all, you know, they fluoridated in Brookline and Newton, and they haven't had a cavity there since. I thought—if that was happening downtown——."

Kennedy guffawed. There was a difference to be made. Churning up the Massachusetts Outback, seeding in his '94 Senate reelection, Kennedy picked up energy steadily bumping around the state. His schedule was packed with opportunities to merchandise what seniority can do for biotech engineers and computer hardware entrepreneurs, to dispense block grant money and ARPA—Advanced Research Products Agency—checks to CEOs across the North Shore.

Between appearances he got to relax. "Hey, big guy," he rounded on his amused driver after a wrong turn. "This is unbelievable. If you were lookin' at the map instead of tryin' to tickle me, we wouldn't be on this side street. And where's the little orange juice can? Have you drunk that already?" Irish humor never dies: The ghost of Jack Crimmins hovers.

When barnstorming like this, refreshment was where you grab the opportunity. A few minutes later, wandering through the laboratories of the Abiomed Company in Danvers, Kennedy plucked up a plastic and titanium artificial heart the size of a cantaloupe and pressed it against the narrow chest of a skinny little local photographer for fit. "Don't get sick," he advised the astonished cameraman. "Me, it's all right."

Kennedy's heft these days was again a concern to staffers in an election year, but he seemed untroubled. There was old pol's ambiance about Kennedy this time around, a degree of comfort that, closing in on sixty-three, he had at last evolved into what he needed to be. The day grew warmer and warmer, but Kennedy rocked in and out of the factory gates and conference rooms and cafeterias of post-industrial Massachusetts, his winter-weight double-breasted dark gray suit badly rumpled, shooting the big gold links in his French cuffs, increasingly red-faced and perspired. His heavy silver hair is cut quite wavy and long. Mature, foreshortened by the decades, he had come to resemble the Toby Mug version of himself.

Still—settled in, listening to the presentations from executives who wanted something from their government, Kennedy betrayed underlying restlessness. He drummed his fingers, drew scimitars on his notepad and inked each blade in slowly, pulled off his big chrome-rimmed bifocals and opened and closed the bows a few times and slid them into his pocket and glanced around balefully from under those grizzled scrollwork brows and pulled the glasses out and smudged them up and put them on and took them off again. When formalities were over, and Kennedy had made his pitch for health care and the crime bill in front of the mandatory assemblage of secretaries and technicians, there remained just one more item: "By the way," he reminded his onlookers, "there is an election this fall. And Vicki here would like to see her husband reelected." Something unexpected was starting to be felt. Ted Kennedy could lose.

Back in the van, Kennedy sidestepped direct questions about the presumptive challenger, W. Mitt Romney, a wealthy venture capitalist and president of the Boston stake, its fourteen Mormon Churches. All through the Commonwealth politics is traditionally retail, tribal, and today is one more investment by Kennedy in the effort to persuade local chiefs that he can indeed do more for Massachusetts—and for them—after which the word was expected to go forth among the Indians. Romney, on the other hand, seemed determined to buy up Kennedy's Senate seat wholesale, through recurrent television blanketings, in expectation of bypassing the ancient constituencies and pulling in voters electronically.

And this was working. After having trailed other candidates prior to the

May 19 preferential primary, Romney bombarded the airwaves with spots which presented him as a breathtakingly clean-cut forty-seven-year-old father of five "healthy" sons, well suited to demolish the exhausted incumbent. Republican delegates promptly conferred on him 68 percent of their votes. There remained the formal Republican primary in September, and aspirant businessman John Lakian intended to square off against Romney one more time. Mitt Romney looked practically unstoppable.

Whereas in the past Ted's "strategy has always been to raise plenty of money early," observed Milton Gwirtzman, a tuner of political pianos for the Kennedys since Jack, "and get the momentum up enough to scare anybody of substance out," the three or four million dollars the Kennedy campaign had raised so far did not look at all intimidating against the $8 million the Romneys had pledged. As the primary dealmaker for Bain Capital, the venture capital arm of Bain and Company, Romney was widely reported to pull in more than $6 million in a successful year, over ten times Ted's income. Romney's approach was forthright: "If people believe the answer to America's problems is more government, then they should vote for Ted Kennedy. He's the expert on government."

Out on the road again and headed toward Peabody, I managed to nudge Kennedy into touching on—reluctantly, and in that notorious semicoherent delivery he resorted to when he was censoring himself—his apprehensions about the Romney candidacy: "You know, in a state that's hard-pressed economically, the situation has powerful forces that are, uh, out there, that are looking for simplistic kinds of responses . . ." He named no names. Nevertheless, "I'm going to welcome the opportunity for people to debate me on these issues if they are serious about them."

3. Battle

The day will come when aficionados of political science will climb all over this most expensive and embattled of Kennedy's reelection campaigns with the kind of game-plan cross-analysis the smart pros hold back until they are dealing with a classic. This fight had everything—religious haymakers above and below the belt, money panics, the drama of youth versus age, lifestyle clash. That summer and into the fall the recession-ridden Commonwealth heaved.

The balance kept shifting. Through June and into July Romney repeatedly reminded onlookers of the bathing beauty who had the contest won until she opened her mouth. In mid-June, attempting to pin up his own positions as contrasted with Kennedy's, Romney recommended a thirteen-point program he labeled "learn-fare," kept rigorous by requiring drug testing for welfare recipients, mandatory employment for "able-bodied adults without dependents," and denial of all benefits to illegal aliens. It had escaped Romney that as matters stood only adults with dependents were welfare-eligible and that in Massachusetts nobody could collect welfare unless registered with the Immigration and Naturalization Service.

For someone who regularly claimed to run for the office, not against the challenger, Kennedy's response was anything but impersonal: "One of my two potential opponents, who made $11.6 million in the last two years, issued his first comprehensive position paper, attacking poor children and poor women—and he got it wrong."

Off on the wrong foot, Romney waded in deeper. In early July Romney characterized Kennedy as opposed to the line-item veto, against the Gramm-Rudman federal budget restrictions, in favor of single-payer health coverage, and soft on crime. In virtually every particular Mitt Romney had Kennedy's voting record backward.

Romney was soon compounding his research problem by attempting to straddle what positions he did take. *The Boston Globe*'s in-house reactionary, Jeff Jacoby, came away from a *Globe* working lunch with Mitt and observed that he "looked good, spoke well, and came down firmly on both sides of almost every issue." Kennedy, weeks earlier, had accepted his party's nomination at the Worcester Centrum by reiterating, "plainly and unequivocally, that I welcome the opposition of the Far Right, the National Rifle Association, the anti-choice lobby, those who resist civil rights and equal rights." Republican columnist John Ellis pronounced the Romney campaign in "full flounder," and wondered whether "Romney isn't playing at a level well above his game." As the month ended Kennedy registered a 16-to-20-point lead in the polls.

Out ahead, Kennedy relaxed. His nephew, Robert Kennedy's son Michael, was responding well as campaign manager to jabs from the Republican aspirants; with luck this campaign might yet hold expenditures down to $2 million–$3 million, roughly what they budgeted. They cut back sharply on television.

Yet Kennedy's own advisers could see that there was a kind of quicksand under voters' perception of the Boss: Once he stopped moving, he was likely to sink. Kennedy's personal approval rating clearly undermined his job approval rating. This took the form of a widespread fixation on Kennedy's appearance, as if the reporters in particular could not forgive him for showing his age. Just after the convention one commentator decided that "The

Old Lion was a little short in the Raw Meat Department," while another pronounced it "a flat, windy, partly recycled effort, delivered with an occasional grandfatherly quaver."

Romney's sound bites played on this. One spot that cycled through the later months contrasted the vibrant Mitt, in rich color, with footage of Kennedy in grainy black and white, disheveled, paunchy and unsure, gingerly attempting to ease his back onto a park bench. This reinforced that summer's cliché identifying Kennedy as a street vagrant in a thousand-dollar suit. Kennedy's own ads regularly showed him hugging the winsome Victoria, as if to invigorate his image with her youth and vitality. "It's not that subtle," commented the *Globe*'s AD-WATCH commentator Renee Loth. "All that's missing from this picture is Lassie."

By then, finally, Mitt Romney had identified his issue. He insisted that Kennedy was soft on crime, and had in fact "porked up" and watered down the $33 billion crime bill while leaving out new police and new prisons. Kennedy's longstanding opposition to the death penalty was hurting him. A belated round of ads featured Kennedy insisting that "The greatest threat we face is no longer overseas, but here on our streets," while a reassuring voiceover intoned: "He wrote the law that abolished parole for federal crimes and denies bail for dangerous defendants."

Romney came back hard. "He's got to be kidding," one ad responded. "For thirty-two years, Ted Kennedy has repeatedly opposed tough crime measures, like the death penalty . . ." Romney's popularity readings surged.

4. Infighting

Back in the District it was a muggy summer. The long-awaited crime bill lost its first time around, caught up in charges that provisions like funding midnight basketball amounted to welfare in disguise. Romney's charges gained more credibility. The omnibus health reform bill that Hillary and her minions had labored over since arriving in the White House never made it to a floor vote in the Senate, its 1,368-page welter of health-care alliances and national health controls easy picking for the insurance industry's hatchet-wielding TV spokespeople Harry and Louise.

The collapse of health reform amounted to a setback for Kennedy on a scale with the 1980 primary. Once Clinton took office the language was waiting in draft at Labor and Human Resources to effectuate at least the rudiments of universal coverage, the Kennedy-Mitchell-Rockefeller proposal. Polls showed how eager the public was to cover the 37 million uninsured, and Kennedy and his co-sponsors had worked the Cloakroom to win over many Republicans, queasy at the prospect of breasting an incoming tide of national expectations. The way was open, had the inexperienced president only moved in expeditiously behind Kennedy's preliminary dealmaking the way he had in the cases of AmeriCorps legislation and student loans and job retraining.

"It would have passed by eighty-five votes in the Senate those early months," one close observer maintains. Even after a year and a half of special-interest sandpaper on the Clinton plan's salient proposals, Kennedy's nose-counters were sure they could have eked out fifty-one supporters. But health by then was definitely a Hillary issue, swelling egos were involved. Worn out by more than a year spent providing close support operations to Hillary's overblown task force, top Kennedy staffers muttered openly about White House ineptitude. "The fact is, Ira Magaziner and to a certain extent Hillary Clinton were politically tone-deaf," one player maintained.

In June Kennedy had shepherded the repeatedly delayed Clinton plan through his own committee 11–6, still agitating to expand coverage for the poor as well as the disabled and women while developing a control mechanism to retard the growth of premiums. Dubbed "Clinton Heavy," Kennedy's version was subjected to public attack from Daniel Moynihan and the Finance Committee, alarmed at the prospective costs. Moynihan promulgated his Lite version. With right-wing PACs and small-business lobbyists stuffing mailboxes and bombarding the media, conservative Democrats gradually started to defect. Panicking, Clinton made it plain that virtually every aspect of his bill was "negotiable"; a stampede began, and by mid-August this opportunity of a generation had turned into a legislative rout.

Rolling around the Massachusetts hustings, Kennedy made it plain how deeply he continued to be invested in the issue. "Many companies now have wellness programs," I watched him explaining that summer of 1994 to a gaggle of flat-panel lithography technicians. "The fact of the matter is that their people live longer and they cost the health system more. That doesn't mean that we ought to hand out cigarettes." To one listener's observation that things weren't looking so good by then in Congress, Kennedy observed bravely that the country was "further down the road than you'd think from the newspapers. Whenever universal coverage actually gets to the floor, there develops this irresistible support for the bill . . . When I get back down there we're going to propose that everybody in Massachusetts have the same program that I have. Let all my fellow members vote, just ask them: Why don't you reject yours? People are paying attention. After all, in 1964 there were more votes for Medicare in the fall than in the previous spring . . ."

All this was whistling in the dark, of course. Universal coverage was dead. Political virtuoso that he is, Bill Clinton was careful to turn up in Massachusetts for a well-publicized signing of the Kennedy-crafted $60 billion Elementary and Secondary Education Act. The president fluffed off his own State Department to let the Sinn Fein's spokesman Gerry Adams into the United States on a visa, arranged by Nancy Soderberg—by now an Assistant National Security Adviser—in good part as a personal sop to Ambassador to Ireland Jean Kennedy Smith. But nothing brought health back.

Sensing a momentum shift, the Romney campaign now went after Kennedy on grounds that he had not brought enough federal money to Massachusetts, that $1 went out for every $.97 federal programs provided. In his desultory way, Massachusetts Republican Governor William Weld bobbed up and risked an opinion: "I'm sure there have been a lot of things he [Kennedy] has done over the years," Weld remarked. "I'm not familiar with them." Just then Kennedy's constituent liaison staffers were very busy prodding along the federally financed $5 billion artery tunnel as well as the $100 million Boston Harbor cleanup project, not to mention the $150,000 they freed up so Weld could fund his own Washington office. But Weld's comment catered to the notion that Kennedy was played out even in Washington, ineffective.

Kennedy's eulogy at Jackie Onassis's funeral in May of 1994 had energized with what the Boston politicos call a "death bump" his expiring reputation. Even then his oration betrayed what was on his mind. "Teddy, you do it," he quoted his sister-in-law as having urged him to greet the Clintons that day they dropped by Jackie's Vineyard estate for lunch. "Maurice [Templesman] isn't running for reelection."

A year later, Kennedy had pointedly abstained from joining the Clintons during their vacation on the Cape. He was not along the week the president visited Ireland. Exchanges with the White House remained amiable—after the disastrous history of family skirmishes with Lyndon Johnson and Jimmy Carter, decent relations with a Democratic president looked like a prerequisite for survival—but distance opened up.

It did not help that 1994 marked the twenty-fifth anniversary of the Chappaquiddick incident. "This has been a tragedy which I've expressed responsibility for and which I live with every day of my life," Kennedy responded in mid-July to one more press-conference sortie. Older voters recalled Chappaquiddick; their descendants, gibed Republican political consultant Todd

Domke, regarded Kennedy as "just an old career pol, a cultural joke . . . To them, he's the oldest living juvenile delinquent in the country." Struggling again with drinking, Joan picked that moment to retain Monroe Inker, perhaps the Commonwealth's scrappiest divorce lawyer, to reopen her 1982 divorce settlement with Ted. Kennedy's poll results slid steadily; a reputable poll taken on September 8–9 gave Romney 43 percent to Kennedy's 42 percent.

This triggered a red alert. With two months left, Kennedy unhappily doubled his campaign budget and hired on several key Dukakis political managers, Charles Baker, John Sasso, and Jack Corrigan. Rick Gureghian, the campaign's fire-eating press aide, told reporters that upcoming Kennedy ads will "thoroughly explore" Romney's "hidden record" as a businessman. A day later Representative Joe Kennedy had jumped in and attacked the Mormon Church for excluding blacks and women from leadership positions while labeling Bain Capital as "a white boy's club." Evidently Massachusetts's lion of liberalism craved raw meat after all.

Eons before, in May, Kennedy waved aside Romney's Mormonism as "not an issue, and it shouldn't be. President Kennedy and the American people settled that issue in the 1960 campaign." But scruples have a way of bending under the pressure of long, close campaigns, and the fact remained that the high-flown Latter-Day Saints could clearly be made to seem at once prim and exotic somehow, uneasy-making to lunchbucket voters. The Kennedy campaign had already retained The Investigative Group, Inc., a detective agency headed by former Watergate deputy counsel Terry Lenzner. Meanwhile, Kennedy brought back the unflappable Jimmy Flug to coordinate opposition research.

Information had been surfacing for months—and leaking into features on Romney in the *Globe*—which tied Bain Capital to questionable backers. Close relatives of Orlando de Sola, a Salvadoran expatriate who had sponsored Major Roberto Aubuisson and his murderous Arena Party, provided seed money to Bain. Through arms-length exchanges, cash came from junk bonds Michael Milken underwrote several months after the SEC had filed suit against him. Other sources of investment ranged from Yale University to Robert Maxwell. All that wasn't easy to translate into attack spots, but certainly it encouraged some hope that claims of Romney's immaculate political conception were overstated.

Kennedy, in early September, had put forth his opinion that the time had come to ordain women as Catholic priests. A local Catholic spokesman roared back within days: "It would have been surprising if Senator Kennedy

had issued a statement to the contrary. It is entirely consistent with his lack
of fidelity to Catholicism . . ." Was Ted running for pope these days?

Still, who lived in which church's pocket was out there for the voters. By
then a summer of coverage was beginning to probe the cracks in Romney's
Oh-golly delivery and do-gooder manner. Appalled at the number of gays in
his own congregation, Romney had as recently as the fall of 1993 reportedly
denounced homosexuality as "perverse and reprehensible," and sex outside
marriage as immoral. Now Mitt would insist that he really meant pedophilia
and sadomasochism. Near the end of August a single mother in Romney's
stake gave an interview to the press in which she maintained that, a decade
before, Romney had dropped by in the midst of her pregnancy to threaten her
with excommunication if she didn't give up the baby for adoption through a
church agency. Romney himself was starting to come across as programmed
to the eyes with "overarching moral imperatives" and calls to "renew moral
fiber." People started to bring up Kennedy's own unfailing compassion, his
manifest concern when face-to-face with human setbacks and weakness.

There had been evidence all along that Romney and his handlers were
notoriously thin-skinned. With Kennedy's "$50 million trust fund," they
groused, how could he "stoop to attack" Mitt's earnings? They bellyached
when the Kennedy campaign retained Doak, Shrum, Harris, Carrier &
Devine, purportedly specialists in negative advertising. Heavy hints were
dropped that Ted Kennedy's personal life was up for exploitation if need
be and that the 460-page Republican dossier on Kennedy was available on
demand. "He will intentionally try to reverse his brother's victory [over big-
otry]," Romney himself announced, "either with self-proclaimed attack dog
Joe Kennedy or by himself . . ." The point was taken—now that it had been
made—and Kennedy backed off.

The realization that Kennedy might in fact be well into the process of
losing produced a crisis meeting in Kennedy's Back Bay condominium on
September 18. Perhaps a dozen of the people closest to the campaign showed
up. Vicki's father, Judge Reggie, sat in, while Vicki herself, as always, took full
notes. Michael Kennedy was there, along with pollster Tom Kiley and strategist John Sasso and publicist Bob Shrum. "We got together and we changed
fields totally," Shrum was frank enough to explain to me. "As regards the
commitment to the campaign, what we were going to do."

It was already obvious that they would have to pump a lot more money
in—estimates were now up from $3 million to $10 million—so that the
debate was "not over how much we were going to spend but what we were
gong to spend it on. As usual, when responding to difficulty, Kennedy was

at his best." The exchanges were heated. "Ted is very different from a lot of people I know in government," Shrum observed. "The quickest way I know to become irrelevant with Ted is to tell him what a great idea he has, or how smart he is.

"We had a couple of testy moments," Shrum remembers. There were inevitably recriminations over having let the television placements slide through July and August. Kennedy finally rounded on Shrum: ' "You can be a pain in the ass. I can be a pain in the ass. But my brother Jack always told me, you've got to have a couple of people around who can make real pains in the ass out of themselves.'

"We ran on who Kennedy is," Shrum says. "We never ran away from that. Health care, education, freedom of choice." Shrum also directed media for several other winning Democratic senators—Paul Sarbanes of Delaware, Chuck Robb (much put to the test in Virginia that autumn by Oliver North)— and pushed them too into hardball exchanges which emphasized traditional party positions. Others backed away, especially from health care, and "overall, it wasn't a good year for Democrats."

Nerved up that summer, Kennedy himself got scratchy about the Contract With America panaceas Newt Gingrich and his acolytes were hawking. "I mean, the balanced budget amendment will solve all our problems," he broke out at one point. "Term limitations, let's all go to the Cape for the weekend. The death penalty will solve our problem on crime." When aides identified difficulties on which they might capitalize in exchanges with the Republicans, Kennedy insisted on solutions. Nobody cuts the welfare rolls without providing for day care, retraining allowances, housing subsidies. Otherwise, tax breaks today bought social chaos tomorrow.

Budgets closer to home already worried the Kennedy advisers. The ten-plus million dollars the campaign ultimately spent required lots of money the campaign did not have. Moreover, it looked to resources even the candidate didn't have, at least at hand.

The era was decades behind them all when bills for leaflets and advance-men's salaries and hotel vouchers and plane tickets would flood in, and Joseph P. Kennedy would grimace and reach for his checkbook. Kennedy managers reminisced fondly about the days when, the candidate solidly reelected, the hotel executives and telephone company managers would queue up outside Steve Smith's office in the Pan Am Building. They'd come in one by one, each with his past-due invoice in a folder in his sweaty palm, and Smith would frown—annoyed at being interrupted—and stub his cigarette out, and listen a few restless minutes before looking up to offer the supplicant $.20 on the dollar. Advising him to take it—reimbursement would be dropping any second now to $.10 on the dollar.

Most took it. But Steve was gone. Political vendors had learned. Payment was by credit card, normally cleared in advance.

Kennedy saw this coming, certainly by the spring. As early as the second of June, *Boston Globe* feature writer Sally Jacobs was trailing Kennedy as he roamed the backstairs White House, hunting for a painting his family had presented to the nation years ago, a Monet. "I should have hung onto that thing," Kennedy muttered, perhaps a little ruefully. "Then I wouldn't be worried about raising money for my campaign."

Cash remained on Kennedy's mind. Shortly after his amble through the White House, I got to bantering with Kennedy about a nightmare I'd recently had, during which I found myself elected to public office. Characteristically, he turned it around. "I feel you might, ah, actually enjoy serving," Kennedy shot back, preparing to administer the needle. "The truth is, in my own mind I've often thought of you as a colleague from New Hampshire."

I said I'd think about that, and once I returned home I wrote Kennedy, indicating that I'd pondered what he said and decided to run for senator. I would, however, require a donation of perhaps $20 million to seed my campaign. Since he'd come up with the idea, a cashier's check would suffice.

Kennedy got back within a week. He'd enjoyed our time together, he wrote. Also: "Vicki agrees with me that if you do run for the Senate from New Hampshire we should definitely give you a contribution. In fact, Vicki says if there is anything left in the campaign kitty after my victory, you are welcome to it. Although I'm not sure that $2.99 will be of much help—but it might stake you to a bumper sticker."

By September the shortfall of cash was serious. They'd raised more than $8 million, and that was not enough. All along Kennedy bookkeepers had refused to get into the details of trust arrangements within the family. But estimates of Kennedy's estate were shrinking: newspaper projections descended from $50 million to $20 million–$30 million, and down from there. Kennedy could still depend on a taxable cash flow of plus-or-minus $500,000 a year, much of it earmarked for office expenses. As advertising bills piled up during the cyclonic weeks before the election, Kennedy took out a second mortgage at Bank of Boston on his house in McLean, Virginia, for $2 million.

Kennedy's lawyers now reached an accommodation with Joan Kennedy, going public with assurances to reporters that the much-bandied-about

$4 million–$5 million settlement of the early eighties was as much as 80 percent too high. Under pressure from all three of her children—who saw the strain under which their father was struggling that fall—Joan dropped her demands for fresh capital in return for provisions in Ted's will to guarantee her income in the event of his death. Nobody in the family had forgotten how strapped Jackie found herself once Jack was murdered, how panics about support money had prompted the Onassis marriage.

Jacking up the ante, Kennedy authorized what local critics characterized as "a virtual miniseries of off-ramp attack ads." Kiley's polls kept showing that Kennedy's favorable/unfavorable ratings lagged Romney's, the warning pattern preliminary to an upset. The problem was—what could they target? Romney himself was young, successful—if not by any means the friendly self-made venture capitalist he presented himself as; Romney's leveraged-buyout maneuvers recalled the previous generation's corporate raiders; Mitt had no cogent political record of his own. His ties to the Republican Party were recent and opportunistic. He admitted quite freely to having voted for Paul Tsongas in the 1992 Democratic primary. The popular Republican governor, William Weld, was leery and reluctant to risk a flank attack on Kennedy in Romney's behalf. Mitt's position on virtually every issue was hard to establish, nebulous—Kennedy himself laughed off Romney's approach to abortion as "multiple-choice."

Once elected, Romney pledged, he would hurry down to Washington to serve as the "jobs candidate." Kennedy was played out, lacked clout, become ineffective. Absurd as this sounded to anybody in touch with business in the Capitol, who understood the ramifications of seniority throughout the Congress, it accorded with the recurrent tabloid fantasy that Kennedy lay bloated in political shallows. Around yuppified Greater Boston there were a good many enclaves where Romney's presentation resonated, his unblemished Stepford-Husband cool roused approval. Here was a man whose handsomely tailored wife, Ann, had divulged that Mitt had not raised his voice to her since the couple were teenagers. This played against the tumult of Kennedy's shaggy personal life for several decades.

Luck favors the prepared mind. In September of 1994 Kennedy's worried handlers moved. Heavy artillery from everywhere in the Democratic Party, from Paul Tsongas to Jesse Jackson, showed up at fund raisers to plug The Big Guy. A selection of all-stars from Kennedy's great staffs over the years pitched in. Ranny Cooper enlivened meetings. The incomparable David Burke, by then the beneficiary of successive golden handshakes from CBS

News and the Dreyfus Corporation, drove up to travel with Kennedy, his wry basso profundo a talisman to ground the candidate. This could easily amount to the Last Great Battle.

On September 21 Romney breezed through the Republican primary. Kennedy's assault grew serious. One theme that Shrum and his cohorts had started to bedevil was Romney's performance as a businessman, his assertion that Bain had generated ten thousand jobs around the Commonwealth. An outspoken Kennedy ally, Rich Rogers, the AFL-CIO's Massachusetts political director, now publicly dismissed Romney as "just another robber baron. If they look deep enough, they'll find his firm destroyed ten jobs for every job they have allegedly created."

Shrum picked this up. "Romney," an attack ad blazed. "In business he made $11 million in two years while his largest company [Staples] provided no health insurance to many workers. The company pays for it for employees overseas, but not for thousands in the U.S . . ."

Behind the scenes, a lot of the coordination was coming from Victoria Kennedy, who talked with Shrum every day. Vicki liked to tease Ted by claiming that he only married her to sanitize his image for the upcoming election. That autumn, insiders were beginning to speculate that Kennedy had tied the knot because it was the only way to guarantee for himself Vicki's extraordinary political instincts.

At that point the Kennedy people got a break that hinted of divine intervention. In July a company Bain Capital owned, Ampad, had picked up an affiliate of SCM Office Supplies in Marion, Indiana. Just as their senior management withdrew, the SCM officers laid off the entire paper products plant's workforce. Ampad quickly rehired most of the jobless, although in many cases at reduced wages and benefits. As affiliates of the United Paperworkers International Union, the workers went out on strike on September 1.

Robert Shrum's partner, Tad Devine, showed up in Marion with a taping crew days after the strike started. They'd prepared some material, comments the workers could read off a teleprompter into Devine's camcorders. But outrage and despondency at Ampad came through so spontaneously that Devine and his crew tossed aside the script and built their sound bites by zooming in on worker after worker and intercutting and splicing afterward. Immediately after the buyout, one of the jobless maintained, "we had no rights anymore." "They cut the wages," another worker asserted. Sharon Alter, a "packer" released after twenty-nine years, hammered in the point: "I would like to say to the people of Massachusetts—You think it can't happen to you? Think again, because we thought it wouldn't happen here either."

Heavily aired in early October, these ads made very plain how calculations in the sterility of a Boston boardroom resonated through decent people's lives a thousand miles away. "We'd run the spots," Shrum now recalls, "and naturally we were focus-grouping, rewriting all the time to show, for example, that Senator Kennedy was behind legislation to correct some of these abuses. A spot like that would run for huge points, because it was driving votes like crazy."

Six striking Ampad workers drove east to plead their case in Massachusetts. Mitt Romney wouldn't really answer the charges. "I'd love to help," he insisted once pickets were in place outside Bain. "But there's a separate management team running the company. I don't work there."

Kennedy's polls picked up. By the end of October the Romney consultants were again on the hunt. They had discovered in a *Boston Herald* flash exposé a remote investment of Joseph P. Kennedy Enterprises in an office building in D.C. Part had been leased to U.S. Government agencies in 1989; Kennedy had been taken out of his .04 percent holding at the time to avoid conflict of interest. Misunderstanding—somebody's calculator needed batteries—Romney launched an ad: "Ted Kennedy. He attacks Mitt Romney's honest record of achievement and makes $10 million for himself at taxpayer's expense." Even Paul Tsongas, never really a Kennedy partisan, was prompt to rebuke the Romney campaign for proceeding on "irresponsible data."

The charge collapsed overnight. Romney moved on immediately to accuse Kennedy of sponsoring judges who were "notoriously pro-criminal." That didn't stick either; such skeptics as Republican consultant John Ellis dismissed the Romney campaign's financial charges as "patently ridiculous. Kennedy knows nothing about money. If his paychecks were lost for four months he wouldn't even know they were missing." Local jurists couldn't deny how picky Kennedy invariably proved with judicial appointments.

After ten months of circling Kennedy, Romney had remained so underinformed and delusional when it came to the incumbent that he was attacking a phantom, meanwhile largely ignoring, for example, such serviceable vulnerabilities as Kennedy's willingness during the previous year to get behind $131 billion in spending measures and only $51 billion in cuts. Campaigning was an expensive way for Mitt to enlighten himself.

While Romney repeatedly reversed himself on abortion and the minimum wage, Kennedy personally remained upbeat. "It isn't just flip-flop, it's flip-flop-flip," he was heard to remark. "If we give him two more weeks, he may even vote for me."

5. Debate

By October the obligatory debate between the candidates was almost upon them. Apart from risking a belated sympathy vote, the Romney campaign's months of attempting to present Kennedy as, in the words of *Globe* columnist Bella English, "a tongue-tied, blowzy aging incompetent," with "enough baggage to keep a bellhop busy for life," now rendered the incumbent the underdog. At this point, Kennedy barely needed to show up sober to astonish the hard-core detractors.

After weeks of chivvying each other over the venues and preconditions of the debates, a combined offer from *The Boston Herald* and *The Boston Globe* proved acceptable to both political camps. To prepare himself, Kennedy assembled the familiar suspects at McLean. A former aide, David Smith, played Romney. Shrum served as moderator, while Sasso, Corrigan, and Carey Parker doubled for the questioners. Kennedy badgered Smith relentlessly over the details of his health care proposals and teased the others for having negotiated an extra-wide podium to mask Kennedy's bulk.

The initial debate was mounted on Tuesday, October 25, in the historic fastness of Faneuil Hall. "The entire national press corps showed up," Shrum reminisced later. "Everybody was there because they thought Teddy was going to do very badly." Romney operatives had been circulating gibes, embellishing for reporters exactly what their man would do to the incumbent now that "the training wheels will be off."

Through much of the opening exchanges it looked as if the detractors were right. Given the candidates' respective history, Sally Jacobs of the *Globe* demanded of Kennedy, "Why is this race even close?" Like almost any lifestyle question just then, it couldn't help but tilt Kennedy onto the defensive. He immediately looked discomfited, his lips pursed. Conditions were not good, he wanted to emphasize, but with his longevity in the Senate he was in a position to help the state——.

Romney cut into that. "Lemme tell ya," he assured the crowd. "This idea of clout gets overstated. Every two years you have a senator who comes here with one of those big cardboard checks . . . All that was just more pork," it was past time that "people realize that those checks are drawn on their bank accounts."

Kennedy attempted to rally; his spread jowls, dusted for the occasion with brick-red powder, inflated as he rambled badly in his effort to explain himself, his raddled baritone dropping from time to time in fleeting transports of stage fright.

They proceeded to welfare. Kennedy cited the workfare legislation that he had overseen through the Senate in the Reagan years, an effort to tighten up the law but not without "a safety net for children . . ."

Romney brushed that off. "One of the great things about our nation, Sally," he instructed the questioner, and at that moment a sharp ripple of the dismissive preppiness no briefing could expunge came through like a whiff of ammonia. The mood was altering. Few across that audience appreciated this display of scoutmastering.

There was a go-around over abortion; then Kennedy pitched into Romney for boasting about having created those thousands of jobs only to have so many part-time and minimum wage. The Romney modus operandi amounted to closing a plant down, throwing everybody out, then hiring back only the younger workers and dumping the older people. Why not retrain everybody?

As Kennedy and his advisers foresaw, this definitely roused Mitt. "Senator Kennedy and his family have a multiple real estate empire around this country," Romney charged, and in the Merchandise Mart, "the jewel of the empire," the part-time employees did not get health insurance either. Kennedy attempted to mutter something about at the very least providing access. Romney cut him off: "I don't know what you're talking about. You don't supply health insurance."

It was a palpable hit. The exchange moved on, with Romney edging into control. Sally Jacobs had another question.

"Senator Kennedy, what is your greatest personal failing?"

This was the sort of query Kennedy detested most, squishy and extremely danger-ridden, but now he made an attempt. He tended to talk about himself, he confessed. Say too much about personal values and personal achievements. And more than that: "I know that I have not lived up to all the expectations of the people of Massachusetts. I have made that statement." But recently, "my life has changed dramatically, I'm trying to be a better father, son, husband. Since my life has changed with Vicki, in personal matters life has been enormously reinvigorating." This was the party line that season, but it was also the truth and obviously it took something out of Kennedy to put himself through even that formularized a mea culpa.

The questioning turned to Romney. His greatest personal failing? Well, Romney opened, as it happened he had given up two and a half years when he was young living with the poor, and even now he spent one day a week "with people less fortunate than myself . . . I've spent hundreds of hours in hospitals across the state, working with sick people, consoling them——."

The moderator, Ken Bode, finally cut Mitt off: "This was a question about your greatest personal failing." The audience broke up.

Romney's failing, it developed, was that he couldn't totally fulfill his "God-given obligations to do more." That he wasn't even more of a saint.

With this the momentum of the evening shifted. In some ineluctable way Kennedy now acquired a centeredness, self-consciousness dropped away, and for the rest of the hour Romney kept jumping at Kennedy, like a suave but too-eager whippet bouncing off a huge old pug. When Romney again attacked Kennedy's "blind trusts" Kennedy stood his ground in solemn tones: "Mr. Romney, the Kennedys are not in public service to make money. We have paid too high a price." That remained in place as Mitt charged that "Marion Barry gave your family a no-bid deal that he wouldn't give to anybody else in this country, and you know it."

They proceeded to health care. Romney attacked the Clinton plan. Kennedy asked him how he would handle the health crisis and Romney cited the Bentsen proposals of the eighties.

That wasn't a health proposal, it was an insurance reform package, Kennedy corrected Mitt. He asked after the impact of incentives in a plan like that on the overall budget; Romney snapped that he did not have the "Congressional Budget Office" at his disposal so he could go through the details "piece by piece."

"That's exactly what you have to do with a piece of legislation," Kennedy volunteered with a delicate asperity. For the remaining minutes Kennedy occupied himself pretty largely tutoring his challenger. When Romney lamented the shortage of fathers in mid-city areas, Kennedy admitted that he did not have "a silver bullet" for needs that profound, although he was involved in initiatives to develop families and communities.

"Women!" Romney came back. "Women are concerned about the glass ceiling."

"When I heard that, I thought, 'Well, we've won the debate,'" Bob Shrum recalls. "It was like pitching a slow ball over the plate to Babe Ruth." Kennedy trotted out a range of legislation he had seen through the Congress, from language which helped implement a woman's right to sue on the job to provisions which allocated money to study women's health problems at the National Institute of Health.

As the debate ended, Romney seemed a little out of breath. "C'mon. Folks, c'mon," he kept exclaiming, like somebody being steadily backed off a cliff.

The return engagement at Holyoke Community College two evenings afterward was friendlier and much, much duller. Within hours of the Tuesday debate the Kennedy campaign had issued a statement specifying that the Merchandise Mart had four hundred employees, seven of whom were part-time. For each it was a second job, and all had health coverage either from other employers, or from others in their families, or Medicare. That disposed of Romney's bombshell.

The town-meeting format in Holyoke further helped defuse rancor. The podiums in the Holyoke auditorium were small and low, and flanked by very high stools. Kennedy's back was clearly torturing him, and he slumped upright whenever he listened to attempt to ease it a little. His big spongy face looked extraordinarily distended around the jawline, perhaps by medication, and many of his responses were halting—if measured—and laden with forbearance that verged on the lachrymose.

When one of the questioners, a Professor Hamilton, referred to having met the senator in 1962, Kennedy justified those exhaustive briefings: "I remember very well. It was in North Adams, at the Fall Foliage Festival!"

Much of what debate there was revolved around welfare. Here, as again and again throughout the months of the campaign, Romney propounded his breakthrough proposals only to discover that Kennedy had been involved for years in attempts to turn formulations all but identical into law. "I couldn't agree more with the need to take care of our children," Romney found himself concurring at one point. "I couldn't disagree more with his ability to get the job done. He's been there thirty-two years. He knows not only the trees and the forest, he knows the leaves one by one." This came through not so much as a complaint about Kennedy's voting record as a wail of frustration at having to contend with the incumbent's encyclopedic legislative grasp.

Each innovation Romney thought he was introducing, Kennedy shrugged off expertly. Tax breaks for employers who hire welfare recipients? "First of all," Kennedy informed him, "there is already a tax credit on the books. It is not working very well . . ." To such standard Republican bromides as "The best social program is a good job" and "We have to have the jail space to be tougher" on criminals who commit crimes with guns or sell drugs to minors, Kennedy somewhat wearily agreed. What kept coming through in Kennedy's intricate responses was the social vision of a lifetime, an enveloping comprehension of how our multifaceted society operated—and should operate—as the millennium ground out its last few years. This vision undoubtedly owed more than Kennedy himself realized to the continuing Catholic inquiry into what promotes social justice, what individuals owe to—and what they should expect from—worldly authority. Moving into his sixties, Kennedy shone at moments with reflected light from the City of God.

Obviously aware that Thursday that the ferocity of his lunges at Kennedy during the earlier debate had damaged his numbers, Mitt worked to gentle out his persona. He came over coltish, more affirmative, a kind of rangier Pat Boone. While lean and hungry-looking still, Romney downplayed the bumptious junior executive clambering toward his deal across the bodies piling up. By legislating according to Kennedy's ideas, he charged at one point, "we'd have kids all over the street, welfare moms at home . . . If this mom has a problem, I want to get her into rehabilitation." Across the political lawns of Romneyland, "moms" substituted that autumn for the traditional welfare queens.

Dramatically, the high point arrived when one of the questioners, a Cambridge small businessman, asked Kennedy to comment on reports in Rick Burke's memoir that Kennedy had shared cocaine and engaged in sexual harassment of female staffers. Onlookers gasped.

Kennedy seemed more resigned than taken aback. "Well, those are old allegations by a disgruntled ex-employee of mine," he observed, "which were reviewed in their entirety by the Senate Ethics Committee. They are completely false . . ."

"I don't want your question," Romney quipped when the businessman from Cambridge homed in on him.

During his short summation, Mitt Romney ventured an anecdote. "I was in Dorchester not long ago," he recalled. "Somebody said, 'This is Kennedy country.' I looked around, and I saw boarded-up buildings, and I saw jobs leaving. And I said, 'It looks like it.'" No politician with sound instincts ventures that close to defaming entire communities, and by extension Mitt was soon giving away precincts all over the Commonwealth.

Edward Kennedy had started out more vulnerable than he ever appeared before. His accomplished and presentable opponent raised $8 million and spent it without restraint. On November 9 Kennedy won again, 58 percent to 41 percent. He'd seen it coming. "Mr. Romney," Kennedy himself announced just before the campaign ended in response to Mitt's characterization of Kennedy country as anywhere in the state troubled by welfare dependency, rising crime, and failing education, "when the votes come in . . . on election night, we're going to board *you* up. We're going to put you out of business." And indeed, they had. Edward Kennedy was back from the dead.

CHAPTER VII

While the Dust Settled

1. The Contract on America

"I think it was a surprise," Carey Parker was willing to admit, with reference to the overall 1994 elections. Parker was a fixture after going on thirty years around Kennedy's back offices: domey, graying, dry as a Presbyterian deacon at this stage, always intellectually rigorous, so identified with Kennedy after decades of discreet Cloakroom negotiations that he was referred to sometimes as the 101st senator. Parker was Harvard Law, a Rhodes Scholar, a PhD from the Rockefeller Institute—all the top-tier academic credentials Edward Kennedy didn't come close to having. "We really didn't see that Republican tide coming. We were shocked that we lost both the House and the Senate. I think with hindsight it was fairly clear what the Republican strategy had been . . . Kennedy was, first of all, proud of the campaign he ran, he wasn't giving an inch to, you know, the Republican alternatives on the issues. Other Democratic Senate candidates, including some good friends of Senator Kennedy, felt they had to trim their sails a bit and move toward the middle, toward the Republicans." Accordingly, many lost. "Inevitably," Parker concludes, "the voters will choose the real thing."

I had been visiting these offices for longer than Parker even had been around, and I was reminded each time of how little anything substantive changes. Out in the waiting room a pair of presentation gloves and an admiring note from Muhammad Ali still hung on the wall, quite near a photograph of Joseph P. Kennedy and his three boys who survived the war. The Ambassador stands bristling with self-assurance with the collar of his trench coat snapped up, that case-hardened grin fixed for the photographer. Those were exuberant times.

By the middle nineties, a rotation of complacent, pudgy interns, usually male, alternated at the front desk over which Melody Miller had long presided. Now deputy press secretary, Melody normally spent her afternoons on the telephone, presiding over a media-strewn desk inside while ushering through her far-flung clientele of journalists and Kennedy acquaintances. As liaison for the world between outsiders and the Kennedy family, Melody had now managed for over a decade to pull some fiendishly overheated chestnuts out of a rolling broil of heavy publicity. Parker's job verged on the executive; what position papers and speeches he did not write he was likely to edit. Still, Kennedy did the final revision, often while he awaited his turn to speak, those steel-rimmed glasses sliding a little at a time down the ridges of his nose.

When anything was important, he made the ultimate decisions. "I remember one meeting in 1980," Bob Shrum says, "when we were asked to help figure out whether Ted should run against Carter. It came out four to four. 'The vote is one to nothing,' Kennedy then told us. 'I'm going to run.'"

Parker held up each day against history. For instance, with the health plan—Obama might have been forewarned—"the big mistake was in delaying so long, letting it spill into the campaign year. My own theory is that the Republicans made a rather cynical decision in the spring of '94 that the best way to make major gains in the fall elections was to prevent any significant achievements by President Clinton. Their strategy was, no bill shall pass. They were willing to bring down the temple. Gridlock worked. The Democrats woke up too late."

Thwarted in 1994, Kennedy and the surviving Democrats struggled into 1995. What they woke up to, along with a Republican Congress, was Newt Gingrich and his horde of right-wing-revivalist hoplites in the House and their big-ticket Contract With America. Panic swept the Hill, but "we felt the 1994 election was not in any sense a mandate for the Contract," Parker maintains. "They had the votes to jam it through the House, but then it got to the Senate, and I think Kennedy played a major, major role in developing the arguments about what Republican cuts in medicine would do, what Republican cuts in education would do, the unfairness of the Republican tax plan, which had a superficial appeal to middle-class families but which was heavily weighted against the average person . . .

"We did a lot in terms of putting together witnesses, held a few forums . . ." By then the Democrats were starting to regroup. Jim Sasser of Tennessee, who had been expected to replace George Mitchell as Majority—

now Minority—Leader, had lost. In the Democratic caucus Kennedy's frolicsome drinking companion, Chris Dodd, went down by a single vote to Tom Daschle of South Dakota, with whom Kennedy quickly fell into a profitable working relationship, pepped up by weekends together in Hyannis Port. The plain-spoken Daschle showed plenty of aptitude from the outset at keeping the Democrats focused and together. Relations with the White House held up, especially since the president now found himself largely on the outside and eager for allies in his attempts to deal with a Congress relentlessly generating a continuing flow of "bad legislation coming over from the House," as Parker saw it.

"Dick Riley and Bob Reich in the administration were very receptive. We never had the sense that we were tugging them. We were working very closely with the administration to put together details and data." Before long the nonpartisan—if avowedly illiberal—polltaker and strategist Dick Morris was on hand to troubleshoot the White House in frantic hopes of bettering the fading president's prospects. Morris constituted "a discouragement" to several of the Kennedyites, with his repeated advice to "triangulate" on policy with Congress. This meant, in effect, to go along with many Republican proposals to shave back entitlement programs and revamp the safety net.

"Obviously, he was talking a different, uh, strategy," Parker acknowledges. "But I think it didn't make a lot of difference on the president's final position on these issues." Seasoned White House insiders like ex-Kennedy staffer Harold Ickes Jr. still exerted considerable drag on Oval Office decision-making. "By the end of 1995, when the Republicans had clearly overplayed their hand, it turned out the country didn't agree. That was the beginning of the end of the Contract With America."

In his matter-of-fact way, what Parker was describing to me highlighted Kennedy's most noteworthy endowment, his instincts as a field commander. Where today's political technicians fixate automatically on numbers, opinion surveys, Kennedy took in individuals, backgrounds, possible shared interests, the potential for fresh coalitions once the frenzy of the battlefield clears. While younger colleagues panicked—nobody cares about health issues anymore, focus groups are budget-obsessed—Kennedy himself had ridden out so many sieges at this point that much of the time the thud of one more Republican battering ram pounds along in concert with his heartbeat. He'd endured this many times, this ambuscade of attack ads, the misery of collapsing polls. People's needs don't change. They come back.

Adversity bucked him up. "There was a certain dispiritedness among the Democrats with the loss of the Senate," Carey summarizes, "losing the majority, and I think Kennedy helped pull all the Senate Democrats out of that by the force of his personality and his leadership. That's his greatest gift."

Melody Miller looked in. It was after six, but both the senator and his staff habitually soldier on into the evening hours whenever the Senate is in session. Kennedy was still tied up on the floor, so we had settled down in his inner office, a vaulting and shadowy rectangle dominated by John Kennedy's big desk and a scattering of cherished memorabilia such as Rose Kennedy's framed note upbraiding her youngest for even suggesting that she got anything less than an A during her schoolgirl days and admonishing him for cusswords. Little in the office had altered: It was still full of serviceable, battered furniture; when I'd stopped by most recently I spotted Kennedy's Jack Russell terrier, Blarney, gnawing on the leg of a coffee table.

"Nick is back," Melody Miller said, referring to Littlefield. "He can't stay terribly long, so here is his room when you get done with Carey, 644 Dirksen Building." Melody has a warm, level, businesslike delivery, which, like her pastel blouses and tailored skirts, imparts a kind of convent-school ebullience and concern with details to everything she does. Melody never seems completely out of uniform. She handed me a buckslip with Nick Littlefield's location on it.

"Should I go now?" I said.

"Welllll. I think if you were here another five to seven minutes, and then head over . . ."

Exactly seven minutes later I shook hands with Carey and started down the echoing corridor toward one of the big, brass-trimmed elevators. Now that—the Democratic majority having been lost in the Senate—Ted Kennedy was no longer the chairman of HELP, his total staff Capitol-wide had inevitably been trimmed: From something around one hundred people, Kennedy's payroll numbered fifty-eight, coming back from forty-six. Nobody had found a way to lower the senator's ambition-threshold, however, so what that meant is that everybody worked twice as hard, the Boss in particular. ". . . it seemed like virtually the consistent figure in every task force at every meeting was Ted Kennedy," Tom Daschle commented at the time. "He was really like this enthusiastic freshman looking for more work."

At this point staff director for the Ranking Minority Member of HELP, Nick Littlefield looked too busy to worry much about anybody's formal drop-in status. If Carey Parker pondered legislation from the strategic heights, Nick Littlefield was Kennedy's aide-de-camp in the hot daily trenches. He relished the shot and shell. A tallish, knobby shirtsleeved ex–federal prosecutor with a curly bristle of stiff gray hair striping back from his widow's peak and the constricted, overfocused face of the unembarrassed policy wonk, Nick Littlefield spent most of his time six or seven days a week striding around in one of those piled-up satellite suites Kennedy maintained for milling out the legislative paperwork.

"I don't think Senator Kennedy has ever had a better sixteen months in the Senate than since the '94 elections," Littlefield opened flatly. "Because he ran as an outspoken progressive Democrat, fighting for working families, around the issues of jobs, education, health care. That was our mantra during that campaign, and that was what got him reelected.

"People around here were very depressed." Kennedy had stepped forward immediately to "define for the president the role he should play on the two key issues of health and education, that he should not permit one nickel to be cut. Then he put together the whole strategy in the Senate to concentrate on working families."

While Newt Gingrich was marshaling support in the rebellious House for nine of the ten measures of the Contract With America—only term limits never got a hearing—Kennedy and Daschle managed to coalesce the forty-seven surviving Democratic senators as well as a shifting handful of Republicans behind a series of bills and amendments intended to stall Gingrich's momentum. Ignoring a chorus of shrill cries from the outraged Right, Kennedy was now embarked on strict class warfare, with emphasis on pointing up abuses and unscrambling the Gingrichian doublespeak intended to camouflage the thrust behind this onslaught of legislation.

As Senate Republicans prepared to draft counterpart language, Kennedy let his presence register. He rounded up ninety-six senators behind a bill to close the longstanding legal shortfall that permitted the extravagantly rich to renounce their U.S. citizenship to avoid taxes, the "Benedict Arnold" loophole. He put together a quorum of thirty-four Democratic senators to pay a call on moderate Republican Mark Hatfield, chairman of the Appropriations Committee, to advise Hatfield that if the anticipated additional billion were stripped from the pending education bill to satisfy the House in conference, legislators could count on a presidential veto. By July 5 articles were appearing in editorial columns under Edward Kennedy's name which identified Republican initiatives "built around lavish tax cuts that primarily benefit the wealthy," already projected at $245 billion, while Medicare budgeting was down $180 billion. Kennedy forged the linkage in the public's mind.

"We made this chart," Littlefield explained to me, dragging it out from behind something and propping it up. It itemized Republican efforts to slash Wages, Medicare, College Opportunities, and Education. With Gingrich wheeling siege machinery into place, "We'd bring that chart down to the Senate floor every Friday afternoon," Littlefield says. "He'd talk for two hours about that stuff. It just picked up momentum. Every time we had a chance we organized amendments around those four issues.

"Whether it was minimum wage or Davis-Bacon or student loans or Medicare or nursing home standards or pensions—these were all Kennedy's issues. Kennedy was constantly beating the drum for taking a stand on Medicare, which was the issue which was really getting through to the public."

Off the Senate floor, Kennedy visited all over town. As early as December of 1994 he'd closeted himself with Clinton before a presidential radio address, urging him to dig in publicly against the proposed rise in Medicare premiums and the expected round of education cuts. "He was at the White House five or six times," Littlefield remembers, "talking to the president about holding the line, sending memoranda, talking with Gore, Ickes, Stephanopoulos. He kept after Vic Fazio, Gephardt, David Bonior in the House. And at the same time, when he found a Republican like Jefford or Campbell who seemed sympathetic on issues like education he kept after them, sometimes on the phone. Last week we were able to restore the three million dollars to education funding, and we won it by six votes.

"The Republicans were always trying for what they called regulatory reform," Littlefield continued. Much of the intent was obfuscated in impenetrable formulations, so "We were always trying to simplify what the Republicans were all about, find some straightforward, easily understandable consequences of what they were up to."

Littlefield broke into a sudden fierce shy grin as he turned over another chart, white letters on faded blue. "What they called the Regulatory Reform Bill, we called The Polluters and Poisoners Protection Act. It seemed to mandate 'unsafe drinking water, unsafe meat, unsafe fruits and vegetables, unsafe baby food.' Meat would be polluted with E. coli bacteria, fruits and vegetables would have cancer-causing pesticides on them if the Republicans managed to remove safety standards. Kennedy made a whole crusade out of this."

Another Gingrich initiative that Kennedy managed to short-circuit in the Senate was the recurrent proposal to take hundreds of thousands of mothers off welfare while allocating virtually nothing for childcare. "We called it the Home Alone Bill," Littlefield says. He chuckles. "We created a big problem for Dole around that. Dole put some more child care money in, which we lost in the House."

Nick had to interrupt the interview to take a call from Kennedy himself.

It was approaching 7 PM. That week—late March of 1996—Kennedy had an amendment in the works to raise the minimum wage. "Well, we've got all the groups ginned up," Littlefield told his boss. "We have to decide what we're going to do. About the workup. We can't object until two hours after he comes in, so that means 11:30. I'll take it to the floor staff in the meanwhile. Yes, well, thanks to your parliamentary experience. I worked the room, and everybody wrote their stories after your press conference. Right. In any event, I'll see you at a quarter of eight."

Littlefield hung up. Even half of the conversation attests to what a three-dimensional chess game lawmaking can be, how moves on every level can advance or stymie a program. Unlike his more linear brothers, Ted Kennedy was able from his first moments on the Senate floor to integrate issues, personalities, and the public mood of the season and forward or block key legislation. "Here we are on the day Dole clinched the nomination for himself in California," Littlefield burst out, exhilarated, "and Kennedy has outsmarted Dole and gotten the minimum wage amendment onto the floor. Right now Dole is so scared of the issue he's going to have to recess the Senate rather than risk a vote!"

Littlefield is so sharp, so ready with statistics and answers, that Kennedy took a particular delight in catching him on the uptake. "That's in the briefing sheet—I'm surprised you didn't pick that up, Nick," he chided his hard-driving aide at an early-morning skull session with a clutch of experts. "Page three!" When Littlefield cut across the ruminations of one of the consultants, Kennedy wasted no time: "Will you let him talk, Nick!" Another overscheduled day was on them all, and Kennedy was already edgy.

So much of Kennedy's time that winter went into containing Republican brainstorms. The effort was afoot to raise $4.4 billion by charging colleges and universities fees in connection with the federal loans they administered. Kennedy stepped on consideration of a measure to permit private companies to tap employee pension funds. ("This is one cookie jar," he was quoted at the time, "that Republican hands are not going to get into.") Republican budgeteers nourished proposals to foreclose on private residences to pay back Medicaid for nursing-home expenses for the elderly, then billing out the surviving heirs for additional charges. Kennedy disposed of that.

By April of 1996 eight of the nine Democratic bills that Minority Leader Thomas Daschle identified as "priority legislation" came directly out of Kennedy's shop. What one year before had seemed an irresistible Gingrich juggernaut had largely fallen apart, shattered by a long winter of presidential vetoes of the wish-list budgets with which the Republicans seemed willing to bankrupt the government. Vetoes, and a primarily Kennedy-led counter-attack in the Senate left the Contract mired down in Republican factionalism exacerbated by heavier and heavier national coverage.

At that point, Kennedy was thinking positive. With the Republican takeover, Nancy Landon Kassebaum replaced Kennedy as chair of the wide-ranging Health, Education, Labor and Pensions Committee. A considerate and reasonable woman, Kassebaum's Senate colleagues appreciated her as a person, and Kennedy took pains over the years to accord her an extra mea-sure of courtliness and warmth. There have been policy differences: Kasse-baum had been adamant in her determination to scale back OSHA and reduce governmental involvement with student loans, and was a principal propo-nent for loading administrative charges on universities which accepted public support. But she worked closely with Kennedy to push through a bill assuring the portability of health care when a worker changed jobs, an important step in introducing universal coverage bit by bit, "incrementally," as Kennedy now liked to say.

Despite the Democratic minority on the committee, Kennedy had been adroit enough at inside politics to frustrate Kassebaum's revisionist prefer-ences. Where they had agreed, they'd several times converted almost the entire Senate. After months of preparation overseen by a young onetime Dukakis-and Weld-administration consultant, Stephen Spinner, Kennedy, and Kasse-baum came to agreement on a bill that consolidated dozens of worker train-ing programs, raised grant levels, and shifted implementation largely out of Washington. By October of 1995, the draft was in place and Spinner was dying at thirty-four of cancer. Two days before he died Kennedy showed up at Stephen's home in Cambridge to hash over last-minute plans for the floor debate. The bill passed the Senate 95–2. Kassebaum stood up on the floor immediately after the passage of the bill to broach a testimonial to Spinner's contribution, and broke down. Not much steadier, Kennedy rose to round out the tribute, which he confessed to sharing with her "heart and soul."

By then Edward Kennedy and Nancy Kassebaum were polishing up the health bill that already bore their names. The finished legislation guaranteed access to insurance to all who lost or left their jobs or suffered from preexist-ing medical conditions. It forbade insurance companies from denying cover-age to employers based on the health status of individual employees. It made the cost of long-term health-care deductible and increased the health-care deduction for the self-employed.

The response at both political extremes was predictable. Labor tended to dismiss the impact as ameliorative, largely a portability band-aid. The conservative ex-governor of Delaware Pete DuPont called it "socialized medicine by the back door."

On April 23, 1996, the Kennedy-Kassebaum health bill passed the Senate 100-0. Kennedy beat back a Dole-sponsored amendment to include "medical savings accounts" for the carriage trade, an up to $4,000 tax deduction against high-deductibility coverage. "For him to pick up the pieces like that is typical of Kennedy," Jack Farrell noted. "Build what you can, then nudge, nudge, nudge. With Kennedy, it's the steps that you take. Kennedy-Kassebaum shows that he's as wily and crafty as ever with half the staff and none of the priorities the chairman can hold in the Senate."

This was a crowning success for Kennedy—potentially. A counterpart version was debated in the Republican House, where, more than Kennedy's, it was *Kassebaum*'s conciliatory tendencies that kept Gingrich's Young Turks suspicious. "In a lot of ways, Orrin Hatch was easier to deal with when he was chairman of the Health Committee," one insider stated frankly. "He was a strong, savvy legislator in his own right, he followed through and got things done. Other conservatives trusted him.

"Kassebaum is more of a moderate. The deals have a way of slipping away from you. We'd had this incredible six years, and now since Kassebaum became the chairman not one bill enacted through this committee has made it into the laws. It's because she can't get along with the Republicans in the House. Kennedy has tried to help: he's resisted the more extreme proposals that have come through, especially in the labor area."

Nick Littlefield echoed a lot of this. Accompanying me out, he started to dream aloud, a devout tactician's reverie: "Long-term, it may turn out that the failure of the Clinton health care bill ushered in the Republican landslide of 1994, and that landslide unleashed such extreme forces that it has turned the country against Republicanism for a generation and regalvanized the Democratic majority.

"If that happens," Littlefield said, his intense visionary's eyes taking on light from the corridor, "then the last laugh on health care belongs to Kennedy, and we'll get it done next time."

While the 1996 elections were not to repudiate the two-party system in America, what did register was the determination of the voters not to relinquish the security of sixty years of remedial social legislation in exchange for some Republican spinmaster's slogan of the moment. Gingrichism imploded. What transfused both parties was a morning-after sobriety about the real issues—the need to deal with the deficit, public demand for Medicare and Medicaid, an awareness that no kind of quick fix or profusion of sound bites or rejiggering in the private sector could hope for long to contain the crisis. Legislators of every orientation now found themselves under pressure to confront the real problems across the health and human welfare spectrum—the place from which Kennedy had been operating for decades.

2. The Coming Storm

Politics is largely timing. At the end of April 1996, Edward Kennedy was clinking champagne glasses all over Washington having somehow convinced all ninety-nine of his colleagues to get behind the landmark Kennedy-Kassebaum Health Insurance Reform Bill. Six weeks later, alarmed that Bob Dole manifestly intended to ignore the recommendations of the Democratic leadership and pack the delegation to the conference committee with the House with members committed to medical savings accounts, Kennedy was backtracking fast to nullify his triumph. This tax break could only drive up premiums for the sick and needy. It was an election year; senators needed to get home to campaign. The Kennedy-Kassebaum bill was sidetracked.

Politics, like Ireland, is a sow willing to eat its farrow. Kennedy's thinking was plain enough. Staff around the White House had indicated that the president would very likely veto any health legislation adulterated with "the killer amendment"—medical savings accounts. Quite possibly, he would. And if the House were to return with a Democratic majority in November, and possibly the Senate too, who could really tell what all-encompassing medical reforms might open up overnight? There were clearly risks, but politics is risky, and when had that ever dismayed Kennedy?

Dick Armey and other hard-right ideologues in the House sometimes attempted to vilify Kennedy for stepping on his own bill, but beyond that it was surprising overall how little heat he took. Both polls and focus groups indicated widespread revulsion with Gingrich. It turned out Medicare really was the third rail of American politics. Ted Kennedy, on the other hand, seemed to have taken on that peculiarly American sanctity that devolves on a reformed sinner. Even the ever-innovative Richard Viguerie, fund raiser to the Right, found receipts falling off sharply whenever he tried to resurrect Kennedy to his time-honored prominence as bogeyman from the Left. A consensus was forming among scholars of the Senate that, as Ross Baker of Rutgers put it, "It's not just occupying a seat—but to have had an influence to varying degrees on important aspects of public policy over nearly forty years ranks with the Henry Clays and Daniel Websters."

In January of 1995 another death bump had bounced Kennedy back into the news. Rose Kennedy died at 104. Until she was wheelchair-ridden by strokes a decade earlier, Rose had continued the regimen of travel and self-discipline that kept her lively and competent if, ultimately, remote within her family as the generations proliferated. Obituaries described her in later years as "carrying her own clubs, played nine holes of golf alone against the biting gusts of sea air" of the autumn Cape. "Mother would have been a great featherweight," her surviving son observed. "She had a mean right hand."

Ted was especially devoted. "After his mother became infirm," a family friend remembers, "the first thing he would do at Hyannis Port was put down his briefcase and go to her room. You'd hear his booming voice: *Hello, Muthah, we're here for the weekend.* And every week he would show her clips and videotapes of what he was doing. They'd bring a priest in and Ted would serve the Mass in the living room. Sometimes somebody would play the piano and they would sing Irish songs and Ted would say things like: "Do you remember, Mother, how Agnes would enjoy this?"

On better days, Kennedy would insist on pushing his mother's wheelchair out onto the beach, he none too steady and she somewhat crumpled to one side and heavily bundled up. Rose was, at best, marginally in and out. There were occasionally moments. She was 102, Kennedy reports, when he stopped by her room just before a tennis match. "So that's where my tennis racket went!" he says she teased him as he loomed in the doorway. "I've been wondering."

Rose Kennedy was laid to rest beside Joe in Brookline. She left behind forty-one great-grandchildren.

Two were Ted's grandchildren. One girl, Grace, was born to Kara, who emerged from a bumpy adolescence to put in time helping run a family philanthropy called Media for the Very Special Arts, a provider of cultural outlets to the mentally challenged, as the phrase goes. Kara was diagnosed with a rare and normally deadly form of lung cancer; her father appeared daily at mass while her exhausting, experimental treatments dragged on. She recovered. Her husband, Michael Allen, is an architect who specializes in historic restorations.

Another grandchild, Kiley, also a girl, was born within a month of Kara's to her sister-in-law, Kiki, nee Gershman, Teddy Jr.'s wife. Kiki is a psychiatrist who teaches at the Yale Medical School, where her expansive husband for some years directed the Welch Center, which identifies and detoxifies children contaminated with lead-based paint. Teddy Jr. moved on to pick up a law degree and heads the Marwood Group in New York City, an investment banking firm that specializes in recently issued securities in the health area.

Most unexpected to Kennedy watchers was probably the career turn Ted's youngest took. Evidently beyond his cocaine problems, still struggling with asthma, after recuperating from a perilous operation to remove a growth from his spinal cord the shy and rather reflective Patrick had run for the Rhode Island legislature at twenty-one and took his seat after expending a record $93,000, $78 per vote. Although Patrick's asthma-threatened personal manner suggested that he must struggle with himself to push a word out edgewise, he developed a reputation for persistence and integrity—especially on the labor issues, as he began showing up on picket lines throughout the little state—and worked out his own stands irrespective of the party bosses. Finishing out six terms, he emerged as chairman of the Rules Committee.

In 1994 he ran for the U.S. Congress from Rhode Island's First District. Even in his mid-twenties, Patrick Kennedy, while tall, what with his big unblinking eyes and English public-school bowl-cut, came over as a kind of throwback, perhaps to the fifties, the sort of novice in a suit and tie who rang your doorbell and pressed a copy of *The Watchtower* into your palm while stammering through his pitch.

In crumbling old Providence, Patrick beat his primary opponent, a convicted sex offender, and proceeded into an extremely nasty campaign against the Republican nominee, Dr. Kevin Vigilante. Both campaigns were heavily financed—Patrick raised and spent just over $1 million and Vigilante approximately $800,000. Vigilante soon found himself trading virulent attack ads with the experienced Kennedy operatives. Lagging in the polls, the increasingly agitated doctor lashed out at his assailant in JFK Plaza: "In the real world, if I had been an alleged witness to an alleged sexual assault committed by my cousin, ran from the press, denied any knowledge—only to admit that I did have knowledge—I could not be a credible material witness. In the real world, if I broke the law by using cocaine, I could not have actually considered running just two years later to become a lawmaker for the state."

But this was not the real world, at least not that summer. Caroline Kennedy flew in by private jet to plump for her cousin; Tony Bennett bobbed up to soft-shoe through a fund raiser. Vigilante responded by surfacing Patrick's eighty-four-year-old landlady, who asserted that the pleasant-spoken young scion had stiffed her for $3,400 in rent.

Patrick won 54–46. He proceeded to Washington, already warding off death threats. There would be lumpy moments; at once point he was cited by the police for driving his car into one of the cement stanchions behind the Capitol while under the influence of something. His father loved to tease him. "Don't tell me you counted the Republican ballots too!" he chided Patrick when his son put time in tallying the vote count in one of the Rhode Island bi-elections.

Both houses were chafing to adjourn by early August of 1996—the prospect of returning to the electorate for the August break as majority members of the "do-nothing 104th Congress" was starting to panic the Gingrich Republicans. By then Kennedy's delaying tactics with the health bill, capped by several days of subcommittee maneuvering to tighten the regulations on insurance companies during job changeovers, was yielding up the sort of legislation Ted was after all along. Gaining momentum from the broad-scale welfare revisions passed the previous week—which Kennedy expressly hated—Congress on August 2 rushed through the updated Safe Water Drinking Act, the long-sought legislation to raise the minimum wage by $.90 over the next two years, and a perfected version of the Kennedy-Kassebaum bill that contained no more than a "pilot program" experiment with medical savings accounts.

Summoned later that day to appear on the *NewsHour* with Jim Lehrer, both Kennedy and Nancy Kassebaum emphasized that their bill addressed only a few of the most urgent problems in our ramshackle health-care system. But, later in the broadcast, pundit E. J. Dionne of *The New York Times* summed up the outcome of two years' control in both houses of Congress by insurgent right-wingers: "This is not the Republican Contract with America, it's Ted Kennedy's Contract With America." Falling back on persistence, salesmanship, and unmatched parliamentary legerdemain, Kennedy had again helped turn the entire flank of American lawmaking.

With the health insurance bill pending, Kennedy decided the winter of 1996 to reconnoiter a new front. The debates with Romney had reminded Kennedy that many of the deepening problems in post–Cold War America traced back to favoritism in the tax laws, the infiltration by generations of lobbyists and special-interest conservatives from both parties of what was now starting to go by the name "corporate welfare."

This wasn't a new issue, and stirred some resonance in Kennedy's touchy family from over a century of agreement that, as JFK once quoted his father, "most businessmen are sons of bitches." The emergence of multinational corporations had intensified the surreptitious recasting of the tax code, increasingly to the detriment of what was left after the Reagan onslaught on organized labor and unaffiliated working people. As factory employment waned in favor of service positions, and jobs moved overseas, ripples reached national politics. By the middle nineties, the phenomenon agitating stump speakers in both parties was the steadily falling spendable incomes of regular working Americans. The middle class was drying up.

As a Democratic Advisory Council founder, Bill Clinton kept attempting to straddle this discomfiting issue. After an extended delay, Kennedy himself had gone along with Clinton and voted for U.S. entry into NAFTA and GATT, which opened American markets to, respectively, North American and worldwide producers. Both treaties had been condemned by longstanding Kennedy allies like Steve Early of the Communications Workers of America for endangering millions of Stateside jobs while making it harder and harder to keep the international corporations answerable. From home-grown militia hotheads to disgruntled John Birchers, the awareness was spreading that wealth was polarizing society, that the indulgence of the international corporations was speeding this disastrous process up. The success of Pat Buchanan's scathing neo-isolationism throughout two cycles of Republican primaries attested to the issue's potency.

Typically, Kennedy abstained from the perennial the-rich-are-killing-us shibboleths of the shopworn left and set his people to dissecting the intricacies of the tax code itself. Kennedy wanted a comprehensive analysis, and then he wanted remedies. Experts and specialists flew in for early-morning brainstorming sessions at McLean. Kennedy added to his staff a prominent New York attorney who specialized in international law, Dennis Kelleher. On February 8, 1996, Kennedy sounded fair warning in a speech at the Center for National Policy in Washington entitled "The Rising Tide Must Lift More Boats."

He summarized the problem: "President Kennedy said that a rising tide lifts all boats," Kennedy asserted, "And for the golden decades after World War II, that was true. But today's rising tide is lifting only some of the boats— primarily the yachts . . . While productivity was rising, real wages were sinking. Corporations laid workers off even in good times. Parents were forced to work several jobs, to the detriment of their children. A storm is coming, and the effects are already being felt by most families."

In fact, the government itself seemed to be colluding in this socially catastrophic process. The Federal Reserve Board, fixated on throttling down inflation, was choking off growth. Kennedy proposed certain remedies. Initiate a new corporate tax rate which rewards companies which create better-quality, higher-paying jobs at home. Such companies should receive better capital gains treatment for their investors as well as preferential treatment when government contracts are awarded. To fund these incentives Kennedy proposed "eliminating costly tax loopholes that encourage layoffs, discourage job creation, and reward companies for moving American jobs overseas. Over the next seven years, corporate welfare, tax loopholes, and tax preferences will cost the federal government over four trillion dollars. In 2002, these tax entitlements will represent a far larger share of the federal budget than Social Security, Medicare, or Medicaid."

Pointing out that in 1991, for example, 73 percent of foreign-based businesses and over 60 percent of U.S. companies paid no U.S. income taxes, Kennedy pinpointed the abuses which contributed to this hemorrhage of revenue:

- The "transfer-pricing loophole," through which multinationals avoid taxes by "shifting income through rigged transactions to overseas subsidiaries."
- The "runaway plant loophole," which permits foreign subsidiaries of U.S. companies to defer taxes on income earned abroad, profits which are ultimately sheltered once they are invested overseas. "The painful, preposterous result is that our tax laws generate new jobs and investments in foreign countries rather than here at home in America."
- The "foreign sales corporation loophole, a paper shell that lets companies shield 30 percent of their income from U.S. taxes."
- The "title passage loophole," which allowed companies to claim that U.S. sales were made on foreign soil, so they could be offset by foreign tax credits.
- The "Benedict Arnold loophole," which permits "billionaires to renounce their citizenship and move to a foreign tax haven . . ."

Even before his speech, Kennedy had been field-testing these tax reforms where he saw openings around the government. At a freewheeling powwow with the leadership in both parties in mid-December of 1995, just as the federal government itself was sliding off-budget, President Clinton personally appeared to be intrigued by Kennedy's exhortations to shut the corporate loopholes down, his demonstrations that "There is real feeding at the trough." The president asked that details be sent to the White House directly. But throughout the hours Kennedy was lobbying his case, aides to Treasury

Secretary Robert Rubin and Chair of the Economic Council Laura Tyson continued to work the room.

"They don't want to do it because they basically are a spokesman for many of these industries," Kennedy grumped to an interviewer. "I would like Bob Rubin to tell me the best ones to cut. I would like him to tell me, and tell the president, how to do it. But he is representing a different kind of constituency. He knows it. I know it. The president sort of knows it. So that makes it a political issue."

It would require a decade before even the insiders would wake up to the extent to which Wall Streeters from both parties were gnawing away at vital safeguards in place since the Depression, starting with the Glass-Steagall Act, with an eye toward magnificent positions and nine-figure bonuses once they retired from government service. Twelve years before Barack Obama stepped out to more than hint that entrenched Democrats were selling out their principles to placate Washington's omnipresent business lobbyists, Kennedy was nailing up Obama's future agenda. Wall Street was in there cutting the deals, no matter who appeared to be in charge.

This was a rare, unguarded breakout of Kennedy's suppressed impatience with the divided administration. Like much of the older and more ethics-driven Democratic leadership, Kennedy was put off by the president's penchant for going soft around the edges whenever principle threatened to collide with politics. Clinton could wobble badly that close to the fall elections. Particularly galling was the president's widely telegraphed readiness to sign the "Personal Responsibility and Work Opportunity Act of 1996," the Orwellian title its Republican sponsors attached to vitiating welfare reform legislation.

The welfare revisions Clinton had been promoting since 1992 would have cranked up the overall cost of welfare in America by $10 billion a year to provide the day care and job training recipients were expected to require. The bill he signed carved $56 billion from existing expenditure levels, with some of what was left having been earmarked, if not very precisely, for vocational and child care purposes as part of the block grant distribution to the states. An additional 1.1 million children were expected to grow up now in unrelieved poverty.

Kennedy let himself be quoted the day the welfare changes went into law as baffled by this "let-'em-eat-cake" approach. The extent of his disillusion crept into his February 1996 speech on corporate welfare. After flogging a wide range of administrative changes, from extending the antitrust laws to restricting new combinations which promote layoffs to better protecting unions and subsidizing additional research and development and simplifying regulatory procedures, Kennedy squared off directly to confront a number of the issues which were bulking up the Buchanan campaign.

We should, Kennedy announced, "do more to defend American workers against low-wage labor and sweatshop practices from overseas. It is not protectionist to refuse to compete on the basis of who can exploit their workers the most. We should declare a pause before entering into new free trade agreements, so our economy and our companies can adjust to NAFTA and GATT . . ."

What had been going around was finally coming around. From the trickle-down theoreticians of Herbert Hoover to Ronald Reagan's supply-side deficit dervishes to exponents of the post-industrial tomorrow which reflected the New World Order, a lot of common economic sense had been out on holiday. A concern for ordinary working Americans had given way to the self-interest of the power elite. From time to time Kennedy himself bought in. Listeners discerned a note of remorse when it came to Kennedy's eleventh-hour support for NAFTA. As with S-CHIP and the No Child Left Behind legislation coming up, his instinct to go along with his president and keep the colleagues happy was starting to compromise Kennedy's better judgment.

As the practical consequences played out, whatever the customary assurances, each phase in implementing the NAFTA treaty had led us deeper into economic quagmires. Despite months of administration insistence that it would hold out for better labor conditions and environmental protections beyond the Rio Grande, in short order NAFTA had produced a collapsed peso, a tremendous loan to the Mexicans to bail out Robert Rubin's friends among the American lenders, a vast trade deficit with Mexico where recently had been a surplus, devastation of the Mexican economy, and the disappearance of what was estimated to amount to a million American jobs, many thousands in agriculture. Ross Perot's Giant Sucking Sound was audible again, and closing.

Kennedy's February 1996 speech had cast a long shadow up Pennsylvania Avenue, one guaranteed to reach the White House. The fight was on for Bill Clinton's ephemeral soul.

The stakes were rising again; nevertheless, Kennedy continued to work both sides of the aisle. Although Congress remained trapped in partisan deadlock, Kennedy managed to coauthor a bill with Bob Dole to authorize a Whaling Park in New Bedford in return for the Nicodemus Historical Site in Kansas. He shamed the majority into supporting a disclosure bill on prescription pharmaceuticals opposed by the drug industry, and cosponsored with arch-conservative Lauch Faircloth successful church arson legislation. Meanwhile, Kennedy protected the high-tech handouts and research grants on which so many Massachusetts corporations battened.

Yet little by little, for all his bipartisan footwork, Kennedy was increasingly aware that a historic crisis was coming. That two Republican parties, as he sometimes joked, was one, at least, too many. That unless deep-seated reforms were instituted, and soon, the game was likely to break up once and for all.

3. Compensating for Gridlock

Much as he liked the president personally, Kennedy recognized all along where principle gave way to panicking around the Clinton White House. "Disillusioned?" one of Kennedy's lieutenants responded to me soon after the election of 1996. "It was always hard to be illusioned. You have to retain the sense that this is somebody who is powerful and effective politically. He represents a chance to get things done. You don't do it with a Panglossian vision of Clinton as a person. You play smart political ball."

Smart and—behind the scenes—at times very tough. "Clinton was made aware," the Kennedy operative continues, "when the budget deal was pending in 1995, and Dick Morris was pushing Clinton to compromise on Medicare with the Republicans, that he wasn't only going to face a lot of open opposition from Senator Kennedy and Dick Gephardt, but that he might well have confronted a primary challenge. That's what his deputy chief of staff Harold Ickes was arguing at the time—it wasn't a set of political maneuvers but rather policy preferences that were going to save the presidency. Clinton didn't really want to make that fight, but then there's always been that problem . . ."

Kennedy himself campaigned hard around the country, for both the president and an assortment of local candidates. Most urgent had been the reelection of John Kerry in Massachusetts. Kerry's campaign floundered badly the summer of 1996. His opponent, Massachusetts Governor William Weld, managed to sell the voters of the Commonwealth on the proposition that he really wasn't that Republican on the social issues—he was demonstrably pro-choice, he favored gay rights, etc. But Kerry was unreliable on crime, welfare, and taxes, and that was the real difference between them.

With Kerry's numbers collapsing, Kennedy got increasingly worried and convinced his colleague that the single most important thing he could do was to let in a number of Kennedy's own key people to refocus the campaign. Bob

Shrum took charge of the media for the duration, and Kennedy technicians like John Giesser were detached from the Clinton-Gore campaign. Charlie Baker came back for the critical later weeks and helped Kerry background himself for the interminable series of public debates with Weld which ran almost until election day. Television spots and the substance of the argument between the candidates were moved inexorably back toward traditional Democratic issues—health, Medicare, education, the environment, minimum wage. John Kerry came back day by day and, in the end, won handily.

The standoff the elections provided left Kennedy and his people circling cautiously to await Clinton's second term. There was a lot of concern about Harold Ickes's bumpy exit from the administration along with the wholesale resignations of left-leaning senior staffers like George Stephanopoulos and Leon Panetta. The ascent of the efficient, pro-business Erskine Bowles to chief of staff had not reassured the Kennedy brain trust. "There's some sort of fight going on for the president's soul and prerogatives," one of them assured me after Ickes was bounced. "The president himself has signaled his own sort of indecision. One day he says he's for the balanced budget amendment, the next day he has his people calling around to say he's not. He's having trouble deciding on the cabinet. Clinton now has a chance to make a difference. But we don't know yet what difference it will be."

There were bruised feelings when Clinton seemed to agree to nominate Stephen Breyer, once on Kennedy's Judiciary Committee staff, to the Supreme Court, then appeared to blow his chance, then reconsidered and picked Breyer for the next court vacancy. Kennedy's staffers had long constituted a seedbed for senior White House appointments—Ron Brown would wind up as Secretary of Commerce, Melody Barnes went into the Obama administration as the president's top domestic policy adviser, the inexorable Kenneth Feinberg set executive salaries, and there would be a raft of Kennedy staffers at policy-making posts around the Obama government—Gregory Craig, James Steinberg, David Blumenthal, and up and down.

Inevitably, there were long second thoughts about Clinton's second campaign itself. "Once all the revelations about John Huang and all the Indonesian money broke, you did see a lot of deflation in the president's numbers," Bob Shrum told me not long before Thanksgiving. "Without that, over the last ten days or two weeks of the campaign Clinton would have gotten 53 or 54 percent of the vote. The difference is, that margin would have produced a Democratic House and probably a few more Senate victories." With gridlock again threatening, "Clinton's second term remains unformed. The Republicans keep sending signals back that basically say, 'Sure, we'll be bipartisan, send us something. C'mon, send us something.' Then, when he sends it, they're going to punch him in the nose.

"The hope is—I know Senator Kennedy's hope is—that the president will wake up some morning soon and realize that this is a transformational time for him. He isn't going to have another election. He's either going to pass things he cares about, or not pass things he cares about. And so he better be careful that what he sends is really something he wants to fight for."

By December 12 of 1994, when I caught up with Kennedy, his normal wary hopefulness seemed pitted as much by concerns about the second-term Clinton agenda as about the carryover Republican majority in Congress. "There's no question but that the budget squeeze, in terms of trying to reach a balanced budget in five years, is going to be much more serious this year than last, yes," he agreed when I referred to the resignations of Ickes and Stephanopoulos and Panetta.

This was an administration of bookkeepers, his heavy forbearance suggested. The god was budget surpluses. The United States was now carrying the lowest percentage of debt compared with its gross national product in the industrial world. "If all we do in the next two years is just debate whether we're five years out or seven years out in terms of a balanced budget, well, that's not a very productive use of the time or talents of this Congress."

There might be $80 billion in new revenue the first year if Congress got serious about corporate welfare reform, Kennedy conjectured, and $35 billion and rising a year after that, and for some reason Congress gave the Pentagon $12 billion last year it hadn't even requested. So money was out there. Meanwhile, "What has been developing in America since 1972 is an enormous disparity, with close to 65 percent of Americans losing ground. So that's the overarching issue as we go into the next century." Kennedy summed it up: "Is the system going to work for a few, or should it work for everybody? It's clear to me that we're just going to have to pull and haul in terms of the priorities."

You're talking about the White House end of Pennsylvania Avenue? I put in.

"Well." There was a pause. "We might. I did it last year on welfare, and I did it last year on habeas corpus—you know, the anti-terrorist bill. We're prepared to work with them all that we can, but I'm prepared at times I think that programs are wrong to . . . to vote no."

"And do you think you're going to get a majority of the Democrats to go along with you?"

"Well, we did last time," Kennedy reminded me. "You know, historically, the Democrats have been the representatives of the public interest. And the others have been the protector and projector of the special, more narrow interests. All along there's been this tension between the role of the corporation as a wealth generator and its responsibility to society. We're basically the empowerment party, we believe in empowering people in terms of bettering education, health, jobs in the economy, a greater sense of optimism. Programs come and go, but values don't. I'm a believer in that." Sometimes even Republicans went along.

You went after whatever was on the plate. In 1997 Kennedy and Orrin Hatch, at that point Kennedy's replacement as Health Committee Chairman, went into their well-advertised soft-shoe behind closed doors and came up with the s-CHIP program, a landmark state/federal program to provide health care to children from low-income families. This amounted to another unfunded mandate imposed on a nation of unhappy governors, but it was to bail out an estimated seven million children of the working poor. Hatch commented whenever he got the chance that, given the extent to which he and Ted came at politics from opposite extremes, wherever they overlapped was likely to sprout legislation. With Orrin's help a lot of footnotes and arcane amendments slipped through—tax credits to pharmaceutical houses for developing medicines for rare diseases which they would otherwise have ignored (the Orphan Drug Act), higher mammography standards, additional money for AIDS, regulation of medical devices and drug advertising . . .

The shade of Hubert H. Humphrey rose behind us as Kennedy went over the breakthroughs. One project Kennedy had been nursing since the Carter years was some kind of intervention to untangle a hundred years of dynamitings and bitter civil resistance in Northern Island against British occupation. In 1977 Kennedy had joined Tip O'Neill, Pat Moynihan, and New York Governor Hugh Carey—the "Four Horsemen"—in urging both the occupiers and the IRA to renounce violence. Nudged hard by Kennedy, Bill Clinton had finally appointed Ted's sister Jean Smith Ambassador to Ireland.

"Jean was no day at the beach in certain matters," admits Robert Healy, who had signed on as part of the American delegation attempting to push the negotiations, "but if she hadn't had her own contacts with the IRA people and the insides to stand up to the key American diplomat in London, who caught the 'British fever,' I don't think Adams would have had the clout he needed to go into the peace process." Once she had settled in, Jean became instrumental in bringing an end to "the troubles," pressure our reluctant

State Department to confer a visa on Gerry Adams, the head of the Sinn Fein, and squeeze a variety of unhappy diplomats in London and Dublin until the Good Friday Agreement of 1998 produced a workable peace.

On up days, somebody close to Kennedy had recently tipped me off, there were again intimations that he might just go for the presidency in 2000. Carey Parker went along to the midterm convention in Chicago with express orders to butter up the delegates. That could be serious, or possibly a feint for leverage with the returning administration. Either way, by now Bill Clinton should have recognized fair warning.

CHAPTER VIII

Endgame

1. Safe Haven

The nineties were disappointing for tabloid editors hoping for something juicy from Kennedy. Where lights were brightest—and dimmest—nobody had seen him recently. The stories one did hear cleave to the domestic. A magnet for youngsters, Kennedy kept things interesting at McLean by competing with his stepchildren, Curran and Caroline, to see who could hold out the longest standing on his/her hands upside down in the pool. He was quietly tutoring a ghetto teenager in English. Even when the Senate was in session all but around the clock, Kennedy slipped out for dinner at home when Vicki was working late and dealt with his share of the carpooling and game attending. One seasoned White House operative during the later seventies, who long had shared the Carter staff's disdain for Kennedy after several years of bitter skirmishes, called up an acquaintance from Ted's entourage to admit, finally: "OK, you win; I really like him a lot. We're having this First Communion class with his kid, Caroline, and he is there at every single session. I've never seen anything like it." Kennedy had started to attend mass, a lot.

This was a different universe entirely from the excruciating non-recognition scenes with Joan, let alone those scorched-earth years as a child at Hyannis Port, where Joe and Rose so often dealt with the children—and each other—at arm's length, through personal secretaries and boarding school administrators, and pudgy little Teddy was ignored, "Biscuits and Muffins," an afterthought for the housekeeping staff to deal with. By 1996, caught by the cameras of C-SPAN gesticulating on the Senate floor roaring "Greed! Greed!" at the recalcitrant Republicans, or nose to nose with *Larry King Live*, a Ted Kennedy unavailable for decades was starting to reemerge. Across that broad yeoman visage the features were gradually working back into place, restored to a semblance of the old proportions. Kennedy's eyes had largely cleared, his color was healthy if florid, and Honey Fitz's solid jawline was again on view.

Congratulated on the weight he'd lost, Kennedy chuckled and credited it to Victoria's excellent Cajun cooking. "I thought since downsizing is in," he tossed off, "I'd better get on the treadmill. I wish I found the treadmill sooner." Not that the indulgences of a lifetime don't expire hard. Trapped on an elevator recently next to a man carrying a slice of pizza, Kennedy reportedly ventured "half-jokingly": "You don't mind if I have a bite of that? I had a fruit salad lunch, and here it's not even 3:30, and I'm hungry."

Something profound was involved. When Kennedy had ventured in February of 1996 that "today's rising tide is lifting only some of the boats— primarily the yachts" he had in mind a good deal more than a variation on President Kennedy's dictum that "a rising tide lifts all boats." All along, for Ted, statements by his brother constituted writ. Now, though gently, what he was implying was that Jack's economics were outmoded, the universe of postindustrial politics had shifted and it was up to him to interpret the working of the world. He'd become the lawgiver.

In somebody of Kennedy's deep-seated need to swaddle his apprehensions in homage to family publicity this constituted a breakthrough. It was a very explicit signal that he was ready to bear the entire weight that came with taking himself seriously. Kennedy's life so far had amounted to debilitating stretches of hard work punctuated by gargantuan evasions and precarious high jinks along the edge whenever overwhelming responsibility threatened. Whatever price he'd paid, he'd unmistakably preferred that to failing before the ghost of his father at a series of roles he suspected he was not competent enough to fill.

He'd taken the long way around, building up his position with year after year of stupefying work and tirelessly pushing out his range until even he himself could no longer downplay the proportions of his accomplishment. It took the whirlwind of exposure that swept over them yet again once the Palm Beach incident broke, the anger and betrayal that even those closest to Kennedy showed openly, to make him understand that continuing to go through the empty motions of his dragged-out Reagan-era bachelor existence amounted to emotional self-immolation.

Unlike his brother the president, Edward Kennedy had proceeded all along on the immigrant's assumption that the game was rigged. He understood his calling as primarily to redeem the promises of the Constitution, to exploit the devices of parliamentarianism to return the system to balance. Long before the phrase ever found its way into vogue, Kennedy had preoccupied himself with empowerment. Many of his sixties initiatives—to guarantee expanded franchise opportunities, to bring justice to our immigration procedures, to guarantee women's rights, to draft the gentry into the Vietnam War—came out of his assumption that once more outsiders began to identify with government, social justice would follow. Even what were derided at the time as Edward Kennedy's flirtations with the conservatives—the deregulation of buses and airlines, federal incarceration without parole of career criminals—came out of an abiding if sometimes misguided impulse to break up monopolistic interest groups, whether mobsters or airline executives. Let the system breathe.

The poor spooked Kennedy; they dogged his awareness like an unpaid bill. Perhaps more than anybody else in public life he felt their eyes, their expectations. Even as a child, well before he volunteered his college hours teaching basketball in settlement houses, Kennedy couldn't help apprehending the meanness, the exasperation that ruined the lives of the poor. Again and again, confronted by the conditions in which millions of Americans subsisted, he would denounce the neglect and abuses he could see were commonplace. Such conditions were repellent, he would announce. They were unacceptable—a refrain over decades, echo of an older aristocracy.

As political generations turned, Kennedy depended with ever-increasing effect on his remarkable talent for evoking political decency among his colleagues, for reducing all argument to irresistible human elements. Slogans came and went—"You can't throw money at problems" was a Reaganite favorite—but in the end that made no sense, money was what you had, and day by day Kennedy held off the worst of the excisions. He hammered on education, and never gave up on health, and stalemated the predatory right until the voters caught on.

Perhaps Kennedy fought so steadfastly over the years for the dispossessed and helpless because in the end he was one of them. Beneath the caustic ribbing and the hit-and-run roistering and all that unceasing competitiveness which disfigured the upbringing of the Kennedy brothers, each developed in isolation. Each was forced to endure an emotional disenfranchisement which kept each of them thrashing around quite wildly much of the time for gratification and support. Each of their wives had fought back differently. Joan was particularly subversive, first establishing her alcoholism, then blaming the weakness for her tendency to disappear for days during a crisis, or tug down her panties to show her tan line to a security guard, or drift in a diaphanous nightie through a political breakfast meeting at McLean. Desperation produced desperate measures.

Internally close to frantic with compounding responsibilities, intermittently racked by loss, Kennedy jumped without apology on whatever relief presented itself. Inside, the loneliness grew year by year more oppressive.

After decades of talking to himself when he wanted to hear from somebody he trusted, throughout final decades he talked with Victoria. "I thought this sort of relationship was impossible for me at this stage," Ted told friends. His uninhibited exchanges with his second wife reportedly date from that first summer of 1991, when she had helped nerve him up to confess before the Kennedy School in October that he was finally able to "recognize my own shortcomings . . . I alone am responsible for them, and I alone must confront them." This was the beginning of salvation, and a step into the void.

By Kennedy's lights, even this indirect mea culpa amounted to taking the pledge—"My name is Edward, and I've been incorrigible." While alcohol had always been a prickly subject around Kennedy, something he continually insisted he had no problem with, his efforts those last years to confine himself to a quiet social highball probably approximated an admission of how often drink had unshackled the furies. Lifetime patterns are hard to expunge, and who can guess how easily a season of frustration and setbacks—or hubris— might have uncorked the bottle again? With Victoria rarely far from view, Kennedy's friends were growing hopeful. "I'm writing a book here about death and redemption," I recently told one of them, "and I would not like to be surprised on publication day by Bad Teddy's reappearance."

He laughed, if warily. "I think you're OK," he assured me after a moment. "The bandages of Lazarus are long since gone."

2. Bush II

In many respects the ordeals of the presidency of George W. Bush were reminiscent of the trials of the Reagan years, except with Dick Cheney crouched ruminating in the closet, sharpening his teeth. Kennedy had maintained easygoing relations with three generations of Bushes, starting with grandfather Prescott, who had come in and lectured at a law school colloquium Ted put together. The prospect of Desert Storm had unsettled Kennedy during the previous Bush administration; he voted against it. The odor of the evangelical rose immediately from this counterstrike, coupled with the suggestion of big protective favors to the oil interests. As things turned out, the battle was quick and surgical. Was he unduly apprehensive?

The cunning younger Bush worked the stops with great care when it came to Edward Kennedy. Shortly after taking office, W hosted the Kennedy family at a White House preview of *Thirteen Days*, a film loosely based on the Cuban missile crisis of 1962. The following November the president solicited a few gratified remarks from Ted during the ceremony at which the new U.S. Justice Department building was named after Robert F. Kennedy. The aging senator appeared to be softening up.

Not that Kennedy's political judgment was yet seriously impaired. Within a few months of taking the oath of office Bush had his legislative managers ramming through—by a simple majority, conciliation, rather than a "filibuster-proof" sixty votes—the Tax Cut Bill which would develop by the end of the decade into the fiscal depth bomb that came very close to blowing up the nation's economy, a long-range disaster which would approach the magnitude of the Iraq war.

From the beginning, Kennedy was not fooled. "The budget resolution on which this $1.35 trillion tax bill is based also eliminates $308 billion of funding for education which had the support of a majority of Senators." Kennedy proclaimed on the Senate floor on May 26, 2001. ". . . the Republican bill gives such a huge windfall to the rich. Four hundred and fifty billion dollars will go to the wealthiest 1 percent of taxpayers . . . The massive tax cut contained in this bill will shortchange an entire generation of children." Kennedy's proposal to reclaim at least a part of these lost funds a year later was dismissed by Right-Wing opinion sheets as "green-eyeshade arguments" intended to undo this "bipartisan tax-relief package" and "maximize the amount of dollars in Washington that he and his big-spending allies can dispense to their friends in the federal bureaucracy."

After 9/11 the new Bush administration was able to hornswoggle the populace into focusing its anger on Iraq. "The great leaders of our country have never turned to the politics of fear, but rather the politics of hope" Kennedy had protested early. But "the politics of fear has been Carl Rove's mantra to win elections." To whip up their base the Republicans had pushed constitutional amendments on "things like same-sex marriage and flag burning."

By 2006 Kennedy was emphasizing that "The best vote I ever cast in the Senate" was against the resolution to go into Iraq: "Well, I'm on the Armed Services Committee and I was inclined to support the administration when we started the hearings. And it was enormously interesting to me that those in the military who had served in war—General Wes Clark, General Zinni, General Hoar, General Nash, a series of distinguished military figures with distinguished records in the Gulf War, in Kosovo, in Vietnam—virtually all of them said, no, don't go, this isn't going to work. And that influenced me to the greatest degree." Iraq was quickly becoming "George Bush's Vietnam."

As for Donald Rumsfeld's insistence that there were weapons of mass destruction "North, East, South, West" in Iraq?—Why weren't the United Nations inspectors finding them? Kennedy wanted no part of the "Crusader State." Warnings that dated back to Old Joe Kennedy reverberated in his refusal to sign on; he stood up with twenty-two other senators—one Republican—against the resolution. The war in Iraq, based as it was on a "quicksand of false assumptions," had been "a distraction from our attack on Al Qaeda," and left us to face "a hydra-headed enemy around the world."

Truth to tell, a lot more than geopolitical analysis had gone into Kennedy's change of heart. Many contacts—I certainly was among them—had papered Melody Miller's desk with long, urgent memos warning Kennedy off on Iraq. By the autumn of 2002 my wide-ranging contacts in the CIA were confiding to me that there were no weapons of mass destruction in Iraq in quantities that might have constituted a cause for alarm.

"As for his original stance on Iraq," David Burke acknowledges, "he was one of the boys, a good vote for going in." After forty years, highlighted by a number of the top jobs in media and finance, the penetrating ex-assistant who taught Kennedy the essence of his liberalism had settled down in an antique house on a promentary overlooking Cape Cod. Burke had provided Kennedy with an ethical weather vane throughout his entire career.

"We had a dinner at my home and I kept coming back to it again and again and again," David told me. "The structure of my argumentation was strong and unrelenting. I didn't know I felt that strongly, but I did that night. I felt a sense of the street to convey what the street was thinking. And he always thanked me for it. I'm not making a case for my eloquence. I just knew from the day I was born the whole thing wasn't on the level. People were lying . . ."

Before Iraq sucked up the national dialogue, Kennedy had tried to collaborate. One theme Bush II banged hard during the 2000 campaign had been that American schools were in disarray, children were not learning, new laws were necessary to bootstrap the public system into the kind of shape our free-enterprise system required. In 2001, collaborating closely with the new administration's educational technocrats, Kennedy had gotten his Health Committee behind the emerging No Child Left Behind legislation. The key here was to be monitoring "All schools now measure performance based not on the achievement of their average and above-average students but on their progress in helping below-average students reach high standards as well." Money from the government would depend on the measurable improvement in test scores.

Kennedy would expand in unusual detail in his 2009 memoirs on his own increasingly sickening ride on the Bush educational express. There was the seductive White House screening of a Missile Crisis film so laudatory to Bobby, screened conspicuously in the White House the first day of Bush's presidency. The new president held out the promise of the long-delayed reauthorization of the Elementary and Secondary Education Act. Before long Kennedy proclaimed himself willing to go along with a trial "block-grant" approach to indulge local governments, a feature, like vouchers, for many years a commonplace of Republican agendas. New Hampshire's immovable Senator Judd Gregg handled the aging Kennedy behind committee-room doors, and when the "bi-partisan" legislation came through in early 2002 it was critically underfunded in important categories.

"They were going to be two best friends," David Burke recalls of the early days after W assumed the presidency. "They were going to tour America together. They'd be down there lookin' at movies together, having a great time. Something must have occurred, because when it ended it was on an angry note. Had to do with the funding. Maybe he felt that he had been taken, he was really upset."

By 2008, Kennedy himself would concede that this "one-size-fits-all approach encourages 'teaching to the test' and discourages innovation in the classroom." The Bush administration was starving out education, ignoring all assurances to Congress when the bill was passed.

Badly piqued in early February of 2008 because Kennedy had turned away from Hillary and endorsed Obama, Bill Clinton recurred in an Arkansas high school to "a deal" Kennedy had made with Bush seven years earlier which was "supposed to be, We will give the schools more money and get rid of two programs that Bill Clinton actually started—hiring more teachers in the early grades which actually does help performance and help schools with construction needs if they are overcrowded," along with withholding money from "after-school programs, which does help . . ." The consequence was ". . . a train wreck that was not intended. No Child Left Behind was supported by George Bush and Senator Ted Kennedy and everybody in between. Why? Because they didn't talk to enough teachers before they did that . . ."

Clinton's outburst gave voice to a developing concern that Kennedy tended

more and more to go along with those persuasive pals of his from across
the aisle on legislation that worked out best for the entrenched interests.
Those bipartisan triumphs tended to go sour, fast. Kennedy would remain
the drummer boy on the Senate floor for traditional liberal initiatives, from
raising the minimum wage to federal research into methods of dealing with
minority and special needs to extending COBRA protections to unemployed
workers and terrorist victims to granting better terms on student loans.
And on and on. But in the clinches, behind closed doors, it seemed to be
Kennedy's impulse now to push legislation through that a lot of Democrats
wished he hadn't. The suspicion was spreading that the Lion of the Senate
was losing his teeth.

I myself was finding Kennedy much more domestically oriented. He and
Victoria had given up the McLean estate and moved to a more convenient
house in Georgetown. Melody Miller finally retired, and her replacements—
it took several—were all business and reluctant to bother the senator with
the likes of writers. When I was rounding out my research for *Bobby and J.
Edgar* in 2006 I was able to arrange a telephone interview with Ted. He called
one Sunday and we talked for a long time. I was interested in such details as
whether he remembered the family row when Bob proposed to the Ambassador in 1956 that he, Bob, spearhead a committee in the Senate to investigate racketeering in America. Joe had blown up—who knew how many of his
business partners could look forward to finding themselves grilled beneath
the lights by this most unpolitic of the Kennedy offspring? But Ted couldn't
remember any of those exchanges. He had recently attempted to write a children's book as told from the viewpoint of a dog, and he wanted to discuss
that.

Conservative New Hampshire Senator Judd Gregg, the senior Republican
on the Health Committee, worked closely with Kennedy on measures like
No Child Left Behind and the Taxpayer-Teacher Protection Act of 2004,
which cracked down on banks profiteering from student loans. Despite
the booming voice, Gregg advised onlookers, it was as well to distinguish
between "that fiery rhetoric" when the media were around and "Kennedy's
behind-the-scenes desire to compromise."

The trade-offs in the days before the Senate overwhelmingly passed the
2007 Food and Drug Administration Improvement Act found Kennedy agreeing to grant the FDA a lot of new authority to monitor drugs but appeasing
industry spokesmen like Gregg and Mike Enzi of Wyoming, both substantial
recipients of pharmaceutical-house payoffs, by narrowing the authority of
the FDA until it was authorized merely to "target drugs only when there's

evidence of harm" and agreeing to "water down a proposal that would have required all clinical studies to be made public after meeting with industry officials." The drug companies would remain in control.

So many initiatives, so much responsibility, so much fine print. Even that last year, Kennedy was working closely with John McCain on one last, inspired effort at immigration reform. Kennedy was "a consummate deal-maker and as close to indispensable as anybody I've known in the Senate," McCain had to allow to reporters. According to *The New York Times*, Democrats on the caucus worried that McCain was taking Kennedy into camp, that "without safeguards" protecting guest worker and citizenship provisions . . . this is headed into an unfair, unbalanced bill." With Orrin Hatch, Kennedy had already rammed into law the Serve America Act, a sort of enlarged VISTA program which would reach into more communities with stipends for volunteers from youngsters to retirees to entrepreneurs with non-profit startups. Collaborating with his uneven son Patrick in the House, Kennedy had wriggled through the Medical Health Parity Bill to assist addicts and the emotionally disabled.

3. The Final Campaign

As late as early June of 2008, on his way to Durham, North Carolina, where neurosurgeons at Duke were to remove a plug of Kennedy's skull and subject his brain to an especially intense form of chemotherapy, lobe by lobe, while he kept responding to questions so that his doctors could determine how much of his brain function was affected by the aggressive glioblastoma that was already afflicting him with seizures—even then, en route to the airport, Kennedy was on his cell phone to deputize Chris Dodd to take over his mental health bill and Barbara Mikulski to watch out for his higher education bill. Kennedy's fundamental commitment ended when he did.

After the Bush years finally ended, Kennedy's susceptibilities were jolted one last time as universal health coverage came back to the top of the political agenda, that Halley's Comet of modern legislative wish fulfillment. The thought of finally bringing this off while he was still around provoked long, late thoughts. Years earlier, Kennedy had reminisced to me about looking in when Jack reappeared after combat in the Pacific in 1944. "I remember my brother coming back when I was about twelve years old," Ted recalled, "the times when he was up in the hospital, and then recovering up in the Chelsea Naval Hospital and the difficulties that he had both from malaria and the wounds that he had . . . I think that as a young person going into hospitals and seeing other people that were facing needs and suffering made a big impression on me. Obviously, with a brother that was so close . . .

Then, "As an older person I'd seen my brother's recovery in 1956. I spent a lot of time . . . my father used to let us go . . . we went down at Christmas and Easter to visit him down there [Palm Beach] but that was really the only time that we were expected to kinda come on home, because everybody was in school and college and working, but after my brother was sick he asked me if I couldn't come down and visit him on the weekends, so most of the weekends I'd come down and spend with him. You could see the impact of pain and suffering on him . . ."

There kept coming through Kennedy's final realization of how atomized "that family" remained behind the walls of the estate, so unceasingly busy, such overpowering expectations. Only illness and death seemed to wake them up momentarily. No wonder that health turned into the touchstone of Kennedy's career. That, fighting to protect others, he little by little contrived to heal himself.

Continuing down his list, Kennedy ticked off the death of his brother the president's infant son from Hyaline's Membrane Disease. Kara's lung cancers. And his own son Teddy's battle with ligament cancer—"It was about $2,700 a treatment for three days every three weeks, and you needed it for two years. Fine, talk to parents whose children were going through similar experiences. They'd do it for five months, or six months, because that's all they could afford. And the burning impression about the fact that the difference between a child living and not living was whether you were able to afford the health insurance . . ."

"I saw it again in my son Patrick, who is a chronic asthmatic, and still has about $2,500, $2,800 a year in terms of prescription drugs . . ." Whether pushing through funds to set up the Institute of Rehabilitation Medicine at the National Institute of Health, or cutting off insurance-industry attempts to game-plan the pool of policy-holders so that the premiums jump out of reach for people at serious risk, or threatening the HMOs with specific "rifle-shot" legislative remedies to deal with overnight birthing requirements or gag rules on doctors or drive-by mastectomies—all this in Kennedy's mind impacted, sooner or later, everybody. Family and Medical Leave? "I was always able to take three days off every three weeks when Teddy was so sick. I told Mike Mansfield I wouldn't be around every three weeks on a Friday . . . I not only never risked losing my job, I was still getting paid while I was doing it. And Massachusetts would not have wanted me to be anyplace else." All politics remained personal.

As his doctors had predicted, Edward Kennedy was to live something over a year after his brain tumor was detected. It amounted to a sort of victory lap. To the Clintons' dismay, he came out fairly early in the 2008 primaries for Barack Obama and brought with him his respected niece, Caroline. Kennedy was still stable enough to address the Democratic Convention in Denver in August, by then a little breathy but still able to affirm that "Barack Obama will close the book on the old politics of race and gender and group against group." Then, one final blast of the familiar trumpet: "The work begins anew. The hope arises again. And the dream lives on."

Kennedy obviously would not. In September he suffered another "mild seizure." He had stayed in D.C.; there would be TV moments from time to time of the senator and Vicki marching up and down the corridors of the Senate, both Portuguese water dogs Sunny and Splash on leads as Vicki tilted backwards to keep them under control. He continued to convene his "work-horse group" on health and romance Max Baucus, whose Finance committee was crucial to obtain effective funding for health care reform. By then Ted had taken to wearing a kind of round-rimmed black parson's hat and shuffled along very slowly. He was suffering now from kidney stones and beginning to lose his eyesight. The British had in effect knighted Ted: an Order of the British Empire.

That winter Kennedy was forced to repair to a friend's estate near Miami, although his staff people told me he was still in constant communication via videoconferencing. He reappeared in Washington to cast his vote on the renewal of Medicare.

Then he began to fade out. By spring he had resettled in the Hyannis Port "big house." Pictures were released which presented Kennedy all bundled up and wearing a baseball cap while purportedly sailing the *Mya*. His office told me that he had resumed racing. Barack Obama presented the Kennedys with a puppy (Captains Courageous, Cappy) but held back any endorsement of Caroline Kennedy Schlossberg when there was a brief flurry of interest in her candidacy to replace Hillary Clinton as a senator from New York; word got around that Kennedy was miffed.

Kennedy survived the summer but he was losing capacity. He was reportedly back to putting down his self-determined "limit" of whiskey nightly along with a deadly mixture of mocha-chip and butter-crunch ice cream all "smooshed together," by the quart. And he was up and tottering around until he died on Tuesday, August 25, 2009.

Most people no doubt remember the rest. There was a memorial service at the John F. Kennedy Presidential Library in Dorchester and a closed mass on August 29 in the ornate Basilica of Our Lady of Perpetual Help—the Mission Church, in a dilapidated corner of Roxbury, where Kennedy himself regularly repaired to pray when Kara was undergoing heavy radiation for lung cancer. The Pope discreetly put aside Kennedy's unwavering support in the Senate for abortion rights and permitted Cardinal Sean P. O'Malley to preside. Kennedy's sons spoke, movingly, Yo-Yo Ma played, and Barack Obama delivered the eulogy. Then Kennedy's body was transported through the adoring mobs lining the streets of the North End and buried, near his brothers, in Arlington.

With Kennedy's passing, at first it was as if not only his life but a lot of the surviving vitality of his inimitable strain of liberalism was spent. Paul Kirk, Kennedy's lawyer and from the beginning of his Senate career a tribune in the family's ranks, was appointed to occupy his seat, a place-holder. In January of 2010, when the interim election was held in The People's Republic of Massachusetts, disgust in both parties with politics-as-usual was such that a vacant, virile-looking Republican attorney named Scott Brown—best known around the Commonwealth for once having stripped for *Cosmopolitan*—beat the listless Massachusetts Attorney General Martha Coakley for Kennedy's hallowed seat. In February Kennedy's openly troubled son Patrick announced that he himself was serving out his last term in the U.S. House of Representatives.

Although Kennedy was gone, as time passed the force and focus he imposed on the legislative process began again to make itself felt. After a year of handwringing and bombast from the alienated Right, the first serious legislative attempt in fifteen years to overhaul and rationalize our predatory medical infrastructure, the Patient Protection and Affordable Health Care Act, was signed into law in the East Room of the White House on March 23, 2010. Hanging over President Obama's shoulder while he signed this landmark measure was Victoria Kennedy, smiling with gratification, the proxy for Edward Kennedy's contented ghost.

4. Requiem For a Minotaur

Edward Kennedy wound up serving forty-seven years in the U.S. Senate. He performed without letup through good times as well as bad. Late in 1993, rummaging around the attic in McLean, Victoria Kennedy's son Curran came across a solicitation from the Green Bay Packers, circa 1956. "It read, 'Dear Mister Kennedy,'" Victoria recalled to me during the nineties, with a laugh, "'you have been recommended for a professional football career. Our scouts have watched you and tell us you have promise.' My son was blown away. He adored Ted anyway, but that really clinched it. Ted tried to tell him it was a form letter, but Curran wasn't buying that. I finally said, 'Ted, you know, maybe the Green Bay Packers could use you. They're havin' a tough time too this season.' Isn't that hilarious?"

Maybe the Packers could have. Kennedy was an established performer, and what he meant—and continues to mean—to the country transcends issue or party. Dick Day, Republican Alan Simpson's right-hand man, probably caught years ago the prevailing feeling throughout many of Kennedy's controversial decades in the Senate best: "Ted Kennedy is one of those guys who, when they have a list of the ten best senators and the ten worst senators around here, would very likely make both lists." Kennedy's lingering death through most of 2009, excruciatingly consecrated by the media, would leave him interpreted more as a national monument than a hard-working politician. That underrates both his limitations and his tremendous accomplishments.

At his staff party for Christmas of 1992, mocking his own reputation around Capitol Hill, Kennedy appeared in horns and a mask while Victoria teased him. "Hello, beast," she opened. "You know you have been a beast at times."

What point in denying that? Beastliness reflects the bloodlines, that inspiration which years ago tempted Lewis Lapham to term Edward Kennedy a "Minotaur," a crossbreed of man and mythology, "a creature who carries within him all the 'opposed principles' that are the family legacy."

In Kennedy's family, and in the end in ours.

ACKNOWLEDGMENTS

This unified biography of Edward Kennedy is the consequence of an involvement that has spanned more than forty years, most of my writing lifetime. While it is not essentially a memoir, which would imply a selective, episodic recounting of very often random incidents, a great deal depends on an ongoing, hit-and-run relationship Kennedy and I somehow maintained throughout the many decades. Along with months and months of research at every stage and the many hundreds of interviews that informed both the predecessor volumes and the magazine pieces which appeared in and around the books, I was able to tag along regularly when Kennedy was out among 'em. During these many jaunts I continually filled my notebooks and taped the human material which produced the more dramatic, impressionistic sections of the text. Beyond that, a great deal of fresh detail that I was unwilling to include while Kennedy was alive or discovered after he passed on has been integrated throughout.

One great advantage that accrued to me over the years was a number of personal friendships that seemed to take shape spontaneously with Kennedy's most trusted aides and/or the journalists who covered him. All of them seemed to understand that, while I would tell the whole story and that nobody was going to get a preliminary look at anything, my intention—no matter what triumph or disgrace was breaking over Kennedy's reputation at any moment—remained to establish the larger truth. To concentrate on the unremitting political ambitions and specific accomplishments of this unique leader and avoid getting all tangled up in that season's scandal.

A great many individuals contributed to the formulation of this book, most—I hope—credited throughout the notes. A handful have remained loyal and supportive all along, even after the 2007 publication of *Bobby and J. Edgar*, which probed what my namesake has labeled the dark side of the Kennedy legacy. While Edward Kennedy himself was not, in the end, completely unaware of his father's underworld connections, his own career tended to move out beyond the universe of political bosses and special-interest trade-offs and CIA cover-ups on which his brothers' careers had in part depended, and permitted Teddy to embark on a vast, integrated body of accomplishment even the most energetic right-wing mud-slingers have never been able to compromise.

I'd like here to thank specifically five individuals who never seemed to worry unduly about whether the truth was likely to help or hurt the senator. David Burke, Jim Flug, Bob Healy, Lester Hyman, and Melody Miller—alphabetical order—have pitched in and helped me out whatever the political weather. If there were lifetime achievement awards being handed out in my universe, they would be first in line. Among Kennedy's academic sponsors, the seemingly indestructible Sam Beer and Arthur Schlesinger Jr., both now gone, always added a historian's perspective and a warm appreciation for the fine line between fairness and frankness.

I would also like to acknowledge a number of sources, some staffers at one point for the Kennedy organizations, some media people, some friends and contemporary politicians and even members of the family, whose contribution enriched this chronicle at many, many points. Some of these contributors survive and a great many do not, more every day.

Beyond the individuals cited below there are a great many dignitaries of earlier eras, from senatorial colleagues to competitors who pushed the Kennedys to staffers to the occasional out-and-out mad-dog hater, all generous enough to confide in me. The reader will find their names in the notes.

Kirk Lemoyne Billings
Jeffrey Blatner
Greg Craig
Jack Crimmins
John Culver
Gerald Doherty
Richard Drayne
James Doyle
Fred Dutton
Peter Edelman
Joseph Gargan
Dun Gifford
Richard Goodwin
Milton Gwirtzman
David Hackett
Dr. Larry Horowitz
Doris Kearns
John Kerry
James King

Paul Markham
Speaker John McCormack
Frank Mankiewicz
Nick Littlefifeld
Ed Martin
David Nexon
Kenneth O'Donnell
Speaker Thomas P. (Tip) O'Neill
Wayne Owens
Carey Parker
Robert Shrum
Daniel Schorr
Steve Smith
Charles Tretter
John Tunney
William Vanden Heuvel
Andrew Vitali
Angelique Voutselas
Helga Wagner

In preparing this comprehensive edition of Edward Kennedy's life, much material from the earlier volumes has very carefully—line by line, word by word—been stripped out of the preexisting texts. In *The Education of Edward Kennedy* many of the opening sections were devoted to laying out in extensive—Lord Save Me, scholarly— detail the background of the family and the evolution of what came to be known as the Kennedy political machine. Writing in the late sixties, interviewing dozens of holdovers from the Honey Fitz era and loquacious coat-holders and old-line political managers, on whom Joe Kennedy relied to build a future for his boys, I recognized a compounding trove for future historians and tended to put everything in. Crafting this edition, I saw right away that a great deal of this background detail would have to be foreshortened to permit the focus to remain, early and throughout, on Edward Kennedy himself. A lot of the style mannerisms left over from the rock-and-roll era needed to be moderated. I moderated ruthlessly.

With Kennedy's entire life now available to contemplate, important themes became apparent. Exchanges with his intimates and my own astonishing late conversations with Kennedy as well as passages from his memoirs and even comments by his children during his funeral touched on the purposes and apprehensions that drove him most of his life. Born last, brushed-off, he was to spend many, many years proving to himself that he even deserved to be Kennedy. A number of Joe Kennedy's private convictions—that it was vital for the more fortunate to take responsibility for the poor, that foreign entanglements, "the projection of American power," were likely to bring down the Republic—these came more year by year to inform this most vulnerable of his children.

Continuing to talk with the senator and a number of the informal advisers who fed him ideas and had been caught up in one crisis or the next, I had discovered that tip-offs of very large historical import had all but escaped me when I originally reported his life. Details of the Chappaquiddick accident, including a revelatory conversation with Helga Wagner, the woman in Kennedy's life when the disaster exploded, will change historians' reading of that shattering event. Why Kennedy defied the Catholic Church and completely reversed his position on abortion in the early seventies, and the upshot inside his family. How paranoia so seized the Nixon White House that Kennedy was forced to conclude that his own survival required him to blow Richard Nixon out of office, and how he wheeled the siege machinery into place to accomplish that. The attempt by George W. Bush to seduce Kennedy into supporting his No Child Left Behind initiatives, and the bitter upshot.

Integrating all this into a coherent, all-encompassing biography meant boiling down and rethinking much of what I'd written. Fortunately, all along, I had a lot of inspired help. My editor at William Morrow for *The Education* had been the legendary James Landis, perhaps the outstanding editor of the era and himself a gifted and original writer. At *Esquire* Harold Hayes and Don Erickson had done me nothing but good, and ran my version of the Chappaquiddick disaster as an entire issue. Jack Limpert of *The Washingtonian* brought out my insider version of Kennedy's misbegotten run at the Democratic nomination in 1980. When a number of these later magazine pieces were fleshed out into book form for Steerforth Press in 1997 as *The Shadow President*, that brooding goblin Thomas Powers reviewed the manuscript.

With this edition, a lot of both vitality and coherence has been lent by the dedicated involvement of Bob Ickes. An editor with credentials, Ickes took many weeks to go through a draft I had already—I thought—worked nicely into shape and contributed what amounted to a running gloss of acute suggestions. All this processed through Counterpoint Press energized by the imagination and encouragement of Charlie Winton, along with Laura Mazer and Roxanna Aliaga, Tiffany Lee, April Wolfe, and Julie Pinkerton, all of whom saw immediately the possibilities in such an edition, and jumped.

Support on every level came, as ever, from Ellen, my wife since time out of mind. Invaluable computer backup depended on Johnny Andrus and Rich Rice, while Cindy Byers' matchless keyboarding and programming skills repeatedly pulled me through.

Shadows grow longer. With Ted Kennedy's passing, it is undeniably time to get it out there.

My hope is that the chapter-by-chapter source note system that follows will prove helpful, provocative, solidly researched, and inclusive. These notes, linked to key phrases and quotations in the text, follow it chronologically; many come from new sources and the round of interviews I conducted with Kennedy insiders shortly after the senator's death. (In many instances here, Edward M. Kennedy is abbreviated as EMK.)

Innumerable statements and projections in the book are drawn from background impressions and a medley of overlapping information too complex and evasive to identify in footnotes; the notes included are expected to function as pinpoint leads for future students of the Kennedy political experience. Many of the source notes—especially those listing only a name and a date—refer to the hundreds of interviews and dozens of notebooks I myself accumulated during the fifty years I researched to collect the material in which the work is rooted. Some sources are deliberately bypassed; others are masked in the interests of a proper confidentiality.

BOOK ONE: THE INITIATION OF THE MINOTAUR

Preface

xiv   That got complicated: Milton Gwirtzman interview, 12/10/69.

xvi   "As your letter suggests": Edward M. Kennedy, letter to Burton Hersh, January 29, 1971.

Chapter I: Origins

5   That night John Kennedy's lunar dream: Inquest into the Death of Mary Jo Kopechne, Edgartown, January 5–8, 1970, Five Volumes, Docket Number 15220, Volume III, Kennedy testimony, p. 472.

6   What the native Yankees: John Henry Cutler, *Honey Fitz*, p. 15, 17, Richard J. Whalen, *The Founding Father*, pp. 7, 8, 12.

7   "The pariah has few choices": Walter Bryan, *The Improbable Irish*, pp. 54, 109 ff.

8   This shows in their earliest purposeful: Cutler, op. cit., p. 10, p. 72, Whalen, op. cit., p. 13.

8   Tom and Rosemary Fitzgerald: Cutler, op. cit., pp. 37, 38, 72.

8   "When I was six years old": Nancy Sirkis, *Boston*, preface by Edward M. Kennedy, p. 9.

9   Anybody interested in how: Cutler, op. cit., pp. 41–43.

10   By the time the effervescent: Bryan, op. cit., p. 77; Walter Muir Whitehill, *Boston in the Age of John Fitzgerald Kennedy*, p. 35; William V. Shannon, *The American Irish*, p. 185.

10   "Many of the rich people of the Back Bay": Cutler, op. cit., pp. 213, 214.

10   It was, in fact, a tarpaper revolution: Bryan, op. cit., pp. 79, 80, Oscar Handlin, *Boston's Immigrants*, p. 114.

11   Alongside the performances of: Cutler, op. cit., p. 50, 69.

12   Fitzie had discovered: Francis Russell, *The Great Interlude*, p. 172–183; Cutler, op. cit., pp. 72–128, 149–157.

14   Rose Kennedy, who remembered: Interview, Sept. 29, 1969, Joseph F. Dinneen, *The Kennedy Family*, p. 5.

14   Mary Kennedy's daughter: Mrs. George Connelly, letters to Burton Hersh, November 3, October 25, 1969.

14   "All the family have self-confidence": *Ladies' Home Journal*, April 1970.

15   There are the reveries in later years: Edward M. Kennedy (ed.), *The Fruitful Bough*. Many sources quoted from *The Fruitful Bough* are kept anonymous at the request of Senator Kennedy.

15   Harvard is her idea: James MacGregor Burns, *John Kennedy: A Political Profile*, p. 14.

15   Overhearing that a German A classmate: Whalen, op. cit., p. 25; E. M. Kennedy, op. cit.

16   Everybody isn't buying: Whalen, op. cit., p. 381.

16   Furious, upset: Ibid., p. 27.

17   "Joe's reaction": E. M. Kennedy, op. cit.

17   Given his mentality: Whalen, op. cit., p. 38.

18   A wit of the period: Cutler, op. cit., p. 213; "The crafty Joe Kennedy:" E. M. Kennedy, op. cit.

18   Rose worked hard: Cutler, op. cit., p. 174.

Chapter II: Political Lullabies

20   Having survived his precocious glamor: Whalen, op. cit., p. 52.

20   After twenty–two months: Ibid., p. 99.

20   Back home in the: Ibid., p. 90.

21   "I was amazed": Victor Lasky, *J.F.K.: The Man & the Myth*, p. 44.

21   After a trial residence: Whalen, op. cit., p. 74, 89.

21   At about this time: Leo Damore, *The Cape Cod Years of John Fitzgerald Kennedy*, pp. 17–19.

22   Early testimony: Kirk Lemoyne Billings, 6/3/69.

22   At breakfast: Evelyn Lincoln, *My Twelve Years With John F. Kennedy*, p. 216.

23   As with the earlier children: Peter Collier and David Horowitz, *The Kennedys;*

pp. 31, 57; Barbara Gibson and Ted Schwarz, *Rose Kennedy and Her Children: The Best and Worst of their Lives and Times*, p. 47.

24   Joe Kennedy–Joe Kennedy's life: Whalen, op. cit., p. 122.

24   Kennedy took hold: Dinneen, op. cit., pp. 40, 41.

24   An awkwardly inquiring telegram: Whalen, op. cit., p. 131.

25   "Years ago we decided": Ibid., pp. 164, 165.

25   An awareness: Joseph Gargan, 5/14/69.

25   At the time of Billings's Christmas: Ralph G. Martin and Ed Plaut, *Front Runner, Dark Horse*, p. 123, 124.

26   That introductory visit: Kirk Lemoyne Billings, 6/3/69.

28   "The Kennedys never shit themselves": Al Novak, 12/11/67.

28   "Carroll, that's a crazy deal": Joseph Gargan, 5/14/69.

28   For all the financier's evasiveness: Hersh, *Bobby and J. Edgar*, p. 68.

28   Close to the beginning: Harold L. Ickes, *The First Thousand Days*, p. 173.

28   "Joe Kennedy unexpectedly came in": Harold L. Ickes, *The Lowering Clouds*, p. 147.

28   He advocated a deal: Kevin Phillips, *American Dynasty*, p. 188.

28   "If Teddy came in second": Martin and Plaut, op. cit., pp. 121, 122.

29   "What is the big idea": Edward McLaughlin, 4/17/69.

29   Once the family celebrity: Edward McLaughlin, 4/17/69.

29   Once he was gone: E. M. Kennedy, op. cit.

29   The archives of family legend: Joseph Gargan, 5/14/69.

30   "If I had slipped": Theodore C. Sorensen, *Kennedy*, p. 31.

30   "Mr. Kennedy had a great generosity": Stephen Smith, 6/3/69.

30   "The father liked to get together": Edward McLaughlin, 4/17/69; Kirk Lemoyne Billings, 6/3/69.

30   "I fixed it so that": Cutler, op. cit., p. 247.

30   "My children won't be able": Joe McCarthy, *The Remarkable Kennedys*, p. 11.

30   "Mr. Kennedy was very understanding": Joseph Gargan, 5/14/69.

31   "My father always made it a point": Edward M. Kennedy, 12/12/67.

31   "I think there was a real sense of direction": Stephen Smith, 6/3/69.

31   Until, in the end: Robert Fitzgerald, 5/14/69.

32   "You'll see a tremendous change": Joseph Gargan, 5/14/69.

32   "Bring up the oldest": *The Concord Monitor*, August 5, 1969, p. 3.

32   The nuns who taught: Damore, op. cit., p. 26.

32   "He had a pugnacious": Ibid., p. 27.

32   "It wasn't their father": Martin and Plaut, op. cit., p. 125.

32   Lem Billings: Kirk Lemoyne Billings, 6/3/69.

33   There were the unavoidable: Robert E. Thompson and Hortense Myers, *Robert F. Kennedy: The Brother Within*, p. 65.

33   In the ideological line: Margaret Laing, *The Next Kennedy*, p. 76.

33   Jack, hoping to slide out from under: Burns, op. cit., p. 30.

33   The honors thesis: John F. Kennedy, *Why England Slept*.

33   "You would be surprised": Burns, op. cit., p. 44.

34   By mid-March of 1938: Whalen, op. cit., pp. 209–211.

34   Backed up to an elephant: *Ted Kennedy: Heir to Greatness* (Universal Publications), pp. 14, 15.

34   "His first day": *Woman's Day*, April 1939, Jerome Beatty article, reprinted in *Reader's Digest*.

34   "Can I hit Romney": Dinneen, op. cit., pp. 66, 67.

35   The historical instant: Cutler, op. cit., p. 278, 279.

35   Joseph P. Kennedy, after months: Ibid., p. 338.

35   The disgusted president: Dinneen, op. cit., p. 84.

35   The years of exuberant: Arthur M. Schlesinger, Jr., *A Thousand Days*, p. 84; George Kennan, Memoirs, p. 92.

35   Teddy, seven, informed: *Esquire*, April 1962, Thomas B. Morgan article.

35   Once the war started: Whalen, op. cit., p. 362.

36   The renown the Ambassador: Hersh, B, *Bobby and J. Edgar*, p. 72.

36   "His worldly success": Ibid., p. 373; John F. Kennedy (ed.), *As We Remember Joe*; McCarthy, op. cit., p. 83.

36   As the lull deepens: Whalen, op. cit., p. 86; E.M. Kennedy, op. cit.

37   When Arthur Krock: McCarthy, op. cit., pp. 53, 54.

37   Private losses mount: Whalen, op. cit., pp. 374, 375.

37   Hanging on: Ibid., p. 376.

37   Property values: Ibid., p. 379.

37   Ennui was setting in: Hugh Sidey, *John F. Kennedy, President*, p. 22.

38   Employees, squeezing: E. M. Kennedy, op. cit.

39   Rest, at last: Cleveland Amory, *Who Killed Society?*, p. 142.

39   He himself would credit: *Esquire*, April 1962, Thomas B. Morgan article.

39   "It was too late": *Redbook*, June 1962.

39   Shortly before he passed away: Edward M. Kennedy, *True Compass: A Memoir*, p. 62.

39   By 1941: Ibid., p. 63.

40   Then, unprompted: EMK interview, 12/12/67.

40   She battered: *Esquire*, April 1962, Thomas B. Morgan article.

40   "I remember him when he was seven": *Redbook*, June 1962.

40   Jack, who doted: *Esquire*: April 1962, Thomas B. Morgan article.

41   Loved–loved: Kirk Lemoyne Billings, 6/3/69.

41   "Even as a child": *Ted Kennedy: Heir to Greatness* (Universal Publications), p. 12.

41   The adult Ted Kennedy: E. M. Kennedy, op. cit., Edward M. Kennedy section, p. 201.

41   There, a walloping: *Redbook*, June 1962.

41 "My father—": Edward M. Kennedy, 12/12/67.

41 "Dear Teddy": E. M. Kennedy, op. cit.; quote from Joseph P. Kennedy, p. 8.

42 Even then the child: Gore Vidal, *Palimpsest*, pp. 18, 19, 340.

42 By 1941, with all the others: Edward M. Kennedy, *True Compass: A Memoir*, p. 20.

42 "One summer": *Redbook*, June 1962.

43 "This is really important": Joseph Gargan, 5/14/69.

43 *Time*, after the Chappaquiddick: *Time*, August 1, 1969, p. 13.

44 "Bob, quite frankly, was interested": Joseph Gargan, 5/14/69.

45 "The old man scared me": Kirk Lemoyne Billings, 3/16/69; David Hackett, 4/21/71.

45 "It was a delight": Joseph Gargan, 5/14/69.

45 It is something one can very nearly: E. M. Kennedy, op. cit.

46 One incident plays: Joseph Gargan, 5/14/69; E. M. Kennedy, op. cit.

47 Edward, writing about: Ibid., Edward M. Kennedy section, p. 207.

48 "I remember Teddy": Kirk Lemoyne Billings, 3/16/69.

48 "When you have older brothers and sisters": *Ted Kennedy: Heir to Greatness* (Universal Publications), p. 14.

48 "We used to sail together": *Esquire*: April 1962, Thomas B. Morgan article; Damore, op. cit., p. 40.

48 Younger, weaker until his growth: Joseph Gargan, 5/14/69.

48 Polo, for example: E. M. Kennedy, op. cit.; Joseph Gargan, 5/14/69.

49 "Eunice started to explain": McCarthy, op. cit., p. 81, 82.

49 "Shortly after Jack": Mark Dalton, 6/23/69.

Chapter III: Whelping the Juggernaut

50 "I got Jack into": Cutler, op. cit., p. 301.

50 Clem Norton, a pal of: Schlesinger, op. cit., p. 90; WBZ television interview, etc.

51 "Sometimes we all have to do things": Martin and Plaut, op. cit., pp. 131, 132.

51 He was forever without cash: E. M. Kennedy, op. cit.

51 "Good God, Jack": Edward McLaughlin, 4/17/69.

51 You could follow Jack: Lincoln, op. cit., p. 85.

51 He had a way of walking around: Mark Dalton, 4/23/69.

51 The Massachusetts district: Burns, op. cit., p. 60.

52 "'Red'" Kennedy's Navy buddy: Fay, op. cit., p. 152.

52 One was Joe Kane: William Sutton, 6/11/69.

52 "Get that sonofabitch": Cutler, op. cit., p. 306.

52 The financier's other find: Cutler, op. cit., p. 306.

52 "Frank's job in life": Edward McLaughlin, 4/17/69.

52 "Morrissey's detractors": Gerard Doherty, 3/18/69.

53 "Morrissey was disgusting": Kennedy intimate.

53 The campaign manager: Mark Dalton, 6/23/69.

53 When a *Boston Post* poll: Whalen, op. cit., p. 398, 399.

53 At the time the idea: Whalen, op. cit., p. 401.

54 "I never thought Jack": Ibid., p. 396.

54 "He was not a speaker": Mark Dalton, 6/23/69.

54 One of the high spots: Burns, op. cit., pp. 65, 67.

54 Weekends, that rare day off: *Ted Kennedy: Heir to Greatness* (Universal Publications), p. 18.

55 "Let's watch our swearing and": William Sutton, 6/11/69.

55 "Trust nobody completely": Thompson and Myers, op. cit., p. 201.

55 About the time Jack: William Sutton, 6/11/69.

55 "Jack tended to be": Stephen Smith, 6/3/69.

55 As the postwar years stretched: *Life*, March 18, 1946.

55 "I remember as kids": Joseph Gargan, 5/14/69.

57 The Truman foreign policy: Whalen, op. cit., p. 407.

58 "Some people have their liberalism": Burns, op. cit., p. 155.

58 He advocated the inclusion: Lasky, op. cit., p. 111, 113, 116, 117, 128.

59 "I'd be very happy": Burns, op. cit., pp. 134, 135.

60 One day on the floor of: Lasky, op. cit., p. 109.

60 "Jack, if I were you": McCarthy, op. cit., p. 98.

60 When, in 1947: Burns, op. cit., p. 92.

61 "Jack was . . . as a congressman": Foster Furcolo, 3/18/69.

61 Lodge was admittedly: James King, 5/12/69.

61 Over the same years: Dinneen, op. cit., pp. 143, 144; Whalen, op. cit., p. 419.

62 John Ford, of the: Mark Dalton, 6/23/69; Whalen, op. cit., pp. 420, 421, 422.

62 "Jack Kennedy in 1952?": Betty Taymor, 3/18/69.

62 Dalton, who remembered the father: Mark Dalton, 6/23/69.

63 All this business about: Laing, op. cit., p. 129.

63 Leo Damore: Damore, op. cit., p. 74.

64 As late as 1952: Laing, op. cit., p. 127.

64 "When Bobby came in": Ibid., p. 130.

64 "Fought like cats and dogs": Helen Keyes, 6/23/69.

64 The pinning figure: Laing, op. cit., p. 97; Kenneth O'Donnell, 5/12/69.

64 Paul Dever had already: Thomas O'Neill, 11/18/70.

64 They threw together: McCarthy, op. cit., pp. 100, 101.

64 Another subtle move: Foster Furcolo, 3/18/69.

65 Kennedy entered the party primary: Burns, op. cit., p. 106.

65 "Six people": Kenneth O'Donnell, 5/12/69.

65 Bobby arrived: Whalen, op. cit., p. 421; Thompson and Myers, op. cit., p. 181.

65 "A cold champion": Martin and Plaut, op. cit., p. 164.

66   The first time Jackie: 6/23/69.

66   "I didn't think": James King, 5/12/69.

66   As early as the first planning: Whalen, op. cit., p. 420.

66   When Pat Jackson: Whalen, op. cit., p. 429.

66   "Bobby is soft": Laing, op. cit., p. 103.

67   "That was, of course": Thomas O'Neill, 11/18/70.

67   "He had a fantastic ability": Edward McLaughlin, 4/17/69.

67   "He used a self-proclaimed": Sorensen, op. cit., p. 72.

67   "Jack absolutely hated": Edward McLaughlin, 4/17/69.

67   John Torney, in time: John Torney, 10/21/69.

68   He was not then: *Look*, March 4, 1969.

68   Albert Norris: Albert Norris, 10/21/69.

69   Rose Kennedy, whose: Rose Kennedy, telephone conversation notes, 10/29/69.

70   Jack Kennedy, recuperating: Thomas Cleveland, 10/21/69.

70   "There was always a lot": Edward Martin, 5/5/69.

70   "Read all you can": John Culver, 6/18/69.

71   "The toughness was important": Schlesinger, op. cit., p. 79.

72   One team member: Edward M. Kennedy classmate.

73   "It was an easy test": William Frate, 12/13/69.

74   "He made no bones about it": Thomas Cleveland, 10/21/69.

74   At home he dated: *National Enquirer*, September 21, 1969, p. 22.

74   "Do the best you're able": Edward M. Kennedy, 12/12/67.

74   "Sixteen of the most worthwhile": Letter to Arthur Perry, Milton Academy files, 10/21/69.

75   "You are exposed as": Edward M. Kennedy, 12/12/67.

75   In fact, Kennedy: *Esquire*, April 1962, Thomas B. Morgan article.

75   Over those military months: Ibid.

75   One of the few: *Time*, July 26, 1960.

75   "He was no aristocrat at college": Milton Gwirtzman, 12/13/67.

75   "He now regarded himself": Martin Doctoroff, December 1968.

76   Fred Holborn: *Redbook*, June 1962.

76   Always a plugger: Victor Lasky, *Robert F. Kennedy: The Myth and the Man*, p. 62.

76   Friends of the period: John Culver, 6/18/69.

76   Robert Wood: Robert Wood, 5/12/69.

76   Kennedy's grades: *Redbook*, June 1962.

76   The regular end: Damore, op. cit., p. 148.

77   "Bobby was more a defensive type": *Esquire*, April 1962, Thomas B. Morgan article.

77   Lamar recalls the next: *Redbook*, June 1962.

77   On a family vacation: McCarthy, op. cit., p. 110.

78   Ted remained well taken: Edward M. Kennedy classmate.

78   Three of Joe Kennedy's sons: Whalen, op. cit., p. 228.

78   Ted, to the Ambassador's joy: E. M. Kennedy, op. cit.

78   "The Army obviously makes": Edward M. Kennedy, 12/12/67.

79   He volunteered to coach: *Esquire*, April 1962, Thomas B. Morgan article.

79   "At least one good friend": Burns, op. cit., p. 127.

79   When the party's rising: Foster Furcolo, 3/18/69.

79   The tendency among: Schlesinger, op. cit., p. 9.

80   It was that same John: Lasky, *J.F.K.: The Man & the Myth*, pp. 112–116, 232; Sorensen, op. cit., pp. 135, 136.

80   In Massachusetts, though: Burns, op. cit., pp. 142, 143.

80   Kennedy voted for: Martin and Plaut, op. cit., p. 207.

80   In fact, back as far: Whalen, op. cit., p. 151.

80   When Stevenson got: also see Burton Hersh, *Bobby and J. Edgar*, p. 202, p. 425.

81   Arvey functioned: Burns, op. cit., p. 136.

81   By 1954: Foster, Ibid., p. 10.

81   As it happened: Leverett Saltonstall, 5/12/69.

81   Before a joint television appearance: Schlesinger, op. cit., p. 96.

81   "Foster, you have a hell of": Burns, op. cit., p. 148.

82   Worse, Kennedy secretly: Sorensen, op. cit., p. 73.

82   "Paul Dever always": Foster Furcolo, 3/18/69.

83   John C. Carr: Burns, op.cit., p. 176.

83   "Bobby and I felt": Kenneth O'Donnell, 5/12/69.

83   The afternoon of the vote: Sorensen, op. cit., p. 80; Betty Taymor, 3/18/69; Thomas Gerber, 3/7/69.

84   The Kennedy forces won: Burns, op. cit., pp. 179, 180.

84   Hubert Humphrey: Lasky, *J.F.K.: The Man & the Myth*, p. 190.

84   Years afterward, Gene: McCarthy, op. cit., pp. 123, 124, 6/10/69.

84   Following the expenditure of enormous: Sorensen, op. cit., p. 88.

84   But the generous-minded: Dinneen, op. cit., pp. 203–205; John McCormack, 2/10/69.

85   "We did our best": Whalen, op. cit., p. 444.

85   The old financier: Martin and Plaut, op. cit., pp. 106, 107.

85   Bobby–never graceful: Ralph de Toledano, *R.F.K.: The Man Who Would Be President*, p. 141.

86   "It really struck me then": Martin and Plaut, op. cit., pp. 106, 107.

86   A silent figure on the Stevenson train: Lester Tanzer (ed.), The Kennedy Circle, A Collection (H. Sidey article), p. 201.

86   "I'd been interested": Edward M. Kennedy, 12/12/69.

87   For Ted Kennedy: John Culver, 6/18/69.

87   "I've got to go at": *Look*, March 4, 1969, interview with Edward M. Kennedy.

87   "Bob had lots on the ball": Laing, op. cit., p. 112.

88   "Ted worked very hard": John Tunney, 12/11/67.

89   "Ted put more energy": *Redbook*, June 1962.

90   "He turns into quite a different": John Tunney, 12/11/67.

90   Between semesters: *Esquire*, April 1962, Thomas B. Morgan article.

90   Thomas Whitten: *National Enquirer*, September 12, 1969, article by George Carpozi.

91   Politicians and newspaper commentators: Lasky, *J.F.K.: The Man & the Myth*, p. 316.

92   "We dry-ran everything": Kenneth O'Donnell, 5/12/69.

92   Listening to the matter-of-fact: Stephen Smith, 6/3/69.

93   "Edward Kennedy is the most": Francis X. Morrissey, 3/18/69.

94   This meant the earliest: Whalen, op. cit., p. 446.

94   The realization of this projected: *Manchester Union Leader*, November 20, 1969, eulogy by William Loeb.

94   For four rugged years: Sorensen, op. cit., p. 100.

94   The mood and tenor: Ibid.

94   Bringing Ted in: Stephen Smith, 6/3/69.

94   "It was obvious from": Kenneth O'Donnell, 5/12/69.

95   "I think I was the one": James King, 5/12/69.

95   Early in a five-week: Damore, op. cit., p. 159.

95   There were the predictable: Ibid., p. 160.

96   Filling in for: Edward M. Kennedy, 12/12/69.

96   "Ted Kennedy was better": Edward McCormack, 5/14/69.

97   Sorensen wrote an aide: Burns, op. cit., p. 222.

97   "It was the old man": Edward McLaughlin, 4/17/69.

98   "Betty, what are you doing": Betty Taymor, 3/18/69.

98   There was an incessant: Lester Hyman, 4/11/69.

98   Out of the older generation's: Betty Taymor, 3/18/69.

98   "I don't believe the president": Edward M. Kennedy, 12/12/69.

99   "From what I understand": Thomas Gerber, 7/7/69. Gerber was the chief of the *Boston Herald-Traveler* bureau in D.C. during the fifties.

Chapter IV: The Castle

101   Theodore Sorensen, aware: Theodore C. Sorensen, *The Kennedy Legacy*, p. 38.

101   Kennedy's Senate performance: Sorensen, Kennedy, p. 58.

101   "He was like that": Thruston Morton, 12/13/67

102   Years earlier: Lasky, *J.F.K.: The Man & the Myth*, p. 309.

102   He appeared to have matured: Burns, op. cit., p. 89; Lasky, *J.F.K.: The Man & the Myth*, pp. 294 ff.

102   James MacGregor Burns: Burns, op. cit., pp. 216–266.

103 "Fifty percent": Ibid., p. 268.

103 "I knew vaguely of": Rose Kennedy, telephone conversation notes, September 29, 1969.

103 As late as the Christmas holidays: *Saturday Evening Post*, January 18, 1936, Joseph P. Kennedy article.

103 "It makes no sense": *The Boston Globe*, November 19, 1969.

104 A month or so earlier: Kennedy source.

104 "All the way through": Edward Kennedy, 12/12/69.

105 Lyndon Johnson's own: *The Boston Globe*, December 26, 1969.

105 As characteristically with: Burns, op. cit., p. 189.

105 "I liked the idea": John McCormack, 12/10/69.

106 "It was on January": Thomas O'Neill, 11/18/70.

106 The financier was ubiquitous: *Esquire*, August 1971, Robert Alan Arthur article.

107 "I had a brief": Fred Dutton, 6/17/69.

107 James Burns had: Burns, op. cit., p. 269.

107 As evocative: *Manchester Union Leader*, November 20, 1969.

108 This is a vision: William Honan, 12/13/69

109 "Do you want a man": *Esquire*, April 1962, Thomas B. Morgan article.

109 Kennedy himself once played out: Edward M. Kennedy, 12/12/69.

111 That afternoon: Theodore H. White, *The Making of the President*, 1960, p. 57.

111 In front of fifteen: *Time*, October 12, 1959.

111 After a post-graduation deferred: *Esquire*, April 1962, Thomas B. Morgan article.

111 "Ted doesn't have exactly": William Honan, 12/13/69.

112 Lumps, streaks: *Teddy, Keeper of the Kennedy Flame* (Macfadden–Bartell Publications), p. 39.

112 "I went to the top": *Redbook*, June 1962; Lasky, *Robert F. Kennedy: The Myth and the Man*, p. 131.

113 March is a lion: White, op. cit., pp. 80–96 ff.

113 Bob Healy: Robert Healy, 5/6/69.

114 "I had gone to school in the East": Edward M. Kennedy, 12/12/69.

115 In Arizona: White, op. cit., p. 143.

115 "There were situations": Edward M. Kennedy, 12/12/69.

116 Throughout the months: White, op. cit., p. 146; Sorensen, Kennedy, p. 160.

116 By far the most absorbing: Evelyn Lincoln, *Kennedy and Johnson*, p. 88.

117 Revisiting the suite: Schlesinger, op. cit., pp. 57, 58.

117 As the convention played through: John McCormack, 12/10/69.

117 From behind the scenes: Edward McCormack, 5/14/69.

118 "Don't worry, Jack": Schlesinger, op. cit., p. 58.

118 That critical Wednesday: White, op. cit., p. 169; Sorensen, Kennedy, p. 183.

118 "We held a review": Edward M. Kennedy, 12/12/69.

118 Edward Kennedy came out of: *Esquire*, April 1962, Thomas B. Morgan article.

119 Some losses were closer: Sorensen, Kennedy, p. 220.

119 What seemed most disappointing: White, op. cit., p. 363.

119 The publisher of: Sorensen, Kennedy, p. 220.

119 Football star and Rhodes: Lasky, *Robert F. Kennedy: The Myth and the Man*, p. 150.

120 Worried, John Kennedy: Sorensen, Kennedy, p. 220.

120 "He had a public relations": William Evans, 6/3/69.

121 "Can I come back": Private source; *Redbook*, June 1962.

121 "Here, too, Ted": George Lodge, 2/19/70.

121 Even the society columnists: *Esquire*, April 1962, Thomas B. Morgan article.

121 It becomes quite evident: *Ladies' Home Journal*, October 1962.

122 "The president used": *Look*, February 26, 1963.

122 There is that oceanic afternoon: *Ladies' Home Journal*, October 1962.

122 There is a naivete: *Redbook*, June 1962.

123 Somebody who was a child: William Honan, 12/13/69.

123 Joan Bennett had married: *Teddy, Keeper of the Kennedy Flame* (Macfadden–Bartell Publications), p. 22.

124 "When I started spending": *Redbook*, June 1962.

124 Joan Kennedy is the sweetest: *Playboy*, June 1969, Gore Vidal interview.

125 "The disadvantage of my position": *Ladies' Home Journal*, October 1962.

125 "We've been married four": *Look*, February 26, 1963.

125 But when the Ambassador: Fay, op. cit., p. 10.

125 "Rose Kennedy is a string saver": *Ladies' Home Journal*, October 1962.

125 "I like to go glamorous at night": *Look*, February 26, 1963.

125 "His main reason": *Redbook*, June 1962, p. 73.

126 Country lawyering: Edward M. Kennedy, 12/12/69.

126 He could have gone: *Ladies' Home Journal*, October 1962; *Redbook*, June 1962.

126 "Nobody forced me to run": Edward M. Kennedy, 12/12/67.

127 "Listen, if you want": Charles Tretter, 6/11/69; also Lester David, *Good Ted, Bad Ted*, p. 67, Edward M. Kennedy, *True Compass: A Memoir*, p. 170.

127 "My father's logic": Edward M. Kennedy, 12/12/69.

127 Furcolo's final term: *Saturday Evening Post*, June 5, 1965, Edward Sheehan article; Damore, op. cit., p. 232.

127 The jostling got serious: Foster Furcolo, 3/18/69.

128 Meanwhile, Ted Kennedy: *Esquire*, April 1962, Thomas B. Morgan article.

128 "He happened to be looking": Ibid.

128 "He's going to run for something": Charles Tretter, 6/11/69; *Esquire*, April 1962, Thomas B. Morgan article.

128 The president calls: Ibid.

129 Al Hutton: Al Hutton, 2/19/70.

129 "I enjoyed the work": Edward J. Kennedy, 12/12/69.

130   As Ted's intention clarified: *Esquire*, April 1962, Thomas B. Morgan article;
      Betty Taymor, 3/18/69.

131   Crimmins, a bachelor: Milton Gwirtzman, Joseph Gargan, et al., 6/17/69.

132   "I knew he was running": John Crimmins, 2/20/70.

132   "You have to know": *Esquire*, April 1962, Thomas B. Morgan article.

132   An extended tour: Murray B. Levin, *Kennedy Campaigning*, pp. 55, 166.

132   He marketed the: *Esquire*, April 1962, Thomas B. Morgan article.

133   Another trip: Levin, op. cit., pp. 11, 12.

133   One companion was: Robert Healy, 5/6/69.

133   The Ambassador, queried: *Esquire*, April 1962, Thomas B. Morgan article.

133   The watchful father: Whalen, op. cit., p. 474.

133   When Ted won: Edward M. Kennedy, *True Compass: A Memoir*, p. 158.

133   "From 1952 on": Thomas O'Neill, 11/18/70.

134   "I think": Edward McCormack, 5/14/69.

134   "Frank was very helpful": Edward M. Kennedy, 12/12/69.

134   "This man knows what": Gerard Doherty, 3/18/69.

134   It turned out: Whalen, op. cit., p. 479.

135   "You can see": Edward M. Kennedy, 12/12/67.

135   "Nobody could possibly": Murray Levin, 12/20/70.

135   "The Kennedys run solo": Maurice Donahue, 12/19/70.

136   "[I]t was sporting": *Time*, March 30, 1962.

136   *The Washington Post*, Ibid.

136   *The New York Times*, Ibid.

136   Advisers well positioned: *Life*, January 15, 1965, Robert Ajemian article.

136   Robert was opposed: Clark Clifford, cited in *The Boston Globe*, May 19, 1971.

137   "I came back to the Boston": Robert Healy, 5/6/69.

137   "I entered Harvard": Levin, op. cit., pp. 13, 14.

138   "Hi, glad to see you": Betty Taymor, 3/18/69.

139   "They were having": Charles Tretter, 6/11/69.

139   "I never held it against": Edward M. Kennedy, 12/12/67.

139   "Reckless . . . childishly": Levin, op. cit., p. 21.

139   When academics: Samuel Beer, 12/18/67; 3/8/69.

139   "Well, you know": Robert Wood, 5/12/69.

140   "I want you to meet": Edward McLaughlin, 4/17/69.

140   The president and the Speaker: John McCormack, 12/10/69.

140   There was talk that: *Saturday Evening Post*, June 5, 1965.

140   On paper: Levin, op. cit., pp. 15, 16.

141   Edward McCormack, who pitched: Edward McCormack, 5/14/69.

141   "Eddie McCormack and Mark": Robert Healy, 5/6/69.

142   "That's the way politics is": Private conversation, spring 1967, Eddie McCor-
      mack, 5/14/69.

142 There is a kind of quirky pride: *The American Scholar*, Autumn 1962, article by Benjamin DeMott.

142 By 1962: Edward McCormack, 5/14/69.

143 Massachusetts congressional: Thomas P. (Tip) O'Neill, 11/18/70.

144 A favorite opening: *The New Republic*, June 4, 1962, Paul Driscoll article.

144 One aide of the: James King, 5/12/69.

144 A holdout in the Nahant: *Newsweek*, June 18, 1962.

145 "All right": *The New Republic*, June 4, 1962, Paul Driscoll article.

145 There were gentler: William Evans, 6/3/69.

145 By now the unsleeping: *The Reporter*, July 5, 1962, Douglas Cater article.

145 "They're cold, they're cold": *Time*, June 15, 1962.

146 However irrepressible: Ibid.

146 "If his name was Edward": Stephen Smith, 6/3/69.

146 The Man in the White House: *The Reporter*, July 5, 1962, Douglas Cater article.

146 Regular contact: Milton Gwirtzman, 12/13/67.

146 "I was present": Murray Levin, 2/20/70.

147 "My concept of a liberal": *Redbook*, June 1962.

147 "He was a little callow": Samuel Beer, 3/8/69.

147 "Lay off": Edward McLaughlin, 4/17/69.

147 "I can't help it, Teddy": *The Reporter*, July 5, 1962, Douglas Cater article.

148 "I was the first": Stuart Hughes, 2/19/70.

148 "His people": Andrew Vitali, 4/2/69.

149 The intriguing melange: Levin, op. cit., p. 130.

149 "He had a magnificent": Ibid., p. 137.

149 Steve Smith—who moved: Stephen Smith, 6/3/69.

149 Hyman, had always: Lester Hyman, 4/11/69.

149 "What sticks in my mind": Edward Martin, 5/5/69.

150 "If you want my vote": Edward M. Kennedy, 12/12/67.

150 "For Christ's sake": Lawrence Laughlin, 5/5/69.

150 "I remember one fine": Charles Tretter, 6/11/69.

151 "I figured": Gerard Doherty, 3/18/69.

151 Before the primary: Betty Taymor, 3/18/69.

151 "In Massachusetts": Gerard Doherty, 3/18/69.

151 "Ted Kennedy doesn't": Milton Gwirtzman, 4/4/69.

152 All over Basic: Andrew Vitali, 4/12/69.

152 "You are going": Boston political operative.

152 Addressing one: *Newsweek*, June 18, 1962.

152 "Fitzy beat Lodge": *Saturday Evening Post*, October 27, 1962.

152 McCormack had hoped: *The Reporter*, June 5, 1962, Douglas Cater article.

153 "Have no fee–uh,": Milton Gwirtzman, 12/13/67.

153 Purportedly to alert: Milton Gwirtzman, 12/13/67.

153   "How are things in Brockton": Robert Healy, 3/6/69.

153   "Now listen": Fay, op. cit., p. 244.

154   McCormack's advisers: Levin, op. cit., pp. 189, 190.

157   Edward Kennedy was by now: James King, 5/12/69.

158   "You just didn't attack": Andrew Vitali, 4/1/69.

158   "Ted told me once": Charles Tretter, 6/11/69.

159   "The guys around the White": Kennedy aide.

159   There was another debate: Levin, op. cit., p. 232.

159   For six more weeks: George Lodge, 2/19/70.

159   "George was a very": Stephen Smith, 6/3/69.

159   "If Father had": George Lodge, 2/19/70.

159   When somebody in the Lodge: Edward Martin, 5/5/69.

160   "Ted ran a perfect campaign": George Lodge, 2/19/70.

160   The vote on November: Levin, op. cit., p. 232.

Chapter V: The Senate

161   The November 22: William Manchester, *The Death of a President*, p. 197.

161   Arriving at the dais: "The Torch is Passed" (Associated Press), p. 20.

162   By the time: Manchester, op. cit., p. 198.

163   Afraid, apparently: Ibid., p. 372.

163   "There's been a bad accident": Ibid., pp. 500–502.

164   To pick the quotes and citations, Ibid., p. 549.

164   George Thomas, a Kennedy: Ibid., p. 576.

166   He took his place: William Smith White, *Citadel*, pp. 20, 2L, 69.

166   "You . . . don't . . . you just": An old congressional hand.

167   "I think Teddy Kennedy's": Milton Gwirtzman, 12/13/67.

167   "This used to be Bobby": Edward M. Kennedy, 12/12/69.

167   "Ted, Ted": Charles Tretter, 6/11/69.

168   The Kennedys were realists: Robert Sherrill, *Gothic Politics in the Deep South*, p. 210.

168   When irate Southern: Fred Dutton, 6/17/69.

169   "Tell your brother": Sherrill, op. cit., p. 195.

169   "I don't agree with Senator": Birch Bayh, 6/16/69.

169   "I appreciate the wisdom": *Newsweek*, January 21, 1963.

170   Even before 1962: *U.S. News and World Report*, December 31, 1962.

170   What Kennedy was doing: *Time*, January 4, 1963.

171   "One characteristic of Ted's": John Culver, 6/18/69.

171   "Charlie and Bill": Kennedy aide.

171   "A lot of the time": longtime Kennedy aide.

171   "He's got one of those": Gerard Doherty, 3/18/69.

171   "He likes to break": Ibid.

172 "Teddy is very good": Ibid.

172 Gerry Doherty: Ibid.

173 The luck was: Walter Bashista, 6/1/69.

173 Edward Kennedy himself: *Time*, June 26, 1964.

174 The excitement that summer: *Saturday Evening Post*, June 5, 1965.

174 Peabody went out handshaking: Lawrence Laughlin, 5/5/69.

175 And all this was working: Betty Taymor, 3/18/69.

175 Hogan had planned: Barnes airport officials, 6/1/69.

175 The five of them: Birch Bayh, 6/16/69.

175 Kennedy himself: Arthur Egan, 3/26/70.

176 "Let's give the pilot": *Ladies' Home Journal*, September 1968.

176 Control 1: Barnes airport records, 6/1/69.

176 The Civil Aeronautics: CAB documents, Docket 2–0058, 1964.

177 Marvella Bayh: Birch Bayh, 6/16/69.

177 People were already: Members of the Bashista family, 6/1/69.

178 There were voices demanding: Arthur Egan, 3/26/70.

178 Arrival at a hospital: *Holyoke Transcript*, June 28, 1965, Michael McCartney article.

178 For eighteen hours: *Good Housekeeping*, April 1965.

179 The first person: Peter Barnes, 12/11/67.

179 When Joan found: *McCall's*, February 1965.

179 Among Ted Kennedy's: William Vanden Heuvel, 11/20/70.

179 "The Kennedys intend": *McCall's*, February, 1965.

180 Edward himself seemed detached: Kennedy associate.

180 "Is it ever going to end": *Good Housekeeping*, April 1965.

180 George Lodge: George Lodge, 2/19/70.

180 The Massachusetts Organization: Lawrence Laughlin, 5/5/69.

180 It made for punishing days: *Good Housekeeping*, September 1969.

180 "Joan's sense of humor": *McCall's*, February 1965.

181 "Chahhr–lee": Charles Tretter, 6/11/69.

181 There was a girlishness: Gerard Doherty, 3/18/69.

181 "You didn't win": James King, 5/12/69.

181 On November 3: *Teddy, Keeper of the Kennedy Flame* (Macfadden–Bartell Publications), p. 58.

181 A fellow female: Betty Taymor, 3/18/69.

181 Another remembers noticing: Fellow delegate.

181 Unable to put it away: Longtime Kennedy associate.

182 "I'm improving": *Good Housekeeping*, September 1969.

182 "I don't do": Ibid.

182 Joan's drop-in lunches: Edward M. Kennedy, 3/15/70; *Good Housekeeping*, April 1965, William Shannon article.

182   Every three hours: *Good Housekeeping*, September 1969.

183   At one point: William Vanden Heuvel and Milton Gwirtzman, *On His Own: Robert F. Kennedy*, 1964–68, p. 64.

183   In October of 1963: Charles Tretter, 6/11/69.

183   "Senator, how's my campaign": *Good Housekeeping*, April 1965, William Shannon article.

183   "In my nearly fifty years": Edward M. Kennedy, *True Compass: A Memoir*, p. 501.

183   The father: Whalen, op. cit., pp. 480, 481.

183   Ted himself was willing: *Good Housekeeping*, April 1965, William Shannon article.

184   Actually, as the Cooley: *Holyoke Transcript*, June 25, 1965, Michael McCartney article.

184   The lump of gristle: Edward Martin, 5/5/69.

184   By early December: *Good Housekeeping*, April 1965, William Shannon article.

184   Noticing this: Longtime Kennedy follower.

184   One day not long: Edward Martin, 5/5/69.

184   Angelique Voutselas: Angelique Voutselas, 4/1/69.

185   Ted did manage: E. M. Kennedy, *The Fruitful Bough*.

185   But, on the emphatic: Robert Wood, 5/12/69.

185   Kenneth Galbraith: *Life*, January 15, 1965, Robert Ajemian article.

185   "I would lie there": *Good Housekeeping*, April 1965, William Shannon article.

186   "In my judgment": Robert Wood, 5/12/69.

186   "I'm not of the opinion": Birch Bayh, 6/16/69.

186   Well before the accident: Samuel Beer, 3/8/69.

187   "I had a lot of time": *Good Housekeeping*, April 1965, William Shannon article.

187   On December 16: Edward Martin, 5/5/69.

Chapter VI: Teddy and Bob—Part One

188   Late in his recuperation: William V. Shannon, *The Heir Apparent*, p. 75.

189   "Well before I": Dun Gifford, 6/12/70.

189   "Whenever Ted": Charles Tretter, 6/11/69; Jerry Marsh, 6/16/70.

189   "I'd sleep nights": Old reportorial hand.

190   There comes to mind: Charles Guggenheim film on Robert F. Kennedy (1964 Democratic Convention).

190   John Kennedy much loved: Kirk Lemoyne Billings, 6/3/69.

191   "You going to come": Peter Edelman, 4/4/69.

191   The "advisers," meanwhile: Vanden Heuvel and Gwirtzman, op. cit., pp. 11 ff.

192   The days when Kenny and Larry: De Toledano, op. cit., p. 165.

192   "Which way do I drive": *Life*, January 15, 1965, Robert Ajemian article.

192   Reporters in the press gallery: Saul Friedman, 3/16/70.

192   Respect for Ted Kennedy's: *Life*, January 15, 1965, Robert Ajemian article.

193   Kenneth Keating: De Toledano, op. cit., pp. 307, 308.

193 "Is this the way I": Vanden Heuvel and Gwirtzman, op. cit., p. 54.

193 "There was a certain competitiveness": John Culver, 6/18/60.

193 "Once Bobby": Kennedy aide.

193 What rubs there were: David Burke, 12/13/67.

194 Worried enough: James Doyle, 12/14/67.

194 The financier had always: E. M. Kennedy, op. cit., Edward M. Kennedy section, p. 204.

194 Whereas John: Shannon, *The Heir Apparent*, p. 86.

195 "If you ask him about": David Burke, 12/13/67.

195 Careful to keep close: *Congressional Record*, 1963, Index.

196 The mandate of the: Jerry Marsh, 6/16/70.

197 Rose Kennedy debated: Rose Kennedy, telephone conversation notes, September 29, 1969.

197 The last book John: David Burke, 12/13/67.

197 Kennedy regarded immigration: Edward M. Kennedy, 12/12/67.

198 A few of the exchanges: *Look*, July 13, 1965, Joseph Roddy article.

198 Ervin's main complaint: Hearings before the Subcommittee on Immigration and Naturalization, Committee on the Judiciary, U.S. Senate on S:500, To Amend the Immigration and Nationality Act, February 10, 24, 25; March 1, 3, 4, 5, 1965—all Robert F. Kennedy quotes March 4, 1965, pp. 227, 237, 248, 249.

200 U.S. Government Printing Offices: *Newsweek*, January 17, 1966.

201 The voting-rights struggle: *The Reporter*, December 15, 1966, Meg Greenfield article.

201 He posed the frame: Eric F. Goldman, *The Tragedy of Lyndon Johnson*, p. 310.

202 Johnson convened: Ibid., p. 319.

202 The goad here: Peter Edelman, 4/4/69.

202 Dirksen demanded and got: *Newsweek*, May 24, 1965, Kenneth Crawford article.

202 This revolutionary legislation: Goldman, op. cit., p. 323.

204 All this came later: David Burke, 12/13/67.

204 "He subjected the": 1965 Voting Rights Act hearings before the Judiciary Committee, March 30, 1965.

204 Why must: Ibid., March 25, 1965, p. 176.

204 Why is there: Ibid., p. 176.

205 How did the administration: Ibid., pp. 294, 295.

205 Judge Leander Perez, Ibid., p. 562.

205 "A fine young Jewish": Ibid., p. 563.

205 He pushes the evasive: Ibid., p. 177.

205 When A. Ross Eckler: Ibid., p. 591.

205 Why not, Kennedy proposes: Ibid., pp. 596, 597, 598.

206 Senator Tydings: Ibid., p. 660.

206 "He was sitting at the table": David Burke, 12/13/67.

206 Kennedy's amendment to: *Congressional Record*, August 13, 1965, p. 7882.

207 Kennedy argued powerfully: *Look*, July 13, 1965, Joseph Roddy article.

207 The administration and: Ibid.

207 This lacked Edward: *Congressional Record*, April 13, 1965.

207 "One day he asked": David Burke, 12/13/67.

207 His office telephone lines: *Time*, May 21, 1965; *Newsweek*, January 17, 1966.

207 With moderates or borderline Southerners: *The Reporter*, December 15, 1966, Meg Greenfield article.

208 He reportedly gave Hubert: *Look*, July 13, 1965, Joseph Roddy article.

208 One member of the: Andrew Vitali, 4/1/69.

208 By then Edward: *Time*, May 21, 1965.

208 Mike Mansfield handled: Senate aide.

209 It came in the middle: *Time*, May 21, 1965.

209 "Frank had a great desire": Edward M. Kennedy, 12/12/69.

209 As early as 1961: Hearing before a Subcommittee of the Committee on the Judiciary, U.S. Senate, October 12, 1965, on the Nomination of Francis X. Morrissey to be a United States District Judge for the District of Massachusetts.

209 Robert Meserve: Ibid., p. 71.

209 As Albert Jenner: Ibid., pp. 52, 53.

210 "There had been": Robert Healy, 6/10/69.

211 The legal establishment: *Time*, October 29, 1965.

211 Coleman, an urbane: Sherrill, op. cit., p. 177.

211 Jim Coleman, of course: Judiciary Committee Hearings on the Nomination of James P. Coleman, July 12, 1965, p. 4, 128–136, 162, 163.

212 That, or something: *The Reporter*, December 15, 1966, Meg Greenfield article.

212 One off-the-record comment: Kennedy aide.

212 Another aide: Charles Tretter, 6/11/69.

213 More fearful day by day: Edward M. Kennedy, 12/12/69.

213 The ineffable: Vanden Heuvel and Gwirtzman, op. cit., jacket copy.

213 Others, like Al Novac: Al Novak, 4/4/69.

213 "Morrissey's crime was": David Burke, 12/13/67.

214 Jim Doyle: *The Boston Globe*, October 12, 1965.

214 Edward Kennedy delivered: Morrissey hearings, op. cit., pp. 2–8, 10, 12, 13, 14–21, 36.

216 Jenner had just referred: Morrissey hearings, op. cit., p. 57, 65, 66, 94, 99–106.

218 It had been an unconscionably: *The Boston Globe*, October 14, 1965.

218 Prodded, Morrissey admitted: Ibid., October 20, 1965.

219 Francis X. Morrissey was: Ibid., October 14, 1965.

219 Bob Healy, back home: Robert Healy, 5/5/69.

219 "You ran in 1934": *The Boston Globe*, October, 18, 1965.

220 He now checked closely: Ibid., October 15, 1965.
220 The bedridden: Ibid., October 16, 1965.
220 By this time: Ibid., October 14, 1965.
220 Kennedy, who had not: Al Novak, 4/4/69.
221 That embattled formal report: *The Boston Globe*, October 19, 1965.
221 "Probably no judicial": Ibid., October 20, 1965.
221 A "veteran Boston politician": Ibid., October 20, 1965, David Wise's column.
221 Hubert Humphrey attempted: Ibid., October 21, 1965, James Doyle.
222 The Kennedys' own: *Newsweek*, January 17, 1966.
222 And now, inevitably: *The Boston Globe*, October 20, 1965.
222 Having answered a 1:30: Ibid., October 21, 1965.
222 The large, very visible: *The Washington Post*, October 15, 1965.
222 Representative H.R. Gross: *The Boston Globe*, October 21, 1965.
222 Dirksen had earlier: Ibid., October 20, 1965.
222 "I'm not interested": Ibid., October 22, 1965.
222 One of the things: Kennedy associate.
222 "At the same time": *The Boston Globe*, October 22, 1965.
223 Just before he withdrew: *Congressional Record*, October 21, 1965, p. 27936.
223 Kennedy saved what face: *The Boston Globe*, October 27, 1965.
223 "It takes something": *Time*, October 29, 1965.
223 "For Christ's sake": Charles Tretter, 6/11/69.
224 When Kennedy got back: David Burke, 3/13/67.

Chapter VII: Teddy and Bob—Part Two

225 "As a sailor": Longtime Kennedy associate.
226 In McLean he authorizes: Klein, *Edward Kennedy*, p. 64.
226 From the beginning: *Ladies' Home Journal*, July 1970, Betty Hoffman article.
226 "Apart from the weakness": Edward Kennedy, *True Compass: A Memoir*, p. 183.
227 "He expressed his appreciation": *Good Housekeeping*, September 1969, Barbara Kevles article.
227 "I cherish": *Ladies' Home Journal*, July 1970, Betty Hoffman article.
227 "Now we know our good": *Ladies' Home Journal*, July 1970, Betty Hoffman article.
228 "He spends a great deal": Life, July 17, 1970, Rose Kennedy interview.
228 "Isn't there another": Kennedy associate.
228 "I'm his worst critic": *Good Housekeeping*, September 1969, Barbara Kevles article.
228 "You know you look": Sylvia Wright, 7/25/69.
229 Milt Gwirtzman: Milton Gwirtzman, 4/4/69.
229 "President Kennedy had a bound": Edward M. Kennedy, 12/12/69.
230 David Burke worries: David Burke, 12/13/67.
232 "He's never flown a jet": David Burke, 3/12/67.

232 "What happened": Andrew Vitali, 4/1/69.

233 We, all the staff guys: David Burke, 3/12/67.

234 "He was forever getting": Gerard Doherty, 3/18/69.

234 Ted preferred to: Milton Gwirtzman, 12/13/67.

235 As a onetime draftee: Edward M. Kennedy, 12/12/67.

235 "Right, yeah": Andrew Vitali, 4/1/69.

236 Ten minutes later: Dun Gifford, 4/1/69.

237 "Then—nobody knows": Dun Gifford, 1/22/69.

238 Flug tends: James Flug, 2/11/67.

239 It was a pounceable: Dun Gifford, 12/14/67.

240 One version of Celler's: *Congressional Quarterly Almanac*, 1967, p. 551, 553, 555.

240 A black politician: *The New York Times*, June 12, 1967, John Herbers article.

240 "Senator, you've just got": James Flug, 12/11/67.

240 The Judiciary Committee: *Congressional Quarterly Almanac*, 1967, p. 554.

241 The most infectious of the arguments: *Congressional Record*, May 25, 1967.

241 After Kennedy's May 25 speech: Ibid., June 6, 1967, p. 14784.

241 Flug and the rest: James Flug, 12/11/67.

243 One quiet breakthrough: Laing, op. cit., p. 287; Vanden Heuvel and Gwirtzman, op. cit., p. 93.

243 Typical was Kennedy's proposal: Dun Gifford, 12/14/67.

244 Kennedy fell back on his reserves: Dun Gifford, 12/14/67.

244 Russell had long before: *Congressional Record*, June 14, 1967, p. 15757; Ibid., June 14, 1967, p. 15772.

245 "It happened that": James Doyle, 4/3/69.

247 Edward Kennedy had put himself: *The Reporter*, December 15, 1966, Meg Greenfield article.

247 "Throughout the Johnson": Robert Wood, 5/12/69.

248 "He had his muscle": Duff Reed, 12/13/67.

248 "There are little things": Thruston Morton, 12/13/67.

248 The astute Meg: *The Reporter*, December 15, 1966, Meg Greenfield article.

248 "I realized only later": Peter Edelman, 4/4/69.

248 "I'd rather see him in": Joseph Dolan, 12/14/67.

249 "RFK started out": Peter Edelman, 4/4/69.

249 There were possibilities: Ibid.

249 "I'm not leaving": Dick Schaap, *R.F.K.*, p. 33.

249 A hesitation reflecting: Peter Edelman, 4/4/69.

250 Robert was never one: Dun Gifford, 12/14/67.

250 His trips to Poland: Vanden Heuvel and Gwirtzman, op. cit., pp. 236, 237.

250 Helping out other Democrats: Dun Gifford, 12/14/67.

250 A reporter recalls motorcades: Meg Greenfield, 12/12/67.

252 I got back briefly: *Congressional Record*, December 13, 1967, pp. 36181 ff.

253 "Move in for the kill": *Time*, December 1, 1967.

Chapter VIII: Cannonball

254 "Robert regarded his younger": Vanden Heuvel and Gwirtzman, op. cit., p. 189.

255 "I remember when I": Fred Dutton, 6/17/69.

255 On tour with: Peter Edelman, 4/4/69.

256 "After he got back": Melody Miller, 4/1/69.

257 Once a prominent hawk, Bob: Schaap, op. cit., p. 17.

258 Beginning with the October: Sorensen, *The Kennedy Legacy*, p. 125.

258 The wisdom: Ibid., p. 127.

259 "There were three or four": Edward M. Kennedy, 12/1/70.

259 "Teddy doesn't think": William Vanden Heuvel, 11/20/70.

259 "You know it's his instinct": Richard Goodwin, 11/30/70.

259 Fred Dutton, whose: Fred Dutton, 11/17/70.

260 Ted Kennedy's reservations: Lewis Chester, Godfrey Hodgson and Bruce Page, *An American Melodrama: The Presidential Campaign of 1968*, p. 115.

260 "Teddy didn't believe": Dun Gifford, 6/12/70.

261 Jimmy Flug, who would be left: 10/5/09.

262 "Bobby's therapy": *The New York Times Magazine*, June 2, 1968, Victor Navasky article.

262 "I don't believe": Duff Reed, 12/13/67.

262 "No one in Washington": Sorensen, *The Kennedy Legacy*, p. 129; Chester, Hodgson, and Page, op. cit., p. 74.

263 In 1964, in a watershed: Vanden Heuvel and Gwirtzman, op. cit., footnote, p. 327; Saul Friedman, 3/16/70.

263 "Gene!": Lester Hyman, 11/17/70.

263 McCarthy wandered up: Vanden Heuvel and Gwirtzman, op. cit., footnote, p. 327.

263 "I'm not a great Kennedy": Eugene McCarthy, 6/17/69.

263 In November of 1967: Lester Hyman, 11/17/70.

265 Whenever he could lure: Ibid., 4/11/69.

265 The breakaway point: Ibid., 11/17/70.

265 Ted Kennedy's own feelings: Witcover, op. cit., p. 39; Peter Barnes, 12/11/67.

266 By the time: Chester, Hodgson and Page, op. cit., p. 83.

266 Bob Kennedy assured: Sorensen, *The Kennedy Legacy*, pp. 127, 139.

266 At the beginning of December: Chester, Hodgson, and Page, op. cit., p. 83; Lester Hyman, 11/17/70.

266 On Friday: Chester, Hodgson and Page, op. cit., p. 119; Robert Kennedy lieutenant.

266 When Bob, who: Arthur Schlesinger, Jr., 11/20/70.

267 First Ted, then Bob: Richard Goodwin, 11/30/70.

267 "I wish there was somebody": Richard Goodwin, 11/30/70; William Vanden Heuvel, 11/20/70.

267 "How do you think": Witcover, op. cit., p. 68.

268   The New Hampshire: Witcover, op. cit., p. 64.

268   Lyndon Johnson himself: Chester, Hodgson, and Page, op. cit., p. 121.

268   Ted called Clifford: Witcover, op. cit., pp. 76–78.

268   "I think Teddy thought": Fred Dutton, 11/17/70.

268   Bobby's transparent: Chester, Hodgson, and Page, op. cit., p. 124.

268   The night of March 15: Richard Goodwin, 11/30/70.

269   A group of: William Vanden Heuvel, 11/20/70.

269   At breakfast: Arthur Schlesinger Jr., 11/20/70.

269   "At stake is": Chester, Hodgson, and Page, op. cit., p. 125.

269   Sorensen is frank about: Sorensen, *The Kennedy Legacy*, pp. 140, 150.

270   "Let's see": Witcover, op. cit., p. 75.

270   Lester Hyman remembers: Lester Hyman, 4/11/69.

270   "We're thinking of Indiana": Chester, Hodgson, and Page, op. cit., pp. 161, 162.; Gerald Doherty, 12/1/70.

271   "I'm sure I was the only": Witcover, op. cit., p. 137; Fred Dutton, 11/17/70.

271   The candidate presumptive: Fred Dutton, 11/17/70.

272   Whatever tentative: Witcover, op. cit., p. 128.

272   Vanden Heuvel, who was with: Vanden Heuvel and Gwirtzman, op. cit., p. 333.

272   The morning after: Chester, Hodgson, and Page, op. cit., p. 160.

272   Senator Birch: Gerard Doherty, 12/1/70.

273   The week before: Witcover, op. cit., p. 123.

273   West Virginia was well: Sorensen, Kennedy, p. 141; De Toledano, op. cit., pp. 153, 154, 155.

273   "When the Indiana guys": Gerard Doherty, 12/1/70.

273   "The Kennedys are": Arthur Schlesinger Jr., 11/20/70.

273   "The Indiana primary": James Doyle, 4/3/69.

274   "There had been": David Burke, 6/16/69.

274   "There were certain people": Gerard Doherty, 3/18/69; 12/1/70.

274   "I told Bobby a long": Richard Goodwin, 10/30/70.

275   This barbered version: Witcover, op. cit., pp. 138, 155–157.

276   Robert Kennedy was: Theodore H. White, *The Making of the President*, 1968, pp. 200, 201.

276   When the votes were: Vanden Heuvel and Gwirtzman, op. cit., footnote, p. 348.

276   On April 4, long: Witcover, op. cit., pp. 171, 177.

276   His responses: Ibid., pp. 142–146.

277   Good Bobby howled: Ibid., p. 169.

277   "I didn't relate to Robert": Gerard Doherty, 12/1/70.

277   "And, through the whole thing": Gerard Doherty, 12/1/70.

278   "Bob went into that thing": Fred Dutton, 11/17/70.

278   "You mean I got more": James Doyle, 4/3/69.

278 "Election night I got a call": Gerard Doherty, 3/18/69.

279 But the days were over: A Washington reporter.

279 "I'm coming out for Bobby": Lester Hyman, 4/11/69.

279 "I think I blew it": Vanden Heuvel and Gwirtzman, op. cit., p. 304.

280 There was a spattering of: David Burke, 6/16/69, Vanden Heuvel and Gwirtz-man, op. cit., p. 362.

280 "If it were you, Teddy": Wayne Owens, 11/17/70.

281 Delegations like that of: Vanden Heuvel and Gwirtzman, op. cit., pp. 362, 335.

281 The critical benevolence: Chester, Hodgson, and Page, op. cit., pp. 316, 317.

282 "It seemed to me": David Burke, 6/16/69.

282 "The major question was": Edward M. Kennedy, 12/1/70.

282 "I don't like that": Lester Hyman, 11/17/70.

282 The Michigan delegate: Vanden Heuvel and Gwirtzman, op. cit., appendix.

283 "We had a very difficult time": Edward M. Kennedy, 2/1/70.

283 Depending on this: Vanden Heuvel and Gwirtzman, op. cit., p. 362.

283 On April 19: Chester, Hodgson, and Page, op. cit., pp. 153, 548.

283 On April 1: Witcover, op. cit., p. 134.

283 "We went to their": Edward M. Kennedy, 12/1/70.

283 Kenny O'Donnell: Vanden Heuvel and Gwirtzman, op. cit., p. 317.

284 "Those were unusual": Joseph Gargan, 3/27/70.

284 Holed up in a Harrisburg: Dun Gifford, 8/6/70.

284 The day after: Vanden Heuvel and Gwirtzman, op. cit., p. 363.

285 "The beginning of the campaign": Arthur Schlesinger Jr., 11/20/70.

285 Instead of showing: Witcover, op. cit., p. 185.

285 Former Lieutenant: Ibid., p. 197.

285 The sustaining explanations: Ibid., pp. 202, 209.

285 At home in Oregon: Chester, Hodgson, and Page, op. cit., p. 300.

285 The demographic: Witcover, op. cit., p. 100.

286 Only by daring always: Chester, Hodgson, and Page, op. cit., p. 304.

286 "Who was running": Dun Gifford, 6/12/70.

286 The polls looked: Vandel Heuvel and Gwirtzman, op. cit., pp. 365–367.

286 Mrs. Green: Witcover, op. cit., p. 201.

286 For all the belated: Witcover, op. cit., p. 216.

287 Teddy, who: William Vanden Heuvel, 11/20/70.

287 "We hit Oregon": David Burke, 6/16/69.

287 Somebody Jack Trusted: Witcover, op. cit., p. 219.

288 The Park Avenue: Chester, Hodgson, and Page, op. cit., pp. 318–326.

289 At the same time: Ibid., pp. 336, 337.

289 California had rigid: Ibid., pp. 317–339.

289 Reports of what: David Burke: 6/16/69.

289 Three days after: Vanden Heuvel and Gwirtzman, op. cit., p. 379.

290   "My brother": Witcover, op. cit., p. 306.

291   Sometimes, pressured: Chester, Hodgson, and Page, op. cit., p. 344.

291   "Why did they do": Longtime close Kennedy friend.

Chapter IX: Two Summers

292   While Robert Kennedy: David Burke, 6/16/69; Witcover, op. cit., p. 277.

292   "I can't let go": Dun Gifford, 6/12/70.

292   "I'm going to show": Edward M. Kennedy confidant.

292   He held on to himself: Witcover, op. cit., p. 308.

293   So that Edward: *Newsweek*, August 5, 1968; Kennedy associate.

293   With Joe cut off: Richard Goodwin, 11/30/70.

293   "When we were boys": Joseph Gargan, 5/14/69.

294   Joe Kennedy wept: *Ladies' Home Journal*, February 1971, Rita Dallas article.

294   Ted made sure: Chester, Hodgson, and Page, op. cit., pp. 565 ff.

294   It became a summer: *Newsweek*, April 5, 1968; Joseph Gargan, 5/14/69.

295   "It's inaccurate": Kennedy social acquaintance.

295   "He was a basket": Kennedy family acquaintance.

296   That part even Joe: Joseph Gargan, 5/14/69.

296   The kind of fun: Fred Dutton, 6/17/69.

296   Without Bobby there: *Life*, November 1, 1968, Paul O'Neil article.

297   "What was unspoken": Edward M. Kennedy, *True Compass: A Memoir*, p. 422.

298   As early as the Rackets Committee: Thomas Gerber, 7/7/69.

299   The threat from Nixon: *Newsweek*, August 5, 1968.

299   At the urging: Joseph Gargan, 3/27/70.

300   The idea of such: *Ladies' Home Journal*, March 1971, Rita Dallas article.

300   "We had lunch": William Vanden Heuvel, 11/20/70.

301   "They'll say he was off": *Newsweek*, August 5, 1968.

301   Kennedy in absentia: Chester, Hodgson and Page, op. cit., pp. 566, 567.

302   It had been Bob: Ibid., p. 351; Richard Goodwin, 11/30/70.

302   Then, on August: Chester, Hodgson and Page, op. cit., p. 567; *Newsweek*, September 2, 1968.

303   "When I started": David Burke, 11/30/70.

303   "He seemed fine": David Burke, 6/16/69.

303   August had already: White, *The Making of the President*, 1968, pp. 325, 326.

304   Humphrey had jarred: Chester, Hodgson and Page, op. cit., pp. 556–557.

305   As if the peace-plank: White, *The Making of the President*, 1968, pp. 339–343.

305   Humphrey was well aware: *Newsweek*, August 5, 1968.

305   Then, disconcertingly: Chester, Hodgson, and Page, op. cit., pp. 570, 571.

306   The Edward Kennedy candidacy: Ibid., p. 563; White, *The Making of the President*, 1968, p. 331.

307   "It all started really": Milton Gwirtzman, 6/17/69.

307   Smith went: Chester, Hodgson, and Page, op. cit., pp. 569, 570.

307   That is: Stephen Smith, 4/19/71.

307   As early as he: Chester, Hodgson, and Page, op. cit., p. 569.

308   "I was at the Conrad": Fred Dutton, 11/17/70.

308   "Steve was extremely": Lester Hyman, 4/11/69.

309   Twelve hundred: *Look*, March 4, 1969, Warren Rogers article; Stephen Smith, 4/19/71; *Look*, August 10, 1971, Warren Rogers article.

309   Intentions were serious: David Hackett, 4/21/71.

309   "There's a big movement": *Newsweek*, September 9, 1968.

309   "He was extremely wary": Fred Dutton, 11/17/70.

309   There were 2, 622: Vanden Heuvel and Gwirtzman, op. cit., appendix, p. 391.

309   A "genuine draft": *Newsweek*, September 9, 1968.

310   Coy Gene appears: Chester, Hodgson, and Page, op. cit., pp. 570–575; Stephen Smith, 4/19/71.

311   "Teddy had the best": Eugene McCarthy, 6/17/69.

311   Even the disgruntled: White, *The Making of the President*, 1968, p. 332; *Newsweek*, September 9, 1968.

312   "I didn't call it": *The Boston Globe Magazine*, May 4, 1969, Richard Stewart article; Edward Kennedy, 12/1/70.

313   Doves like: George Wilson, summer 1970.

313   Lyndon Johnson: White *The Making of the President*, 1968, p. 332.

313   "The delegates": Arthur Schlesinger Jr., 11/20/70.

313   "On the one hand": Edward M. Kennedy, 12/1/70.

314   "We're going to have to climb": William Vanden Heuvel, 11/20/70.

314   "I found it especially difficult": David Burke, 4/19/71.

314   "This was Bobby's year": Chester, Hodgson and Page, op. cit., p. 575.

314   The Vietnam peace: William Vanden Heuvel, 11/20/70.

314   By now the convention: *Newsweek*, September 9, 1968.

314   "Teddy called me": Fred Dutton, 11/17/70.

315   "I think": Lester Hyman, 4/11/69.

315   On September 10: *The Boston Globe*, September 11, 1968.

316   Kennedy opened: Ibid., September 20, 1968.

316   A week could disappear: Thomas Cleveland, 10/21/69; *Look*, March 4, 1969, Warren Rogers article.

316   Grabbing the Assistant: *The New York Times Magazine*, February 23, 1969, William Honan article.

317   Long–whose demagogue: Drew Pearson and Jack Anderson, *The Case Against Congress*, pp. 144, 145 ff.

317   Among the more moderate: Wayne Owens, 11/17/70; *The New York Times*, February 23, 1969.

318   "At least Ted Kennedy": Southern colleague.

318   "Christmas was the first": *Newsweek*, January 13, 1969.

318   First responses sounded: *The Boston Globe*, January 3, 4, 6, 1969.

319 Mansfield, while prevented: Ibid., January 6, 1969, Evans and Novak column.

320 "There was no time": *Time*, January 10, 1969.

320 "Just as the Kennedys": Fred Dutton, 6/17/69.

320 By Thursday afternoon: *The Boston Herald-Traveler*, January 3, 1969.

321 "I don't know": *Time*, January 10, 1969.

321 McCarthy had refused: Eugene McCarthy, 6/17/69.

321 Weeks afterwards: *Look*, April 1, 1969, Joseph Roddy article.

321 Kennedy was actively promising: *Time*, January 10, 1969.

321 Question marks: Wayne Owens, 11/17/70.

322 "I had Kennedy outgunned": *The Boston Globe*, January 4, 1969.

322 Denied the austere: Ibid., January 6, 1969, Evans and Novak column.

322 "I do not": Ibid., January 4, 1969.

323 Staggered out: *The Reporter*, December 15, 1966, Meg Greenfield, et al.

323 "The [Whip] job": *The Boston Globe*, January 4, 1969.

323 "He felt that": Andrew Vitali, 4/2/69.

323 Interviewed a few weeks: *The New York Times*, February 23, 1969, William Honan article.

324 While disclaiming: *The Boston Globe*, January 4, 1969.

324 The Subcommittee Chairman: Pearson and Anderson, op. cit., p. 118.

324 Eastland—unwilling: James Flug, 6/17/69.

324 Then Kennedy began: Hearing before the Subcommittee on Administrative Practice and Procedure, Senate Judiciary Committee, S. RES. 39, March 27, 28, 1969.

325 "The Boss": David Burke, 6/16/69.

325 "As near as I can tell": Wayne Owens, 11/17/70.

325 It had been Kennedy's hope: David Burke, 6/16/69.

325 The generation of senior: *The New York Times Magazine*, February 23, 1969, William Honan article.

325 To help offset: Wayne Owens, 11/17/70.

326 "Teddy's got it locked up": *Newsweek*, March 17, 1969, Stewart Alsop article.

326 "At first": Ralph Yarborough, 6/17/69.

327 "He's far more decisive": David Burke, 6/16/69.

327 "He has a remarkable": *The New York Times Magazine*, February 23, 1969, William Honan article.

328 The showcase hearings: Equal Employment Opportunity Procedures Hearings, before the Subcommittee on Administrative Practice and Procedure, Senate Judiciary Committee, March 27, 28, 1969, pp. 14–24, 128, 146–148.

330 Kennedy's heretofore inflammatory: *Newsweek*, June 2, 1969, Stewart Alsop, et al.

330 He reactivated: James Flug, 1/23/69; *The New Yorker*, December 14, 1968, Richard Harris article.

330 Kennedy introduced a bill: *The Boston Globe*, February 19, 1969, March 6, et al.

331   The day the Senate: *The New Yorker*, December 14, 1968, Richard Harris article.

331   As that Republican spring: Richard Harris, *Justice: The Crisis of Law, Order, and Freedom in America*, p. 42.

332   Tapping and bugging were: Richard Harris, *The Fear of Crime*, p. 64; *The New Republic*, July 5, 1969; *The New Republic*, April 17, 1971, Nathan Lewin article.

332   On January 23: *The New York Review of Books*, October 22, 1970.

332   Mike Mansfield: Ibid., Herbert Packer article.

332   Perhaps it was his own sense: De Toledano, op. cit., pp. 220, 221.

333   "Do you know a lot": White, *The Making of the President*, 1968, footnote, p. 159.

333   After some heavy references: *The Washington Star*, June 18, 1969.

333   By that time Jim: James Flug, 6/17/69.

334   As recently as 1968: *The Boston Globe*, February 2, 1969.

334   Or was he really: Dun Gifford, 1/22/69.

335   On February 19: *The Boston Globe*, February 20, 1969.

336   Russell Long: Ibid., February 21, 1969.

336   Then, on March: Ibid., March 15, 1969.

336   The liberals, who "want you": David Burke, 6/16/69.

336   Insisting at the time: *The Boston Globe*, March 15, 1969.

337   He released his: *Newsweek*, May 12, 1969.

337   When headlines detailing: Ibid., March 24, 1969.

337   Vietnam was dragging on: Ibid., June 2, 1969.

337   "It hit everybody": David Burke, 6/16/69.

338   In mid-April: Ibid; *The Boston Globe*, April 11, 1969.

338   The touring: *Time*, April 18, 1969.

338   Alaska's own: Ibid.

339   As the strain tightened: *Life*, August 1, 1969.

339   "Look Look": Sylvia Wright, 7/26/69.

339   At Arctic Village: Brock Brower, 11/20/70.

339   "He started whackin'": Newsman.

340   John Lindsay, 4/22/71.

341   Ed Muskie, Newsman.

341   As early as 1963: Richard Goodwin, 11/30/70.

341   "I think he knew": Burke Marshall, 4/18/71

341   What many among: Robert Kennedy intimates.

343   "Do you know": Associated Press reporter.

343   "People criticize Jackie": *Ladies' Home Journal*, July 1970, Betty Hoffman article.

343   "No I have to wear this": Kennedy social acquaintance.

344   "If you get drunk": Kennedy affiliate.

344   "I think": Arthur Schlesinger, Jr., 11/20/70.

344   "In a sense": Richard Goodwin, 11/30/70.

346   Fixated on: Gerard Doherty, 12/1/70.

346   She traveled in his behalf: Charles Tretter, 4/15/70.

346   Writing over Robert Kennedy's: *McCall's*, September 1970, Mrs. Joseph Kopechne.

347   During the 1968 campaign: *Newsweek*, August 4, 1969.

347   What remains: Subsequent material drawn from informal conversation over successive two years with John Crimmins, Edward M. Kennedy, Charles Tretter, Joseph Gargan, Paul Markham, and several others. Many details drawn from January 5–8, 1970, inquest testimony.

347   "*Goddammit Jack*": My notebook, 13.

348   On Chappaquiddick: *Inquest into the Death of Mary Jo Kopechne*, Massachusetts, Edgartown, January 5–8, 1970, Five Volumes, Docket Number 15220, Volume III, p. 333.

348   By Thursday Ray: *Time*, September 5, 1969.

349   By July: Paul Markham, 12/1/70; *The Boston Globe*, July 22, 1969, et al.

350   "The girls that were there": Paul Markham, 12/1/70.

350   "I knew": Edward M. Kennedy, 12/1/70.

351   "The drill that night: David Hackett, 4/21/71.

351   Arriving on the island: Kennedy associate.

351   Jack was grumbling: Charles Tretter, 4/15/70.

351   Meanwhile Crimmins used: Inquest, Volume III, p. 338.

352   All afternoon Paul: Ibid., Volume II, pp. 287–289.

352   At eight-fifteen: Ibid., Volume II, pp. 214–216.

353   Gargan, already legendary: Charles Tretter, 4/15/70.

354   By shortly after eleven: Inquest, Volume II, p. 221.

354   Crimmins, not mollified: Ibid., Volume III, p. 347.

354   "As parties go": Edward M. Kennedy, 12/1/70.

355   By his own admission: Inquest, Volume I, pp. 38–39.

355   The emotion: Ibid., Volume I, p. 39.

355   The report of Kennedy's local: Ibid., Volume IV, exhibit 27.

356   Swept out and away: Ibid., Volume I, pp. 53–57.

356   ". . . better get Paul, too": Ibid., Volume I, pp. 57, 58.

356   "There was been a terrible": Ibid., Volume II, p. 298.

356   A lot of this trembles: Ibid., Volume II, pp. 226–231.

357   Kennedy himself, respectfully: Ibid., Volume I, pp. 35–38.

358   "The unsatisfactory thing": Kennedy associate.

358   A matter of weeks: Matthew Storin, 11/18/70.

358   Two bumpy minutes: Inquest, Volume IV, p. 595.

358   "I knew Mary Jo, yes": Edward M. Kennedy, 12/1/70.

359   "Senator Kennedy," Gargan: Inquest, Volume II, p. 237, 238.

359   Gargan and Markham: Ibid., Volume II, pp. 306, 307, 308, 241, 242.

360   Robert Kennedy, who: David Hackett, 4/21/71.

360 Driving to the ferry: Inquest, Volume I, pp. 63, 64.

362 "Our first concern": Stephen Smith, 4/19/71.

362 With that, as Gargan: Inquest, Volume II, p. 243.

362 "Pretend you weren't": Markham associate.

363 "I don't want you people": Inquest, Volume II, p. 327.

363 Not long before: Ibid., Volume IV, pp. 507, 498.

363 Charlie Tretter and Cricket: Charles Tretter, 4/15/70.

363 Speculation among: Inquest, Volume V, pp. 650, 656.

364 Markham, slumping: Ibid., Volume II, pp. 313–317.

364 Edward Kennedy slept: Ibid., Volume I, pp. 65, 67, 72.

365 Not long after the tragedy: Edward Kennedy, 12/12/69.

365 Several calls: Helga Wagner, 1/28/2010.

366 Five hours after: Ibid., Volume II, pp. 259–261.

367 There are circumstances: Ibid., Volume II, pp. 320–322.

367 At that moment: Charles Tretter, 4/15/70.

367 Steered now by Markham: Inquest, Volume II, p. 250.

368 Kennedy roughed: Ibid., Volume II, p. 324; Richard Drayne, 4/21/71.

368 By early evening: James Wieghart, 3/16/70.

368 By that time: Inquest, Volume IV, pp. 548, 560; John Farrar, Richard Hewitt, 7/26/69.

369 The episode: Charles Tretter, 4/15/70; Inquest, Volume II, p. 197.

369 The two played: Ibid., Volume IV, pp. 579, 580.

370 Reminded of that: The Boston Globe, July 20, 1969.

370 At a quarter to three: Inquest, Volume III, p. 487.

371 "The Boss drove": William Honan, 12/13/69.

371 "I sat there": Richard Drayne, 4/21/71.

371 The assassination: William Vanden Heuvel, 11/20/70.

372 Burke reached Dun: Dun Gifford, 6/12/70.

372 By the time Gifford: Inquest, Volume IV, pp. 515–519.

372 Even before Gifford: Ibid., Volume IV, pp. 521, 522.

372 By that time the newspaper: The Boston Globe, July 30, 1969.

372 Kennedy himself reportedly: Citizens' Voice, William Kashatus, July 19, 2009.

373 Edward Kennedy was subsequently: Inquest, Volume I, p. 73.

373 If, in his way, Marshall: The Boston Globe, July 22, 1969.

373 "I told him I'd": Burke Marshall, 4/18/71.

373 He had made his name: The Boston Globe, July 22, 1969.

373 "When I talked at first": Burke Marshall, 4/18/71.

375 Another avatar: Richard Goodwin, et al., 11/30/70.

375 "Never would have happened": Lyndon Johnson intimate.

375 "The week afterwards": Edward M. Kennedy, 12/1/70.

376 "By the time": Dun Gifford, 6/12/70.

376 By Tuesday: The Boston Globe, July 23, 1969.

376   Marshall, who: Burke Marshall, 4/18/71.

377   Goodwin left: *The New York Times*, July 27, 1969.

377   "Our prime concern": Stephen Smith, 4/19/71.

377   John Farrar: John Farrar, 7/26/69.

378   By midweek *Newsweek*: *Newsweek*, July 28, 1969.

378   *Newsweek* reporter: John Lindsay, 4/22/71.

378   He decided, against: *Boston Record American*, July 26, 1969.

379   Boyle, fatherly: *The Boston Globe*, July 25, 1969.

379   After securing: Burke Marshall, 4/18/71; Richard Drayne, 4/21/71.

379   "Who am I": Kennedy associate.

379   Dave Burke: Kennedy aide.

379   "Almost anything": Richard Goodwin, 11/30/70.

379   "Teddy needed some people": Gerard Doherty, 12/1/70.

380   As a device: *The Boston Globe*, July 26, 1969.

380   "He was like a baby": Sylvia Wright, 7/26/69.

380   He deleted most: Compare bound galleys, printed version of Sorensen, *The Kennedy Legacy*.

Chapter X: Human Size

381   "Come here": *The New York Times*, July 29, 1969; *The Boston Globe*, July 29, 31, 1969.

381   "Can you imagine": Kennedy confidant.

383   The anxiety, the sadness: David Burke, 4/10/69.

383   "He was the best": James Flug, 12/10/69.

383   Now, to whom: *Life*, October 3, 1969, Sylvia Wright article; *The Boston Globe*, September 13, 1969.

383   That helped give character: James Flug, 12/10/69.

384   "You must be pleased": Lester Hyman, 12/11/69.

384   On August 5: *The Boston Globe*, August 6, 1969.

384   Nevertheless, the Pentagon's: *The New York Times*, August 10, 1969.

385   Amending when the: *Congressional Record*, October 13, 1969, S 12351; *Congressional Record*, September 29, 1969, S 9471; *The Boston Globe*, January 24, 1970.

385   Wary as ever: *Congressional Record*, October 1, 1969, S 11713.

385   After bearing down: *The Boston Globe*, September 30, 1969.

385   Very skeptical: Ibid., November 9, 1969.

385   "The D.C. Crime Bill": James Flug, 12/10/69.

386   While losing: *Congressional Record*, January 22, 1970, S 417.

386   After that initial: *The Boston Globe*, August 8, 1969.

387   In 1962: *Newsweek*, August 25, 1969; Massachusetts Democratic leader.

388   "The press kept giving": Edmund Dinis, 4/23/71.

388   Whatever hope the Edgartown: *The Boston Globe*, July 23, 24, 1969.

388   Everything seemed withheld: *Boston Record American*, July 25, 1969.

388 "This is just an automobile case": *Newsweek*, September 8, 1969.

388 The word was already: *The Boston Globe*, July 23, 1969; *Boston Record American*, August 1, 1969.

388 On July 31 his office: *The New York Times*, August 3, 1969; *Boston Record American*, August 7, 1969.

389 Cornered publicly: *The Concord Monitor*, August 20, 1969.

389 By ordering up: Edmund Dinis, 4/23/71.

389 This could be more: Damore, op. cit., p. 40.

389 Judge James Boyle: *The Boston Globe*, August 6, 1969.

389 Therefore, there was to be: *Time*, September 5, 1969; *The New York Times*, August 3, 1969.

389 So lawyers wrangled: *Boston Record American*, September 3, 1969.

390 The advisers congratulated themselves: *The Boston Globe*, August 23, 1969; *Newsweek*, September 1, 1969.

390 Kennedy personally had argued: *The Boston Globe*, September 4, 1969; *Boston Record American*, September 2, 1969.

390 On October 20–21: *The Boston Globe*, October 31, 1969; Leslie Leland, 7/24/71.

390 An assortment of experts: *Boston Record American*, October 22, 1969.

390 The Massachusetts police chemist: John McHugh, 7/27/31.

390 Dinis himself testified: *Boston Herald-Traveler*, October 22, 1969.

390 An assortment of townspeople: *The Boston Globe*, April 7, 8, 1970; 3/27/70

390 After two days: *Boston Record American*, April 7, 1970; Inquest, Judge James Boyle's summation, p. 12.

391 "That was the hook": Edmund Dinis, 4/23/71

391 In fact, whenever counseling Leland's: Private source.

391 There were a number of discrepancies: *The Concord Monitor*, May 29, 1970.

391 Such skeptical reporters as: Arthur Egan, my notebook, 19; *Manchester Union Leader*, "Egan's Many Probes," August 13, 1969, January 7, 8, 9, 10, 1970, June 11, 1970; *The Concord Monitor*, April 2, May 29, 1970.

392 Hanify himself had: Massachusetts court records, 342 Mass. 119, 1961; Al Hutton, my August 17, 1971, interview.

392 "She died and I got": Edmund Dinis, 4/23/71.

392 "The core of his extended: Edward M. Kennedy, *True Compass: A Memoir*, p. 293

393 "Wouldn't it be possible": Winthrop House Forum, Harvard University, my notebook, 18.

393 The abashedness: Roger Woodworth, 6/17/69

394 After an autumn of exchanges: *The Boston Globe*, December 17, 1969.

395 Having proposed to rip: James Flug, Joseph Onek, et al., 11/18/70

395 As if Russell Long: *Congressional Record*, December 8, 1969, S 16099, 16101.

395 Kennedy's popularity among: James Flug, Joseph Onek, 11/18/70.

395 This was the sort: *Congressional Record*, February 10, 1970, S 1638.

397 Aware of Kennedy's: Carey Parker, et al., 11/18/70.

398 The House voted the Senate: *Congressional Record*, June 17, 1970, H 5679.

398 Nixon, with an unhappy: *The Boston Globe*, June 23, 1970.

399 Getting involved in: James Flug, 11/18/70.

400 The strategy that recommended: *Time*, April 20, 1970.

400 Between January 27: *Newsweek*, March 16, 1970; *The New Yorker*, December 5, 1970, Richard Harris article.

400 Carswell had himself: Hearings before the Committee on the Judiciary, U.S. Senate, on the nomination of George Harrold Carswell, January 27, 28, 29, February 2, 3, 1970.

400 Griffin, broke in: Ibid., p. 28.

401 "No fair, I will not let": James Flug, 11/18/70.

401 Marian Wright Edelman: James Flug, 11/18/70; *The New Yorker*, December 5, 1970, Richard Harris article.

403 That winter of 1970: *The New York Times Magazine*, May 24, 1970, William Honan article.

403 Other times: Ibid., p. 75.

403 Would the traumas: Ibid., p. 27.

403 Kennedy's most profound: "Lecture by Edward Kennedy before the College Historical Society Bicentenary," Trinity College, Dublin, Ireland, March 3, 1970.

403 "I worked weeks": Edward M. Kennedy, 3/15/70.

403 "At first glance": Trinity College lecture, op. cit., pp. 1–6.

405 "Each day in the nation's": *The Boston Globe*, June 13, 1970. Succeeding material drawn largely from my notebook for that day, 10/26/70.

412 "Nobody really knows": David Burke, 11/3/70.

412 Seasoned Kennedy organizers: *The Boston Globe*, October 24, 25, 1970, Matthew Storin article; Gerard Doherty, 12/1/70.

412 There was no mushroom: James Doyle, 1963 reports in *The Boston Globe*; Murray Levin treatment in *Kennedy Campaigning*.

413 "I just wrote my story": Privileged newsman.

413 Mr. Byrd: *Congressional Record*, November 16, 1970, S 18271.

414 "This has been going": *Newsweek*, February 1, 1970.

414 For Bobby Byrd: *The Boston Globe*, November 9, 15, December 30, 1970.

415 "I've thought about": *The New York Times Magazine*, May 24, 1970, William Honan article.

415 "It's still a": Wayne Owens, 4/20/71.

415 "You have that contract": 10/26/70.

416 When the president: *The Boston Globe*, November 4, 1970.

416 In Europe to attend: December 23, 1970; *Manchester Union Leader*, November 30, 1970.

416   It all looked: *The Boston Globe*, December 30, 1970, Evans and Novak column; Ibid., November 22, 1970, Robert Healy.

416   When Nixon took advantage: Ibid., December 27, 1970.

416   He hailed the December 21 Supereme Court acceptance: Ibid., December 22, 1970.

417   No opportunity: *Newsweek*, February 1, 1971.

417   Conversely, Kennedy assistants: Kennedy aide; *Congressional Record*, December 21, 1970, S 42959.

417   Kennedy remained: Wayne Owens, 4/20/71.

417   Nobody's umbrage: *Congressional Record*, December 30, 1970, S 44113; December 31, 1970, H 12578; *Newsweek*, November 23, 1970.

417   Meanwhile, Kennedy seemed to want: *The Boston Globe*, November 15, 1970.

417   "Much as he": Kennedy aide.

418   "It's subtle": James Flug, 11/18/70.

418   Stuart Symington: *The Boston Globe*, January 22, 1971.

418   "He's built it on courtesy": *The New Republic*, December 12, 1970, Paul Wieck article.

418   "Bob Byrd would do": *Newsweek*, February 1, 1971.

418   "[Kennedy] really": *The Boston Globe*, January 22, 1971.

419   The unforgiving Russell: Washington cognoscenti.

419   From his seat: *The New Republic*, December 12, 1970; *The Boston Globe*, November 12, 1970, Evans and Novak column.

419   "Ideologically, Bobby": *The New Republic*, December 12, 1970.

420   In November he startled: *Newsweek*, November 30, 1970; *The Boston Globe*, November 29, 1970.

420   Robert Byrd was forever: *The Boston Globe*, November 12, 1970, Evans and Novak column.

420   One minute Byrd was: *Congressional Record*, December 28, 1970, S 43691.

420   Above-ground, Kennedy: *The Boston Globe*, November 15, 24, 1970.

421   Furthermore, checking around: David Burke, 4/19/71.

421   Still, Dick Drayne remembers: Richard Drayne, 4/21/71.

421   Adlai Stevenson III: *The Boston Globe*, January 22, 1971.

421   Alaska's Mike Gravel: *The Boston Globe*, November 12, 25, 1970, Evans and Novak column.

422   Harrison Williams: Washington insider.

422   Kennedy was "rejected as Whip": *Look*, August 10, 1971, Warren Rogers article.

422   There is sound reason to believe: Southern senator.

422   Kennedy appears never to have: *The Boston Globe*, January 22, 1971.

423   "Once I pick the liberal": *The New Republic*, February 6, 1971.

423   "At least in Vietnam": Kennedy friend.

423   After venturing, with strained: *The Boston Globe*, January 2, 1971.

BOOK TWO: THE SHADOW PRESIDENT

Notes for the earlier version of The Shadow President *are limited; the text of this section has perhaps doubled, and contains a great deal of new material. There is much detail concerning Kennedy's private life that would have been inappropriate to include while he was still alive. I have now included details crucial to any final historical judgment. These range from Edward Kennedy's reversal on the abortion issue, to the dominant behind-the-scenes role he played during the Watergate proceedings that resulted in the destruction of the Nixon presidency, to his involvement in the peacemaking negotiations over Northern Ireland, to his hard-won Iraq vote and his previously unrevealed feud with George W. Bush after Bush sandbagged Kennedy subsequent to the passage of No Child Left Behind. Here, all are dealt with fully. The notes below reflect a text that has been radically revised and expanded and reorganized; I hope they at least suggest the amazing range of the sourcing involved.*

Between the Acts

427   Daniel Webster had staying power: *Encyclopedia Britannica.*

Chapter I: The Comeback

The background material for this chapter comes from standard newspaper sources and private interviews, many off the record.

429   Yet at the same time: *The New York Times*, Aug. 27, 2009.

435   The day Ted finally: Aide to Senator Hart, 12/14/67.

436   "This is quite a day on another front too!": J. Anthony Lucas, *Nightmare*, pp. 16, 17.

436   "You see this?": Edward Kennedy, 3/15/70.

437   "Even more than Jack or Bobby": Saul Friedman, March 16, 1970.

439   "Bobby never really wanted any": Mankiewicz papers, Kennedy Library, RFK Collection.

439   Typical was a grilling: FAA hearings, March 16, 1970.

440   "When I came down here to work for Kennedy": Feinberg, 9/12/78.

Chapter II: Finishing Nixon

443   Kennedy's blonde young: Melody Miller, 1/15/2010.

445   In 1971 he had: Catholic Action League news release, via Pharmacists for Life International website, pfli.org, Aug. 29, 2009.

446   "I recall the frustration": David Burke, 9/22/09.

447   "Rarely, I think": Christopher Matthews, *Kennedy and Nixon* p. 289; *Larry King Live* (rebroadcast of EMK interview), September 9, 2009.

447   From Kennedy's point of view: Matthews, op. cit., p. 512.

448   Days after George: Adam Clymer, *Edward M. Kennedy*, p. 191

448   Going through Kennedy's 2009: Flug, 10/5/09.

448   Once Arthur Bremer: *The Haldeman Diaries*, p. 318.

449 Kennedy's first real shot: Dita Beard IT&T material best reported in Matthews, op. cit.

449 Archibald Cox's astute aide: James Doyle, *Not Above the Law*, p. 50.

449 Kennedy brought Flug along,: Edward M. Kennedy, *True Compass: A Memoir*, p. 326.

449 Nixon, alarmed: Adam Clymer, op. cit., p. 191.

449 "Kennedy thought Kleindienst": Flug, op. cit.

451 The president, he announced: Matthews, op. cit., p. 300.

451 "Should this Kennedy mafia": Lucas, op. cit, p. 181.

452 "I know the people around": Carl Bernstein and Bob Woodward, *All the President's Men*, p. 374.

452 Robert Dole, reading: Matthews, op. cit., p. 319.

452 "White House tapes of": Kennedy, op. cit, p. 333.

452 "When Richardson was nominated": Flug, op. cit.

453 While Jackie: Gore Vidal, *Palimpsest*, p. 310.

454 He succeeded in presenting: Edward Kennedy, op. cit., p. 340.

454 Rick Burke, a stiff, pallid: Richard Burke, *The Senator*, p. 42.

455 How reckless things: Ibid, pp. 44, 87, 98.

456 One day I looked in: Edward Kennedy interview, early November 1973.

457 "The ACLU performed": Parker, November 1979.

462 "The senator would like": Bo Burlingham, *Esquire*, November, 19, 1975.

Chapter III: The Brass Ring

465 "I don't have to kiss his ass": *The Boston Globe*, May 28, 1978.

465 Kennedy brooded all spring: *The New Republic*, April 29, 1978.

466 The president was guilty: *The Boston Globe*, July 29, 1978.

467 "We went down there just to fire a shot across the bow": *Newsweek*, December 5, 1978.

467 "special aura of appreciation": Ibid.

468 "He was a major player": Jan Kalicki, November 1979.

468 "Whereas the United States": "Cranston/Kennedy Joint Resolution on Taiwan," February 1, 1979.

469 "The president . . . asked me the other day": *The Boston Globe*, February 18, 1978.

469 With time and politics: Edward Kennedy speeches at Grinnell, Iowa, November 13, 1979; Manchester, New Hampshire, November 21, 1979.

470 On May 2: *The Boston Globe*, May 3, 1979.

471 "various labor people were going around": John Durkin, November 1979.

471 "If I were to run, which I don't intend to": *Time*, June 25, 1979.

471 Virtually from the day: Richard Whalen, *The Founding Father*, p. 218.

471 "FDR . . . sent Joe Kennedy to London": Ted Morgan, *F.D.R.*, p. 497.

471 By 1940 Joe was divulging: Nigel Hamilton, *JFK*, p. 368.

473   By early spring: *The New York Times Magazine*, June 24, 1979.

474   Mudd set Kennedy up: Quotes from broadcast itself, also *The Boston Globe*, October 31 and November 6, 1979.

475   A Democratic National Committee straw poll: *The Boston Globe*, November 2, 7, 20, 1979.

476   "I look forward very, very enthusiastically": *The Boston Globe*, November 8, 1979.

476   "It was like, I want to be president": *The Boston Globe*, October 4, 1981.

477   "The Shah had the reins": *The Boston Globe*, December 3, 1979.

477   Shortly afterward Kennedy press spokesman: *The Boston Globe*, December 14, 1979.

477   "Ted Kennedy is the worst politician": Robert Shrum, 12/16/93.

478   Kennedy's polls slipped: *The Boston Globe*, January 13, 1980.

478   "Kennedy had been drafted": Carey Parker, 11/3/1993.

479   Smith declined to designate: *The New York Times*, May 18, 1980.

480   "More than anything else Steve": Shrum, op. cit.

480   By April: *The Boston Globe*, May 6, 1980.

481   "a loud plaid suit": *The Boston Globe*, May 29, 1980.

481   If Ted did win: *The New York Times*, February 24, 1980.

482   "One of the side effects": *The Boston Globe*, April 19, 1980.

483   "We had no budget whatsoever": James Flug, 11/29/93.

484   Kennedy's speech lifted: *The Boston Globe*, August 13, 1980.

Chapter IV: The Politics of Counterinsurgency

485   "Goddamn it": Shrum, op. cit.

486   "That's one thing about being Leader": *The Boston Globe*, August 1, 1986.

486   "I know what you guys are thinking": Tom Rollins, 12/1/93.

487   Although denied the chairmanship: For details of EMK's legislative initiatives, search "Accomplishments of Senator Kennedy 1962–2009" at realclearpolitics.com.

487   "After the '80 campaign": Edward Kennedy, 12/2/93.

487   On Labor and Human Resources: George Will, *The Boston Globe*, January 29, 1980.

488   Over his five decades: *The New York Times*, Adam Clymer, August 27, 2009.

489   "Tree ripe with the richest": *The Boston Globe*, July 17, August 14, September 25, 1981.

489   Aghast at the "jellybean economics": *The Boston Globe*, May 17, November 11, 1981.

489   "He doesn't steal credit": Raleigh (N.C.) *News & Observer*, November 17, 1987.

489   Kennedy was already criticizing: *The Boston Globe*, June 5, 1982.

490   "I've pulled Casey's nuts": Joseph Persico, *Casey*, pp. 373–75.

490 "You are a valuable member of the committee": *The Boston Globe*, July 8, 1984.

491 "Instead of cutting off food stamps": *The Boston Globe*, June 28, 1982.

491 "Some people have even written": *The Boston Globe*, October 18,1982.

491 "The decision that Joan and I have made": *The Boston Globe*, December 2, 1982.

491 "Jobs, a nuclear freeze": *The Boston Globe*, January 23, 1982.

491 "Much increased my effectiveness": Edward Kennedy, December 2, 1993.

493 "You know where he stands": *The Boston Globe*, November 16, 1984.

493 But Kennedy himself: Rick Atkinson, *The Washington Post Magazine*, April 29, 1990.

496 "C'mon Strom": Ibid.

496 Once Reagan was reelected: *The Boston Globe*, March 30, 1985.

496 "Congress is not only part of": *The Boston Globe*, October 11, 1985.

496 "You know, I liked you a lot": *The* Boston *Globe*, April 14, 1985.

496 "I admire him so much": *The Boston Globe*, February 20, 1982.

497 Nine of the eleven: *New York Post*, January 5,1987.

497 "When we took the Senate back": Rollins, op. cit.

497 "If you want to find Ted Kennedy": *The Washington Post Magazine*, April 29, 1990.

498 "Compounded out of equal parts emotion": Dick Day, 12/2/93.

498 "They had totally opposite senses of humor": Jerry Tinker, 11/30/93.

500 "Energetic, focused, and relentless": Jeff Blattner, 11/29/93.

501 When Daniel Ortega came: Greg Craig, 12/1/93.

502 "The feel-good invasion": *The Boston Globe*, January 24, 1990.

503 "I had always been somewhat reluctant": Edward Kennedy, 12/2/93.

504 "My brothers had a relationship": Ibid.

505 Yet at the same time: *The Boston Globe*, March 28,1990.

Chapter V: Bush I

506 "Will murder you": Michael Kelly, *GQ*, February 1990.

506 "You can talk to Ted": *The Boston Globe*, July 16,1989.

506 "Holds office but doesn't know what to do with it": *The Boston Globe*, March 7, 1989.

506 Two years later the 101st Congress: See John Broder, *The New York Times*, Aug. 28, 2009.

507 "Major themes of the Clinton campaign": Nick Littlefield, 11/30/93.

507 "Many of the liveliest stories": See heavy tabloid coverage. For example, *National Enquirer*, April 14,1992.

508 The news break in Damore's book: *The Boston Globe*, January 24, 1988.

508 "Substantive, fortyish women": *Newsweek*, December 9, 1991, etc.

508 Throughout much of the seventies: Helga Wagner, 1/28/2010.

509 "I went out there thinking": Shrum, op. cit.

510 Ted Kennedy reportedly cut off John Culver: Evan Thomas, *Newsweek*, December 9, 1991.

510 "You can bring anyone, or anything": Tinker, op. cit.

511 The two were close enough: Edward Kennedy, 12/2/93.

511 Mourners at Steve's funeral: Melody Miller, 1/15/10.

512 "And we were visiting in the patio after dinner": *The Boston Globe*, December 7, 1991.

512 "Many large parties": John Ney, *Palm Beach*, p. 28.

513 Kennedy's personal income in 1972: Richard Burke, *The Senator: My Ten Years With Ted Kennedy*, p. 60, also Edward Klein, op. cit., p. 180.

514 "Noticed both Patrick": *The Boston Globe*, December 7, 1991.

514 "Was not the first night that week": John Aloysius Farrell, April 30, 1994.

514 "A Eurotrash kind of place": *The Boston Globe*, April 4, 1991.

515 Patrick—who overcame: *The Boston Globe*, December 10, 1991.

515 "What a comedown!": *The Concord Monitor*, July 27, 1988.

515 "He's my life": *The Boston Globe*, April 10, 1991.

515 "Patrick looked like he was having a terrible time": *The Boston Globe*, May 15, 1991.

516 "Big families and scuba diving": *The Boston Globe*, April 7, 1991.

517 "Does your father embarrass you?" *The Boston Globe*, April 6, 1996.

517 "Pulled out": *The Boston Globe*, May 15,1991.

517 Originally Bowman ostensibly asserted: *The Boston Globe*, September 13, 17, 1991.

517 A number of objets d'art: *The Boston Globe*, April 17, May 11, 1991.

517 Nevertheless, the family did not waste time: *The Boston Globe*, April 3, 4, 1991.

518 "What I didn't anticipate": Farrell, op. cit.

518 "Kennedy stated that he was simply enjoying": *The Boston Globe*, April 9,1991.

519 The following July: *The Boston Globe*, August 2, 3,1991.

519 "Palm Beach boozer": *Time*, April 29,1991.

519 "The living symbol": *Newsweek*, December 9,1991.

520 "Have to be a little more attentive": *The Boston Globe*, June 9, 1991.

520 "Disagreement with Ted": *The Boston Globe*, October 18,1991.

521 "In my family and among my friends": *The Boston Globe*, October 7, 1993.

521 "I recognize my own shortcomings": *The Boston Globe*, October 26, 1991.

521 Touching on a litany: Edward Kennedy, 12/12/94; Barbara Gibson, op. cit., p. 73.

522 "You can have a serious": Edward Kennedy, op. cit., p. 40.

523 "Are we an old boys' club?": *The Boston Globe*, October 16, 1991.

523 "The vanishing views": *The Boston Globe*, September 13,1991.

524 "In hindsight": Jeff Blattner, 11/29/93.

524   "Even during the rape trial": David Nexon, 11/30/93.
525   Victoria Reggie was frank: See background profiles in *The Boston Globe*, April 2 and September 27, 1992, and September 24, 1993; *People* magazine, March 30, 1992.
526   "She's smart": Peter Edelman, 11/28/93.
526   "We saw each other": Victoria Kennedy, 12/2/93.
527   Victoria usually cooked: *The Washington Post*, March 20, 1992.
527   With reelection in 1994 coming up: *The Boston Globe*, September 13, 28, 1993.
528   In a short biography: Klein, op. cit., pp. 167, 168.

Chapter VI: Back From the Dead

529   "Don't really have a relationship": *The Boston Globe*, December 8, 1992.
530   "Invitation to drive the epidemic underground": *The Boston Globe*, September 22, 1987.
530   "Your private sector role": *The Boston Globe*, April 28, 1992.
531   "The senator decided early on": David Nexon, op. cit.
531   "Every effort to bring the American people together": *The Boston Globe*, June 20, 1993.
532   He worked a complicated: Pamela Barnes, *The Boston Globe*, September 9, 1993.
532   When Clinton returned to Boston: *The Boston Globe*, October 30, 1993.
533   By then it hadn't gone unnoticed: *The Concord Monitor*, May 9, 1994.
533   A *Boston Globe* poll that spring: *The Boston Globe*, March 12, 1993.
534   "The fun goes out of it": *The Boston Globe*, August 3, 1986.
534   The senator cranked a window down: Paul Donovan, 11/30/93.
534   By October of 1993: *The Boston Globe*, October 6, 1993.
535   Only 38 percent felt that he merited: *The Boston Globe*, May 14, 1994.
535   "My God, what weather!": Edward Kennedy, June 20, 1994.
538   "Strategy has always been to raise plenty of money early": Milton Gwirtzman, 4/1/94.
538   "If people believe the answer": *The Boston Globe*, June 22, 1994. Many of the details and statistical material throughout this 1994 senatorial election were gathered by the outstanding political reporters of *The Boston Globe*. In general, only major features or controversial details will be attributed.
539   "Learn-fare": *The Boston Globe*, June 17, 1994.
539   "One of my two potential opponents": *The Boston Globe*, June 18, 1994.
539   In early July: *The Boston Globe*, July 3, 1994.
539   "Looked good, spoke well": *The Boston Globe*, July 12, 1994.
539   "Full flounder": *The Boston Globe*, July 23, 24, 1994.
540   "Raw Meat Department": *The Boston Globe*, June 8, 14, 1994.
541   "Many companies now have wellness programs": Edward Kennedy, op. cit.
542   "I'm sure there have been a lot of things": *The Boston Globe*, June 3, 1996.

542 Not to mention the $150,000: *The Boston Globe*, October 11, 1994.

542 "Teddy, you do it": *The Boston Globe*, May 24, 1996.

542 "This has been a tragedy": *The Boston Globe*, July 19, 1996.

543 "Just an old career pol": *The Boston Globe*, June 2,1994.

543 Retain Monroe Inker: *The Boston Globe*, September 9,1994.

543 A reputable poll: *The Boston Globe*, September 17,1994.

543 The campaign's fire-eating press aide: *The Boston Globe*, September 21,1994.

543 "Not an issue, and it shouldn't be": *The Boston Globe*, May 22, 1994.

543 Orlando de Sola: *The Boston Globe*, August 8, 1994.

543 All that wasn't easy: *The Boston Globe*, September 7, 1994.

543 A local Catholic spokesman: Ibid.

544 "Perverse and reprehensible": *The Boston Globe*, July 15, August 7, 1994.

544 Near the end of August: *The Boston Globe*, August 26, 1994.

544 "$50 million trust fund:" *The Boston Globe*, June 18,1994.

544 "He will intentionally try": *The Boston Globe*, September 28, 1994.

544 "We got together and we changed": Robert Shrum, 3/27/96.

545 "I mean, the balanced budget amendment": *The Boston Globe*, July 7, 1994.

546 Sally Jacobs was trailing Kennedy: *The Boston Globe*, June 2, 1994.

546 "I feel you might, ah": Edward Kennedy, op. cit.

546 "Vicki agrees with me": Edward Kennedy letter to Burton Hersh, July 6, 1994.

546 As advertising bills piled up: *The Boston Globe*, October 22, 1994.

546 Kennedy's lawyers now reached: *The Boston Globe*, September 29, November 10, 1994.

547 "Multiple-choice": *The Boston Globe*, September 22,1994.

547 Here was a man: *The Boston Globe*, October 20, 1994.

548 "Just another robber baron": *The Boston Globe*, September 23, 1994; *The Boston Globe*, September 30, 1994.

549 "We'd run the spots": Shrum, op. cit.

549 "I'd love to help": *The Boston Globe*, October 10, 1994.

549 A remote investment of the Joseph P. Kennedy enterprises: *The Boston Globe*, October 24, 25, 1994.

549 "Patently ridiculous": *The Boston Globe*, October 29, 1994.

549 Kennedy's willingness during the previous year: *The Boston Globe*, November 4, 1994.

549 "Flip-flop-flip . . .": *The Boston Globe*, October 21,1994.

550 "A tongue-tied blowzy": *The Boston Globe*, October 31,1994.

550 "The entire national press corps": Shrum, op. cit.

550 "Why is this race even close": Most of this material comes from the videotapes of the two debates.

553 Within hours of the Tuesday debate: *The Boston Globe*, October 26, 1994.

554 "Mr. Romney," Kennedy himself announced: *The Boston Globe*, October 31, 1994.

Chapter VII: While the Dust Settled

555 "I think it was a surprise": Carey Parker, 3/26,96.

556 "I remember one meeting in 1980": Shrum, op. cit.

558 Kennedy's payroll numbered fifty-eight: Lloyd Grove, *The Washington Post*, July 9, 1996.

558 "It seemed like virtually the consistent figure": Adam Clymer, *The New York Times*, August 11, 1996.

559 "I don't think Senator Kennedy has ever": Nick Littlefield, March 26, 1996.

559 He put together a quorum: *The Boston Globe*, May 14, 1995.

559 "Built around lavish tax cuts that primarily benefit the wealthy": *The Boston Globe*, July 5, 1995.

561 "That's in the briefing sheet": *The Washington Post* , op. cit.

561 The effort was afoot: *The Boston Globe*, September 21, 1995.

561 "This is one cookie jar": *The Boston Globe*, October 28, 1995.

561 By April of 1996 eight: *The Boston Globe*, April 26, 1996.

563 "Socialized medicine by the back door": *The Boston Globe*, April 20, 1996.

563 "For him to pick up the pieces like that": John Aloysius Farrell, March 26, 1996.

564 Six weeks later: *The Boston Globe*, April 28, 30, 1996; May 6, 1996.

564 Richard Viguerie: *The Boston Globe*, April 26, 1996.

565 "Carrying her own clubs": *The Boston Globe*, January 23,1995.

566 The shy and rather reflective Patrick: Most of the material here comes from Joshua Seftel's 1996 cinéma vérité film *Taking On the Kennedys*.

566 He developed a reputation for persistence and integrity: *The Boston Globe*, June 19,1995.

567 He proceeded to Washington: *The Boston Globe*, November 10, 1994. Also see *The New York Times*, May 6, 16, 2006; *The Boston Globe*, June 19, 1995.

567 By then Kennedy's delaying tactics with the health bill: *The New York Times*, August 4, 1996.

568 Kennedy allies like Steve Early: *The Boston Globe*, November 21, 1994.

570 "They don't want to do it because they basically": *The Boston Globe*, July 9, 1996, part of a three-part series on corporate welfare.

571 Congress remained trapped in partisan deadlock: *The Boston Globe*, May 19, 1996.

571 He shamed the majority: *The Washington Post*, op. cit.

573 Shrum took charge: 3/27/96.

573 There were bruised feelings: *The Boston Globe*, Aug, 27, 2009.

575 In 1997 Kennedy and Orrin Hatch: *USA Today*, Aug. 27, 2009.

575 One project: EMK, op. cit. pp. 354, 464: Robert Healy, 9/15/09.

Chapter VIII: Endgame

578 "I thought since downsizing is in": *The Boston Globe*, May 11, 1996.

578 Trapped on an elevator recently: *The Washington Post* , op. cit.

581 "Well, I'm on": *Larry King Live*, Sept. 9, 2009 (rebroadcast).

582 "As for his original stance": David Burke, 9/22/2009.

583 "They were going to be": Ibid.

583 By 2008: *The Washington Post*, Jan. 7, 2008.

583 Badly piqued: ABC News, Feb. 1, 2008.

584 He had recently attempted: Edward M. Kennedy and David Small, *My Senator and Me: A Dog's Eye View of Washington, D.C.*, 2006.

584 Despite the booming voice: *USA Today*, John Fritze, Aug. 27, 2009.

584 The trade-offs: *History Commons*, May 9, 2007.

585 "A consummate deal-maker": *USA Today*, editorial, Aug. 27, 2009.

585 According to *The New York Times*: *New York Times*, Apr. 12, 2006.

585 As late as: *The Washington Post*, David Broder, Aug. 21, 2009; *The New York Times*, July 29, 2008.

587 Kennedy was still stable: *USA Today*, Aug. 26, 2008.

587 He continued to convene: *The New Republic*, Jonathan Cohn, June 10, 2010.

588 "It read, 'Dear Mr. Kennedy,'": Victoria Kennedy, op. cit.

589 Dick Day: Dick Day, op. cit.

BIBLIOGRAPHY

The following presumes in no way to constitute a true survey of the already monumental Kennedy bibliography; it represents, in fact, barely a sizable fraction of my own reading. It is largely an effort to identify the books this text draws upon particularly; a few additional have slipped in sideways, because they seem—to me, at least—to bear especially strongly on my own thinking throughout these slow years of preparation and drafting. For a wider–ranging selection of sources pertaining to Edward Kennedy and his family see the bibliography of my book Bobby and J. Edgar *(New York: Carroll and Graf, 2007).*

Acheson, Dean. *Present at the Creation.* New York: W. W. Norton & Company, Inc., 1969.

Adler, Bill. *The Robert F. Kennedy Wit.* New York: Berkley Publishing Corporation, 1968 (paperback original).

Adler, Bill, ed. *A New Day: Robert F. Kennedy.* New York: The New American Library, 1968 (paperback original).

Alsop, Stewart. *The Center.* New York: Popular Library, 1968 (by arrangement with Harper & Row, Publishers, Inc.).

Amory, Cleveland. *Who Killed Society?* New York: Harper & Brothers, Publishers, 1960.

Bernstein, Carl, and Woodward, Bob. *All the President's Men.* New York: Simon and Schuster, 1974.

Bryan, Walter. *The Improbable Irish.* New York: Ace Books, Inc., 1969.

Buck, Pearl S. *The Kennedy Women.* New York: Cowles Book Company, Inc. 1970.

Burke, Richard. *The Senator.* New York: St. Martin's Press, 1992.

Burns, James MacGregor. *John Kennedy: A Political Profile.* New York: Harcourt, Brace and Company, 1959.

Burns, James MacGregor. *Edward Kennedy and The Camelot Legacy.* New York: W.W. Norton, 1976.

Canellos, Peter S., ed. *Last Lion.* New York: Simon and Schuster, 2009.

Chayes, Abram, and Wiesner, Jerome B., eds. *ABM: An Evaluation of the Decision to Deploy an Antiballistic Missile System.* New York: The New American Library, Inc., 1969 (reprint of hardcover edition published by Harper & Row, Publishers, Inc.).

Chester, Lewis; Hodgson, Godfrey; and Page, Bruce. *An American Melodrama: The Presidential Campaign of 1968*. New York: The Viking Press, 1969.

Clymer, Adam. *Edward M. Kennedy*. New York: William Morrow, 1999.

Collier, Peter, and Horowitz, David. *The Kennedys*. New York: Summit Books, 1984.

Crown, James Tracy, and Penty, George P. *Kennedy in Power*. New York: Ballantine Books, 1961 (paperback original).

Cutler, John Henry. *"Honey Fitz": Three Steps to the White House*. Indianapolis and New York: The Bobbs-Merrill Company, Inc., 1962.

Damore, Leo. *The Cape Cod Years of John Fitzgerald Kennedy*. Englewood Cliffs, N.J.: Prentice-Hall, Inc., 1967.

Davis, John. *The Kennedys*. New York: McGraw-Hill, 1984.

De Toledano, Ralph. *R.F.K.: The Man Who Would Be President*. New York: G. P. Putnam's Sons, 1967.

Dinneen, Joseph F. *The Kennedy Family*. Boston and Toronto: Little, Brown & Company, 1959.

Doyle, James. *Not Above the Law*. New York: William Morrow, 1977.

Exner, Judith. *My Story*. New York: Grove Press Paperback, 1977.

Fay, Paul B., Jr. *The Pleasure of His Company*. New York: Harper & Row, Publishers, Inc., 1966.

Frady, Marshall. *Wallace*. Cleveland and New York: The World Publishing Company, 1968.

Gershenson, Alvin H. *Kennedy and Big Business*. Beverly Hills: Book Company of America, 1964 (paperback original).

Gibson, Barbara. *Rose Kennedy and Her Family*. New York, Birch Lane Press, 1995.

Goldman, Eric F. *The Tragedy of Lyndon Johnson*. New York: Alfred A. Knopf, Inc., 1969.

Goodwin, Doris Kearns. *The Fitzgeralds and The Kennedys*. New York: Simon and Schuster, 1987.

Goodwin, Richard. *Remembering America*. Boston: Little Brown, 1988.

Halberstam, David. *The Making of a Quagmire*. New York: Random House, 1965.

Halberstam, David. *The Unfinished Odyssey of Robert Kennedy*. New York: Random House, 1968.

Haldeman, H. R. *The Haldeman Diaries*. New York: G. P. Putnam's Sons, 1994.

Hamilton, Nigel. *JFK, Restless Youth*. New York: Random House, 1992

Handlin, Oscar. *Boston's Immigrants*. Cambridge, Mass.: Harvard University Press, 1941.

Harris, Richard. *The Fear of Crime*. New York: Frederick A. Praeger, Publishers, 1969 (paperback original).

Harris, Richard. *Justice: The Crisis of Law, Order, and Freedom in America*. New York: E. P. Dutton & Company, Inc., 1970.

Ickes, Harold L. *The First Thousand Days*. New York: Simon & Schuster, Inc., 1953.

Ickes, Harold L. *The Lowering Clouds*. New York: Simon & Schuster, Inc., 1954.

Inquest into the death of Mary Jo Kopechne, Massachusetts, Edgartown, January 5–8, 1970, Five Volumes, Docket No. 15220.

Ions, Edmund. *The Politics of John F. Kennedy*. New York: Barnes & Noble, 1967.

Kennan, George. *Memoirs*. Boston: Atlantic-Little, Brown, 1967.

Kennedy, Edward M. *Decisions for a Decade*. New York: The New American Library, 1968 (reprinted by arrangement with Doubleday & Company, Inc.).

Kennedy, Edward M. *True Compass: A Memoir*. New York: Twelve/Hachette Book Group, 2009.

Kennedy, Edward M., ed. *The Fruitful Bough*. Halliday Lithograph Corporation, printed in the U.S.A., 1965.

Kennedy, John F. *Profiles in Courage*. New York: Harper & Row, Publishers, 1955 (reprinted by arrangement with Harper & Brothers).

Kennedy, Robert F. *Apostle of Change*. New York: Simon & Schuster, Inc., 1968 (reprinted by arrangement with Harper & Row, Publishers).

Kennedy, Robert F. *The Enemy Within*. New York: Harper & Brothers Publishers, 1960.

Kennedy, Robert F. *To Seek a Newer World*. New York: Bantam Books, 1968 (reprinted by arrangement with Doubleday & Co., Inc.).

Klein, Edward. *Ted Kennedy, The Dream That Never Died*. New York: Crown, 2009.

Laing, Margaret. *The Next Kennedy*. New York: Coward-McCann, Inc., 1968. Lasky, Victor. *J.F.K.: The Man & the Myth*. New York: The MacmHlan Company, 1963.

Laing, Margaret. *Robert F. Kennedy: The Myth and the Man*. New York: Trident Press, 1968.

Leamer, Lawrence. *The Kennedy Men*. New York: William Morrow, 2001.

Levin, Murray B. *The Compleat Politician*. New York: The Bobbs-Merrill Company, Inc., 1962 (paperback original).

Levin, Murray B. *Kennedy Campaigning*. Boston: Beacon Press, 1966. Bibliography 499.

Lincoln, Evelyn. *Kennedy and Johnson*. New York: Holt, Rinehart, and Winston, 1968.

Lincoln, Evelyn. *My Twelve Years with John F. Kennedy*. New York: David McKay Company, Inc., 1965.

Lippman, Theo, Jr. *Senator Ted Kennedy*. New York: W. W. Norton, 1976.

Lucas, J. Anthony. *Nightmare*. New York: Simon and Schuster, 1993.

MacManus, Seumas. *The Story of the Irish Race*. New York: The Devin-Adair Company, 1944.

Manchester, William. *The Death of a President*. New York: Harper & Row, Publishers, 1963.

Markmann, Charles Lam, and Sherwin, Mark. *John F. Kennedy: A Sense of Purpose*. New York: St. Martin's Press, 1961.

Martin, Ralph G., and Plaut, Ed. *Front Runner, Dark Horse*. Garden City, New York: Doubleday & Company, Inc., 1960.

Marvin, Richard. *The Kennedy Curse*. New York: Belmont Books, 1969 (paperback original).

Matthews, Christopher. *Kennedy and Nixon*. New York: Simon and Schuster, 1996.

McCarthy, Joe. *The Remarkable Kennedys*. New York: Popular Library, 1960.

McNamara, Robert S. *The Essence of Security*. New York: Harper & Row, Publishers, 1968.

Neustadt, Richard E. *Presidential Power*. New York and Toronto: The New American Library, 1960 (reprinted by arrangement with John Wiley & Sons, Inc.).

Newfield, Jack. *RFK: A Memoir*. New York: E. P. Dutton & Co., Inc., 1969.

Ney, John. *Palm Beach*. Boston and Toronto: Little, Brown & Company, 1966.

Olsen, Jack. *The Bridge at Chappaquiddick*. Boston and Toronto: Little, Brown & Company, 1970.

Opotowsky, Stanley. *The Kennedy Government*. New York: E. P. Dutton & Company, Inc., 1961.

Pearson, Drew, and Anderson, Jack. *The Case Against Congress*. New York: Simon & Schuster, 1968.

Persico, Joseph. *Casey*. New York: Viking, 1990.

Phillips, Kevin. *American Dynasty*. New York: Viking, 2004.

Quirk, Lawrence J. *Robert Francis Kennedy: The Man and the Politician*. Los Angeles: Holloway House Publishing Company, 1968 (paperback original).

Russell, Francis. *The Great Interlude*. New York: McGraw-Hill Book Company, 1964.

Salinger, Pierre. *With Kennedy*. Garden City, New York: Doubleday & Company, Inc., 1966.

Schaap, Dick. *R.F.K.* New York: The New American Library, 1967.

Schlesinger, Arthur M., Jr. *A Thousand Days*. Boston: Houghton Mifflin Company, 1965.

Shannon, William V. *The American Irish*. New York: The Macmillan Company, 1963.

Shannon, William V. *The Heir Apparent*. New York: The Macmillan Company, 1967.

Sherrill, Robert. *Gothic Politics in the Deep South*. New York: Grossman Publishers, 1968.

Sidey, Hugh. *John F. Kennedy, President*. New York: Atheneum, 1963.

Sirkis, Nancy. *Boston*. New York: The Viking Press, 1965.

Sorensen, Theodore C. *The Kennedy Legacy*. New York: The Macmillan Company, 1969.

Sorensen, Theodore C. *Kennedy*. New York: Harper & Row, Publishers, Inc., 1965.

Stone, I. F. *In a Time of Torment*. New York: Random House, 1967.

Swift, Jonathan. *Gulliver's Travels*. New York: American Book Company (Selective English Classics).

Tanzer, Lester, ed. *The Kennedy Circle*. New York: Robert B. Luce, Inc., 1961

Thompson, Robert E., and Myers, Hortense. *Robert F. Kennedy: The Brother Within.* New York: The Macmillan Company, 1962.

Vanden Heuvel, William, and Gwirtzman, Milton. *On His Own: Robert F. Kennedy, 1964–68.* Garden City, New York: Doubleday & Company, Inc., 1970.

Vidal, Gore. *Palimpsest.* New York: Random House, 1995.

Whalen, Richard J. *The Founding Father.* New York: The New American Library, 1964.

White, Theodore H. *The Making of the President, 1960.* New York: Atheneum Publishers, 1961.

White, Theodore H. *The Making of the President, 1968.* New York: Atheneum Publishers, 1969.

White, William Smith. *Citadel.* New York: Harper & Brothers, 1957.

Whitehill, Walter Muir. *Boston in the Age of John Fitzgerald Kennedy.* Norman, Oklahoma: University of Oklahoma Press, 1966.

Wicker, Tom. *JFK and LBJ.* New York: William Morrow & Company, Inc., 1968.

Wicker, Tom. *Kennedy Without Tears.* New York: William Morrow & Company, Inc., 1964.

Wills, Garry. *The Kennedy Imprisonment.* Boston: Little Brown, 1981.

Witcover, Jules. *85 Days: The Last Campaign of Robert Kennedy.* New York: G. P. Putnam's Sons, 1969.

PHOTO CREDITS

1. Courtesy of Margaret Burke
2. Courtesy of Margaret Burke
3. United Press International Photo
4. Courtesy of Bradford Bachrach
5. Wide World Photos
6. *Life Magazine*, Property of Time Incorporated
7. Black Star, Owen (W.W.)
8. Courtesy of Paul Fay
9. United Press International Photo
10. United Press International Photo
11. United Press International Photo
12. United Press International Photo
13a. Wide World Photos
13b. Wide World Photos
14a. Courtesy of Walter Bachista
14b. United Press International Photo
15. *Life Magazine*, Property of Time Incorporated
16. *Life Magazine*, Property of Time Incorporated
17. United Press International Photo
18. United Press International Photo
19. Courtesy of *The Boston Globe*
20. MUTO
21. Courtesy of *The Boston Globe*
22. United Press International Photo
23. United Press International Photo
24. Black Star, Jack Hubbard
25. United Press International Photo
26. United Press International Photo
27. Photo. No. Px 76–71:2 in the John F. Kennedy Library
28. Ken Regan, Camera 5
29. AP/Wide World Photos
30. Photo. No. NLK 90–C49L #26A in the John F. Kennedy Library
31. Photo. No. 91–C34D #26 in the John F. Kennedy Library
32. Photo. No. NLK 92–C54B #7 in the John F. Kennedy Library
33. *The New York Times*, Stephen Voss
34. Photo. No. NLK 01–C17F:23 in the John F. Kennedy Library
35. AP Photo, Jim Rogash
36. Photo. No. NLK 92–20C # 11A in the John F. Kennedy Library
37. *The New York Times*